AF372089

PHILANTHROPY IN
VICTORIAN SCOTLAND

For

Edith Philipson

Robert Fraser Anthony

In Memoriam

PHILANTHROPY IN VICTORIAN SCOTLAND:
Social Welfare and the Voluntary Principle

OLIVE CHECKLAND

JOHN DONALD PUBLISHERS LTD
EDINBURGH

ISBN 0 85976 041 3

Phototypesetting by Burns & Harris Limited, Dundee
Printed in Great Britain by Bell & Bain Ltd., Glasgow

Contents

		Page
List of Tables		xi
List of Abbreviations		xiii
Preface		1
	1. A study in supply	1
	2. The nature of charity	1
	3. The phasing	3
	4. The organising principle	4
	5. The motivation	4
	6. The range	6
	7. Charity and the public sector	7
	8. The sources	7
	9. Thanks for charity received	9
Part I The Traditional Basis		11
Chapter 1. Pre-Victorian Charities		12
	1. Provision from the past	12
	2. Charity and poor relief	12
	3. Knoxian education	14
	4. Early orphanages; charity hospitals	16
	5. Charity for the old	18
	6. The infirmaries (general hospitals)	21
	7. The benevolent societies	21
	8. The renovations	26
	9. The continuities	27
Part II The Philanthropy of Piety		29
Chapter 2. Piety as a Programme		30
	1. Clergy and churchmen as philanthropists	30
	2. Evangelical philanthropy	30
	3. The Church Extension Movement	32
	4. Bible and Tract Societies	39

5. Religious Institution Rooms   41
6. Organisations to preserve the Sabbath   43
7. Sunday Schools   46
8. The Young Men's Christian Association   50
9. From Sunday School to Boys' Brigade   54
10. The attempt by the Church of Scotland to regain the welfare
    initiative   59
11. The rise and fall of piety   61

Chapter 3.   The Home Missionary Impulse   65

1. Middle versus working class recipients   65
2. The mission call   66
3. City missions   66
4. Missions to seamen   71
5. Mission work in the Highlands   73
6. Missionary staff   77
7. The forms of retreat   78

Chapter 4.   Piety and Medicine   80

1. Health as an evangelical aid   80
2. The Medical Mission Societies   80
3. Mission staff; the women's role: the Deaconesses   84
4. The Deaconess Hospital, Edinburgh   88
5. Healing and preaching   88

Chapter 5.   Piety and Temperance   90

1. Piety and sobriety   90
2. Early temperance   91
3. Government intervention   93
4. Campaigns for legal restraint, 1858-1914   95
5. 'Counter-activities'   98
6. Success?   99

Part III   The Philanthropy of Education   103

Chapter 6.   Formal Teaching: Schools and Universities   104

1. The continuum to 1872   104
2. The Dick Bequest   105
3. The charity hospitals (boarding schools)   108
4. The Education Act of 1872   112
5. The Endowed Schools and Hospitals (Scotland) Commission,
    1872   116

6. Higher education: grammar schools 118
7. Higher education: technical schools 121
8. The universities 126
9. The philanthropists as educators 130

Chapter 7.   Education for Life and Leisure 132

1. The challenge of savings and leisure 132
2. Savings banks 132
3. Public libraries 137
4. Art galleries 143
5. Parks and recreation grounds 146
6. The susceptibilities of councillors 147

Part IV   The Philanthropy of Health 151

Chapter 8.   The Poor and the General Hospitals 152

1. The philanthropic-medical empathy 152
2. The hospital in the community 152
3. The Royal Infirmaries in Edinburgh and Glasgow 155
4. The doctor as philanthropist 158
5. The philanthropist as financier and manager 160

Chapter 9.   The Care of Lunatics 165

1. The philanthropists' mental block 165
2. The problem of lunacy in England and Scotland 165
3. The philanthropic initiative: the seven Royal Lunatic Asylums 168
4. The professionals: the problem of therapy 172
5. The public commitment after 1857 174
6. The supremacy of the Royals 176

Chapter 10.   The Specialist Hospitals 178

1. Philanthropists at the core and the periphery of health 178
2. The use of specialisms 178
3. Maternity hospitals 183
4. Hospitals for and by women 187
5. Children's hospitals 188
6. Eye and ear hospitals 191
7. Hospitals for venereal disease 194
8. The dental hospitals 196
9. Later specialisms 197
10. The sources of motivation 198

Chapter 11.   The Dispensaries 200

  1. The dispensaries as a 'putting-out' system 200
  2. The general dispensaries 202
  3. The Infirmary dispensaries 205
  4. The specialist hospitals' contribution 206
  5. The medical missions 206
  6. The provident principle 206
  7. The dispensary debate 207
  8. The passing of the dispensaries 207

Chapter 12.   Supportive Services: Cottage Hospitals and Convalescent Homes 209

  1. Village hospitals 209
  2. Post-hospital care 214

Chapter 13.   The Nursing Revolution 219

  1. Old-style nursing 219
  2. Recruitment 221
  3. Training in the hospitals 222
  4. The nursing associations 224
  5. The Queen's Golden Jubilee 226
  6. The female aspect 227
  7. The sociology of the emergence of a profession 228

Part V   Residence and Remedy 231

Chapter 14.   The Prostitutes 232

  1. Residence as a basis for remedy 232
  2. The philanthropic attack on prostitution 232
  3. The publicists 233
  4. The Magdalene Asylums in Edinburgh and Glasgow 235
  5. Life in the Asylums 238
  6. Prostitution and the Police Acts 241
  7. Employment, wages, marriage and prostitution 242

Chapter 15.   Reformatories, Ragged Schools, Industrial Brigades and Training Ships 245

  1. The challenge of abandoned or fugitive children 245
  2. The Ragged Schools 246
  3. Sheriff Watson in Aberdeen 246
  4. Rev. Dr. Thomas Guthrie in Edinburgh 247
  5. The Glasgow House of Refuge for Boys 249

6. Government intervention 251
7. The Industrial Brigades 253
8. Training ships 254
9. Voluntary effort and government takeover 256

Chapter 16.   Orphanages 258

1. A new beginning 258
2. William Quarrier 258
3. The Orphan Homes of Scotland, Bridge of Weir 260
4. Into the Homes: Out to Canada 263

Chapter 17.   Remedial Homes for the Disabled 266
1. Residential homes for the deaf 266
2. The training and education of the blind 273
3. Homes for the mentally and physically disabled 275

Part VI   The Philanthropy of Housing 279

Chapter 18.   The Transient Tenant 280

1. The two challenges 280
2. The housing crisis 280
3. The Night Asylum and the Strangers' Friend 281
4. The Model Lodging House 285

Chapter 19.   The Housing Debate 290
1. Permanent housing: the philanthropic response 290
2. Building societies 292
3. Workmen's dwellings 293
4. A philanthropic failure? 294

Part VII   The Philanthropist Challenged 297

Chapter 20.   The Approach to Professionalism 298
1. The need for a new beginning 298
2. The Charity Organisation Society 298
3. The Kyrle Society 302
4. The University Settlement movement 303
5. Women in social work and the advent of professionalism 309

Chapter 21.   Civic Action and the Question of Rationalisation 311

1. The civic contribution 311
2. The challenge of rationalisation: the voluntary versus the
   municipal principle 314

Part VIII   The Voluntarist Balance Sheet   317

Chapter 22.   How Successfully Was Need Met?   318

    1. Provision versus need   318
    2. The philanthropy of piety   319
    3. Education   321
    4. Health   323
    5. The residential principle   326
    6. Housing   329
    7. The philanthropic outlook and performance   331

Chapter 23.   Lessons Learned and Lessons Lost   333

    1. The continuity question   333
    2. The components of continuity   335

Appendices   341

    I. The Old Man's Friend Society: Treasurer's Accounts; Legacies   342
   II. The Glasgow Sailors' Home: Regulations   345
  III. Foundation Ceremony of the Glasgow Asylum for Lunatics   346
  IV. West of Scotland Convalescent Seaside Homes, Dunoon:
     Grand Bazaar   349
   V. Gifts to the Mission Coast Home, Saltcoats   351
  VI. The Glasgow Boys' House of Refuge: Regulations   353
 VII. Industrial Brigades: Regulations   361

Bibliography   365

Index   391

Tables

		Page
Table 1	Urban Assessments in Scotland, entered into and not revoked	13
Table 2	Mixed Endowments available in Scotland in 1875	19
Table 3	Regional and family name societies active in Glasgow in 1881	25
Table 4	Church Extension programme in Scotland, 1835-1839	35
Table 5	Societies based on the Religious and Charitable Institution House, Glasgow	42
Table 6	Sunday School enrolments and density in Great Britain, 1851-1911	50
Table 7	Glasgow YMCA Annual City Hall Lecture Programme, 1861	52
Table 8	Statement of Income and Expenditure of Glasgow Medical Missionary Society in 1872 and 1890	83
Table 9	Course of Medical Study at the Medical Training Home for Lady Missionaries, Glasgow	87
Table 10	Votes of Scottish Members on the Permissive Bills	96
Table 11	Heriot's Day Schools, Edinburgh, in 1859	110
Table 12	Heriot's Day Schools: occupations of fathers, 1859	111
Table 13	Table of the Endowed Hospitals in Edinburgh, 1872	113
Table 14	Table of the Endowed Hospitals in Scotland in 1872 (excluding Edinburgh)	114
Table 15	General Endowments available in Scotland for Education in 1875	116
Table 16	College of Science and Arts, Glasgow: students and their courses, 1881	123
Table 17	Annual revenue received in 1875 by the Scottish universities from endowments made between 1808 and 1875	128
Table 18	Deposits at Ruthwell Savings Bank between 1811 and 1814	133
Table 19	General Hospital provision in Edinburgh and Glasgow in 1899	159
Table 20	Glasgow Royal Infirmary: a comparison between annual subscriptions (from private citizens) and contributions from workmen in public works, 1842-1858	162
Table 21	Lunatic Asylums in Scotland in 1839	168
Table 22	Lunatics in Scotland at 1 January, 1858	174
Table 23	Local Authority Lunatic Asylums in Scotland in 1899	175
Table 24	Specialist Hospitals in Edinburgh in 1899	179
Table 25	Specialist Hospitals in Glasgow in 1899	180
Table 26	Specialist Hospitals in Aberdeen, Dundee and Greenock in 1899	182

Table 27 Patients at Glasgow Dental Hospital, 1886-1888 196
Table 28 Scottish Dispensaries in 1899: a select list 200
Table 29 Patients treated at the New Town Dispensary, Edinburgh, between September 1815 and December 1842 203
Table 30 Cases dealt with at Glasgow Central Dispensary, 1893 205
Table 31 Cottage hospitals in Scotland at 1880 211
Table 32 Cottage hospitals in Scotland at 1899 212
Table 33 Convalescent homes in Scotland in 1899 214
Table 34 Number of patients admitted to the Mission Coast Home between 1866 and 1878 217
Table 35 Visits to houses of ill-fame in Glasgow, 1842 234
Table 36 Ages of girls admitted to Glasgow Magdalene Asylum between 1851 and 1859 237
Table 37 Glasgow Magdalene Asylum: admissions and discharges between 1851 and 1858 241
Table 38 Number of boys from training ships who went to sea in 1893 and 1894 255
Table 39 Source of funds for industrial training ships in 1893 and 1894 255
Table 40 Quarrier's Orphan Homes, Bridge of Weir: Cottage Homes built before William Quarrier's death in 1903 261
Table 41 Night Asylum, Glasgow: total overnight stays, 1838-1902 284
Table 42 Night Asylum, Glasgow: place of origin of people admitted, 1838-1902 284
Table 43 Glasgow Corporation Model Lodging Houses in 1891 287
Table 44 Outgoings at the Women's Lodging House, Glasgow, in 1872 288
Table 45 Glasgow Workmen's Dwelling Company Limited: new houses built 293

Abbreviations

AR	Annual Report
AUL	Aberdeen University Library
BA	British Association
BMA	British Medical Association
COS	Charity Organisation Society
EBS	Edinburgh Bible Society
EHR	Edinburgh Hospital Reports
EMAM	Edinburgh Magdalene Asylum Minute Books
EMJ	Edinburgh Medical Journal
EMMA	Edinburgh Medical Mission Association
ENAM	Edinburgh Night Asylum Minutes
EPL	Edinburgh Public Libraries
ERI	Edinburgh Royal Infirmary
EUL	Edinburgh University Library
GAFCS	Proceedings of the General Assembly of the Free Church of Scotland
GALH	Glasgow Association of Lodging Houses
GAMLH	Glasgow Association for the Establishment of Model Lodging Houses
GBCL	General Board in Lunacy for Scotland
GBCLS	General Board of Commissioners in Lunacy for Scotland
GBS	Glasgow Benevolent Society
GCM	Glasgow City Mission
GFBRS	Glasgow Foundry Boys Religious Society
GLH	Glasgow Lying-in Hospital Minute Book 1834-1856
GMA	Glasgow Magdalene Asylum
GMCHP	Glasgow Municipal Commission on the Housing of the Poor
GMJ	Glasgow Medical Journal
GMMS	Glasgow Medical Missionary Society
GRI	Glasgow Royal Infirmary
GSSU	Glasgow Sabbath School Union
GUA	Glasgow University Archives
GUL	Glasgow University Library
GULH	Glasgow University Lying-in Hospital Minute Book, December 4, 1834 — August 29, 1878
GUYMCA	Glasgow Union of Young Men's Christian Associations

HC	House of Commons
HL	House of Lords
NAPSS	National Association for the Promotion of Social Science
NBR	North British Review
NSA	(New) Statistical Account of Scotland, 1845
OMFS	Old Man's Friend Society (Glasgow)
OSA	(Old) Statistical Account of Scotland, 1795
PSHR	Philanthropic Society House Records, Edinburgh
QMCSA	Queen Margaret College Settlement Association
RC	Royal Commission
RCLAS	Report of HM Commissioners on Lunatic Asylums in Scotland, 1857
RCUS	Royal Commission of Inquiry . . . the Universities of Scotland
RCESH	Royal Commission on Endowed Schools and Hospitals (Scotland)
RSHW	Royal Samaritan Hospital for Women
SC	Select Committee
SDS	Society . . . for the Destitute Sick (Edinburgh)
SLC	Scottish Lunacy Commission
SPBTA	Scottish Permissive Bill and Temperance Association
SSCP	Social Science Congress Proceedings
SSPCK	Society in Scotland for the Propagation of Christian Knowledge
SSGS	Society for the Support of Gaelic Schools
TNASS	Transactions of the National Association for the Promotion of Social Sciences
UMS	University (Glasgow) Missionary Society

Preface

1. A study in supply

THE present book is, in essence, a study in the supply responses of a society. It is concerned with the welfare provision made in Victorian Scotland to meet social need. It is thus an investigation of the operation of the voluntarist principle as it responded to those who, under the market system of emerging and maturing capitalism, required, or were thought to require, assistance. It is the first real attempt to take a comprehensive view of what was provided, and the circumstances that evoked it. It may therefore be read as a history of the social services in Scotland down to 1914. Moreover, a good deal of light is incidentally thrown upon the general social history of Scotland.

Though the philanthropists were the means of providing so much, including both the educational and the health systems, they are not directly studied as a social phenomenon in their own right. It is hoped, however, that some incidental light will be thrown on the sociology of philanthropy. There are certain omissions, as for example the church charities directly to members, the whole of the Roman Catholic charitable activity, and the infinity of un-organised and private givings. The role of philanthropists as bringing pressure to bear on the state to improve conditions of work and life is also omitted. The philanthropists indeed helped to bring the state itself into action, but this is a separate story. Here they are treated only as the providers and sponsors of services. These gaps are partly due to limitations of space. And yet, in the matters treated, there is an inescapable need for detail about persons and institutions, for only through it can we savour the reality of things.

Quantification is almost impossible, at least in any aggregative sense. The resources of particular charities can sometimes be discovered but philanthropy as a totality cannot, at least as yet, be measured. We are left with statements such as that made in the Report of 1897 of the Annual Conference of the Charity Organisation Society: 'Glasgow charities are computed to amount to something like £1,000,000 per annum, Edinburgh £250,000.' There is no way of knowing what was included in such a computation, though it may say some-thing about proportionalities as between Glasgow and Edinburgh.

2. The nature of charity

A charitable act is a unilateral one, undertaken on behalf of another person, intended for his good, whether moral, physical or social. It can take many forms, involving financial aid, time, energy or technical expertise, but it does not necessarily receive or expect any response.

The terms charity and philanthropy embrace at least two different concepts. Charity is an essential element of many religious faiths involving care and concern for others. Most world religions incorporate such a concept; certainly the Christian faith, rooted in Judaism, adopted the ancient beliefs of the Middle East in the value of charity. But Christian charity was often a social observance, designed rather for the re-assurance of the giver than for the good of the receiver. It was regarded as a thank offering made by those with a surplus to those less fortunate than themselves. It was, indeed, one of the conditions upon which the medieval schoolmen justified the owning of private property. Philanthropy, on the other hand, is a broader concept, based on humanitarian considerations, for it is concerned to better human conditions. It should not be involved with making moral judgments of the recipients.

There are many Biblical references to charity, extolling it as an essential Christian virtue. St. Paul, following his exhortation 'concerning spiritual gifts', stressed its importance:

> Charity suffereth long and is kind
> Charity envieth not, charity vaunteth
> not itself, is not puffed up
>
> Charity never faileth
>
> And now abideth faith, hope and charity, these three;
> but the greatest of these is charity.
>
> (First Corinthians, 13)

In a society so Bible-based as that of Victorian Scotland it is not surprising that much was made of the need for charity, and of its social desirability. Charity in Victorian evangelical terms was inextricably linked with the poor, for St. Paul's injunction was clear:

> and though I bestow all my goods to feed the poor . . . and have not charity, it profiteth me nothing.

Although the elevation of the poor may have been an admirable intention, charity in Victorian times was often heavily impregnated with moral judgments of those who became its objects. In consequence charity came to be looked on by cynics and recipients as mean and grudging. Phrases like 'as cold as charity' were commonly used.

Moreover the Scottish church, whether Established or not, was conservative. Old forms of charitable endeavour were preferred, for society was seen in terms of the past. There were no strong groups of Quakers or Unitarians or other independently minded nonconformists active in Scotland, willing to experiment with new forms of social service.

In economic terms charity has always been difficult to construe. Because it is a one-sided action, expecting no *quid pro quo*, it is a misfit in the economic structure of modern society, which rests upon the principle of exchange. In consequence, economists have tended to ignore the impact of charity on the economy. But when these large voluntary transfer payments were disbursed they must have made some impact upon the economy. Moreover the nineteenth century classical economists were hostile to charity, inveighing against it and the (English) Poor Law because it vitiated the working of economic laws by providing sustenance for the able-bodied in defiance of those laws. In particular it reduced the incentive to work, as well as distorting the wage pattern. But a real question lay behind the economists' fears, namely how far does philanthropic provision sap the initiative of the individual to provide for himself and his family? To achieve the perfect system, balancing the meeting of the needs of the indigent against the operation of the rules of society, has never yet proved possible.

Sociologists have concerned themselves with voluntary giving. They have distinguished between charity given directly, from the donor to the recipient, and charity passed from hand to hand anonymously. The social bond which involved a direct handing of charity from the one person to another may have implied a moral obligation on the part of the donor, recognised by society as a whole. This created a sort of social cohesion, albeit on the donor's terms. Anonymous charity was impersonal and implied no such link. And yet it was presumably the larger part of the whole.

3. The phasing

Three general phases of philanthropic philosophy can be discerned.

In the first of these an ill-defined but nevertheless real interpretation of the social bond philosophy was strong. It led Thomas Chalmers to undertake his social work in St. John's Parish, Glasgow, in 1819. References to it run right through Scottish Victorian philanthropy. Chalmers' ideas were wrong-headed in that they were based on assumptions derived from the pre-industrial economy and society, and thus took insufficient account of unemployment and other suffering-inducing circumstances in an industrialised world. But insofar as Chalmers' followers organised volunteer labour and instituted enquiries into the cases of individual families in need, they represented an axiom of charity, namely that individuals must give their own time at significant cost to themselves to caring for those less fortunate than themselves. From this it followed that Victorian philanthropists could only be from the upper and middle classes, members of those groups who commanded leisure, a privilege in which working men did not share.

The 1870's began a second phase. Efforts were made to rationalise the charitable world. The Charity Organisation Society tried to bring some order into charitable giving and spending, but with little success. The state did the same, in a limited way, with its Royal Commission (Scotland) on Endowed Schools, reporting in 1873, 4, 5. New techniques were introduced to place social enquiry on a 'scientific base', to find out more exactly where the short-falls occurred, and where charities overlapped. New developments were undertaken to correct these faults. They demanded a steadily increasing commitment of time. This in turn led to the advent of the professional social worker. Trained women and men were now needed who could make enquiries of individuals and families on behalf of society, and who could take action to alleviate the distress of those found in need.

From the 1890's the emergence of the Fabian Society and other socialist groups marked the third phase. It was characterised by the introduction of more radical ideas. Socialists of various definitions argued that large areas of social provision, heretofore charitable, should be within the public sector. Such pressure was being exerted well before Victoria died in 1901. But it came to the fore in 1905 when the Royal Commission on the Poor Laws was set up with Beatrice Webb and George Lansbury as members. Socialism brought new ideas of the support the working men were entitled to from the state. In socialist theory charity should be largely obviated by comprehensive state provision. Over many areas of need this was indeed happening in whole or in part. But as the state has taken over areas of social provision formerly within the province of charity, so philanthropic endeavour has discovered newly generated areas of social need. Modern charities are pace-setters for the societies in which they live, discovering casualties, taking initiatives, and, where necessary, invoking the state.

4. The organising principle

The work is not, however, set out on a chronological plan. Instead it is concerned with objectives and functions. Beginning with the evangelical impulse to convert to Christianity (with the profusion of incidental 'causes' thus adopted), it embraces education and health (the two great core concerns of philanthropy), passes through the use of the residential principle in attempting remedies for many conditions (prostitution, youthful criminality, orphanhood and disablement), to the attempt to improve housing for both transients and the settled population. The final concern is with efforts to bring order and economy into the system while, at the same time, it was beginning to be augmented by civic action. The book concludes with an assessment of the voluntarist achievement and its relevance to the present day. In a sense a chronological progression is indeed present, as we move forward in time from an intensely evangelical community to a humanist-secular one.

5. The motivation

It is easy to patronise the motivations of charitable givers, but less easy to substitute anything in their place. The state's action was limited by the funds that electors were willing to pay in taxes, either national or local. The Victorian state collected relatively little revenue and assigned only an infinitesimal part of that for social purposes; most of the burden fell on the local rates.

The more notable philanthropists were activists, forcing people to consider the needs of society. They became precipitators, men and women who persisted until the necessary action was taken. The study of such driven and driving people has a peculiar fascination. But most wealthy Victorians did not involve themselves at this level, they waited to be solicited, when they gave money only. This second type of action was more properly 'ritual' giving, whereby the rich paid an accepted 'debt to society'; men like Sir Charles Tennant were in this category. They gave, as was expected of them, but their real interest was engaged elsewhere.

In the charitable world of the Victorians there was much which emphasised and underlined status. Standing in the community was in this sense related to the part played in the charitable world. Men and women were flattered to be invited to collect subscriptions, to serve on committees, to inspect homes and hospitals. Indeed the precipitators became expert in operating a kind of honours system, which by publishing donors' names and amounts, served as an almost costless incentive to givers. Those who were keen to spend a considerable proportion of their time in these ways were often those newly established in a level of society where free-time was the ultimate achievement. Leisure was indeed a philanthropic hall-mark, as well as a necessity. Much of the giving thus confirmed social success. Such ritual givers and collectors were numerous among those solid respectable citizens whose fortunes were improving, enabling and requiring them to give more money.

But with the bankruptcy courts kept busy, the middle classes too generated their casualties. In the large extended families of middle class Victorian Scotland any family group could include elements of both givers and receivers, as for example in the wake of the failure of the City of Glasgow Bank in 1878.

The activist philanthropists were behind most campaigns for social amelioration by the state. Some of the doctors, for example, were committed through their professions to improvement. Other givers were self-impelled by what they saw around them in the society of their day. It is satisfying to glimpse, albeit fleetingly, the names of so many honourable and dedicated Scotsmen and women. The work of Susan Carnegie for lunatics, Sheriff Watson and Thomas Guthrie for the ragged children, William Quarrier for the orphans of Scotland, William Smith and Henry Drummond for the Boys' Brigade, Beatrice Clugston for the Convalescent Homes, and many others and their causes, command respect. Many of such men and women who campaigned for their chosen objectives also pressed reluctant governments into action.

Those who wanted the state to do more had to campaign ceaselessly. They were influential in promoting Royal Commissions and official enquiries into the state of the 'lower orders' in nineteenth century Britain. Some such enquiries included Scotland, others of them were confined to Scotland. The reports published presented masses of evidence invaluable to historians. But such reports and their recommendations depended heavily on the attitudes of the commission members, who often rode away on their favourite hobbyhorses or made ineffectual proposals. Only rarely did such reports propose radical changes. The philanthropists, in consequence, were often left with unresolved problems.

The roots of much charitable work, especially in its first phase, lay in the evangelical movement of the nineteenth century. It was primarily concerned with personal salvation leading to eternal life. Although sometimes humourless and insensitive, this type of charity was transformed into good practical social work through organisations like the YMCA and the Boys' Brigade. The temperance movement seemed to many observers to be narrow and bigoted, but it gave encouragement to many earnest working men who used its organisations to give discipline and direction to their lives, and as stepping stones to educate themselves and gain business experience. It is not enough to dismiss these men and women as egoists and self seekers. Nor is any simple class approach adequate, treating them as motivated by fear and guilt. They responded to need as they saw it, and in so doing often gave a demonstration of what could be done.

6. The range

The Victorian philanthropists tackled an enormous range of social problems. Their drive, confidence and optimism enabled them to embark on ambitious schemes of social amelioration, supported as they were by their Christian faith.

A significant proportion of the church-based education of Scotland had traditionally relied on charitable benefactions. Even when a good deal of elementary education became rate-supported from 1872, the government deliberately left higher, technical and university education to the care of the voluntary principle. Throughout Victoria's reign and for more than a generation later blind, deaf and crippled children relied almost entirely on charitable initiatives. Savings banks, libraries, art galleries, parks and recreational facilities all resulted from their zeal and generosity. In partnership with the medical profession they helped to establish hospitals and dispensaries of all kinds in the towns. They were indeed the providers of health services to the public. Most of the hospitals they financed are still in use, supplemented by more recent foundations, though since 1948 part of the National Health Service. Striking Victorian buildings stand as memorials to their founders. In the country they set up convalescent homes and cottage hospitals. And to service all these growing medical facilities they worked equally hard at organising the newly emergent nursing profession in the form of Nursing Associations. They explored various ways of meeting the housing needs of the working classes. The responses were not so effective as they hoped, partly because of the immensity of the housing problem and the growth rate of the population; in the end philanthropic housing made little impact and municipal housing was increasingly favoured. But the philanthropists had been active in provoking public interest and in investigating the practicalities of housing provision and management for the working classes.

7. Charity and the public sector

Down to the middle of Victoria's reign charitable effort was expected, in Scotland as elsewhere, to supplement the only official outlay, namely that made through the poor law. Indeed in Scotland charity was especially important, for in contrast to England, official provision of poor law relief was restricted to the old, the young and the disabled; a strict interpretation of the law did not permit support for the able-bodied however great their need. But it is to be remembered that these laws were based on a pre-industrial society where provision for the old or the young often did not make excessive demands. In a largely agrarian world a child had been an asset which could be expected to be productive from an early age; the old rarely lingered on.

Magistrates and town councils were perforce involved with almost all local charitable initiatives, once the philanthropists had established them. For voluntary efforts not only reflected creditably on their town, they also provided facilities which made slight demands on the rates. Any charitable institution was thus a bonus for the city authorities. Not surprisingly they could gain official approval and support. Indeed one of the fundamental incentives of philanthropic action was pride of place, or civic action. The civic authorities also had overall responsibility to provide adequate forces for law and order; they therefore welcomed the establishment of those institutions, philanthropically founded, which helped to keep the peace and reduce social costs. Reformatories, Magdalene Asylums and venereal disease hospitals, and boys' clubs all relieved the magistrates in their task, making it possible for them to assign troublesome elements to care and cure, philanthropically provided.

Indeed so well understood was this that the magistrates of Edinburgh, Glasgow, Aberdeen or Dundee often took a direct and active part in the establishment of charities. Any such officially approved initiative could expect to attract wide support. Most charitable societies had a list of patrons: they were a kind of local Who's Who.

8. The sources

The principal primary source materials for the study of philanthropy are the annual reports of charities, treasurers' accounts and minute books. Annual reports circulated in large numbers; historians must rely heavily upon them. But they were subject to a series of complex and contradictory biases. They had to stimulate the interest and generosity of the putative subscriber by alternately over-emphasising the seriousness of the social problem, and encouraging the giver to believe that the society whose report he was reading offered the best chance of solving it. Reports usually had on the front paper cover the name of the society, its date of founding and its Biblical motto if appropriate. It was not only mission societies which proclaimed their evangelical urge. But as the century progressed such declarations became rarer. William Quarrier always highlighted the religious nature of his enterprise by carrying the legend 'Naked and ye clothed me', appropriately illustrated, on the front cover of the annual report of the Orphan Homes of Scotland. Inside the cover of a typical report was the list of patrons (mostly honorary and mostly landed), and directors or managers. But Glasgow was different. There the Lord Provost usually headed the list, for society in the industrial capital was markedly independent, seldom seeking the great aristocratic names. Perhaps Glasgow's charitable organisers were shrewd, anticipating a more generous response from their own sons than from the landed wealth which knew little of urban poverty. Glasgow's own landed gentry were the merchant princes, newly risen to such status, such as John Burns of Castle Wemyss, Charles Tennant of the Glen and James Campbell of Tulliechewan. In this respect Glasgow was unique in Scotland and true to its mercantile tradition. Edinburgh and Aberdeen in much greater measure sought the aristocratic cachet.

In the body of a typical report a fine balance was achieved, as the successes of the society were stressed and any societal disagreements were glossed over. Only rarely did a major conflict come to the attention of the contributors. Then followed the treasurer's report and the annual statement of the funds. Many societies were run on very small budgets. But some church charities had large ones compared for example with small hospitals and dispensaries. The largest element in the report consisted of long lists of contributors, together with their addresses and the size of their contributions. The greatest general interest in the report often lay in the emulative giving thus publicised.

The minute books of charitable societies are another important source. Relatively few survive as complete series, for when societies were wound up and offices vacated, secretaries rarely realised the value to historians of their primary source material. Minute books are usually more revealing than annual reports, for they record matters withheld from the public gaze. Occasionally they give financial details which do not appear in the treasurers' annual statements. In general, early minute books are more charming and revealing, giving insights into attitudes and behaviour as the charitable venture is created and passes through its early phase. Later minute books are more formal, less indicative of the real problems and their solutions. This change in format often reflected the move from a voluntary unpaid amateur to a paid official. The new kind of secretary was often more discreet, less gossiping, and more concerned only with recording decisions. Some societies have also kept correspondence, usually in the form of letter books. But these, alas, are comparatively rare.

As there were (and are) no Charity Commissioners in Scotland there are no reports directly concerned with the charitable world. The Royal Commission on Endowed Schools and Hospitals made important enquiries in the 1870's, as a result of which the funds of many educational charities were re-assigned. For other purposes the scholar must hunt among the Royal Commissions which enquired into social conditions. The evidence given to such Commissions by those working for voluntary bodies reveals much of the motivations and achievements of such men and women.

The survival of source material certainly causes a bias toward the larger cities, especially perhaps to Glasgow. But it was in such places that social problems were most acute and answers to them most eagerly sought.

9. Thanks for charity received

In undertaking a study of Scottish Victorian philanthropy the extent of the commitment only became apparent as the research progressed. The philanthropists were everywhere, bringing an immediacy to social problems which no one else would tackle. The very breadth of their involvement has posed problems. Little monographic work has been done on them, so that the lack of detailed individual studies has been sorely felt. It is necessary, therefore, in the scope of a single study, to try to encompass a large and diverse field.

Sincere thanks are due to librarians throughout Scotland for their efficient and kindly help. Those of the University of Glasgow in particular have eased my path frequently and pleasantly. My thanks are due to the Trustees of the Nuffield Foundation for financial aid in the early stages of the research. John Tuckwell of John Donald has given much encouragement and dealt with many difficulties. I am grateful to Margaret Lamb, Callum Brown and Carolyn Pennington for critical reading of parts of the Mss. Mrs. Aileen Forbes Ballantyne has prepared the index. My thanks also to many colleagues, including M. T. Baikie, Dorothy Black, Stewart Brown, Margot Butt, Robert Cage, Alec Cheyne, Derek Dow, A. A. M. Duncan, Neil Evans, Colin Galloway, Matthew Garrey, Ann Good, R. J. M. Hart, Lindy McLean, Mary Manchester, John Moore, Rhona Morrison, Michael Moss, Ian Muirhead, David Orrock, Jean Robertson, John Shaw, Elspeth Simpson, Alan C. Tait, J. R. Waddington, and David Walker. Isabel Burnside has worked with me long and loyally; her secretarial skills combined with her flexibility and adaptability have made her an indispensable part of the household. My husband has encouraged his erstwhile research assistant into ever more demanding tasks with a patience and understanding which has not always been deserved. He has also the distinction of being the *non-pareil* of house-husbands. I thank him for all his efforts, for without him there would have been no book.

5 The University,
Glasgow.
E. O. A. Checkland,
1980.

PART I

The Traditional Basis

1

Pre-Victorian Charities

1. Provision from the past

OF the profusion of Scottish Victorian charities, some dated as far back as the seventeenth century. We begin with these products of pre-industrial society. They were a mixed lot, arising from a wide range of motivation. Humanitarianism had its part, as did conscience, together with an urge to be favourably remembered and a need to dispose of one's earthly estate somehow. But the most powerful and sustained impetus came from the desire, under the urging and indeed sanctions of church teaching, to make provision for the needy.

Pre-industrial charities in their various manifestations extended well into the nineteenth century, and thus provided a continuity between the traditional and the moral-evangelical. Many eventually withered because they were irrelevant to industrialisation, and many were adapted to new uses.

There were six principal manifestations of traditional charity. There was that element of voluntary giving dispensed by the Church of Scotland, operating in conjunction with its parish poor law responsibilities (the unestablished churches also supported their own needy, but with no poor law functions). The second great role of the philanthropists lay in education. Other functions were discharged on a lesser scale. Specific provision was often made for orphans by the establishment of special funds or institutions. The old could also benefit from designated benefactions. The sick too invoked their own provision in the form of infirmaries, the first medical institutions for the caring of in-patients. Finally there was a range of benevolent societies for the discharge of particular philanthropic functions.

The object of the present chapter is to introduce this range of pre-Victorian philanthropic action. It is convenient, also, to carry the story of some of these pre-industrial provisions through to their demise or re-organisation, thus clearing the ground for the initiatives typical of the Victorian age.

2. Charity and poor relief

In Scottish parishes before the industrial revolution funds for the relief of the poor were composed, in the main, of church door collections, together with charitable monies either as bequests or gifts. If these two sources were inadequate the heritors (landowners) were required voluntarily to assess themselves. If they failed to do so the statutes provided that a legal assessment could be imposed upon them. The sums involved were very small. A distinction between money for poor relief and for charity was not always made. The essence of the old Scottish poor relief system was its voluntary nature; compared with England this automatically elevated charity to a more important status.

The kirk session of the Scottish parish, whether urban or rural, preferred the old voluntary system. It was cheap and forestalled the imposition of a legal assessment. There were, when the Poor Law Amendment Act of 1845 was passed, many parishes (especially in the North and West), which had no permanent legal assessment. Times of crisis could produce temporary or voluntary assessments, but these could be abandoned once the bad seasons were over. As Robert Peel Lamond remarked, 'The people preferred a voluntary assessment, as a sort of rate in aid of church funds, mortifications and other charitable sources of supply, to the legal assessment sanctioned by the Statutes. They regarded it only as a *dernier ressort*, a thing to be avoided at all hazards. Nor, . . . did they act illegally. It was not, as in the English Statutes, absolutely compulsory.'[1]

Indeed as late as 1839, of the 900 parishes in Scotland only 236 had legal assessments.[2] These assessed parishes were mainly in the south and east. In the larger towns, legal assessments were resorted to at various times, thus:

Table 1

Urban Assessments in Scotland, entered into and not revoked

Edinburgh	1660's (during Charles II's reign)
Glasgow	1735? certainly by 1774
Dundee	1810
Dumfries	1834
Aberdeen	1836
Inverness	After 1845 Act

Source: Cage, R. A., Poor relief in Scotland, Glasgow Ph.D., 1974, 166-167.

The money raised went to support the town's hospital (1735) in Glasgow, and the charity workhouse (1742) in Edinburgh; in Aberdeen, however, the poor's hospital (1739) was funded until 1836 without recourse to a legal assessment. Glasgow and Edinburgh also instituted general sessions (representative groups of the kirk sessions) to administer poor relief. There were also out-relief pensions paid to widows and those who qualified on grounds of age. The compounding of poor relief monies and charitable monies was less frequent in the towns than in the country; rural parochial kirk sessions disbursed money from the church door collections and charitable sources (like mortifications) without distinction.

In 1845 the Poor Law (Scotland) Amendment Act obliged the Scots to re-organise their poor relief. Even so the scene changed but slowly. In theory poor relief and charity were no longer to be intermingled, but in practice much of the symbiosis remained, with poor relief and charity continuing to reinforce one another. The church's position was weakened by the 1845 Act; its members could still organise and control much of the charity provided by its congregations, but the provision of poor relief passed over time to secular hands, namely a new system of lay parochial boards.

Charitable assistance was usually given to the same categories of casualties who could claim poor relief, that is to say the old, the dependent young and the disabled. In addition widows were frequently relieved, partly because they often had young children and few widows could manage on what they could earn. Charity was also frequently given in Scotland to the able-bodied especially in times of dearth, even when, as before 1845, they had no legal entitlement. No doubt considerations of maintaining the civil peace were important.

As accounting systems were casual and rudimentary, confusion between the various monies was inevitable. Its extent became clear only after the 1845 Act had replaced the old kirk sessions with the new parochial boards. Secular authorities such as magistrates and town councils who saw themselves failing to gain control of valuable charity funds still in the hands of the church (now relieved of poor law responsibilities) took action to acquire such funds. Banff Town Council, for example, 'claimed for themselves the right of independent administration'[3] in order to repossess themselves of their charity funds.

Aid given was either in the form of pensions or payment in kind. Where there were regular pensions from charity they were usually paid as a reward to the independent poor, namely those who accepted the life-long struggle to remain off the poor roll. It was widely believed by the parish authorities before 1845 that a bag of meal was less likely to be misapplied than money, which was more negotiable. Relief in Scotland was usually 'out door', although occasionally the old could obtain places in almshouses and the young in orphanages.

3. Knoxian education

Education was the subject of one of the nine chapters of the *First Book of Discipline*, issued by the Commission of the Church of Scotland on 20 May 1560. It projected a comprehensive provision of popular education, including parochial schools, grammar schools and universities; this sytem came to be the pride of Scotland. John Knox, the dominant member of the Commission, stated the case: 'Seeing that God hath determined that his Church here on earth shall be taught not by angels but by men . . . it is necessary that your Honours be most careful for the virtuous education and godly upbringing of the youth of this realm . . . For as the youth must succeed us, so ought we to be careful that they have the knowledge and erudition to profit and comfort that which ought to be most dear to us, to wit, the Church and Spouse of the Lord Jesus.'[4] Scottish education was thus church-based and church-inspired. By the nineteenth century this control still existed, but it was threatened.

Much of Scottish educational provision, all the way to the Act of 1872, depended on educational endowments which had existed since the reformation to help Scottish children to obtain education in Scottish schools or colleges which they could not otherwise have afforded. Such endowments were usually intended to 'supplement teachers' salaries; to pay the fees in whole or in part; to provide school salaries or prizes to encourage (children) to undertake secondary education; to provide books'. Few sums were ever left to maintain the fabric of the school buildings, for these responsibilities were placed firmly (by law) on the shoulders of the heritors and the kirk session. Many benefactors also distinguished between poverty and pauperism. Poverty was honourable; pauperism was not. Poor candidates were often favoured, but members of families who had had to resort to parish relief were discriminated against. Archibald Miller was acting within the strict convention when in the regulations for his charity school of 1795 he decreed that 'the children whose parents or guardians receive parish charity are not to be admitted to the benefit of the institution.'[5]

The conditions of the deeds of foundation varied according to circumstance. But there was a following of standard models which underlined the lack of originality among benefactors: almost all wished to benefit 'founder's kin'; relatives of the philanthropist, however remote, were to be preferred to strangers. Indeed the trust deeds usually included a list of the family names of the kinship group. This often proved a condition difficult to meet, and conscientious trustees found themselves in after years perplexed as to how to locate possible recipients of the bounty. Indeed, later legislative enactment often swept aside the founder's kin provision, judging it inefficient and cumbersome and bearing no relation to categories of need. In the towns many bequests and endowments were designed to benefit 'children of Burgesses'; again the category of burgesses, meaningful in earlier times, was no longer relevant. Where substantial trust funds remained, men (and women too) could and did buy themselves into the burgess roll in order to gain some entitlement for their children. Indeed this burgess benefit principle was successfully challenged in the nineteenth century when 'The Edinburgh ratepayers had got an Act of Parliament declaring that in the sense of George Heriot's deed, all citizens were Burgesses who paid rates'.[6]

But though the principle of founder's kin lost favour with the passage of time, the other notion, namely benefiting the parish of the giver, was more acceptable, and so lasted longer. Almost all endowments gave preference to those living in the parish or town of origin of the benefactor. Indeed where the benefactors failed to name a parish the law usually recognised that it would

have been his intention to nominate his own parish of origin, and the benefits
therefore went to that parish.

4. Early orphanages; charity hospitals

There were many homeless orphans in pre-industrial Scottish towns, for few
had relatives who could afford to rear them. But charity involving the young
could be very appealing to givers. The sponsors of the Edinburgh Orphan
Hospital did not fail to exploit this attraction when they wrote in 1833 that
'One primary advantage . . . is that it has to do with the young, and in this
respect it occupies one of the most hopeful of all the provinces of charity.'[7]

There was much diversity of practice between Scotland's cities. Edinburgh
was early in the field with a separate orphan home, founding it in 1733. In
Glasgow as late as 1830 orphans were 'Boarded at a cheap rate with decent
families in the country.'[8] In Aberdeen orphans remained resident in the poor's
hospital, although a separate boys' hospital and girls' hospital were built later,
in 1818 and 1828 respectively. These homes were originally charitable and
retained their status as subscription-worthy institutions, but they did in time
become the official local authority provision and were partly rate-supported.
In Dundee an orphanage was established in 1815; a Royal Charter was
obtained in 1870, by which date it had become the Royal Orphan Institution
(at Craigie Terrace, Ferry Road). In addition out-door pensions were paid by
the Dundee authorities to orphans or their guardians. From this mixture of
provision it would appear that where, as in Edinburgh, a philanthropic
initiative could be generated to found an orphans' home, this was the principle
adopted. Where this was absent, as in Glasgow, the boarding-out principle, or
the provision of orphans' pensions, being free of capital cost, would operate,
or the children simply lived with the rest of the indigent in the poor house.

Early orphanages relied on gifts and endowments, often augmented by some
finance from the town council, together with the proceeds of the industrial
production of the inmates (when this was not negative). Optimistic managers
embarked on ambitious training schemes in anticipation of high productivity.
Despite the outlay of substantial sums on raw material and specialists to teach
difficult and complex processes like the manufacture of wool and linen, 'in
course of time so many difficulties and disadvantages were found that it was
ultimately abandoned'.[9]

The orphanage initiatives of Edinburgh and Aberdeen were notable. The
Orphan Hospital, Edinburgh was originally sponsored by Andrew Gairdner
who succeeded in 1733 in opening a small house for orphans at Bailie Fife's
Close. Gairdner was Treasurer of the Trinity Hospital, an ancient foundation
(established in 1461 by Mary of Gueldres), which was then falling into decay.
His efforts were supported by the Society in Scotland for Propagating
Christian Knowledge, which supplied the first teacher. The Orphan Hospital

was later moved to the north of the Old Town near the site of the present General Post Office, at the end of North Bridge. But with the expansion of the town it came to be overshadowed by larger buildings. The location and condition of the hospital deteriorated so badly and 'the mortality of the children became at length so appalling'[10] that active steps had to be taken to remove it to a more salubrious place. A site at Dean was obtained and in 1834 the hospital removed to its new premises. The managers, having made a large unbacked investment, were financially embarrassed, for the endowment was not sufficient to finance such a large new building as well as to meet the expense of running it. But a further public appeal was successful and the Edinburgh Orphan Hospital could continue to rear children as it had done for over 100 years.

Aberdeen was especially noted for its orphanages. The city authorities had long since channelled into them resources from both pre- and post-reformation foundations. In early Victorian times two more initiatives were taken: the Aberdeen Female Orphan Asylum begun in 1840 by Mrs Mary Emslie, and the Orphan and Destitute Female Children's Hospital of 1849. The Aberdeen orphanages were the only ones to come under the scrutiny of the Royal Commission (Scotland) on Endowed Schools and Hospitals which reported in 1873, 4, 5. The Commissioners were highly critical.

They disliked the idea of isolating children from the community of which they should be a part. Most orphanages were like the Aberdeen Female Orphan Asylum where 'they are never allowed to go home at all.'[11] The atmosphere of such an institution can be best conveyed by what the girls wore, as late as the 1870's: 'a mob cap indoors — the old fashioned white linen cap that old ladies in France wear. All the girls wear that and they are most anxious to get rid of it.'[12] It was complained that pride had caused Mrs. Emslie to build too grandly for her orphans; one witness remarked, 'It is a large and very fine house — perhaps too fine for the purpose.'[13]

Mrs. Emslie's intention was to produce good and reliable domestic servants, although some girls may have been trained for more demanding roles. One witness claimed that, despite the fact that 'the deed of foundation and bequest by Mrs. Emslie is so short and definite as to defy all innovation', a few pupil teachers, dress-makers and nursery governesses were trained at the Aberdeen Female Orphan Asylum.[14]

The criticisms of the Commissioners appeared justified, for the traditional Scottish orphanage as exemplified in Aberdeen was no longer relevant to late Victorian society. By 1873 Mrs. Emslie's orphanage for example had a serious shortfall of applicants, for there were then only 6 applicants for 60 vacancies. As a witness commented: 'The girls are tempted to go into mills and manufactories, of which there are a great many in Aberdeen, because they can earn more money there.' Mrs Emslie's orphanage was closed on 27 July 1891. After its purchase by the School Board, it was enlarged and re-opened as the Girls' High School.[15] Girls were admitted on the grounds of ability (with scholarship provision), and as fee-paying pupils.

Other small orphan institutions which were eventually assimilated into the school system as a result of the Commissioners' actions included the Scott Institution, Greenock (1838), Muirhead's Hospital, Dumfries (1753), Wood's School, Newburn by Largo, Fife (1659), Samuel Douglas Free School, Newton Stewart (1789) and Speyside Charity School (1795). These were all small trusts providing for a few children; once the Board schools were established after 1872 they had little purpose.

There were other charitable bodies of long standing running homes for girls which did not come under the scrutiny of the Commissioners of the 1870's. These relied on annual subscriptions rather than endowments, and so were outside the Commissioners' brief. They were all similar to the Glasgow Institution for Orphan and Destitute Girls. This was opened in November 1825, and became an important addition to the residential accommodation available for needy girls. Its training was for domestic service, to provide 'useful employment and honest maintenance in life'.[16] The lives of the girls revolved around a three-week rota of duties as kitchen maid, laundry maid and housemaid. In the early days perhaps dairy work was also done. The tight control of the girls extended to their rewards; girls who saved were made to use the Savings Banks. In the early years the managing committee of the Glasgow Institution hoped that another category of girl would be sent to them, paid for by family and friends. This may well have been an oblique reference to the placement of illegitimate girls. Few girls of this category ever appeared.

In addition to the orphanage as such there were also from the seventeenth century large charity hospitals (e.g. boarding schools) in the principal cities. These were often well-endowed, offering facilities for orphans far superior to anything available in the orphanages. But they were not accessible to the orphans of the mass of the population, being provided by men of the middle classes for sons (age 8-14) of 'decayed burgesses', often with a preference for founders' kin. These eighteenth and early nineteenth century hospitals were usually small, of classic Georgian style, looking rather like lesser country houses. Edinburgh was particularly rich in them, with George Heriot's, John Watson's, Donaldson's, Fettes College and others (see chapter 6, section 3 below).

5. Charity for the old

There had been for centuries hundreds of small pensions available for the aged independent poor through charitable organisations. But only a small proportion of the elderly men and women could benefit. The rules were strict, so that by no means all of the aged qualified for benefit. These moneys were almost always intended for the poor who did not accept poor relief. They were considered a reward for those whose pride or resourcefulness had kept them independent throughout their active lives.

Many of such endowments had also been intended to benefit orphan children. Most of such moneys were to go to burgesses and members of Trade Corporations or their dependants, yet these categories had by Victoria's accession ceased to be meaningful. Full and public enquiry was long overdue. Eight of these mixed endowments were examined by the Commissioners in the 1870's:

Table 2

Mixed Endowments available in Scotland in 1875

(Roughly half of the funds to go to the old and half to the young for educational purposes)

Name	*Place*	*Annual Revenue (£'s)*
Hutton Bequest	Dumfriesshire	900
Gillespie's Hospital	Edinburgh	1,700
Hutcheson's Hospital	Glasgow	14,000
Allen's Hospital	Stirling	700
Cowane's Hospital	Stirling	2,000
Cunninghame's Hospital	Stirling	210
Spittal's Hospital	Stirling	750
Ferguson Bequest	Counties of Dumbarton, Renfrew, Lanark, Ayr, Wigtown & Kirkcudbright	16,080
		36,340

Source: RCESH, Appendix to 3rd report, Vol. II, Statistics 345.

Ferguson's Bequest was used primarily to supplement ministers' and missionaries' salaries and to maintain church buildings; little was going (by 1875) to the aged poor. The others were giving regular pensions to the old, but in practice this meant great diversity: whereas a fair proportion of the old and needy in Stirling could expect to receive a pension, in other places there were very few such supplements available.

Perhaps Hutcheson's Hospital, Glasgow is the most useful of such charities to look at more closely, not only because of the large income which it had at its disposal, but because a closer examination reveals some of the problems facing the trustees. The brothers George and Thomas Hutcheson of Lambhill, Glasgow left money and land for a hospital and a school in 1639 and 1641. The original benefaction was modest: a sum of about 68,700 marks Scots, with a 'tenement of land' and 'a barnyard on the North Side of Trongate'. George and Thomas envisaged a small almshouse for 11 men and a school for 12 boys, but residential accommodation was rapidly given up and money pensions were paid to the successful applicants. In 1737 the trustees decided to allow pensions to females. This was a serious breach of their trust, but no one challenged them and women came to occupy an increasingly important place on the pensions roll. It was a sensible move; widows of all ages, but especially those with dependant children, represented a large category in extreme need. By 1869 there were seven times as many females on the roll as males (about 618 females and 80 males).

In the seventeenth and eighteenth centuries the trustees had regularly bought land in Glasgow, usually contiguous to that which they already owned. With Victorian prosperity and the expansion of the city the land was feued and the trustees found that they were administering a fortune which annually increased at an embarrassing rate. Indeed as the Commissioners commented, '. . . Hutcheson's Hospital Fund, Glasgow, has increased since the Commission began its sittings from £11,000 to £14,000 a year', that is between 1872 and 1875. Even in 1874 'the Hospital is possessed of 116 acres in a locality towards which the city is rapidly extending, and the feuing of this land will add materially to the income of the institution.'[17]

By the 1860's (and before the Commissioners on Endowed Schools were appointed), the trustees of Hutcheson's had obtained an Act of Parliament to enable them to re-organise their charity. Under this Act (in 1873) the patrons spent 'on pensions £6,808, on education £2,341, out of net revenue of upwards of £10,240'. The Commissioners, intent on seeking out funds which could be released for education, criticised the amount payable to the pensioners and feared that it would 'degenerate into a system of indiscriminate doles, injurious to the independence of the recipients and to the community'.[18] Eventually the trustees bowed to pressure and produced a new scheme giving much more emphasis (and money) to education. The Hutcheson's trustees had, in terms of their trust, always excluded from their rolls anyone who had received parochial relief. Other societies took a different view. The Old Man's Friend Society was established in Glasgow in 1812. By 1839 it was committed to aiding men over the age of 60 who 'after due enquiry, are found deserving of its care, and so destitute as to need its aid'. In contrast to most charities intended to help the old, all its pensioners 'must have applied for, and obtained parochial relief'.[19] The relief payments were paid to the Society; these, augmented by benefactions, paid for the operation of the Society's Asylum. Although the society remained a voluntary charity, it was in fact supplementing the official poor law provision. The Asylum was built about 1837 in Rottenrow, with accommodation for about 30 old men where 'health, cleanliness and comfort have in many cases gladdened those who were before subjected to disease, neglect and want.'[20] The residents were employed at 'picking cotton yarn cops, an occupation at once easy and light'. A new Asylum was built and occupied in 1840, also in Rottenrow. The Society, in addition, had (in 1839) 220 'outdoor' pensioners in regular receipt of aid:

> 57 between 60-70 years of age
> 98 between 70-80 years of age
> 45 between 80-90 years of age
> 10 between 90-100 years of age

The Society employed John Wood, M.D., and J. G. Fleming, M.D., who, as honorary officers, undertook the medical attention of the Asylum residents.

Their medical reports were full and helpful and stressed the infirmities of the resident and out-door pensioners. The two doctors made reference to their inability to visit all the non-resident pensioners, although they did examine 150 of them.

The comforts of the new Asylum included a type of central heating which worked by means of 'the introduction of heated air through flues from a stove in the ground floor, the temperature of all the dormitories can, in the course of about three hours, be raised to 65°F; and the nature of this heated air is most agreeable and salubrious.' Treasurers' Accounts reveal that the sums for the upkeep of their old men from the parochial boards were substantial, namely £420 in 1838 and £866 by 1878. Subscriptions were £283 in 1838 and £203 in 1845 and £407 in 1878 (see Appendix I). In June 1877 the Society opened an Old Woman's Home, in Dean Street, which initially accommodated 28 women. In the next thirty years the Society's budget tripled; with the two buildings they had to maintain, this was essential. The Society remained active until recent years when it was re-created in the form of Balmanno House in the west end of Glasgow.

The existence of the Old Man's Friend Society was perhaps a standing rebuke to the normal poor relief system. It may be that the organisers believed they were catering for a different class of aged from those normally associated with the Town's Hospital; nevertheless they were running a philanthropic poor house, annually supplementing the basic poor relief money with a substantial injection of gifts and donations.

6. The infirmaries (general hospitals)

The systematic in-care of the sick in Scotland began with the infirmaries or general hospitals; these were later, in most Scottish cities, to become the Royal Infirmaries. Edinburgh was the pioneer in 1729. By the beginning of Victoria's reign all major Scottish cities and many minor ones had infirmaries, totalling eleven. In all of them the philanthropists played a major part in founding, financing and managing. Just as the philanthropists had to evolve a relationship with the church in terms of the poor law and charity, so too they had to come to terms with the medical profession in the supply of these basic facilities (see chapter 8 below). But the infirmaries, though of great importance to the development of medical practice, were remote from most of the labouring people.

7. The benevolent societies

Much closer to the lives of most of the population were the benevolent societies. Some of them were formed by members of the middle classes, with a view to helping the working class. These involved one class sitting in beneficent judgment on another. Others were created as a form of insurance or self-help. They proliferated from the later eighteenth century. By Victorian times there were hundreds of them in Scotland, all seeking to assist the poor in one way or another. But they were hampered by two difficulties, namely the lack of effective outlets for their energies and the dangers of harmful giving. A variety of tests was introduced in the hope of discouraging the undeserving. The benevolent societies were always faced with the irreducible dilemma of very limited resources to be applied to unlimited needs. Examples of such societies were the Edinburgh Benevolent and Strangers' Friend Society, the Glasgow Society for Bettering the Condition of the Poor, the Glasgow Benevolent Society for the Destitute Sick, the Gorbals Benevolent Society and the Female Benevolent Society.

But one of the most important was the Edinburgh Society for the Relief of the Destitute Sick, founded in 1785. It illustrates the working of such a body. It was to continue throughout the Victorian period. It was cast in the heroic mould of moral exhortation for, as its report of 1844 put it, 'its agents, while they care for the body, its wants and ailments, moreover care for the soul, its necessities and diseases.'[21] It is somewhat surprising to read of 'the happiness that is often spread through the homes of the poor by the visits of their wealthier neighbours', for by the 1840's the poor were becoming hostile to such interfering visits. The Bible and Tract activity of the Society is described as 'that nursling of providence'. The Society was also giving practical aid. In the first year of operation it spent some £62 on relief; this had increased to £320 in 1800, £1,942 in 1837 and £2,000 in 1865.

Thousands of visits were paid annually, and by 1867 printed schedules were available on which applications for relief had to be made. The schedules included the following questions addressed to the sick:

1. How long have you been confined?
2. What is your employment? and with whom last employed?
3. What is the number of your family? and how many are dependent upon you?
4. How long have you resided here? or, where for the last three years?
5. Did you ever receive aid from this Society before?
6. Have you any relief from the Parish? and how much?
7. Have you ever applied for relief from the Parish, and been refused?
8. Are you a member of any benefit society? or do you at present receive any support from any source?
9. Have you any friends able to assist you?
10. Are you a member of any church? or do you at present attend any place of worship?

Clearly the visitors of the Society acted as social workers of the most inquisitional kind 'to detect the deceit and impositions which are too frequently attempted'.[22] The bounty of the Society was to be paid out only in certain circumscribed cases; the painful decisions which visitors had to make with respect to the unemployed and the sick come out very clearly.

The Society continued to try to reverse the movement of the population into

Edinburgh by invoking Settlement laws; visitors were encouraged to persuade individuals and families to apply to the Strangers' Friend Society to obtain their fares to return home. The visitors of the Destitute Sick Society were in these cases authorised to add to the provision made. The list of instructions to visitors is a reminder of the complexity of such visits; number 14 brought the list to an end by reminding the visitor of his charge 'that he shall embrace every opportunity of speaking with them about spiritual and eternal things, and pray with them if desired'.

The Glasgow Benevolent Society 'for the relief of the destitute sick and others in extreme poverty' was founded in 1832. It did not however set up its own enquiry agency. By the 1870's (and probably much earlier) it had become a money-collecting agency only, employing only a Collector for, 'The city, parochial and congregational missionaries are still your almoners.'[23] The funds were disbursed by the missionaries in cash or in penny and sixpenny tickets for bread, provisions and coal. There was much anxiety as to the corrupting effect of this on the poor. The Rev. Dr. D. McLeod dismissed these arguments on the grounds that as the average amount of money expended by each missionary was somewhere about 5 shillings a week, or about 3d. a family per week of those who were assisted, 'it could do little damage'. But the timid subscriber was always fearful of 'indiscriminate charity'; he preferred to give charity in kind rather than in cash. This was done by means of tickets with which provisions could be bought from accredited grocers. Of an annual budget of £1,676 in 1875-6, £1,485 was in this way paid for provisions. The system of grocery tickets is still in use today.

The North Parish Washing Green Society[24] is an example of Glasgow initiative, with a strong element of self and mutual help. It collected money from those willing to contribute, and allocated small pensions to deserving citizens to increase the comforts of old age. It was founded in 1792 by the heritors of the North Parish of Glasgow, who owned land adjacent to the Molendinar Burn by the Cathedral and Royal Infirmary. Their objectives were twofold, firstly to provide washing green facilities where local residents could, for a small charge, do their laundry. Secondly, the fees collected were then used for charitable purposes. The Society provided the green, the wash-house, hot water tubs and stools and other facilities. Eventually the committee judged that with the expansion of the city their washing green was no longer a viable proposition and they sold their land in 1873 to the Royal Infirmary for £3,005.[25] The Society continued to function, inviting life membership at one guinea. Such a modest sum has enabled many humble residents of the parish to become members, and to become eligible in old age for the Society's pensions. The Society attracted generous gifts and legacies, placing substantial funds at its disposal. It still continues to provide extra pensions for a number of old people in the city.

It is difficult to make any judgement of the value and efficacy of the general benevolent societies. They remained an active (but increasingly criticised) philanthropic presence. Their organisers volubly sought to impress upon the public the underlying Christian ethic which inspired their work. They constantly encouraged their contributors with Biblical exhortations, such as 'For the poor shall never cease out of the land; therefore I command thee saying, thou shalt open thine hand unto thy brother, to thy poor and to thy needy in the land' (Deuteronomy XV, II), and 'Naked and ye clothed me: I was sick and ye visited me' (Matthew XXV, 36).

It was easy enough for the recipients of benefits to be cynical. Dr A. M. Adams created in 1835 the character of the Edinburgh slum woman, Lucky Mackintosh, whose neighbour commented freely on the activities of the philanthropists and their charities. Her views on the benevolent societies were particularly biting:

> for if ye gang tae a benevolent society, ye'll be sent back again for a line o' recommendation, an' maybe's folk may get that, an' maybe's no. An' if we dae chance to get it, we're ordered tae gang an lea' it wi' the treasurer o' the society until the veesitor o' the distric' comes roun', which he very aften forgets tae dae; but su'd he come, he has then tae gi'e in his report, as he ca's it, tae the committee, after which, aiblins, on the Seterday they'll gi'e ye a peck o' meal; but no afore ye hae studden at their door lang enough for a' the folk that passes tae see ye, an' tae ken, o' course, that ye're stannin' as an advertisement o' the godly folk i' the inside; an' o' ye're ain humiliatin' siteation i' the outside; so that a' this application in' an' veesitin', wi' a hantle o' praying an' admonishin' for a nievefu' or twa o' meal, isna worth a body's pains.[26]

Perhaps the couplet from the pen of the Irishman, J. B. O'Reilly, sums up criticism most accurately:

> The organised charity scrimped and iced,
> in the name of a cautious and statistical Christ.[27]

There was a further range of benevolent societies for incomers to the cities, based on place or county of origin. They were part of a support system that had a strong mutual element which new arrivals organised for themselves. They combined both the aspects of a friendly society and those of a charitable society. While primarily for social purposes, giving a cohesion to those regional groups nostalgic for people and places long abandoned, they were also operating as insurance schemes, members contributing during their good years of high earnings, confident that if in their years of infirmity they needed aid they could apply successfully to the society. For example, the Perthshire Charitable Society in Glasgow was 'to afford relief to persons in indigent circumstances, natives or widows of natives of Perthshire, or their children . . . unexpectedly falling into distress'. Some societies also had separate sums ear-marked for helping with the schooling of members' children. If funds permitted, societies sometimes instituted an educational bursary fund, which would at least provide one award of say £25 a year. Bursaries and school prizes could also be established at schools in the county of origin. There were twenty-four regional societies in Victorian Glasgow:

Table 3

Regional and family name societies active in Glasgow in 1881

Date of Founding, if known

	Argyllshire Society
1769	Brown's Society of Glasgow
1725	Buchanan Society
1837	Fife Kinross and Clackmannan Charitable Society
1858	Glasgow Aberdeenshire Association
1761	Glasgow Ayrshire Society
1837	Glasgow Caithness Benevolent Society
1856	Glasgow Celtic Society
	Glasgow Dunbartonshire Benevolent Society
	Glasgow Dumfriesshire Society
	Glasgow Eaglesham Friendly and Educational Association
	Glasgow Galloway and Dumfriesshire Society
	Glasgow Moray and Banffshire Friendly Society
1836	Glasgow Northern Highland Benevolent Society
1837	Glasgow Orkney and Shetland Benevolent Society
	Glasgow Stirlingshire and Sons of the Rock Society
	Graham Charitable Society
1727	Highland Society of Glasgow
1855	Kilmarnock Benevolent Society of Glasgow
1825	Kintyre Club
	Lochwinnoch Benevolent Society
	Perthshire Charitable Society
1844	St. George Benevolent Society in Scotland
1813	Tweedside Charitable Society

Source: Handbook of Glasgow Charities (Glasgow 1881).

They reflected the high proportion and the diversity of recent incomers. They could not command indefinite fidelity from successive generations. With time, incomers became integrated with the community to which they had moved. Such societies survived as dining clubs, and indeed sometimes produced whole books of rhyming verse in praise of their native heaths. The men of Morayshire were well served by *The Lintie o' Moray*, a book containing much nostalgia and starting with *Elgin and Forres for Aye*:

> Come fill up a bumper each Morayshire lad,
> And drain your glasses quite dry,
> I'll gie you a toast, will make your hearts glad—
> Here's — Elgin, and Forres for aye.[28]

The Highland Society of Glasgow was established in 1727 by 17 gentlemen 'who had come from the Highlands and settled in Glasgow'. It had a more ambitious programme than most regional societies and was especially important in stimulating education for children. The Society was incorporated by Seal of Cause by the magistrates of Glasgow in 1751 and a scale of entry money was fixed, which gave a life membership. For sixty years (until 1861) the entry fee was a minimum of 42s., although wealthier members were encouraged to pay more.

Its objects were 'in educating and putting out to trades, boys born in the

Highlands, or descended from, and branches of Highlanders, whether in this city or country, without distinction, and for other charitable and laudable ends'. The Society from the beginning continued to apprentice boys to various trades; as early as 1788 it opened its own evening school where apprentice boys received an education. It continued to expand its commitment to educating members' children (a girls' school was added in 1827). In 1831, following the expansion of its responsibilities, it purchased ground in Montrose Street and there erected 'very commodious and elegant buildings'. By 1861 the schools, with 396 boys and 424 girls, were 'divided into five departments — three for English, one writing and arithmetic, and one girls' school of industry. Each department is presided over by a teacher assisted by two or three pupil teachers.'[29] But the schools were not so efficient as the Society thought, and received unfavourable reports from inspectors. After 1872 they were under serious pressure from the new Board Schools. The managers decided to close them and sell the property. But the Society continued to pay school fees for children in ordinary or advanced classes and bursaries for likely boys at the University of Glasgow. With the integration of the Highland population with that of Glasgow, men and women no longer needed so much support from other Highlanders. With the provision of Board Schools the children were better placed with the rest of their age groups in the ordinary schools. Societies like the Highland Society remained in existence primarily as a focus for social activities and so they have continued into the twentieth century.

There were also clan societies run on benevolent society lines. As with the regional benevolent societies they were concerned not only to support their poor members but also to educate 'such young men as give indications of talent and genius'.

8. The renovations

As the various surviving parts of pre-industrial welfare provision passed through the Victorian age, some underwent official revision. The first to be brought under systematic review was the poor law. The Act of 1845 was a recognition that the voluntary principle could no longer sustain the burden of the needy, hence the setting up over time of quasi-official agencies in the form of the parochial boards. The traditional orphanages and boarding schools for orphan boys (and some girls) had by 1872 reached such a state of inadequacy as to help to inspire the setting up of the Royal Commission.

In consequence of its review such institutions were radically reorganised (see chapter 6, section 5 below).

But the other three forms of pre-industrial philanthropy escaped governmental scrutiny. Charity for the aged continued largely unchanged, on a piecemeal and unco-ordinated basis. The infirmaries rose from their humble beginnings to thrive mightily as the great force of Scottish medicine (see below, chapter 8), entirely free of the state. The benevolent societies too could thrive, free of official attention.

9. The continuities

Many of the traditional charitable societies have long since disappeared. But in many cases moneys still remain. Where this is so, trustees have two possible courses of action. They can continue to disburse funds in the old way to supplement state provision, or they can seek to broaden their terms of reference, endeavouring to disburse their funds to deserving causes of a related nature, or they may experiment with new ventures. The availability of these moneys, the most important of which are possibly those held by the Merchants House and Trades House in Scottish cities, enables the system to retain a certain flexibility (albeit a fairly conservative one), without which many charitable initiatives would fail.

NOTES

1. Lamond, 1870, 30.
2. Saunders, L. J., 1950, 197.
3. RCESH, 1875, 153.
4. Knox, J., *A History of the Reformation of Religion in Scotland* (Glasgow 1761), 493.
5. Anon., *Rules of Archibald Miller's Charity School for girls* (Glasgow 1812), 5.
6. Walker, A., 1886, 29.
7. Anon., *An historical account of the Orphan Hospital of Edinburgh* (Edinburgh 1833), 30.
8. Anon., *Town's Hospital of Glasgow* (Glasgow 1830), X.
9. RCESH, 1875, 61-62.
10. Anon., *Statement relative to the Orphan Hospital* (Edinburgh 1838), 2.
11. Walker, A., 1883, 47.
12. RCESH, 1873, 90.
13. RCESH, 1873, 89.
14. RCESH, 1873, 88-89.
15. *Aberdeen Journal*, 29 July 1891.
16. *The Glasgow Institution for Female Orphans and Destitute Girls Report*, 1838, 1.
17. Menzies, T., 'The Royal Incorporation of Hutcheson's Hospital in the City of Glasgow', TNASS, 1874 (London 1875), 473.
18. RCESH, 1875, 151-2.
19. OMFS, AR, 1839, 8.
20. OMFS, AR, 1839, 6.
21. SDS, AR, 1844, 6.
22. SDS, AR, 1867, 30.
23. GBS, AR (Glasgow 1876).
24. I am grateful to Mr. R. J. M. Hart of McOmish Hart for the use of these records.
25. *The North Parish Washing Green Society*, n.d., 5.
26. Adams, A. M., 1835, 206.
27. O'Reilly, J. B.. *In Bohemia* (Boston 1888).
28. Anon., *The Lintie o'Moray* (Forres 1851).
29. *The Glasgow Highland Society* (Glasgow 1861), 7.

PART II

The Philanthropy of Piety

2

Piety as a Programme

1. Clergy and churchmen as philanthropists

THE Scotland of Victoria's reign saw a remarkable phenomenon, namely the attempt by the Church of Scotland and the other churches in Scotland to stay the tide of secularism and to recall the nation to God and to his worship. In this the philanthropists (both clerical and lay) were the driving force. By an extraordinary range of initiatives they sought to resist the incipient secularism of the industrial age and to create, perhaps in a somewhat renovated form, a life in which the Christian religion was the principal part. But in so doing they found themselves, in their efforts to attract and retain support, moving in the direction of a mixture of entertainment and welfare. With their Church Extension Movement, Bible Societies, Sabbath Defence, Sunday Schools, the Young Men's Christian Association, the Boys' Brigade and the Church of Scotland's own welfare programme, churchmen exerted themselves mightily, and with some degree of success, both in religious and in welfare terms.[1]

For this reason the clergyman is reasonably regarded as a philanthropist when he makes a serious commitment to the betterment of his fellow men over and above the daily and weekly duties of his charge, and when he embraces causes at a communal or local level. The case for the lay churchman as philanthropist is even clearer. He goes far beyond what his duty as a member of a congregation would require, both in the promotion of piety and in supporting general welfare.

2. Evangelical philanthropy

Piety was the great prop and stay of Scottish Victorian philanthropy. It drew its strength from the evangelical movement, especially in the first half of the nineteenth century. It is necessary therefore to glance back into the religious history of Scotland, for it is there that the roots of the Victorian system of social values lay. The pietistic urge must be seen as a whole, a profound continuum whereby the inheritance of the Scottish Reformation could pervade Victorian life, in the first phase largely to dominate it, and from the 1870's to be increasingly brought under challenge.

The Presbyterian church in Scotland was originally established in 1560 by the inspiration of John Knox. It was based on a Calvinist philosophy which concerned itself with all aspects of the life of the people, whether spiritual or temporal. It was a church organised by presbyteries, giving power and authority to men of substance which in turn reinforced their success within the community. Calvinism was ethically well suited to Scotland where there was little wealth available and most people had to be satisfied with a modest portion. Austerity was the essence of Scottish Calvinism, for while 'the Middle Ages had insisted upon an asceticism away from the world; Calvin introduced an asceticism in the midst of the world'.[2]

This harsh doctrine, applied in a country as economically backward as Scotland, produced a remarkable people. Almost everyone lived parsimoniously. The doctrine of pre-destination repudiated with theocratic authority any attempts to make the lives of the poor, or anyone else, easier. As it was believed that man's eventual fate after death was pre-ordained by God, it was useless to make life comfortable on earth; indeed to seek to do so directly negated God's will. But it was a duty to care for men's souls.

The Scottish churches produced their evangelicals who, shocked by the loss of souls in the urban industrial slums, sought to bring working people to the 'great Christian doctrine of sin, grace and redemption'.[3] Their campaigns were aimed at raising the moral tone of the workers. Evangelical teaching urged patience and humility; for in this way men and women could confront their problems more successfully, or at least bear them without moral collapse.

But even this evangelical interpretation did little to soften the Calvinist orthodoxy of the time, for almost all church ministers believed that all evil and injustice (caused by the wickedness of man) was a positive expression of God's will. This rigid determinism prevented any fundamental challenge in the attitudes of the church to deteriorating social conditions, indeed it enjoined passive acceptance. At no time did any group of churchmen in Scotland challenge the existing basis of the social order, that graded hierarchical pyramid with power and privileges at the top. The social attitude taken by the church and its churchmen was basically ameliorative; it never suggested a fundamental change in the *status quo*.

By Victorian times charitable work organised by the church was of two main types. In the first place church congregations were marshalled to undertake benevolent work. Much of this activity centred on collecting money from members, a status-conscious activity which encouraged generous donations. The paraphernalia of collecting subscriptions, with its visiting and social display at soirées and the like, constituted a self-rewarding element in life for many church-goers. In a different category came the work of church-goers directly related to the labouring classes. Benevolent activity included schemes aimed at making the church more attractive to those already committed to church attendance and membership. Much of such effort became increasingly difficult. Missionaries who carried promises of heavenly salvation to semi-starving slum dwellers became more and more dispirited as the responses elicited became increasingly apathetic and eventually hostile.

The second form of charitable work produced schemes for the Christianisation of the working population, the 'unchurched masses'. There were missions of all kinds, Bible and Tract Societies with staff like the Bible Women and the Colporteurs to convert men and women to the faith. Then there were medical missions which combined prayer with healing; these reflected the activities of evangelical doctors and their ancillaries who offered free medical treatment as an incentive to get people to attend prayer meetings in the dispensaries. Some of these religious charities were of a hybrid nature, combining assistance to those who were already church members (or who were at least responsive to organised religion), and those outside the churches.

Pietistic charities enabled church congregations to organise various fund-raising schemes, as well as to marshal missioners and Sunday School teachers to go and teach the poor. The churches thus attempted to reach those large numbers who had no church allegiance or, as Chalmers graphically put it, busied themselves 'excavating the heathen'.

There were hundreds, indeed thousands, of such small missionary efforts based on church congregations. Sums of money, great in aggregate, were subscribed over long periods. Such efforts may have been misguided, but many people felt they were making a real contribution to the social improvement of their fellow men by giving generously to church funds for missions conducted with so much devotion.

3. The Church Extension Movement

The Church Extension Movement of the 1830's was an attempt to re-establish the Church of Scotland in urbanised Scotland. The government firmly declined to assist the established church by providing further money for a church building programme. Its only hope lay in the philanthropists among its members. The response was impressive: a notable range of evangelical philanthropists answered the call of their church.

Their activism reflected the success in 1834 of the evangelicals in gaining control of the General Assembly of the Church of Scotland. Leaders like Thomas Chalmers, Thomas Guthrie and Robert Candlish were determined to challenge the passivity of the Moderates in the face of the increasing problems of the ever-growing industrial cities. They believed that the industrial masses were in all senses deprived, but it was spiritual destitution rather than physical poverty which so stirred them. The siting of churches reflected out of date patterns of population distribution, for there were few in newly built up areas. The machinery for creating new churches was cumbersome and time-consuming; even the opening of a chapel of ease was a major undertaking. The members of the newly dominant evangelical arm of the Church of

Scotland resolved to apply themselves to the problem. They planned to build churches all over Scotland where they were most needed. They made a sustained appeal to church congregations for large funds to be voluntarily subscribed.

Those involved in extending church accommodation were not only concerned with the task of persuading 'the men of handicraft and hard labour' (as Chalmers designated them) to rent seats in their churches from the proceeds of which ministers were paid; they were also anxious to re-establish the church's influence at the centre of family life. But those sensitive to the church's position knew that the 'pastoral superintendence' of earlier times no longer existed.

The struggle to bring the church to the town labourer was fundamental. It was basically concerned with the churches' role in controlling education, as well as in providing the number of seats in churches necessary to serve the masses. Parish schools had traditionally been in clerical hands. It was in large measure the hope of recovery of the power this gave which inspired those who involved themselves in the Church Extension movement, launched in the mid 1830's. The first small state grant was given in 1833; it made the re-instatement of the church in the centre of the educational scheme imperative. As Chalmers pleaded, 'We solicit the aid of Government to carry a scheme into effect for the Christian education of now unprovided thousands.'[4]

The two great exemplars of the early Church Extension movement were Thomas Chalmers (1780-1847) and William Collins I (1789-1853). They had had a very close relationship since Chalmers' first essay into urban industrial problems with the St. John's Parish experiment in Glasgow between 1819 and 1822. Collins was a devoted disciple from that time. He was well established as a printer and publisher, handling all of Chalmers' voluminous output.

Chalmers became convener of the Church of Scotland's committee on Church Extension in 1834; he boldly involved himself, showing his usual enthusiasm by writing and speaking.[5] The Association for Promoting the Interests of the Church of Scotland was founded in 1832; its object was to provide more churches in newly populous areas of Scottish towns. In Glasgow Collins became secretary of the Glasgow Church Building Society, and started to organise a massive campaign to build twenty new churches in the city. The story is that he was sitting by the side of his dying daughter Elizabeth explaining to her the problems of the unchurched masses. Her response, 'Can nothing be done?' encouraged her sorrowing father to pledge his resources and his organising ability to the cause.[6]

Collins and Chalmers believed that charitable effort from already existing congregations could be marshalled to pay for the new churches. It was hoped that the government would then make a substantial contribution. Chalmers made this dual approach quite clear: 'by our scheme of Church Extension, the work is partitioned between church or country, and the Government — the former party providing the fabric; the latter solicited, and we hope at length prevailed upon, to grant an endowment for the maintenance of the clergy-man.'[7] The pressure put upon the government for this purpose was not new. In 1824 it had been persuaded to vote £100,000 to erect and endow new churches, the provision being especially ear-marked for new expansion in urban areas. The agitation for further action was very great in the mid 1830's. On 9 May 1836 the government, harassed but unwilling to concede, agreed to set up a Royal Commission.[8] The reports of this Commission[9] were often known as 'of the Commissioners of Religious Instruction in Scotland'.

There was a flurry of activity to provide evidence for the Commissioners.[10] The Church of Scotland relied on its spokesmen, William Collins and Thomas Chalmers. They were not disappointed. Collins, as publisher and publicist, was never more important than at this time. He wrote briefly under the title of the *Church of Scotland the Poor Man's Church*, arguing that the establishment was deeply concerned at the plight of the uneducated impoverished workman who could not afford a church seat. In addition, as secretary of the Glasgow Church Building Society, Collins prepared another long pamphlet originally for submission to the Royal Commissioners but subsequently published. He set out the aims of the Society in terms to appeal to the public and (it was hoped) the Commissioners. They were:

—that churches shall be erected in the poorest and most destitute districts of the city and suburbs

—that no church shall contain more than 1,000 sittings

—that 300 sittings in each church shall be let at a rent not exceeding 2s. annually

—and that 200 more at a rent not exceeding 4s. annually

—that in letting the seats a preference shall always be given to parishioners

—and they record it as their earnest desire, that in poor districts the parish shall not contain more than 2,500 souls.[11]

Collins also provided the drive behind the enormous collecting agency which persuaded church-goers to subscribe generously to the church-building funds. He ceaselessly negotiated for sites, examined plans, instructed builders, and supervised the work from start to finish. Thus Collins became the stone and mortar man of the movement; his dedication ensured that 'by 1841 the last of the twenty churches had pierced the city's smoky skies, and all stood in their allotted space.'[12]

Chalmers also gave a great deal of his time to this work. As convener of the Church of Scotland Committee he rose nobly to the challenge. His message was clear and simple: 'What we aim at is not accommodation only but cheap accommodation — so cheap as to congregate the lower orders in the House of God, not by individuals only but to congregate them in families, that the men of handicraft and hard labour . . . may be enabled to possess themselves of whole pews, both for themselves and their children.'[13]

Chalmers estimated in 1837 that 40,000 individuals in Edinburgh were without church facilities and that while 9 churches had already been built, there were still as many as 30 churchless congregations in the capital. Things were even worse in Glasgow where his calculations revealed 60,000 with no place of worship. 'With the population increasing at the fearful rate of 8,000 a year', Glasgow needed 50 churches to supply its immediate needs. As far as the members of the congregations of the Church of Scotland were concerned, Chalmers' words did not fall upon deaf ears. Large sums were collected and quickly disbursed to the church building programme, thus:

Table 4

Church Extension programme in Scotland, 1835-1839

Year	Churches built	Cost
1835	62	£65,626 1 11¾
1836	26	32,359 12 5¾
1837	67	59,311 6 0
1838	32	48,683 1 4¾
1839	14	25,959 14 9¾
	201	£231,939 16 8

Source: Chalmers, T., *Works*, Vol. XVIII, On Church Extension (Glasgow n.d.), XXVII.

In his pamphlet prepared for the Royal Commissioners, William Collins gave figures for church seats available before the Glasgow Campaign for Church Extension of

Seats in Church of Scotland Churches in Glasgow	34,524
Seats in 'other churches that hold the principle of an establishment'	9,917
Seats in Dissenting Churches	34,965[14]

This calculation inevitably drew fire from the Dissenters, who viewed Collins' campaign with a jaundiced eye. They challenged the position of the Church of Scotland as the established church. They resolved that the grievances of Dissenters could only be redressed by 'an immediate total and eternal separation of Church and State'. In short, they opposed the whole Church Extension campaign as a plot of the establishment. Their organisers quickly rallied: the Voluntary Church Association was re-organised in 1834 and renamed the Scottish Central Board of Dissenters. Courses of lectures and sermons were arranged and given to crowded audiences and congregations. Their arguments were powerful, based as they were on criticism of the Church of Scotland for claiming for itself further endowment and thereby demanding further special privileges for the established church. By trying to foist a legal commitment on the state to provide for a new batch of ministerial stipends, the Church of Scotland was especially vulnerable to the charge of inconsistency, for it had always insisted on the benefits of the voluntary principle in all dealings with the poor. Rev. Alex. Harvey made much of this point: 'It is curious to witness the confidence which some churchmen repose in voluntary contribution for the supply of the temporal wants of the poor, and to contrast it with their want

D

of faith in its efficiency for their external interests. They can deplore the evils of a "compulsory pauperism" while they are perfectly fascinated with the spectacle of a compulsory Christianity.'[15] Various ministers of dissenting churches in their evidence to the Commissioners challenged arguments breezily introduced by Chalmers. He liked to suggest that there was not much difference between several of the dissenting groups and the established church. Rev. Dr. John Ritchie commented tartly, 'There is all the difference in the world between us. We believe that there should be no State Church.'[16]

The Church Extension movement was inextricably involved with the agitation in Edinburgh against the Annuity Tax.[17] The salaries of the Edinburgh clergy of the Church of Scotland were paid from 'a personal tax of 6% levied on the occupiers of houses and warehouses'. The tax had first been imposed during the reign of Charles I. It caused particular offence because there were large numbers of exemptions, enabling, for example, the whole of the legal profession to avoid payment. In 1809, under guise of a Bill to extend the boundaries of the Royalty of Edinburgh, 'a smuggled clause' had been included, increasing the numbers of ministers whose salaries were paid by the tax from 6 to 18. The obligation of Dissenters to pay for salaries for the established clergy angered many and added fuel to the opposition to the Church Extension movement. But the tax continued, being finally commuted only in 1870.

The Dissenters in their opposition to the Church Extension scheme made considerable impact on public opinion. Objective witnesses told the Commissioners that almost all churches in the industrial towns had numbers of empty seats, which the working classes did not take up. Chalmers appeared before them and provided them with more and more material; but they found his arguments unconvincing when he wrote: 'The cause of endowments, rightly understood, is essentially popular. The common conception of them is not the true one. Their proper and original object is not to aggrandize the clergyman, but to cheapen the Christian education of the people . . . Ministers are the fishers of men; and the effect of an endowment is to lengthen their line, and enable them to reach downwards to the lowest graduations of the commonwealth.'[18]

When the Commissioners reported, it was clear that they had rejected the call of the Church of Scotland for financial aid. They judged that opinion in general in the country was against it. Although they agreed that 'the opportunities for public religious worship and the means of religious instruction and pastoral superintendence at present existing and in operation are inadequate', they would only recommend to the government that money might be made available for further church building only in rural areas. A Bill was introduced to this limited end, but was subsequently withdrawn. Such a solution was not acceptable to the church or churchmen. The Commissioners were undoubtedly right in refusing government financial aid in the cities to a single denomination. Church Extension was not a popular cause, although once the churches were built (with subscribed money), congregations were not hard to find. The Church of Scotland was a church among churches rather than the accepted church of the whole of Scotland. The Church Extension movement represented the last attempt of the established Church of Scotland to re-state its authority over all the people.

The year 1843 was fast approaching: it was to bring the greatest disruption of the Church in Scotland. Chalmers himself and many others of evangelical persuasion then left to found the Free Church. Ironically Chalmers, the first Moderator of the Free Church, took upon himself the immense task of duplicating for the Free Church a provision of churches equal to its needs. The last four years of his life were devoted to raising money for the Free Church Sustentation Fund and the Manse Fund.

It was not only the established church which recognised that it was failing to reach the people. The Reformed Presbyterian Church, among others, embarked upon a similar, albeit more modest programme, supported by members like Thomas Binnie, who had established himself as a building contractor in Glasgow during the 1830's. He not only undertook the work of erecting new churches, but also helped to finance the poorer congregations. As his son explained, 'He in this way assisted in the erection of chapels in Ayr, Greenock, Rothesay, Darvel, Airdrie, Dundee, Glasgow, Girvan, Lochgilphead and Laurieston . . . he lent to various congregations between two and three thousand pounds . . .'[19]

The dismissal by the Commissioners of the campaign of the Church of Scotland for Church Extension was not the end of the matter. For though after the Disruption there was great danger that defeatism and apathy would prevent any further moves, there were still powerful activists. The Rev. James Robertson left his parish at Ellon in 1844 to move to the Chair of Ecclesiastical History at Edinburgh. The appointment was perhaps a curious one, as Robertson was no scholar, but he did have a mission. He was devoted to the cause of Church Extension, and by his enthusiasm he did much from the elevation of his chair to arouse the Church of Scotland from that torpor which it threatened to sink into following the catastrophe of 1843. Between 1846 and his death in 1860 he succeeded against all the odds in raising almost £400,000 and in adding 60 *quoad sacra*[20] parishes to the church, making him perhaps the greatest philanthropic money raiser in Scotland.

The Church Extension movement was furthered in the latter years of Victoria's reign by another form of missionary extension work. Wealthy congregations could establish missions in poor areas and there set up modest chapels. If the work was successful a proper church could be built. For example, in Glasgow the Rev. David Watson entered on a charge at just such a church. St. Clements, 'an excellent example of Church Extension',[21] was begun as a mission in 1872. The inspiration and money for the mission came from Sandyford Church encouraged by its minister, Dr. Elder Cumming. A small mission chapel was built in Sister Street. There, in addition to the missionary,

Sandyford provided a part-time missionary and a Bible Woman. By 1886 St. Clements was sufficiently well established to attract David Watson, an energetic and thoughtful new minister, and in March 1888 the parish was officially designated a *quoad sacra* parish. David Watson was drawn to the place because of its social problems; under his guidance much welfare work was done. St. Clements was particularly proud of its crèche, organised to accommodate infants while their mothers worked in the mills of Glasgow. A great many other initiatives were taken, including District Social Meetings, a Band of Hope, a Boys' Brigade, a Men's Social Institute, a Women's Guild, a Girls' Club and a Mothers' Meeting.

The Church Extension movement attracted an enormous amount of philanthropic money. Considerable numbers of churches were established and large congregations were built up by sincere and hard-working ministers. The movement offered a programme for protestant church congregations, especially where new communities were being built up. At the present time the churches built with such pride as 'extensions' by Victorian congregations on inner-city sites are being sold at greatly enhanced values and the proceeds used to build new churches in suburban or New Town Scotland.

But for all the argument and effort, the masses remained unchurched, intent on daily survival. To the poor working man and his family questions of seat rents, pew places and Church Extension remained unreal. Verses were penned in Edinburgh in the 1830's which put the anti-church case:

The Poor Christian and the Church[22]

'How glorious Zion's courts appear,'
The pious poor man cries:
'Stand back, you knave, you're in arrears,'
The manager replies.

Poor Christian
'The genius of the Christian code
Is charity, humility;'

Manager (in a rage)
'I've let your pew to ladies, Sir,
Of high respectability.'

Poor Christian
'And am I then debarred the house
Where erst my father pray'd?
Excluded from the hallowed fane
Where my loved mother's laid?'

Manager
'Their seat-rent, Sir, was never due;
The matter to enhance,
As duly as the term came round,
They paid it in advance.'

Poor Christian
'The temple of the living God
Should have an open door,
And Christ's ambassadors should preach
The Gospel to the poor.'

Manager
'We cannot, Sir, accommodate
The poor in their devotions;
Besides we cordially detest
Such antiquated notions.

'We build our fanes, we deck our pews
For men of wealth and station;
(Yet for a time the thing has proved
A losing speculation).

'Then table down your cash anon
Ere you come here to pray;
Else you may wander where you will,
And worship where you may.'

Poor Christian
'Then I shall worship in that fane
By God to mankind given;
Whose lamps are the meridian sun,
And all the stars of heaven;

'Whose walls are the cerulean sky,
Whose floor the earth so fair,
Whose dome is vast immensity:—
All nature worships there.'

The success of the Church Extension campaigns is difficult to assess. Large sums of money were raised and quickly applied to stone and mortar. The churches thus built ensured that everyone lived within a short distance of a place of worship. They attracted considerable numbers of skilled workers. In some cases from these men and their families new congregations were created which included a fair social mix. But by and large Church Extension failed to attract the unskilled and the very poor, leaving the Church of Scotland largely composed of the middle classes and the respectable artisans.

4. Bible and Tract Societies

But there was another and more general attempt to bring about the Christian salvation of the people. It lay not through institutional religion, but through the dissemination of the divinely inspired word of the Bible. Even where men and their families failed to attend church (much less rent pews), declined to listen to sermons or to join in collective prayer, it was hoped that the Bible, especially the New Testament which spoke for Christ, would in the privacy of the home effect the spiritual redemption that was so earnestly desired by the evangelicals. Perhaps it was recognised by the evangelicals, albeit subconsciously, that the new industrial masses could hardly fail to be suspicious of a Christianity that spoke with so many voices; accordingly they organised their Bible distribution campaign interdenominationally, thus seeking to suggest the underlying unity of the churches.

Bible and Tract Societies were the organisations of dissemination. They were primarily money-collecting agencies run by church congregations in order to supply religious books to the poor, either free or at subsidised prices. They remained important throughout the nineteenth century. The saintly messages of cloying piety which dominated tract writing became less popular toward the end of the century, but even when the tract market had contracted, the demand for Bibles remained strong.

The British and Foreign Bible Society was founded on 7 March 1804. It was an essential part of the evangelical awakening of the early nineteenth century, reflecting the concern of men and women who wished to extend to others less well off than themselves the benefits of Bible study. It advocated education for the sole purpose of teaching men and women, boys and girls to read in order to make the Holy Scriptures directly accessible.

David Dale of Glasgow is credited with establishing the first Bible Society in Scotland, when in July 1805, 'delighted with the grandeur and simplicity of the idea', he called a public meeting in the city and founded the first Auxiliary Society to the British and Foreign Bible Society in London. Dale died within a year, and his early initiative failed. But later, when the Glasgow Bible Society was resuscitated in 1811, it claimed Dale as its founder. The Auxiliary Society in Edinburgh was set up in 1809, as were the Scottish Bible Society and the East Lothian Bible Society. In the succeeding decade nearly 50 other Auxiliaries were started. Between them they had by 1817 contributed a total of over £35,000, all of which was transmitted to London. Although all these Scottish Societies were 'Auxiliaries', several of them claimed 'freedom of action and the right of independent initiative'.[23] The Society in Edinburgh was particularly explicit: its objects were to be the same as those of the British and Foreign Bible Society, but it determined to 'act in concert with it, or separately, as circumstances shall require'. In Greenock, Port Glasgow and West Lothian similar rights were preserved, so that these Societies were 'Auxiliaries' only when head office policy continued to please them.

Moreover, both the Glasgow and Edinburgh Societies quickly established themselves as regional centres for Bible Society purposes. By 1816 there were 31 Branches and Associations linked to the Glasgow Society, and at the same date Edinburgh had 22 Associations and 40 Auxiliaries. In the decade between 1816 and 1826 the number of Auxiliaries and Associations continued to increase. But by the mid-1820's the co-operation between Scottish and English Societies was seriously threatened.

The progress of the Bible Society movement was sorely affected by the Apocrypha controversy in the 1820's. It generated a quarrel of impressive dimensions which threatened all the Bible Societies in England and Scotland. The dispute centred on the propriety of circulating Bibles with the books of the

Apocrypha bound in with them. The holy books of the Apocrypha represented additional knowledge, and it seemed to many, especially on the continent, that it was better to bind these books in with the Bibles circulated all over the world. To the Scots this proposal was rank heresy and as such was bitterly opposed. An enormous pamphlet war took place, as a result of which the whole Bible Society world was severely shaken. The Scots could not accept that anything but the Bible, which was, they believed, a text directly inspired by God, should be circulated.

After much bitter argument the Scottish Bible Society seceded from the British and Foreign Bible Society; from 1826-7 the Edinburgh Society became the head of the Scottish Bible Society movement. Most local Societies were not in fact Auxiliaries of Edinburgh and had direct control over their own funds, although usually they continued to send them to Edinburgh. There followed a remarkable growth in women's Auxiliaries. These were in effect collecting societies based on church congregations, giving a focus to much female endeavour.

The setting up of the Free Church of Scotland in 1843 did no damage to the Bible Societies, for their appeal to both denominations was great, receiving support from all evangelical elements of the protestant church in Scotland.

Glasgow, with its increasing following of Auxiliary Societies, became a rival focus for the movement, but the National Bible Society of Scotland was founded in 1861 to co-ordinate all activities.

Bible Societies prided themselves on their efficiency in circulating great quantities of Bibles. Every respectable family had its Bible, in which births and deaths were carefully entered. Each member of the family had his or her own copy, bought for him or her as a child by parents or god-parents. Most of these would be bought at regular shop prices. But in addition there were many thousands of Bibles bought at the rate of 1d. a week through the good offices of the Societies' missioners, or colporteurs, many of which were provided at subsidised prices.

It is extremely difficult to know how far such Bible Society missionary ministrations reached. In any event there were Bibles in almost every Scottish home excepting the very poorest. In later Victorian times, as workers' incomes rose, the element of subsidy became more important for heathens overseas rather than at home.

5. Religious Institution Rooms

Many Scottish Victorian cities had a building, often large and impressive, in which the pietistic societies came together. It was used for offices and to provide rooms for meetings, as well as a base for the Bible and Tract Societies where they maintained their stocks of publications. Much later the lantern and lantern slides used in lecturing were also housed here. Both Edinburgh and

Glasgow set up such centres in the early nineteenth century, known as Religious Institution Rooms or Philanthropic Institutes.

Glasgow took the most striking initiative. Its Religious and Charitable Institution House was established in 1821. David Nasmyth (1799-1839) was appointed secretary at the Institution Rooms (59 Glassford Street) in October of that year at an initial salary of £60 per annum. This was provided by some of the Societies then occupying the rooms (at £2 12s. 6d. each).[24] Nasmyth nominally acted as secretary to many committees, all of which were based in the Institution Rooms. It is difficult to see how he could have done justice to them all, viz:

Table 5

Societies based on the Religious and Charitable Institution House, Glasgow

1. The Glasgow Auxiliary Religious Tract and Book Society for Ireland
2. The Glasgow Auxiliary Scotch Missionary Society
3. The Glasgow Bible Society
4. The Glasgow Auxiliary Bible Society
5. The Nile Street and George Street Chapels Sabbath School Society
6. The Glasgow Missionary Society
7. The Glasgow Auxiliary Moravian Society
8. The Glasgow Society for Promoting Christianity among the Jews
9. The Glasgow Auxiliary Hibernian Society
10. The Glasgow Seamen's Friend Society
11. The Glasgow Continental Society
12. The Glasgow Auxiliary Baptist Society
13. The Glasgow Auxiliary London Missionary Society
14. The Glasgow Auxiliary Irish Evangelical Society
15. The Glasgow Religious Tract Society
16. The Glasgow Naval and Military Bible Society
17. The Glasgow Young Men's Auxiliary Society for the support of Gaelic Schools
18. The Glasgow Auxiliary to the Irish Society for Native Schools
19. The Glasgow and West of Scotland Temperance Society
20. The Glasgow (established church) Society for Promoting the Religious Interests of Settlers in British America
21. The Glasgow Auxiliary to the British Society for Promoting the Religious Principles of the Reformation
22. The Glasgow Auxiliary Gaelic School Society
23. The Glasgow City Mission (for Bibles, Tracts, and Testaments, and for Education of Adults and Poor Children)
24. The Glasgow Infant School Society
25. Committee for Promoting the Better Observance of the Sabbath
26. The Glasgow Society for Benevolent Visitation of the Destitute Sick, and others in extreme poverty.

Source: Cleland, J., *Enumeration of the Inhabitants of Glasgow* (Glasgow 1823).

Later, in 1877, the great Christian Institute in Bothwell Street, Glasgow was opened and took under its wing a large number of religious bodies. It became the centre of the religious and cultural life of many people in the city.

Rooms and Institutions of the kind formed in Glasgow represented a conscious concentration of effort by philanthropic societies, coming together in order to reduce their operating costs and to promote mutual reinforcement, rather as retailers were doing as they formed shopping concentrations in suitable streets. Common facilities were provided, as with reading rooms where periodicals were available, together with annual reports, religious communications, and news of charitable societies both at home and abroad. By such means a city clearing house for pietistic effort could be constituted.

6. Organisations to preserve the Sabbath

Much zeal, as well as philanthropic money, went into the movement to protect the Sabbath, with the organisation as early as the 1830's of Committees for Promoting the Better Observance of the Sabbath, and the like. Those who supported the movement in Victorian Scotland were anxious, as they put it, to 'stem the tide of irreligion' as it affected personal and family behaviour. The movement was perhaps a rearguard action taken by those who regretted the weakening of church authority and clerical discipline. The argument of the protagonists rested on the 'fourth commandment of the moral law contained in the Decalogue', which was regarded as 'a perpetual moral obligation'. The Commandment was explicit and beyond argument: 'Remember the Sabbath day, to keep it holy. Six days shalt thou labour and do all thy work, but the seventh is the Sabbath of the Lord thy God . . .'[25]

Those who wished to preserve the Sabbath inviolate, confining it to church-going, prayer and meditation, quoted the authority of Luther, Calvin and Beza. They reinforced theological arguments with Biblical quotations. Those who opposed this view with its insistence on church attendance and rigorous Bible-reading claimed that the Sabbath was a Jewish holiday wrongly applied to Christian communities and that healthful out-door pursuits were permissible once church service had been attended. A degree of anti-Semitism manifested itself among those who attacked the Sabbatarian idea.

The Sabbath protection movement coincided with the acceleration of industrialisation. But although it sought to preserve the principle that 'every man is entitled to the rest of the Sabbath', there is scant evidence to suggest that this was connected with movements to achieve a shorter working week. Campaigns to protect the Sabbath were philanthropically financed, but they also received much support from working men. The Working Man's Sabbath Protection Association in the 1850's, with strong Free Church affiliations, agitated with great determination. It promoted many meetings, pamphlet distributions, and other publicity campaigns.

Seamen and their masters, and owners of ships were much involved in the movement. By 1834 there was in Scotland a Society on Sunday Sailing which was sufficiently strong to persuade Sir Andrew Agnew to introduce a Bill to parliament to prevent by law the departure of ships on Sunday. The Greenock Seamen's Friend Society was jubilant that such action should be taken, and circulated all the Seamen's Societies in the United Kingdom to urge support.[26] But Agnew's Bill failed. The Glasgow ship-owner George Burns resisted Sunday sailing by his steam passenger ships plying between Glasgow and Liverpool. In 1829 Burns' Liverpool partner sarcastically suggested that if he was so sensitive about their ships sailing on Sundays he should provide chaplains to sail on them. This Burns henceforth did. Captain Hepburn, in command of the second Burns vessel with a chaplain on board, was jeered by the people on the Broomielaw as he sailed away, the local wits bantering him on 'sailing in a steam chapel'.[27] Between 1829 and 1843, when the Disruption 'made such a draft upon licentiates that operations had to be suspended', chaplains sailed on Burns Line ships. The Seamen's Societies in the 1830's had a clear understanding that the 'Sabbath bestows on the poor man that rest which, both physically and morally, is indispensable to his temporal welfare, while its importance is past reckoning, religiously considered.'[28]

With the railway building boom of the 1840's there was strong pressure to run trains on Sunday, which was becoming more of a day of leisure than a holy day. Excursion trains were popular and profitable. How were railway boards to respond to the campaigns appealing to them not to run trains on Sundays when there was such a steady demand?

In 1865 the Presbytery of Glasgow took a firm stand on the Sabbatarian side. It prepared a pastoral letter maintaining the churches' position on Sabbath observance, which was to be read in all the churches under its care. But Dr. Norman MacLeod (1812-1872)[29] was directly opposed to the view expressed in the letter; he vigorously addressed the Presbytery to express his disagreement. His violent attack on the traditional Scottish Sabbath, or at least on its traditional basis in the Fourth Commandment, very nearly caused him to be charged with heresy.[30] MacLeod maintained that in place of rigid Sabbath Observance should be substituted a Christian Lord's day. On Sundays church attendance should take up part of the day, but healthful outdoor walking with the family and other innocent occupations should also be part of the day's activities. It was the workman's Sunday, taken as a day of rest and relaxation, that he was anxious to elevate into a day set apart. He pointed out that on Sundays 'Our servants do servile work, light fires, make beds, clean out our rooms, cook our dinners and probably drive those to church who have carriages.'[31] The inconsistency of many middle-class Sabbatarians seemed to him too much.

MacLeod's 'Lord's Day' speech made a tremendous impact, coming from a man so distinguished in church affairs. A pamphlet war ensued. Most of the writers deplored the proposed liberalising of Sabbath observance. A few voices were raised in MacLeod's defence, urging that 'The Sabbath was made for man, not against him, and from this it follows that it is not to be regarded as a burden, but accepted as a boon.'[32]

Although MacLeod had many opponents within church circles, nonchurchmen throughout Scotland warmly applauded his courage. A long and

vigorous rhyme, in twenty-four verses, in the style of a traditional ballad, was
published in 1866 extolling Norman MacLeod's vision of a Lord's Day for the
working classes:

Norman's blast[33]

What stour is this that stirs the Wast,
And scours the kintra far and fast,
That's set the auld Kirk folks aghast,
The Free Kirk stormin'?
Norman MacLeod has blawn his blast!
Brave, honest Norman!

Your fair 'Good Words' had cleared the way
To rid us o' the Sabbath Day,
Besides commandments twa or three mae
I needna name
I fear this haste may spoil the play
And lose our game

But troth, he's little cause to fear
Wha's hand and glove wi' the premier
And at the Palace mony a year
Has winged and bowed—
The Queen's ain chaplain! wha daur steer
Norman MacLeod?

All praises to Tulloch and to Lee[34]
But, Norman, you're the lad for me
You've ta'en the start o' a' the three
You've beat them hollow
From 'Jews old clothes' you've set us free
The rest will follow

So, Doctor Norman, fare you weel
Gang on your gate, you pawky chiel',
Head not McTaggart's whine and squeal
Dr. Charteris' weepin'
But, speak the truth, and shame the Deil,
And — keep your stipen'

Now all fast lads and lasses free,
Who love a lark and Sunday's spree
Let's drink to him who bears the gree
Amang the crowd;
Fill up a bumper — three times three—
Norman MacLeod!!!

The urge to replace the old-fashioned Sabbath with its gloom and repression
was part of a movement to liberalise the Church of Scotland. But much time
and energy were given to resisting a change which came in the end to be irresis-
tible. The Glasgow Presbytery later recognised the need for the trams to run
on Sunday, thus indicating an acceptance of new thoughts and new ideas.

7. Sunday Schools

Nowhere can the evangelical urge to bring salvation be seen more clearly than in the Sunday School movement. It was a major manifestation of active evangelism, and one of its widest and most sustained. Bringing working class children out of their homes, even temporarily into the Sunday School, exposed them to values and influences foreign to them and their families. The Sunday Schools carried the evangelicals' greatest hopes, for that movement was concerned with the young, the responsive and the malleable. Starting from them, a Godless society could be redeemed.

It has been argued by E. P. Thompson that the Sunday School was the organisation which confirmed for the working class child his place in the order of things, in a society which required primarily a disciplined work-force. 'Once within the school gates,' Thompson writes, 'the child entered the new universe of disciplined time.'[35] No doubt the Sunday School taught many things convenient for the middle and employing classes. But most Sunday School teachers themselves differed little from their pupils and were perhaps only marginally better educated. The Thompson thesis is too simple; more persuasive is the argument of Walter Laqueur that 'The Sunday School was . . . tightly integrated into the working-class community. When children left the home and entered the very different atmosphere of the school they came into contact with the most literate of their class and imbibed the values of artisan respectability taught there. Though the potential for intergenerational change was great, it was not of a kind generally repugnant to working class parents.'[36]

Before compulsory education for all in Scotland was made possible by the Education Act of 1872, the Sunday Schools were the only educational facility available to all the children of working families. Their strength rested on their ubiquity, for Sunday Schools were everywhere, and on the involvement of elements of the working classes, sometimes only marginally better off than those they sought to help. This immense effort was provided by men and women who wished to serve. Perhaps this was the great attraction of the Sunday School movement, for it gave to the layman a recognisable role and function both in the churches and in society generally.

In Scotland as elsewhere the Sunday School movement was spontaneous; individual examples appeared in various places from the 1770's. In one sense the Sunday School was not a new initiative, for the Scottish church had always taken responsibility for the education of the people. The organisation of a more formal 'school' on Sundays reflected the need of the church to ensure that this responsibility was properly carried out. These early Sunday Schools were not necessarily the product of evangelical enthusiasm, for moderate church leaders also took such initiatives.

Some children paid, others attended their Sunday Schools free. Gratis Sunday School schemes involved congregations in bearing the expenses. This was usually willingly done because of the good which was expected to accrue.

In addition some teachers were paid, although in general Sunday School teaching was thought of as a form of voluntary service.

Dr. John Burns[37] (minister of the Barony Church, Glasgow from 1774 to 1839) launched a scheme of Sunday Schools at Calton in the east end of Glasgow in 1775. Sunday Schools in the expanding Scottish cities were a necessary innovation, for the burgh schools were never able to accommodate the growing school population. As momentum was gained, the Society for the Support and Management of Sabbath Schools in Glasgow was founded as early as 1787. It was one of many ephemeral organisations for the co-ordination of Sunday Schools. Perhaps Sunday Schools (and evangelicalism) were suspect during the period of political unrest in the 1820's. The Glasgow Sunday School Union was not established on a permanent basis until 1837.

The Rev. Dr. Thomas Chalmers epitomised that evangelical element of the Church of Scotland which became deeply involved with Sabbath Schools. When he arrived as minister of the Tron Church in Glasgow in 1815, he found little parochial work. He outlined his plans, which involved 'a comprehensive system of Sabbath Evening Schools to counteract in some degree the deplorable ignorance he had discovered among the wynds and allies'.[38] Later he invited a few picked members of his congregation to form themselves into a society for the purpose of establishing such schools in various districts of his parish. On 13 December 1816 the first of these schools was opened with 13 in attendance; within two years 1,200 children were under religious instruction.

Paradoxically the Sunday School movement was much invigorated by the secession of the Free Church of Scotland in 1843. The outburst of energy from the new church, whose officers insisted upon duplicating all the institutions of the old, brought new vigour to Sunday Schools. Dr. Robert Buchanan (1802-1875), minister of Glasgow's Free Tron Church between 1843 and 1857, initiated a new attack. He determined to inculcate Christian faith into the disreputable Old Wynds area in his parish. To this end he organised Sunday Schools with over forty teachers and innumerable other missionary enterprises.

By 1853 the Glasgow Sabbath School Union had 115 Sabbath Schools on its books and claimed a total attendance of 34,000 children taught by 3,300 teachers. In addition, almost half of these Sabbath Schools claimed to organise further day or night schools at which reading and writing were taught. By 1870 the Glasgow Sabbath School Union claimed that there were 187 Sabbath School Societies with 6,692 teachers and 69,022 scholars. All the protestant religious denominations in the city and environs were involved, including the Church of Scotland, the Free Church of Scotland, the United Presbyterian Church, the Reformed Presbyterian Church, the United Original Seceders, the Congregational Church, the Baptists, the Wesleyan Methodists, the Primitive Methodist Church, and the Episcopalian Church.

To deal with such large numbers there were arrangements for training teachers, Scripture lessons were demonstrated, and a journal was issued full of moral homilies, rhyming verses and other teaching devices. An example of the moral lesson can be seen in this little poem:

Waste[39]

> I must not throw upon the ground
>   The crust I cannot eat
> For many little hungry ones
>   Would think it quite a treat
>
> For wilful waste makes woeful want
>   And I may live to say
> Oh, how I wish I had the crust
>   That once I threw away.

Also typical was the alphabet rhyme used to teach Biblical stories to the children:

Moral Alphabet[40]

> A stands for Adam, of mankind the first
> B stands for Balak, who would Israel curse
> C stands for Canaan, the Jews' promis'd rest
> D stands for David, whom God often bless'd
> E stands for Esau, his birth-right he sold
> F stands for Famine, once mighty we're told
> G stands for Gallio, who car'd not for God
> H stands for Herod, who shed infant's blood
> I stands for Israel, good Jacob's new name
> J stands for Joseph, his son of great fame
> K stands for Korah, of Moses' line
> L stands for Laban, whom Jacob did find
> M stands for Moses, he Israel did guide
> N stands for Nebo, the mount where he died
> O stands for Olives, where Christ was oft found
> P stands for Pharao, who in the Red Sea was drown'd
> Q stands for Quails, on which Israel were fed
> R stands for Rachel, who mourned for her dead
> S stands for Samuel, a prophet from youth
> T stands for Thomas, who doubted the truth
> U's for Uriah, who in battle did fall
> V stands for Viper, that fasten'd on Paul
> W's for Wisdom, bestowed on a King
> X stands for Christ, whose praises we'll sing
> Y stands for youngest, the prodigal son
> Z stands for Zimri, and now we have done.

The manner of using these Alphabets is, for a child to stand in the rostrum, having 26 squares of wood, on which are painted the letters of the alphabet, great and small. The child then holding up the square, on which the letters A.a are drawn, calls aloud — 'A stands for Adam, of mankind the first'; which the children, looking at the letters, repeat after him. He then holds up B.b., and so on throughout the whole 26 squares. Thus the children become familiarised with the letters, and at the same time their little minds are stored with Scripture truths; which, under the teaching of the Holy Spirit, may lead them 'to a knowledge of Him, whom to know is life everlasting.'

Sunday School teachers were a voluntary force. But they required training. In Glasgow Dr. Chalmers, with characteristic energy, started organising classes for his Sunday School teachers from 1816. David Nasmyth of the Philanthropic Institute recognised the role of the Young Men's Religious Societies in training teachers for Sunday Schools when he wrote, 'Many of our most *intelligent* sabbath-school teachers have been drawn from Young Men's Associations; in fact they are the training schools for teachers.'[41] A self-reinforcing process was set up whereby the Young Men's Religious Society provided Sunday School teachers who trained youths who in their turn joined the Young Men's Religious Society; thus: 'a youth being admitted to membership in Young Men's Societies . . . presents hope to the sabbath school teacher, who is working with prayerful anxiety upon the advanced boys of his class . . .' The problem of discipline within the Sunday School was not apparent before the 1850's. Education was a scarce commodity, and those who attended Sunday School in the earlier days were in general keen to learn as much as they could. This, of course, made things easier for the teachers.

Sustained efforts went into the improvement of the quality of the work done by Sabbath School teachers. These included lectures on the duty and deportment of a successful teacher, how to achieve a well-ordered school, the method and manner of teaching, the best means of retaining senior scholars, the management of infant classes and the aims of Sabbath School teaching. Model lessons were given and well received. A Glasgow teacher reported: 'I also beg to state that by attending Mr. Muncie's model lessons I have been enabled to teach more efficiently and I have been greatly edified myself. My experience in Sabbath School teaching is not great, this I can say, that unless I pray most earnestly for my class, I never teach successfully. It is of the utmost importance to prepare the lesson most carefully, to speak very plain, so as to make the lesson suit the children's capacities, to secure order in the class, to be firm and kind, to show no partiality, to endeavour to study the children's dispositions, and to set a good example before them.'[42]

But by 1850 there were regular and repeated complaints about the shortage of Sabbath School teachers and the difficulty of recruitment. Efforts at training and attracting teachers were further extended, perhaps in an attempt to lower the pupil/teacher ratio. Schemes of Lessons and Notes for teachers were published, along with the *Sunday School Magazine*, emphasising the need for effective teaching (in the 1850's and 1860's). These reflected the increasing problem which the church and its agents were having in recruiting teachers to cope with restless and unruly young people on Sundays at school meetings. The enormous numbers of children enrolled in Sabbath Schools may have convinced organisers and onlookers alike that the Schools were flourishing, but a closer look at the reports is a reminder of the problem of morale of those working in the Sabbath School movement.

It is very difficult to gauge the success of the Sunday School movement. Children who attended Sunday Schools in their youth did not necessarily become church members in their maturity. But the churches were optimistic about the role of the Sunday School at the mid-century. The General Assembly of the Church of Scotland reported in 1852: 'In admirable keeping with all the parts of our parochial economy, the Sabbath School is the nursery of the church, enabling the minister of the parish, through means of teachers in whom he can replace confidence, to address individually the younger members of his parish, and maintaining that close connection between him and the families over whom he has the spiritual oversight; which cannot fail to strengthen his hands and to advance the cause of righteousness in the vineyard where he labours.'[43]

The churches' hopefulness about the Sunday School movement was not misplaced, at least until 1881. Enrolments for Great Britain doubled in the 30 years after 1851. But in the following 30 years they hardly increased at all, and indeed from 1881 fell as a percentage of population:

Table 6

Sunday School enrolments and density in Great Britain, 1851-1911

Year	No. of Students	Percentage of population in England, Scotland and Wales enrolled in Sunday Schools
1851	2,614,274	13
1881	5,762,038	19
1901	5,952,431	16
1906	6,178,827	16
1911	6,129,496	15

Source: Laqueur, T. W., *Religion and Respectability* (London 1976), 246.

Though membership was static after 1881, and the disciplinary problems were more serious, the Sunday Schools responded to the challenge, widening their scope and undertaking a new range of activities, including outdoor activities, sports, camping and the Boys' Brigade (see section 9 below).

These activities were funded from a variety of sources. The children and young people in the Sunday Schools made some contributions themselves, and parents and others in the various church congregations also worked hard to raise money for all these worthwhile church initiatives.

8. The Young Men's Christian Association

In any period of revival whether social, religious or political, it is likely that young men will meet together to discuss matters of common interest. For this reason the growth of young men's societies during the nineteenth century was not surprising; shop assistants, clerks, apprentices and tradesmen were imbued with a spirit of mutual improvement. Their gathering together in societies for religious and educative purposes was likely therefore to develop simultaneously in several places at about the same time. The founder of the movement in Glasgow was undoubtedly David Nasmyth (1799-1839), a man of much energy and many evangelical distinctions: 'Our young men,' he insisted, 'must be trained for the Lord.'[44] He first made reference to a young men's society in 1823 when he wrote, 'It has been proposed to form an association among the young men, which is likely to take place. I hope to have the pleasure of the company of the whole to breakfast on the morning of New Year's Day . . .'[45] The Glasgow Young Men's Society for Religious Improvement was established in 1824 and Nasmyth's initiative spread widely. Nasmyth claimed (writing on 8 February 1826), 'Since the close of 1823, the privilege has been granted to me, of forming about 70 Young Men's Societies in the United Kingdom, France and America.' He also insisted in the same letter on 'the great importance of their young men combining attention to the soul and eternity with a diligent application to literary pursuits.'[46] These societies reinforced the evangelical leanings of many young men between the ages of 14 and 35, who were 'of good moral character, and professing no opinions subversive of evangelical principles'. Meetings were to be 'for the purposes of mutual improvement and benevolent exertion. The Bible is considered as their rule, and all political discussion is prohibited.'

There was a direct link between Nasmyth's societies and the renamed Glasgow Young Men's Christian Association, founded in Glasgow in 1841, which pre-dated the 'original' YMCA established by George Williams in London on 8 June 1844.[47] Its objects were 'to afford facilities for the Intellectual, Moral and Religious Improvement of the Young Men of Glasgow'. Within the Association in 1861 there were fourteen Congregational Young Men's Mutual Improvement Societies, representing three parish churches of the Established Church, five Free Churches and five United Presbyterian Churches. Thus the Association was firmly rooted in interdenominationalism.

At first Bible Classes and prayer meetings were the basic fare, but associations soon discovered that a more varied intellectual diet was necessary and that their success depended on the diversity of their appeal. Young men (dissatisfied with the traditional Sunday School) were stimulated by more challenging YMCA lecture programmes. Moreover the active young Christian member was more useful to the Sunday School for, with his newly acquired education, he could better attract and maintain the interest of his Sunday School class.

The YMCA lecture courses were based on Christian teaching, but by 1861 the Annual City Hall Lectures in Glasgow (held between 7 October and 23 December) were of general interest (see Table 7).

In 1865, 1,397 members subscribed, paying 2s. 6d. each (ladies paid 1s. and platform tickets cost 5s.). These sums (together with some small amount for single lecture tickets) brought in just over £240. Expenses were heavy and the Glasgow Association was glad to have £200 in annual subscriptions to keep its budget balanced.

The lecture of the Rev. John Anderson D.D. on 'The Sciences and

E

Table 7

Glasgow YMCA Annual City Hall Lecture Programme, 1861

October 7	Rev. Wm. Landels	Hero of the Scottish Reformation
October 14	Rev. Sam Coley	Books: what they are and how to read them
October 21	Sheriff Tennant	Glaciers
October 29	Rev. Henry Allan	Church Song, in relation to church life
November 4	Rev. John Anderson D.D.	The Sciences & Revelation, not at variance
November 12	Rev. Wm. Brock	The Burning Bush
November 18	Professor Kelland	Lives and Labours of Astronomers
November 25	Rev. Wm. Arnot	Human footprints on the sands of time or Man's Work on God's World
December 2	Rev. John Edmond	Modern Spiritualism
December 9	Rev. Sir H. W. Moncrieff, Bart., D.D.	Perseverance and Trustability
December 16	Dr. Daniel	Cardinal Richelieu
December 23	Henry Lancaster Esq., Advocate	The Constitution between Scotland and England since 1707

Source: YMCA, AR (Glasgow 1861), 4.

Revelation, not at variance', is a reminder of the challenge posed by Charles Darwin who had in 1859 published *The Origin of Species*. The Glasgow YMCA could not ignore the Darwin controversy, for item VIII of its constitution stated: 'That none shall be eligible for election as Directors or Representatives, except such as hold the doctrines of the Divine Inspiration of The Holy Scriptures — the Deity and Atonement of Christ — the Work of the Holy Spirit in the Conversion and Sanctification of the Sinner — and the Justification of the Sinner by faith alone.' David Mure MP, in his address at the Annual Soirée of the Glasgow YMCA held on 9 January 1865, expressed his anxieties about the impact of Darwin upon Christian philosophy.

In England the YMCA was founded as a result of a meeting on 6 June 1844, in London. It was proposed to form an association of 'converted men in the different drapery Establishments in the Metropolis' who wished to respond to 'their obligation and responsibility as Christians in diffusing religious knowledge'. George Williams, who emerged as the leader of the growing YMCA movement, was an evangelical member of the Church of England. He succeeded in attracting many philanthropic supporters including Lord Shaftesbury. Although the YMCA was, and remained, a religious movement (carefully eschewing politics), because it had a great many shop assistant members it became involved with the Early Closing Association whose members were campaigning for weekly half-day closing and some control on shop opening hours.

In 1877 the Glasgow Young Men's Society for Religious Improvement (established by Nasmyth in 1824) and the Glasgow Young Men's Christian Association (1841) amalgamated under the name of the Glasgow United Young Men's Christian Association, with the objects of 'The Religious, Moral,

Intellectual and Social Improvement of Young Men.' Following the merger the new society could muster a large membership and organise an impressive programme of activities. By 31 December 1878 there were, in and around Glasgow, 180 branches (associations) with 5,550 members. Each association was based on the church which sponsored the group, where 'many young men are being disciplined for the battle of life by the reverent study of the Bible in these Sabbath meetings.'[48] In addition the City Hall Lectures continued as a focal point of the autumn programme, with an ever wider range of subjects including (in 1878) The North Pole and Sir Walter Scott as well as Post Office and Telegraph Service with Experiments.

The reading room and libraries of the associations were 'of the greatest value to the large numbers of Members who are constantly engaged in the systematic study of the Bible'. The Lodgings and Employment Committee was heavily used after October 1878 when the City of Glasgow Bank failure must have thrown many YMCA members out of work and so out of their lodgings.

Membership of the Association made good sense to those who sought a course of educational improvement. Over 1,300 members committed themselves to some form of study, although many of the courses were probably at an elementary level. Classes in 17 subjects were offered including Grammar and Composition, Arithmetic, Mathematics and Writing and Book-keeping. The numbers studying Latin, Greek, French and German suggest that many were keen to broaden their education without special reference to their jobs. Some of the best scholars submitted themselves for the annual examinations of the Science and Art Department, South Kensington, London (which at that date provided a yard-stick against which provincial students could gauge themselves). The results reported seem modest enough. But clearly some of the students and teachers were working well, although the proportion of men proceeding to the examinations was very low. Mathematics and Machine Construction and Drawing as well as Inorganic Chemistry and Animal Physiology attracted some successful candidates.

The role of the YMCA in providing educational opportunities was very important. At a time when public education was confined to the elementary grades and when more advanced education was not easy to find, the YMCA played a notable part in providing good courses at very modest fees. Indeed the YMCA organisation throughout Scotland, while never neglecting its Christian duties, continued to extend its activities. In addition to providing varied educational courses, it opened hostels for working boys and girls at very modest charges. The YMCA continued to be an organisation sensitive to the changing needs of the young and so remained flexible. But despite the charges it made to its members, it required regular injections of philanthropic money.

9. From Sunday School to Boys' Brigade

By the 1850's it had long been obvious that older boys could no longer be occupied successfully in the traditional Sabbath School. Perhaps fewer children were now illiterate, and so more attractive fare was needed. Certainly the old Sabbath School docility and obedience were increasingly hard to generate. Most boys had been subjected to work or school discipline all week and their natural energies and exuberance were hard to repress on the day of rest.

The inspiration for the necessary renewal of the Sunday School movement came from the army. Some time after 1859 there was an extraordinary revival of the Volunteer movement in Britain. After the Crimean War (1854-56) Britain had hoped to return to a peaceful pre-war security, unassailable in her industrial supremacy and in the protection of her Royal Navy. Unfortunately, the France of Napoleon III took on a war-like posture and seemed likely to disrupt the *Pax Britannica.* The new emperor of the French embarked upon his Italian adventures to prove that he was as great in war as had been his uncle Napoleon I. The French press, as eager as ever to talk of avenging Waterloo, startled a complacent British public by a campaign (zealously reported in the British press) proving to their own satisfaction that it would be easy to invade Britain and plant the Imperial Eagle on the Tower of London.[49]

As a result of this posturing, the government was put under pressure by men wishing to re-establish the Volunteer movement. Perhaps such a reaction was inevitable; the Volunteer movement had always been important during times of crisis, as during the Napoleonic wars. Older men thought back to those brave days. The government responded by sanctioning such volunteer forces (for which provision was already on the statute book).[50] But they also made it clear that no financial assistance would be given.

Despite this lukewarm official response, hundreds of volunteer corps were founded in England and Scotland. Most of these were charities: 'In the majority of cases the funds were supplied by subscription lists and by the contributions of what were called Honorary Members.'[51] Many were founded by the gentry who organised their tenants, and others by industrial employers who marshalled their workmen. The gentleman organisers often made themselves responsible for the cost of uniforms and equipment. Astonished by the extraordinary response, the government reluctantly agreed to supply arms at a rate of 25% of the men enrolled; subsequent Secretaries of War bowed to the inevitable and agreed to arm all enrolled Volunteers.

In Glasgow and the West of Scotland enthusiasm was great. *The Reformers Gazette* reported a meeting on 7 May 1859.[52] Thereafter the Glasgow Volunteer Rifle Corps was established. The 'Gallant west-enders', not to be outdone, commenced drilling on 27 July when 'Drill became the passion of the hour, all other amusements gave way before it — the lawyer wheeled his clients to his right or left, as suited his whim, — the banker balanced step, without taking ground, while he balanced his cash, — the clerk numbered his office associates, odd and even numbers, while he told off his 4s, and all assumed a head-up, — look to your front — get out of my way — military air.'[53]

This sort of thing was enormously appealing. Perhaps city-dwellers whose sedentary life gave them no real chance of exercise or outdoor sport were glad of an outlet at once so patriotic and so pleasantly martial. Extraordinary parades were held involving enormous numbers of men. Perhaps the most famous in Scotland was that of 7 August 1860, held in Holyrood Park and attended by the Queen.[54] 'In all 348 companies marched past Her Majesty; and as each company consisted of sixty men — besides officers and sergeants — the grand total cannot have been under 22,000 men. Of these, from 1,800 to 2,000 were Volunteers from the North of England, thus leaving about 20,000 as the total number of Scots Volunteers who took part in the Review.'[55]

With this extraordinary upsurge in martial ardour the sequel is not perhaps surprising. Many of the officers of the Volunteer units were keen churchmen already working in the Sunday Schools. The outrageous behaviour of some boys at Sunday Schools was notorious. The need to provide some means of taming them was urgent. It was a happy thought that if the boys' energies could be marshalled into drill, parades and such pursuits they would be healthfully occupied as well as remaining within the influence of the church.

The first initiative of this kind came from the Glasgow Foundry Boys' Religious Society. The boys working in the iron foundries had first been approached by Mary Ann Clough, a factory girl who worked in a mill on the northern outskirts of the city near the foundries (on the banks of the Forth and Clyde Canal and in Maryhill and Possilpark). She was particularly concerned with the moulders' assistants, rough boys in an ugly world, who 'soon picked up all the vices and were a by-word for hooliganism and profanity'. She decided to try some remedial work; she began to talk with them, and from this beginning she in effect organised a Sunday School. She emigrated to New Zealand in 1862 and her work came to an end. But her efforts were not forgotten. In May 1865 attempts were made to pursue her initiative, and to extend it: the boys were not only given religious instruction but were also drilled 'on one evening a week, much to their own enjoyment'. On 21 November 1865 the Glasgow Foundry Boys' Religious Society was founded. The initiators were Alexander MacKeith, William Martin, William Hunter and Ian Hunter. The objects of the Society were 'religious classes and meetings on the Sabbath, together with educational classes, drill exercises, banking and other provident facilities, and musical and social meetings during the week'.[56] In order to organise these activities properly the work was divided into four departments: Religious, Educational, Social Reform and Provident. All meetings began and ended with prayer; rousing hymns were sung. But the real appeal to the boys was the physical exercise and the military drill with the discipline which it imposed. To the organisers of the Glasgow Foundry Boys' Religious Society is due credit for this, a successful initiative: for the first time in Britain or elsewhere they drew together boys whose lives were formless into a framework of co-ordinated effort and expression.

The Society flourished, alternating indoor winter drill and entertainments with summer outdoor drill and excursions and field-week trips. The Duke of Argyll became Honorary President of the Society in 1869 and encouraged the organisers to hold their summer camps at his seat at Inveraray. The greatest annual effort was made before the Fair Week trip, because the boys had to save carefully to have the money to buy boots and blankets and put by 'the 5/- of their trip money, which sum, thanks to the assistance of a few friends, included passage to and from and board and lodging at Inveraray'. Branches of the Society were established all over Glasgow. Boys (and later girls) were encouraged to join, who had no connection with foundries, thus greatly widening the Society's social scope. The religious element of the work was always important, but the real strength of the Society lay in the widening of the children's horizons and the attraction of vigorous outdoor pursuits. By 1870 there were 36 separate groups with 12,000 boys and girls and 1,200 workers. In 1871, during the visit of the Earl of Shaftesbury to Glasgow, Mr. John Burns informed him and the public that the Glasgow Foundry Boys Society 'has organised a system of Sabbath Religious meetings, week-day education classes, drill exercises, savings banks, summer excursions, winter evening exhibitions, soirees, musical, social and temperance meetings, singing classes'.[57]

But the Society was encumbered by its name. Although attempts were made to remove the word Foundry, loyalty demanded that these be resisted. The Glasgow Foundry Boys' Religious Society, though it had performed a pioneering role, was to be surpassed by a new and more general organisation.

This was the Boys' Brigade. Its founder was William Alexander Smith (1854-1914). Although he was born near John O'Groats, he had strong family connections with Glasgow. On 12 February 1874 he heard Moody and Sankey for the first time, and was much affected by the popular missionary work which they and their followers were then doing in Scotland. Like many young men of the period, Smith was anxious to commit himself to evangelical service. In 1874 he noted in his diary that he had called on 'Mr. Reith re proposed Young Men's Society', which he ran on Sundays at the Free College Church Mission, North Woodside Road.[58] Like everyone else, Smith encountered among the children problems of discipline and behaviour. As he explained, 'As is usual in Sunday schools, and perhaps in Mission schools especially, much of the time that should have been given to teaching was wasted in efforts to secure order and attention. The boys attended because they were sent there by their parents, and their lack of interest was obvious.'[59] Smith's business partner is reputed to have said to him, 'Can't you make some use of your volunteer methods in the Sunday School?' The Foundry Boys were already being drilled in Glasgow in imitation of the volunteer units; elsewhere temperance organisations were also drilling and parading children. After much thought and prayer Smith decided he would try to form a group of boys with a programme based on elementary drill, physical exercise, punctuality and cleanliness. Permission was granted, albeit reluctantly, by the Free College Church Mission authorities. On 4 October 1883 the Boys' Brigade was launched, with three officers and twenty-eight boys. Smith himself was captain and James R. Hill and John B. Hill were lieutenants.

Some 59 boys enrolled. By December the officers were sufficiently confident of their success to organise examinations for promotion. The first test was a practical one of drilling; as a result, the first twelve boys entered for a written examination, after which 'Marks were added by the officers according to their estimate of the candidate's character and general suitability to wield authority and bear responsibility.' The first non-commissioned officers thus selected were sergeants Wm. H. Wylie and George Mill, corporals John R. Jarvie and John Tennant, and lance-corporals Robert Paterson and Alex. Dowie.[60] The Boys' Brigade took as its motto *Sure and Steadfast*, with an anchor incorporated in its crest. The stress on the text, 'Remember now thy Creator in the days of thy Youth', clearly reflected the emphasis on reliance upon God. The object was stated as 'The Advancement of Christ's Kingdom among Boys, and the promotion of habits of Reverence, Discipline, Self Respect and all that tends towards a true Christian manliness.' The word 'Obedience' was added in October 1893. The Constitution laid down that 'all boys between the ages of twelve and seventeen shall be eligible for membership of the Brigade . . . agreeing to comply with the rules of the Brigade, and expressing a desire to be true to Christ in their lives, and to help other boys to do so. Strict discipline shall be enforced, and all members must submit to the authority of the Officers and Non-commissioned officers placed over them.'[61]

By the beginning of 1885 there were five companies or brigades. On 26 January 1885 Smith called a meeting to regularise the organisation. In October 1885 the first annual meeting was held. Carfrae Wilson was elected President and William Smith secretary. By the end of the second year there were seven companies and by the end of the third year there were 44. These consisted of:

25 companies in Glasgow	2 companies in Kilmarnock
5 companies in Edinburgh	1 company in Alexandria
3 companies in Beith, Ayrshire	1 company in Dundee
2 companies in Ayr	1 company in Inverness

and one company each in London, Manchester, Armitage Bridge and Penzance.

By 1887 the Boys' Brigade could proudly announce the formation of the 1st St. Louis Company, U.S.A., and the 1st Auckland Company, New Zealand. The Brigade went from strength to strength; hundreds of companies were established. It was suggested that the head office would be better in London, but in 1895 the Annual Meeting declined the proposal, preferring Glasgow as the base.

The success of the Boys' Brigade was quite astonishing. William Alexander Smith (knighted by Edward VII in 1909) had most certainly met a long-felt want when he inaugurated the first Glasgow Brigade in October 1883. The creation of the Brigade, giving a sense of purpose to boys at a time when the passive occupations of the average Sunday School were being increasingly challenged, was a master stroke. The simple name, Boys' Brigade, could embrace all, of whatever race, creed or colour. The alliteration produced initials destined to become a household symbol. From the beginning the Boys' Brigade was interdenominational and so was accepted by many branches of the Christian church.

But some philanthropists preferred to form independent organisations. These included W. M. Gee, Secretary of the junior branch of the Church of England Temperance Society; in 1890 he started the Church Lads' Brigade. The Catholic Boys' Brigade, the Jewish Lads' Brigade, the Boys' Life Brigade (1889) and the Boy Scouts (1908) followed.

There was a strong case for organising girls. The Girls' Guildry was founded in Glasgow in 1900 by a B.B. officer, Dr. W. F. Somerville.[62] The Girls' Life Brigade was formed in 1902 by Dr. Paton as a sister organisation to the B.L.B. within the Sunday School Union. The Girls' Guildry became strong in Scotland, as did the Girls' Life Brigade in England.

There was controversy over the para-military side of the movement. It had been deliberately imitative of the Volunteer Companies, with rules and regulations based on military models. Indeed its success depended on the strictness of its rules, instilling into its members obedience and self-discipline. The boys in Scotland did not wear a uniform, but the accoutrements with which they equipped themselves, belt, bag, hat and small wooden rifle, were certainly of direct military derivation. The implications caused much concern and provoked a substantial volume of criticism. The B.B. was under constant attack by the Peace Society, whose members were urged 'in season and out of season to do their utmost to crush this young praying and fighting monster'. The Brigade was attacked as 'the master-stroke of Mars . . . dragging true religion into the gutter of corruption'.[63]

One of the most celebrated of those associated with the Brigade was Henry Drummond (1851-1897). He had been elected the first Professor of Natural Science in the Glasgow Theological College on 31 May 1884. He seems to have become involved with the B.B. in 1885, about two years after its foundation; from then on he became its prophet and publicist. Drummond was rather a quixotic character, with many gifts as a populariser, making a great impact with his speeches and sermons. He took up the cause of the Boys' Brigade and made it his own. Talking to Harvard University students, he developed the theme 'One way to help Boys.'[64] He explained the Boys' Brigade thus:

It is a new movement for turning out boys, instead of savages. The average boy . . . is a pure animal. The Sunday School cannot handle these boys. The old method was for somebody to form them into a class and try to get even attention from them. Half the time was spent in securing order. The new method is simply this. You get a dozen boys together . . . you get them into some little hall and put upon every boy's head a little military cap that costs in our country something like 20 cents, and you put around his waist a belt that costs about the same sum, and you call him a soldier . . . You can order that boy about till he is black in the face . . . If he likes it you are coming next Thursday night . . . Military discipline is established from the first moment . . . You have taught him instant obedience, punctuality, intelligence, and attention for a year for one cent. Then you have taught him courtesy. He salutes you and feels a head taller.

But Drummond urged that these manoeuvres were only the trappings. As he explained, 'That is the outward machinery; but it is a mere take-in . . . The real object is to win that boy for Christianity.' Drummond set out to show that 'The Brigade inculcates a martial but not a war-like spirit', although as he explained, 'the first year they have a military drill, and the second year bayonet exercises — an absolute copy of army drill.'

The Boys' Brigade has remained part of the churches' organisation for Christ long after Drummond's death. Its success represents the new efforts to provide a wider range of activities for young people, linking them with the churches; it has opened new horizons for thousands of boys and young men, especially by providing leisure occupations for those otherwise enclosed in the towns.

10. The attempt by the Church of Scotland to regain the welfare initiative

Towards the end of the nineteenth century dedicated men of the established church refused to concede that the church was no longer central to the community. The Rev. David Watson (1859-1935) was a leading example. He resolved to launch a counter-offensive. In 1901 he founded the Scottish Christian Social Union. Its object was 'to claim for the Christian law the ultimate authority to rule social practice, to affirm and to put into effect the social mission of the church, to investigate and study social problems, and to take actions furthering specific reforms'.[65] Watson had become minister of St. Cuthbert's in the east end of Glasgow in December 1886. He had been running District Social Meetings since 1889, and had been extremely active in building up a large and loyal congregation in a poorer part of the city.

Watson and his supporters (including A. H. Charteris and James Paton) were anxious to re-instate the official church as the provider of social policy. There had been much debate on the wisdom of the church organising homes for drunkards, labour colonies and rescue homes for women. These questions were then discussed variously by committees of the General Assembly of the Church of Scotland, such as those on Temperance, Life and Work and Home Missions. In 1904, at the General Assembly in Edinburgh in May, at the urging of men like Watson and Charteris, it was agreed to set up the Committee on Social Work. As a result of the Committee's initiative a number of new projects were undertaken.[66] By 1910 there were Church Labour Homes in Ayr, Dundee, Perth, Peebles and Paisley. A feeding station under a railway arch at

Bridge-gate, Glasgow, was opened, where 500 men a night were supplied with hot soup and bread. Lodging Homes were established in various parts of Scotland, beginning with one in Edinburgh in 1907: by 1911 there were others in Glasgow, Peebles, Perth and Dundee. For destitute men from an agricultural background, farming work was made available. Cornton Vale Farm, Bridge of Allan, was bought in 1907. This venture accepted 'ex-prisoners, moral degenerates, and inebriates'. Some of the men subsequently emigrated to Canada where they became farmers. The Cornton Vale Farm was used by the Board of Agriculture after the first world war to train discharged soldiers. Later the church used it to train delinquent lads for settlement overseas. After the second world war the Scottish Home Department purchased the farm for an experiment with selected Borstal lads.

For boys, other homes were started to give them cheap clean lodgings. The first venture was the Humble Agricultural Labour Home for Boys which Lord Polwarth had started in 1865, and which the Church Social Work Committee took over in 1905. At Aberdeen in the same year the Committee started the Maberly Street home for working lads. By 1912 there were similar homes in Glasgow (at Herbert Street), Govan and Paisley.

A good deal was done for women, including a bureau in Edinburgh (1905) to help unemployed women find work. This was still apparently operating in 1953. The Glasgow employment bureau was set up in 1929. In 1907 the church's first Rescue Home for Women was begun at Morham. In the same year the church's Social Work Committee took over a large Industrial and Lodging Home for 100 women, formerly run by the City of Glasgow. This was moved first to Uddingston, and later (1914) to Pollokshaws. In 1917 and 1919 such homes were opened in Edinburgh and Paisley respectively. Work with girls and women in police hands was started in 1908. A flat in Atholl Place, Edinburgh was obtained to allow the Deaconess Hospital to give overnight shelter if necessary. A hostel for working girls was opened in Glasgow in 1912, and others in 1913 in Edinburgh, Dundee and Aberdeen. An orphanage for girls was established by the early Church Life and Work Committee, followed in 1913 by an orphanage for boys at Morham. Lodging House Mission was begun in Glasgow in 1908, taking over a station in the Candleriggs to begin rescue work among the women inhabitants of lodging and farmed-out houses. Attempts to establish Homes for the Aged proved abortive until 1926, when the Powfoulis Home for Aged Persons was opened; in 1931 Belmont Castle, Meigle was opened by the Duchess of York; many others have been established over more recent years. The Eventide Homes represent nowadays a very important element of the Church of Scotland's social work. Indeed it is here, with the residential home for those in need, that the church has found its principal social role in modern times.

In spite of the outstanding work done by men like David Watson in trying to restore the Church of Scotland at the hub of social policy, over the years it has had to accept a lesser role. The task has been too great; the secular power and resources of the state have inevitably been invoked to meet the many challenges of welfare. In spite of all the activism, Victorian times saw a long and irreversible retreat; the central role of the church as the provider of social facilities has long gone and cannot be resumed.

11. The rise and fall of piety

In pre-industrial Scotland the churches had remained quiescent, making little or no response to problems of the day. The changes brought by the industrial revolution caused the relocation and disorientation of large numbers of people; it was to respond to their needs that new initiatives were taken. The activists, clergymen and laymen, recognised that the church was rapidly losing ground; they were determined to give people opportunities which were being denied them.

The Church Extension campaigns were attempts to provide new and commodious physical plant to accommodate the newly urban proletariat. They were a response to a spatial distribution problem and could be undertaken as a spatial exercise. The attack upon this problem of geographic fit was perhaps the most successful campaign that the various churches undertook, for its ambitions were modest and easily understood. It was comparatively simple to launch a campaign for money for such an object, and to find sites and instruct builders.

The Bible and Tract Societies were also concerned with education, for in consequence of their efforts even those who would not leave their homes to attend church could assist in their own salvation by Bible study at home. Bible Societies attempted to ensure that no-one was unable to have a Bible because of poverty. They were subsidising agencies paid for by the middle classes. The organisers of such activities were concerned for individual souls, but there was also a growing fear among many of a secularised, godless proletariat. The religious institution rooms acted as administrative centres and depots for much of the Bible Society work, as well as providing premises for meetings, socials and soirées.

The struggle over Sabbath Observance was provoked by the demand for more and wider recreational facilities for working people. Most members of the working classes had only one day per week for leisure; the rigid rules applied to Sundays ensured that the only course acceptable to the church was regular and sustained church attendance on that day. But the widening of facilities available on Sundays, chiefly through railways, steamships and trams, threatened the old Sabbath. Norman MacLeod's response, in time adopted by most churches, was a compromise: the church recognised the need for recreation but insisted upon a programme which was non-labour generating. But even this safeguard was later discarded, for members of Church of Scotland presbyteries argued successfully that it was necessary to use public transport (on which men were employed on the Sabbath) to get to their places of worship. But the Sabbath was still hedged about by constraints when Victoria died.

The primary and compelling aim of the evangelicals was to bring the people to salvation. For this, Christian education was believed to be a fundamental requirement. The Sunday Schools gave to many the only education they would ever have. Before 1872 the church, by its provision of Sunday Schools, enabled the people to obtain the rudiments of education, although most of the learning related to reading the Bible. After 1872, when the School Boards were created to provide elementary education where it was lacking, the Sunday Schools were threatened; they re-organised themselves to provide wider opportunities for older boys and girls in the form of boys' and girls' clubs or the Boys' Brigade.

The trend of pietistic philanthropic endeavour was, over the whole of Victoria's reign, to take account of the critical responses of men and women who demanded more and better opportunities from their churches. For many people their religious faith remained central to their lives; their churches could in this sense be judged to have made a successful response. Many were able to find a church which suited them near to their home, attend the services, and send their children to Sunday School and later to the Boys' Brigade. In addition there was ample scope for them to serve, either by philanthropic sub-scription to a wide variety of good works, or by offering their own time and energy for the good of others. For these people the church had successfully made the transition from the eighteenth century authoritarian institution to a church appropriate to the nineteenth century, equally supportive but much more tolerant. But at the same time it had been necessary to cease to rely upon pietistic appeal alone; the churches had been obliged to think in terms of attraction and recreation. Even more secular, perhaps, was the attempt to adopt new functions in the field of social welfare.

NOTES

1. I am grateful to Callum Brown, who has allowed me to use his as yet unpublished material.
2. Bieler, 1964, 60.
3. Burleigh, 1960, 328.
4. Chalmers, T., *Works*, Vol. XVIII, n.d., 146.
5. Chalmers was always fascinated by economic problems, and the Church Extension movement seemed to him to epitomise these. As he wrote, 'It has happened to us according to a universal law in Political Economy. Along with a cheapening of the goods there has been a widening of the market. We have found our way to poorer customers, than before; but unless the goods be further cheapened, by what in commerce is termed a bounty, and in Christianity is termed an endowment, we shall inevitably stop short, before we can find our way to the great mass and majority of the unprovided population.' Chalmers. T., *Works*, Vol. XVIII, preface XXIV.
6. Keir, 1952, 105.
7. Chalmers, T., *Works*, Vol. XVIII, n.d., X.
8. The terms of reference were as follows: A Commission to inquire into the opportunities of religious worship, and means of religious instruction, and the pastoral superintendence

afforded to the people of Scotland, and how far these are of avail for the religious and moral improvement of the poor and of the working classes, and, with this view, to obtain information respecting their stated attendance in places of public worship, and their actual connexion with any religious denomination, to inquire what funds are now and may hereafter be available for the purpose of the Established Church of Scotland, and to report from time to time, in order that such remedies may be applied to any existing evils, as Parliament may think fit, 29 July 1835.

9. The Earl of Minto was the chairman. Both the Church of Scotland and the Dissenters objected to the composition of the Commission, believing it to be already prejudiced. See Chalmers, T., *Works*, Vol. XVIII (Glasgow n.d.), 315.

10. See *Reports of Commissioners to inquire into opportunities of public religious worship.*

1st	1837	(31) XXI	9		6th 1839	(153) XXIV	1
2nd	1837-8	(109) XXXII	1		7th 1839	(154) XXV	1
3rd	1837-8	(113) XXXIII	1		8th 1839	(162) XXVI	1
4th	1837-8	(112) XXXIII	273		9th 1839	(164) XXVI	607
5th	1839	(152) XXIII	1		(P. 156, General Index Accounts & Papers, 1801—52.)

11. Collins, W., *Statistics of the Church Accommodation* (Glasgow 1836), Appendix.

12. Keir, 1952, 107.

13. Chalmers, T., *Works*, Vol. XVIII, n.d., VI.

14. Collins, W., 1836, 17.

15. Harvey, A., *On the Voluntary principle in relation to National Responsibility and the Religious Instruction of the Poor* (Glasgow 1835), 28. This was the 8th of a series of lectures given under the patronage of the Glasgow Voluntary Church Society in the first 4 months of 1835 in the Relief Chapel, John Street, Glasgow.

16. *Report of Commissioners to inquire into opportunities of public religious worship.* Popularly known as *The Commissioners of Religious Instruction in Scotland*, 1st Report. Evidence by Rev. Dr. John Ritchie, Minister of the United Associate Synod Congregation, Potterrow, Edinburgh, Appendix, 282.

17. See Mackie, 1888, Chapters VIII and IX.

18. Chalmers, T., *On the Distinction between parochial and congregational and between endowed and unendowed churches* (n.p., n.d.), 4.

19. Binnie, 1882, 80.

20. *Quoad sacra* parishes were for ecclesiastical purposes only, and were thereby distinguished from civil or *Quoad omnia* parishes.

21. Watson, D., *A Mile-end Chronicle* (Glasgow 1903), 19.

22. Chalmers, T., *Works*, Vol. XVIII (Glasgow n.d.), 173. Chalmers quoted the 'poor Christian verses' as part of an attack he was making on the Magistrates and Town Council of Edinburgh who controlled the seat rents of established churches in Edinburgh and had recently raised them, substantially, as Chalmers believed, against the poor.

23. Canton, 1904-1906, Vol. I, 96.

24. Campbell, J., 1844, 74.

25. Anon., *Sabbath Traffic on the railways* (Glasgow 1865), 11.

26. *The Greenock Seaman's Friend Society*, AR (Greenock 1834), 12.

27. Hodder, 1890, 159.

28. *The Greenock Seaman's Friend Society*, AR (Greenock 1834), 12.

29. The prestigious and influential minister of the Barony Church, Glasgow, and one of Her Majesty's chaplain's for Scotland. See MacLeod, Donald, *Memoir of Norman MacLeod* (London 1888).

30. Burleigh, 1960, 381.

31. MacLeod, N., 1865,12.

32. Ross, W., 1865, 12.

33. Anon., *Norman's Blast* (Edinburgh, Glasgow & Aberdeen 1866).

34. Robert Lee, Professor of Biblical Criticism at Edinburgh from 1847, and minister of Greyfriars Church, had been severely criticised for his attempts to modernise practices at church services. John Tulloch, principal of St. Mary's College, St. Andrews, taught a mild liberalism.

35. Thompson, E. P., 'Time, Work, Discipline and Industrial Capitalism'. *Past and Present*, No. 38 (1967), 84.

36. Laqueur, 1976, 192.

37. Hodder, 1890, 33.
38. *Ibid.*, 81.
39. Caughie. 1869.
40. Bilby and Ridgway, 1835, 22-23.
41. Campbell, 1844, 97.
42. *GSSU, Sabbath School Instruction*, 17th AR, 1854, 32.
43. *Report of the General Assembly on Sabbath Schools in connection with the Church of Scotland* (Submitted to the General Assembly, May 1852) (Glasgow 1852), 5.
44. Campbell, J., 1844, 99.
45. *Ibid.*, 83.
46. *Ibid.*, 94-95.
47. Binfield, 1973, 120.
48. *GUYMCA*, AR, 1879, 10.
49. Crawford, J., 1878, Vol. 1, 90, 91.
50. Act 44, George III, cap. 54 (5 June 1808).
51. Crawford, J., 1878, Vol. 1, 90, 91.
52. *Ibid.*, 99.
53. *Ibid.*, 101.
54. 'Her Majesty wore a pale lilac silk dress, a green silk bonnet, with Maltese lace trimmings and green feathers, a Stuart Tartan shawl, and a white parasol with white fringe. This last she changed for a dark green one, some say in compliment to the riflemen, others, with more show of reason, as a better protection against the clouds of dust which swept across the parade.' Vernon, 1860, 15.
55. *Ibid.*
56. *GFBRS*, 1st AR, 1866, 14.
57. Anon., *Shaftesbury*, 1871, 41.
58. These halls are no longer owned by the church. They were called the Reith Halls as a tribute to Sir John Reith's father, who was minister of the Trinity (Free Church) College Church at Lynedoch Street, Glasgow, at this time.
59. Gibbon, n.d., 32.
60. *Ibid.*, 44.
61. *Ibid.*, 40.
62. *Ibid.*, 138.
63. *Ibid.*, 83.
64. Drummond, H., 1900, 77.
65. Watson, D., 1901, 1.
66. See Bishop, D. H., thesis, 1953. Much of this section is based on Dr. Bishop's valuable work.

3

The Home Missionary Impulse

1. Middle versus working class recipients

HOW far is it possible to make a distinction between two kinds of middle-class pietistic effort, namely between the initiatives taken by the middle classes largely in the interests of their own kind, and the efforts they made to assist the working classes? In a general way such a duality is represented in the distinction between piety as a programme (chapter 2 above), and the present chapter's concern: the missionary impulse.

Much of what is dealt with in chapter 2 seems to remove this distinction. Church extension cut across class boundaries, undertaking as it did to fill gaps in church provision in many different parts of the cities, including those containing large working-class populations. Bible Societies strove to provide holy books for all sorts and conditions of people. Sunday Schools and companies of the Boys' Brigade were organised in church and mission halls throughout the cities, concerned as they were with widening the educational and social opportunities for young people regardless of social class. There would thus seem to have been a considerable merging of recipients from middle and working classes.

But as working class indifference or even hostility grew, together with alternative (especially state) provision, there was a sense in which the middle classes withdrew from pietistic effort in the direction of the workers. The most striking example of this was perhaps in the case of the Sunday Schools as the most important element in working class educational provision.

On the other hand there were certain groups that were so distinctively working class that the efforts directed at them were specific, and not of a nature to be shared by middle class people. First, there were the 'dark' areas of the cities, where need of all kind was greatest, the slums and near slums. To redeem them for Christ was the object of the city missions. Within the working class component of the cities certain specific groups attracted attention, the police, the cabmen and the seamen in the ports. Finally there was a group that was not urban at all, but which seemed to need special aid, namely the Highlanders.

2. The mission call

The modern missionary movement in Britain stemmed from William Carey (1761-1834), a journeyman cobbler from Northamptonshire who was inspired by the command, 'Go ye therefore and teach all nations and baptise' (Matthew 28, 15). Brought up within the Church of England he was, as an impressionable 17-year-old, taken to a nonconformist prayer meeting where he found the preaching service there much to his taste. He became fired with a vision of 'The World for Christ', and launched a campaign for overseas missions to convert the heathen. 'If Baptism concerns us, the world missions must no less' was one of his most telling phrases. The world mission campaign was launched with some hesitancy, but it gained rapid momentum and swept through the land. Carey succinctly stated his programme for establishing a missionary society, 'Pray, plan, pay.' The effect of this on church congregations was impressive. Given something positive to do, they were galvanised into activity.

In Scotland as well as in England the church in the later eighteenth century was in a somnolent phase, with abuses abounding. But the missionary movement allowed congregations to involve themselves more fully. Individual congregations responded warmly to the need for money for missionary endeavours. This was something practical they could do well.

But there was strong opposition to this kind of activity within the established Church of Scotland. The quietists were unimpressed by emotional arguments to convert the heathen. The more extreme Calvinist view was that it was quite wrong to interfere with the Lord's intentions; if He had wanted missions He would have organised them. Nevertheless the chance for action was welcomed by many. Those who were eager to embrace the idea of mission work found it unacceptable that men should organise such work overseas, channelling large resources there, when there was so much ignorance at home in the now rapidly expanding industrial cities. Thus the home mission was born out of the overseas mission movement: indeed many of the missionary societies were dual in character, funnelling their resources both to overseas and home missions. But our concern is with home missions.

3. City missions

The city mission movement was part of the redemptive activity launched by the evangelical wing of the Church of Scotland. The challenge of the industrial revolution seemed to those involved to require a spiritual response. By 1832 both Glasgow and Edinburgh had their city missions. Later many other such mission societies were launched, some by individual churches, others by variously named evangelical societies. They were all charitably funded, devotedly supported and earnestly worked.

The Glasgow City Mission was founded on 1 January 1826. It was the inspiration of David Nasmyth, who took as his maxim 'Blessed is he that considereth the poor' (Psalm XLI, 1). Nasmyth and other members of Greville Ewing's Independent Congregational Church were eager to involve themselves in local redemptive activity. Theirs was one of the earliest home missions. As such it epitomised pious philanthropy, the evangelical Christian response in Scotland to deteriorating conditions in the industrial towns. As James Cleland remarked in 1831, 'The Want of Church accommodation and the total inability of the clergymen of the city to attend to the religious wants of a numerous class of the community . . . led to the formation of the City Mission.'[1] Its object was 'to promote the spiritual welfare of the poor of this City, and its neighbourhood, by employing persons of approved piety, and otherwise properly qualified, to visit the poor in their own house, for the purpose of religious discourse; and to use other means for diffusing, and increasing amongst them, a knowledge of evangelical truth'.[2]

The Edinburgh City Mission opened in February 1832 with the objects of 'taking the glad tidings of salvation to the poor, and such others as may receive them — to form meetings for prayer, reading the scripture and exhortation — to distribute the Bible — to circulate religious tracts and books — to send people to church — to increase the attendance on week day, Sabbath and Infant Schools — and in every possible way to contribute to the souls of the destitute'.[3]

David Nasmyth's enthusiasm had also set up, in the spring of 1825, the London City Mission.[4] There the missioners, well-trained and organised, offered 'a moral police institution. In its admirable discipline, benevolence and humanity are beautifully blended with order and law.'[5]

City Missions were often interdenominational. In Glasgow, of the eight missioners working in the 1820's, four belonged to the established church, two were independent, and one each was from the United Associated Synod and the Relief body. In both Glasgow and Edinburgh the town was divided into districts, and missionaries were apportioned to each. The Edinburgh missionaries were instructed 'to visit the inhabitants of the district assigned to you, for the purpose of bringing them to an acquaintance with salvation through the Lord Jesus Christ, and of doing them good by every means in your power'.[6] In Glasgow missioners were brusquely advised, 'As your visits must be short, generally not exceeding fifteen minutes, avoid secular conversation.'[7] Missioners worked five hours a day for six days, and studied on Sundays.

The eight Glasgow missionaries employed in 1826 were sorely overworked; in consequence more were appointed. 'In December 1831 there were 22 licentiates, or students of divinity, employed at salaries of £40 each, 20 of these were on full-time (four hours a day) and the other 2 on two-thirds time.'[8] There were 52 missionaries in 1864, but by 1892 this figure had dropped to 33.

Missionaries had an unenviable job, with large areas to cover; conscientious men, aware of their responsibilities, must have been hard-pressed to visit so many people. They were not welcomed in many homes and it is clear from

F

guarded remarks in the annual reports that they received many rebuffs. Lucky Mackintosh expressed her disapproval of such men:

> What is ye're hame missions, as the're ca'd, but the agents o' a clamjamfry o' heepocrites . . . Some auld broken-down sodger . . . wha can flatter a curran o' ye're 'aimables' — a fallow wha aiblins can squeak a stave or twa o' the psalms o' David and drawl ower some drone o' a prayer he has teach'd himself.[9]

In general, families whose allegiance was to one of the many dissenting sects would not allow the City missionary over the doorstep. Later, with the influx of Irish families, many other doors would be closed to them. In addition, men and women whose basic struggle was with poverty and even starvation were not inclined to receive spiritual comfort. Even from the annual reports (which are notable for their skilful glosses), it is clear that the work was often distasteful.

The missionaries were constantly faced with problems of the most abject poverty. They would indeed have been men of stone if they had found preaching the word easy in these circumstances. Every year they wrote their reports under sectional heads entitled Ignorance, Indifference, Drunkenness and Destitution. Their recitations are evocative and harrowing. But were they exaggerated? It is difficult to know. It was the missioners' bounden duty to present in their statements material from which an annual report could be written, calculated to bring a generous response from the contributors.

Cleland reported in 1831 that 'During the year 1830 the agents spent 16,747 hours in the service of the Mission. In that time they visited 40,269 families, held 1,880 meetings among the people, which have been attended by 67,850 hearers. 4,012 visits have been paid to the sick and 1,916 to the infirm.'[10] The precision of these figures brings a sceptical reaction now, but they were judged persuasive by the writers of the time (and Cleland was an accomplished statistician).

But evangelical enthusiasm was really not enough. By the 1830's missioners were almost certainly relieving the poor by practical means, handing out bread tickets, small sums of money, directing them to a Benevolent Society, and taking susceptible Directors with them on their rounds. Possibly the general mission work became increasingly unrewarding. Were the families in the slums even less welcoming than before? In any event these special welfare services began to occupy more space in the Annual Reports and more missionary time.

From early in its history the City Mission in Glasgow was providing special services for groups other than the destitute. By 1830 these could include services at the Seamen's Chapel on Sabbath afternoons, and regular visits to the Police Office to expound the Scriptures 'during the interval of public worship on the Lord's Day'. The expansion of this work does suggest that missionaries were keen, whether consciously or not, to find outlets for their evangelism which would be more fruitful than working with the destitute. During the latter half of the century this work rapidly expanded. Separate mission work was — by 1879 — being done for cabmen, the police force, the Old Man's Asylum, Broomhill Homes (Kirkintilloch), the Fever and Smallpox Hospital (Belvidere), the Eye Infirmary, and the Dunoon Convalescent Homes. The emphasis upon work in the residential homes suggests a desire for work in a controlled situation where the missionaries would be sure of a respectful hearing.

The City Mission organised a special approach to cabmen from about 1854, with the Rev. Peter Anderson as missioner from 1862. Cabmen were thought to be especially at risk, for they were away from their homes and out at work at all hours. Although they were poorly paid (in 1862 wages were about 12s. or 13s. per week but could be made up by tips), they had a cabmen's Friendly Society and Temperance Society with a cabmen's library. Some of the men were sufficiently keen on self-help and self-improvement to enter an essay competition on the subject of Domestic Happiness in 1864. The missionary held Sabbath meetings in the stable-yards for the men, although Sabbath working was deplored.

Many people responded sympathetically to the obvious discomforts of the cabmen's lives. Cabmen's shelters were built in Scottish cities in the 1870's. Mrs John Burns, in Glasgow, interested herself in this work and defrayed the expenses of at least one 'Rest'. In 1879 a Glasgow merchant built and equipped a 'handsome and commodious Rest at the Caledonian Railway Station, Buchanan Street'. Here 'Well cooked food at a low price' could be bought. This Rest was handed over to the City Mission to administer. In Dundee the cabmen's shelter 'somewhat resembles a huge omnibus in appearance', and was 'well lighted and ventilated, had seats all round, with nags (pegs) on which to hang coats and hats'.[11]

By 1864 the Mission was undertaking 'with vigour' work with the city's police force. This was done on the grounds that 'Much of the sin and debauchery of a great city he (a policeman) must see, and familiarity with vice is no help to religion.'[12] The total force was about 600 men, based on the Central, Southern and Eastern Districts. The missionary claimed to visit 200 police families every month. It must have been heart-warming to be received into policemen's homes 'with great cordiality'. In addition, the missionary held meetings for the men in the various police halls, as well as Sabbath meetings for wives and families. The police themselves did not attend readily but their families usually did. In 1862 the Mission reported, 'Thanks are due to Captain Smart and the Superintendent, Inspectors and Sergeants, for their kind feelings and services toward the Missionary and his work.'[13] Notwithstanding the support given by those in authority, one missionary reported in 1879 that 'I have found the soil to be not of a very fertile kind.' The policemen themselves believed that they were 'much exposed to temptation and to evil influences of one kind and another', and that this excused them from responding seriously to the preaching they received. The instructor resignedly reported that 'They are not much inclined to anything of a spiritual nature.'[14]

From the 1850's the missionaries visited the Old Man's Asylum in Rottenrow (see chapter 2 above). The charities founded by Miss Beatrice Clugston all received missioners who were encouraged to visit at the Broomhill Homes (Kirkintilloch) and the Convalescent or Seaside Homes at Dunoon (see chapter 12, section 2 below). Indeed at Dunoon special accommodation was provided for a resident missionary who preached to and prayed with the patients and so enjoyed an annual holiday. For the evangelists this was pleasant work; as one reported, 'Conducted worship daily, morning and evening; all the inmates attended.' It must have been balm to the gospeller to have a ready-made audience sitting silent and attentive, for many patients convalescing after serious illness were receptive to salvationist ideas.

At the time of Lord Shaftesbury's visit to Glasgow in August 1871 to receive the Freedom of the City, the Glasgow City Mission laid before him an impressive array of figures. It claimed in the previous year to have made visits in the evenings totalling 55,664 hours (with 11,654 people), and had held 5,454 meetings attended by 289,407 people. Its Bible classes were well supported:

Young men over 14	19,702
Young women over 14	34,752
Children younger than 14	22,782

Unfortunately this report does not state how many missionaries undertook this mountain of work. By 1871 the income for the year was £3,225 and outgoings totalled £3,055.

The objectives of the Glasgow City Mission did not change. The missionaries continued to pray and preach. They were able to attract funds and were often referred to for guidance by charitable organisations during times of hardship. After the financial crisis of 1878 they received appeals from the relief committees 'to furnish information regarding real cases of poverty, and to become almoners of the bounty of the charitable'.[15]

The difficulties and disappointments of the missionary's life were offset by successes with Bible Classes. The development of a Bible Class as a regular educational and social occasion perhaps crowned the work of the successful missionary, for he found the basic mission work 'hard, depressing and discouraging'.

From time to time new waves of enthusiasm were generated. The Grove Street Institute was founded in 1859 following a new outburst of Christian energy. It was the Glasgow branch of the Evangelisation Society of London, a body which provided 'preachers to preach the gospel' on request. Some £7,000 was raised by subscription to build the Grove Street Mission Halls in 1865. From this base a wide variety of activities was undertaken. In 1892 Grove Street claimed to be employing 200 volunteer workers in 'General Evangelistic, Medical Mission, Benevolent and Temperance Work'.[16]

The Glasgow United Evangelical Association was founded in 1874, taking advantage of the stir caused by the Moody and Sankey campaign of the same year. Its work was not confined to the east end of the city although the Tent Hall, Steel Street was one of its centres. Noonday prayer meetings and fellowship meetings were held in the large hall of the Christian Institute, as well as services at several venues in the city. Perhaps the most entertaining performances were given by the Mizpah Band which did Gospel Temperance Work at eight different centres in the city.

Like other mission bodies, the Association was not satisfied with its spiritual work. It compensated by undertaking a wide variety of useful ameliorative work. On every Lord's Day morning at 8 a.m. it provided a 'free breakfast' (for about 1,200 in 1891), with a Gospel address to follow. Later the same day the children's Sabbath dinner attracted about 1,000 children at which 'A Bible lesson, with blackboard, is given.' Children's day refuges were also organised, in which board school children were provided with three meals a day and with clothing and footwear where needed. The Association also had a home for girls at risk. Finally, it ran the Saltcoats Homes for children and fresh-air fortnight schemes (see chapter 12; section 2 below).

4. Missions to seamen

The British people have always held their sailors in warm regard, whether they carried 'the meteor-flag which burns so terrific in war' or 'the white flag of commerce which waves so beneficently in peace'.[17] The nation depended upon both types of sailors, and they were a popular cause for the benevolent. The aid which they were offered in the early days of the nineteenth century was invariably spiritual and homiletic, in the form of Bibles, tracts, sermons and prayers. These were intended to help them overcome the moral hazards of their calling, particularly during their long absences from home and family. The development of practical aid sprang from the obvious needs of men on shore for unsettled periods with no homes or friends. Seamen's Homes were a practical response to the vivid temptations which were believed to lie in wait for them.

Not surprisingly it was in the busy port of Greenock that the first Scottish Seamen's Friends' Society was established. The Society was initiated in 1819 'to promote the temporal and spiritual interests of Seamen trading to, or connected with, the port'. The objectives were:

1. To furnish seamen with Bibles;
2. To distribute tracts on board ship;
3. To establish and encourage Prayer meeting on board ships in the Harbour;
4. To solicit Clergymen to preach to Seamen occasionally;
5. To recommend well-regulated Boarding Houses to stranger Seamen, on their arrival in Port.

In time item 5 took precedence; seamen's hostels became the chief focus of the work.

By the 1830's, in addition to services on board ship and in chapel on shore, the Greenock Society had placed about 45 portable libraries on vessels, and they ran a Seamen's School for seamen's children. The Greenock Society was also very actively involved in encouraging 'Temperance Ships'. It tried to persuade masters and men to refuse to drink spirits while on board. This was to fly in the face of a tradition which had always allotted spirits to men undertaking heavy duties in bad weather. The Committee was also active in support of the Sabbath Observance Movement. In 1850 the Sir Gabriel Wood's Mariners' Asylum (later Home) was opened in Greenock for retired mariners. This splendid building remains in use, although its purpose has recently been altered to make it a more general residence for old people.

In Glasgow the Seamen's Friend Society was established in 1822. The American master of the *Morning Star* was the inspiration for this initiative, offering his vessel 'for the purpose of performing public worship'.[18] By 1825 a Seamen's Chapel had been built near the harbour; this was serviced through the good offices of the kirk session of St George's. Other ministers undertook the duties from time to time. In spite of their avowed aims 'to promote the temporal and spiritual interests of seamen trading to this port', this Society was at first primarily interested in the spiritual welfare of seamen and their families. A school was built for seamen's children, and cheap (and sometimes free) education was given. For the rest the Directors visited ships in the harbour every Sunday morning to persuade crew members to come to chapel.

The Glasgow Sailors' Home was opened on 26 January 1857 at the corner of James Watt Street and Broomielaw. For the first few years it had a struggle to survive. There were two special difficulties. In the first place the Managers had included shops when building the property, anticipating that these would be let quickly and would bring in good revenue, but the shops did not at first attract tenants. In addition the Superintendent found that men 'left without settling their accounts at all, and others gave their advance notes in payment, which were useless from the men either deserting, or never joining their vessels'.[19]

A second Sailors' Home was established at 150 Broomielaw (with William Euing as Secretary) at the end of 1869. The homes were frequented by thousands of men. In 1872, 3,483 men stayed at 150 Broomielaw. Most of them were British (Scottish 1,456, English 934, Irish 276, and Welsh 74), but at least fourteen other nationalities made up the total. In 1884 the New Bethel Reading and Recreation Rooms were erected at a cost of £6,000 to cater for those men whose ships were tied up at the docks nearby.[20] In Dundee a Sailors' Home was opened in 1879 after £12,000 had been subscribed.

The main function of the Sailors' Homes was to provide comfort and security. It was often difficult for seamen, especially foreigners, to find suitable places to live. Sailors were paid off at the end of their voyages with substantial sums of money, and so the Superintendents provided an important service, acting as banker for the men and ensuring that at least some of the money was posted to wives and dependants, or placed in the Savings Bank. The homes undoubtedly provided a focal point for men's lives while on shore. They were paternalistic and demanded high standards of behaviour, but nevertheless they attracted many seamen.

The Shipwrecked Fishermen and Mariners' Royal Benevolent Society was founded in 1839 with Queen Victoria as patron. Its motto was, 'There is sorrow on the sea.' The Glasgow Auxiliary Society was probably of later date. It was a practical body, without religious connection. Shipwrecked men were recovered and brought home and bereaved dependants given practical financial aid in their distress. In accordance with the spirit of the age, there was 'a Thrift-encouraging Self-help Section, in which some 40,000 Fishermen and Mariners are providently enrolled, at nominal payments, as Beneficiary Members'.[21]

5. Mission work in the Highlands

Home missionary work similar in nature to overseas work was undertaken in Scotland in the Highlands.[22] There was in both cases the problem of a language other than English and the difficulty of coming to terms with it and the culture that had produced it.

The Society in Scotland for the Propagation of Christian Knowledge was founded in 1709 with the financial support of Queen Anne. The risings of 1715 and 1745 did a great deal to remind interested parties of the need 'towards the farther promoting of Christian Knowledge, and the increase of piety and virtue within Scotland, especially in the Highlands, Islands and remote corners thereof, where error, idolatry, superstition, and ignorance do mostly abound, by reason of the largeness of the parishes and scarcity of schools'.[23] This missionary project was philanthropic and salvationist; it aimed at converting the inhabitants to the protestant religion. But it was also concerned with weaning them from Stuart allegiance, 'wearing out' or destroying the Gaelic language and making the area safe for the Hanoverians.

The work in the Highlands was financed by church congregations from all over England and Scotland. Ministers spoke to congregations in England and Scotland on the plight of the Highlanders and the need to proselytise them. The money so given was administered by the SSPCK in Edinburgh and its Auxiliaries in Glasgow and Port Glasgow.

The SSPCK had good reason for entering the field. In some places pockets of pre-Reformation catholicism remained; elsewhere it was sometimes difficult to distinguish any but primitive pagan beliefs. In some areas, especially in east coast parishes, ministers had reclaimed their territory for the Church of Scotland, but these were exceptional. It seemed an admirable objective to establish schools in which Highlanders could be taught to read English. Moreover the people could be weaned from their old ways by interposing the

English translation of the Bible between them and the past. It seemed obvious
to many educated people in England and the Scottish Lowlands that Gaelic
was an outmoded language and that all would benefit by its demise. English
was the language of industry, commerce and the law.

These objectives sounded simple enough, but to achieve them was a
complex and difficult assignment. The Bible itself was not the simplest of
books to master; other and more elementary readers had to be introduced for
preliminary learning. Only fluent scholars could expect to graduate to Bible
reading for themselves. Another difficulty was the superimposition of English
on a Gaelic culture. To a people unused to receiving formal education the com-
plexities of learning to read in a foreign (and alien) language were baffling and
defeating. Nor could these isolated people necessarily see the need to learn to
read at all, let alone in English. They did not appreciate the precariousness of
their economy in the overpopulated Highland valleys and had no premonition
of the new economy by which they would be thrust out. The chiefs of the
Clans resented any interference with their people, regarding education as an
unsettling and unnecessary luxury.

The SSPCK eventually recognised that it would have to use Gaelic (or Irish
as it was usually called) as the medium through which to teach English. But
there were very few English books translated into Gaelic and even fewer
acceptable religious texts. In 1773, when Boswell wanted some Gaelic texts for
Dr Johnson, he approached the SSPCK in Edinburgh who provided him with
five, consisting of the *New Testament*, the *Confession of Faith*, *The Mother's
Catechism*, *The Saints Everlasting Rest* and a *Dictionary*. But until 1801 there
was no complete edition of the Bible in Gaelic. The paucity of the tools in this
field meant that success was limited.[24]

SSPCK schools were all circulatory ones, remaining for one or two winters
on one site and then moving elsewhere. Most schools worked from October to
May; education could not compete with other commitments during the long
spring and summer days.

By the beginning of the nineteenth century conditions in the Highlands had
become well known. There were more travellers, intercourse between Highlands and Lowlands was commonplace, and the sense of isolation was passing.
Perhaps there was also some understanding of the challege of expecting highlanders to respond to teaching in an alien tongue. More particularly (despite
rosy reports from the ministers and others who examined the pupils in the
schools for the SSPCK), there was a realisation that the rate of progress was
discouragingly slow.

After the Disruption in 1843 the SSPCK sought guidance in the Courts, in
order to establish its relationships with the churches. Was it necessarily linked
with the Church of Scotland or could it work with the new Free Church? In
1846 it was declared that the SSPCK was indissolubly linked with the Church
of Scotland, and that teachers, catechists or missionaries who were appointed
by that Society had to be members of that church.

The attack on the highlanders' language and culture had been modified in 1811. The Society for the Support of Gaelic Schools was established in Edinburgh, with a formidable list of aristocratic patrons. The office-bearers were for the most part landed highlanders, though representatives from London and other parts of the country were also listed. Mrs Gladstone of Liverpool was one of the governors (by subscription), as were several of her Mackenzie of Seaforth relatives. By 1811 Gaelic was not regarded with the same suspicion as it had been earlier. Many ministers and others serving in the Highlands recognised the insuperable barrier which learning to read English imposed upon the scholars there. These men and women felt that to teach the people in their own language was a realistic practical objective which would give the taught an entrée into education. They knew that:

> . . . hundreds of children might be found in schools, who could read English as accurately as Highlanders can read, and yet who did not understand one word of what they read.[25]

Even the SSPCK in 1817 introduced a Gaelic spelling book as part of its teaching.

The Gaelic Schools' Society was anxious to associate itself with the SSPCK, as the activities of the latter 'for a century past, have been highly beneficial, as a means of promoting civilisation and Christian Knowledge'.[26] But 'although (in 1826) the said Society maintains 290 schools at which nearly 16,000 young people are taught, it is a melancholy fact, that many parts of the Highlands and Islands continue in a state of great ignorance, and that only a small proportion of the inhabitants can read in any language'.

For financial reasons the Gaelic Schools' Society had to pin its faith on circulating schools. Its sole object was 'to teach the inhabitants to read the Holy Scriptures in their native language'. The Society was unwilling to agree to the establishment of a school unless the people locally would bestir themselves and provide 'a suitable school house'. 'No allowance whatever,' it was insisted, 'shall be given from the funds of the Society for the erection of a School-house, or for the rent of it.'[27]

By 1835 the Society had 79 Gaelic Schools on its books, but as there were only 57 teachers it was clear that many teachers had to remove themselves from one 'station' to another during the year. The Society claimed that since its founding in 1811, with an average number of teachers of 60 and 540 stations, nearly 70,000 people had been taught to read the Scriptures 'in the vernacular tongue'. In 1835 the Society maintained that it had provided, since 1811, 167,800 books, 97,600 elementary books and Scripture extracts, 70,200 Bibles, New Testaments and Psalm Books. The Society believed that the total population of the Highlands and Islands was between 400,000 and 500,000. The Rev. Dr McLeod of Campsie, who had long experience of the Highlands, claimed that everyone benefited from the Gaelic Society's activities. As he put it: 'English reading and English-speaking have made greater progress in the Highlands and Isles of Scotland since the system of Gaelic speaking has been acted upon, that is during the last twenty years, than it did for centuries before then.'

The Society continued to serve the northern isolated communities throughout the middle years of Victoria's reign. It received great financial support from all over Scotland and substantial donations from England and beyond. By 1879 there were 20 Auxiliaries, including one in Little Skye, Victoria (Australia).

But with the passing of time everyone (including the highlander) became convinced that English was the language to learn. No one wanted to learn to read Gaelic, with the result that the Society's arguments that it was easier to learn English through the medium of Gaelic were no longer convincing. The SSPCK felt it was again on strong ground in teaching directly into English. As might have been expected, Glasgow was not content merely to follow the Edinburgh leadership. The Glasgow Auxiliary Gaelic Schools' Society, founded on 5 March 1812 as an auxiliary to Edinburgh, became increasingly independent. It not only collected money to send to the capital, but it also launched work on its own behalf. Glasgow objectives were wider than those of Edinburgh: they went beyond merely supporting the Edinburgh Society which was only teaching in Gaelic, to promote a wider education including English, writing and arithmetic. These wider ambitions of the Glasgow Society raised the educational aspiration on to an entirely different plane. The financial contribution which the Glasgow Society made to the Edinburgh one was generous; Glasgow furnished £500 out of an annual budget of £1,250 in 1816. But later, when it was organising its own schools, its contributions to Edinburgh were less. The Inverness Society founded in 1818 worked for many long years along similar lines.

Following the passing in 1872 of the Education Act providing for compulsory School Board education, both the SSPCK and the Gaelic Schools' Societies had to reconsider their position. The Act made no provision for teaching in Gaelic.

In 1878 the annual income of the Gaelic Schools' Society was £650, a drop of almost £300 from its income of £948 in 1872. The Society was then supporting 24 schools with an attendance of 936 pupils. It claimed that in 1878 the government was spending £482,000 in Scotland on state education, none of which was devoted to teaching Gaelic. It maintained that, given £15 a year for the teaching of Gaelic in each school in the Gaelic third of the country (costing say £3,220 a year), each Gaelic-speaking child in Scotland could be taught to read the Bible in his or her native language.

Gaelic was by this time a lost cause, for neither the teachers nor the taught in Highland schools wanted to be involved with it. Increasingly the teachers came from other parts of the country and did not know the local language. Pupils were more conscious than ever of the need to know English in their changing world. Thus the Society for the Support of Gaelic Schools was finally forced to retreat. But a new movement was beginning to assert itself, namely Scottish nationalism. Conferences were called in 1905 and 1906 to consider the future of the language. Representations were made to the Secretary for Scotland for support, with the result that an annual grant of £10 was made to each Gaelic-speaking teacher. The original objectives of the SSPCK were only too successful. Gaelic and indeed Gaelic cultural values had been reduced to a low level, from which recovery would be very difficult.

Certain philanthropists of the eighteenth century and the first decade of the nineteenth, in their concern for the future of the Highlands, had played a powerful part through the SSPCK in the destruction of its language and culture. Other philanthropists from 1811 had sought to arrest this trend through the Gaelic Schools' Society. They were finally reinforced by those who had become Scottish nationalists. In all this the state had played no part; the external influences brought to bear on Highland culture were entirely voluntarist. Any judgement on this rare example of the ethnic impact of philanthropy depends, of course, on one's value judgements concerning cultural preservation.

6. Missionary staff

Missionary work involved visiting people in their homes for the purposes of prayer, admonition and exhortation. It was no new departure for ministers, probationary ministers and church elders who had always claimed the right to enter the homes of parishioners to undertake these spiritual duties. The use of missionaries for these purposes was therefore an extension of a principle well understood in Scotland.

Missionaries, as distinct from parochial visitors, were first introduced with the founding of the Glasgow City Mission in 1826. They were often men who believed they had a vocation for the church ministry, but who were unable for financial reasons to complete their training and therefore entered mission work *faute de mieux*. Many spent a life-time in the service of the poor. Theirs was arduous work, demanding long hours of visiting, often in conditions of great discomfort. Missionaries were primarily involved in rendering spiritual support although some may have assisted in obtaining practical assistance for the relief of acute poverty.

It was not always easy to find missionaries who would work in the urban slums 'with acceptance'. By the 1850's attempts were being made to find missionary workers from another source, namely women. Bible Women were usually working women (often widows) who could hope to effect entry to houses by appealing to the mothers of families. It was relatively easy to recruit them. Once convinced of their own ability to do the job, they were eager to share their spiritual redemption with others worse off than themselves. The Bible Women represented a new beginning in two ways. They entered an area of male activity, and they did so from the working-class level.

But working-class male missionaries were also recruited from the 1850's. The Colporteurs' Society in Scotland was formed in the late 1850's. As Rev. William Boyd explained, 'The Colporteurs were got without difficulty from the working-classes, and to each was allotted the care of 5,000-8,000 people — upon whom they were expected to call monthly — offering them for sale Bibles, Testaments and a great variety of religious books and periodicals and distributing tracts.'[28] The Colporteurs were also 'catechists in their districts, holding prayer-meetings, praying with the sick and infirm'.[29] In 1857 ten were employed, but by 1863 there were one hundred and twenty-five. Each man cost the Society about £60 per annum, of which £40 or £50 was his salary. By 1863 the Society was selling a wide range of religious literature valued at £11,000 per annum. Rev. William Boyd concluded on a sanguine note: 'The advantage of the system was, that it had developed a taste for pure and good literature among those who had never read at all before, or had read only cheap and pernicious periodicals.'[30]

In the Highlands of Scotland the SSPCK and the Gaelic Societies also employed school-masters who had to have a strong streak of missionary zeal. Theirs was a rough life, housed as they often were with some of their pupils' families. The school-house was usually a room in someone's home or a part of the church, for only the most favoured places had a proper building.[31] The school-master was expected to be 'a person of piety, loyalty, prudence, gravity, competent knowledge and literature.'

Missionaries, Bible Women and Colporteurs had an arduous and often unpleasant task. But to some it was an opportunity to seek a fulfilling role, and to acquire respectability.

The value of Home Mission work is difficult to assess. It was done for others who did not invite it, and who may have suffered resentfully under its ministrations. It could be insensitive, for the missionaries' concern for the spiritual welfare of those they sought to serve could mean ignoring physical hardships. The work continued throughout Victorian times, although perhaps at a lesser pace, with the missionary evolving into a social worker, though still with a Christianising function.

The efforts of some at least were appreciated, witness the memorial stone in an Edinburgh cemetery to a city missionary:

> In Memory of William Mitchell, Missionary, died 10th April 1878, Aged 63 years. Full of zeal for the spread of the Gospel, his labours were unceasing. Profound in learning, he was always ready to impart his great knowledge to others. His Amiability and Christian piety won the love and respect of all who knew him. 'Christ in me the Hope of Glory.'
>
> Erected by the West Fountainbridge Working Men's Mutual Improvement Association and a few friends.[32]

7. The forms of retreat

Home Missions, as we have seen, were aimed by the middle classes at the working classes, both generally and in terms of particular groups. They eventually attracted a considerable element of working-class participation in the form of Bible Women and Colporteurs, but there was always the problem of maintaining the dynamic of such activity. Discouragement could all too easily overtake the missionary worker, especially when confronted with a large and difficult district. One form of adaptation (or retreat) was to do as those concerned with churches and Sunday Schools had done, namely try to add other attractions to the plea for piety, with entertainments, soirées and the like. The other response was to recede from the general, as represented by the district, and concentrate upon particular groups, like police families or cabmen or seamen, where a specific approach could be made, and continuous, though limited, contacts be maintained.

NOTES

1. Cleland, 1832, 46.
2. *Report of the Society for Promoting the Religious Interests of the Poor of Glasgow and its vicinity, or Glasgow City Mission* (Glasgow 1827).
3. Anon., *Edinburgh City Mission* (Edinburgh n.d. c. 1832), 1.
4. Other early city missions were Dublin (1826), New York (1830) and Liverpool (1839).
5. Campbell, J., 1844, 462.
6. Anon., *Edinburgh City Mission* (Edinburgh n.d. c. 1832), 2.
7. *GCM*, Instructions to Agents.
8. Cleland, 1832, 45.
9. Adams, J. M., 1835, 208-9.
10. Cleland, 1832, 45.
11. *Handbook to the Charitable Institutions of Dundee* (Dundee 1875).
12. *GCM*, 38th AR, 1864, 11.
13. *Ibid.*, 36th AR, 1862, 11.
14. *Ibid.*, 53rd AR, 1879, 21.
15. *Ibid.*, 6.
16. *Glasgow Charitable and Philanthropic Institutions* (Glasgow 1892), 27.
17. Fleming, W., 1836, 9.
18. *Ibid.*, 16.
19. *Glasgow Sailors Home*, 4th AR (Glasgow 1862), 6.
20. Nichol, 1885, 232-233.
21. *Glasgow Charitable and Philanthropic Institutions* (Glasgow 1892), 17.
22. The inhabitants of Orkney and Shetland knew no Gaelic.
23. Anon., *State of the SSPCK* (Edinburgh 1741), 8.
24. Campbell, H. F., 'Notes on the County of Sutherland in the 18th century', *Gaelic Society of Inverness*, Vol. XXVI (1904-1907), 478.
25. *SSGS*, 24th AR, 1835, 36.
26. *Ibid.*, 1826, Resolution No. 1.
27. *Ibid.*, AR, 1826, 65.
28. Boyd, W., 'Colportage in Scotland', *SSPCK*, 1863, 236.
29. *Ibid.*, 237.
30. *Ibid.*
31. Kerr, J., 1913, Chapter XIII.
32. Mitchell, W., 1874, 109.

4

Piety and Medicine

1. Health as an evangelical aid

THE two greatest ancillary services that could be undertaken in conjunction with the primary aim of drawing men and women to God were to provide education and medical care. The Sunday Schools were the great vehicle of the former; in medicine, piety and healing were combined in a range of organisations. The Medical Mission Societies in Edinburgh and Glasgow, operated by male doctors and medical students aided by Bible Women nurses, perhaps made the largest contribution. But there were also ventures wholly for the training of women, especially in Edinburgh the Deaconess Hospital and, in Glasgow, the Medical Training Home for Lady Missionaries and the Lady Missionaries Training Home. Apart from the Deaconess Hospital, all these ventures took the form of dispensaries, treating the poor as out-patients (see chapter 11 below).

2. The Medical Mission Societies

Medical missions in Edinburgh and Glasgow had a dual purpose: to train men (and later women) for medical missionary service overseas, and at the same time to bring free medical treatment to the poor at home. The first medical mission in Britain was established in Edinburgh in 1841 where the medical school was already training men as doctors whose ambition was to enter the overseas mission field. The idea of a medical mission was first developed by Dr. Peter Parker, an American;[1] Dr. Parker visited Edinburgh briefly and impressed an influential group of university medical teachers there with 'a new and challenging vision of what medical science, allied with the Christian spirit might accomplish overseas'.[2] Edinburgh took the British initiative, and has remained a focal point of such work ever since.

The founding meeting was held in Edinburgh on 26 July 1841, with the Lord Provost as chairman; it resolved to support the Medical Missionary Society in China. On St. Andrew's Day (30 November) of the same year the committee convened a further meeting at which the Edinburgh Association for Sending Medical Aid to Foreign Countries was founded (the title was later changed to the Edinburgh Medical Mission Society). The first President was Dr. John Abercrombie, 'the acknowledged leader of the medical profession in Scotland'; his two Vice-Presidents were Dr. Thomas Chalmers and Dr. W. P. Alison. The practical day-to-day work of the organisation was carried out by Dr. John Coldstream, who was later described as 'virtually the founder'. In the 1840's there were similar societies in London, Liverpool and Glasgow, but they were short-lived.

In spite of strong Edinburgh support, entering the field abroad with a body of medically trained missionaries proved a difficult task. It was in the course of considering the implications of this that several members of the committee, including Dr. Peter Handyside (1808-1881), began to see the possibilities of a Home Medical Mission to feed and service the Overseas Medical Mission. Dr. Handyside started the work at Main Point, Edinburgh, and later took premises at 39 Cowgate, in a very poor part of the town, where in 1858 a dispensary was opened. Dr. Handyside remained a powerful influence on the medical mission. His philosophy was expressed in the annual address of 1871: 'The fundamental ideas which unite us in this institution [are] that the study of medicine is a noble pursuit, that the practice of medicine is a noble employment and that both the study and practice ought to be conducted, under the authority of God, for the good of our suffering fellow creatures.'[3]

But the real initiator of home medical missions was William Burns Thomson (1821-1893). He came 'to Edinburgh to prepare for the ministry, intending, when his studies were finished, to go as a missionary to China'.[4] As a young man he had undertaken missionary work in Edinburgh; there he had discovered how resistant the people were to Christian proselytisation. In a moment of desperation while visiting an unwelcoming family he offered medicine (in this case castor oil!) and was astonished at the change in the attitude of the family. Thus inspired and emboldened, he entered as a Prize Essay to the Edinburgh Missionary Society, *Medical Missions.*[5] He decided to substitute home mission work based upon medicine for his earlier ambition of overseas mission work. His first task was to obtain a medical qualification. This he did. When in 1859 he was appointed superintendent of the dispensary at 39 Cowgate he was promised the assistance of medical students who wished to work overseas and who were eager for experience among the poor. But he found their attendance erratic and unsatisfactory. Therefore in 1866 he persuaded the committee of his dispensary to allow him to open a hostel (run at his own expense) at 39 Cowgate, where the senior students could live, with more junior men living in George Square. No. 39 Cowgate became a home and work centre for these young men, led by Burns Thomson. When he married, he and his wife debated whether to live in such surroundings. They decided to do so. The move of the Thomsons to 39 Cowgate was deplored by many friends. 'The locality was so unhealthy,' they urged, 'the approach so filthy; your mind will never be off the strain; if your wife should die you will get the credit of dragging her into the Cowgate to her grave.' Within a few years 'ten students, three doctors, five Bible Women-nurses, two servants and mistress', making 21 in addition to the Burns Thomsons, were in residence.[6] This was the effective beginning of Scottish home medical missionary work.

One of the eminent doctors who supported the Medical Mission wholeheartedly was James Miller (1812-1864), Professor of Surgery in Edinburgh University. He became a director in 1847 and wrote warmly of the Medical Mission, which 'shew(s) how we may profitably blend the healing of the sick with the teaching of the gospel, the cure of the body with the care of the soul'.[7] As a result of his help the Edinburgh Medical Missionary Society's training scheme for nurses was launched, later based on Chalmers Hospital in the city, of which body Professor Miller was also a director. Dr. Thomson was able to send his nurses to train there.[8]

Burns Thomson's Training Institution at 39 Cowgate flourished, the dispensary became famous in that area of Edinburgh, and the inspiration and dedication of the man himself led to much emulation not only in Glasgow and Aberdeen but also in London and on the Continent. But Burns Thomson did not always work in harmony with his committee. Matters came to a head when, in 1870, a recalcitrant student appealed to the managing committee against an edict of Burns Thomson, and the committee supported the complainant. Thomson resigned and removed to St. John's Street in the Canongate. There he endeavoured to supply a comprehensive medical service for working families, including a small hospital. He retired in 1880, having lived long and arduously amongst the poor, doing a residential job which implied being 'on call' for twenty-four hours a day.

During the second half of Victoria's reign the premises at 39 Cowgate became increasingly unsatisfactory. At the time of David Livingstone's death (1873) there was a tremendous interest in and financial support for overseas medical mission work. The Board of Management of EMMA took the opportunity of launching an appeal. As a result the original building was demolished and a splended new complex constructed. The foundation stone of the new building was laid by the Rev. Dr. Moffat, Livingstone's father-in-law, on 9 June 1877, bearing the name of the 'Livingstone Memorial Medical Missionary Training Institution'. As well as a dispensary and offices, the facilities included a hall for evangelistic meetings.[9]

The Edinburgh Medical Mission survived in its old form until the National Health Service was introduced in 1948. The University of Edinburgh later took over the premises (now the Department of General Practice), and the Overseas Medical Mission moved to Malcolm Kerr House, 12 Mayfield Terrace, Edinburgh, where the Church of Scotland still maintains an active presence.

In Glasgow about 1868 a new initiative was taken to establish medical mission work. The objects of the Glasgow Medical Missionary Society were:

1. To encourage a Missionary spirit among Medical Students in Glasgow;
2. To co-operate with kindred Societies in training and supporting Medical Missionaries;
3. To carry on medical Mission work among the poor in Glasgow.

A dispensary was established at 68 Nelson Street where 'It endeavoured to encourage a missionary spirit among medical students in Glasgow.'[10] An advocate of a wider application of the principle was the Reverend James Johnston (St. James Free Church, Glasgow), who wrote: 'Instead of one medical mission in Glasgow, we should have ten, or at least six or seven thoroughly trained Christian physicians and surgeons, with all the appliances for medical and missionary work.'[11] But his ideas were never taken up and the Glasgow Medical Mission staff remained small and were probably seriously overworked. In the early 1870's the staff consisted of a superintendent and an assistant who was at one time a female, together with a dispenser and 'two Bible Women nurses' and no doubt domestic and janitorial staff.

With this modest complement of officials an enormous number of cases were undertaken. In addition to the crowds coming to the dispensary, the staff visited 640 patients at home between December 1870 and August 1871, as well as holding 229 prayer meetings. The Bible Women paid 1,925 visits. The ministrations of Dr. Lyell at this time were described thus: 'At one o'clock he reads to all who have assembled in the Mission Hall, a suitable portion of Scripture, carefully explains it, earnestly invites them to accept its precepts in simplicity, and then commends the passage to them for private meditation and prayer. This service occupies about half an hour, after which he prescribes for their bodily ailments and sufferings.'[12]

At Whitsunday 1872 the Glasgow Medical Mission moved to the Society's

Table 8

Statement of Income and Expenditure of Glasgow Medical Missionary Society in 1872

	£	s	d	£	s	d
By Balance due the Treasurer at 1st Dec., 1871						
,, Salaries— Dr. Lyell	£300	0	0			
Mr. Black, to 5th Oct.	45	0	0			
Mr. Nairn	4	0	0			
Dispensers	26	0	0			
Bible Women Nurses	63	0	0			
				438	0	0
,, Rent of Hall				50	0	0
,, Rent of Religious Institution Rooms for Meetings				3	6	0
,, Cleaning and Heating Hall, Hall Keeper, &c.				25	1	6
,, Printing, Advertising, Stationery, Tracts, &c.				30	11	7
,, Mrs. McLaren, Bible Woman Nurse, from London three months				11	7	6
,, Mrs. McLaren, Travelling Expenses, from London and back				4	0	0
,, Medicine and Sundries				79	0	0
				£643	17	1

Source: GMMS, 5th AR (Glasgow 1872), 33-34.

Income and Expenditure in 1890

INCOME

Year	Subscriptions	Investments	Miscellaneous Receipts	Legacies	Total	Ordinary Expenditure
1890	£1,151	£5	£20	£163	£1,339	£1,372

Source: Nicol, J., *Vital, Social & Economic Statistics of Glasgow* (Glasgow 1891), 35

New Hall, in Havannah Street. In September 1875 it opened another dispensary at 19 South Coburg Street.[13] By 1890 the work in Glasgow was being conducted from two addresses, at Moncur Street (25,000 annual visits) and Oxford Street (16,000 annual visits). These figures indicate a rate of 68 and 44 each day at Oxford Street and Moncur Street respectively. Such numbers of patients treated suggests that, with limited staffs, examination and diagnosis were necessarily cursory. The dispensaries also undertook 'much work . . . at the home of the poor by medical superintendents, nurses and medical students'.

The budgets of the Glasgow Medical Missionary Society were slender. Two examples remain. In 1872 their annual receipts and expenditure totalled £643, and by 1890 had risen to £1,372. A good deal of the working of such a society is indicated by its financial statement (see Table 8).

The Grove Street Mission in Glasgow (see above, chapter 3, section 3) also ran a comprehensive Medical and Surgical Department. When it took possession of its new wing in 1895 it was able to allocate more space to the medical work. Dr. J. Anderson Robertson was Superintendent of the Medical Mission and he had five medical colleagues assisting him, including Dr. J. G. Connal who specialised in throat and nose cases. They were open five afternoons a week and (in 1894) had over 4,000 consultations and paid over 200 visits to the homes of the poor. The doctors were supported both at the Mission and in the home visits by lady missionaries based at the Lady Missionaries' Training Home, 15 Burnbank Gardens.

3. **Mission staff; the women's role; the Deaconesses**

The ability of women to undertake a philanthropic role was determined primarily by their general status in society. Because they were thought incapable of major roles as organisers, they were left with only minor philanthropic functions. Their attempts to extend their sphere of action were accompanied by an urge to serve and a willingness to do so in minor roles and without payment; this self-effacement and altruism made them acceptable, but only under male aegis.

It would have been surprising if women had not sought a wider role directly through the church and its institutions. The Roman catholic church had always used women as nurses and teachers, but the protestant churches had not drawn upon such labour. During the second half of Victoria's reign the movement to recruit women for professional duties as Christian workers gathered momentum and by the end of the century several new and important initiatives had been taken, though still using women only at a lowly level. Some of the work undertaken by women was paid, but often only minimally; women undertaking such employment were recognised by society as acting altruistically, as 'angels of mercy'.

There are signs that during the generation before 1887 members of the Church of Scotland were searching for a wider role for women. But effective action was not taken until then. The Reverend Professor A. H. Charteris (1835-1908), in his Baird Lectures in 1887, traced the recognition of women's work from Phoebe, the deaconess of the early church commended by St. Paul (Romans, XVI, 1). He proposed a pyramidal structure which would encompass all facets of women's work within the church. The base would be the Women's Guild, 'tapering upwards through the Guild leaders and associates to the deaconesses'.[14] The Church of Scotland, increasingly uneasy at the threats which the new humanism had produced, and seeking to confirm the allegiance of the women, was prepared to accept Charteris' plan. It was the more eager to do so because it needed trained women for overseas mission work, as well as for tasks at home.

A period of experimentation had begun in the 1850's involving initiatives both religious and medical. The most obvious field for women's service was in nursing. During the Crimean War (1854-1856) the dreadful losses inflicted by disease rather than by battle gave a tremendous impulse to the movement to develop nursing services based on cleanliness. Those operating medical missions were eager to use women. They gradually developed, from the Bible Woman, the Bible Woman Nurse. The missions attempted to ensure that their Bible Women Nurses were hospital-trained. Burns Thomson in Edinburgh sent his to Chalmers Hospital; there was a similar arrangement in Glasgow. But there was friction when the general hospitals started to organise their own training schemes (see chapter 13, section 3 below).

The Bible Woman Nurse served in the mission itself and also made a great many home visits. She was warmly regarded by the doctors who employed her. Burns Thomson had one, notable for her 'piety and gumption', at 39 Cowgate from about 1861. Dr. Lyell, of Glasgow, was enthusiastic, remarking on 'the amount of practical good which a number of prudent Christian women, with a thorough knowledge of nursing can bring to this society'.[15]

But despite the welcome which the Bible Woman Nurse received, she was not given enough training to become a professional. Partly as a result of this, her role as a ministering angel dispensing Christian piety as well as medicine was increasingly called in question. It was therefore inevitable that a more professional approach to nursing would eventually squeeze her out.

The Deaconess movement was an attempt to assert a new effectiveness for women. It developed along lines similar to those established in Germany at Kaisersworth in 1836. Deaconesses were, in this context, Christian women social workers who had varying responsibilities either within the community or more specifically as trained nurses in a hospital. The Mildmay Mission for Deaconesses was founded in 1860 in London as a nurses' training establishment for such women. Later, in 1877, a small hospital was opened in an old factory at Bethnal Green.[16] After an appeal for funds a proper hospital was opened in Austin Street in 1892. Women were trained there for a dual role, either at home or overseas. As Deaconesses they either became qualified nurses or they trained for congregational work visiting in the parish; in either case their roles were secondary and supportive under the authority of men.

Following Professor Charteris' initiative in 1887, steps were taken to work out the practical details of a Deaconess movement within the Church of Scotland. It was recommended that the Deaconesses should be drawn from two classes:

1.   Those who have been active workers for seven years;
2.   Those who underwent two years' training and service within the Institution.

Once set apart they were to have the right to append the letters D.C.S., Deaconess of the Church of Scotland, to their names. The scheme was accepted by the Assembly and all seemed in order and approved. There was a slight flurry, however, when the Edinburgh Presbytery raised the matter of the Deaconess's status, believing that she would rank higher than the elder if she were to be 'set apart' by the presbytery. As a result it was agreed that a Deaconess would be set apart by her own kirk session, which would then inform the presbytery. The way being clear, Lady Grisell Baillie, the first Deaconess, was set apart at Bowden on 9 December 1888. She was a distinguished senior lady, and had in effect performed the functions of a Deaconess for many years. As first Deaconess she also became the head of the Women's Guild, founded in 1887.

By giving a role to the Guild the church encouraged a strong response from the women. The Guild undertook many philanthropic concerns such as 'Health visitation of Infants, Charity Organisation, Red Cross Movement, Cripples Leagues, Guilds of Play, and Mission Study Circles'.[17] Naturally the Guild was also keenly involved in supporting overseas mission work; it financed the building of the Charteris Hospital at Kalimpong in 1893, which had Deaconesses on its staff.

The co-ordination of women's missionary work under the Deaconess banner meant that much progress could be made. In Edinburgh a house was rented at 33 Mayfield Gardens (opened on 16 December 1887). Subsequently 41 and later 27 George Square were purchased. The centre in Edinburgh was intended to become the mother-house, handling all applications and co-ordinating activity under the Deaconess Board. It in turn came under the Church Life and Work Committee of the General Assembly of the Church of Scotland.

Glasgow produced its own new initiatives, enabling women to train for medical missionary work both at home and abroad. They were based on the Missionary Nurses Training Home (at 8 Westercraigs, Dennistoun), later known as the Medical Training Home for Lady Missionaries. Dr. Charteris inaugurated a lecture series in Glasgow in 1889. On these courses women spent a total of three years training, a long time for those days. There was a three-month probationary period in the training home, studying 'biblical instruction and evangelistic training'. Thereafter candidates committed themselves to a 2½-

year medical course. Finally there were six months of 'further practical training in evangelistic work'.[18] The medical courses consisted of the following:

Table 9

Course of Medical Study at the Medical Training Home for Lady Missionaries, Glasgow

First Summer	*First Winter*	*Second Summer*	*Second Winter*	*Last 3 months*
Anatomy (3 months)	Anatomy (6 months)	Surgery		
Materia Medica	Physiology Medicine		Medicine	Practical Midwifery in Maternity Hospital
		Diseases of the Eye	Diseases of Women	
Clinical Medicine	Clinical Medicine	Clinical Medicine	Clinical Medicine	
Clinical Surgery	Clinical Surgery	Clinical Surgery	Clinical Surgery	

Source: Prospectus of the Medical Training Home for Lady Missionaries (Glasgow n.d. c. 1894).

Such a course of three years, with so comprehensive a teaching programme, must have raised the Lady Missionaries who qualified to a level well above that of nurses in general, approaching that of doctors themselves.

A second Glasgow venture was the Lady Missionaries' Training Home at 15 Burnbank Gardens. It was established at the behest of the Grove Street Institute as a base for 'Christian Young Women of any evangelical denomination' who desired to become missionaries either at home or abroad, who 'wish one or two years Biblical and Medical instruction'.[19] The young women do not appear to have received any formal lectures, although the 'Practical Christian Work' embraced 'Nursing and visiting the Sick, District Visiting, Teaching the Young, Dispensary work, etc.'

Thus, with the Deaconesses in Edinburgh and the women trained by missionary organisations in Glasgow, new opportunities for education and service were created. But these women, when their course was finished, were nurses, not doctors. Their training represented a half-way house; they had received some serious medical education, the purpose of which was to enable them to cope in foreign mission stations where they could expect to be isolated and only rarely in contact with a male doctor. The relatively poorly trained Bible Woman Nurse was bound to be pushed out by the new professionalism. While in some cases she may have transferred to further training, her basic education was rarely sufficient for her to compete with other better qualified women. The medical training of the Lady Missionaries in Glasgow represented a curious hybrid between the status of doctor and nurse, which could not maintain its position, especially in the face of the demand for full and equal medical training for women doctors.

The role of the Deaconess remained a valuable outlet for women largely due to the powerful support given by the Church of Scotland. Because a Deaconess was either a trained nurse or a trained social worker she emerged as a significant part of the new professionalism of middle-class women.

4. The Deaconess Hospital, Edinburgh

The work of the Deaconesses was centred on the Pleasance, a district of Edinburgh which belied its name. There were one hundred and eleven 'Deaconettes' enrolled, most of whom were able to pay their own expenses, especially as the terms for board in the Deaconess House were very reasonable. Initially nurses' training for these women was in the Edinburgh Royal Infirmary and its counterpart in Glasgow, but there were difficulties. It was suggested that Deaconesses were being wrongly trained to work in large hospitals when their careers would be in small ones. This may have been the case, but more likely there were conflicts of divided authority.

Such difficulties quickly led to plans for the Deaconess Hospital with the motto 'Christo in pauperibus', where the women would receive training suitable to their role. Funds were raised with great enthusiasm. The Hospital[20] was opened at the Pleasance, on 11 October 1894, a memorial to Lady Grisell Baillie. Professor Charteris was eloquent on the Deaconess training: 'It is the Christian visitor,' he said, 'and not the mere nurse that we educate here.'[21] He explained that 'a special sub-division, Deaconess-Nurses' was envisaged: 'We are a home for teaching sick-nursing as part of the education of Christian workers.' The hospital had 22 beds and much ancillary accommodation for the Deaconesses and other staff. The whole establishment cost rather less than £4,000. It was presented free of debt to the Church 'as a means of furthering her usefulness to the Scottish people'. The Deaconess Hospital is still at work in the Pleasance, although it was taken over in 1948 as a part of the National Health Service.

5. Healing and preaching

To the medical men and women serving in a home medical mission or in the Deaconess Hospital, their mixture of faith dispensed with medicine seemed unassailable. Others were less favourably impressed. Some responded angrily, annoyed that medicine was sometimes only available if the recipients accepted the religious observances of the medical mission.

However, the Webbs' gibe, inspired by the English medical missions, of 'mixing up medicine with religion'[22] may not have been a justified criticism in Scotland. Many medical teachers in the universities were ardent Christians who regarded service in a medical mission as an important commitment. As a result their medical contribution was a very real one, whatever its religious significance. In addition they could anticipate finding cases of special medical interest among the patients.

Medical mission dispensaries epitomised the evangelical spirit of the nineteenth century uniting Christian teaching with healing. As Burns Thomson urged: 'Pray that both the medical and theological student may be taught and trained . . . to labour together in the same work.' The Webbs, from their rationalistic atheist viewpoint made some of their most biting comments on these institutions, partly because they so distrusted the idea of effective medical treatment being associated with Christian proselytisation. But the medical mission dispensaries were a unique and valuable phenomenon. To men like Burns Thomson they were a means of merging medicine and the evangelical call. As he wrote, 'It was the heaven directed, heaven approved method of Christian aggression — Heal and Preach.'[23]

NOTES

1. Parker, 1842.
2. Garlick, 1943, 32.
3. Mss Volume *EMMS* possibly by Dr. Handyside.
4. Burns Thomson, 1895, 19.
5. *Ibid.*, 1857.
6. *Ibid.*, 1895, 11.
7. Anon, *Lectures on Medical Missions*, 1849, 4.
8. *Chalmers Hospital* AR, 1866, 3.
9. *EMMA* 100th AR, 1941, 7 and Taylor, H. F. L., 1941.
10. Anon., 1871, 60.
11. Johnston, 1871, 26.
12. *GMMS* 5th AR, 1872, 5.
13. Russell, 1876, 38.
14. Gordon, A., 1912, 355.
15. *GMMS* 5th AR, 1872, 7.
16. The Bethnal Green Medical Mission is still in existence. It conducts a general medical practice, run by three Christian doctors, as well as religious mission services.
17. Gordon, A., 1912, 359.
18. *Medical Training Home for Lady Missionaries*, prospectus (n.p., n.d.), 5.
19. *Grove Street Institute, Glasgow*, AR 1895, 50.
20. Gibson, G. A., 'The Deaconess Hospital, Edinburgh', *EHR*, Vol. III (Edinburgh 1895), 7-12.
21. Charteris, A. H., 1894.
22. Webb, S. & B., 1910, 134-5.
23. Burns Thomson, 1854, 46.

5
Piety and Temperance

1. Piety and sobriety

THE evangelical piety of the Victorians, as we have seen, covered a wide spectrum. At the one end there was the objective of inducing piety in a 'pure form', through Church Extension, Bible Societies, Sabbath Schools and the like. But piety had increasingly to be associated with a wider programme which included secular diversions and help. The diversions included bodies like the Boys' Brigade and the YMCA. The help took the form of medical services through the mission dispensaries, together with welfare advice and aid.

There remains one further area in which piety expressed itself but had to come to terms with the real conditions of working-class lives. This was the matter of temperance. Philanthropists, largely of the middle class, made an immense effort to deal with the problem of drunkenness that was so appalling in Scotland in Victorian times. For the evangelical, true piety was only possible in the sober; only a man in full possession of his faculties could be responsible for himself to God.

But among the churches there was some equivocation. In the eighteenth and early nineteenth centuries ministers of religion drank with the rest of their social class; relatively few were prepared, before mid-century, to take a stand in favour of temperance. Yet within the churches there was a minority of pious men and women who pressed for an attack on this dreadful problem. When the Free Church came into being after the Disruption of 1843, composed as it was of ardent evangelicals it became the focus of the Scottish temperance movement. Gradually support spread through the churches, so that by the later nineteenth century the link between piety and temperance was very strong. But, as in other areas of pietistic activity, it was necessary to provide something more. As a result men and women who had entered upon philanthropy through temperance found themselves seeking to improve the quality of working-class social life so that recourse to drink might be lessened. There was thus a three-part progression: from piety, through temperance, to the provision of social facilities.

2. Early temperance

Tho' serpent drinks that dim our fame
And send afar our island's shame
O! Britons! Britons! give them up
Dash down the foul deceiving cup

From the frontispiece of *History of Temperance*, 1855, by Edward Morris, a clerk in the Canal swift-boat passenger office, Port Dundas, Glasgow.

The temperance movement probably aroused more passion than any other of the campaigns for social improvement in Victorian Scotland. It was seen by many as a salvationist cause, to rescue the working-class male from himself, from frittering away his income on strong drink and from a path leading inevitably to moral degradation. Its supporters launched many campaigns. First there were appeals for particular forms of abstinence (from beer, or whisky or brandy), then teetotalism, then prohibitionism in various forms. The success of these campaigns is difficult to judge. But there is no doubt as to their widely based philanthropic intent, liberally and voluntarily financed as they were by substantial sections of Scottish society. Especially after 1850, temperance, in one form or another, was attracting support from men and women at almost all levels of society, encouraging an inter-class relationship which did much to increase social cohesion. Temperance in any form was, indeed, associated with religious commitment, requiring the individual to be self-disciplined. The churches insisted that drunkenness diminished self-control and self-respect, and led eventually to the drunkard's neglect of himself, his family and his community. The churches of Victorian Scotland, in urging elements of society towards temperance, were powerful proponents of self-help.

The idea of controlling drink was a revolutionary one. Even the hospitals dosed their patients with large quantities of alcohol, assisting many of them to drunkenness. To the community in general, and to employers in particular, heavy drinking was a wasteful and destructive pastime. Whether men were driven to drink because of their poverty or their drinking habits caused their poverty was a constant argument. The early reformers optimistically believed that it would be possible to persuade a whole people to abandon strong drink and banish the problems of drunkenness with all its attendant tragedy from Scotland. Later leaders proposed more modest and more attainable objectives. Attempts were made to alter the laws, to control the trade by restricting the number of licences, to fix the opening hours of public houses, and to give local residents the power of local veto. These campaigns to achieve an acceptable level of control of the drink trade represent an important part of Victorian life, a movement which affected all classes.

Temperance agitation was always troubled by definitional difficulties. Whether temperance, moderation or abstinence were the favoured words, the necessary extent of personal commitment to improved behaviour was always difficult to define. The most common form of promise to remain teetotal was by taking the 'pledge', whereby an individual vowed absolutely not to take intoxicating liquor. As a later refinement the 'pledge' could either be 'long' or 'short'; with the former the individual would neither drink intoxicating liquor himself nor offer it to others; with the latter he committed only himself. Opponents of the pledge criticised the emotional meetings, so often combining a plea for religious conversion, after which most pledges were taken. It was widely believed that many pledgers regretted their commitment and became backsliders with an additional burden of guilt.

The nineteenth-century temperance movement appeared spontaneously in several regions, first in North America, and later in Northern Ireland and Scotland. John Dunlop founded the first temperance society in Scotland in Greenock in October 1829. He moved quickly into Maryhill, Glasgow, and gained the support of William Collins I. The first abstainers forswore spirits, 'the scorching brandy, the burning rum, the fiery whisky and the stinging gin'. But other drinks were permitted, so that as the sales of spirits fell those of beer and wines went up: 'The brewers of ales and porters, and the wine merchants, said . . . that the pledge of the first movement did them good, it worked into their coffers.'[1]

Although John Dunlop had a modest success with his first temperance societies, he was advocating an extremely unpopular course. Early Victorian social usage in Scotland demanded that any friendly intercourse between neighbours, businessmen, workmates or friends, or even clergy and their charges, should be celebrated with a drink. This social compulsion was very demanding. As Dunlop himself expressed it in 1839, 'There has been constituted with us a conventional and artificial connexion between liquor and courtesy and business; and this unnatural conjunction is not . . . occasional but universal.'[2] In consequence there were few converts to temperance in the West of Scotland in the early 1830's. Many clergymen and doctors, among other professional men, ridiculed the idea. Working men remained indifferent to a cause the acceptance of which would cut them off from their friends and associates.

Temperance meetings could indeed be successful in the short term, but support soon fell away. The dedicated of Glasgow, Messrs Dunlop, Collins, Kettle, Wardlaw, Reid, Drs. Ritchie, Beattie and others, struggled on, but clearly some change of tactic was necessary. In Preston, Manchester and Liverpool, Joseph Livesey and his friends were making steady progress with a teetotal movement, on joining which all members pledged themselves to abstain from all intoxicating liquors (unless specifically prescribed by a doctor).[3] Temperance in Glasgow was so moribund in 1836 that the Glasgow pioneers had the mortification of receiving an emissary from Lancashire, sent by Joseph Livesey, who wished to vitalise the movement in Glasgow by transforming it into one of total abstinence. Mr. John Finch, an iron merchant from Liverpool, rallied the discouraged men of Glasgow and on 16 September 1836 initiated a new movement based on total abstinence centred upon the Glasgow Radical Temperance Society.[4] Of the 37 members named, the occupations of

11 are given.[5] Mr. Morris was the only name well-known in temperance circles who gave his support to the total abstinence movement. But his modest job and status may have made it difficult for him to carry conviction with Collins and Dunlop, who belonged to a superior class of civic leaders. The new Society offered an uncompromising platform: it was too strong for the 'moderation' party. Collins reconsidered his position and withdrew. This was less surprising because he was already deeply engaged in other good works, including the Glasgow Church Extension movement. In 1838 the Glasgow Abstinence Society was formed. In September of that year the various Scottish elements joined forces as the Scottish Temperance Union (later re-named the Scottish Temperance League in 1844).

Succeeding waves of the temperance agitation brought new men into the campaigns with novel objectives and fresh energy. After 1850 the emphasis changed; the stress on moral suasion of the individual remained, but not in the forefront. Temperance campaigns now aimed to change the law of the land in order to bring the drink trade under more stringent controls. The individual pledge remained an essential part of the personal commitment of many, but most temperance workers recognised that the additional force of the law was required.

Nevertheless a vociferous minority within the movement opposed the shift of temperance policy towards legislative enactment. The strife between the factions was long and bitter. As one observer lamented, some 'kindled the fires of dissension and strife; and, with a terrible fidelity to a wrong cause, they have continued to fan them with unflagging zeal'.[6] The Scottish Temperance League became the focus of the opposition to the campaigns for legal control of the drink trade. Within the churches the League was commended for its vigour, for 'It was pointed out that it had distributed temperance literature to the extent of 19½ million pages.'[7]

3. Government intervention

There was separate provision for control of the liquor trade in England and Scotland. Legislation to this end in England dated from the seventeenth century. It began in Scotland in 1756 with an Act to ensure that retailers of alcoholic liquors obtained licences. It was based on an English statute, and mention was made of 'ale, beer or other exciseable liquors', a categorisation which apparently excluded whisky. In 1793 a further Act rectified this omission and required those who sold whisky to obtain a licence and pay stamp duty on it. From 1808 a licence provided by the Excise authorities for retail sale was conditional on a publican obtaining a 'certificate' from the justices.

The interest of the central government was primarily in revenue raising; it was not at this time concerned with the social problems caused by heavy and continuous drinking. In an attempt to simplify a complicated and widely by-passed duty system the government in 1824 reduced the duty on spirits from 7s. to 2s. 10d. per Scotch gallon. As a result consumption rocketed from some 2 million gallons to almost 6 million gallons by 1830, although smuggling may have artificially depressed the earlier figure.

In response to deteriorating public behaviour in the towns, and to public pressure for more information, a Select Committee on Intoxication was set up in 1834. This was chaired by James Silk Buckingham, an enthusiastic temperance advocate. The witnesses from Scotland included William Collins I, John Dunlop and Sheriff Substitute Campbell. Collins in evidence noted that in 1832 Glasgow 'contained 19,467 families with 1,360 spirit dealers'.[8] John Dunlop reported that in 1829 within the Royalty of Edinburgh 'in 1833 the number of licences was 736', an astonishing figure for a population of 55,232.[9] Sheriff Substitute Campbell of Paisley explained that 'I have been perpetually met with objections on the score of its being an encroachment upon the liberties of the subject to refuse a licence to every person certified as of decent character . . . who, . . . desires to earn a living by acting as land lords of tippling houses'.[10]

Despite the impact of evidence strongly in favour of control, much of it from the philanthropists, the government was unconvinced of the need for strong action. The duty on a Scots gallon of spirits was raised to 3s. 8d. in 1840, but this was not enough to affect consumption, and public disquiet continued. By the 1850's the city authorities in both Edinburgh and Glasgow were sufficiently concerned at the threat posed by drunkenness to the civil peace to consider taking steps to limit excesses within their own boundaries. In both places constraints were placed on the hours of licensed premises, which had hitherto been open or not at the choice of the licensee. The Lord Provost of Edinburgh between 1851 and 1854 was Duncan McLaren;[11] himself deeply convinced of the need for temperance, he was determined to enforce some control on the drink trade. The regulations which he imposed in the city became the basis of the Forbes Mackenzie Act of 1853.[12] It was the major piece of temperance legislation in Scotland before 1903, carefully regulating the times of opening of public houses, and giving the magistrates the power to withdraw licences where the prescribed hours were breached. Each major Scottish burgh had its Police Acts; these Acts often contained powers that could be used to regulate the drink trade, as McLaren had done in Edinburgh. In Glasgow local regulations had been passed in 1839 and 1850 requiring public houses to be closed on Sundays.

The advocates of consumption controls for the liquor trade were well satisfied with the effects of the Forbes Mackenzie Act. But others deplored any campaigns which effectively curtailed free choice. James Stirling, an active pamphleteer of the day, wrote persuasively against the Act: 'The State has no right to compel morality. Self-ennoblement is the end of man's existence; and to force virtue on him, even were it possible, is to do him wrong'.[13] But despite

James Stirling's Rousseau-esque arguments, temperance advocates, aware that the government would require to be strongly lobbied before any further legislation might be forthcoming, were moving steadily towards ever more urgent campaigns to control legislation. To this end new philanthropic organisations fed by new funds with new campaigns were necessary.

4. Campaigns for legal restraint, 1858-1914

From the 1850's there were two distinct campaigns organised by temperance societies in Scotland. The less spectacular was that mounted by the Scottish Temperance League[14] (allied to the British Temperance Association in England). The League's campaigns were based on educating the people towards self-discipline and self-control. To do this it was assiduous in organising lecture campaigns in church and public halls, and provided a wide range of temperance literature at modest (and subsidised) prices.

Its rival, the Scottish Permissive Bill and Temperance Association, founded in 1858, based its strategy on legislative enactment to regulate and reduce the liquor trade, through strict control of the issuing of licences. The Association's work focused on the 'local veto', by which the inhabitants of whole areas in Scotland could vote, by a majority, to exclude the sale of all liquor in their area. The Association's programme was much more newsworthy than that of the League and drew more attention from the public press. The League sought to convert to temperance, through church and chapel meetings and other social activities. The Association sought to use the power of its members and supporters to alter the rules of life of everyone else in the community through legislative action.

The temperance movement in Scotland followed with interest campaigns being waged elsewhere. Delegates travelled widely for this purpose. There was especial interest, after 1850, in various forms of prohibition. Two developments in the United States and in Sweden were especially remarked. Under the terms of the Maine Law, liquor traffic was totally prohibited; many temperance workers in Scotland were advocates of this. Indeed in Edinburgh in the spring of 1853 the Maine Liquor Law League was formed 'to agitate for the total legislative Prohibition of the liquor traffic'. The Gothenburg system,[15] based upon licensing, seemed to many others in Scotland to offer a satisfactory way forward.

On the frontispiece of the annual reports of the Scottish Permissive Bill and Temperance Association was the stated objective, 'to assist in procuring the suppression of the liquor traffic by the power of the national will and through the form of a legislative enactment'. Elsewhere in the report this aim was described as 'the promotion of Total Abstinence from all intoxicating beverages — not as a matter of expediency, but as a duty, based upon Christian morals and sound philosophy . . .'[16] The Association was remarkable for the skill with which it harnessed support from all levels of society. Lord Kinnaird represented the landed aristocracy and there were several parliamentary members who were prepared to devote their time to temperance. These included Mr. A. Cameron Corbett, member for Tradeston, Glasgow, Mr. John Wilson, member for Govan, Mr. Alex. Findlay, member for Lanarkshire N.E., and Mr. P. McLagan, member for Linlithgowshire. The Association's campaigns ran parallel to those organised by the United Kingdom Alliance (founded 1853), whose 'praiseworthy efforts to secure the enactment of a permissive bill, conferring upon the ratepayers of cities, burghs, parishes, and townships, the power to prohibit the traffic within their respective boundaries' were emulated in Scotland. There was much co-operation between the two bodies. Although many members of the Association in Scotland would have preferred to outlaw the drink trade absolutely, for practical reasons ambitions were focused on the possibilities of what came to be known as the 'local veto'. Because such an objective required legislation, the Association needed an active voice in Parliament. This it found in Sir William Lawson (1829-1906) of Brayton (the member for Carlisle), who presented a series of Permissive Bills, all of which failed, to the House in the 1860's and 1870's. The Permissive Bill Association took careful note of the voting record of all Scottish M.P.'s:

Table 10

Votes of Scottish Members on the Permissive Bills

	1864	*1869*	*1870*	*1871*	*1873*	*1874*	*1875*	*1876*
Ayes	10	12	16	24	18	16	19	18
Noes	24	18	12	14	20	19	24	16
Absent	19	30	32	22	22	25	17	26
	53	60	60	60	60	60	60	60

Source: SPBTA, AR (Glasgow 1876), 6

At no time did the advocates of the Permissive Bill get more than 24 of the 60 Scottish members of parliament to vote in favour, and there were large numbers of abstentions. The Association was jubilant in 1876 when it was discovered that 18 Scottish M.P.'s had voted in favour and 16 against the Bill. They subsequently campaigned even more energetically, convinced that success was imminent.

Legislative control of the drink trade could produce many variants of legislative proposals. A wide range of Bills was presented to Parliament from the 1870's to 1914. The Association in its Annual Report methodically discussed these other measures. 'There were seven Liquor Bills, two Sunday-Closing Bills, two Suspensory Bills, an Assimilating Bill, a Licensing Boards Bill and the Permissive Bill[17] introduced during the Parliamentary Session 1875-6.' These other Bills represented attempts to control the drink trade through licences and other means. The amount of Parliamentary time and energy devoted to this question reflects the amount of interest in the country at large.

Out of this welter of schemes the most hopeful for legislation seemed to be the 'local option' or local veto. It was not difficult for protagonists to find evidence from police reports and other sources of the advantages in an area with no public houses. As William Kidston reported in Glasgow in 1875, 'With regard to the district of Hillhead . . . it was entirely free from crime . . . The reason for that very satisfactory state of things was the entire absence of public houses. Hundreds of working men passed through the burgh, on the Great Western Road, and in consequence of there being no public houses they went straight to their homes.'[18] In 1890 Glasgow promoted a private Police Act which enabled the populations of wards to keep pubs out of their areas altogether, by refusing to issue licences. Indeed when large areas were covered with local authority housing in the inter-war years, no pubs at all were built in these parts of the city.[19] The move which Glasgow made to obtain the power to enforce a local veto was not at this time national to Scotland.

The British government, whether Liberal or Tory, had continued to regard temperance as a sectional and divisive issue. Both parties in Scotland (though not in England) received support from the brewery interests, although the Liberals were in part 'captured' from time to time by temperance interests. In 1896 the government temporised by setting up a Royal Commission on Liquor Licensing Laws for Britain as a whole, 'to enquire into the operation and administration of the laws relating to the sale of intoxicating liquors, and to examine and report upon the proposals that may be made for amending the aforesaid laws in the public interest, due regard being had to the right of individuals'. The Commission of 23 men was headed by Viscount Peel, with eight representatives of the liquor trade and eight on the temperance side; the other members were neutral. The Commission produced a majority report, deploring the situation but not offering solutions, and a minority report recommending local option as a solution. One of the vexed problems was related to compensation for the licensees in the event of arbitrary curtailment of licences.

The Temperance Association hoped to build on the proposals of the minority report. But in the meantime came the Licensing (Scotland) Act, 1903. As a codifying Act it was not hailed with any great enthusiasm by the temperance movement, but it proved valuable for it tidied up and clarified a number of confused matters.

The campaigns for local veto continued with increasing fervour. There were further attempts to legislate in favour of the veto, but these continued to be unsuccessful until 1913. In that year the Temperance (Scotland) Act was passed. Thereby powers were given to local communities to make themselves 'dry'. But no veto polls were to be held until June 1920.

5. 'Counter-activities'

During Victoria's reign temperance campaigners launched a wide range of what they called counter-activities designed to wean men away from convivial drinking. This positive policy was of great importance, not only for men but for women and children, offering a programme of social activities which carried on throughout the year. It was often organised through the church and gave families a new focus for their lives. In the winter, meetings, soirées and entertainments, with singing and recitations, were held. In summer excursions to the sea and to the country were arranged. Many cocoa and coffee houses were opened; temperance hotels and bowling greens were other forms of social response from the temperance movement.

No one was more successful in organising counter-attractions than Mr. Thomas Corbett, a businessman working in Glasgow, with his Great Western Cooking Depot.[20] He was 'a philanthropist of the most practical kind'; one who did not 'distribute his means like milk spilled upon the ground'. He and his wife were impressed with the idea of providing pure food, well prepared and cooked, for the working population of Glasgow. By so doing they would keep working men out of the pubs in their lunch hour, as well as improving the diet of them and their families. After consulting various people in London and else-where, they resolved to open a depot where each item of cooked food would if possible be served for 1d: 'A bowl of porridge, . . . a plate of potatoes, an egg, a cup of coffee, cost no more.'[21] The project was an extraordinary success. The Corbetts established a larger cooking depot in Pitt Street (the original one had been in the Broomielaw adjacent to the Sailors' Home), and from this centre enormous supplies of victuals were sent out every morning to all parts of the city. By 1872 there were 28 branches of the Cooking Depot in operation. Although the principal ones were in Jamaica Street and Mitchell Lane, 'most of them are in the immediate vicinity of public works'; so that hundreds of workmen obtained their dinner each day from this source. Indeed from August 1871 the various branches had between 10,000 and 12,000 customers every day.[22] The Great Western was a profitable venture despite its modest charges. This was achieved by making 'a farthing of profit on every pennyworth sold', and Corbett himself 'received a certain interest for his money'. But apart from his modest return, all the remaining profit was re-invested in other charitable ventures; by 1872 over £7,000 had been so allocated.

All over Scotland there were many anti-drink initiatives, albeit on a lesser scale. At Dundee the British Workman, a 'public-house' without drink, was opened in the Overgate, with 'a free reading room for all-comers, . . . and refreshments may be purchased at a cheap rate, . . . in premises which had previously been used as a public house for seventy years, and is intended to be a counter active to the evils of the ordinary public house.'[23]

In addition to their Sabbath Evening Discourses, the Glasgow Abstainers' Union arranged Saturday Evening Concerts by which they 'endeavoured to suit all tastes, meet the wants of all classes, and offend none'. Twenty concerts and ten 'entertainments' were organised each year. 'Three Opera recitals were given, and one oratorio, the choruses being rendered respectively by Mr. H. A. Lambeth's Select Choir, Mr. W. M. Miller's Select Choir and the Glasgow Tonic Sol-fa Choral Society.' The Union quaintly referred to its entertainments as 'operating negatively', while the Sunday discourses were 'positive'! The success of the Glasgow Abstainers' Union rested significantly on its social activities. Men, and especially women and children, were glad to have such diversions laid on either free or at a modest cost. By 1860, in addition to the City Hall concerts on Saturday evenings, there were Soirées or Social Tea Parties, Lectures and, most enjoyable of all, Excursions 'every Saturday afternoon during the summer months to places of Historic Interest and Natural Beauty'.

The Glasgow Abstainers' Union also took the initiative in providing homes for those convalescing from accident or illness. It opened the Kilmun Sea-Side Convalescent Home for the Poor. The Directors were delighted to report that it 'has proved a most valuable and direct Temperance Agency; from 30 to 40 weekly living in a Temperance Home, receiving Temperance Teaching, for your Matron is also a Temperance Missionary, practising the principles and experiencing the benefits . . .' (see chapter 12, section 2, below).

The energy and initiative of temperance organisations in providing counter-attractions was important. They undertook work at so many levels, organising fairs and 'hoppings' as counter-attractions to horse-race meetings. Their activities provided new interests for working-class families, occupying the leisure time of people never before catered for. The use of free time by pleasurable temperance occasions was an educational experience opening new horizons in an informal way to people living drab and dull lives. Many had much for which to thank the Temperance Movement.

6. Success?

The Temperance Movement made a great impact on the lives of men, women and children in Victorian Scotland. There can be little doubt that the leisure pursuits it provided helped to popularise the movement and its objectives. Women and children stood to gain most from the success of temperance, because the home of the abstainer was much more comfortable and secure than that of the heavy drinker, and because contact with the movement brought a widening of social and cultural horizons. Temperance organisations took to publishing improving works of fiction or non-fiction with women in mind.[24] Until the mid-century the professional and employing classes approached temperance gingerly and with little enthusiasm. Perhaps only after the counter-activities movement was well established did the middle class activists emerge in strength to throw their very important influence behind temperance.

H

The attitudes of the churches to the temperance movement reflect the change, for success was cumulative. Churchmen and their congregations became increasingly involved in all aspects of temperance. Indeed by 1900, as David Paton remarks, 'the Temperance Movement had become much more closely identified with the church at a time when the church itself was on the point of becoming a "failing force"'.[25]

In the second half of the century temperance campaigns, supported by men and women of power and influence in the community, became more aggressive and demanding. Although the signing of the pledge remained an important feature of temperance meetings, the limited nature of this device was realised. The main aim of the campaigns altered; complete prohibition of the drink trade was increasingly advocated. The claims made on behalf of systems of prohibition such as the Gothenburg System and the Maine Law were seriously challenged and brought into disrepute. The dangers of complete prohibition came to be acknowledged by many temperance authorities.

Their really effective campaign was that in favour of the local veto. By the time it was organised, the professional classes (including the might of all the churches in Scotland) were lined up in support. The passage in 1913 of the Temperance (Scotland) Act gave the local communities the chance (to be first exercised in 1920) of taking a poll of the inhabitants to see whether licences in their area should be banned. The Act required that 35% of those on the electoral register should vote (as a minimum) and that 55% of those voting should be in favour of the No-Licence resolution.

The local veto campaigns brought prohibition to some areas of Scotland for more than 50 years. These were the better-off suburban areas and some rural places where the necessary votes could be obtained. This sort of action was strongly opposed by Socialist thinkers as a class measure. They argued that only in strong middle-class areas of good housing could the 'local veto' vote be successfully organised and that men and women in working-class areas had no hope of mounting a successful vote to make their part of the city dry.

In one important sense Socialism was inimical to temperance, for the latter relied almost entirely on appeals to the individual to control himself and was strongly against government interference. Socialists, however, believed in greater official involvement and more public support for each person. But the inconsistency was not perceived, and when large areas of Glasgow were covered with local authority housing in the inter-war years no pubs at all were built in these parts of the city. For in those days the Labour administration was also strongly pro-temperance and had no hesitation in imposing an authoritarian solution.

The 'success' of the Temperance Movement in Victorian Scotland is hard to evaluate. The achievement of the local veto Act of 1913 and the subsequent well-heralded achievement of local veto campaigns may have convinced people. But increasingly temperance became an affair dominated by the churches and supported by women and children. To the male philanthropist seeking a cause to espouse, it seemed increasingly irrelevant to the problems of Scotland.

NOTES

1. Morris, 1855, 50.
2. Dunlop, 1839, 4; and see Dunlop, 1836.
3. Large quantities of liquor were prescribed in hospitals and in homes for all patients.
4. Morris, 1855, 55.
5. In addition to Edward Morris there were two weavers, one painter, teacher, saddler, missionary, clerk, druggist, sail maker and mechanic.
6. *Glasgow Abstainers' Union* (Glasgow 1873), 6.
7. MacGregor, M. B., n.d. c. 1949, 42.
8. *S.C. on Intoxication*, 1834, 323.
9. *Ibid.*, 533.
10. *Ibid.*, 175.
11. Mackie, J. B., 1888.
12. An Act for the regulation of public houses in Scotland, 16 and 17 Victoria, cap. LXVIII (August 15, 1853), in operation from Whitsunday 1854.
13. Stirling, J., 1859, 4.
14. See Scottish Temperance League collection, GUL.
15. Goadby, 1895.
16. *SPBTA*, 18th AR (Glasgow 1876), 3.
17. *Ibid.*, 18.
18. *Proceedings of the General Assembly of the Free Church of Scotland* (Edinburgh 1875), report of Committee on Temperance, 5.
19. Council estates in Glasgow remained publess until 1969, for churches, tenants' associations (with a high proportion of women members), trade unions and Labour party branches all campaigned against the removal of the veto. See Checkland, S. G., *The Upas Tree* (Glasgow 1976), 69.
20. 'These were so successful, that they not only served their first purpose of feeding the hungry but made a profit of £30,000 all of which, I believe, he gave to found the Saltcoats Convalescent Homes.' Rowallan, 1976, 5.
21. Jeans, S., 1872, 184.
22. *Ibid.*, 186.
23. *Handbook to the Charitable Institutions of Dundee* (Dundee 1875).
24. Reid, W., *Woman's Work for Woman's Weal* (Edinburgh 1860); Wood, Mrs. Henry, *Danesbury House* (Glasgow 1902), both published by the Scottish Temperance League.
25. Paton, D. C., Edinburgh Ph.D., 1977.

PART III

The Philanthropy of Education

6

Formal Teaching: Schools and Universities

1. The continuum to 1872

BY the beginning of Victoria's reign it was apparent that the old Scottish system of education was no longer adequate for an industrial nation. As Alexander Morgan has pointed out, 'Even in rural districts, out of some 4,450 schools there were only 1,130 parochial schools, the others such as General Assembly schools, schools maintained by the Society for the Propagation of Christian Knowledge, subscription schools, and proprietary and private adventure schools, being supplied by voluntary efforts.'[1] In the new urban areas, a large parish needed as many as twenty schools and had perhaps one. In Scotland there were about 500,000 children of school age (between 5-13); of these, 90,000 did not attend school at all, and of the remainder about one half attended schools with no inspection at all. The old system, by 1837, had become woefully inadequate.

Despite much pietistic philanthropy in the provision of schools, there was never any hope of educating all the children under church aegis. After the Disruption of 1843 the idea of church-based education became even more of an impossibility. Indeed all the religious groups tried to provide schools for their own children, which made the confusion worse. During the 1850's and 1860's several attempts were made to get a comprehensive elementary education Act for Scotland onto the statute book at Westminster, but passions ran high and opposition lobbies, mainly clerical, succeeded in defeating each such attempt.

Meanwhile the administration of hundreds of philanthropic endowments, involving tiny sums of money, baffled administrators in towns and villages. They either altered the terms of the trust (which was illegal, but usually passed unnoticed), or they ceased to administer the fund so that money accumulated unused for many years. Reform was long overdue, for these mortifications reflected old-fashioned standards and regional differences long out of date (see chapter 1, section 3, above). The 1872 Education Act swept these sums into the coffers of the School Boards, although a handful of especially useful bequests were exempted from this takeover.

2. The Dick Bequest

One such exemption covered the Dick Bequest, one of the most interesting of the educational endowments in Victorian Scotland. Its objective was to encourage schoolmasters to improve their qualifications and their performance in parochial schools and thereby raise the standards of education throughout the counties of Scotland to which it applied. James Dick (1743-1828), a Morayshire man, left a fund of over £113,000, which, when invested in land securities in Scotland, brought in an income of between £3,300 and £5,500 per annum. It operated from 1833.

Mr. Dick's Bequest was to apply to the Counties of Aberdeen, Banff and Moray (excluding the Royal Burghs of those Counties). The Trustees were 'to encourage active school masters, and gradually to elevate the literary character of the Parochial Schools, and School Masters'. The Dick Bequest money came at an important time. It encouraged schoolmasters to improve themselves; increasingly the three 'Dick' counties attracted a higher proportion of able teachers with high qualifications. Such men, once they had passed the diet of exams, could be sure of secure and relatively high earnings. The Dick Bequest thus came to occupy a singularly significant role in the Scottish educational system in the North-East, contributing to the high standing achieved by many schools there.

Schoolmasters in Victorian Scottish schools were usually men who had ambitions to enter the church. Many of them limped through universities, attending when funds permitted, but supporting themselves otherwise as schoolmasters. Many never succeeded in completing their courses and were destined to begin and end their careers, reluctantly, in education. Others struggled through and may have graduated M.A., until they were licensed by their presbyteries to preach. Such licensees still had to await a call from a parish; many spent years preaching around, in the hope that their preferred occupation would open to them, only to find themselves once more relegated to schoolmastering, which seemed to some to be a second best.

From the beginning of the Dick Bequest in 1833 most of the schoolmasters who presented themselves for its benefits were graduates in Arts, and were 'with rare exceptions, either Licentiates of the Church, or Students of Divinity'.[2] Only such qualified men could contemplate undertaking the arduous diet of examinations which the professional judges of the Bequest devised.

The judges recognised the need especially to encourage scholarship and good teaching. To this end they organised an examination for intending schoolmasters in the three counties. The first was introduced in 1835 under the direct guidance of three academic examiners, Dr. Pyper, Professor Macdougall and Professor Kelland.

In 1853 the diet consisted of twelve subjects:

English (Literature & Language)	Arithmetic
History & Chronology	Algebra
Latin (Livy)	Geometry
Latin (Horace)	Trigonometry
Greek (New Testament)	Physics
Greek (Arrian)	Geography

There seems no doubt that the requirements appeared formidable to many aspiring schoolmasters. The Trustees assumed, erroneously, that all the candidates would present themselves for all twelve papers in any one year, but candidates, on discovering that there was no rule requiring them to do this, began to draw the procedure out over several years. From 6 February 1849 candidates had to present themselves for at least five subjects at any one sitting, and these subjects had to include English, Arithmetic and Latin. Of course no payment could be made until the complete diet of exams had been passed.

The report of the Dick Bequest of 1854 gave the papers and the answers of one candidate. These are of great interest, revealing as they do the educational philosophy of the Trustees. The English paper was based on Hooker's *Ecclesiastical Polity* (Book I), but was more particularly concerned with English history and grammar. The study of general history and chronology was particularly focused on the Old Testament and Greek and Roman history. The Latin and Greek papers consisted of translations into and from these ancient languages, together with various other pertinent grammatical and historical questions. The arithmetic paper demanded long and arduous answers, all carefully set out. The physics paper was introduced in 1853, and was in that year optional. In geography the candidates were asked some interesting questions requiring rather more information than knowledge of 'capes and bays'. The series of papers was certainly a demanding two-day programme. The examiners were not content merely to examine the candidates, however rigorously. They witnessed a lesson taught by the candidate. Finally they required a report from the candidate's presbytery, and then conferred with the minister of his parish. They saw their role as the raising of standards, and they were determined to achieve this. When these many hurdles had been passed, the successful schoolmaster could expect to receive an additional £30 or so a year as a reward for his efforts. In 1863 the figures of such a schoolmaster's income were quoted as follows:

Statutory Salary	£43 4 11
Value of House & Garden	10 0 0
Fees actually received	28 9 8
Session Clerk Register	9 0 0
Dick Bequest	31 11 8
	£122 6 3 [3]

There was therefore much eagerness among intending schoolmasters to present themselves as candidates to the Trustees. The reward over a life-time of teaching service was substantial and well worthwhile. Between 1844 and 1853, 99 candidates presented themselves for the examination for the first time, and 67 passed. Thirty-seven candidates re-submitted and passed at a second attempt.

The Trustees of the Dick Bequest were fortunate in securing the services of Professor Allan Menzies (of the Chair of Conveyancing in the University of Edinburgh) and of Professor S. S. Laurie (the first holder of the Chair of Education at Edinburgh). Both men had vision and imagination. They established the Dick Bequest as a real instrument for improvement in the parochial schools of the North-East. But they were also conservative in outlook, preferring the old Scotch system of education, church — rather than state-controlled. In a sense, it could be argued that the success of the Dick Bequest scheme acted as a brake on the change to state education.

When the turning point came in 1872 with the Education Act, the greatest care was taken to maintain the Dick Bequest as a separate charity. But in the years after 1872 the emergence of the School Boards was bound to cause changes. Especially after 1890, the nature of the Dick Bequest altered. In that year the Trustees adopted a new scheme which effectively ended the direct relationship between the individual schoolmaster and the Trustees. Under the new arrangement (clause 27), grants after 1890 were to be available on two counts, either 'paid to the School Boards on condition that the teacher be a university graduate, and that the teaching staff was sufficient to enable the principal master to give time to the higher branches', or 'special grants of not less than £60, and not more than £200 annually, to assist certain selected centres in developing the higher department of their schools, . . . they further take into consideration (1) the number in Latin, Greek and Mathematics, (2) the extent to which efficient instruction is given in Mechanical Drawing and Science subjects, (3) the adequacy of the staff'.[4] Thus the Dick Bequest Trustees relinquished part of their brief — the direct stimulus of incentives to suitably qualified school teachers. But they clung to their other commitment, to encourage the public (parochial) school to continue to teach beyond the elementary level. In 1904 Laurie reported that in 1903 the Dick Bequest had been helping schools at which over 21,000 children attended. Of these, 2,609 were in Advanced Classes. He revealed that the number of Government Leaving Certificates gained (a test intended primarily for Secondary Schools) was:

Junior	935
Higher	417
Honours	6
	1,358

But even with such modest success, the slow take-over of the Trustees' functions by the School Boards meant a gradual weakening of their usefulness. Professor Laurie could not hope to stem the tide of public provision.

The Milne Bequest was confined to the parishes of the county of Aberdeen, together with one parish in Kincardine. It was established under the will of Dr. Milne, President of the Medical Board in Bombay, who died in 1841. By 1875 the net income per year was about £2,000. Under its terms parochial school-masters were entitled to apply for an annual grant of £20 per annum, provided they were teaching efficiently and had on their books 25 scholars of poor families who paid no fees. The Milne Bequest, unlike the Dick, was never regarded as particularly effective. Once a schoolmaster had obtained the £20, he continued to receive it as an augmentation. The Commissioners (on Endowed schools) were not impressed, and compared the Milne Bequest un-favourably with the Dick Bequest.

3. The charity hospitals (boarding schools)

The term hospital could be used to describe a residential establishment either for pensioners or for orphans, or for a mixture of both (see chapter 1, section 4, above). A hospital operated on pre-industrial principles of charity; its organisation and character reflected the needs of an earlier urban society. The fact that old-style hospitals continued to be founded well into the nineteenth century reflects the innate conservatism of the donors and not the needs of society.

At the time of the Education Act of 1872 there were 23 hospitals in Scotland where boys (and a few girls) were boarded (usually between the ages of 8-14), educated and subsequently apprenticed. The prototype was George Heriot's Hospital in Edinburgh. George Heriot had followed King James VI to London on his becoming James I of England in 1603. The resultant fortune came back to Scotland on Heriot's death. His hospital was modelled on Christ's Hospital in London. Others, in turn, were based on principles similar to those of Heriot's.

The purpose of Heriot's foundation as prescribed in George Heriot's will was 'for the maintenance, relief, bringing up, and educationne of puire fatherless bairnes, friemen's sonnes of the Towne of Edinburgh'. The word 'fatherless' was subsequently dropped so that the Governors could accept a wider range of applicants. Boys were admitted to Heriot's between the ages of 7 and 10 and left at the age of 14. A few 'hopeful scholars' were kept on and assisted to go to College.

The large hospitals in Edinburgh were George Heriot's, the Merchant Company's Hospitals (which included George Watson's, Daniel Stewart's, James Gillespie's and Merchant Maiden), John Watson's, Donaldson's, Fettes College (as originally — 1864 — endowed), Trades' Maiden Hospital and the Orphan Hospital. Outside Edinburgh there was Hutcheson's Hospital[5] in Glasgow (which provided for the old as well as the young), and Robert Gordon's in Aberdeen — both large and wealthy bodies. There were fifteen other smaller hospitals in various places, for example the Scott Institution in

Greenock, which in 1873 had six foundationers and an income of about £184.

Hospitals were for the most part funded by money invested in urban land. Governors and trustees had, generation after generation, bought small parcels of land, often contiguous to areas already owned. By the nineteenth century the land was increasingly feued for new houses, factories and offices, and the hospital funds began to increase. The process continued rapidly; hospital Governors found themselves administering funds which grew year by year, which they could hardly use for their hospitals, however lavishly they provided for their foundationers.

Nor could this be kept to themselves; the wealth of the hospitals became a matter of public knowledge and soon of public scandal. In the 1840's Dr. Guthrie, the advocate and publicist of the Ragged Schools in Scotland, made much play of the splendid buildings of the hospitals and contrasted the privilege of their scholars with the destitution of the orphans on the streets.[6]

In addition there was increasing unease about the whole system of residential schools. Almost all hospitals accepted children on condition that they would enter the establishment and remain within the walls, without any holidays or home-leave, for very long periods and even for the whole period of their stay. This was known as the Monastic System; it became the object of much adverse criticism on the grounds that when the pupils were ultimately released into the outside world they found it difficult to adapt themselves to everyday life. In addition doubts were expressed as to the choice of pupils; the question was asked, were some parents who were well able to afford to rear and educate their young evading responsibilities which should rightfully be theirs? Furthermore, as was subsequently discovered, 'Deviations from the regulations laid down, or the purpose contemplated by the founder, have almost universally taken place.'[7] The attack on the hospitals was long and sustained.

Many governors resisted all suggested changes. At Robert Gordon's Hospital in Aberdeen in 1849 even the proposal that boys should be allowed out of the hospital on Sunday afternoons aroused 'fierce discussion'. Legal opinion was sought from an Edinburgh Counsel, which did not contribute in any way 'to the calming of the discord'. But in the end 'The relaxation is conceded, and no evil follows.'[8] In other cases small changes were made; children were sometimes allowed to go home for weekends, half-holidays and vacations.

There were no Charity Commissioners in Scotland, so that changes could only be made by an Act of Parliament. This was a difficult and expensive process. Other changes could be made (without taking proper legal steps), provided the governors agreed among themselves. But then they risked being challenged by interested parties who might claim they were in breach of their trust. The most extraordinary widening of interpretation which succeeded and was not challenged was that at Donaldson's. It was suggested that the hospital should accept applications from deaf mutes as well as from normal children.

This was agreed on the grounds that although James Donaldson had not mentioned deaf mutes as a category to be included in his hospital, he had not excluded them either. From 1850, when Donaldson's opened, it accommodated about 200 children of whom as many as half could be deaf.

The Governors of Heriot's Hospital, anxious about their increasing income, acted timeously and, urged on by one of their number, Duncan McLaren (later Lord Provost of Edinburgh), obtained an Act of Parliament[9] in 1836 to establish day schools in Edinburgh. The Governors wished to use up their surplus funds, but also to spread their bounty more widely and provide education for poorer day-school pupils. In the years following, Heriot's set up twelve foundation schools for 3,000 day pupils[10] in the poorer parts of the town. These schools were:

Table 11

Heriot's Day Schools, Edinburgh, in 1859

Name of School	Date of Opening	Accommodation	Principal Class-room		Juvenile Class-room		Sewing School		Writing School	
			Length	Breadth	Length	Breadth	Length	Breadth	Length	Breadth
Heriot Bridge	1838	318	58	31			31	16		
Broughton Street	1855	270	34	22	21	12	26	19	26	18
Borthwick Close	1840	290	60	28	29	18	29	21		
Old Assembly Close	1840	285	60	28	29	18	29	21		
Cowgate Port	1840	336	54	29	29	17	29	20		
High School Yards	1840	336	54	29	29	17	29	20		
Brown Square	1846	255	47	24	24	16	24	16		
Rose Street	1848	326	42	37	22	20	28	21		

Infant Schools	Date of Opening	Accommodation			Large Class-room				Small Class-room	
Old Assembly Close	1841	213			41	28			16	16
High School Yards	1840	185			30	27			17	11
Rose Street	1848	204			43	27				
Broughton Street	1855	160			34	21			21	12
		3,178								

Source: Bedford, F. W., *George Heriot's Hospital* (Edinburgh 1859), 212.

The Governors took their duties seriously, visiting the schools 'in rotation, as indicated in the printed list of Committees'. They also took part in the annual examination of the schools, which must have been daunting occasions for teachers and taught. Not content with this type of internal examination by amateurs, they also requested Her Majesty's Inspector of Schools to inspect the Heriot's Schools; in 1842-3 they had the satisfaction of receiving a glowing comment from the Inspector, who wrote: 'Upon the whole, it is not too much to say that these Schools form by far the most valuable elementary educational machinery existing in this country. The course of instruction is extensive, . . . The teachers are thoroughly qualified to conduct it with efficiency . . . The superintendence is . . . effective.'[11]

The Governors, in establishing their day schools, had anticipated receiving large numbers of applications from children of Edinburgh burgesses, for to this extent they would still be acting within the old provisions. In the event only 4% of applications came from burgess children, and even then this reflected the proportion of those parents who had troubled to take out burgess tickets only because they intended to use the Heriot's day schools as a stepping stone to Heriot's Hospital. Paternal occupations show a remarkable range:

Table 12

Heriot's Day Schools: occupations of fathers, 1859

Children of:		Children of:	
Labourers	78	Smiths	32
Shop and Street Porters	71	Washerwomen	28
Wrights and Upholsterers	61	Footmen and Waiters	20
Cab-drivers, Coachmen and Grooms	61	Brassfounders	18
Tailors	60	Needlewomen	18
Shoemakers	56	Hawkers	14
Bakers	45	Masons	14
Printers	42	Clerks	14
Painters	34	Soldiers	13
	508		171

Total 679

Source: Bedford, F. W., *George Heriot's Hospital* (Edinburgh 1859), 225.

The Governors of the Edinburgh Merchant Company were responsible for George Watson's, Daniel Stewart's, James Gillespie's and Merchant Maiden Hospitals. They too were convinced of the need for change. In 1852 they attempted to 'introduce day scholars into George Watson's Hospital and paying pupils into the Merchant Maiden so as to some extent to leaven these schools'.[12] But legal authorities demurred and nothing was done. The Argyll Commission reported on Burgh and Middle Class Schools in 1868; it made a point of emphasising the anomaly of the hospitals having such wealth to educate so few children, when secondary education in Scotland was so inadequate and starved of funds. Encouraged by this public declaration, the Merchant Company commissioned Professor Laurie to prepare a report on their schools and on the hospital system. Laurie advised that he did not think the system 'a wholesome one, either morally or intellectually', that the children were denied 'the most powerful of all the building moral forces', the influences of home and family. Pressure was put on the Lord Advocate in Scotland to legislate to ease the way for the trusts to broaden their scope. In 1869 the Endowed Institutions Scotland Act[13] was passed, by which it was hoped that the hospitals could re-allocate their resources in a more meaningful way to benefit the children of Scotland.

The Merchant Company hastened to take advantage of the new law. Their main proposals were:

1. All foundationers to live with their relatives or friends (and the aged beneficiaries of Gillespie's Hospitals to receive pensions and live with their relatives);
2. The four buildings formerly used as Hospitals to be converted into 'great day schools' for pupils (whose parents would pay moderate fees) and for foundationers;
3. Open examination to be the basis of choice for foundationers;
4. Bursaries and travelling scholarships to be available for post-school education;
5. The endowment of a Chair of Commerce in the University of Edinburgh;
6. The Establishment of Industrial Schools for the neglected children of Edinburgh.

Almost all their proposals came to pass. James Gillespie's became an elementary school (and because of lack of endowment was handed over to the Edinburgh School Board in 1908); the other schools all became secondary schools. George Watson's Boys' School took over the Merchant Maiden Hospital. The Educational Institution for Young Ladies was opened at Melville House, George Square, and Daniel Stewart's specialised in teaching technical education. The Merchant Company had reason to be pleased with their progress: 'Previous to 1870, 428 pupils in all were taught in the three Hospitals and in the Free School; for the session 1871-2, 4,100 boys and girls were enrolled and many had to be refused.'[14]

The Governors of Heriot's Hospital, encouraged by the success of the Merchant Company in re-organising their schools so successfully, worked out a scheme for themselves. But the Home Secretary declined to accept it. The law officers of the Crown came to believe that the 1869 Act was not adequate. After further hesitation it was decided to subject the educational endowments of Scotland to a comprehensive official scrutiny, although both Heriot's and the Merchant Company in Edinburgh had already attempted to respond to criticisms of the hospital system by re-allocating their resources. The Royal Commission on Endowed Schools and Hospitals was set up in 1872. The Commissioners' enquiries produced Tables 13 and 14 showing the resources of the hospitals at that time.

4. The Education Act of 1872

The Education Act (Scotland) was passed in 1872. It was one of the most significant measures of the Victorian age; it brought the state into the lives of the people in a way hitherto unheard of. It provided an administrative structure through the School Boards — the School Boards were abolished in 1918 — and provided them with rate collecting authority. It was to be the forerunner of many other educational measures.

Did it mean that the philanthropic donor was in retreat? Although almost all those gifts and endowments which had supported the parochial schools passed to the School Boards, the government continued to urge the benevolent

Table 13

Table of the Endowed Hospitals in Edinburgh, 1872 [1]

Designation of Hospital	Date	Locality	Foundationers	Revenue	Cost per Head		
					Education	Maintenance	Total
Donaldson's	1830	Edinburgh	220	£8,980	£5 2 0	£30 0 0	£35 2 0
Heriot's	1624	Edinburgh	180	18,950	11 10 0	43 8 0	54 18 0
Fettes College	1836	Edinburgh	50	7,000	—	—	—
Merchant Company { *Merchant Maiden*		Edinburgh	65	4,880	—	—	—
Watson's (George)		Edinburgh	55	7,127	—	—	—
Stewart's		Edinburgh	37	3,453	—	—	—
Orphan	1727	Edinburgh	90	2,063	2 8 0	23 18 0	26 6 0
Trades' Maiden	1704	Edinburgh	48	1,772	9 15 0	26 0 0	35 15 0
Watson's (John) Institution	1759	Edinburgh	100	4,555	7 12 0	32 12 0	40 4 0

1. Those which were by now also public or day schools are printed in italics: in these cases the capitation cost of the Foundationers cannot be precisely estimated.

Source: RCESH (Scotland), C.1123, 226-227.

Table 14

Table of the Endowed Hospitals in Scotland in 1872[1] (excluding Edinburgh)

Designation of Hospital	Date	Locality	Foundationers	Revenue	Cost per Head		
					Education	Maintenance	Total
Boys' and Girls'	1739	Aberdeen	100	£1,758	£1 9 0	£15 2 0	£16 11 0
Gordon's	1732	Aberdeen	176	5,611	7 7 0	17 18 0	25 5 0
Orphan and Destitute Female Children's	1849	Aberdeen	50	917	1 2 0	15 11 0	16 13 0
Orphan (Female) Asylum	1849	Aberdeen	46	1,075	1 13 0	19 6 0	20 19 0
Shaw's	1807	Aberdeen	10	285	1 4 0	22 18 0	24 2 0
Spier's		Ayrshire		1,500	—	—	—
Muirhead's	1753	Dumfries	10	342	1 2 0	15 11 0	16 13 0
Morgan's	1861	Dundee	90	2,505	4 2 0	24 1 0	28 3 0
Orphan Institution		Dundee	55	995	3 6 0	14 7 0	17 13 0
Cauvin's	1833	Duddingston	26	990	5 4 0	36 0 0	41 4 0
Elgin Institution	1815	Elgin	43	1,800	3 0 0	25 0 0	28 0 0
Scott Institution	1838	Greenock	6	184	1 0 0	27 16 0	28 16 0
Brookland's		Kirkpatrick-Durham	8	180	6 15 0	16 0 0	22 15 0
Douglas Free School	1798	Newton-Stewart	12	480	6 17 0	28 5 0	35 2 0
Schaw's	1781	Prestonpans (East Lothian)	11	740	10 1 0	32 7 0	42 8 0
Stiells	1812	Tranent (East Lothian)		764	—	—	—
Speyside Charity School	1795	Grantown	22	339	0 16 0	11 4 0	12 0 0

1. Those which are now also public or day schools are printed in italics: in these cases the capitation cost of the Foundationers cannot be precisely estimated.

Source: RCESH (Scotland), C.1123, 226-227.

to espouse the cause of education at all other levels, where no state money was to be available.

The Act made education compulsory for children from 5-13. Small fees were paid by their parents.[15] The state took over the statutory parochial schools and replaced the old managers (usually the heritors and the minister) by School Boards, democratically elected. The Act established the right of the School Boards to levy rates for educational purposes. It thus set up a proper and complete network of schools over the whole country. The Scots had never been indifferent to education; families had long taken advantage of opportunities offered through the schools. As the Royal Commissioners reported in 1865, 'The poor Irish immigrant, the Highland Crofter in Ross and Sutherland, the weaver of Maybole, or the fishermen of Cellardyke, as classes, are all actuated by an appreciation of the benefits of education, and would gladly see their children better able to read or write than themselves.'[16] The Act provided the basis for what the majority of people in Scotland wanted, namely an efficient, uniform and generally available system of elementary education. Yet there was a real continuity with what had gone before.

The Scots had prided themselves on the fact that the parochial school under a good schoolmaster was not confined to elementary education, but could and did prepare boys for university entrance. The Act of 1872 made provision for Higher Class Public Schools, hoping that the true continuity in Scottish education would appear here. But these schools were to receive no support from the School Rate money. Their finances were to come from school fees, the 'Common Good' fund of a Burgh, and any endowments and bequests which the school had previously had or could attract. Indeed the Lord Advocate spoke explicitly: 'It is not in accordance with the views of this house, to give imperial money, or to authorise local taxation in order to provide for higher class education, and therefore I can only provide for the higher class education otherwise than pecuniarily.'[17] It was perfectly clear from remarks made by Sellar, the Lord Advocate's Secretary, that 'Now, however, that they (the Higher Class Schools) have a recognised position in the educational system of the country, there is some probability that they will be selected as objects of private generosity.'[18]

Elementary education was thus the only type to be funded from the education rate in 1872. All other schooling was to continue to depend upon philanthropy. It was a particular satisfaction to Gladstone's Liberal governments that the urgent financial needs of the country's four universities had been met by major public appeals to the nation by 1872, bringing in substantial sums to allow the universities to expand. It seemed not unreasonable to hope that private giving would provide for secondary education as well.

After the 1872 Act there were some general educational endowments reserved for various reasons intact and separate; these brought in an income of over £17,000 a year. They often became an addition to funds for Higher Class Schools all over the country. These funds were of considerable significance before 1908. In that year the government finally gave ground and started making proper provision for Higher Schools.

Table 15

General Endowments available in Scotland for Education in 1875

Name	Place	Annual Revenue
Dick Bequest	Counties of Aberdeen, Banff and Moray	£4,300
Milne Bequest	Aberdeenshire	1,900
Philp Bequest	Fifeshire	2,380
Bell Bequest, Residue	Scotland generally	770
Society for Propagating Christian Knowledge	Scotland generally	6,500
Maclean Bequest	Scotland generally	670
Other Funds	Scotland generally	598
		£17,118

Source: RCESH (Scotland), C.1123, Appendix to the 3rd report, Vol. II statistics (Edinburgh 1875), 345.

5. The Endowed Schools and Hospitals (Scotland) Commission, 1872

On 12 September 1872 the Endowed Schools and Hospitals (Scotland) Commission was empowered to 'inquire into the nature and amount of all Endowments of Scotland, the funds of which are wholly or in part devoted, or have been applied, or which can rightly be made applicable to Educational purposes . . . and also to inquire into the Administration and Management of any Hospital or Schools supported by such Endowments, and into the System and Course of Study respectively pursued therein, and to Report whether any and what changes in the administration and use of such Endowments are expedient, by which their usefulness and efficiency may be increased'.[19]

The speed with which the government acted was a response to the vigorous campaign which had been going on in Edinburgh against the hospital system. In spite of the establishment of the Heriot's Day Schools and the reorganisation of the Merchant Company schools, most hospitals were carrying on as they had always done. Critics argued that the large financial resources of the Scottish educational endowments were being ill-advisedly used (if not squandered) for the benefit of a few hundred children. The money, it was urged, was sufficient to educate several thousand children if differently applied. The strength of the opposition to the old-style charity school can be judged from the protagonists who entered the field. One of the most distinguished (and eloquent) was Sir Alexander Grant, Principal of the University of Edinburgh. He launched a fierce attack in 1870. Grant disliked these 'imitations of imitations' and listed them as follows:

Merchant Maiden's Hospital	founded 1695
Trades Maidens Hospital	founded 1704
The Orphan Hospital	founded 1727
George Watson's Hospital	founded 1738
John Watson's Hospital	founded 1759
James Schaw's Hospital	founded 1789
Daniel Stewart's Hosptial	founded 1814
George Stiell's Hospital	founded 1822
James Donaldson's Hospital	founded 1830
Louis Cauvin's Hospital	founded 1833

His list, to be complete, should have started with the original 'imitation', namely Heriot's (1624). Grant claimed that 'The original bequest of George Heriot amounted only to £23,625, the revenue now derived from the investment of this sum, less the cost of the building, is upwards of £16,000 per annum! The original bequest of Daniel Stewart, who died in 1814, was £13,000 by the accumulation and investment of which the property of Stewart's hospital is now estimated at £120,000.' Grant also reminded his readers that the Argyll Commission of 1868 which had enquired into Burgh and Middle Class Schools remarked that hospital funds 'point to the necessity of some enquiry, in order to ascertain whether more economy might not be introduced into the administration, and whether the inmates of the hospitals might not be more economically educated and boarded'.[20]

The Commissioners of 1872 were Thomas Edward Colebrook (Chairman), Lord Rosebery, William Stirling-Maxwell, C. S. Parker, John Ramsay, Henry H. Lancaster and A. Craig Sellar, with Professor Simon Somerville Laurie as Secretary. Critics claimed that this was a 'Whig' commission, consisting of men who 'know nothing of the endowments of Scotland'. Subsequently in 1878 another Commission was appointed. But although the personnel were different, the conclusions were broadly similar.[21]

There seems no doubt that the government was seeking to release much of the resources of the residential hospitals for other types of education. Having introduced a local education rate for elementary education, it was concerned with the financial difficulties of other educational establishments. The government believed that though it was necessary to fund elementary (i.e. working class) education from the rates, it was unjustified to finance Higher Class Public Schools (or any other more advanced education) in the same way. This followed from the belief that it would be improper to subsidise middle-class education. It was taken for granted that secondary education was for the middle classes, and that they should pay for it by philanthropy and fees.

The Commissioners sent out questionnaires and interviewed, collected and collated information. They received reports from all the endowed grammar schools (some 40 in all), and all the hospitals (some 25). They also sought the views of the universities. They concluded that 'In all cases where an endowed school occupies ground which would otherwise be supplied by a public school under the Education Act, the community have a right to exercise as much supervision as may afford security for the efficiency of the schools.'[22]

With regard to hospitals, the main burden of their recommendations was:

1. Charity foundationers should in general be boarded out in families;
2. Hospital Schools should be thrown open to all, at moderate fees, as day schools, the instruction being adapted to the circumstances of the locality in which each foundation is placed. Where convenient Foundationers should attend Public or other Elementary Schools;
3. The number of Charity Foundationers should generally be reduced, and in some cases contributions towards their maintenance should be required;
4. A considerable proportion of the places on each foundation should be thrown open to competition among boys who have completed a course of Primary instruction, either in schools connected with the foundation or elsewhere.[23]

For the encouragement of endowments for higher education they made two recommendations:

1. That where the reasonable objects of any foundation can be attained without expending the whole revenue, the surplus should be applied to promote Higher Instruction.
2. Bursaries at Secondary Schools should be the reward of merit.

The implementation of these recommendations, coming as it did immediately after the 1872 Education Act, was of great significance. The re-organisation of the great endowed hospitals ensured that middle-class children (in fact descendants of 'burgesses' and no doubt 'founders kin') remained the beneficiaries of the endowments. For it was the middle-class parents who instilled educational ambitions into their children. The bursaries, as 'the reward of merit', would go to children who had received good elementary education and whose families were pushing them toward high achievement. The new-look endowed schools (formerly the hospitals) became schools where small fees were paid by parents, fees which were largely subsidised from the endowment funds.

6. Higher education: grammar schools

The former parochial schools were intended to form the basis of the new comprehensive system of education for the working men's children of Scotland after 1872. Some School Boards were also to manage a range of secondary schools, designated Higher Class Schools, but sometimes known as Higher Grade Schools, 'with a view to promote the higher education of the country'. The advantage of handing over Higher Class Schools to the School Boards was primarily an administrative one, although it could be an important step towards eventual state financing. These schools were starved of funds, remaining impoverished for many years. The later Education Act of 1878 gave a little aid by providing funds to pay examiners' fees and pensions for retired schoolteachers, but did not meet the basic deficiency.

There were some fifty secondary schools (variously named Grammar

School, Academy or Institution) in Scotland in 1872. They had all been funded by charitable monies, and all relied on endowments and fees for their continued existence. Some were well endowed, but many were not, and limped along from one financial crisis to the next. At best the secondary schools provided a good education embracing the teaching of classical and science subjects. At worst they were burgh schools similar to poor parochial schools, with little or no pretension to teach the higher branches of education.

But some of them were to come under the administrative control of the School Boards. The Treasurer of the School Boards was to keep separate accounts for these schools; this measure was intended to ensure that no funds from the school rate passed into the Higher Class Schools; but it would also reveal the parlous state of their finance. It seems probable that Lord Young, the Lord Advocate, and Craig Sellar, his Secretary, had done their best in difficult circumstances to ensure the future involvement of the state in more advanced education but were only partly successful. Some Higher Class Schools were thus made part of the School Boards structure, although expressly excluded from any financial benefits by being so linked. Indeed, of the fifty or so secondary schools in existence, eleven only were scheduled in the Act to come under the School Boards. These could be called Statutory Secondary Schools. The eleven schools officially embraced were : Aberdeen New Grammar School, Ayr Academy, Dumfries Academy, Edinburgh High School, Elgin Academy, Glasgow High School, Haddington Burgh School, Montrose Academy, Paisley Grammar School and Academy, Perth Academy and Stirling High School. The other forty remained independent, outside any official scheme and in the voluntarist sector, left to administer their endowments as efficiently as they could. Originally Dundee High School, Inverness Academy, Greenock Academy and Madras College, St. Andrews were also on the list, but during the passage of the Bill through parliament local representatives persuaded the House to remove them. Local pride was probably less of a feature here than a good financial competence which the trustees preferred to keep in private hands rather than pass to the School Boards.

The miserable supply of secondary schools in Scotland after 1872 did not go unnoticed. The government hoped and expected that philanthropy would provide further foundations. The School Boards, who had some responsibility for the eleven 'designated' Higher Grade Schools, were ambivalent in their attitude toward them, being already almost overwhelmed by the task of providing elementary education for every child in their area. The universities were dissatisfied; they had long had to admit schoolchildren as undergraduates whose education did not fit them for university study, and they deplored the continuance of a system which forced them to undertake the secondary education of their students.

It fell to the Commissioners for Endowed Schools to attempt an examination in some detail of the plight of the Higher Class Schools in the post-1872 period. They regarded the failure of the Education Act of 1872 to provide some form of uniform finance for secondary education as unfortunate. They did what they could by sending their assistants to investigate and by making some constructive comments.

They noted that 'Secondary Schools . . . can scarcely be said to have any place in the educational economy of Scotland.'[24] They wished to ensure that at least the eleven Statutory Secondary Schools 'would be adequately endowed and fully equipped'. To do this they recommended that any foundation which had a surplus should allocate it to higher instruction as far as possible. They also, like the government, made a plea for further private endowment so that every sizeable town in Scotland would have a secondary school. Where bursary funds existed (which could be earmarked for higher education), they wanted them dispensed as 'rewards of merit', limiting competition to pupils of Public Schools. This recommendation stemmed from their discovery that money already available was misapplied or under-used. Their enquiries in Dundee produced evidence of inefficiency bordering on peculation. There the Webster Bursary boys always attended a private school, the main asset of which was the steady income which came from the Webster Trust. Under the traditional system it was likely that trustees, following the old rules of preference being given to founders' kin and such like, benefited less able boys. Under the Commissioners' recommendations merit was to replace outdated privilege. They also argued for a categorisation of schools so that everyone knew which type of education (infants, elementary or secondary) was being taught in any particular institution. As a result of the Commissioners' published comments, no one could deny or remain ignorant of the fact that the Higher Education Schools in Scotland were being disgracefully neglected.

A new phase began when in 1885 Mr. (later Sir) Henry Craik was appointed Secretary of the re-organised Scotch Education Department. He maintained a constant and concerned interest in Higher Grade Schools seen as an integral part of a comprehensive educational provision. He instituted inspection of Higher Grade Schools in 1886, and in 1888 introduced a standard leaving certificate. These measures encouraged timid School Boards to allocate resources to education other than elementary. Due primarily to Craik's concern, new Higher Grade Schools were opened at the end of the century which would take clever pupils from poorer families beyond the elementary stage. Thirty-one such schools opened between 1900 and 1901.

The 1908 Education Act in Scotland finally dealt with the thorny problem of financing the Higher Grade Schools. It set up the Education (Scotland) Fund, which 'became the central bank account of the department'.[25] The Fund was sustained by £40,000 per annum from the Local Taxation (Customs and Excise) Act 1890 and £60,000 from the Education and Local Taxation Account (Scotland) Act 1892, together with other small sums from various sources. But until this was done, secondary education in grammar schools in Scotland had been left in large measure to the philanthropists.

7. Higher education: technical schools

By and large Scottish scientific and technical education, like grammar school education, remained throughout the Victorian period a matter for the philanthropist. It is true that after 1872 the government allowed some public money to filter through at various levels. But officially government policy remained to provide no 'imperial money' for education other than elementary.

From the beginning of the nineteenth century many fruitful initiatives had been taken by concerned and benevolent persons to ensure that Scottish cities had their classes in scientific and technical education. These, reinforced by a great deal of further activity in the post-1872 period, had to suffice until the government took steps to provide a more uniform and officially financed coverage.

In Scottish cities, especially in Glasgow where engineers, scientists and technicians abounded, there was much concern at the inadequacies of technical and scientific education. Perhaps in Glasgow feelings ran especially high. As Montgomerie Neilson wrote in 1880: 'Comparisons instituted between the industrial products of Great Britain and of the Continental States, at the International Exhibitions since 1851, together with investigations recently prosecuted by competent inquirers throughout the industrial communities of Europe have led to a general conviction that this country is not keeping pace with her Continental neighbours in many of those departments of trade in which hitherto she has been unrivalled. The same inquiries have forcibly directed attention to the fact that the nations which are successfully emulating Great Britain in the various departments of mechanical engineering, and of chemical and textile manufactures, and which surpass her in the arts of mining and metallurgy are precisely those in which adequate provision had been made for Technical Education.'[26] Exhibitions in Paris in 1867 and 1878 revealed the extent of the British shortfall. Gladstone's government, frightened by the implications, set up the Samuelson Commission on Technical Education in Britain, which reported in 1884. Its report revealed the weakness of both secondary education and technical education, neither of which was funded by the government. It further emphasised the need for an 'essential unity' of secondary education, and for a good technical education. Stung by the implications of this report, the government passed the Technical Schools (Scotland) Act of 1887, which allowed certain funds held by local authorities to be applied to technical education. More generally for Britain as a whole, there were the Technical Instruction Acts of 1889 and 1892. Neither was very effective in Scotland. The Bryce Commission in 1895 went over the ground again and reminded Britain that secondary and technical education should go hand in hand.

Notwithstanding the failure of successive governments to provide adequately for advanced education, progress was made. In at least five major urban centres of Scotland new initiatives were taken. Glasgow, Edinburgh,

Dundee, Aberdeen and Paisley all developed institutions where a high quality of technical education and training were taught. The new moves were possible for three main reasons. First, there were men in positions of power in Scottish education (including Sir Henry Craik) who encouraged new and extended ventures in technical education. Secondly there were the experts in Scottish technical education including Henry Dyer (1848-1918), David Sandeman (1814-1887) and E. M. Dixon (1829-1889),[27] who campaigned ceaselessly for improved facilities. In addition the Royal Commissioners on Endowed Schools in Scotland had powers to re-fashion old endowments and to adapt them to the needs of the 1880's; one of their priorities was undoubtedly to extend and improve opportunities for technical and scientific education.

Glasgow had a distinguished history of technical education starting with the initiatives of John Anderson, an eminent professor of Natural Philosophy at Glasgow College who on his death in 1796 left ambitious instructions for the establishment of Anderson's College. Dr. George Birkbeck (who became Professor of Chemistry and Natural Philosophy at Anderson's) founded the first of the Mechanics' Institutes in Glasgow in 1823, to ensure that 'men should be taught the principles of the arts they practise'. In 1879 the Mechanics' Institution in Glasgow became 'the College of Science and Arts'.

Allan Glen's Institution, Glasgow[28] was opened in 1853, as a result of a benefaction from Allan Glen (1778-1850). Glen, a wright by trade, was a member of the Unitarian church in the city; he left his money to provide a school 'which should be for the education and fitting for business of children of respectable parents of the industrious classes who were unable to give their children a suitable education'. If funds permitted, he also wished to establish 'an Industrial School of a plain but useful description . . . for the purpose of educating the unfortunate and destitute children who are wandering about the streets'. This was never done. Allan Glen's School was opened in a new building on land owned by Glen on the corner of North Hanover Street and Cathedral Street, in May 1853, with some fifty boys. While the education was to be along practical (and secular) lines, there was no sign at the beginning of the school's later scientific distinction. For Allan Glen was inspired by the old ideas of benevolence, anxious to repeat in his school some of the successes achieved by the Highland Society and Hutcheson's Trust in their already well-known and reputable schools in Glasgow (see chapter 2). There is no evidence that in the early years the Governors were especially concerned with scientific education. In 1876 the Governors obtained Allan Glen's Institution Act,[29] which enabled them to extend their charity by expressly educating necessitous boys (by providing free education and clothing) and to pay for older boys to go on to university at Glasgow or elsewhere.

In 1876 George Gilbert Ramsay[30] was appointed a Trustee of Allan Glen's School by the University of Glasgow. Shortly thereafter, Edward Maxwell Dixon, a mathematician, was appointed headmaster of the school. Ramsay and Dixon between them began the vital switch to technical and scientific education. Dixon remained headmaster from 1878-1889, a zealous and effective guardian of the pioneering school. The Royal Commissioners on Technical Education wrote in 1884, 'We consider that Allan Glen's School is one of the very best examples of a secondary technical school (except for the buildings which are poor) that we have met with in the course of our investigations.'[3] Dr. John Guthrie Kerr succeeded him in 1890. Kerr too was a distinguished headmaster who built up the reputation of the school and the number of boys in it. But there were severe financial constraints. The reserves available to the Managers in the 1880's had evaporated by 1900. The Governors negotiated with the School Board of Glasgow to see if a formula for transfer could be agreed. The hand-over eventually took place in 1912.[32] The main provisos were that the school would retain its name, and 'be carried on as a Science High School, *pari passu* with the High School' (of Glasgow). Under the School Board, Allan Glen's name was carried on with distinction in his native city.

The College of Science and Arts, Glasgow had been reconstructed in 1879 as a Technical School (and the arts classes largely dropped). By 1881 it had 1,265 students studying 23 courses in day and evening classes:

Table 16

College of Science and Arts, Glasgow: students and their courses, 1881

Practical, Plane and Solid Geometry	138
Machine Construction and Drawing	97
Mechanical Engineering	43
Building Construction and Drawing	46
Freehand or Perspective	15
Mathematics (Junior)	105
Mathematics (Senior)	28
Theoretical Mechanics	57
Applied Mechanics	53
Steam	52
Magnetism and Electricity	73
Electrical Engineering	67
Chemistry (Theoretical)	115
Chemistry (Practical)	30
Chemistry (Practical Advanced)	34
Botany	49
Botany (Ladies' Day Class)	9
Geology	32
French	45
German	7
Phonography	50
English Grammar and Literature	39
Writing, Arithmetic and Book-keeping	81
	1,265

Source: College of Science and Arts, Glasgow, 59th AR (Glasgow) 1882), 7.

Sessional fees ranged between £31 10s. and £5 5s. for each day class; evening classes were between 2s. 6d. and 20s. depending upon the subject. Some employers were keen: 'The Tharsis Company continue to send students for Chemistry, twenty-one being present last session.'[33]

In 1886 a range of Glasgow institutions, all involved in some way with technical teaching, were brought together, by the actions of the Commissioners, as the Glasgow and West of Scotland Technical College. These were Anderson's College, the College of Science and Arts, the 'Young' Chair of Technical Chemistry (founded by Dr. James Young) and the Atkinson Institution. Allan Glen's Institution was placed under the jurisdiction of the new Technical College, but continued as a school intended to provide pupils for the College.

After the amalgamation of 1886 there was a strong move to house the Glasgow and West of Scotland Technical College in buildings appropriate to the foremost college of its kind in Scotland. An appeal was launched, endowments to the value of £225,000 were raised, and a splendid new edifice was built and equipped in George Street in the city centre. In the booklet prepared for the opening of the first section of the new buildings in 1895 it was noted that students came from a wide area: 'The day students are drawn from nearly every county in Scotland, from England, Ireland, the Continent, India and the Colonies, while practically all the important works within twenty-five miles of Glasgow contribute their quota of evening students.' This institution became the Royal Technical College and finally emerged in July 1962 as the University of Strathclyde.

In Edinburgh similar moves were made to refurbish and regenerate older colleges to make them suitable for modern scholarship. The Edinburgh School of Arts (founded in 1821 by Leonard Horner) became part-owned by the subscribers to a memorial to James Watt; it was re-named the Watt Institution and School of Art. As a result of the Educational Endowments Act of 1882, part of Heriot's endowment money passed to the College, which became Heriot-Watt College, and in 1966 Edinburgh's second university.

At Aberdeen a scheme was pushed through as a result of the enquiries of the Commissioners into Endowed Schools and Hospitals whereby Robert Gordon's Hospital was transmogrified into Robert Gordon's College (the Provisional Order came into force on 1 August 1881). Aberdeen's technical college has continued to maintain Robert Gordon's name with distinction and is known now as Robert Gordon's Institute for Technology.

In Dundee, although there had been scientific and technical classes in connection with the Mechanics' Institute, modern teaching began in 1871. A serious problem was the confusion of standards. Sir David Baxter had envisaged courses in his Mechanics' Institute for 'working mechanics and other craftsmen', and yet other classes were at an entirely different and more advanced level. In addition, some classes were in the evening and some during the day. The Dundee example highlights the classic dilemma posed by a system provided by the private donor, namely lack of uniformity on the one hand and duplication of some services on the other.

The difficulties in Dundee were only resolved after 1908 when the Scotch Education Department was authorised to take responsibility for evening class instruction in Scotland. The classes from the High School and those of the YMCA were taken over by the Managers of the Technical Institute, where much of the technical and scientific teaching was based. After the Act of 1908, finance was available to improve technical education. The Scotch Education Department offered help for a new Dundee Technical College, provided local generosity could be tapped once again. This formula, of offering a grant of £1 per £1 donated, proved popular. The Dundee Technical College and School of Art was opened early in 1911 to provide classes for those working in Dundee's various industries. Courses in engineering, textile and building trades were also provided, together with instruction for men going to sea as engineers or ships' officers, or seeking to qualify as naval architects, druggists, lithographers, as well as others.[34]

The government's position was not easy; it was clearly ambivalent about overall policy. On the one hand it knew that the money going from whatever source to technical and scientific education was not enough. On the other it knew how determined was the resistance to increases of local rates for whatever purpose however good. The government settled for compromise arrived at over time. Local authorities were encouraged to allocate small sums to technical education. Legislation of a permissive kind was passed. Under the Technical Instruction Act of 1889 local authorities in Scotland were entitled either to allocate funds raised by the Local Taxation (Customs and Excise) Act 1890 to technical education, or to apply such funds to the relief of the rates. When the first return was assembled it was discovered that of the 82 Burghs and 105 Police Burghs in Scotland, only 31 and 39 respectively were using such funds to finance technical and other educational 'extras', while 51 and 66 respectively were passing on the bonus directly to the relief of the rates. Of the cities, Edinburgh (1890-1) was applying the full amount received (£4,235) to 'Manual Instruction' (including £250 to Heriot-Watt College), and to a wide variety of practical classes including cookery, horticulture, applied art and dentistry. Glasgow in the same year applied about half its allowance of over £6,000 to the relief of the rates, but £1,500 went to the Glasgow and West of Scotland Technical College and £327 to Glasgow School of Art and Haldane Academy. The sum of £2,000 went to support the Mitchell Library (see chapter 7, section 3, below). In Aberdeen £300 went to Robert Gordon's College and £70 to Gray's School of Art (although over £500 went to the relief of the rates). Dundee had a total of £1,380 to dispense, of which over £550 went to lessen the rates, but the Technical Institute received £630, the YMCA £150 and the High School for Evening Science and Art Classes £50.[35]

In addition, and fully in line with apparent policy, other public money was used to encourage technical students. From 1873 the Royal Society of Arts was offering grants to schools for students who passed their scientific and technical exams, and at least by 1878 small amounts of government money were available for 'Certified Lecturers' who presented successful students for exams outside those of the Royal Society of Arts. It was a payment-by-results system. It worked well in the sense that lecturers and students were so keen to make progress that they willingly accepted the conditions offered.

But the whole scheme was on a very small scale. Indeed the country as a whole took an uninformed view of the need for technical education. When Parliament debated these matters, M.P.'s prevented any effective leglislation being passed. The spectacular rise of local rates had frightened many and caused good and necessary measures to be put aside.

In 1908 the government finally grasped the nettle. It took over the proper financing of technical and scientific education by the Education Act of that year.

8. The universities

The three pre-reformation universities of Scotland, namely St. Andrews (1411), Glasgow (1451) and Aberdeen (1494), were foundations of the church; after 1560 they were incorporated into the educational structure of the reformed (presbyterian) church. The University of Edinburgh was established by the initiative of the Town Council and received its charter in 1582. All four depended on traditional charitable money for their finance. But the upheaval occasioned by the reformation resulted in serious loss of income for the three church foundations because of the unscrupulous annexations of their revenue by the more powerful men of post-reformation Scotland.

The pre-reformation universities were primarily bodies for teaching and training churchmen, their funds came from kirk, mortcloth dues or from endowments and benefactions. The latter were most often in the form of teinds (tithes) or other church revenues; the sums involved were tiny, and the universities remained small and poor. Professors depended upon student fees for their income and so competed for class enrolments. But though professors could sometimes be in conflict with one another over class demarcations, they banded together and formed a barrier against any sort of expansion, or the institution of new chairs, fearing for their fees. Payment by results thus generated a strong conservatism, which prevented the Scottish universities from expanding and adapting readily to the changing needs of the nineteenth century. Whereas in the eighteenth century the Scottish universities had represented the acme of European academic achievement, by the middle of the nineteenth century they were falling seriously behind.

In the eighteenth century, benefactions from the Crown were of considerable importance. The Crown endowed five new chairs in Glasgow between 1713 and 1760: the Practice of Medicine, 1713; Civil Law, 1713; Ecclesiastical History, 1716; Anatomy and Botany, 1718; and Astronomy, 1760. The establishment of the Regius Chairs remained a bone of contention within the University, primarily because of the chronic shortage of funds. But whereas in Oxford professors 'were almost superfluous to the system of education . . . at Glasgow the professors were almost the entire teaching staff'.[36]

In Edinburgh great hardship was caused by the peculiar dependence of the University on the Town Council. The latter had in the eighteenth century commuted the University's funds into a lump sum, which remained fixed. On the other hand the philanthropic contribution became more important, for some of the endowments grew at a remarkable rate, owing to the increases in land values. Even so, however, the University was greatly constrained by its poverty.

When the Scottish Universities Commission (1826-30) reported, it made no comments on the very serious financial situation. The Scottish Universities Act of 1858 brought relief when, as a result of a further enquiry, major changes were made. The Scottish Universities Commission was established and it was given extensive powers, including those 'to grant additional parliamentary funds to provide for retirement allowances for aged or infirm professors, to pay the fees of outside examiners, to increase the salaries of existing professors or other university officials, and to endow new chairs'.[37]

Through these powers the Commissioners granted an annual sum of £1,805 to Glasgow, £4,043 to Edinburgh, £1,680 to Aberdeen and £1,094 to St. Andrews; the relatively large amount awarded to Edinburgh acknowledged the unfair burden placed on that University by the Town Council's substitution of a fixed sum for the old endowments of the College. By 1858, therefore, the government was accepting some part of the financial burden of the universities of Scotland. Its financial commitment thereafter steadily increased, taking the form of sums annually allocated for the salaries of the principals, the professors, the assistants and the examiners, together with provision for pensions, bursaries and libraries. In Glasgow these sums totalled almost £7,500 in 1889. By 1895 the government was providing almost £21,000 of the £55,000 total expenditure of that University.[38]

Notwithstanding these very considerble sums from central government (far in excess of those then being allocated to English universities), it was by no means government policy to encourage reliance upon state provision. The Victorian ideal of self-help was never more earnestly invoked than in the case of the universities. The declared view of the government was that the community as a whole should take responsibility for increasing the financial security of the universities through appeals for philanthropic giving. The forms which these appeals took varied; they were primarily aimed at establishing bursaries (both for undergraduate and graduate students), and professorial chairs (to ensure that new subjects entered the curriculum). In a sense the government was right, for all the Scottish universities benefited greatly from private gifts. In 1864 the Association for the Better Endowment of the University of Edinburgh was founded, marking the beginning of a period of great activity. As Craig Sellar explained in 1872: 'Individuals have of late years gifted or bequeathed large sums of money to the Scotch Universities. An association for the better endowment of the Universities has met with considerable success.'[39] As a result of this generosity the University of Edinburgh acquired £142,000 for scholarships and £90,000 for bursaries in the post-1864 period. Even so, however, as Horn remarks, 'Edinburgh remained much less well provided, in proportion to student numbers, with bursaries than Aberdeen, where in 1872 two-thirds of the Arts students were bursars, or St. Andrews of which it was popularly, but perhaps erroneously, believed in Edinburgh, that there were more bursaries than students.'[40]

The degree of provision made for the Scottish universities under the philanthropic principle to 1875 is shown below:

Table 17

Annual revenue received in 1875 by the Scottish universities from endowments made between 1808 and 1875

	Chairs	Bursaries	Scholarships and Prizes	Total
St. Andrews	£ 215	£ 674	£ 560	£ 1,488
Glasgow	2,291	1,748	2,268	6,307
Aberdeen	2,235	1,328	423	3,986
Edinburgh	3,392	2,034	3,322	8,748
Common to one or more		892	640	1,532
	£8,133	£6,676	£7,211	£22,020

Source: RCESH C.1123 Vol. II Statistics (Edinburgh 1875), 346.

These sums, together with student fees, were enough to relieve the most serious stringency until the state was prepared to enter upon university finance as part of its accepted obligations.

Finance, of course, was not the only problem. Even more difficult was the question of the content of university education. The struggle to bring the Scottish universities into line with the English was a long and hard one, generating increasing bitterness during the middle years of the century. Matters were resolved in the Universities Acts of 1858 and 1889; by the late 1880's the 'progressives' had forced the Scottish universities to accept a new curriculum and new subjects on the English model. Under the old Scottish formula pupils in schools took a general Arts (Classics) course; even those who proceeded to university continued in Arts and Philosophy. Only when this thorough grounding had been successfully mastered did young men move on to specialities such as medicine, science or law. This time-consuming process, although ideal perhaps for producing the all-round cultured man, was ill adapted to the bustle of the commerce and industry-orientated society of nineteenth-century Scotland. It came under attack notably from Englishmen or from English-educated Scotsmen who felt that Scots ideas on these subjects were outmoded. Under the 'English' system, a greater concentration on a narrow range of subjects was encouraged in order to allow a high standard of education to be developed.

The role of the philanthropists at this level of university educational policy is not easy to discern. In any case, though they might endow chairs for more 'modern' subjects, it would appear that the struggle over educational content was largely fought out among the academics.

An important part of the content question lay in the need to improve standards of technical and scientific education in the universities. But progress was slow. Benefactors set up several chairs such as (in Glasgow) the John Elder Chair of Naval Architecture (1883). In Edinburgh Thomas Carlyle 'Directed that of the ten bursaries he founded in memory of his wife, five were to be awarded for proficiency in mathematics, and especially in pure geometry, and the other five for proficiency in classical learning.' Carlyle's singling out of mathematics is a reminder of the need for special encouragement in this subject, where Scottish universities had fallen behind.

Perhaps the greatest philanthropic achievement in the field of Scottish university education lay in the removal and renovation of one of the largest of the Scottish universities. In 1870 the University of Glasgow was moved from its 400-year-old site on the ancient High Street to Gilmorehill in the new West End.[41] The new beginning was a remarkable demonstration of communal determination and generosity. The amount of government money involved was small.

The Principal set up a committee for obtaining subscriptions. Dean of Guild Archibald Orr Ewing of Ballinrain presided over a Joint Subscription Committee which harnessed the energies of Scotland, and especially of Glasgow and the West. As a result of their very successful organisation no less than £159,705 was contributed from private subscriptions by the end of 1867. The Treasury had promised £120,000 in 1867, provided a like sum was raised by private subscription. The University's total bill in the end was £427,856, towards which it had accumulated no less than £397,204 (including government matching funds), leaving a shortfall of only £30,000. It was an astonishing achievement, for most of the basic accommodation required by the University was built and was free of debt. In 1882 generous bequests from the Marquis of Bute, Mr. Charles Randolph and later Mr. Andrew Cunningham (in 1888) allowed the Bute Hall, the Randolph Hall and the tower to be completed. John Oldrid Scott was the architect of these later buildings completing the Victorian University of Glasgow which his father Sir George Gilbert Scott had created.

At the same time strenuous efforts were being made to build the Western Infirmary, vitally necessary for the Medical Faculty of the University now that the Royal Infirmary was three miles away to the east. The sum of £85,000 was raised, again by private subscription, for the new hospital which opened in 1874.

Once the University of Glasgow was established in its new home, many new developments took place requiring considerable expansion. In 1901, when the University celebrated its 450th birthday, Principal Story, recognising that the University needed yet more space and more facilities, launched a new appeal. This brought in a further £75,000 before he died in 1907.

The other great Scottish success story is that of the University College of Dundee, founded in 1881. There a private donor contributed £350,000 for its foundation. The College was virtually the sole creation of the Baxter family in the persons of Dr. John Boyd Baxter and Miss Mary Ann Baxter whose fortune had come from a large local flax, jute and hemp importing and manufacturing company.[42] Andrew Carnegie, when rector of the University of St. Andrews, paid for a physics laboratory at the Dundee College, which still bears his name. As the Dundee College was so near to St. Andrews it was inevitable that there should be a close relationship between them. In 1897 the College was united with the University of St. Andrews, from which it was again separated on 1 August 1967. There was some duplication of classes, but at the Dundee campus of the University of St. Andrews more emphasis was given to science, engineering and clinical teaching.

9. The philanthropists as educators

The philanthropist was an essential feature of Scottish education throughout Victorian times. He must be credited with a wide range of educational initiatives which benefited generations of Scottish children. For the first three-quarters of the nineteenth century the state left the entire field of education to charity and to private ventures. Only by the Act of 1872 did the state take its first major step towards requiring the provision, by local taxation, of facilities for elementary education for all children. With compulsory education thus provided came the beginnings of a state elementary system. The state could now seek to remove the random idiosyncratic features of philanthropic education. In Scotland, much of the elementary system thus passed to the School Boards. But even here philanthropy played its part, for men and women gave freely of their time in serving on the Boards.

As to secondary education, the state was loath to relieve the philanthropists. Its role, right down to 1908, was largely confined to bringing about a rationalisation of endowments. At university level also the state was able to leave the principal responsibility to others. It made some minor sums available, and it intervened in university government, but it went no further. After all, both secondary and university education were largely affairs for the middle classes; it did not seem unreasonable to continue to leave them to the voluntarist principle.

NOTES

1. Morgan, 1927, 164.
2. Menzies, 1854, 26.
3. Laurie, 1865, 340.
4. *Ibid.*, 1904, 13.
5. Anon., *An account of Hutchesons School* (Glasgow 1867).
6. Guthrie, 1847.
7. *RCESH* (Scotland), C.1123, 3rd Report (Edinburgh 1875), 67.
8. Walker, A., 1886, 28.
9. An Act to explain and extend the powers of the Governors of the hospital in Edinburgh, founded by George Heriot, jeweller to King James the Sixth, 14 July 1836. See *Steven's History of Heriots Hospital* (Edinburgh 1859), Appendix XV; also J. B. Mackie, *The life of Duncan McLaren* (Edinburgh 1888), Chapter VI.
10. Bedford, F. W., 'On the Hospital System of Scotland', *TNASS, Edinburgh 1863* (London 1864), 340-347.
11. Bedford, 1859, 214.
12. Harrison, 1920, 25.
13. 32 and 33 Victoria, c. XXXIX.
14. Harrison, 1920, 32.
15. 'Poverty is no excuse;' poor parents who could not pay fees had to approach their parochial boards for aid: Sellar, A. C., *Manual of the Education Act* (Edinburgh 1872), xliv. Fees were abolished in time after 1889; see Morgan, 1929, 224.
16. Wright, A., 1898, 200.
17. Sellar, 1872, XII.
18. *Ibid.*
19. *RCESH* (Scotland), C.755, Introduction to 1st Report (Edinburgh 1873), ii.
20. Sir Alexander Grant, 'The endowed hospitals of Scotland', *Recess Studies* (Edinburgh 1870), 117-150.
21. Mackie, 1888, Chapter 22.
22. *RCESH* (Scotland), C.1123, 3rd Report (Edinburgh 1875), 220-223.
23. *Ibid.*, 220.
24. *Ibid.*, 97.
25. Scotland, J., 1969, 36.
26. Neilson, 1880, 10.
27. Henry Dyer, M.A. & B.Sc. Glasgow 1873, D.Sc. Glasgow 1890, Principal of the Royal College of Technology at Tokyo from 1873-83; David Sandeman was Chairman of the Weaving branch of the Technical College and E. M. Dixon, B.Sc. Headmaster of Allan Glen's Institution, Glasgow (1878-1889).
28. Rae, 1953, 19.
29. Allan Glen's Institution Act, 1876, 39 & 40 Victoria Cap. X/V. Perhaps the Act had to be obtained to secure the legal status of future trustees. The last of the original trustees, Robert Jameson, had died on October 31, 1874.
30. Professor of Humanity (Latin) in the University of Glasgow from 1863 to 1906.
31. *Royal Commissioners for Technical Education*, C.3981, 2nd Report, Vol. I (London 1884), 489.
32. On 25 June 1912 Royal assent was given to the Allan Glen's School Order Confirmation Act, subsequently confirmed by Act of Parliament.
33. *College of Science and Arts, Glasgow*, 59th AR (Glasgow 1882), 7.
34. *British Association Handbook* (Dundee 1912), 229.
35. *Abstract of Returns furnished to the Department of Science and Art* (London 1893), C.7112.
36. Robertson, P. L., 'The Finances of the University of Glasgow before 1914', in *History of Education Quarterly*, Winter 1976, 452.
37. *Ibid.*, 461.
38. *Ibid.*, 464.
39. Sellar, 1872, X/i.
40. Horn, 1967, 187.
41. Mackie, 1954, 282.
42. Sanderson, 1972, 171 and Kidd, 1909, 94-100.

7

Education for Life and Leisure

1. The challenge of savings and leisure

THE growth of the savings bank movement, the provision of parks and recreation facilities, and the building of libraries and art galleries all reflected the urge of various groups to extend opportunities to all, including working-class people. The pressure for progress on these fronts was often philanthropically motivated and powered, usually but not necessarily by middle-class activists.

The ownership of savings opened a way to independence and a widening of choice over time. With the support and confidence which savings could encourage, men and women could budget and plan their finances, moving away from the traditional hand-to-mouth existence of the poor. A deposit in the savings bank represented security, provision for the 'rainy day' and possibly protection from unemployment. Some savers were able to buy their houses with substantial savings, but this option was available only to a few.

Education as continuing throughout life, especially for the working classes, was a concept only dimly perceived in Victorian times. The idea of leisure as a necessary prerequisite to extended education was equally remote, although the campaigns for shorter working hours were indirectly related to this ambition. Libraries, art galleries and parks all offered stimuli to mental and physical development. The broadening of the mind was a worthy Victorian objective. For many philanthropists the library, filled with books for earnest study, was easier to accept than the art gallery with its apparently frivolous pictures. The park offered an outlet for physical exercise, but decorous perambulations and small children's games were preferred amid protected grass, with borders and beds glowing with beautiful blossoms.

2. Savings banks

The founders of savings banks were hardly aware of their long-term advantages; they concentrated on more immediate gains. Such banks were begun as philanthropic institutions in order to encourage the poor to save, in the firm belief that 'there was a causal sequence between the increase in deposits and the diminution in poor rates'.[1] This relationship between savings banks and poor relief was much stressed in Scotland by those who approved the old Scots system of minimal allowances for the poor.

The pioneer of the movement was the Rev. Henry Duncan (1774-1846).[2] He opened a savings bank in his parish of Ruthwell, Dumfriesshire (population 1,100) in May 1810. The bank chest had three different locks, with three keys held by three authorised officers. In this way Duncan hoped to allay the suspicions of the subscribers. The Ruthwell bank had a complicated constitution, based on rules similar to those usual to friendly societies. But it was well supported, as the table shows:

Table 18

Deposits at Ruthwell Savings Bank between 1811 and 1814

Date	Deposits
1811	£151
1812	£176
1813	£241
1814	£922
1814	£1,164

Source: Mss at Ruthwell Savings Bank Museum.

The association between the church and the savings bank in the early years was close, for as George Rose explained, 'The pulpit had been a very efficacious means for giving furtherance to the measure of the Banks, . . . it being considered as one tending to the advancement of religion and good morals, as well as to great temporal advantages.'[3]

The Edinburgh Savings Bank was founded in December 1813 by J. H. Forbes, second son of Sir William Forbes (in his day the doyen of Scottish private bankers). Forbes produced a simple business-like constitution, modelled on that of a commercial bank. Unfortunately the acrimonious dispute between Forbes and Duncan as to the primacy of their respective banks has tended to obscure the contribution which the Edinburgh bank made to the savings bank movement. Savings banks were ultimately modelled upon the bank in Edinburgh, the main feature being that it was an *ordinary* bank. Moreover, neither the complicated constitution nor the questioning of putative depositors (as to their moral standing), which were part of the Ruthwell procedure, was necessary.

The philanthropic persons involved in the savings banks were the trustees, men of good repute in the community, usually with sound business experience, who were prepared to give service. Trustees were also expected to make contributions to the savings bank to ensure that the cost of management did not fall on the depositors. The trustee principle proved a sound one; such stewardship continued throughout Victoria's reign and beyond. The concept of trusteeship was an élitist notion; depositors had no voice in the management of the savings bank (as in Duncan's original).

But savings banks could do little for the destitute, in spite of early hopes. The Edinburgh Savings Bank was indeed founded as a branch of the Edinburgh Society for the Suppression of Beggars, while at Aberdeen the organisers arranged that 'the Bank was to have the use of a room in the Poors Hospital as an office'.[4] But the men and women who were to make the savings bank movement widespread and successful were not likely to associate themselves with the very poor, but with the deserving. Fortunately other savings banks had premises in church halls and other offices and the taint of the poor law was soon erased.

By 1818 there were, in addition to the savings banks in Glasgow and Edinburgh, 130 popular savings banks in Scotland with about 1,000 members and £30,000 in deposits.[5] The first banks were opened to receive deposits for a few hours once a week. Withdrawals were discouraged, and notice of intent had to be given, thus delaying repayments. As the historian of the savings bank in Aberdeen wrote: 'No sums under 2s. (it was usually 1s.) or above £5 were to be received in deposit; no interest was to be allowed on any payments until they amounted to £1, on which interest at 5% was to be allowed; and every additional sum of £1 lodged was to bear interest in the same manner, the interest to be calculated by months.' Another rule in Aberdeen provided, 'as the object of this institution is to encourage the deposit of small sums which a Bank will not receive, and which might otherwise be squandered away, unsafely deposited or lost altogether, whenever the sum amounts to £25 the owner will be required to withdraw it, and a new account will be opened for the small sums of his savings as formerly'.[6]

It was vital that savings banks should find a safe place for their funds which would also give a satisfactory return. The Scottish banks were keen to encourage the infant savings bank movement; they offered a generous rate of interest. The Ruthwell Bank invested with the British Linen Bank, which gave 5% interest on all sums deposited. In Glasgow, when the first Glasgow Provident Bank was established (3 July 1815), the administrative costs were borne by the Royal Bank: 'The deposits are lodged in the Royal Bank of Scotland, whose directors, very much to their honour, allow the Provident Bank such a sum over and above the usual interest, as enables them to transact the business of the depositors without any charge whatsoever.'[7]

The position in England was different, for the country banks there, although numerous, were unstable. The infant savings bank movement required some secure depository for its funds. George Rose, who had long been interested in friendly societies and the poor law, recognised that the savings banks, properly protected, could become a form of security for the poor. Rose introduced a successful bill on 5 February 1817. This contained two vital provisions. The government agreed to allow the savings banks to pay their funds into the Bank of England, into the account of the Commissioners for the Reduction of the National Debt. The fund was to be known (as it still is) as the 'Fund for the Banks for Savings', and on these investments the government was to grant a generous rate of interest. In addition, 'The voluntary nature of the management was also clearly defined in the Act — no treasurer, trustee or manager was to derive any benefit whatsoever from his office.'[8]

Dr. Duncan insisted that Scotland be excluded from George Rose's Act. He believed that the Scotch banks would continue to support the infant savings bank movement. The Scottish joint-stock banks were stable, but they were not protected from the fluctuations of interest rates, so that Scottish savings banks were sometimes paid as little as $2\frac{1}{2}\%$ on their deposits, often forcing them to try and obtain a higher return on their investment, to make private arrangements, or to invest with municipalities, or on heritable security, or even on personal security. Such returns were not necessarily secure. Although Duncan was unwilling to have the Scottish savings banks protected by George Rose's Act, he knew they needed some legal protection. To this end he introduced a Bill which became law on 2 July 1819. But the Scottish savings banks continued to have difficulty in finding satisfactory investment outlets. Even Dr. Duncan 'began to wonder whether the English system with a less fickle rate of interest combined with a government guarantee might be an advantage'.[9] Duncan suggested an 'optional clause' which would have enabled Scottish savings banks to join the government scheme, but the government required 'uniformity and compulsion' and the matter dropped.

Eventually in 1835 an Act was passed which allowed Scottish savings banks to take advantage of the investment facilities available in England. They then became part of the 'National Security' now known as the Trustee Savings Bank system. All new foundations after 1835 were bound to register under the new Act. The older ones were permitted the option of changing. In both Edinburgh and Glasgow the original provident savings banks were allowed to die. In 1836 both established new 'National Security' Savings Banks under the 1835 Act. In practice the Glasgow Savings Bank deposited its funds with the Western Bank and transferred larger sums, in excess of immediate requirements, to the Bank of England and the account of the National Debt Commissioners. The interest differential between these two enabled the Savings Bank to cover the expenses of management.

The early savings bank movement thus flourished. But there were difficulties. The government had timeously provided satisfactory machinery for investment, but there were not sufficient checks and safeguards at the managerial level. There were a series of major peculations in the 1840's (in both Ireland and England) which caused consternation. They frightened the government which, egged on by timid trustees, had removed liability from them by an Act of 1844 without substituting other safeguards. The lack of confidence encouraged a re-examination in the early 1860's of Samuel Whitbread's ideas for a government-organised savings bank (first outlined in a Bill of 1807 to establish a 'Poors Fund and Assurance Office'). There was substantial opposition, but W. E. Gladstone was determined, and on 17 May 1861 the Act establishing the Post Office Savings Bank received the Royal assent. An important motive with Gladstone was the desire to provide the government with a source of borrowing independent of the London money market.

Yet a further initiative, the penny-savings bank movement, started in Scotland in the late 1840's and 1850's. It was an important attempt to bring into the savings movement a poorer class of men, women and children, whose savings were counted in pennies. Home visiting was an essential feature of the scheme. Men and women knocked on doors every week to collect the pennies of the poor, in an attempt to instil the laudable principles of thrift and self-help. Sunday banks, church banks, Sunday school banks, local street banks were all penny banks, and were to become a useful under-pinning of the savings bank movement.

William Meikle, actuary of the Glasgow Savings Bank and a great servant of the movement, recognised the importance of the penny banks as 'institutions of great public utility, managed gratuitously by benevolent individuals under the superintendence of local trustees, who sign a constitution guaranteeing depositors against loss'.[10] The most famous penny bank in Glasgow was probably that in the Old Wynd (1850),[11] where educational and social work had been going on for many years. But the movement was much broader: within twenty years of the opening of the Old Wynd bank, 102 banks had been opened, at which 39,071 depositors had accounts. These banks — likened to the 'small pipes which conducted to the central reservoir the surface water which would otherwise have been evaporated'[12] — 'steadily increased in number and scale of operations until by 1881 the 60,000 depositors of the 213 Penny Banks in and around Glasgow were transferring to the Savings Bank about £20,000 per year, figures which had grown to 297 banks, 80,123 depositors, and transfers of £30,751 in 1914'.[13] The penny bank, by providing a neighbourhood deposit centre, encouraged the fragile resolve of the poor (and the young) to save, and provided a critical link in the chain of self-help.

Industrialists also organised penny banks at their works, although workmen sometimes regarded such initiatives with suspicion. Horne gives as examples Hood's Cooperage and Glasgow Glass Works (1834), Monkland Iron and Steel Works (1840), and Kerr and Co.'s Nailery (1841). The money was often saved for seasonal expenses, such as rent and winter fuel. Sometimes very little would go into longer-term savings, although at Kerr and Co.'s Nailery a small agency of the National Security Savings Bank was operated.

The savers can be roughly divided into two main classes. There were those who needed to be persuaded to save; for them the door-to-door collecting schemes and the penny banks were organised. Those who were intent on self-improvement needed little encouragement to save in the Trustee Savings Banks. As P. L. Payne explains of the Glasgow Bank, 'In the year 1856 . . . of every hundred active depositors, there were 15 domestic servants, 23 mechanics, 16 miners, 9 clerks and warehousemen, 7 labourers, carters and porters, 5 female warehouse workers and servers, and 4 shopkeepers and small traders'.[14] Many members of the middle classes were equally glad to take advantage of favourable savings schemes. The savings bank movement benefited many classes of men and women other than those rural poor of whom Duncan originally thought.

The philanthropic organisers also manifested a duality. For the penny bank the collectors were usually philanthropically motivated, perhaps linked with Sunday school or church or temperance society. At the other end of the scale the trustees remained as benevolent overseers of a movement, the management of which had largely passed into professional hands.

3. Public libraries

The provision of books for the people was not considered a high priority, even by the most ardent advocates of a participatory society, until the 1870's when 'education for all' became a common cry. Libraries, as an arm of general learning, were not thought of until the mid-nineteenth century. Even then there was no rush to provide them.

The interplay between the benevolent donor and the local authority is nowhere more vividly seen than in the case of libraries. Because early legislation was permissive,[15] and required that a majority should vote in favour of levying a penny rate for library purposes, it was comparatively easy to obtain a negative vote. Interested donors were thus obliged to offer incentives, in the form of library buildings, or book collections, to local authorities, making it a condition that the voters would accept the 1d. rate. This practice, a long and arduous one, proceeded slowly in the second half of the nineteenth century. But with the involvement of Andrew Carnegie (from 1890) it was much speeded up. By 1907, 77 authorities in Scotland had adopted the Libraries Acts.

There were, however, other kinds of libraries in Scotland charitably founded long before public provision was thought of. In a society where the minister often had a monopoly of local learning it was natural that many early libraries should be church-based. Some private libraries allowed free public access, but this was of limited value although the occasional bright boy, moving from parochial school through to university, would be encouraged to use them.

The most interesting library pioneer in Scotland was James Kirkwood of Dunbar (1650-1708), who about 1700 advocated a comprehensive national system of parochial libraries for Scotland.[16] Kirkwood graduated from the University of Edinburgh in 1670 and became chaplain to the Earl of Caithness. His duties took him to the North of Scotland, where he was greatly distressed at the ignorance of the people. He added to his parochial library scheme a visionary plan for a local printing works so that each library could command a constant supply of books. Later Kirkwood, deprived of his benefice in Scotland, had a church at Astwick in Bedfordshire. There he became associated with the Society for the Propagation of Christian Knowledge founded in London in 1699. The SPCK received monies from Queen Anne, during whose reign the Scottish SPCK was founded (in 1709). This was for the express purpose of proselytising in the remoter Highlands and Islands. Kirkwood's ideas of parochial libraries (later modified to county libraries) became part of a larger movement involving both peripatetic schools and libraries.[17]

Perhaps the first 'publick liberarie' in Scotland was that bequeathed by William Baikie[18] in 1684; it formed 'the Bibliotheck of Kirkwall'.[19] It was under the control of the kirk session; during the eighteenth century it remained a clergyman's library of theological books. In 1815 the original collection was incorporated into the Orkney Library, a subscription library, but the right of public access was preserved for the Baikie collection. This library was finally incorporated into the Kirkwall Free Library when it took advantage of the public library legislation of 1890.

Another remarkable library was that established by David Drummond, Lord Madertie. His testimony is dated 1680, but the library (at Innerpeffray near Crieff in Perthshire) may have been opened about 1694 'for the benefit and encouragement of young students'. Burgh libraries were also established by the Rev. John Gray in Haddington (1729), by the Rev. Dr. Robert Henry in Linlithgow (1790) and by the will of Walter Stirling (merchant), who died in Glasgow in 1791.

Two of the earliest libraries in Scotland were those organised for and by lead miners at Leadhills and Wanlockhead. The Miners' Library, or more accurately the Leadhills Reading Society, was established in 1741. Perhaps James Stirling, a remarkable innovator, suggested the idea to the miners.[20] It was a subscription library and not apparently endowed. The Wanlockhead library may have been different; founded as it appears to have been by the Duke of Buccleuch in 1756. Both libraries were run by committees of members. Despite complicated and cumbersome rules they were no doubt of great use and benefit to their members.[21]

By 1837 there were four distinct types of library available in Scotland. These were: institutional libraries (including university and professional libraries), Mechanics' Institute libraries, philanthropic libraries established by gift and endowment, and subscription and circulating libraries. Most libraries, including those of universities and Mechanics' Institutes, reflected the professional interest of their members whether clerical, legal or technical, while subscription and circulating libraries responded to the demands of paying customers. The philanthropic libraries occupied a middle ground; although most of them started as individual personal book collections, they often came to form the nucleus of the public library in their town of origin.

With the spread of popular education there was pressure to pass legislation to allow local authorities to provide a public library service. A Select Committee of the House of Commons reported on public libraries in 1849 and legislation swiftly followed. But the enabling Act reflected ambivalent attitudes towards public libraries. Under the terms of the Public Library Act (Scotland) 1853, burghs could raise a 1d. rate for library services only if they had canvassed the matter among the ratepayer-voters and had secured a majority vote. Public library facilities, which would have involved only a modest outlay in any case, became the butt of local political campaigns fought over the issue of the 1d. rate. In these battles the role of the private philanthropist often became crucial. Early library endowments enabled unwilling burgh councils to defend their own inactivity by pointing to the 'public' library privately provided. Some new endowed libraries were accepted by grateful town councils eager to defer the unpopular step of levying the 1d. rate. All over Scotland the controversial issue of the public library was resolved repeatedly by the action of philanthropists. They made generous gifts in one form or another and so forced the hand of reluctant councils who found themselves obliged to provide matching funds.

Glasgow had a particularly rich legacy of libraries from donors at different times. Walter Stirling died in 1791 and left his own personal library, together with money and other property, to the burgh of Glasgow for a public library. Unfortunately the resources were not enough. But the trustees eventually succeeded in altering the terms of the trust so that they were able to establish a subscription library. It was hoped that the fees from subscriptions would subsidise the 'free' library, but only after 1848 were some free reference services available. After 1871 Stirling's Library, a private subscription library which had been founded in 1804, was amalgamated with the Glasgow Public Library. The latter continued until 1912 when it was finally incorporated into the City Public Library system and became the Central Lending Library.[22] In view of Stirling's objectives, it is appropriate that his name should be preserved.

Stephen Mitchell (1789-1874), a Unitarian, left £70,000 'to form the nucleus of a fund for the establishment and endowment of a large public library in Glasgow, with all the modern accessories connected therewith'.[23] The civic authorities must have accepted eagerly this bequest which enabled them to withstand the lobby campaigning for the city to adopt the Free Public Libraries Acts which had been passed in 1853-54. Mitchell's Trust Disposition was reasonable and sensible. His remarks on censorship are of special interest. He insisted, 'That to the Library, Books on all subjects not immoral shall be freely admitted, and which word immoral shall not mean books which simply controvert present opinions on political or religious questions.'[24] The Mitchell Library opened in a building at the corner of Ingram Street and North Albion Street on 1 November 1877 with a stock of over 14,000 volumes and 130 current periodicals. The membership of the library grew very rapidly. Although the city authorities were delighted at the success of their new venture, the accommodation was clearly inadequate for the demands made upon it. The Library's usefulness continued to increase and the premises became more and more crowded. The frustrations of the staff and users were only relieved after the new Miller Street premises were opened on 7 October

1891. The expense involved in their purchase and necessary alteration cost the Mitchell Bequest £25,845, which reduced the Fund to £40,000. The interest from the remaining sum was by no means sufficient for the running costs of the Library, and when the rate of interest on the endowment fell from $4\frac{1}{4}$% to 3% the position became critical. From 1891 Glasgow Town Council provided about half the revenue required to keep the Mitchell Library going. Various surpluses were allocated from time to time from the Gas Trust and Local Taxation (Customs and Excise) Act 1890.[25] Thus for more than nine years before Glasgow was legally entitled to charge a library rate, public monies were going year by year to the upkeep of the Mitchell Library. Indeed not until 1904-5 was any charge (visible in the accounts) made for the Mitchell Library on the rates of the city.

The Mitchell received bequests of money and books. James Moir left money for purchasing old and rare books; David Logan willed money for buying books (fund exhausted 1917-18). Donald McPherson was a less usual benefactor: he was a journeyman painter who, having enjoyed the privilege of using the Mitchell Library, left his small savings for its benefit. Louis E. Campbell left property and money to the library; Robert Jeffrey's name is perpetuated in the Jeffrey Reference Library (he died in August 1902). There were bequests also from Alexander Macdonald (1897) and Arthur J. Taylor (1960).

The premises in 21 Miller Street soon proved too small; when the present site of the Mitchell Library (fronting North Street) became available, the corporation decided to build a really splendid library there. By this time, however, it was plain that a building worthy of its purpose could not be philanthropically funded: the corporation had to find the money. The building was opened to the public on 16 November 1911. The move brought the Mitchell Library from an east-end site near the original business core of the city to the west, within easy reach of the University of Glasgow.

George Baillie's Library was specifically provided for the working man. In 1863 he made a trust deed 'to contribute to the moral and intellectual culture of those who have to struggle with poverty and prejudice in their early years'.[26] Baillie's objectives were:

1. To aid the self-culture of the operative classes, from youth to manhood, and old age by furnishing them with warm, well-lighted, and every way comfortable accommodation at all seasons, for reading useful and interesting books, in apartments of proper size attached to one or more Free Public Libraries provided for them; and
2. To afford to the children, male and female, of the operative classes, the means of unsectarian moral and intellectual instruction, and industrial training in one or more School and School Grounds either gratuitously, or for such small consideration in the form of school fee as my said Trustees may think advisable . . .[27]

The form of George Baillie's Trust Deed was of particular interest. He was an aged man, a lawyer, who looked back with pleasure to the old days and old ways, and decided to model his trust on that of George and Thomas Hutcheson,[28] with both libraries and schools as his objectives. Within a decade the Education Act Scotland (1872) made elementary schooling compulsory for all children and so his provisions for schools were never carried out; in any case there was insufficient money for schools and library. After Baillie died in 1873 his trustees, the Faculty of Procurators, cast around for a way of implementing his wishes. There seems no doubt that they were puzzled. The deed was based on outmoded ideas difficult to implement. The Public Libraries Act had been on the statute book since 1853-5 and but for the Glasgow ratepayers' intransigence, public libraries could have been introduced in Glasgow at any time.[29]

To add to the problems of Baillie's trustees, the government, having taken the irreversible step of legislating for elementary education for all, was faced with the question of what to do with all the multifarious educational institutions, some duplicating the work of the new School Boards. It had set up Commissioners under the Educational Endowments (Scotland) Act of 1882. The powers of the Commissioners were designed to encourage obsolescent endowments to refashion themselves; the trustees of George Baillie thus found themselves under scrutiny before they had succeeded in establishing anything at all.

Professor Ramsay suggested that Baillie's trustees should join forces with those of Allan Glen's School (planning to concentrate on scientific education). This seemed appropriate in view of the Unitarian background of both benefactors. But the need to preserve Baillie's name proved a drawback; his trustees were also thirled to the idea of a Baillie's Library. In the end the trustees approached those responsible for Stirling's Library, and they came to an arrangement that Baillie's would occupy part of their building at 48 Miller Street, where Baillie's Institution finally opened in September 1887.

The libraries of the Mechanics' Institutes were primarily book collections for working men bent on self-improvement; there were no novels on their shelves. But the rate of serious book production increased during the century, making it very difficult for Institute libraries to keep up to date, given their narrow resources. Most of them therefore were suffering almost certain eclipse by the 1850's when the first enabling public library Acts were passed.

Aberdeen was fortunate in having a remarkably flourishing Mechanics' Institute (1824). It had as part of its provision a valuable library of 16,000 volumes. This was widely used and seemed to the citizens of Aberdeen (who declined to implement the adoption of the Free Public Library Acts in 1871 and 1872) to be provision enough. The Aberdeen Mechanics' Institute, in providing technical and scientific teaching, had been of sterling service, although it had suffered something of an eclipse after Robert Gordon's College started organising evening classes. But in 1845 the Institute took possession of a large new building in Market Street and was thereby given a new lease of life. In 1884 the Directors of the Institute offered the city the Mechanics' Institute building together with its library as a gift, on condition that the Free Public Libraries Acts be adopted. At a public meeting on 25 March 1884 the citizens agreed (by a majority of 891 votes to 264) to adopt the Acts and to accept the gift of the Institute building and its contents. The readership of the Institute library had been about 800; from the beginning the public libraries had about 8,000 readers.

At first glance, Victorian Edinburgh was well provided with libraries, for many professional bodies held book collections of a technical nature for their members. The Edinburgh Mechanics' Institute Library (1825) was important in providing books for others. Indeed the Edinburgh publishers were generous in their gifts to the Mechanics' Institute Library, which was probably one of the best in the country. When the public library Acts were passed and the Edinburgh authorities were permitted to open public libraries, it was a comparatively easy matter for the opposition to rally their forces on the grounds that Edinburgh was already well provided with library services. When the matter was first put to public vote (that the libraries Acts be *not* adopted), the motion was carried by 1,025-68. In 1881, when the matter was again put to the vote, the figures were 15,708 against adopting the Acts and 7,619 in favour.[30] Edinburgh was only persuaded to vote for the public library Acts after the philanthropic intervention of Andrew Carnegie in 1888.

In Dundee public subscriptions had been collected as a memorial to Prince Albert who had died in December 1861. It was decided to establish the Albert Institute of Literature, Science and Art with the money collected. Partly because of the commitment of the people of Dundee to the Albert memorial, there was no difficulty in adopting the public library Acts in 1866, and the library opened in the Albert Institute on 1 July 1869. Dundee was the second burgh in Scotland to adopt the Acts, Airdrie in 1853 having been the first.

In spite of various successes, the general progress towards public provision of free libraries was somewhat halting until the 1890's. The intervention of Andrew Carnegie (1835-1919) marked a new beginning. Carnegie had left his native Dunfermline for America with his family (who were linen hand-loom weavers) in 1848. In his later years he attempted to disburse his vast fortune on both sides of the Atlantic. He had a great reverence for education. But finding the School Boards already occupying the field, he determined to associate himself with libraries. He offered the local authorities of Scotland a tantalising package. He would supply the library buildings (and sometimes the fittings and furnishings), provided that they adopted the library Acts and undertook the maintenance and continuation of the service. As a result, whereas 'by 1889 only seventeen authorities had adopted the Acts in Scotland, by 1911 there were 77'.[31] Carnegie made no provision for staff or books; in this way he satisfied himself that he was not sapping the initiative of local authorities but encouraging it. Impressive Carnegie Libraries were erected all over Scotland, distinguished by their quality and size, sometimes indeed dwarfing the more modest provision of neighbouring public buildings. The formula which Carnegie adopted was that the local authority would agree to maintain the library at an annual charge of 10% of the Carnegie grant for the building. Unfortunately Carnegie's calculation disregarded the fact that, legally, local authorities could only levy a rate of 1d. In almost every case this was not enough to stock and staff the splendid library Carnegie had gifted.

It is a curious reflection that Carnegie's relatively over-lavish provision should in the short term have proved an embarrassment. The Carnegie trustees eventually came to recognise the difficulty. 'Dr. Aitken reports that in Scotland, Carnegie grants were given to 40 Scottish libraries . . . and of these 40 libraries only 3 had a rate income of or exceeding the 10% of the grant received . . . In many cases the grants — and the buildings erected with them — were out of all proportion to the library's income.'[32] That Carnegie succeeded in stimulating the movement for public libraries in Scotland there can be no doubt, but it is curious that with all his hard-headedness he allowed so much over-building to take place. Perhaps he was deceived by his American experience, where standards were higher and provision more lavish, into supplying libraries which were beyond the resources of Scottish local authorities to maintain.

Between 1890 and 1911, of the 77 authorities which had adopted the library Acts, 56 had received Carnegie grants either to establish libraries or to improve facilities already available. Carnegie thus greatly accelerated the coverage of Scotland by a library service.

All the Carnegie libraries were burgh libraries; there was virtually no rural library provision, although the legislation would have permitted parishes to unite for library purposes. In 1913 the Carnegie United Kingdom Trust was established at Dunfermline with a capital of $10,000,000. To formalise Carnegie's arrangements the Trustees were charged with 'the future oversight and extension of certain experiments to which he had already set his hand, and notably among these, the provision of public libraries'. The Trustees, conscious of the need to establish priorities, asked Professor W. G. S. Adams of the University of Oxford to conduct an inquiry. Adams produced two main conclusions: that although urban areas were reasonably well provided with library services, rural areas were not; and that the Carnegie grant system had produced a great deal of overbuilding.[33] As a result, the Trustees discontinued urban building grants and instead developed a series of valuable experimental schemes in rural areas. The North of Scotland scheme for the supply of books to people in Orkney, Shetland and Lewis was a pioneering venture in this field. In these ways the Carnegie United Kingdom Trust moved from the spontaneous generosity of Carnegie to well thought out schemes.

4. Art galleries

Art as a cultural experience, both 'educative and humanising', which ordinary men and women could enjoy, was remote from the lives of Victorian Scots, largely bent as they were on more mundane matters. Art galleries were prized only by a few, for it was mainly artists' societies which concerned themselves with the display of paintings and sculpture. In Scotland, galleries for exhibitions were more commonly used to mount displays of scientific and technological items. But travel in Europe and especially Italy became a popular holiday pursuit among the leisured classes in the second half of the nineteenth century. The broadening of cultural interests led to the acquisition of pictures, sculptures and *objets d'art*. Those who became connoisseurs sometimes preferred to keep their collections whole rather than disperse them among family members. In this way most civic collections started with a nucleus of pictures bequeathed to them. Individuals were able to purchase almost any type of painting: Rembrandt, Franz Hals and Van Dyck were all available for comparatively modest sums of money. Purchasers could also be attracted by poor quality works, or fakes; most collections contained items which have subsequently had to be weeded out.

In terms of national resources, the collecting of pictures in Scotland, based on the nation's capital at Edinburgh, was slow. The Royal Institution (1819) had been looking for 'ancient pictures as a nucleus of a national collection'. The Royal Scottish Academy[34] (1826) was also in the market; it bought 'old masters' as well as contemporary works such as canvasses by William Etty. Such collections were not available for public view.

In 1845 Sir James Erskine of Torrie bequeathed 'his fine cabinet of pictures, principally of the Dutch school' to the University of Edinburgh, with the proviso that they must be publicly displayed. After a good deal of manoeuvring, the government decided that there should be a Scottish national collection, and that a gallery to house it should be built. The city of Edinburgh granted for a nominal sum a site on the Mound. There the National Gallery of Scotland was opened to the public in 1859. Erskine was the catalyst; he was the first philanthropist to give his collection on condition that there was public viewing. The National Gallery was very short of money and expanded its collection only slowly. The Vaughan bequest (1900) of thirty-eight Turner water colours was a marvellous addition.

The Glasgow civic collection owed its existence to Archibald McLellan (1796-1854).[35] Between 1835 and 1850 he amassed an astonishing collection of pictures at a time when discerning buyers of modest means could purchase works now far beyond the purse of any but the wealthiest. McLellan, anxious to exhibit his pictures for the benefit of his fellow citizens, built the McLellan Galleries in Sauchiehall Street; these were ultimately bequeathed together with the pictures 'for the behoof of the citizens of Glasgow in all time coming'. This munificent gift encouraged others to come forward; William Euing's collection passed to the city in 1874; in 1877 the Graham Gilbert collection was also bequeathed (including Rembrandt's 'Man in Armour').

In the early 1880's attempts were made to discover the value of the Glasgow collection, and in the end Sir Charles Robinson, Her Majesty's Surveyor of Pictures, was consulted. He reported that 'I apprehend that the aggregate in Glasgow constitutes the most interesting and valuable provincial public collection in the Kingdom; nor do I think I am exaggerating when I say that I think the Glasgow Gallery, when better known, will rank as a collection of European importance.'[36] The Glasgow International Exhibition of 1888 was held in Kelvingrove Park. This proved a spur to those who wished the city to build a museum and art gallery. The exhibition produced a surplus of £55,000. They launched an appeal for a museum and art galleries and raised a further £130,000. In 1896 the corporation took over the whole project (including the money already raised), although it continued to consult with the Association for the Promotion of Art and Music. The building the corporation produced was a magnificent example of Glasgow's civic pride and confidence. It was opened (at a total cost of £258,000) on 25 October 1902. The completion of the Art Gallery was followed by a rush of generous gifts including those from James Reid, the Donald Collection, and the Hamilton Bequest.[37] In 1944 Sir William Burrell's collection, one of the most remarkable in existence, was gifted to the city, although this requires a separate gallery for its display.[38]

In Aberdeen the original Art Gallery was opened in 1885. It was primarily used for exhibitions by the Aberdeen Artists' Society and for industrial displays. In 1900 the city was pushed into more active participation in the art world by receiving the Alexander Macdonald bequest, which added greatly to its collection. When Sir James Murray was appointed chairman of the Art Gallery Committee, he determined to involve the city more closely. After a re-organising of the galleries (in 1905), the city authorities took over the art galleries in 1907.

In Dundee the city Museum and Art Gallery began in 1872. It was largely concerned with scientific and technical exhibits. The collection of the Watt institution later reinforced the emphasis on technology. The gallery built up its collection steadily, although it was not formally taken under the direct control of the city until 1957.

Those who favoured the development of art galleries were frequently opposed by groups within the community who regarded art with a philistine eye. Genre paintings, especially rather sentimental subjects, were approved, but much of art, especially nudes, was severely censured.[39] The art galleries of Scotland owed their existence to those in society who wished to share their enjoyment of art collections with others. Although there was no general artistic appreciation in Victorian Scotland, there was a growing sense of the significance of an art collection to a community. As Edward Pinnington wrote (of the Glasgow collection) in 1898, 'The pictures and statuary comprise both a property and an instrument of the municipality. While art makes a universal appeal, . . . the Glasgow collection has a direct bearing upon popular rule and popular pleasure. It is a recognised means of democracy.'[40]

When the Prince Consort laid the foundation stone of the National Gallery in Edinburgh in August 1850 he had summed up the Victorian attitude to social progress, saying: 'Gentlemen, the history of this grant exhibits to us the picture of a most healthy national progress: the ruder arts connected with the

necessaries of life first gaining strength, then Education and Science supervening and directing further exertions; and lastly the Arts, which only adorn
life, becoming longed for by a prosperous and educated people.'[41] In this culminating process the contribution of philanthropists was very important both
in supplying pictures and buildings, for it was through their generosity that
municipal authorities became pledged to committing their own resources.

5. Parks and recreation grounds

The acquisition of parks for Scottish Victorian cities was a matter for both
private donors and civic pride. Most cities had open spaces like Edinburgh's
royal parks, Glasgow's Green and Aberdeen's Links. These were usually
ancient undeveloped common lands available for various recreational
purposes. But with the expansion of the Victorian city a more active policy
was required than the protection of traditional open spaces. Parks were a
popular cause with civic leaders. Town councils themselves often acted as
developers, buying areas of land for parks and selling off the perimeter plots
for housing, thereby obtaining funds with which to embellish the park.
Glasgow was active in this respect, purchasing Kelvingrove Park in 1852-4,
Queen's Park in 1857, and later Alexandra Park in the east end.

A Public Parks Act was passed in 1859, making it possible for town councils
to take over and run pleasure grounds and pay for them from the rates. This
encouraged a great extension of such facilities. But the whole matter of public
use of the parks was bedevilled by the thorny problem of Sabbath observance
(see above, chapter 2, section 6). The long working week allowed men to be
with their families only on Sundays. But the Sabbath was the day for church
attendance rather than for idling in parks. Indeed such parks as there were
were often closed on Sundays, the only time when many could use them. Dr.
Norman MacLeod's attack on the sterility of the Lord's Day included these
comments: 'We get parks for these working men — men who rise at five
o'clock in the morning . . . and come home weary at night — and we have,
hitherto, practically said to these men, in the name of the Sabbath of the Lord,
Kennel up into your wretched abodes.'[42] But after the great controversy over
the proper keeping of the Lord's day in the mid-1860's, parks became more
generally recognised as good and necessary lungs for the cities.

The Glasgow authorities were especially active in buying plots of land, especially to provide open spaces in the more populous areas. By 1900 the city
had over 1,000 acres of park space, almost all of which the corporation had
bought. Only some 70 acres had been provided benevolently. Some 49 acres
had been gifted by James Dick at Cathkin Braes, on condition that the land
remained in its natural state, and 21 acres had come from Sir John Stirling
Maxwell in the form of Maxwell Park. Dundee by 1912 had 266 acres of parkland, mostly provided by civic initiative, although Baxter Park of 37 acres had

been presented by Sir David Baxter in 1863 and Lochee Park of 23 acres by Messrs. Cox Brothers in 1899.

Paisley was enriched by the presentation of the Fountain Gardens by the Coats family in 1886. Mr. Thomas Coats of the cotton firm bought the land and proceeded 'to hand over the same to the community, to be used as a place of healthful recreation and resort'.[43] The grounds were transferred to the ownership of the community of Paisley on 26 May 1868. A splendid ceremony was held at the Gardens, attended by some 4,000 persons representing all the societies and trades of the town. In the grand procession artisans were garbed to represent their trade, carrying banners and models. The tobacconists' banner bore the message, 'This plant will end in smoke, but Coats' gift will last for ever.' The masons put in a political plea: 'We recommend the nine hours movement.' The fishmongers brought goldfish in a glass bowl to be released into the grand central fountain, the proud product of the Sun Foundry of Glasgow.

One of the most interesting and important benefactors in the field of education for leisure was Isabella Elder, widow of John Elder,[44] who enriched the lives of many in Govan.[45] She perhaps epitomised the well-funded bene-factress whose loyalty was attached to a place of work. Her husband's ship-building yard, the Fairfield works, was in Govan; it was her late husband's workpeople that she wished to benefit. To this end she gave the Elder Park in 1885. From the deed of gift the park was to provide the inhabitants of the burgh of Govan with 'healthful recreation by music and amusements'. Mrs. Elder's recognition of the need to provide comfort of a secular kind through books and outdoor activities reflected a broadening of the objectives of the Christian philanthropist. In one corner of Elder Park, twenty years later, she built the Elder Free Library.

The city fathers could take pleasure in viewing the parks they had provided as they travelled about their daily affairs. Censuses of users were taken and the figures were noted with satisfaction. As James Nicol, city chamberlain of Glasgow reported, on Sunday, 2 August 1885, 188,283 citizens entered and enjoyed the facilities of either Glasgow Green, or Kelvingrove, Queen's or Alexandra Park.[46] The identification of common public interest with the pro-vision of parks lessened the need for philanthropic prodding.

6. The susceptibilities of councillors

The opportunities for education and leisure which are discussed here added a further dimension to the Victorian philanthropic achievement. With the savings banks the aim of the benevolent was to gather in the money to strengthen the position of the saver, so that the independence of the individual benefited both him and society. In addition a worker-saver was not likely to call on the state for help in times of difficulty, for he was protected by his nest egg and by the self-respect it had engendered. But the philanthropic function of gathering savings was not enough; the state had to step in and provide both security for the funds saved and sound investment opportunities through the Bank of England.

In the case of libraries and art galleries the philanthropists acted as precipitators, providing books or pictures, or libraries or art galleries, and thereby challenging the local authorities to match them. Philanthropic action thus forced demands upon civic leaders, from men and women of their own class, which civic pride could not ignore.

Public parks were provided both by philanthropic gift and by civic initiative, but the latter greatly predominated. Their provision and upkeep by public money was a much more popular cause than either libraries or art galleries. Councillors could readily identify themselves with the need to get their fellow citizens into the open air. Citizens who would never dream of walking through the forbidding portals of an art gallery or library (which led to an alien world which they did not understand) would readily walk through the ornamental cast-iron gates of the park into an open and welcoming space. The invisible barriers between the classes were much less formidable in the parks; the ordinary councillor, seeing this, responded to the need for a programme of park development.

NOTES

1. Fishlow, A., 'The trustee savings banks, 1817-1861', *Journal of Economic History*, Vol. XXI, No. 1 (March 1961), 26, quoting Lewins, W., *A History of Savings Banks* (London 1866).
2. In England Mrs. Priscilla Wakefield (in Tottenham) and Rev. Joseph Smith (in Wendover) are credited with introducing savings banks there. See Horne, H. O., *A History of Savings Banks* (Oxford 1947), 26.
3. Rose, 1816, 33.
4. Anon., *Aberdeen Savings Bank*, 1967, 8.
5. Mechie, 1960, Chapter 3.
6. Anon., *Aberdeen Savings Bank*, 1967, 6.
7. Cleland, 1823, 125.
8. Horne, 1947, 77.
9. *Ibid.*, 54.
10. Meikle, W., 'On Savings Banks, Penny Banks and School Banks', *TNASS, Glasgow 1874* (London 1875), 933-935.
11. Walker, 1877, 507-8.
12. *Glasgow Savings Bank*, 28th AR (Glasgow 1863), 4.
13. Payne, 1967, 156.
14. *Ibid.*, 159.
15. Public Library Acts which affected Scotland:
    1853 Public Libraries (Scotland and Ireland) Act
           (16 and 17 Victoria Cap. 101);
    1854 Public Libraries (Scotland) Act
           (17 and 18 Victoria Cap. 64);
    1864 Public Libraries Act (an English Act), but two important modifications applied to Scotland
           (29 and 30 Victoria Cap. 14);
    1866 An Act for England, Scotland and Wales;

1867 An Act to amend and consolidate the Public Libraries Act (Scotland)
(30 and 31 Victoria Cap. 37);

1871 Public Libraries Act
(34 and 35 Victoria Cap. 59);

1887 Public Libraries Consolidation (Scotland) Act
Has remained principal Act for Burgh Libraries ever since;

1894 Public Libraries Act;

1899 Amended. Public Libraries Consolidation (Scotland) Act.

16. Anon. (James Kirkwood), *An Overture for Founding and Maintaining Bibliothecks in every Paroch throughout the Kingdom* (1699). Anon. (James Kirkwood), *An Account of a Design about Erecting some Libraries in the Highlands of Scotland for the use chiefly of Ministers and Probationers* (Edinburgh 1702).

17. Kelly, T., 1966.

18. Craven, J. B., *Descriptive Catalogue of the Biblioteck of Kirkwall (1683) with a notice of the founder, William Baikie, M.A., of Holland (in Stronsay, Orkney)* (Kirkwall, privately printed, 1897). Only 25 copies of this were printed. GUL.

19. Some of the original books in this collection are now deposited as 'The Bibliotheck of Kirkwall', AUL.

20. James Stirling (1692-1770) was called 'the Venetian' because he had lived in Venice for ten years where he became interested in glass making. Subsequently he was brought in to save the mines from financial collapse. He was an extraordinary man who reorganised the whole community, cutting the work day to 6 hours and introducing exceptional social benefits. (See *Scotland and Scotsmen in the 18th Century Mss of John Ramsay of Ochtertyre*, 2 vols. (Edinburgh 1888), II, 306-25).

21. Crawford, J., 'Two miners' libraries in the '70s', *Library Review*, 1971-72, Vol. 23, 14-17.

22. Stirling's Library was first sited in Surgeons' Hall in St. Enoch Square. Between 1805 and 1844 it was in Hutcheson's Hospital, Ingram Street. Later it was at 48 Miller Street, in the building erected at the site of Walter Stirling's own mansion, where it remains.

23. Anon., *Glasgow Public Libraries, 1874-1966* (Glasgow 1966), 10.

24. Stephen Mitchell Trust Disposition and Settlement (5 January 1866), quoted in Anon., *Glasgow Public Libraries, 1874-1966* (Glasgow 1966), 12. Stephen Mitchell, George Baillie and Allan Glen were all members of the Unitarian Congregation in Glasgow. All three trusts (Mitchell and Baillie establishing libraries and Glen a charity school) included injunctions against narrow sectarian interests.

25. £2,000 in 1890-91 from Local Taxation (Customs and Excise) Act 1890. (*Abstract of Returns*, Department of Science and Art) (London 1893). C.7112, 71.

26. Baillie, G., *Trust Deed:* recorded . . . at Edinburgh, 15 December 1863. In Baillie's Library.

27. Baillie, 1864, 7.

28. '. . . considering the admirable example set in former times by two members of my own profession in Glasgow, George and Thomas Hutcheson, whose pecuniary bequests though amounting only to Three Thousand, Four Hundred and Twenty-Eight pounds Sterling . . . have by being judiciously invested in land near Glasgow . . . become one of the largest and most useful institutions for benevolent objects in the City . . .' *Ibid.*, 3.

29. The four failed attempts to persuade the ratepayers in Glasgow to vote for public libraries were: 17 April 1876, rejected by 1,779 votes to 993; 9 May 1885, rejected by 29,946 votes to 22,755; 1888 rejected; 1897 rejected.

30. See Anon., *Edinburgh Public Libraries* (Edinburgh 1951).

31. Tyler, W. E., 1967, Thesis, 4.

32. Aitken, W. R., *A History of public library provision in Scotland to 1955* (Glasgow 1971).

33. Adams, W. G. S., 1915.

34. Caw, J. L., *The National Gallery of Scotland* (Edinburgh n.d.), V.

35. A coach-builder and harness-maker who became town councillor and magistrate.

36. Pinnington, 1898, 29.

37. Anon., *The Hamilton Bequest* (Glasgow 1977).

38. In the spring of 1978 a start was made on the building to contain it in the grounds of the Pollok estate.

39. See appendix to J. D. Bryce (Glasgow 1859).

40. Pinnington, 1898, 1.

41. Anon., *Catalogue of the National Gallery of Scotland under the management of the Board of Manufactures* (Edinburgh 1895).
42. Macleod, 1865, 15.
43. *Inaugural Ceremonies in Honour of the Opening of the Fountain Gardens*, Paisley, 1868, 9. GUL.
44. See Craig, A., 1912.
45. Govan was an independent burgh between 1862 and 1912.
46. Nicol, 1885, 134.

PART IV

The Philanthrophy of Health

8

The Poor and the General Hospitals

1. The philanthropic-medical empathy

ONE of the primary responsibilities imposed upon the philanthropic evangelical by Christ was the care of the sick. This was perhaps the most deeply felt obligation, and one which encountered no dispute. For all of the sick were, by virtue of their condition, 'deserving'. But the philanthropists could not respond directly. They lacked the necessary skills. On the other hand those who had the skills did not have the means: the doctors could not, on their own, generate a hospital and health service. The commercial principle, under which the service might have paid for itself, was irrelevant, for those who needed the service, namely the working classes and the poor, could not pay an economic price. The task of the philanthropists, therefore, was to provide the resources framework within which the professionals could operate. This they did by paying up themselves, and by persuading others to do so, using powerful appeals to conscience and religion.

2. The hospital in the community

In order to identify the philanthropic contribution to the care of those sick in body and mind in Scotland, it is necessary to enter pretty largely into the general history of hospital provision.

Medical care of any sort, other than that provided locally by interested amateurs, was of recent origin. The earliest elements of the present health service date back to the eighteenth century when the first Scottish hospitals were founded. After these initial steps, lunatic asylums were built to house mentally ill people who were not suitable as patients in ordinary hospitals. Later specialist hospitals concentrating on treatment for some particular ailment or part of the body took their place in an increasingly complex system. After 1870, largely because of increasing surgical skills and the demands of an urban population, the number of hospitals grew and subsidiary services such as convalescent homes were added to the provision. In country areas a new movement to provide cottage hospitals sprang up, giving rural patients their first opportunity to experience hospital treatment. The whole of this expansion and development depended not only upon the doctors and their skills but also

152

upon the competence of members of the newly trained cadres of nurses, without whose intelligent interpretation of doctors' instructions progress would not have been possible.

All these advances depended upon charitable initiative; it was philanthropists who precipitated extensions of medical care, whether residential in hospitals or domiciliary in people's homes. Neither the local authority nor the central government took any direct action to bring about these changes, although local powers could be encouraging and supportive. These amateur activists were often local businessmen; the professionals were of course doctors. The Victorian philanthropist took upon himself the complex functions involved in founding, funding and managing hospitals and medical services in Scotland. An attempt will be made here to show how philanthropists and doctors stimulated each other to provide a system which survived without government interference until 1948.

The involvement of municipal government in hospital development stemmed from the fever epidemics of the nineteenth century. Following Chadwick's Sanitary Report of 1842, and the legislation which resulted, industrial cities were forced to take more active responsibility in matters of public hygiene. Public health authorities slowly gained in authority and prestige. In Glasgow where, because of its size, socio-medical problems were acute, the authorities opened the first purpose-built municipal fever hosptial at Belvidere in 1877. They were the first town council in Scotland to take such an initiative. In Edinburgh in 1871 the authorities bought the Canongate Poorhouse as a fever hospital. It proved to be too small, and in the 1890's steps were taken to acquire a site outside the built-up area of the city. The Colinton Mains Fever Hospital was opened in May 1903. Medical Officers of Health were appointed in Edinburgh and Glasgow in 1862 and 1863. Early basic poor law provision was also expanded to provide a safety net for the indigent.

These three elements, the philanthropic, the municipal and poor relief, made up the hospital provision of Scotland.

At the time of Victoria's accession Scotland had general hospitals (infirmaries) in at least eleven different centres. These were Edinburgh, Glasgow, Aberdeen, Dundee, Greenock, Perth, Dumfries, Montrose, Paisley, Leith and Inverness. Almost without exception these hospitals have survived, expanded and prospered; and since 1948 they have been the basis of the National Health Service. They provided the only place of residence for the sick, other than the poor house; during the fever epidemics of much of the nineteenth century they were flooded with patients. Local authorities, usually parochial boards from 1845, showed the utmost reluctance to take any effective epidemical action, although fever hospitals were built later in the large cities.

The first hospitals in Scotland were, as elsewhere, medieval, prereformation foundations involving small-scale service by the church and churchmen[1] (see chapter 1, section 5, above). They concentrated their efforts on succouring the old, the young and the sick; they were 'hospices' and gave shelter, food and aid and whatever medical remedies they could. After the reformation a few foundations survived, such as the Hospital in Aberdeen, St. George's in Dunkeld, and the Magdalene Hospital in Edinburgh, but these were not 'hospitals' in the modern sense.

Scotland had three powerful medical bodies dating from before the Union of the Parliaments in 1707. They controlled entry to the medical profession, and indirectly affected hospital development. The Royal College of Physicians[2] (1681) and the Royal College of Surgeons[3] (1505) in Edinburgh and the Royal College of Physicians and Surgeons[4] (1599) in Glasgow provided important nuclei of medical education in Scotland. With three medical colleges, and two universities at Glasgow and Edinburgh,[5] foremost in scientific education and research, it is not perhaps surprising that from the eighteenth century Scotland attained a remarkable pre-eminence in medical matters. Edinburgh's early emergence as one of the most distinguished centres of medical education in the world (with enormous influence on new medical schools elsewhere) is an absorbing success story, of which the development of Edinburgh Royal Infirmary is an integral part. Although good medical education gradually became available in Glasgow, strife between the Faculty of Physicians and Surgeons and the University absorbed a great deal of medical energy.

The only residential institution publicly provided under the terms of the poor law was the municipal hospital for the old, the orphans and the disabled. Glasgow opened a Town's Hospital in 1733, Edinburgh a Charity Work-house in 1744, and Aberdeen a Poor's Hospital in 1741, while Paisley, Perth, Dundee, Dumfries and Leith all made some shift to house dependent categories. Although there was some overlap and confusion, usually the Poor's Hospital was distinct from the Town Infirmary. The old, the orphans and the disabled lived in the Town's Hospital. Orphan boys were apprenticed and girls sent out into service. Compensatory labour (perhaps in the form of domestic help) was expected, although inmates resisted this type of imposition.

In the North of Scotland, for example in Inverness and Elgin, the Poor's House was supported by a variety of means, including private charity and official monies from the town authorities. Poor-law assessments there were not undertaken until after the Poor Law Amendment Act of 1845. In Glasgow the Town's Hospital was maintained jointly by the Town Council, the Merchants' House, the Trades' House, and the general Kirk Session. The building was originally in the centre of the town (on Clyde Street overlooking the river), but the Town's Hospital removed about 1844 into the abandoned Lunatic Asylum premises on Dobbie's Loan. In Edinburgh the Charity Work-house was established on the North Back of Canongate, behind Canongate Church and church-yard. It was difficult to finance it, for there was bitter controversy over its funding, the proposed rate assessment being actively resisted. In Aberdeen the original suggestion that the Infirmary and the Poor's Hospital should be one and the same foundation was rejected.

3. The Royal Infirmaries in Edinburgh and Glasgow

The Royal Infirmaries[6] in Edinburgh and Glasgow became the great teaching hospitals of Scotland. On them rested much of the responsibility for the development of medical care, teaching and training in Victorian Scotland. The great distinction of the medical faculty of the University of Edinburgh lay partly in the facilities for clinical teaching provided by the Royal Infirmary.

The Town Council[7] and the Colleges of Physicians and Surgeons played their parts in establishing the medical faculty in the University of Edinburgh. In 1720 Alexander Monro (already appointed as teacher of Anatomy by the Royal College of Surgeons at Surgeons' Hall) became 'Professor of Anatomy in the City and College', with an initial 57 students. The Royal College of Physicians was barred by its charter of 1681 from founding a College, and therefore had no option but to organise teaching through the medium of the Town's College. In 1726 four professors (two in Theory and Practice of Medicine and two in Medicine and Chemistry) were appointed by the College on the recommendation of the Royal College of Physicians, so that by 1726 no fewer than five professorial medical appointments had been made, all of Edinburgh men trained at Leiden.[8] Thus, from the beginning the Edinburgh School of Medicine was established as an integral part of the University. From these Leiden-trained men came the initiatives which led to the foundation of the Edinburgh Royal Infirmary.

The Infirmary opened on 6 August 1729[9] in 'a small hired house' with six beds, at the head of Robertson's Close. The idea that patients should live in a hospital for their cure rather than their care was new. The curative powers of doctors were at this time very limited, although students were trained in the Edinburgh Royal to use the techniques then available.

The international fame of the Edinburgh medical school in the nineteenth century was built up partly at least by the successful interrelationship between the Royal Infirmary at Edinburgh and the University medical school. The managers wrote as early as 1788, 'A school of Medicine having been for many years established in Edinburgh . . . the managers of the infirmary resolved to spare no pains in cherishing it as far as the hospital could serve that purpose; and foreseeing that its interests would soon be interwoven with that of the University, they resolved to adopt every measure that would tend to facilitate medical education and to render it compleat.'[10]

In Glasgow the medical profession had been given status and authority by James VI who, in 1599, had granted rights and privileges to the Faculty of Physicians and Surgeons,[11] following representations made by Maister Peter Lowe.[12] The Faculty had a monopoly of entry both to surgical and to general medical practice in Glasgow and a large area of the West of Scotland. But it also came to believe it had a monopoly of medical education, for the Faculty acted as a College and organised all the medical teaching there was. But Glasgow University revived its chair of medicine[13] in 1712; Queen Anne later endowed it and in 1714 John Johnstoun was appointed. Unhappily Johnstoun neglected his great opportunities.[14] Dr. William Cullen was appointed to the Professorship of Medicine in 1751, but in 1756 he went to the Chair of Chemistry at the University of Edinburgh.[15] The strong ground occupied by the Faculty of Physicians and Surgeons in Glasgow, doing most of the effective medical teaching in various 'schools'[16] in the city, made the University's position difficult when that body did decide to attempt to organise a medical Faculty. There was wasteful conflict between the Faculty and the University as to which body was to control medical education. By the Universities Act of 1858 the University's rights to involve itself in medical education were secured.

The Royal Infirmary in Glasgow was founded in 1792 on a site, which it still occupies, north of, but adjacent to, the cathedral. It was a relatively late beginning, reflecting the modest attainments of medical teaching in the city. The Infirmary owed its start to George Jardine (1742-1827), Professor of Logic in Glasgow College, who 'with all that zeal and philanthropy which so much distinguished him' determined to provide hospital facilities for Glasgow. The first organising meeting was held on 5 June 1787 and on 8 June 1787 Jardine wrote to a friend, 'You can expect a very magnificent Infirmary . . . already £5,000 is subscribed for erecting it.'[17] The first patient was received on 8 December 1793. In the interval the site was secured, funds subscribed, the Adam brothers engaged as architects and builders, and the hospital erected.

In the nineteenth century the Royal Infirmaries came to occupy a special place in their respective cities. In Glasgow in 1821 an admirer of the Infirmary wrote a long poem extolling both the hospital and its inmates:

The Royal Infirmary, Glasgow[18]

Stanza XXIV: Philanthropy laid out the area vast
That was in former days the Castle yard
Whereon to build the Infirmary surpast
By none —'tis like a royal palace air'd
From ev'ry side, with rails the green in front to guard.

Stanza XXV: Praiseworthy citizens conceiv'd the plan
That call'd Benevolence to action forth
To mitigate the pains of suffering man
Uniting private aid with public worth
Poor patients from the east, west, south and north
Are guided here with hospitable care.

Medically too the Infirmaries became prestigious institutions. They held a tight monopoly and offered the only patient care, the only facilities for student teaching, and the only outlet for the ambitious doctor who wanted to instruct students. They were managed by the leading citizens of their respective cities. They became very conservative institutions, resisting change and resenting the appearance of other hospitals, whether specialist or general.

The Glasgow Royal Infirmary's position was seriously affected by the removal of the University to Gilmorehill in 1870. The Western Infirmary (opened in 1874) was an integral part of the new University complex, and the University students left the Royal Infirmary and migrated to the Western in a body. The medical professors of the University at last came into their own, with a hospital adjacent to the University built for teaching purposes, and with most of the city's medical students. The alliance of the Royal Infirmary and the Faculty had received a rude shock. Their response was to re-organise the Royal Infirmary Medical School from 1875. A new College was formed, named after St. Mungo (1889). But it rarely attracted many students (who prepared generally for the triple qualification of the Faculty in Glasgow and the two Colleges in Edinburgh). In 1910 the breach between the University and the Royal Infirmary was finally healed by the establishment in the Royal by the University of four chairs, of Medicine, Surgery, Pathology, and Obstetrics and Gynaecology; the teaching facilities of both the Royal and the Western In-firmaries were made available to all medical students.

In spite of these turmoils, Glasgow made striking contributions to the progress of world medicine, pioneering the surgical revolution of the later nineteenth century. Joseph Lister (1827-1912), a Quaker, was born in Essex and educated in University College, London where he qualified in medicine. He came north to work under James Syme at Edinburgh. Syme was a dis-tinguished surgeon and from him Lister learned a great deal. But Syme's reputation notwithstanding, surgery remained a hazardous business and mortality was high. On 28 January 1860 Lister was elected to the Chair of Surgery in the University of Glasgow. His chair, however, did not guarantee access to the Royal Infirmary,[19] and his appointment as surgeon there was delayed until 5 August 1861; it was not until November that he performed his first operation there in public. When he arrived in Glasgow from the compara-tively healthy wards of the Edinburgh Royal Infirmary he was confronted with rampant septic disease. This was one of the great inhibitors of surgical success. Lister determined to deal with it.[20] He introduced his principle and practice of antiseptic surgery (basically by introducing a solution containing carbolic acid into the open wounds).[21] The antiseptic principle was fundamental to the surgical revolution which transformed hospitals and patients' expectations of them. Lister returned to Edinburgh in 1869, assuming the chair there. Of his antiseptic treatment he said, 'Its effects upon the wards lately under my care in the Glasgow Royal Infirmary were in the highest degree beneficial, converting them from some of the most unhealthy in the Kingdom into models of healthi-ness.'[22]

After Lister's departure another remarkable choice was made. William Macewen (1848-1924) was appointed as Surgeon to the Glasgow Royal Infirmary in 1876, at the age of 28. He had been a student under Lister, whom he greatly admired. When he became a surgeon himself, 'He observed that wounds, if not infected, healed better if not continuously drenched in carbolic.'[23] He became one of the pioneers of aseptic surgery, by which every-thing concerned with the patients and the operation was kept clean and sterilised. Macewen was the man who put doctors into white coats.

It is clear that the introduction of antiseptic or aseptic surgery, together with general anaesthetics, made a major alteration in time to the attitude of the public to hospitals. Accident cases which came into the Glasgow Royal Infirmary could now be more successfully treated; working men soon knew that the best thing that could happen to them would be to be carried into the Infirmary. Once the Infirmaries in both Edinburgh and Glasgow had been established as centres of excellence, rather than as places of last resort, a crucial transition had been effected: such hospitals could now become famous for their curing qualities as well as their care.

The breaking of the Glasgow Royal Infirmary's local monopoly by the opening of the Western Infirmary in 1874 encouraged the southsiders to demand their own hospital. During the 1870's funds were collected and active steps were taken to secure a site and establish the Victoria Infirmary; it was opened in 1881. In Edinburgh there was no new general hospital founded, although after a bitter struggle the Edinburgh Royal Infirmary was moved from Infirmary Street to a new and more spacious site on Lauriston Lane where a more commodious hospital was built. The two other general hospitals in the city were Chalmers Hospital[24] and the Deaconess Hospital (see chapter 4, section 4, above), both of which were small, and neither of which offered any sort of alternative to the Edinburgh Royal Infirmary. The fully developed system as at 1899 is given in Table 19.

4. The doctor as philanthropist

Members of the medical profession regarded themselves as philanthropists, for they had traditionally assisted 'their poor and afflicted fellow creatures', in many instances regardless of the prospect of payment. This attitude was encouraged by the respective professional bodies in Edinburgh and Glasgow. When the Royal Infirmaries were set up, it was natural that the Managers would turn to the organised medical bodies for staffing and general assistance.

In the Edinburgh Royal Infirmary three groups of medical functionaries emerged in the eighteenth century. The day-by-day work was attended to by the two Physicians in Ordinary, elected by the Managers (in addition the College continued to elect senior men, called extraordinary physicians, as consulting physicians). Secondly, the Managers also appointed four Surgeons in Ordinary. These were to be supervised by the more senior surgeons of the city (there were probably 32 surgeons resident in Edinburgh, members of the College, in the mid-eighteenth century). The third tier in the hierarchy consisted of the medical professors of the University of Edinburgh. By 1778 the Managers of the Infirmary had granted the sole privilege of giving courses of clinical instruction to the University professors of medicine and allocated to them wards for this purpose.

Table 19

General Hospital provision in Edinburgh and Glasgow in 1899

	Edinburgh		Glasgow	
	Official Provision	*Voluntary Provision*	*Official Provision*	*Voluntary Provision*
	1742 Charity Work-house Poor Law Hospital Fever Hospital City Hospital for Infectious Diseases, Infirmary Street 400 beds 302 occupied on average 1896 2,745 in patients 6 staff nurses 74 probationers	1729 Royal Infirmary 740 beds 40 cots 703 on average occupied Admission free 190 nurses Probationers trained 1864 Chalmers Hospital 42 beds 29 on average occupied 249 in patients 3,046 out patients Admission by recommendation by responsible persons Private wards (male and female at 5/- per diem.) 1894 Deaconess Hospital Lady Grisell Baillie Memorial, 142 Pleasaunce, Church of Scotland Committee on Christian Life and Work 24 beds 3 cots 20 on average occupied Admission free	1733 Town's Hospital Poor Law Hospital Fever Hospital 1853 Barony Parish Hospital Barnhill, Springburn 400 beds 343 on average occupied 12 nurses 22 probationers 1865 Kennedy Street Fever Hospital 1870 Belvidere Hospital London Road 1887 Fever and General: 800 beds 651 occupied 1896 4,606 patients 50 charge nurses 100 nurses 50 probationers, training 2 year course, certificate 1900 Ruchill Fever Hospital	1792 Royal Infirmary 584 beds 554 on average occupied 6,703 in patients 22,799 out patients Admission by recommendation 1874 Western Infirmary 400 beds 386 occupied 4,548 in patients 14,761 out patients 123 nurses, 3 years' training course. Admission by letter 1881 Victoria Infirmary 150 beds 138 occupied 730 in patients 230 out patients Hospital 4,884 at Infirmary Dispensary 27 probationers training given Admission by letter

Source: Various, annual reports and H. C. Burdett.

In Glasgow matters developed differently. The existence of a single strong medical body, the Faculty of Physicians and Surgeons, enabled the medical profession to strengthen its monopoly and use the Glasgow Royal Infirmary as an extension of itself, and so to resist the claims of the University. The professors of the University had no standing in and no entry to the wards of the Royal Infirmary of Glasgow, except and unless an individual from the University was appointed to a medical post there.

Critical to the power structure of medicine in Glasgow was the management of the Royal Infirmary, in which the Faculty of Physicians and Surgeons and its members were dominant. The President of the Faculty was an *ex officio* member and was often the Senior Physician. In addition there were elected annually three Faculty representatives. Against the Faculty presence that of the University was weak. It is true that the professors of medicine and anatomy were both *ex officio* members of the management, together with a third representative of the University, usually non-medical. But the professors were slack in their general duties and remained aloof from the Management, leaving the Faculty in effective possession.

Medical men had a vested interest in the hospitals and in working there. Hospital appointments led to a substantial broadening of income opportunities. Moreover hospital teaching attracted students, and students bought either apprenticeships with substantial honorariums for pupillage, or paid student fees (which at the Glasgow Royal Infirmary were divided equally between the consultant and the hospital). In addition, hospital work involved co-operation with the lay managers — usually influential businessmen — eager to obtain good medical advice for their families. In the course of Victoria's reign hospitals became renowned for the quality of their treatment, and the doctors associated with them were consequently advantaged.[25]

5. The philanthropist as financier and manager

Once the philanthropic effort to establish the hospital had been made, the founders had to ensure that sufficient finance was coming forward on a regular basis. They also had to undertake managerial functions which would enable the hospital to function efficiently and economically. It was essential to build up a loyal group of subscribers whose contributions could be counted on. In addition donations, legacies and endowments had to be sought, for substantial sums of investment income were a useful hedge for all such voluntary hospitals.

Some subscribers were especially active in the affairs of the hospital and became hospital managers. But hospital managers were themselves divided into two groups. There were those who for prestige reasons served on the management committees, and there were those who took a more active part in management. All were gentlemen who for professional or business reasons had come to the notice of the influential members of the community. Each generation of managers seemed to produce a few who would undertake many duties on behalf of the hospital and devote a considerable part of their leisure time to these pursuits.

The bridges between the doctors and the philanthropists in the case of the infirmaries were the Boards of Management, standing, as the Annual Report of the Royal Infirmary in Glasgow put it in 1795, 'as stewards for the diseased and miserable'. The Board had an *ex officio* membership, with the Lord Provost originally as Chairman. Later the Chairman of the Board was a businessman of power and influence in the community. The Honorary Treasurer, usually another businessman, was almost as important. Both men were often eloquent in encouraging more generous subscriptions, donations and legacies from leading citizens. There were other subscribers' representatives also on the Board; they provided, in one character or another, a potentially powerful philanthropic presence. The permanent administrative office of an infirmary was run by the Secretary. From the late 1830's there was a Medical Superintendent in charge of the medical side.

The philanthropists of course deferred to the doctors in the daily running of the infirmaries. But there was a range of issues in which their role could be important, namely matters of general policy, the arbitrament of internal conflicts, the question of admissions, the control of ward budgets and the appointment of staff. The staff question was difficult to deal with: in an age of patronage and solicitation, canvassing for appointments by doctors among laymen could not be excluded. But perhaps the most important internal matter was the control exercised by the boards of management over wards and beds. Access to these was crucial for any doctor wanting to teach or to conduct observations. Decisions on these questions were of the greatest importance within the teaching hospitals, and as between them and the universities.

Public policy had two main aspects. One was the question of extensions to the infirmaries: how to finance and site them. Here business experience could give the entrepreneurial philanthropists real standing. Secondly there were those issues that came to the public attention, the occasional scandal or *cause célèbre*, as in the furore about the employment of Catholic nurses at the Glasgow Royal Infirmary in the 1870's (see chapter 13, section 3). In such situations the lay members of the board stood between the infirmary and general public opinion. They also heard complaints made by one element of the staff against another, or by students against their teachers. In 1821 some of the surgeons and physicians in the Glasgow Royal complained to the managers that 'Pupils have secretly tampered with patients, by telling them that they are merely the subject of experiment in the hands of the Surgeon; that they have been improperly treated, and that they will be maimed for life.'

Hospital finance was based on the 'subscriber's line'. The subscriber had the right to send patients to the hospital in proportion to the amount of his subscription.[26] In 1894 at the Glasgow Royal Infirmary the regulation was:

7. Contributors of not less than £10 10s. and Annual Subscribers of not less than £1 15s. shall be entitled to recommend one patient annually for every £10 of subscription, and for every £1 1s. of annual subscription.[27]

Many subscribers made their contributions to the Infirmary funds with the full intention of using their lines for the benefit of the known poor, domestic servants and related persons. Hospitals did sometimes encourage contributions from patrons on the grounds that subscribers could send their servants as in-patients when necessary. But it was also common for non-medical charitable bodies to appeal to hospital subscribers to 'donate' their lines.[28] It was an extraordinary situation, that those who had the lines, namely the better-off, never wished to nominate themselves for treatment. For hospital patients were charity patients and so exerted no control over the treatment they received, or the doctors who administered it. This was the underlying weakness of a system which remained dominant for more than a century at most infirmaries in Scotland. The persistence of this unsatisfactory practice is a reminder of the inability of the hospital authorities to remove a privilege once granted, for fear of losing subscriptions.

The difficulties of linking subscribers' and doctors' preferences in the matter of patients remained a bottleneck. It had to be by-passed, and other sources of revenue found if the hospitals were to develop their services. The most interesting and important development was the liaison between factories and works and the hospitals. From the 1840's workmen's subscriptions became of

Table 20

Glasgow Royal Infirmary: a comparison between annual subscriptions (from private citizens) and contributions from workmen in public works, 1842-1858

Years	Subscriptions	Public Works	Total
1842	£2,508 4 6	£345 12 2	£2,853 16 8
1843	2,391 8 11	576 6 11	2,967 15 10
1844	2,486 4 0	697 13 7	3,183 17 7
1845	2,465 6 0	709 16 7	3,175 2 7
1846	2,555 7 0	758 11 1	3,313 18 1
1847	2,748 8 6	1,164 2 1	3,912 10 7
1848	2,637 2 6	771 2 1	3,408 4 7
1849	2,521 8 0	1,014 0 6	3,535 8 6
1850	2,440 3 0	773 14 4	3,213 17 4
1851	2,412 3 0	909 3 6	3,321 17 4
1852	2,920 13 0	1,064 17 4	3,985 10 4
1853	3,233 12 6	1,398 18 5	4,632 10 11
1854	3,428 14 6	1,480 8 11	4,909 3 5
1855	3,314 7 0	1,749 0 9	5,063 7 8
1856	3,434 2 0	1,851 14 0	5,285 16 0
1857	3,441 12 6	1,705 3 2	5,146 15 8
1858	3,417 13 0	1,960 16 0	5,378 9 0
Totals	£48,353 9 11	£18,931 1 5	£67,288 2 1

Source: Glasgow Royal Infirmary, AR, 1858.

increasing importance to the Glasgow Royal Infirmary. In 1842 the contributions from workmen to the Glasgow Royal Infirmary funds were about $\frac{1}{16}$th of those of ordinary subscribers. Thirteen years later in 1857, as the Table shows, workmen were contributing about half as much as the traditional subscriber.

In Edinburgh, which had always claimed to be a national hospital for the whole of Scotland, and where all beds were free, no such scheme to tap workmen's contributions was mounted. Edinburgh had a smaller industrial base and possibly was not suited to such a scheme, although money problems there remained acute and several wards were from time to time closed because of financial stringency.

This harnessing of funds from what was called 'the public works' was important, not only because it circumvented the restrictions of the subscriber's note, but it also provided help for those men most likely to need it. As the Managers of the Glasgow Royal Infirmary reported,

> The greater relative proportion of accidents to chronic cases of surgical diseases is one of the distinguishing features of your infirmary, as compared with the other large hospitals of this country.

The rule at Glasgow Royal Infirmary was that accident cases were always to be admitted promptly,[29] an appropriate provision in a mining, manufacturing and shipbuilding district.

It was inevitable that the power balance in the infirmaries should shift away from the philanthropists and toward the professionals.

By the 1870's lay philanthropic initiative in the hospital world was channelled along certain familiar and diminishing lines. Hospital subscribers continued to exert their influence occasionally through their representatives on boards of management; the board as a corporate body administered and controlled the hospital, but did so through the permanent paid secretariat. Only the chairman of the managers and the treasurer as individuals (holding honorary office) were able to exert any real personal influence on the hospital: they represented the surviving and diminishing elements of philanthropic participation in policy making. The infirmaries were great conservative institutions, by the later nineteenth century dominated by their medical mandarins, from which the philanthropic presence had been largely extruded.

But the philanthropic authority could revive in times of crisis, where there was a public controversy, or when a large addition to the funds was required. The philanthropists usually retained power when hospital appointments were being made, although their influence no doubt depended upon both circumstances and the personalities involved.

M

NOTES

1. I am indebted to Margaret Lamb for the use of her as yet unpublished material. See also Durkan, J., 'Care of the poor: pre-reformation hospitals', in McRoberts, D., ed., *Essays on the Scottish Reformation, 1513-1625* (Glasgow 1962).
2. Craig, 1976.
3. Cresswell, 1926, 4.
4. Duncan, A., 1896.
5. Aberdeen and St. Andrews did not develop serious medical teaching until later.
6. Logan Turner, A., 1937; Buchanan, M. S., 1832; Patrick, J., 1940.
7. The University of Edinburgh was founded in 1582 on the initiative of the Town Council: it was often known as the Town's College.
8. Underwood, 1977.
9. A charter was granted on 25 August 1736.
10. Logan Turner, A., 1927, 139, quoting the *History and Statutes of the Royal Infirmary of Edinburgh* (1778).
11. The Faculty of Physicians and Surgeons (1599) of Glasgow was granted the title of Royal (1910) and in 1965 became the Royal College of Physicians and Surgeons of Glasgow.
12. Duncan, 1896, chapter IV.
13. Fergus, 1911, 12. The College had had a chair of the Practice of Medicine between 1637 and 1646.
14. See Mackie, 1954, 224; and Underwood, 1977, 124-5.
15. Thomson, J., 1859. It is tempting to suppose that medical education in Glasgow would have been different had Cullen remained there.
16. Groups of lecturers used the same premises which became known as 'schools', e.g. College Street School and Portland Street School. In addition there was later the medical school of Anderson's University.
17. Letters of George Jardine, GUL Ms. Gen. 507.
18. Harriston, 1824, 37.
19. See Cameron, Sir Hector Clare (Glasgow 1927), 9, note.
20. Anon., *Lister and the Lister Ward* (Glasgow 1927), 43-45.
21. See Cameron, Sir Hector Clare (Glasgow 1927).
22. Lister J., 'On the effects of the Anti-septic system of treatment upon the salubriety of a Surgical Hospital.' *The Collected Papers of Joseph, Baron Lister* (London 1909).
23. Jennett, B., 'Sir William Macewen 1848-1924, pioneer Scottish Neurosurgeon', *Surgical Neurology*, Vol. 6, No. 2, August 1976, 57-60.
24. Boog Watson, W., *Chalmers Hospital 1868-1968* (Edinburgh 1968).
25. Waddington, I., 'General practitioners and consultants', in Woodward, J., Richards, D. (eds.), *Health care and popular medicine* (London 1977), 171.
26. There was, however, at Glasgow Royal Infirmary a refusal book; subscribers who sent 'unsuitable' patients might have them refused and their 'lines' returned. See *Rules and Regulations of Glasgow Royal Infirmary* (Glasgow 1894), 22. GUL.
27. *Ibid.*, 23.
28. 'It would be of great assistance if friends who have lines for public institutions would kindly place them at our disposal. In doing so they may feel assured that they will be well bestowed.' *The Glasgow Kyrle Society* (Glasgow 1895), 12. 'It is not easy for poor people to secure these (hospital lines) for themselves and many demands are made on us so that if friends who have such at their disposal will send them to us they will confer a favour.' *Orphan Homes of Scotland, Glasgow, Narrative of Facts* (Glasgow 1885), 59.
29. 'The Accident Porter shall attend the Accident Gate from 6.30 a.m. to 7.00 p.m. and shall be ready to answer any summons when required during the night.' *Rules and Regulations of Glasgow Royal Infirmary* (Glasgow 1894), 76.

9

The Care of Lunatics

1. The philanthropists' mental block

IN a sense lunacy was not so immediate a challenge to the philanthropists as was physical illness. For throughout the eighteenth century and well into the nineteenth the status of the mad was equivocal in the middle-class mind. Serious mental derangement suggested in these times that no personality existed; there was no mind, or a seriously damaged one within the body. Moreover, there was no therapy that could lead to the engendering or revival of personality. The seriously mad were thus not really human, but seemed closer to the animals. As such they were excluded from Christian care, for it could do them no good. These barriers of identity and treatment had to be broken through before the lunatic could come under philanthropic care. In this the philanthropists played their part. For it was because a few sensitive men and women were able, from the later eighteenth century, to think of the insane as human beings that concern and responsibility for them could grow.

The founding of lunatic asylums in England and Scotland, for these reasons, came significantly later than that of the infirmaries. In Edinburgh the Asylum was not opened until 1813, over eighty years after the Royal Infirmary. In Glasgow the Lunatic Asylum opened in 1814, some twenty years after the Glasgow Royal Infirmary was launched. But the awakening of energy, when it came, was quite striking. The chronology of philanthropic effort for the sick in Scotland was therefore as follows: first came the infirmaries for the physically ill (often however congested with lunatics), then came asylums for mental cases, followed by the specialist hospitals for specific ailments of the body and specific categories of persons (women and children). The setting up of dispensaries, those great auxiliaries of the infirmary system, was, on the other hand, spread over most of the period from the later eighteenth century onward. In all of these the philanthropists were a major force.

2. The problem of lunacy in England and Scotland

Until the last quarter of the eighteenth century there was little or no sympathy for the insane in Scotland or elsewhere. In terms of the law there was no definition of madness. 'Mad' people were treated as public nuisances and vagabonds disrupting society, sometimes requiring to be confined. The medical profession was not able to differentiate effectively between various kinds of deviant behaviour. Perhaps a simple rule of thumb applied: those lunatics who, because of their nuisance value, came to the notice of the authorities, were incarcerated. Other individuals, passive and not violent or destructive, remained in their native communities and were tolerated and supported by friends and neighbours.

In England the aim of the law was to protect the public from the insane, rather than to guarantee the rights of the afflicted. To this end the law permitted the deranged to be bound and chained.[1] An insane person could fall foul of the law in several ways. He could be labelled as a criminal lunatic. If he were unable to maintain himself, he became a pauper lunatic dependant on the parish; if he wandered about and made a nuisance of himself by begging he became a vagrant lunatic. In addition to these three categories there were those lunatics of a better class who spent their lives in the seclusion of their own homes. These patients of the 'middling and upper ranks' did not come to the attention of the authorities. They certainly appealed as a class to the novel writers of the period, especially those of a 'Gothic' bent. The harshness of the law could weigh heavily on the three first categories, for they were without family support, but it rarely affected the insane members of wealthier families.

The madness[2] of King George III in 1788 and recurrently thereafter focused public attention and sympathy on mental illness. When the King suffered an attack, he was treated as any other mad patient. 'The unhappy patient . . . was no longer treated as a human being. His body was immediately encased in a machine which left it no liberty of motion. He was sometimes chained to a staple. He was frequently beaten and starved, and at best he was kept in subjection by menacing and violent language. The history of the King's illness showed that the most exalted station did not wholly exempt the sufferer from this stupid and inhuman usage.'[3] As Kathleen Jones states, 'The matter had one good and lasting effect: for the first time, insanity and the treatment of insanity, formed a burning topic of public discussion. The subject had been brought out of concealment in a way which defeated the conspiracy of silence.'[4] Perhaps even more significant was the King's recovery in March 1789. This improvement in the royal health must have confirmed to a sympathetic public that if the King could recover, so could others similarly affected. For no one really believed that the King was possessed of the Devil, or that he was being punished because of his sins or evildoing. The King finally withdrew into blindness and insanity in 1811 and died in 1820.

In Scotland a good many sensitive citizens had been affected by the fate of Robert Fergusson, the young Scots poet who in the 1770's suffered from attacks of 'furious insanity'. When his behaviour became uncontrollable he was committed to the Edinburgh City Bedlam, which was part of the Charity Workhouse. There he was housed in a small stone-floored cell and there he died in 1774. Fergusson had been treated by Andrew Duncan, M.D. (1744-1828). In 1792 Duncan, deeply affected by Fergusson's sufferings, published a pamphlet urging that a lunatic asylum should be founded in Edinburgh.[5] But the public would contribute only £100, so the project failed.

The most notorious repository in Britain for the insane was Bethlem Hospital in Moorfields, London, founded as long before as 1247. It was commonly known as Bedlam, and had a horrifying reputation. Visiting Bedlam was an outing until 1770, when frivolous visits were forbidden, although the management regretted the change, fearing the loss of about £400 a year which visitors paid. In addition to Bethlem Hospital there was a variety of private madhouses. In 1751 St. Luke's Hospital was established in London as a rival to Bethlem. It had the good fortune or good judgement to appoint Dr. William Battie, M.D., a medical philanthropist and a pioneer in the treatment of mental illness. In 1758 he published his *Treatise on Madness*. This book marked the beginning of a new, gentler and more humane treatment of such patients. Battie, from the beginning of his study, recognised the ignorance which surrounded the subject. 'Madness,' he wrote, 'is perhaps as little understood as any (illness) that ever afflicted mankind. The names alone usually given to this disorder and its several species, viz. Lunacy, Spleen, Melancholy, Hurry of the Spirits etc. may convince any one of the truth of this assertion, without having recourse to the authors who have professedly treated on this subject.'[6] Under Dr. Battie, St. Luke's represented the first British attempt to achieve a more positive regimen for the mad patient. The old 'treatments' were intimidating and debilitating, consisting of violent vomiting and purges, together with a 'lowering diet' intended to make the patient manageable by loss of energy. Dr. Battie advocated a simple wholesome diet and 'diversions' to occupy the minds of his patients. John Howard, the prison reformer, approved of Dr. Battie's constructive programme.[7]

The Retreat was established in 1792 at York by the Society of Friends, on the initiative of William Tuke (1732-1822). The Latin inscription on the foundation stone read, 'The charity and love of friends executed this work in the cause of humanity.'[8] Tuke's hospital was based on 'Christianity and commonsense'. He hoped to banish force and intimidation from lunatic asylums by proving that the application of humanitarian principles not only cured patients but made the organisation and running of the asylum much easier for everyone.

The various charitable asylums in England continued to undertake much of the work of housing lunatics, whether paupers or not. Some effective legislation was passed in 1853, when the Lunatic Asylums Act (England) empowered local authorities to build asylums for their lunatic paupers. This was the beginning in England of comprehensive provision for the insane.

Lunatics in Scotland were perhaps treated even more harshly than those in England. It was popularly believed that their behaviour was affected by the moon, or that they were possessed of the devil, requiring that help be sought for them at holy wells and crosses.[9] If found wandering as vagrants, they were often taken up and immured in cellars or dungeons and chained. Lack of understanding of the problems ensured that as late as 1841 Richard Poole, M.D. could remark with brisk detachment, 'In Scotland, having no Bedlam, we commit the better sort of mad people to the care and training of chirurgeons, and the inferior to the scourge.'[10] But the increased humanitarianism stemming from the eighteenth century was beginning to be reflected in a new concern.

The law in Scotland relating to lunatics was originally based on the principle that 'the Prince, as *pater patriae*' was responsible for such a person and that he appointed a tutor-in-law (usually the nearest male relative) to act for each lunatic. If no close relative was willing to act, then a tutor-dative could be appointed to ensure that someone had responsibility for the lunatic and his property. In the nineteenth century it became more usual to appoint judicial factors, alternatively known as 'curators bonis', as guardians of the person and property of the insane. These appointments were intended to be temporary until the tutor-at-law was assigned, but by common practice this subsequent step was rarely taken.

3. The philanthropic initiative: the seven Royal Lunatic Asylums

The plight of lunatics in Scotland, incarcerated as they often were behind bars, in town houses and bridewells, sometimes in public view, attracted the attention of a number of persons in Scotland in the later eighteenth and early nineteenth centuries who had come to believe that some other way must be found of looking after such people. The humanitarian response to this unpopular cause was remarkable, for lunatic patients were unpleasant and sometimes dangerous people. Over the sixty years before 1840 eight Lunatic Asylums were founded in Scotland, solely to provide for mentally deranged patients:

Table 21

Lunatic Asylums in Scotland in 1839

1782	Montrose
1800	Aberdeen
1813	Edinburgh
1814	Glasgow
1820	Dundee
1827	Perth (James Murray's)
1835	Elgin Pauper Lunatic Asylum, philanthropic in origin
1839	Dumfries (Crichton Royal)

Source: SLC, Appendix to the Report (Edinburgh 1857).

Two of these asylums were begun by remarkable women, in Montrose Susan Carnegie, and in Dumfries Elizabeth Crichton at Crichton Royal. In

Perth James Murray's was also founded by money from a single donor. At Aberdeen, Dundee and Elgin initiative came from the managers of the infirmaries. At Edinburgh and Glasgow philanthropists made general financial appeals.

In Montrose, as elsewhere in Scotland, lunatics had been contained in cells at the rear of the Town House, fully visible to the public, lying in straw like pigs and fed through the bars.[11] Susan Carnegie[12] (1744-1821) was the first person in Scotland to take action on behalf of such unfortunates. She gave two reasons for her intervention: 'My view in this undertaking was merely to rid the town of Montrose of a nuisance — that of mad people being kept in prison in the middle of the street — and the hope that, by providing a quiet and convenient Asylum for them, some of these unfortunate persons might be restored to Society. The plan was set agoing by the liberality of the public, powerfully excited by the unwearied exertions of my worthy assistant the late Provost Alexander Christie,[13] and soon rose to a degree of consequence unthought of in the beginning.'[14]

The influence of Mrs. Carnegie was strong along the North-East coast. In 1800 and 1805 the managers of the Royal Infirmaries at Aberdeen and Dundee resolved to found lunatic asylums in their towns, partly to relieve the infirmary of lunatic patients. At Aberdeen the sponsors were fortunate in having legacies from Baillie John Cargill and John Forbes (a close friend of Mrs. Carnegie). At Dundee the managers obtained a splendid site overlooking the Tay, engaged William Stark as architect, and had the foundation stone laid in 1812. But they had difficulty in raising the necessary money, so that their Asylum was not opened for patients until 1820.

In 1806 Duncan's project for an asylum for Edinburgh was revived. A parliamentary grant of £2,000 was allocated from the revenue of the forfeited estates. A charter was granted in 1807, and a site obtained at Morningside. The building was finally opened in July 1813. But it was always short of funds. The young Queen Victoria in 1840 agreed to become patron of the Royal Edinburgh Lunatic Asylum. She made a generous donation which allowed the managers to expand onto a newly acquired 50-acre site.

The original sponsor of the Glasgow Lunatic Asylum was Robert McNair of Belvidere. As a manager of the Town's Hospital he was profoundly shocked and distressed by the cruel plight of the insane who were kept there. In the early 1800's, supported first by other managers but later by an active and energetic committee, he collected some £7,000. A wider range of appeals was made; lists of likely contributors were drawn up and by 1810 £10,000 had been pledged. By 1822 the committee had collected £22,704 19s. 3d. Generous Glasgow had responded so well that the committee were able to proceed with their plan to build the Asylum complete. They bought a site of some three acres to the north of the city, between Dobbie's Loan and Parliamentary Road. William Stark, the architect, was sent to tour English asylums before embarking on his task. He was interested in the methods and treatment of the

Retreat at York, but came back converted to something rather different. He resolved to build a Panopticon.[15] This was an ingenious new prison plan developed by Jeremy Bentham consisting of a round building with arm-like extensions of cells, like a hub and spokes. The superintendent could, in theory, from his position of vantage at the hub, see into and thus supervise the inmate of each cell.

The foundation stone was laid on 2 August 1810 (see Appendix III); on it was inscribed:

> To restore the use of Reason
> To alleviate Suffering and lessen Peril
> Where Reason cannot be restored
> The Glasgow Asylum for Lunatics
> Was erected by Public Contribution.

The Reverend Stevenson Macgill gave a stirring address, declaring: 'If our friends thus helpless and unhappy, must be removed from us, to what places are they to be taken? Do you desire nothing better for them than a gaol? Would you treat them as the refuse of their species; prepare for them only chains and bolts, a floor of stone, and a bed of straw?'[16] The Asylum opened on 12 December 1814. Forty-one patients were transferred from 'the cells of the Hospital to apartments in the Asylum'. It became Royal in 1824, continuing on the increasingly congested site at Dobbie's Loan for twenty-seven years, with the city encroaching on all sides. By 1841 it was clear that the Asylum must be re-sited. Sixty-six acres were bought from the lands of Gartnavel, some three miles to the west of the city, and in June 1843 some 240 patients were transferred to the new building, designed by Charles Wilson in the Tudor Gothic style.

The James Murray Royal Asylum at Perth[17] owed its existence to the East Indian fortune of Mr. William Hope, whose heir, James Murray, conveyed his whole inheritance to trustees for the purpose. They bought a splendid site, 'situated in a park containing twelve acres, on the acclivity of Kinnoull Hill . . . and (with) a delightful view of the Grampian Mountains, the River Tay and the surrounding country'.[18] William Burn of Edinburgh was the architect, and the Asylum was opened on 28 May 1827.

At Elgin the trustees of Gray's Hospital, harassed by the number of pauper lunatics wrongly committed to their care, themselves offered to make a bargain: 'If the landholders will contribute liberally to the erection of a Pauper Lunatic Asylum . . .,' they said, 'the Trustees will grant a sufficient extent of ground, in a very eligible situation, for the site, and courtyard of an Asylum, give a handsome subscription for the building, and assist in paying the wages and maintenance of a keeper.'[19] The necessary matching contributions were forthcoming. The Elgin Pauper Lunatic Asylum opened in 1835 with accommodation for about 40 patients. But it was too small within fifteen years.

Crichton Institution for Lunatics at Dumfries was perhaps the most notable of the Scottish asylums. Its founder, Mrs. Elizabeth Grierson Crichton, was the widow of James Crichton[20] who left his fortune, once various legacies had been taken care of, to be used for some philanthropic purpose chosen by his widow. The childless Mrs. Crichton entered into her responsibilities with some enthusiasm. It was not her original intention to found a lunatic asylum. In June 1829 she wrote to her fellow trustees 'that nothing can so happily correspond with my husband's intention . . . than to appropriate . . . the largest proportion of the residue of his fortune in founding and endowing a college at Dumfries for the education of poor scholars and others resorting thereto.'[21] But it was necessary that the 'government shall be prevailed upon . . . to take charge and direction of the proposed college so as to give it from the first the station and advantages of a university.' She envisaged a campaign throughout South-West Scotland to raise more money and 'secure to the proposed institution the status and privileges of a university'.

When Mrs. Crichton first approached the Rt. Hon. Robert Peel, her proposal was 'graciously received' and 'referred to the consideration of the Commission just now sitting on the Scotch Universities . . . the Commission were most favourably disposed towards it, and had remitted to a committee of their number to digest the plan of the college.'[22] The Royal Commissioners recommended to His Majesty that he accede to the proposal. They believed that 'The establishment of a University of Dumfries would conduce to the propagation of sound Academical Instruction in Scotland.'[23] Approval was given, but the University of Dumfries was not to be: the four established Universities, jealous of their rights and privileges, and afraid of competition from another College which might drain away their student fees, objected strenuously to a fifth Scottish university, and Lord Melbourne informed Mrs. Crichton of the government's decision that 'the plan of a College at Dumfries be abandoned'.

Although no doubt disappointed, Mrs. Crichton quickly rallied. She proposed 'that a certain part of the fund should be appropriated towards founding and endowing a lunatic asylum in the neighbourhood of Dumfries upon the most approved plan and capable of accommodating 100 patients.'[24] Her husband had left a legacy of £1,000 to the Lunatic Asylum, Edinburgh, which perhaps encouraged her to make her second choice. After some initial difficulties Mrs. Crichton succeeded in buying the Hillhead estate, on a beautiful site overlooking the Nith, on the outskirts of Dumfries. But there were difficulties: 'There existed at one time such prejudice against the introduction of an institution for lunatics into this part of the country, that the public voice was against it — neighbouring proprietors became alarmed that the value of their properties might be deteriorated; and the press were even employed as an engine to write it down.'[25] But Mrs. Crichton prevailed. The building was entrusted to William Burn (architect also of the Edinburgh Royal Asylum at Morningside, and Murray's Asylum, Perth), and he designed a handsome dark-red sandstone building. Like Stark, he was attracted by the idea of a Panopticon, but did not implement it. The first patients were received on 5 June 1839.

4. The professionals: the problem of therapy

Even the new lunatic asylums were at first primarily places of imprisonment; they incarcerated patients just as before, although the buildings were, by early nineteenth-century standards, larger and more spacious. The lay philanthropist was concerned on humanitarian grounds to make patients more comfortable; he was not competent to go further. Only a few of those actively concerned in establishing the seven Royal Lunatic Asylums had any thought of positive medical care. Susan Carnegie was one of the exceptions; she had long advocated a resident medical superintendent, writing, 'By this arrangement a man would have leisure and time to study this particular branch of physic which for the good of mankind it is much to be wished were further advanced.'[26]

Members of the medical profession were becoming involved in attempts to cure mental illness by enquiring into its nature, defining the problems and then applying treatment to individual patients. The first doctors to do so were French, Philippe Pinel (1745-1826), and J. E. D. Esquirol (1772-1840). Pinel pioneered the 'moral' treatment of the insane by which lunatic patients were 'liberated'. Esquirol, his pupil and disciple, carried on the work. Pinel instituted careful enquiry into the symptoms of each patient, and endeavoured to build up close doctor-patient relationships. The foremost medical men of Scotland were in close contact with their French colleagues, the links between Edinburgh and Paris being particularly strong. Andrew Duncan and Alexander Morison (1779-1866) were pioneers inspired by the French example. Morison had a distinguished career in London as well as in Edinburgh and, like Duncan, he lectured on lunacy. His book, *Lectures on the Nature, Causes and Treatment of Insanity*, was first published in 1848 and was widely read in the medical profession.

But it was not until the 1850's-60's that the foundations of modern psychiatry were laid. The Enlightenment of the eighteenth century had tried to penetrate the recesses of the mind by observing conduct and theorising about it. Men like Friedrich Anton Mesmer (1743-1815) were aware of the dark depths of the subconscious. In 1836 the Scottish philosopher Sir William Hamilton wrote that 'Latent agencies — modifications of which we are unconscious, must be admitted as groundwork of the phenomenology of mind.'[27] But the theoretical foundations remained slight and unstable: it was impossible to base an operational therapy on them. There was little that could be done, other than to provide occupations of various kinds — athletics, games, expeditions, magazines, work on the asylum farm or elsewhere. Such activities, by exercising the body and sometimes the mind, were indeed a partial therapy for some, though middle-class patients at the Royals often resisted manual effort as beneath them. There were, too, experiments in shock treatment, as with the revolving of patients in the 'whirling chair'. In the treatment of lunacy in Victorian times there was no 'revolution' in therapy analogous to that in surgery. It may be that mental illness exercised a fascination over philanthropists, drawing them into involvement with it.

Notwithstanding the work of men like Duncan and Morison, most Scottish lunatic asylums remained without any supervising medical authority, although doctors had been appointed to visit regularly. In Glasgow, from 1814 Dr. Robert Cleghorn and Dr. John Balmanno were the visiting physicians, but not until the 1830's did the Royal Lunatic Asylums in Scotland appoint medical superintendents to their staffs.[28] Once these appointments had been made, there were changes in the cure expectation rate, for these men had volunteered to involve themselves in this particular branch of healing and were keen to develop new treatments. The seven Royal Lunatic Asylums, in spirit pre-Victorian foundations, thus became much more effective institutions; their medical superintendents instituted systematic enquiry into the case of each patient as Pinel had done, and attempted to classify the conditions from which each suffered. This of course was difficult, given the then state of theory, but certain hypotheses, as for example heredity, were available.

Perhaps the career of Dr. W. A. F. Browne (1805-1885) is indicative of the type of man who, for professional and humanitarian reasons, was attracted to this work. Dr. Browne had been appointed to the Montrose Asylum in 1834. There he had lectured staff and his managers on the classification and treatment of mental illness. His work was subsequently published.[29] Perhaps it came to the attention of Mrs. Elizabeth Crichton; at all events Mrs. Crichton came to believe that Dr. Browne would make a good medical superintendent for her Crichton Royal. According to a charming story, Mrs. Crichton bowled along to Montrose in her yellow and black carriage and enticed Dr. Browne to Dumfries. He remained medical superintendent at Crichton Royal for twenty years. In 1857, with new government action imminent, he was appointed one of the five new Commissioners in Lunacy.

Apart from the work being done at Dumfries, perhaps that in Edinburgh and Glasgow was of greatest significance. In Edinburgh Dr. David Skae was an able medical superintendent from 1846, working on the problem of classification, and seeking the links between mental disorder and physical disease and malfunction. His efforts, although primitive, did much to encourage essential research into aetiology. Skae was a link with the University, lecturing there to medical students. When Thomas Smith Clouston (1840-1915) succeeded him as medical superintendent in 1873, he too was also appointed as Lecturer in Mental Diseases in Edinburgh University.

5. The public commitment after 1857

The seven Royal Asylums and the Elgin Pauper Lunatic Asylum remained
the main provision for lunatic patients in Scotland, together with some private
accommodation, until 1857. Before that year the Scottish legislation had consisted of three permissive Acts, those of 1815, 1829 and 1841 to 'regulate Madhouses in Scotland'.[30] Between 1847 and 1857 there had been a Board of Supervision which, under the able chairmanship of Sir John McNeill, had repeatedly
pointed out the difficulty under existing conditions of doing anything for
pauper lunatics in Scotland. In 1848 a Bill had been brought forward which
involved the takeover of the Royal Asylums as part of the state provision. The
indignant Directors of the James Murray at Perth petitioned the government
against the Bill, powerfully assisting in its rejection. By the Lunatic Asylums
(Scotland) Act of 1857,[31] based on the English Act of 1853, a General Board of
Commissioners in Lunacy was set up with five Commissioners, and an office
in Edinburgh. It was their responsibility, as civil servants, to 'provide for the
building of district asylums for the reception of pauper lunatics, and to insure
the proper care and treatment of lunatics generally, whether placed in asylums
or left in private houses under the care of relatives or strangers'. A 'district' for
this purpose was a group of parishes controlled by a Poor Law Board; the
finance came from the poor law provisions made in the Act of 1845. The state
was thus moved to set up basic minimal provision for the working-class and
pauper mentally ill.

When the first official count was taken there were 5,748 lunatics visible to
the authorities.

Table 22

Lunatics in Scotland at 1 January 1858

	Male	Female	Total	Private	Pauper	Total
The Royal Asylums	1,226	1,154	2,380	786	1,594	2,380
Private Asylums	330	415	745	219	526	745
Poorhouses	352	487	839	6	833	839
Private Houses	810	974	1,784	—	1,784	1,784
Total	2,718	3,030	5,748	1,011	4,737	5,748

Source: GBCL, 1st AR (Edinburgh 1859), iii.

The five Commissioners had an enormous task; they were faced with a wide
variety of hospitals, poor houses and privately run homes in which lunatic
patients were kept, many of them in deplorable conditions. As all the Royal
Lunatic Asylums had discovered, the law of immediate saturation applied, for
once good facilities became available, lunatic patients appeared to take up and
indeed overcrowd them. In addition, many of the patients, once admitted,
were there for life, as they were either incurable, or not curable by the treatment of the day. The managers of James Murray's at Perth expressed the views

of everyone associated with Lunatic Asylums when they wrote of 'our yearly increasing accumulation of incurables — the class that impedes and clogs all the curative machinery of an hospital . . . the class which is gradually, but inevitably, causing the degeneracy of all our public hospitals for the insane into mere receptacles or retreats for the hopeless'.[32]

In Edinburgh the Royal Asylum at Morningside had been difficult to fund and so wards were built for private patients only. The retention of the pauper lunatics in the Charity Workhouse, part of which bore the title of the 'City Bedlam', had become something of a scandal, and in 1836 the town council negotiated an agreement with the managers of the Asylum. New buildings were to be provided at Morningside, to which pauper lunatics belonging to the city parish, St. Cuthbert's, and Canongate, as well as those of the parishes of North and South Leith and Duddingston would be admitted, the respective parishes paying the necessary fees.

At Crichton Royal the managers were faced with the same problem. Together with the Crichton trustees, they built a twin establishment, the Southern Counties Asylum, on their own grounds at Hillhead, at a cost of some £11,000. When this was opened in 1849 the pauper patients from the Crichton Institution were transferred to it. The original Asylum then accepted only private paying patients.

The Commissioners were not only responsible for the building of new

Table 23

Local Authority Lunatic Asylums in Scotland in 1899

1863	Argyll and Bute District Lunatic Asylum, Lochgilphead
1869	Ayr District Asylum, Ayr
1864	Banff District Asylum, Ladysbridge and Woodpark
1832	Elgin District Asylum, Elgin
1866	Fife and Kinross District Asylum, Cupar
1896	Gartloch Asylum and Hospital for the Insane, Gartloch, Glasgow
1875	Glasgow District Aslyum, Woodilee, Lenzie, Glasgow
1881	Glasgow Kirklands Asylum
1895	Govan District Asylum, Hawkhead, Paisley
1873	Govan Parochial Asylum, Merryflats, Govan
1879	Greenock Parochial Asylum, Smithston
1866	Haddington District Asylum
1864	Inverness District Asylum
1895	Lanark District Asylum, Hartwood, Shotts
1874	Midlothian and Peebles District Asylum, Roslin Castle
1851	Paisley Parish Council Poorhouse (1849) and Asylum
1876	Paisley Burgh Parochial Asylum, Riccartsbar, Paisley
1864	Perth District Asylum, Murthly
1872	Roxburgh, Berwick and Selkirk District Asylum, Melrose
1869	Stirling District Asylum, Larbert
1853	Baldovan Asylum for Imbecile Children near Dundee
1862	Larbert, Stirlingshire, Scottish National Institution for the Education of Imbecile Children

Source: Burdett, H. C., *Hospitals and Charities 1899* (London 1899), 591-593.

asylums; they also had to inspect existing places of deposit, including the surviving lunatic wings of the poor houses. They set about their task of inspection
to ensure that abuses were eliminated as timing and resources permitted, and
under their influence general conditions slowly improved. Local authority
lunatic asylums were built all over Scotland. This new provision gradually
took care of the large category of pauper lunatics who had earlier threatened
to swamp the Royal Lunatic Asylums. Over half a century from the 1860's,
some nineteen new District or Parochial Asylums were built (see Table 23).

6. The supremacy of the Royals

Just as the Royal Infirmaries were to remain the core and centre of medical
provision in Scotland, so too the Royal Lunatic Asylums dominated in their
sphere. Once unembarrassed of the pauper poor, they had scope for thought
and research on mental states. The Royals never lost their leadership, and,
indeed, over the years increased it. Thus, though philanthropic initiative in
terms of founding ended with the Crichton Royal in 1839, initiative in the
development sense never flagged. Each Royal evolved its own tradition. Each
still has its early nineteenth-century central buildings, standing monuments to
philanthropic concern for this most challenging form of sickness. Such
buildings also in their architectural idiom reflect the outlook of their creators
as it related to public service. Their medical superintendents were as gods in
their little universes, very well provided for by their philanthropist-managers,
who understood the need to attract good men. The Commissioners in Lunacy
in Scotland were largely chosen from among the superintendents. Indeed
something of a career structure came into being.

The District, or Pauper Asylums, on the other hand could be little more
than places of human deposit. Overwhelmed by the numbers they were
obliged to take in, and lacking the *cachet* of the Royals, they were depressing
places. The surviving lunatic wards of the poor houses were even worse.
Statistics of cure are notoriously a matter of interpretation but, for what they
are worth, the Royal Lunatic Asylums claimed in 1891 to cure 46% of their
patients every year; the district parochial asylums claimed a recovery rate of
42%, while the surviving lunatic wards of the poor houses reckoned on only a
4% rate.[33]

NOTES

1. By the Act of 1743, lunatics might be 'safely locked up and put in chains'.
2. It is now widely accepted that the King suffered from Porphyria, a hereditary deficiency
   disease. See McAlpine, I. and Hunter, R., *George III and the Mad Business* (London 1969).
3. Quoted in Jones, K., *Lunacy, Law and Conscience* (London 1955), 42, from Jesse, *Memoirs of
   Life . . . George III*, Vol. III, 257.
4. Jones, K., 1955, 42.
5. Duncan, A., 1792.

6. Battie, 1758, 4.

7. Howard, 1789, 140.

8. The Retreat was intended to be 'a refuge, a quiet haven', Hack Tuke, D., *Early History of the Retreat, York* (London 1892), 20.

9. Cormack, 1966, 271.

10. Poole, 1841, 2.

11. Cormack, 1966, 272.

12. Susan Carnegie of Pittarrow and Charlton, Montrose was a daughter of David Scott, a Treasurer of the Bank of Scotland. She had been born over the bank in Edinburgh.

13. The first Unitarian Group to assemble in Scotland was that in Montrose in 1792 at the instigation of William Christie, merchant there. The Christies of Ormiston and Luncarty, of Aberdeenshire descent, were Quakers. It would be tempting to believe that these connections first involved Provost Christie with Susan Carnegie in humanitarian work. See Marwick, W. H., 'Studies in Scottish Quakerism', *Records of Scottish Church History Society*, Vol. XIII (1959), 92. Also Burnet, G. B., *The Rise, Progress and decline of the Quaker movement in Scotland*, Glasgow Ph.D., 1937.

14. Cormack, 1966, 275.

15. See Bentham, J., *Management of the Poor* (Dublin 1796), *Panopticon or the Inspection House* (London 1791), and Stark, W., *Remarks on Public Hospitals for the cure of Mental Derangement* (Edinburgh 1807).

16. Macgill, 1810, 3.

17. Chambers, 1927.

18. Anon., *James Murray's Royal Asylum for Lunatics* (Perth 1828), 16.

19. *RCLAS* Appendix (Edinburgh 1857), 94.

20. James Crichton (1765-1823), a medical graduate of the University of Edinburgh, had served in India and the Far East. He returned home in 1810 with a substantial fortune. He married Elizabeth Grierson in 1813.

21. James Crichton's Trust Sederunt Book (May 8, 1823-September 16, 1839), 88 (at Crichton Royal Hospital, Dumfries).

22. *Ibid.* (October 31, 1829), 112.

23. *RCUS* (London 1831), 85-89.

24. James Crichton's Trust Sederunt Book (October 31, 1833), 143.

25. Crichton Royal Institution Minutes, 26 November 1840, 2.

26. Cormack, 1966, 289.

27. See McAlpine, I. and Hunter, R., 1962.

28. Henderson, D. K., 1964, chapters V and VIII.

29. Browne, W. A. F., 1837.

30. In 1815 (55 George III cap. 69), 1829 (9 George IV cap. 34), and 1841 (4 and 5 Victoria cap. 60).

31. An Act for the regulation of the Care and Treatment of Lunatics, and for the Provision, Maintenance and Regulation of Lunatic Asylums in Scotland, 20 and 21 Victoria, cap. 71, 1857.

32. *James Murray's Royal Asylum for Lunatics*, 36th AR (Perth 1863), 8.

33. Burdett, 1891.

10

The Specialist Hospitals

1. Philanthropists at the core and the periphery of health

THE philanthropists did not confine their efforts to the provision of resources and management for the Royal Infirmaries and the Royal Asylums. Strong though they were at the heart of the medical system, their role was no less important at what might be called the periphery, namely the supply of specialist hospitals. These were much smaller institutions, often indeed minute. They both challenged and augmented the Infirmaries. This meant that some philanthropists concerned with the hospitals were centralists, and others were decentralists. This implied profound involvement in the politics of medicine. The Royal Asylums, too, were a core element, with respect to mental health. The peripheral aspect in their case lay in the public provision of District or Parochial Asylums.

2. The use of specialisms

The rapid multiplication of specialist hospitals in Victorian Scotland had to await improved nursing services after the 1880's, for no special treatment could be competently undertaken earlier. Benevolent individuals and groups responded warmly, joining with specialist doctors in organising new small hospitals. Both parties could claim both practical and altruistic motivation. Ambitious doctors were eager to develop treatment in their own specialism, for 'specialism was a form of self-advertisement';[1] after say 1860 'specialists' were in the market for patients willing to pay for their services. Specialist hospitals, being much later foundations than the Infirmaries, did not rely so heavily on the subscriber's note of recommendation. They were much more likely to have schemes for fee-paying patients. Fees of 7/6d. or 10/- a week were paid by residents, so that subscriptions and donations covered only about half or even a quarter of the cost of running the hospital. Specialism, by concentrating on one part of the body, implied better treatment than that available in the general hospitals. Once accepted by the profession, a specialist hospital could also attract medical students to work with the senior medical staff. The fees of such trainees were a useful source of income when divided between hospital and consultant.

Table 24

Specialist Hospitals in Edinburgh in 1899

Hospitals for Women	Hospital for Children	Eye and Ear Hospital	Consumption and Cancer Hospital	Dental Hospitals
1793 *Edinburgh Royal Maternity and Simpson Memorial Pavilion* 34 beds 338 in patients 622 out patients A midwifery training school is attached. 53 nurses (who pay for their own board) and over 250 students admitted for training in 1897. 1878 *Edinburgh Hospital and Dispensary for Women and Children* 6 Grove Street, Fountainbridge 5 beds 4 usually occupied 35 in patients 121 out patients 71 casualties Admission: provident members 5/- a week others 10/-. Medical Officer: Sophia Jex-Blake. Resident: Mary McDougall.	1859 *Royal Edinburgh Hospital for Sick Children,* Sciennes Road 120 beds 1,243 in patients 5,134 out patients 6 sisters, 4 nurses 24 probationers (probationers trained: 3 year course: certificate given).	1834 *Edinburgh Eye, Ear and Throat Infirmary,* 6 Cambridge Street, Lothian Road 6 beds 54 in patients 1,968 out patients Nursing staff, Matron: Miss Ramsay. Admission free or according to means.	1894 *Victoria Hospital for Consumption and Diseases of the Chest,* Craigleith. Out patients—26 Lauriston Place 15 beds 15 average occupied 91 in patients 732 out patients	1860 *Edinburgh Dental Dispensary* leading to 1880 *Edinburgh Dental Hospital,* 30 Chambers Street

Sources: Various, including annual reports, Burdett, H. C., *Hospitals and Charities* (London 1899).

Table 25

Specialist Hospitals in Glasgow in 1899

Hospitals for Women	*Hospitals for Children*	*Eye and Ear Hospitals*	*Cancer Hospitals*	*Dental Hospital*
1792 *University Lying-in Hospital* in College Open, High Street incorporated into *Western Infirmary* after 1874	1883 *Royal Hospital for Sick Children,* 45 Scott Street, Garnethill	1824 *Glasgow Eye Infirmary* 104 beds 73 occupied 1,420 in patients 20,340 out patients Matron, 7 nurses and 1 probationer. In patients admitted by subscriber's line, out patients free.	1886 *Glasgow Cancer and Skin Institution,* 409 St. Vincent Street 6 beds 230 in patients 1,128 out patients Paying patients at £2 to 5 guineas a week.	*Glasgow Dental Hospital* 6,577 patients (no further details)
1805 *Lock Hospital* 81 beds Admission free	1888 Dispensary, 11 West Graham Street 77 beds 67 occupied 768 in patients 6,402 out patients 715 home patients 4 sisters, 10 nurses, 5 probationers Admission by subscriber's line. Dispensary free.	1868 *Glasgow Ophthalmic Institution,* 126 West Regent Street since 1896 Ophthalmic Department of Glasgow Royal Infirmary 30 beds 692 in patients 3,350 out patients Admission by recommendation. Lectures and Clinical Instruction for medical students given.	*Glasgow Cancer Hospital* (Free), 132 Hill Street, Garnethill. Dispensary 22 West Graham Street. 42 beds 73 in patients 45 home patients 1 sister, 4 nurses, 2 probationers who are trained; certificate given.	
1834 *Glasgow Lying-in Hospital* after 1874 called *Glasgow Maternity Hospital* 34 beds 482 in patients 2,138 out patients 5 nurses, 16 probationers Admission free				
1877 *Glasgow Hospital for Diseases peculiar to Women,* 29 Elmbank Crescent 9 beds 320 patients Admission free by subscribers' recommendation; also some paying patients				

Table 25 (continued)

Hospitals for Women	Hospitals for Children	Eye and Ear Hospitals	Cancer Hospitals	Dental Hospital
1886 *Glasgow Samaritan Hospital for Women and Agnes Barr Dispensary*, Victoria Road (rebuilt 1895-6) 30 beds 271 in patients 755 out patients Admission by recommendation 8 nurses		1880 *Glasgow Ear Hospital* 12 beds 69 in patients 1,369 out patients Admission by subscriber's line. Out patients free.		

Sources: Various, including annual reports.

Table 26

Specialist Hospitals in Aberdeen, Dundee and Greenock in 1899

Place	Date of founding	Name	Beds	Patients	Other information
Aberdeen	1835	Ophthalmic Institution	8	75 in 3,127 out	Free admission
	1877	Royal Aberdeen Hospital for Sick Children, Castle Terrace	85 81 occupied	678 in 988 out	Probationers trained, diphtheria and typhoid admitted
Bridge of Weir (part of Quarrier's provision)	1896	Consumption Hospital for Scotland	26	31	Admission free
Dundee	1896	Private Hospital for Women	11		Hospital staffed entirely by women
Greenock	1880	Eye Infirmary	20	183 in 2,905 out	

Sources: Various, including annual reports.

The specialist hospital usually depended upon the initiative of one or two men. If the doctor who wanted to practise and to teach others to practise his speciality was sufficiently keen and affluent, he could establish a hospital, perhaps in his own home, completely under his own control, and at his own expense. If, however, he could gain the support of wealthy friends, he could encourage them to launch an appeal and set up a hospital, philanthropically financed. In either event it would be modest, perhaps in a former house, with as few as four beds. It may have been that some specialist hospitals were founded by doctors who did not rate highly their chances of breaking into the exclusive cadre of general hospital consultants.

Before 1850 specialist hospitals existed for women in childbirth or for those suffering from venereal disease, as well as from illnesses or defects of the eyes, ears and throat. After 1850 the number of special hospitals greatly increased, providing care for children, and later for cancer and for tuberculosis patients.

The Royal Infirmaries in Edinburgh, Glasgow, Aberdeen and Dundee, proud and powerful in their role as sole providers of philanthropic medical care, resisted proposals for specialist hospitals. For although they themselves 'refused to make adequate provision for special cases',[2] they were jealous of threats to their reputations and their subscriptions, donations and legacies. But their case, as caring for the working population, was vulnerable. They frequently refused entry to difficult classes of patients; from time to time they rejected cases of venereal disease, women in labour, and children. Venereal patients were mostly women of a very low class who were refused admission on moral grounds. Women in labour were a risky category to take in, for they were prone to puerperal fever and often died under care, raising the hospitals' mortality statistics in an invidious way. Children were liable to catch any infection going, as well as being troublesome patients. Not surprisingly, the Royal Infirmaries were charged from time to time with a selectivity which derived from their own interests and biases.

A general view of the provision of specialist hospitals in Scotland is given in Tables 24, 25 and 26.

3. **Maternity hospitals**

The first specialist hospitals in Scotland were for maternity cases. As early as the 1790's, lying-in hospitals were established both in Edinburgh and Glasgow where a small number of working-class women were delivered of their babies.[3] These two hospitals were the creations of male doctors anxious to usurp the position of female midwives and ensure that maternity and obstetrics should be the subject of special study and care. They were attempting to establish midwifery as a proper subject for academic study. They held university appointments but were obliged to launch their ventures on their own initiative. The impulse had to come from such professional men, for working-class mothers, often unmarried, were not a popular object of philanthropy. But by the 1830's the atmosphere was changing. A second 'Public' lying-in hospital for Glasgow was begun in 1834: as the result of philanthropic action. In other Scottish cities such initiatives were long delayed: Aberdeen got its Maternity Hospital in 1896 and Dundee in 1899. Both had strong philanthropic backing.

When Dr. Young was appointed Professor of Midwifery in Edinburgh in 1756, 'A ward in the attic storey of the Royal Infirmary, by the permission of the managers but at Dr. Young's expense, was fitted up for four lying-in women, or as many as Dr. Young could accommodate, each exceeding the number four paying 6d. a day to the house.' Only thus could Dr. Young provide himself with patients on whom he and his students could practise. He also gave notice that women could be delivered in their own homes 'free of expense'. Dr. Young was probably the first in Scotland to lecture in midwifery to university medical students. Previously, some teaching had been done in Edinburgh by Joseph Gibson and Robert Smith, who were employed to instruct female midwives, but there had been no lectures for intending doctors. The activities of the professor of midwifery, and his assumption of the practice of lecturing to male medical students, was eventually to eliminate the female midwives from any but a subsidiary role.

Dr. Alexander Hamilton succeeded Dr. Young in the chair of midwifery. He longed for a hospital of his own and published proposals for one. It was his son and successor, James Hamilton, who finally brought the project to fruition when, in 1793, the Edinburgh General Lying-in Hospital was founded. It was established at Park House in Park Place and remained there for fifty years. In 1843 the property had to be sold by Dr. Hamilton's trustees and the Hospital entered a difficult period.[4] It was not until May 1879 that the new purpose-built hospital was opened, bearing the name of the Royal Maternity and Simpson Memorial Hospital. In the later years of Victoria's reign the hospital was delivering about 265 mothers a year as internal patients, and about 600 mothers a year in their own homes.

The Glasgow (University) Lying-in Hospital was established about 1792 by Dr. James Towers. He solicited the patronage of the Principal and Professors of Glasgow College, asking to be allowed to lecture on midwifery. The Senatus agreed. In 1792 Towers reminded the Senatus that he had incurred expense 'for a Lying-in Ward which he had opened and maintained for the more effective instruction of students.' In response to this strong hint, the University granted him £25 a year towards his expenses. Towers must therefore be credited with the foundation of the Glasgow (University) Lying-in Hospital. It continued to exist, probably without interruption, from the early 1790's until amalgamated with the Western Infirmary in August 1878.

James Towers remained Waltonian Medical Lecturer in Midwifery until 1815, when he was appointed to the newly founded Regius Chair of Midwifery. He was succeeded in 1820 by his son, John, who held the chair until his death in 1834. Relations between the University and the Regius professors were strained, as the University resented the government's action in foisting on it the Regius Chairs. The financial support which the University had given to the Waltonian Medical Lecturer for 'the Lying-in Ward' was withdrawn when the Waltonian Lecturer became the Regius Professor. John Towers claimed in 1827 that he had 100 students in training and that to enable them to gain enough experience of patients in labour he had to continue to organise and take responsibility, financial and administrative, for the Lying-in Hospital.[5] Towers handled about 60 patients each year. The willingness of the Magistrates and the Trades House to support his efforts suggests that they regarded the Hospital as a welcome facility in the town.

Lying-in hospitals were not a popular charity. Difficulties arose regarding the marital status of the patients. Only 'indigent married women' were to be accepted, but unmarried women *in extremis* could not be turned away. Indeed the only women who would enter such hospitals were those who had nowhere else to go. Subscribers full of moral righteousness refused to contribute if they discovered that unmarried women were being admitted.

There was a further difficulty. The attendance of women in child-bed continued to be the preserve of female midwives, for as was said in 1827, 'Midwifery was an act foreign to the habits of a gentleman of enlarged academic education.'[6] But the teaching of midwifery in the universities and the founding of lying-in hospitals meant that the midwife function gradually passed from women to the male doctors, for the old untrained service in the home was more and more challenged by the doctors and their facilities.

But because of the danger of infection, it was considered foolhardy by many to bring women into infirmaries or lying-in hospitals: 'It was continuously observed that puerperal women in Lying-in Hospitals were highly susceptible to the poison of contagious fevers and sensitive to those conditions on which pyeremia and erysipelas depend.'[7] Thus many believed (as did Florence Nightingale) that there should be no hospitals at all for women in childbirth. Doctors who wished to work with such women would not accept this. The controversy over bringing mothers into a maternity hospital for their confinement continued over many years, for puerperal fever continued to take its toll, and many persisted in their belief that mothers and babies were safer at home. The maternity hospital was vigorously defended by James Matthews Duncan, an Edinburgh obstetrician of some renown. In his book, *Mortality of Childbed* (1870), he criticised the statistics of those charitable societies in England which claimed to deliver mothers in their own homes with very little loss of life. He pointed out that infection in the home was no less common than in hospital.

That the Edinburgh Royal Maternity Hospital became a prestigious institution was primarily owing to the efforts of its distinguished medical staff. Sir James Y. Simpson added new lustre to its reputation. Yet as late as 1879 it was difficult to raise philanthropic funds for its support.

In Glasgow, after Towers' death his semi-private venture was taken over by the University, remaining under the medical management of the Regius Professor of Midwifery.[8] Indeed matters probably continued very much as in Towers' day until 1870 when — the College having by then removed to Gilmorehill — the University Lying-in Hospital was left homeless. Following protracted negotiations, the proposal to join forces with the Glasgow Lying-in Hospital was abandoned and attempts were made to link the Glasgow University Lying-in Hospital with the new Western Infirmary. These were successful and the assets were handed over to the Western which incorporated all that remained of the University's Lying-in Hospital.[9]

But Towers' death in 1834 had had a further consequence. A public meeting was held in the Town Hall, Glasgow to found a Public Lying-in Hospital, 'for affording the necessary accommodation and assistance to indigent married females under circumstances which are at all times attended with suffering and frequently with danger and where the want of such accommodation and assistance has often proved fatal to the mother, to her offspring or to both'.[10] In less than a year the hospital opened in 'the second flat and garrets' of the Old Grammar School. But finance continued to be difficult. Some nine years later a move was made to even cheaper premises in St. Andrew's Square. The hospital authorities were forced to adopt 'the most rigid economy — an economy bordering on the penurious, and which the Directors feel satisfied the charitable would desire to see abated'. Morale was low, as a rival hospital was planned (November 1843), although nothing came of it. By the 1850's there were signs of greater financial stability, perhaps because Victorian prosperity was making benefactors more generous. In any event the Glasgow Lying-in Hospital adapted[11] a more impressive building on the corner of North Portland Street and Rottenrow (January 1860); there the Directors congratulated themselves on 'having reared a hospital quite adequate to the requirements of the city'. However, within a few years the building proved unsatisfactory and eventually, in January 1881, a completely new one was opened on the site of the old. Its style was (and is) early English Domestic Gothic, no doubt very grand in its time, but inconvenient and difficult to adapt to twentieth-century demands.

Until later in the century the Lying-in Hospital was troubled with epidemic disease; wards were constantly being closed for cleansing. But medical skill was becoming greater and the Hospital was increasingly used by general practitioners. Also, the social tone was raised: Dr. Jardine commented, 'The vast majority of patients sent in by practitioners are married.' But they were 'all very difficult cases and some of them hopeless'.[12]

The existence of two lying-in hospitals in Glasgow between 1834 and 1878 is not perhaps so surprising, for the University Lying-in Hospital was the personal sphere of the University's Professor of Midwifery and was run primarily for teaching purposes. Perhaps uniquely, Glasgow University Lying-in Hospital planned to train midwives as well as medical students.

The women who were received into lying-in hospitals were those in most urgent need. Many patients were brought to such hospitals by the police and others in authority who were anxious to see them housed before the onset of labour. Until at least 1870, and probably much later, women who had safe and secure homes (however lowly) preferred to have their babies at home. The women who occupied the beds of the lying-in hospitals in Scotland continued to be those to whom choice was denied.

In Aberdeen from 1781 to 1834 the Royal Infirmary attached a midwife to each of the city's districts. Thereafter the managers of the Infirmary, because of the state of its funds, stopped their allowances to midwives. Maternity cases might then apply directly to the Infirmary, but few did so.[13]

Dundee may perhaps serve as an example of late nineteenth-century developments outside Edinburgh and Glasgow. There were no separate facilities for maternity patients there until 1899, when the Forfar Medical Association collected £10,000 for the purpose. It was intended that the hospital should be under the aegis of the Dundee Royal Infirmary. But J. K. Caird, a prominent businessman in the city, 'generously offered to erect Wards and a Maternity Nurses Home'.[14] The result was an independent entity. One of its features was the teaching school for nurses and students. It has been very successful, partly because of the large numbers of patients who applied both to the Hospital and the outdoor department.

By the end of Victoria's reign, then, the Scottish cities had a basic maternity service. It was still tiny in relation to need, but it provided scope for the study of maternity cases, together with the principal means of training for their care.

4. Hospitals for and by women

The later nineteenth century saw a number of new initiatives in medicine as related to women. As surgeons became more skilled, with the spread of anti-septic and aseptic surgery, the care of women could improve. Hospitals specialising in female disorders were opened; they played an important part in improving the health care of working women. Secondly, the new breed of women doctors were seeking to penetrate a male profession. They opened hospitals run by women for women.

The Glasgow Samaritan Hospital for Women[15] was started at a meeting held on 4 January 1886, 'in the first humble premises of the Institution in South Cumberland Street'. There the Hospital remained under the medical care of Dr. Stuart Nairne for its first four years. The premises, on the first floor over some shops, were obviously inadequate. A subscription was opened, and a short lease of Kingston House, Tradeston, was obtained; it was converted 'into a good temporary hospital with Wards for ten in-patients, a Dispensary for out-patients, Operating Theatre, Boardroom and waiting rooms'.[16] New premises were available off Victoria Road in 1896, and the Dispensary was re-sited (1892-98) in a house in Paterson Street, Tradeston, thanks to the generosity of Miss Agnes Barr of Carphin.

With the new building, 1600 patients a year were being treated at a total cost of £2,400 a year. The Hospital had been fortunate in attracting a great deal of influential support, notably from a very strong Ladies' Auxiliary Association, formed in 1887. In 1890 these ladies, led by Lady Stirling Maxwell, organised the first of the great bazaars. As a result of their efforts (and £2,000 from the Bellahouston Trustees) the new building opened free of debt. Two women Directors of the Board were elected annually from 1900.

The Glasgow Hospital for Women (1877) was first established in Elmbank Crescent, but on 10 March 1921 it moved to Burnbank Terrace (off Great Western Road). About one third of the Directors of this Hospital were (in the 1920's) women.[17]

Once women had qualified as doctors, it was not always easy for them to get jobs. They tended to be forced into the least desirable posts among the poorest patients. Specialist appointments were especially difficult to come by, and so it was not unreasonable that they should attempt to circumvent their difficulties by founding hospitals of their own. Small hospitals for women and children were established in both Edinburgh and Glasgow, where by the end of the century there was a steady stream of young women qualified as doctors and apparently a steady supply of women patients preferring their services.

The Edinburgh Hospital for Women and Children was founded by Sophia Jex-Blake, M.D. (1840-1912) in 1878 at 6 Grove Street, Fountainbridge. This was not primarily a maternity hospital. It remained very small, with five beds and an annual budget of £241. About 1883 Dr. Jex-Blake removed her hospital to Bruntsfield Lodge, where in a 'roomy rambling old house'[18] the hospital has remained and flourished. Although Dr. Jex-Blake retired in 1899, her work carried on. In Glasgow the Women's Private Hospital was opened at West Cumberland Street in April 1903, with eight beds, one of its features being the 'modified fee' paid by patients, covering roughly half the cost. It was controlled by a committee of ladies.

The Private Hospital for Women in Dundee was opened in 1896 in a private house, with accommodation for eleven beds. The patients were women who could not afford the fees of the private nursing home, but who were able to pay part of the cost, the rest being met by subscriptions. It too was staffed entirely by women.[19]

Hospitals for women patients run by women doctors have always remained a rather special case. Their establishment reflected the fear of male prejudice and exclusiveness, and not without justification.

5. Children's hospitals

Of all the specialist hospitals founded in Scotland during Victoria's reign, none were more controversial that those for children. It was widely believed that young children should not be separated from their mothers. As Dr.

Henderson of Aberdeen explained in 1822: 'Infant children cannot be properly cared for in an infirmary, and they require the tenderest care and attention of a mother.'[20] Children were vulnerable to many infections and could easily succumb to cross-contagion. For these reasons initiatives taken elsewhere were not pursued in Scotland. L'Hôpital des Enfants Malades opened in Paris in 1802, and subsequently similar institutions were opened in other European capitals including Berlin, Vienna and St. Petersburg; London did not follow until February 1852. In Scotland the first children's hospital came in 1860 and the second in 1877. Perhaps above all others the children's hospital depended on the growth of the nursing profession. Paediatrics as a specialism could go forward only if skilled nursing staff were available to reinforce medical treatment. But once the initial prejudice against such hospitals was overcome, subscriptions did come in freely. Children were a popular charity, so that children's hospitals could attract substantial endowments and legacies.

The Edinburgh Hospital for Sick Children[21] opened in 1860 in Lauriston Lane. From about 1840 Dr. William Campbell (Lecturer in Midwifery at the Argyle Square School of Medicine) had lectured in Edinburgh on the diseases of children.[22] Later Dr. Charles Wilson (1804-1884) wrote persuasively in the *Edinburgh Medical Journal* (May 1856 and March 1858) on the 'expediency of founding a hospital for the diseases of children in Edinburgh'. His writing subsequently reached a wider non-medical audience when it was published in pamphlet form. Dr. Wilson stressed the wide difference in mortality rates between 'ill-fed and ill-clad mites' and wealthier children. Wilson's pamphlet concluded, 'The establishment of a better system of investigation and instruction for the diseases of children is now a matter in which, in this country, we must either aspire to lead, or be constrained to follow.'[23] There followed in March 1859 a correspondence in the *Scotsman*, Dr. Wilson again pressing persistently. A meeting was called for 5 May 1859. During the preliminary stages the managers of the Edinburgh Royal Infirmary, always uneasy at the thought of any category of patients (and the philanthropic money subscribed for them) going elsewhere, argued that they could easily set aside an agreed and sufficient number of beds for children if the necessary funds were provided. But this was not what the organisers of the proposed Children's Hospital wanted. The Infirmary's offer was declined and an influential body of Directors were elected and funds raised. In due course small premises were leased in 7 Lauriston Lane where the Hospital opened on 15 February 1860, with twenty-four beds crowded in. 154 patients were admitted during the first year and 985 out-patients were seen at the Dispensary.

The objects of the Children's Hospital were:

1. To provide for the reception, maintenance and medical treatment of the children of the poor during sickness, and to furnish with advice and medicine those who cannot be admitted into the hospital;
2. To promote the advancement of medical science with reference to the diseases of childhood, and especially to provide for the more efficient instruction of students in this department of knowledge;

> 3.   To diffuse among all classes of the community, and chiefly among the poor, a better
>   acquaintance with the management of infants and children during health or sickness, and
>   to assist in the education and training of women in the special duties of children's
>   nurses.[24]

By 1861 the Directors felt sufficiently confident to buy Meadowside House, at the foot of Lauriston Lane. The price was £2,150, of which £1,300 was raised in December 1861 at a bazaar in the Music Hall. The enlarged premises were opened there on 18 May 1863, with beds for 40 patients and a separate fever ward. Here 323 in-patients and 4,075 out-patients were treated in the first year. In 1889 a new surgical department was added, enabling 610 child in-patients (in the surgical and medical wards) and 7,038 out-patients to be treated.

Notwithstanding this expansion, the Hospital had a bad record of fever. A nurse died of typhoid in 1890; patients and staff were moved temporarily to Plewlands, Morningside, and Meadowside House was pulled down. The managers of the Children's Hospital had intended to rebuild on the site, but the Royal Infirmary required the ground. After further negotiations the Children's Hospital was rebuilt in Sciennes Road at Rillbank Terrace (formerly on the site of the Trades Maiden Hospital). The new Hospital, designed by Mr G. Washington Browne, was of course purpose-built; it had 120 beds. The building was beautifully placed, facing south and close to the Meadows. It was in an E shape, the Administrative offices 'being in the centre and the wards in the two arms, cut off from the centre by cross-ventilated corridors'.

The out-patients department was transferred from Lauriston Lane to the new building on 8 December 1903. Here the small patients and their mothers or grandmothers waited in the large central hall. Most patients arrived in their mother's arms, both enveloped in traditional large black knitted shawls. Small babies undressed by nurses invariably wore the 'broad heavy, navy serge binder' which, as everyone knew, was supposed to give 'strength to the spine'.

The old ideas about treating children as small adults died hard. Dr. John Thomson (1856-1926),[25] an Edinburgh physician, after spending some time on the Continent and in London, returned to Edinburgh with the express intention of dealing only with the diseases of children. In 1898 he published *The Clinical Study and Treatment of Sick Children* and in 1900 was appointed Physician to the hospital.

The Royal Aberdeen Hospital for Sick Children was opened in 1877 in a house on the Castlehill. It was extended in 1885, 'ample funds always being forthcoming from charitable sources'. Later, cottage homes were provided and a nurses' home was built in 1898. The hospital has had a distinguished record of service.

In Glasgow, although it was a controversial matter, there were many eager to establish a Sick Children's Hospital.[26] The managers of the Royal Infirmary were hostile to the proposal, and claimed in 1857 to have instituted a vaccination department where in three years nearly 3,000 children had been vaccinated. The managers also denied that they refused child patients; they claimed that of the 170 accepted in the previous year, 'only about 6% died'. The Infirmary managers did not recognise the need for a children's hospital and disliked the suggestion that they neglected children as a class of patient. At no time did they appear to recognise the view that children constituted a special category and should not be admitted to the general hospital, to sights and sounds from which they should be protected.

An appeal was launched in January 1861 at the behest of 'the most eminent men in the city', and by 1865 over £2,000 had been subscribed. Nevertheless, long delays and difficulties occurred; not until 8 January 1883 did the Glasgow Sick Children's Hospital open in Scott Street, Garnethill. It became 'Royal' in 1889. The Duchess of Montrose and Lady Campbell of Blythswood 'and many other ladies of rank and influence' organised a 'Fancy Fayre' at the end of November 1884; it was so successful that on 1 October 1888 the Duke of Montrose opened the Children's Hospital Dispensary at 11 West Graham Street, completely free of debt.[27]

The skill of those who made appeals on behalf of children was considerable. One approach was through the susceptibilities of middle-class children and their parents, thus:

The Little Brick Builders[28]
By Robert Bird.

But, there are ither bairns as sweet,
Wha scarce can lift their little feet;
In hopeless plight, they sit and greet
   And cry in vain,
For some cool hand to cool their heat,
   And soothe their pain.

My bonny rosebud! are ye willing,
A modest bairnie's part fulfilling—
To beg for love? your wee heart thrilling,
   To help the sick—
Well pleased that ilka guid white shilling,
   Should build a brick!

Published in *The Glasgow News* in 1907.

Children's hospitals were of great importance for accident cases, since burns and scalds were common. There were also numbers of children with bone damage needing long-term medical treatment. The children admitted were poor, and suffered from a variety of serious ailments and also from malnutrition. The reports from both Glasgow and Edinburgh stress, unconsciously perhaps, that the prime function of the children's hospital was to feed up half-starved children. But numerically the provision was tiny.

6. Eye and ear hospitals

The Glasgow Eye Infirmary[29] was established in 1824 on the initiative of William MacKenzie (1791-1868) and George C. Monteath (1788-1828). Mac-

Kenzie was not only an ambitious man but a distinguished ophthalmologist. The early foundation of this hospital may reflect the spread of eye diseases like glaucoma and Egyptian or military ophthalmia after the wars against Napoleon (both in the Peninsular War in Spain and Portugal and in the Middle East). MacKenzie believed that the small but important specialisms were often lost sight of in the large infirmaries.

The Eye Infirmary opened at 19 Inkle Factory Lane, North Albion Street, on 7 June 1824. 209 out-patients were treated in the first six months and some seven operations were performed, but there was no accommodation for resident patients. In March 1835 the hospital removed to 14 College Street. These premises proved to be cramped and unhealthy, and after some worry the Eye Infirmary removed in 1852 to 76 Charlotte Street, formerly David Dale's house, a more satisfactory location on the edge of Glasgow Green. It was dependent in part on its proximity to the University. Students could only attend hospitals near the University, where compulsory classes were held. The removal of the University to Gilmorehill resulted in a serious fall in the number of students attending the Eye Infirmary, and the Managers decided to move westwards also; the site at the corner of Berkeley Street and Claremont Street was chosen. The neo-gothic building was designed by (Sir) John Burnet and occupied in 1874, and like the Glasgow Maternity Hospital, the Eye Infirmary is an example of expansion being hindered by the inflexibility of proud Victorian buildings.

After 1860, treatment in the Eye Infirmary was much improved by the adoption by the eye surgeons of the ophthalmoscope, invented in 1851 in Germany. The new treatments of antiseptic and aseptic surgery greatly stimulated the activities of eye surgeons and many new cases could be treated. The out-patient clinic became very busy, putting pressure on the hospital to provide more beds. Whereas 20 beds had been sufficient in Charlotte Street, with about 11 occupied, in Berkeley Street there were 40 which rapidly increased to 60.

The Eye Infirmary was also involved in treating conditions which had their origin in venereal disease, although there was no special clinic for these until 1920. Philanthropically the Eye Infirmary was warmly regarded by the subscribing public, which may not have realised the connection with venereal disease. It remained a feature of the Glasgow hospital services until its takeover in 1948.

In Edinburgh the Eye Hospital in Cambridge Street was founded in 1834. Cases were also treated at the Royal Infirmary, but it did not have an eye pavilion until 1903, when one was built with the proceeds of a legacy received in 1898. In Aberdeen the Ophthalmic Institution was begun in 1835.

The Glasgow Ophthalmic Institution (1868-1892) was started by and presided over for the whole of its independent life by John Reissburg Wolfe. J. R. Wolfe was one of the most colourful medical specialists to serve in Victorian Scotland. He was born in Breslau but graduated M.D. from the University of Glasgow in 1856. Subsequently he went to Salonika (then still part of the Turkish Empire), which he left after some 2½ years to pursue a career as an ophthalmologist in Paris. He became Senior Surgeon to Garibaldi and also an Inspector of Military Hospitals in the Italian Army. Later he returned to Scotland to a post as Ophthalmic Surgeon and Lecturer in the Royal Infirmary, Aberdeen. About 1868 he moved to Glasgow, and shortly thereafter founded the Ophthalmic Institution. Wolfe was undoubtedly a controversial figure. He was unacceptable to many since his wide experience of eye surgery techniques was continental, and as such they were regarded by Glasgow practitioners as new, untried and dangerous. He was quickly dismissed by some as a fake and charlatan. But he had friends. The only way to make it possible for him to practise was to launch a separate institution, which was done in 1868 when he opened consulting rooms in Bath Street and was appointed Lecturer in Ophthalmic Surgery in Anderson's University. Wolfe received private patients who paid, as well as poor patients who could not. As the result of an appeal at Whitsuntide 1870, a new hospital was opened at 146 West Regent Street and in 1872 the final move was made to 126 West Regent Street.

But Wolfe's detractors were still active. An animated correspondence took place in *The Lancet* following a complaint about him and his advertising. Friends rushed to his defence and eventually the protests died away. When Wolfe himself wrote to *The Lancet*, he explained that his Institution 'is the clinique of the chair of Ophthalmic Medicine and Surgery of Anderson's University. It has beds and nurses, and is conducted in every respect on the same principle as the Parisian Special Hospitals.'[30] Wolfe would seem to have brought to Glasgow 'a modification of the operation for extraction of cataract', together with special skills in healing wounds by skin grafting.[31] He worked away in West Regent Street until 1892, when he succeeded in having the Glasgow Royal Infirmary adopt the Ophthalmic Institution as its Eye Department. Having brought his hospital directly under the care of the Infirmary, he departed at once for Australia, where he became Surgeon-oculist to the then Governor of Victoria, the Marquis of Linlithgow. Returning to Glasgow, he died there in 1904. The Institution which he had founded had 35 beds by 1888, and it has continued to be a viable unit. Wolfe stands as an example of the kind of strong-minded man, who by his own energies and persistence, and supported by philanthropic friends, could operate within the medical politics of his day to bring his own institution into being.

Concern for diseases of the ear arose a good deal later than was the case with the eye; only in the 1870's was serious action taken. The Glasgow Ear Dispensary was founded in 1872, and in 1880 a Hospital followed. Small private dispensaries had operated earlier in the century, and by the time the Hospital opened, treatment for ear troubles was being given both by the Ear and Skin Dispensary in John Street and by the dispensary run by Dr. D. Dewar. The Western Infirmary and the Royal Infirmary opened aural departments in 1877 and 1878 respectively. When Dr. Andrew Buchanan opened the Glasgow Ear Hospital in 1880, he declared it available to 'those of every tongue and clime, of every faith, and to those who have no faith, providing they are suffering from Ear Disease'. Notwithstanding this generous stipulation, patients were admitted in one of two ways, either by medical transference *via* the Dispensary, or by the recommendation by a £1 1s. subscriber. The costs were thus met largely by philanthropic subscriptions.

In the year until 29 February 1887, 846 patients were seen by the Dispensary staff over 4,910 visits; this suggests about six attendances by each patient. During the same year 57 patients were admitted to the Hospital. The medical staff were under the control of the aural surgeon, with two medical men acting as clinical assistants. In addition, two medical students were appointed every six months to perform the duties of clinical clerks. During the winter session of 1877-8, 75 students attended a course at the Hospital and saw something of its work. In 1877 it had an income of £425, of which it spent £343 on running costs. It was originally in Buchanan Street, but in 1885 removed to more commodious premises at 28 Elmbank Crescent.

7. Hospitals for venereal disease

Cases of venereal disease were treated in the Lock[32] Hospitals. They were unattractive to philanthropists, who feared that to cure venereal disease was an encouragement to vice and immorality. The inhibitions that hung over the care of prostitutes and the operation of lying-in hospitals were at their strongest here. Where there were no Lock Hospitals, venereal disease cases were treated in separate wards of the Infirmaries, or in a different building in the Infirmary grounds. Their managers, representing the opinions and prejudices of the community as a whole, blew hot and cold with bewildering rapidity, alternating between acceptance of an unwanted duty and refusal of venereal disease cases. It was in one of the periods of rejection that support for a separate Lock Hospital in Edinburgh arose.

In general, the occupants of the Lock Hospitals were women involved in prostitution. The Glasgow Lock was intended 'for the cure of unfortunate females'.[33] The Lock Hospitals both in Glasgow and Edinburgh never accepted male patients. Men of a better rank of society were treated privately in their own homes. The situation was different in the ports, where sailors were often in urgent need of treatment; male patients were admitted to Greenock Hospital for this purpose.

The Glasgow Lock Hospital was established in 1805[34] and remained in continuous existence in Rottenrow until the second world war. With the advent of penicillin and changing attitudes to venereal disease, it was not re-opened after the war. The purpose-built Hospital had buildings which were 'plain, and so completely enclosed, that the patients can only see into the spacious courtyards'.[35] Although not legally under restraint, the 'fallen women' were kept as if they had been committed to a reformatory. In 1805 the Hospital had 11 beds, but by 1810 these had increased to 20. A new site was acquired in 1846, still in Rottenrow, and the new hospital had seven wards with 45 beds, extensible to 80 beds should they be required.

Until 1855 applicants had to have a subscriber's line before they could be admitted, but thereafter this was not required, anyone applying at the door being freely admitted. In the early 1880's about 330 girls were in residence in the course of each year; 220 of these were reputed to be 'very young girls'. About 28 were in residence at any one time. Although there were a number of subscribers, the Hospital was mostly given over to pauper or police cases; it was regularly supported by annual grants from the City, Barony, and Govan parochial authorities. By 1876 it had 81 permanent beds, which made it the largest specialist hospital in Scotland.[36]

In Edinburgh, Andrew Duncan argued for a separate Lock Hospital in 1825, when he claimed it would 'properly regulated be the best possible preparation for the Magdalene Asylums'.[37] The only provision for venereal cases was in the Royal Infirmary which kept a separate house for them in the grounds. But in 1837 a fever epidemic forced the managers to oust the venereal disease cases and use the space for fever patients. Meanwhile a philanthropic initiative had begun. A Lock Hospital was established in Surgeons' Square in 1835, with the Lord Provost as President of its board of management and Sir George Ballingall as consultant surgeon. The impressive list of subscribers' names quoted in the Edinburgh Almanacs of the day suggests a well-founded institution. But at its busiest it accepted only forty patients a year. The case for it was plainly weakening; it was closed in 1847, after only 12 years, and venereal disease patients reverted to the Royal Infirmary. There they had separate but inferior accommodation. Francis Cadell in 1861 complained that the consequence of merging the Lock Hospital patients with those of the Royal Infirmary was to cause deterioration in the care of venereal patients.[38] There were only 16 beds for them, a provision described by Cadell as 'miserably inadequate'. There remained a strong body of medical opinion which believed that more and better treatment for venereal disease patients would be available if there were a separate institution, but the necessary initiatives were not forthcoming.

Diagnostically it was difficult to recognise and distinguish venereal disease.[39] Syphilis and gonorrhea appeared in many forms, but other diseases produced similar symptoms. The sores and ulcers of venereal diseases were often confused with leprosy; hence the term Lock for this type of hospital. Curiously enough, at Greenock Infirmary, where there was plenty of experience of venereal disease, syphilis and sibbens were listed in separate categories until 1815, after which they were wrongly put into the same category.[40]

The principal early treatment for venereal disease was mercury. A mercurial vapour bath was erected at the Glasgow Lock Hospital in 1854. It is possible that the women in the Lock Hospitals, isolated as they were from society, may have recovered by means of rest and plain feeding as much as by treatment. Students were sometimes allowed to train by attending on venereal disease wards. This again was a controversial matter, some taking strong exception to the idea that young medical students should have contact at all with such women.

8. The dental hospitals

Care of the teeth was a primitive business, at least until the 1880's, even for wealthy people. For the working classes there was virtually no provision — they had to accept decay and toothache as part of life. Dentistry was not a status occupation; it derived from the barbers and surgeons who pulled out teeth; the physicians who dominated the Infirmaries would have nothing to do with it. The dentists had therefore to establish themselves as a profession, working from below in the pyramid of prestige. They did so by eliciting philanthropic support.

The Dentists' Act of 1878 was intended to set standards for the profession. Under its terms the Faculty of Physicians and Surgeons in Glasgow and the Royal College of Surgeons in Edinburgh were empowered 'to institute examinations in dental surgery and grant diplomas to successful candidates'.[41] The first courses in Glasgow for men wishing to prepare for such dental exams were organised by Anderson's College in 1879, but with the amalgamation of Anderson's College with other institutions to form the Glasgow and West of Scotland Technical College in 1886, dental instruction was re-organised.

Two or three devoted dentists provided a new initiative: they raised subscriptions. The Glasgow Dental Hospital and School was opened on 4 May 1885 on a top floor at 56 George Square. It was entirely dependent for finance upon philanthropists. Its services were given free of charge. It was open every evening, Monday to Friday (from 5-7 p.m.) and on Saturday morning. It soon provided a substantial service with, not surprisingly — given working class health — extractions predominating:

Table 27

Patients at Glasgow Dental Hospital, 1886-1888

Date	Patients	Extractions	Fillings	Other preservative operations
1886	6,825	5,309	1,185	208
1887	8,242	6,629	1,522	222
1888	8,267	6,676	1,525	280

Source: Henderson, T. B., *The history of the Glasgow Dental Hospital and School, 1879-1959* (Glasgow 1960), 13.

The teaching programme was extended to allow Glasgow dental students to take any appropriate examination organised in Britain. Although patients were plentiful, subscriptions were always tight.

Reflecting its poverty, the Hospital had an almost itinerant existence; it moved to Chatham Place in 1889, to St. Vincent Place in 1896, to Dalhousie Street in the West End of the city in 1903, and finally to 211 Renfrew Street in 1932. Staffing was provided largely by men giving short-term service in an honorary capacity. A new era began when in 1947 the University of Glasgow accepted the affiliation of the Dental Hospital.

Dentistry for the poor, together with training and experimental services based upon their treatment, were thus the achievement of devoted practitioners of a low-status profession who summoned resources and managerial interest from among the philanthropists.

9. Later specialisms

Two diseases attracted attention late in the nineteenth century, namely tuberculosis and cancer. For neither was there any cure. But both became the subject of care and study. Because of their universality, and the fear they inspired, they could attract philanthropic money.

The tubercle bacillus was isolated in Berlin by Robert Koch in 1882. Robert Philip,[42] an Edinburgh graduate, brought home the knowledge to Scotland and made the treatment of tuberculosis his life's work. In 1887 he opened the Victoria Tuberculosis Dispensary in Edinburgh where he introduced new ideas of a healthy regimen for his patients and important precautions for the members of their families. The Victoria Hospital for Consumption was opened in 1894 at Craigleith House, Edinburgh, with a dispensary for a time at 13 Bank Street. During the 1890's, between 30 and 87 patients were attending its dispensary each afternoon. In addition its medical officer was paying about 140 home visits every month.

The Glasgow Cancer and Skin Institution[43] was begun in 1890; it accepted patients suffering from skin diseases, not necessarily cancerous. Out of it grew the Cancer Hospital, housed from 1890 at 163 Hill Street, Garnethill; in 1896, to gain more space, a move was made to 132/138 Hill Street. There was a new appeal in 1906 and a new hospital, including a research department, was opened in 1912 by Princess Louise as the Royal Cancer Hospital.

In cases of both tuberculosis and cancer the medical specialists were seeking for cures. They therefore wished to have patients in the early stages of the disease. Inevitably there were many. The authorities attempted to keep patients in the terminal stages of either tuberculosis or cancer out of their hospitals.

10. The sources of motivation

The specialist hospitals and their dispensaries (see chapter 11 below) were perhaps unique among the many social provisions made in Victorian Scotland. In all other cases the philanthropists were the originators — in missions, in temperance, in education, in the care of prostitutes, in the establishment of reformatories, industrial brigades and orphanages and in housing, it was they who initiated action. Even with the infirmaries and the lunatic asylums it was they, very largely, who set things going. But with the specialist hospitals it was different. With them it was the various kinds of doctors who were the driving force, men who insisted upon developing their own specialisms. But they could do so effectively only if each could draw upon a sector of the middle classes sympathetic to their aims. This was true over the whole range of specialisms — maternity, women's diseases, care of children, eye and ear treatment, venereal diseases, dentistry, tuberculosis and cancer.

The specialists, with the backing of the philanthropist, could thus promote the advance of medical science by developing defined areas of research for intensive study leading on to new techniques of therapy.

NOTES

1. Abel Smith, B., 1964.
2. Rivington, 1879, 341.
3. London had the British Lying-in Hospital (1748), and the General Lying-in Hospital (1752), and Dublin the Lying-in Hospital (1745).
4. Simpson, A. R., 'Sketch of the history of the Royal Maternity and Simpson Memorial Hospital', *EHR*, Vol. 1 (Edinburgh 1893), 42-47.
5. RCUS, University of Glasgow (London 1837), Professor Towers, 11 October 1827, 200.
6. The President of the Royal College of Physicians in 1827, quoted in Abel Smith, B., *The Hospitals* (London 1964), 22.
7. *Ibid.*, 23.
8. The Lying-in Hospital was accommodated in the College Open, which was part of the University buildings but distinct from the College proper or Close: Mackie, J. D., *The University of Glasgow* (Glasgow 1954) (see map p. 240). It is worth noting that when the organisers of the Public Lying-in Hospital were seeking premises in 1834 they also tried to establish themselves in the College Open (GLH, 22 October 1834, 21).
9. GULH Minute Book 1834-1878 (GUA 191, 79).
10. GLH Minute Book 1834-1856 (GUL.Gen.Ms.76) and *GMJ* July/December 1888, 32.
11. In 1874 the name was changed to Glasgow Maternity Hospital. The King agreed to the addition of 'Royal' to the title in 1914.
12. Jardine, R., 'Statistics of thirty years' work 1869-1898, in the outdoor and indoor departments of the Glasgow Maternity Hospital', *Glasgow Hospital Reports* (Glasgow 1901).
13. Milne, G. P., 'History of Midwifery in Aberdeen', *Medical History*, April 1978, 205-206.
14. BA, *The Dundee Handbook* (Dundee 1912).
15. See Charles Dickens, *All the year round*, 19 November 1859, 'Good Samaritan', for an account of the London Samaritan Free Hospital for Women and Young Children (1847).
16. *Book of the Bazaar*, Royal Samaritan Hospital for Women (Glasgow 1924), 33, GUA.
17. BMA, *The Book of Glasgow* (Glasgow 1922), 119-120.
18. Todd, 1918, 476.
19. BA, *The Dundee Handbook* (Dundee 1912), 51.
20. Henderson, W., 1822, 34.
21. Guthrie, D., 1960.

22. Balfour, G. W., 'How the Royal Hospital for Sick Children was founded', *EHR*, Vol. I (Edinburgh 1893), 35-41.
23. Wilson, Charles, 1859, 14.
24. Carmichael, J., 'The Edinburgh Royal Hospital for Sick Children', *EHR*, Vol. 4 (Edinburgh 1896), 1-10.
25. See Craig, W. S., 1968.
26. See McGeorge, A., 1889, and Robertson, Edna, 1972.
27. The observant can still see the plaque on the building which commemorates this notable Fancy Fayre.
28. Robertson, Edna, 1972, 82-83.
29. Wright Thomson, A. M., 1963.
30. *The Lancet* (24 July 1869), 150.
31. Riddell, 1968, 8.
32. Lock derives from 'Loke', a house for lepers. Medieval authorities were not able to distinguish some ulcerous conditions of venereal disease from leprosy.
33. Cleland, 1816, Vol. I, 100.
34. It was thus the third oldest in the country. The other Lock Hospitals were London (1746), Westmorland (1792), Newcastle (1813), Manchester (1819), Liverpool (1834), Leeds (1842), Edinburgh (between 1835 and 1847), Bristol (1870), and Birmingham (1881).
35. Cleland, 1816, Vol. I, 256.
36. *GMJ*, 1 July 1888, 48.
37. Duncan, A., 1825, 6.
38. Cadell, 1881, 6.
39. Duncan, Andrew, 1772.
40. Ferrier, 1968, 29.
41. Henderson, T. B., 1960, 1.
42. Philip, R. W., 'The Victoria Hospital for Consumption, Edinburgh,' *EHR*, Vol. 3 (Edinburgh 1895), 13-20.
43. BMA, *The Book of Glasgow* (Glasgow 1922), 118-119.

11

The Dispensaries

1. The dispensaries as a 'putting-out' system

THE Infirmaries and the specialist hospitals were costly to set up and run; they were growth points for study and teaching, but their throughput of patients was small. They were also highly expensive per patient, requiring heavy subsidy from the philanthropists. Because of the limitations of philanthropic revenue, the system had to develop a cheaper aspect of itself which was more extensive and less expensive. It did so in the form of the dispensary. Costs were kept down by the fact that the turnover of the dispensaries was high, consisting of working-class people passing through the 'hall', with the use of much free student labour. The cities of Scotland were gradually covered by these medical outposts where working-class people could receive some sort of medical advice, together with fairly simple treatments. These were provided free, except in the case of provident dispensaries. Although this form of the 'putting-out' system was so much cheaper per patient treated, nevertheless it could not have come into being without philanthropic initiative and money. For most of the people of Victorian Scotland the dispensaries were their health service, insofar as they had one. At no time did the Victorian middle classes ever seriously consider following the recommendations of the Rev. James Johnston who in 1871 advocated that 'Each well ordered congregation should have a medical man wholly or partially employed for the benefit of her poorer members.'[1] A list of Scottish dispensaries in 1899 is given in Burdett.

Table 28

Scottish Dispensaries in 1899: a select list

In addition to those listed below, most general hospitals also organised dispensaries, later out-patient departments. Figures are for 1897.

Name	Date of Founding	Entry	No. of Patients	Other Information	Income £	Expenditure £
Aberdeen Vaccine and Lying-in	1823	Free	10,139	2,250 attended in own homes	1,377	
Banff Dispensary	1842	Free	723		61	61
Dumbarton Eye			908		193	194
Dundee Eye	1836	Free	3,312			

Table 28 (continued)

Name	Date of Founding	Entry	No. of Patients	Other Information	Income £	Expenditure £
Edinburgh						
Skin Diseases	1890	Free	580		142	72
Hospital and Dispensary Women and Children	1878	Paying	121 cas. 71	Founded by Dr. Sophia Jex-Blake, small fees paid by all attending dispensary or admitted as in-patients	265	241
Eye	1822	Free	1,600			
Homeopathic			1,198		54	82
Lying-in Institution		Free	114		88	73
Medical Missionary Society	1841	Free	10,641			504
New Town	1815	Free	9,170		391	441
Royal Dispensary and Vaccine Institution	1776	Free	5,906	Patients vaccin- ated...... 456 Home visits. 2,942 Midwifery cases 146	723	605
Women's Dispensary	1887	Free	800	Private ? dispensary		
W. Dispensary Chalmers Institute	1870		4,200		151	157
Glasgow						
Bellahouston Dispensary	1892		4,884	Attached to Glasgow Victoria Infirmary		285
Central Dispensary	1889	Free	7,673	1d. charged each prescription	264	300
Skin Diseases	1861		1,599	All patients transferred to Western Infirmary	502	404
Public Dispensary	1874	Free	4,140	Nursing Depart- ment with 7 beds @ 12/6d. per week	429	449
Inverness						
Forbes Dispensary	1832	Free	2,200		407	312
Jedburgh						
Dispensary	1807	-	100			
Kelso						
Dispensary	1777	Free by letter	123	1 in-patient, nurse visited 70 patients	301	253

Source: Burdett, H. C., *Hospitals and Charities* (London 1899), 553-554.

Treatments were usually laxatives, ointments, or dressings for wounds, although later some lessons in hygiene were given by nurses demonstrating how to wash cuts and abrasions and keep wounds and dressings clean. Poor patients crowded into the dispensary halls in large numbers so that medical officers saw a wide range of cases. In terms of economy it was certainly charity on the cheap. The two famous examples in Edinburgh, the Royal Dispensary and the New Town Dispensary, claimed in 1897 to treat over 9,000 patients every year, at a cost of about 1/- per patient.

There were no fewer than five types of dispensary at work in Victorian Scotland. General dispensaries were established by combined charitable and medical initiative in working-class areas to serve the local populations. Secondly, hospital dispensaries were opened on the premises of the Infirmaries. Thirdly, the specialist hospitals also provided such services. Fourthly, there were dispensaries attached to the medical missions, and finally, there were provident (and not charitable) dispensaries, run by individual doctors, to which working men made regular payment. All the dispensaries had difficulty in getting their patients into the Infirmaries, except those attached to the Infirmaries themselves, or having Infirmary connections.

2. The general dispensaries

The Royal College of Physicians in Edinburgh and the Faculty of Physicians and Surgeons in Glasgow had a long tradition of providing medical care for the poor at their respective halls. When vaccination became standard medical practice at the very end of the eighteenth century, both bodies quickly offered to provide this service free to the poor. They continued to make vaccination available; indeed in 1803 the doctors made a plea to the clergy to remove 'the religious prejudice' which existed against vaccination.[2]

The first[3] dispensary in Scotland was probably the Edinburgh Royal Public Dispensary and Vaccine Institution, founded in 1776.[4] The Kelso Dispensary was started by the Earl of Haddington in 1777. There were probably other short-lived dispensaries in other parts of the country, depending upon the initiative of doctor or philanthropist; there are references to such in both Glasgow and Aberdeen.

The Royal Public Dispensary, a conservative but highly respected institution, worked in Edinburgh without rivals until 1815. In that year the Edinburgh New Town Dispensary[5] was established by a group of distinguished medical men, including John Thomson, M.D. (Consulting Physician), W. P. Alison, M.D. (Physician),[6] J. H. Davidson, M.D. (Physician), J. W. Turner (Surgeon), D. MacLagan, M.D. (Surgeon), Ja. Murdoch, M.D. (Physician Accoucheur), B. B. Buchanan, M.D. (Physician Accoucheur). The managers were chosen by the subscribers, in contrast to the Royal Public's strong medical control; indeed the new dispensary was Whiggish as opposed to its older rival's Toryism. The New Town Dispensary offered a much wider range of services than did its rival. The following was reported in 1817: 'that the names of 8,062 persons have been entered on the books during the first 18 months of its existence, and that of these 3,754 have been entered during the last 6 months . . . In visiting 2,401 patients who have required to be visited in their own homes . . . 984 children have been inoculated for the Cowpox, . . . 369 pregnant women have applied, 299 women have been delivered and cared for.'[7] The success of the New Town Dispensary was regarded sourly by the Public Dispensary. The latter deeply resented the intrusion of such an aggressive body. Henry Cockburn relished the resultant squabble when he recollected much later:

> Any such institution seems at least harmless; yet this one was assailed with a degree of bitterness which is curious now. It was a civic war. Two of its principles were, that medicines and medical advice, including obstetrical aid, were to be administered to patients at their own homes, and that the office-bearers were to be elected by the subscribers; which last, though not absolutely new, was then rare in Edinburgh. All the existing establishments had the usual interest to suppress a rival. But they disavowed this, which however was their true motive, and raised the cry against these two peculiarities. A mob selecting a doctor! The Lying-in Hospital was eloquent on the danger and the vice of delivering poor women at their own houses. The Old Town Dispensary, which did not then go to such patients as could not come to it, demonstrated the beauty of the sick poor being obliged to swallow their doses at a public office. Subscribers choose managers! Impracticable, and dangerously popular! However, common sense prevailed over even this political bugbear, and the hated institution rose and flourished, and has had all its defects imitated by its opponents.[8]

Edinburgh exemplifies the process whereby rival establishments, both strongly supported and both highly respected, learned over time to tolerate one another and divide the dispensary work between them. Their geographical locations fortunately allowed them to draw patients from the two principal

Table 29

Patients treated at the New Town Dispensary, Edinburgh, between September 1815 and December 1842

	Average per annum	Average per month	Average per week	Average per day
Total Number of Medical & Surgical patients since Sept.1815 to 31st Dec. 1842	197,711	7,255	605	140	20
Total Number of Vaccinations...	12,815	470	39	9	1.3
Midwifery patients (since May 1836)	1,132	172	14	3	0.5
Making a Grand Total of Poor admitted since Sept. 1815 up to 31st Dec. 1842, being a period of 27 years 3 months of	211,658	7,897	658	152	21.8
Total Number of patients visited at their own houses (incl. Midwifery patients).................	88,108	3,233	269	62	8.9

Source: New Town Dispensary, AR (Edinburgh 1843), 107.

areas of the city, without any serious overlap. The New Town Dispensary continued very active. But though its aggregate figures were impressive, they did not greatly expand (see Table 29).

The two great Edinburgh dispensaries continued with their work throughout the nineteenth century. It seems likely that the Edinburgh medical establishment, serving in an honorary capacity on the boards of the two dispensaries, would ensure a reasonable standard of treatment. Presumably they encouraged dispensary patients in need to pass on to the Royal Infirmary as inpatients.

Other general dispensaries came into being. One operated at 32 Fountainbridge Street, adjoining the canal basin, from 1 June 1830. The Port Hopetoun Public Dispensary and Humane Society was operating at the same time under the distinguished patronage of His Grace the Duke of Hamilton and Brandon and the Earl of Hopetoun. Later the Edinburgh Fountainbridge Dispensary was opened in 1870 at 7 Brougham Street. Dispensaries at Richmond Street and Rose Street were in operation by 1875. The Edinburgh Provident Dispensary in Marshall Street was founded in 1878. The city thus had a fairly complete coverage. In 1876 Dr. J. B. Russell, Medical Officer of Health of Glasgow, made a very favourable report about Edinburgh dispensaries when he wrote:

> . . . a physician attends for an hour daily, each one having one or two days in the week. The patients who are able to apply personally for advice are examined by the students under the physician's superintendence, and the names of those who are not able to attend are taken down, and each student gets his share of them to visit. He has a visiting book and prescription forms supplied to him. When the student has a serious case on his visiting list, he calls in the physician under whom he is acting . . . I may add that dispensing is done gratis, . . . The Edinburgh plan of visiting patients at their houses is . . . an admirable one for developing students' resources . . .[9]

The use of medical students to extend dispensary service not only kept costs down, but may well have ensured that 'The poor people seem to be well looked after and to be duly grateful.' But this type of 'cheap medicine' produced criticism at a later date.

In Glasgow the pattern of general dispensaries was different. The beginnings of provision were later and less dramatic. Indeed there was no general dispensary in the city until after mid-century. There seem to have been a number of small and short-lived foundations, but because of their size and transience the evidence is scanty. The first sign of real initiative came in 1853 with the founding of the Glasgow Western Public Dispensary at 11 Main Street off Holm Street, Anderston. Its object was to provide for the sick poor from the south-west corner of the city. It catered for 1,010 patients (336 males and 674 females) in its first year, doing so on the astonishingly low budget of £56 15s. 10d. It was run on the slenderest resources and with the maximum economy:

> It will probably surprise many and will certainly gratify all of the Subscribers to hear that at an annual expense of barely Sixty Pounds, One Thousand persons have received Medical Advice and Medicines suitable to their diseases during the past year.[10]

J. B. Russell was critical in 1876 of the failure of Glasgow relative to Edinburgh. Why was Glasgow's performance so inferior to that of Edinburgh? Why did the philanthropists and the doctors in this most working-class of Scottish cities fail to provide the most effective form of medical aid for the masses, namely dispensaries? It may well have been that Glasgow, because of the size of its population, and its lesser attractiveness, was under-doctored; the number of medical students per unit of population was also less. There may, too, have been a lack of interest among the more powerful members of the Glasgow medical profession, though many of the city's doctors rendered unpaid medical services to the less fortunate.

It was Russell himself who generated a wider movement for general dispensaries in Glasgow. He did so from his base as Medical Officer of Health. The Glasgow Central Dispensary was founded in 1889 at 78 George Street, and Russell became its chairman. Although its budget was only £343 in 1894, it had a very ambitious programme, offering advice and treatment on General Diseases both medical and surgical, as well as on specialist problems:

Table 30

Cases dealt with at Glasgow Central Dispensary, 1893

I *General Diseases*		II *Special Diseases*	
Medical	3,120	Diseases of Women	489
Surgical	577	Diseases of Children	997
	———	Diseases of the Eye	37
	3,697	Diseases of the Ear	205
		Diseases of the Throat	443
		Diseases of the Skin	1,791
		Urinary Diseases	210
			———
Grand Total—7,869			4,172

Source: Glasgow Central Dispensary, 5th AR (Glasgow 1894), 3.

In later Victorian times Lady Visitors bearing 'simple comforts', and no doubt good advice, used the general dispensary as a base. Later still, when nursing services became available, volunteer bodies organised nursing care through the dispensaries.

3. The Infirmary dispensaries

Several of the Scottish hospitals had dispensaries, but there was always the danger of the facilities being abused by their patients. The Managers of Montrose Infirmary complained on 6 August 1822 about 'the great number of paupers who are constantly supplied with Medicines, Flannel and Wine at the Dispensary and receive Medical Advice Gratis as well at the Dispensary as at their own house, amounting in some years to nearly one Thousand'.[11] In Aberdeen the Royal Infirmary organised a Dispensary from 1781 (which did not close its doors until 1948) but there were difficulties about supporting both an infirmary and a dispensary. When times were bad the managers considered casting off the Dispensary.[12]

By 1867, at the Dispensary of the Royal Infirmary in Glasgow there were over 12,000 patients — 6,000 medical and 6,000 surgical — being treated each year. Numbers steadily increased, so that by 1873 there were over 14,000 patients annually, of whom 3,400 were under 15 years of age.

There were several advantages in attending a general hospital dispensary. Hospital dispensary cases could become in-patients. By the last quarter of the nineteenth century the quality of treatment at the Infirmary dispensaries was attracting ever-increasing numbers of patients, making them an important aspect of working-class life.

4. The specialist hospitals' contribution

For the specialist hospitals the dispensary was an essential part of their system, bringing patients to them and widening their field of observation. Indeed for them the dispensary was the out-patients' department. This was true of maternity cases, sick children, the eye and ear hospitals, cancer and consumption hospitals, dental hospitals and indeed generally (see chapter 10 above).

5. The medical missions

Among the most dedicated of dispensary providers were the medical missions (see chapter 4, section 2, above). Indeed their missions and their dispensaries were almost identical, with the dispensary and evangelistic halls side by side, or the same hall serving for both. For them healing of the body was a necessary preliminary to therapy for the soul. Edinburgh's most outstanding example was the Medical Mission Dispensary in the Cowgate, which was rebuilt as the Livingstone Memorial Mission's Training Institution in 1877. From about 1868 the Glasgow Missionary Society provided a similar service in Nelson Street, and in 1875 it opened a second dispensary at South Coburg Street. In the same year the Anderson Medical Mission provided a dispensary at 45 North Street, as did the Cowcaddens Medical Mission in Maitland Street. The Grove Street Mission also provided a dispensary service.

6. The provident principle

The 'provident' dispensaries were different from all the rest in one essential: they were not charitable arrangements, but were run on the combined principles of self-help and a form of insurance. Provident Societies of working men collected subscriptions from their members and then paid these to a doctor. Such a doctor would then have his 'panel' of patients who would go to him when ill and receive treatment without further payment. Men only were involved, though women and children, through them, could form contacts with doctors. Under this system the working classes made their first acquaintance with the notion of a family doctor.

7. The dispensary debate

In spite of the minimal cost involved in dispensaries, and their great service to the working classes, they were severely criticised. As early as 1835 Dr. Adams claimed in parody that 'puir folk can only gang tae the dispensaries, whar a curran o' hafflins laddies pay for leave tae try experiments upon us! Deil experiment them.'[13] The patients' fears of doctors who 'practised' on them remained strong for many years. In 1910 the Webbs delivered a diatribe against the dispensary system: 'In our opinion, all these centres for the gratuitous, indiscriminate and unconditional dispensing of medical advice and medicine, far from meriting encouragement, or offering opportunities for extension, call imperatively — at any rate where they involve the gathering of crowds of sick persons in halls and passages — for systematic inspection and supervision by the local Medical Officer of Health, in order to ensure that they are not actually spreading more disease than they are curing.'[14] The Webbs were intent on preparing the way for socialist medicine, and therefore saw charitably funded dispensaries in a poor light. Whether Scottish dispensaries were better than their English counterparts, it is not possible to say.

8. The passing of the dispensaries

The bad press which the dispensaries received, mostly as a result of the publicity given to the Webbs' criticisms, certainly had its effects. General dispensaries gradually disappeared. Those attached to Infirmaries and specialist hospitals became explicitly out-patient departments. The passing of the dispensaries was hastened by Part I of the National Insurance Act of 1911. It made the 'panel' doctor the centre of the new health service offered to certain categories of working men. Many dispensaries did not survive the first world war, which drained away young medical officers. But as a range of interim improvisations the dispensaries were an essential component of Scottish Victorian working-class life.

NOTES

1. Johnston, J., 1871, 26.
2. Anon., *Address . . . to the clergy of Scotland . . .* (Edinburgh 1803).
3. Owen, D., *English Philanthropy* (London 1965), gives the General Dispensary in Aldersgate (dated 1770) as the first such in England.
4. In Gibson, H. J. C., *History of Dundee Royal Infirmary*, 1948, 7, there is a reference to a Dispensary in Dundee in 1735; it has not proved possible to substantiate this.
5. It was also known as the Thistle Street Dispensary, based at 17 East Thistle Street; but its first annual report was addressed from 12 North James Street.
6. Alison probably learned much about urban poverty from his close association with this Dispensary. See Alison, 1840, 1844.
7. *New Town Dispensary*, 1st AR (Edinburgh 1817).
8. Cockburn, H., 1856, 283. The reference to the election of office bearers reflects Cockburn's Whig beliefs. All the old-established institutions of the capital, whether charities or banks, were tight oligarchies with self-perpetuating boards of directors. It was often a hard battle to liberalise the boards and make them more representative.
9. Russell, J. B., 1876, 39.
10. *Western Public Dispensary*, 5th AR (Glasgow 1858), 5.
11. Poole, R., 1841, 35.
12. Porter, 1958, Chapter 3.
13. Adams, A. M., 1835, 206.
14. Webb, S. & B., 1910, 134-5.

12

Supportive Services: Cottage Hospitals and Convalescent Homes

1. Village hospitals[1]

ALTHOUGH the part played by the philanthropists in the management of the Infirmaries was fading by the latter part of the nineteenth century (see chapter 8, section 5, above), the humanitarians, not content with their diminishing role, continued to innovate. No longer so potent at the core of medicine, they proceeded to provide it with peripheral and supportive services. By their efforts the village (later the cottage) hospital brought skilled medical and surgical treatment to farming communities and the smaller towns. Secondly, the convalescent homes they sponsored were a useful extension, taking some of the pressure off the hospitals by caring for those whose need was for re-cuperative facilities. The cottage hospitals were resisted by the Infirmaries and so had to be forced upon the system; the convalescent homes were welcomed.

Albert Napper was an English country physician who succeeded in 1859 in establishing a village hospital at Cranleigh (Cranley) in Surrey. His objectives were twofold: to give patients (especially workmen) good, prompt local treatment, and to broaden the experience of the local doctor. From the 1860's village hospitals sprang up rapidly in England. Many of these were memorial hospitals built either by subscription or donated. The cottage hospital was indeed an ideal memorial, for it was within the means of families of substance. The first cottage hospital in Scotland appears to have been that at St. Andrews in Fife, pioneered in 1865 by Dr. John Adamson.

The initial hostility of the Infirmaries stemmed from the same fear that had inspired their opposition to the specialist hospitals, namely that of competition for philanthropic giving, which would threaten their subscription income as well as diverting patients from them. But these arguments were absurd in view of the acute shortage of hospital beds in Britain as a whole. As Dr. Waring explained, 'It appears that there are no less than 9 million people in Great Britain unprovided with hospital accommodation. To meet this state of affairs 9,000 more beds are required; and allowing 6 beds on an average there is scope for 1,500 Cottage hospitals.' The suggestion was also made that the cottage hospital should act as a depot for medical services, so that subscribers in their

209

own residences could have the use of 'surgical instruments and appliances of the best quality'. As far as is known, this idea was never implemented in Scotland.

The mandarins of the medical profession were also prejudiced in favour of size. To many of them the term 'cottage' conjured up a picture of dirt and disease. As one metropolitan surgeon wrote: 'Everyone knows by this time how inferior the arrangements for nursing, cleanliness and ventilation in cottage hospitals are to those in our great city hospitals.' But the advocates of the smaller institution were not to be put down: 'The cottage element should never be lost sight of. The building should in all cases be a cottage — a model cottage if circumstances permit, with all the advantages of efficient drainage, good ventilation, and a cheerful exterior, but still essentially a cottage in character and pretension . . . Homeliness (combined with cheerfulness and the strictest attention to cleanliness) should be the predominant features throughout.'

One of the medical controversies involving the cottage hospitals related to the death rate of patients who underwent amputations there; it was claimed to be much higher than in large city hospitals. This was taken as a reflection not only on the cottage principle and its nursing provision, but also on the doctors working there. It was charged that local doctors were encouraged by the existence of the facilities to undertake operations better performed in one of the large general hospitals. One commentator regretted 'the absence of any attempt to estimate the real sanitary condition of cottage hospitals as tested by the prevalence and spread of erysipelas in these institutions'.[2] But the dangers of cross infection were not limited to small hospitals.

The cottage hospital movement came late to Scotland and spread slowly. It must have required unusual circumstances and determined sponsors to launch a cottage hospital in a small town when the whole tenor of life in rural Scotland was against such a development. The Cottage Hospital, St. Andrews, was perhaps typical of such hospitals in Scotland. It took as its motto: 'I was sick and ye visited me.' Although St. Andrews was the home of the most ancient university in Scotland, it had never in modern times had a hospital of its own. The initiative was owing to three people: Dr. John Adamson, M.D., a local doctor, Lady William Douglas of Grangemuir and Dunino, and Professor Oswald Home Bell, M.D., Professor of Medicine at the University. The Hospital began in Abbey Street but moved to Abbotsford Place House in 1880. By 1896 it had accommodation for '6 adult patients, 3 male and 3 female, and four children, for whom a special ward is set apart'.[3] Patients requiring medical or surgical treatment were admitted, but none of an infectious nature. Medical men or clergymen from the adjacent rural areas were requested to write to the hospital regarding the admittance of country patients '— awaiting a reply before sending the patient'. A Ladies' House Committee took responsibility for 'domestic details and service'. Nursing services were undertaken by Miss Binford, 'our matron, of whom we can hardly speak too highly', and a nurse.

In 1896 the income received by the hospital was £410, of which £390 was spent during the year. Subscribers of £5 were entitled to name a patient a year, although those other than subscribers' nominees were asked to make a payment of 5/- a week in advance. There were small subscription funds to provide 'free beds', and for these there was no charge. 60 patients were accommodated in 1896, of whom 37 were women, 23 were men and 5 were children. Two died, but all the others were either cured or 'relieved'. Of the women patients, 16 were housewives and 10 were domestic servants (including one cook, one nursery maid and one lady's maid). There were also three female farm-servants and one female strolling player and her child. Male patients included the following occupations: cabinet-maker, quarryman, joiner, farmer, paper-maker, labourer, ploughman, mason and baker. More than half the patients came from outside St. Andrews. The places mentioned included Anstruther, Pittenweem and Cupar. There can be no doubt of the importance of the Memorial Cottage Hospital to its community and district.

In some cases cottage hospitals were encouraged by Poor Law Unions who were unwilling to commit themselves to providing such facilities, but were glad of the opportunity of having hospital beds for their pauper patients. The Cottage Hospital at Alloa, Clackmannanshire (with 15 beds) received a steady if small income from those responsible for the upkeep of sick paupers. It was certainly run most economically.

Table 31

Cottage hospitals in Scotland at 1880

Name	Date of Founding	No. of Beds	Average No. Occupied	No. of Patients 1878-79	Other Information
Crimond, Aberdeen	1866	—	—	—	Stated to be still in existence in 1880 but no information available.
Alloa near Stirling N.B.	1868	15	—	—	Patients pay 5/- & under. Union sometimes sends pauper patients.
Dingwall, Ross (Ross Memorial Hospital)	1873	8	2	27	No medical officer. Six parishes subscribe £5 annually; patients do not pay.
Forgue, Aberdeen (No rent paid)	1875	8	4	17	£10 to medical officer, males 3/6d, females 2/6d, boys & girls 2/- to 3/-. No paupers admitted.
Fyvie, Aberdeen	1879	—	—	—	Not yet built, will be completed end of year.
St. Andrews, Fife (Rent paid)	1866	7	—	31	No fee to medical officer; 5/- to 7/- for servants.

Source: Burdett, H. C., *Cottage Hospitals, their progress, management and work* (London 1880), 462-476.

During the 1870's three hospitals were established in the North of Scotland. At Dingwall the Ross Memorial Hospital opened in 1873 with 8 beds. It had two wings, with accommodation for fever patients in one and non-fever patients in the other. The entrance, kitchens and operating room were centred between the two wards and were therefore common to both. This hospital was praised by Henry C. Burdett in 1880, when he published *Cottage Hospitals*, although he complained that there was no mortuary and that 'This should at once be provided.' The Cottage Hospital at Forgue in Aberdeenshire was established in 1875 with 4 beds. During the year 1878-79 it treated 17 patients. £10 per annum was paid to the medical officer and payment was made (varying from 2/- to 3/6d.) by patients. As no paupers were admitted, this was probably a genuine cottage hospital for the working poor. The Fyvie Hospital (also in Aberdeenshire) opened its doors to patients in 1880. The position in that year was as in Table 31.

The movement to establish cottage hospitals gathered momentum in the 1880's and 1890's. By the end of the century there were 33 in Scotland, with something over 350 beds and cots as shown in Table 32. The largest had 24 beds (at Johnstone in Renfrewshire, and Keith in Banffshire), the smallest two, on Mull. This tiny 'hospital' was initiated and operated by the North Argyll Nursing Association. Some hospitals were gifted outright. Haddo House Cottage Hospital was one such, with seven beds. Several were memorial hospitals or were otherwise named after their major benefactor.

The cottage hospitals not only survived but thrived. They were ideally suited to small-scale effort, and were small and friendly. The initial grumblings by the Infirmaries and doctors in the cities faded away as standards improved and more nurses became available. There seems no doubt that the cottage hospitals, though the total number of beds they could provide was small, provided a valuable addition to rural medical services in Scotland, reassuring farmers and fishermen and sustaining the skill and morale of local doctors.

Table 32

Cottage hospitals in Scotland at 1899

Place	Date of Founding	Type of Hospital	No. of Beds	Other Information
Aberchirder, Banffshire	1892	Rose Innes Cottage Hospital	13	
Aberlour, Banffshire	1895	Fleming Cottage Hospital		In course of erection
Castle Douglas, Galloway		Cottage Hospital		In course of erection
Coldstream, Berwick	1888	Cottage Hospital and Dispensary	12	
Cumnock	1883	Cottage Hospital	14	Built by Lord Bute
Cupar, Fife		Cottage Hospital		Proposed
Denny, Stirling		Cottage Hospital		

Table 32 (continued)

Place	Date of Founding	Type of Hospital	No. of Beds	Other Information
Dufftown, Banffshire	1888	The Stephen Cottage Hospital	10, 1 crib	Founded by Lord Mountstephen
Dumbarton	1890	Cottage Hospital	12	
Dunfermline	1894	Cottage Hospital	28	
Falkirk	1887	Cottage Hospital	15, 22 cots	
Forgue, Aberdeenshire	1875	Cottage Hospital	8	
Forres, Leanchoil, Moray	1892	Cottage Hospital	14	
Fyvie, Aberdeenshire	1879	Cottage Hospital	10	
Galashiels, Tweed Road	1893	Cottage Hospital	14, 1 cot	
Grantown	1884	Ian Charles Cottage Hospital	10	
Hawick	1884	Cottage Hospital and Dispensary	18	
Huntly, Aberdeenshire	1889	Jubilee Cottage Hospital	18	
Jedburgh	1896	Sister Margaret Cottage Hospital		
Johnstone, Renfrewshire	1893	Cottage Hospital	24	
Keith, Banffshire	1880	Turner Memorial Hospital	24	
Kirkcaldy, Fife	1890	Cottage Hospital	10	
Kirkcudbright	1897	Cottage Hospital		
Langholm, Dumfriesshire	1896	Thomas Hope Hospital	14	
Moffat, Dumfriesshire		Cottage Hospital		
Mull	1892	Cottage Hospital	2	Initiated and operated by the North Argyll Nursing Association
Oban	1896	West Highland Cottage Hospital	13, 2 cots	
Rothesay, Buteshire	1894	Victoria Cottage Hospital	10	
St. Andrews	1865	Memorial Cottage Hospital	10	
Skye		Mackinnon Memorial Hospital		Not yet built
Stornoway	1896	The Lewis Hospital	13	
Stranraer, Wigtown	1892	Garrick Cottage Hospital, Dalrymple Street	10	
Tarves, Aberdeenshire	1883	Haddo House Cottage Hospital	7	Governing body Earl & Countess of Haddo

Total hospitals = 33   Total beds = 359

Source: *Burdett's Hospitals and Charities 1899*; see also Burdett, H. C., *Cottage Hospitals* (London 1880).

2. Post-hospital care

The move to provide post-hospital care for recuperating patients started about 1865. The convalescent home was especially attractive to those who did not wish to be associated with the medical profession, and who found an outlet in such residential establishments. This type of rest home also appealed to evangelicals, who made it a favourite field for their redemptive work. By 1899 there were in Scotland about 1,070 beds in some 23 convalescent homes, most of which were near to the urban centres of Glasgow and Edinburgh (see Table 33). The large Homes were:

Glasgow Convalescent Home, Lenzie	(1865)	85 beds
Corstorphine Convalescent Home, Edinburgh	(1867)	100 beds
Dunoon, West of Scotland Convalescent Homes	(1869)	250 beds
Saltcoats Mission Coast Home	(1866)	100 beds

These contained more than half of the convalescent beds then available. Such homes were often built for the exclusive use of patients from one particular hospital, and occasionally the mother hospital accepted financial responsibility for the daughter institution. The Western Infirmary and the Victoria Infirmary, Glasgow did so with respect to the Lady Hozier Convalescent Home at Lanark and the Largs Home respectively, both of which were specifically designed to accommodate their convalescing patients.

The managers of the Edinburgh Royal Infirmary became involved with the rest home at an early date because of an enquiry which they undertook in 1854-55.[4] They discovered that their costs appeared to be higher per patient than those of the Glasgow Royal Infirmary. Patients remained resident for longer periods in Edinburgh, they cost more to keep and, inevitably, the waiting list became longer. In order to improve the patient turnover figure,

Table 33

Convalescent homes in Scotland in 1899

Aberdeen Convalescent Hospital, Hillhead of Pitfodels, Cults, near Aberdeen, 1897, in connection with Aberdeen Royal Infirmary. Nursing Staff: 1 nurse, 1 probationer. Beds 20-25. Expenditure £472.

Aberdeen — Eidda Convalescent Home, Culter, in connection with the Royal Hospital for Sick Children. Patients 54.

Arbroath Convalescent Home, Jennyswell, 1891, in connection with the Arbroath Infirmary. Beds 10. Patients 73. Income (1897-8) £145; expenditure £198. Free to patients from Arbroath Infirmary; others 5/- per week.

Busby Convalescent Home (in connection with the Glasgow Training Homes for Nurses) proposed.

Corstorphine Convalescent Home (1867). A branch of the Edinburgh Royal Infirmary. Beds 100. 5 nurses. Income £2,003. Expenditure £2,229. Duration of stay 3 weeks. A limited number of paying patients received.

Duddingston — Hawthornbrae Convalescent Home. In connection with the Edinburgh Medical Missionary Society. Patients (1897-8) 226. Income £307. Expenditure £299.

Table 33 (continued)

Dundee Convalescent Home, Barnhill, branch of the Royal Infirmary. Average number of beds occupied, 59. Patients 1,061. Income £1,436. Expenditure £1,559.

Dunoon — West of Scotland Convalescent Seaside Homes (1869). Beds: adults 200, children 50, patients (1897-8) 4,065. Admission by letter of recommendation or during December and January payment of £1 for 2 weeks. Open all year.

Edzell N.B. In connection with the Royal Infirmary and Dispensary at Montrose. Admission by subscriber's line unless transferred from Infirmary. Income £188. Expenditure £188.

Gilmerton (Edinburgh) Children's Convalescent Home (1881). Patients 320. Income £243. Expenditure £296. Duration of stay, 2 or 3 weeks.

Gilmerton (Edinburgh) Ravenscroft Convalescent Home (for adults) (1878). Beds 20. Patients 304. Income £470. Expenditure £513. Stay 14-21 days.

Glasgow Convalescent Home, Lenzie near Glasgow (1865). Matron Miss Smith and 1 nurse. Beds 85. Patients 1,740. Income (1898) £2,418. Expenditure £2,540. Terms of admission: free with subscriber's letter. 30 beds reserved for patients from Glasgow Royal Infirmary; 10 for Western Infirmary. Subscriber's letter not required for Infirmary patients. Subscribers' privileges: subscribers are entitled to recommend 1 patient annually for every £1 1s. subscribed. Donors of £10 = subscribers of £1 1s. Duration of stay 3 weeks. Open all year.

Glasgow — Schaw Convalescent Home, Bearsden. A branch of the Glasgow Royal Infirmary erected at a cost of £30,000 and presented to the Infirmary by Miss Marjory Shanks-Schaw. Matron, Miss Scott and 1 nurse. Beds 60. Patients 824. Open to all patients from the Glasgow Royal Infirmary over 3 years of age. Duration of stay 3 weeks. Open all year. Expenditure £1,458.

Kilmarnock — Dundonald Convalescent Home. Matron Miss Barlas.

Kilmun Seaside Home for Convalescent Poor (1867). Conducted by the Directors of the Glasgow Abstainers' Union. Beds 80. Patients 1,168. Income (1897-8) £1,136. Expenditure £1,151.

Lanark — Lady Hozier Convalescent Home. In connection with the Western Infirmary of Glasgow. Beds 43. Patients 796. Income (1897-8) £753. Expenditure £1,383; deficiency made up by Infirmary.

Largs (Ayrshire) — Victoria Infirmary of Glasgow Convalescent Home, Brooksby (1897). Lady Superintendent, Miss Campbell and 1 nurse. Beds 24. Patients 360. Open to patients from Infirmary only. Income £23. Expenditure £732; deficiency met by Infirmary.

Lochend, Inverness — Convalescent Home of the Northern Infirmary, Bona Lochend. Now a ward of the Northern Infirmary, Inverness. Beds 12. Matron Miss Keir.

Nairn — Northern Counties Convalescent Homes, Tradespark, Nairn N.B. (1882). Beds 9. Patients 62. Income (1896) £125. Expenditure £129.

Ochiltree (Ayrshire) Convalescent Home (1881). Beds 16. Patients 144. Income (1897-8) £327. Expenditure £337. Subscriber's line.

Paisley Convalescent Home, West Kilbride, Ayrshire (1886). Beds 92. Patients 947. Income £1,256. Expenditure £1,383. Admission from Paisley Infirmary, otherwise by subscriber's recommendation. Children between two and five years charged 2s. 6d. per week.

Ravenscraig Children's Convalescent Home, established Eaglesham 1890, transferred to Ravenscraig May 1898. Owned by Trinity Congregational Church. Beds 12. Admission free by ticket, age 2-12. Duration of stay 2-8 weeks.

Saltcoats Mission Coast Home, Saltcoats N.B. Established 1866. Beds 100. Patients 1,511. Admission free by ticket, tickets issued by Secretary to cases considered suitable. Stay 2 weeks. Special feature: 'The mode of treatment is hydropathic combined with the use of acetic acid.'

Source: Burdett, H. C., *Hospitals and Charities* (London 1899), 621-652.

'certain benevolent persons' formed themselves into a committee and arranged for a 'few convalescent houses' to be made available in the city; these were to act as a halfway house between hospital and home. From these stemmed the more formal institution of the convalescent home. In July 1864 William Seton Brown offered the Edinburgh Royal Infirmary a convalescent home on condition that the managers would take it over and maintain it. Of course they agreed, and a site at Corstorphine was chosen. In July 1867 the Home was opened, accommodating 50 independent ambulant patients. The original structure cost about £12,000. Another benefactor appeared in 1893: James Nasmyth, the celebrated engineer, gave £13,000, which made it possible for other wings to be built with room for a further 40 patients.

In the West of Scotland there were several wealthy patrons whose interests focused on the convalescent home. But the real driving force was Miss Beatrice Clugston (1827-1888).[5] She was responsible for founding the Glasgow Convalescent Home at Lenzie[6] and the West of Scotland Convalescent Seaside Homes at Dunoon. Miss Clugston turned to the time-honoured device of using the aristocracy as an attractive front for her fund-raising. Her promotional abilities were indeed impressive (see Appendix IV). She appealed to Queen Victoria's daughter, the Princess Louise (who had recently married the son of the Duke of Argyll and become Marchioness of Lorne), and also to Florence Nightingale. Both approaches were successful. Miss Clugston was able to present in her publicity pamphlet a gracious letter, addressed from Windsor Castle, agreeing that a stall at the bazaar should be named 'the Argyll and Lorne', and promising that the Princess and Lord Lorne would make every endeavour to attend. As a bonus the Duchess promised to ask the Queen to donate something which could be sold. Florence Nightingale wrote a long, kind but ponderous letter declining to be patron but praising the proposal.

Premises suitable for the West of Scotland Seaside Homes, Dunoon, fell into Miss Clugston's hands by a fortunate set of circumstances. A Hydropathic Home built by a gentleman who died before he could carry out his purpose became available; in addition there lay adjacent a small private dwelling house belonging to the same estate. Miss Clugston was able to take over these houses and much of their furniture and thereby obtained a ready-made convalescent home for £6,000. Treatment appears to have been given in the form of hydropathy, which used a great deal of acetic acid which the Home received gratis from Messrs F. Coutts and Sons. Dr. Kinnear of Saltcoats gave his services free to the patients 'whenever circumstances seemed to require the presence of a regular medical practitioner'.[7] Miss Clugston's work was strongly evangelical in tone. Rooms were reserved in her establishments for missionaries who were encouraged to take a holiday there, but they were required to undertake a full programme of mission work.

A direct link between the missionary movement in Glasgow and recuperative provision was established when the Mission Coast Home, Saltcoats was opened in 1866. This Home usually took patients for a four-week stay. It was not linked to any hospital, but recruited patients recommended by missionaries working in Glasgow or elsewhere. It was sponsored by the Glasgow United Evangelical Association. It made a growing contribution:

Table 34

Number of patients admitted to the Mission Coast Home between 1866 and 1878

	Persons admitted	Income to nearest £
1866	156	64
1867	490	182
1868	230	302
1869	387	505
1870	717	697
1871	736	973
1872	731	1,038
1873	692	1,183
1874	832	1,389
1875	997	1,136
1876	938	1,341
1877	1,064	1,575
1878	1,241	1,055

Source: Mission Coast Home, Saltcoats, 13th AR (Ardrossan 1878).

The total expenditure for 1878 was £1,244. The substantial elements in the budget included £770 for provisions and £140 for wages. The organisers calculated 3s. 2½d. per week as the cost of food per head in 1877. Total cost per head was 4s. 4d. (see Appendix V for the range of gifts to the Home).

The temperance movement in the West of Scotland also established a convalescent home. The Glasgow Abstainers' Union was anxious to associate itself with 'positive temperance'. To this end it opened the Kilmun Seaside Home for the poor in 1866, with about 35 beds. By 1873 the Directors wrote that the home 'has proved a most valuable and direct Temperance Agency'.[8] They embarked upon a rebuilding programme which enabled them to accommodate 80 beds.

Later developments included the Lady Hozier Home in Lanark (with 43 beds), founded in 1891. It was linked to the Western Infirmary, and with the Schaw Home at Bearsden (with 60 beds), established by Miss Mary Shanks-Schaw for the Royal Infirmary.

At the other end of the scale there were some very small homes. Some of these were run on a self-help basis which must have been hard for the patients and the staff to sustain. Dr. Burns Thomson (of the Edinburgh Medical Mission) (see chapter 4, section 2, above) was keen to give his patients from the Cowgate, Edinburgh a period of recuperation in the country. In the early stages he was able to have the use of houses rented by supporters in Elie, Fife and Polton, East Lothian where his patients could have summer residence. A mission nurse was sent out, and she and the patients between them did all the work including cleaning and food preparation. Of all the results of Dr. Burns

Thomson's mission work '. . . The Convalescent Home stood highest of all. It yielded a clear profit of from 70% to 80% and this I consider a first class investment, better even than the Tharsis Sulphur and Copper Mine.'[9] Later a home was opened, perhaps more adequately staffed, at Hawthornbrae, Duddingston.

The Glasgow Poor Children Fresh Air Fortnight Scheme was a way of getting poor children into the country. Under this scheme children were originally to live 'in the houses of respectable cottars', but the supply of willing cottars proved inadequate and the children may have been sent to the Mission Coast Home at Saltcoats.

Thus, although it may be argued that the philanthropists were being extruded from power in the citadels of medicine, namely the Infirmaries, there was still a store of unexpended energy and inventiveness among them. They brought it to bear on provision of these extensions of the general system.

NOTES

1. Napper, A., *On the Advantages derivable to the medical profession and the Public from the Village Hospital* (London, 3rd Ed., 1886); Waring, E. J., *Cottage Hospitals, their Objects, Advantages and Management* (London 1867); Swete, H., *Village Hospitals and their position with regard to County infirmaries, unions and the professions* (London 1866).
2. Burdett, 1880, 36.
3. *St. Andrews Cottage Hospital*, 31st AR (St. Andrews 1896).
4. Logan Turner, 1937, 174-7.
5. Of Prospect Villa, Lenzie junction, by Glasgow. Buried at Old Aisle Cemetery, Kirkintilloch, where her memorial reads 'Beatrice Clugston, 1827-1888. Dunoon Homes, Broomhill Home, Glasgow Convalescent Home. Charity, Mercy, Humility.' See Watson, T., *Kirkintilloch, Town and Parish* (Glasgow 1894), 123.
6. Clugston, B., *West of Scotland Convalescent Sea-side Homes, Dunoon, being a short account of their present position and capabilities of extension and use, printed for circulation for the purpose of stirring up the community of Glasgow and the West of Scotland to greater efforts for the working classes in times of sickness and distress* (Glasgow 1871).
7. *West of Scotland Seaside Homes*, AR (1878), 7.
8. *Glasgow Abstainers' Union*, 19th AR (Glasgow 1873).
9. Burns Thomson, W., 1895, 135.

13

The Nursing Revolution

1. Old-style nursing

THERE was a second and even more important direction in which the philanthropists undertook new medical initiatives in the later nineteenth century. It had to do not with the periphery of medicine, as with cottage and convalescent homes, but its very heart. Progress in medicine and health was more or less at a halt because of the abysmal condition of nursing. The philanthropists had much to do with raising nursing to new levels in terms of training, prestige and numbers.

The modern profession of nursing for women owes its existence almost entirely to Florence Nightingale.[1] As Joseph Bell, Conan Doyle's model for Sherlock Holmes, and assistant to Professor Syme, the distinguished Edinburgh surgeon, recollected:

> Without apparent exaggeration, it is almost impossible to convey to this generation, the depths of disgraceful ignorance and neglect in which nursing lay in hospitals in 1854. In October of that year the Alma had been fought and the Balaclava charge had aroused the enthusiasm of the nation. Inkermann in November, and cold, exposure and disease all through that awful winter, had opened the eyes of the public to what services needed for their sick and wounded were, and what Florence Nightingale and her staff had tried so nobly to do. The impetus of that work and that woman gave the profession of nursing its first real start in the world, and by a reflected energy at last aroused the hospital authorities all over the Kingdom to action.[2]

Miss Nightingale's extraordinary demonstration in the Crimea, when she had routed not only incompetent doctors but also bungling army personnel, was a sharp reminder to the nation that assumptions of feminine incompetence and frailty were no longer tenable.

The earliest modern nursing training programme originated in Germany at the time of the wars of liberation against Napoleon (1813-14). The Institution at Kaisersworth, under the guidance of Theodor Fliedner and his wife Fredericke, became the Mecca for all women who were concerned to improve standards of nursing. In England the Quakers were the first in the field; it was Elizabeth Fry who (towards the end of her life) consulted Fliedner and set up the first nursing association in 1840.[3]

In 1860 Miss Nightingale applied the £50,000 presented to her by a grateful nation to found the Nightingale Training School for Nurses at St. Thomas's

219

Hospital in London. Her reputation and dedication, together with the nature of the training course, were sufficient to attract girls of better education and to transform the nursing profession within a generation. At St. Thomas's, 'pupil nurses were carefully selected and supervised. Their training lasted a whole year and, like their board and lodging, was free; moreover, although still pupils they were paid into the bargain'.[4] For Florence Nightingale was the first to distinguish between the 'educational and service commitments of the probationer nurse'.[5] As she herself explained, 'An uneducated man who practises physic is justly called a quack, perhaps an impostor. Why are not uneducated nurses called quacks or impostors? Simply because there are few who think a man can understand medicine and surgery by instinct. But till the last ten or twenty years people in England thought every woman was a nurse by instinct.'[6]

Under the old regime nurses and nursing techniques were not considered important by hospital managements. There are one or two rare insights into conditions at both the Edinburgh and Glasgow Royal Infirmaries. Joseph Bell commented:

> For the 72 patients . . . the nursing staff consisted of nine women, aided in an emergency . . . by a drunken old porter . . . The nine women were — two staff nurses each with about thirty-six beds to look after and seven so-called night nurses who had also to do the scrubbing and cleaning of the wards and passages. The two nurses, Mrs. Lambert and Mrs. Porter, were wonderful women of natural ability and strong Scotch sense and capacity, of immense experience and great kindliness . . . but the other seven — poor old useless drudges half-charwomen, half field-worker, absolutely ignorant, almost invariably drunken, sometimes deaf, occasionally fatuous.[7]

In Glasgow the Managers of the Royal Infirmary were pushed unwillingly into improving the condition of the nurses by the upheaval resulting from the removal of the University to Gilmorehill in 1870. The possibility of losing their medical students had sharpened the Managers' responses in a remarkable way. By 1880, having improved the condition of nurses, they were able to write eloquently about earlier conditions, comparing them with the improved state of things:

> In 1861 when the new Surgical Hospital was opened, the number of nurses in the infirmary was 44, the number of wards being then, as it still remains 31. The wages were from 15/- to 17/6d. per month. The women were not adequately fed, no regular meal, not even dinner, being provided for them. Their food consisted of such articles as herrings, chops, eggs or cheese which they cooked in their respective wards, and as this diet hardly satisfied the requirements of nature they were under great temptation . . . of adding to their own scanty fare from the diet supplied for the patients.

> Now instead of 44 there are 62 nurses on regular duty. These . . . are divided into two classes — day nurses and night nurses. One of each class is appropriated to each ward . . . to which she belongs and from which she is never transferred, except for some good reason . . . Besides these regular nurses there are 29 probationer nurses, who may be called floating staff.

> The former practice was for the nurses to do the scrubbing, cleaning and washing . . . but as the imposition of these duties was found to be a hindrance in getting a superior class of women, . . . (there are) two new classes of women consisting of 20 scrubbers and cleaners, and 16 washerwomen and laundry maids.

Not only has the number, but the wages also of the nurses have been much increased since 1861. A probationer coming in to learn is now paid £12 a year. After she is qualified she receives £20 which is increased at the rate of £2 a year until it reaches £30 a year.[8]

2. Recruitment

The unenviable reputation of nurses as a group made it difficult to elevate nursing into a profession. Hospitals were still charitable establishments, primarily intended to accommodate the poor. As such they were considered unsuitable workplaces for respectable girls. Girls who wanted to train had to break through conventions and barriers set up by family and friends. But nursing as a career did have an attraction for Victorians, offering a girl a popular 'angel of mercy' image based on the concept of 'sublime drudgery'. This had the advantage (for men) of reaffirming women's dependent place in the medical world.

Members of the medical profession recognised this problem. As one commentator wrote: 'One of the greatest difficulties met with at the commencement was to persuade suitable persons that they were not degrading themselves by becoming nurses, but that they were really entering a profession to which any woman, however lofty her station, might feel it an honour to belong.'[9]

Recruitment took place at two levels. Both 'ladies' and working women were attracted by the possibilities. The integration of two such widely divergent types was not easy. 'Ladies' were useless if they followed the conventions of their upbringing and jibbed at doing domestic work, although they could often be successful administrators and organisers. Working women were well able to cope with the domestic work, but often did not have the experience or the confidence to exercise authority.

The problems of recruitment to the profession had curious and unexpected consequences. In 1877 there was a bitter row between the Managers of the Glasgow Royal Infirmary and the West of Scotland Protestant Association in the person of their Secretary, Mr. A. M. Stewart, which illustrates the sort of difficulties which could arise. Mr. Stewart[10] accused the Managers of the Royal Infirmary, when appointing nurses, of 'preference given, or at least partiality shown to those of the Roman Catholic persuasion'. The Managers responded rather grandly, that 'The Glasgow Royal Infirmary has been conducted on strictly unsectarian principles and . . . neither in the case of nurses or patients has there ever been any preference shown or religious test applied.' Later the Managers were more explicit, remarking that they 'have for many years past experienced great difficulty in getting a sufficient number of women of good character for the arduous duties required of them'. This dispute became a *cause célèbre.* Several statements and pamphlets were produced and the conflict was reported fully in the newspapers. The Managers' condescension vanished when they discovered that whereas in 1876 they had received subscriptions of £5,815 from workers and workshops, in 1877 these had dropped to £4,400. It seems clear that Irish Catholic nurses were willing to take on nursing duties while Protestant women were not.

Accommodation had to be made available. No respectable family of any class would allow a daughter to go and train as a nurse unless proper arrangements were made for safe and comfortable residence. Hospital authorities who ignored this were undoubtedly the losers when recruitment drives were made. The provision of nurses' homes was made on a charitable basis: hospitals could not finance such large investments out of their annual budgets and were forced to search around for generous patrons. A number of nurses' homes were built in Scotland around 1900. Perhaps the Alice Mary Corbett Memorial Nurses' Home built for the Glasgow Samaritan Hospital for Women may be taken as an example. It was a memorial to Alice Mary Polson, gifted by her mother and opened in 1906. Situated on the corner of Coplaw Street and Victoria Road and built of 'Corncockle Quarry dressings, which harmonise with the yellowish rubble from Fallowhill Quarry', the Home had accommodation for 28 nurses.[11] Each nurse had a room of her own, while a suite of rooms was reserved for the matron. The total cost of site, building and furnishings was over £10,000.

3. Training in the hospitals

Despite the public acclaim which greeted the nascent profession of nursing during the Crimean War, hospital authorities in Scotland did not rush to re-organise and expand their nursing staffs. Charitable hospitals were always very budget-conscious and kept expenses to a minimum. In addition, by the 1850's the Royal Infirmaries of Edinburgh and Glasgow were institutions of much power and a good deal of inertia. Managements had no difficulties, initially, in ignoring any suggestions that nursing staff should be re-organised. One medical writer pointed out in 1878: 'Skilled nursing . . . had scarcely received any attention in Scotland, till within the last few years.'[12]

Nurses had always been poorly paid and miserably housed. They could exert no pressure on managements. Consequently the cost of nursing services remained low. Subscribers naturally applauded keeping costs down. As long as there was no outcry from the public, hospital managements were not likely to undertake expensive reforms, although doctors in hospitals were increasingly dissatisfied with the level of nursing services.

There were, however, other reasons for delay. Doctors in hospitals were anxious about possible clashes of authority if well-trained nurses did appear. As Brian Abel-Smith has explained: 'If the new matron was to undertake what she considered to be her duties, she had to carve out an empire of her own. She had to take over some of the responsibilities of the medical staff and some of the responsibilities of the lay administration. In addition she had to centralize the administration of nursing affairs.'[13]

The Managers of the Royal Infirmary in Edinburgh set up a Committee of Enquiry which reported in March 1861. They 'were unanimously in favour of higher salaries to attract a better class of woman to the profession, a probationary period of training, the creation of a special training fund, and the appointment of a superintendent of nurses'.[14] A Mrs. Taylor was appointed to take charge of the nurses under the new Association for the Training of Nurses; she received permission to use three wards for her training programme. The Association was a philanthropic body which took responsibility for the salaries of the apprentice nurses, while the Royal Infirmary Managers were responsible for both bed and board. This initial arrangement lasted for over a year (1863) before the strains of dual authority proved too much. The Association asked permission to withdraw Mrs. Taylor from the wards, and the Managers thankfully acceded to the request, which saved them the embarrassment of suggesting it themselves. Later the Managers organised their own training scheme, and a Lady Superintendent of nurses was appointed.

At the Edinburgh Royal Infirmary until the beginning of the 1890's the nurses lived in 'the scattered quarters provided in dormitories in the attic floors of several of the pavilions of the hospital'.[15] The Managers inaugurated a special fund for a New Nursing Department, and in due course there were sufficient subscriptions to enable building to go ahead. Early in 1892 the home was opened; it was built of red brick and was known as the 'Red Home'. Each nurse was able to have a room to herself, with communal rooms and services also provided.

At the Glasgow Royal Infirmary lectures for nurses given by physicians and surgeons were introduced about 1875. But there were difficulties: lecture times were awkward, they removed nurses from the wards, and without any follow-up they may not have been of much use. In July 1878 the Managers appointed Mrs. Rebecca Strong (1843-1944) as Matron. Mrs. Strong was then a young widow who had trained at the Nightingale School at St. Thomas's Hospital, London — and then had gone as a pioneer nurse to various hospitals in the south. In 1867 she was appointed Matron to the Dundee Royal Infirmary. Her arrival in Dundee may have been engineered by the new Medical Superintendent, Dr. Sinclair, who was very keen to produce an efficient body of nurses for the Dundee Royal. Under the guidance of Dr. Sinclair and Mrs. Strong, Dundee developed some teaching for nurses, and a nurses' home was founded and built.

When Mrs. Strong arrived at the Glasgow Royal Infirmary in 1878, she found matters in a state of sad neglect. There was a 'lack of domestic help on the wards, poor feeding arrangements, nurses sleeping in nooks and crannies connected with the wards'. As a charming and persuasive woman of 36, she found the Managers willing to act. As she wrote, 'It was most encouraging to find how heartily they set to work to remedy matters as far as was in their power . . . things went on from step to step.'[16] But the Managers' co-operation stopped when she asked for a nurses' home. She knew that 'the work could not advance without it', and so resigned. She remained in Glasgow, running a nursing home for private patients, and considering the content of a proper educational course for the nurse 'if she was to meet the great advance that was being made both in medicine and surgery'. She had an ally in Professor (later Sir William) Macewen, with whom she discussed her plans.

The Managers of the Glasgow Royal Infirmary perhaps recognised that they had lost a good matron, for they built a nurses' home. In 1892 when the matron's post was again vacant, Mrs. Strong[17] was invited to apply and was re-appointed. In January 1893 she launched her preliminary training course lasting about three months. It was organised within the Glasgow Royal Infirmary, but was nevertheless independent of the hospital, its nursing certificates being granted by St. Mungo's Medical College.[18] Mrs. Strong's pioneering work in running training courses for women at Glasgow Royal Infirmary was a significant step forward in the development of the nursing service. But she herself never forgot the benevolent aspect of the work; she hoped that her girls would have 'grace to make these nameless sacrifices which must adorn each day'.[19]

Nurses were also being trained by some of the other Scottish voluntary hospitals by 1881. The Glasgow Maternity Hospital organised and ran its own scheme, admitting about 30 to 40 women a year 'as ladies' nurses and mid-wives'. These trainees paid an entry fee of £5, plus 8s. per week for board. The course lasted for four months, at the end of which there was an examination and a diploma for successful candidates. The course combined theory and practice: 'Three lectures by the physicians are delivered to the nurses during each week.' Practical training was in the care of the Matron. Each nurse had to attend 30 cases of labour, both indoor and outdoor, before she completed her course.[20]

In the Glasgow Sick Children's Hospital by the late 1880's nurses were divided into four classes: pupils, probationers, staff nurses and sisters. The pupils paid for their training. At the end of their period of service they could become probationers and serve as such for two further years. They could be taken on as salaried staff nurses and later become sisters. Over all the nursing and domestic staff presided the Lady Superintendent. In this Hospital the nursing staff's social status was explicit: 'All the nurses are ladies, who have been well educated, and in the hospital they are all on the same footing.'[21]

4. The nursing associations

Scotland was rather slow to organise nursing associations. All were philanthropically inspired. In England the initiative had been taken in 1859 when William Rathbone VI[22] had started the District Nursing Association in Liverpool. Under this scheme women were trained to be nurses with a view to working with patients in their homes. In Scotland in 1872 the Edinburgh Royal

Scottish Nursing Institution was founded and the Glasgow Training Home for Nurses was set up in the following year. From about 1875 both the Glasgow Sick Poor and Private Nursing Association, and the Association for Providing Trained Nurses for the West of Scotland, were functioning,

The aim of all these bodies was to teach women of a reasonable educational standard to nurse in patients' homes. The Association for Providing Trained Nurses for the West of Scotland had as its objects:

1. To provide trained and experienced women of high character to attend the sick poor in their own homes, and midwifery nurses to attend the very poor gratuitously, and the working classes at a moderate fee.
2. To provide thoroughly qualified nurses for private families who are able to pay for their services.
3. To improve the moral and professional qualifications of nurses for the sick among the poor, and in private families, by providing them with training in the wards of an hospital, with the regulations and comforts of a Home, in charge of a Lady Superintendent.[23]

The Glasgow Training Home was unusual in that two women sat on its council of 35 members and on the executive council of 13. One of these was Mrs. James S. Higginbotham (Mary Orrell Higginbotham) and the other was Miss Spence. The Glasgow Training Home for Nurses was a necessary initiative because the Royal Infirmary in Glasgow was so slow in adopting a modern pupil-nursing programme. Temporary premises were rented at 58 St. George's Road, Glasgow, and opened on 9 February 1874. Miss McAlpine was Lady Superintendent and Honorary Secretary.[24] The Glasgow Sick Poor and Private Nursing Association ran in harness with the Home. It administered the whole scheme, although there must have been conflicting demands on its services, making it difficult to allocate the nurses.

Those nurses who went to patients' homes brought to them a standard of care previously unknown. They reassured frightened people and reduced the demand for resident hospital care. But the exhausting nature of the work must have been discouraging to many. One of them confided to her diary the course of her day:

Tuesday, 10 a.m. — Margaret C. — Cancer of Breast. — Very ill today; suffering great pain; had restless night. Refilled water bed, gave hypodermic injection of morphia, dressed sores.

F.M'C. — Dressed ulcer; left dressings.

Mrs. T. — Cancer of Breast. — Made bed, washed patient, &c. Dressed sores with charcoal, linseed, and opium poultices, there being an offensive smell, and patient in great pain. Soaked bandages and poultice cloths, gave medicine, and showed little girl what to do during the day.

W.M. — Patient washed, bed made, room perfectly clean, dressings nicely prepared. Complaining of tenderness and heat in back — Washed it with spirits of wine, poulticed thigh, dressed foot with carbolic oil. Patient suffering from diarrhoea — Gave arrowroot and chlorodyne. (When first visited, patient was lying on a bare board on the floor, wrapped in rags and swarming with vermin, as were all the family. The house is now changed into one of the cleanest in the district.)

M.D. — Dressed leg; recommended warm bath, open windows, and general cleanliness.

James M. — New patient, twelve years old — Dropsy, Abscesses, Bedsores. Deserted by father and mother; kept by grandmother, who drinks. Had to borrow a neighbour's key to get in, the woman being in the habit of locking the child in by himself for hours, with nothing to eat but a few bits of stale crusts, soaked in water — even this often placed far beyond his reach. Room in horrible confusion; most offensive smell.

Home to lunch 1.30.

3 p.m. — Went back to James M. — Grandmother at home; exceedingly anxious to convince us that all in the house were teetotallers; very talkative, making many excuses for the state of matters on the score of her own health, which to us appeared anything but delicate. Washed child; put on a very old woollen shirt (which we brought with us) (no temptation to grandmother to pawn it), dressed sores, &c. Coaxed the grandmother to have clean sheets for us the next morning, and to keep the window open.

T.S. — Quite better. Off books.

G. — Suspicious case. Write to Sanitary Inspector.

Agnes. — Foot much worse. Take down line for Infirmary to-morrow.

J.C. — Called with dressings and whisky. Found patient lying dead — quite stiff and cold. Must have been dead a long time. Mother keeping the other children quiet, thinking he was having a good sleep. One of our oldest patients — felt very sad.

J.M.* — Changed under sheet; he has confidence in us now, and was not at all frightened, and was moved without any pain. When we were going away, M — said, 'It is not like being hanged now, is it?' He grasped her hand saying, in his poor weak voice (with the tears running down his cheeks), 'How is it that the likes of you spend your time helping the likes of me?'

Margaret C. again — Been very restless all day; Doctor been; left orders for second hypodermic injection; gave it; made beef tea; left it and brandy ready for night.

The following footnote was later added:

*John's right leg has been amputated at the thigh, for disease of the bone, which has now appeared in the left knee joint; he is dropsical, and so weak that the slightest movement causes intense agony. His father and mother are kind, and try to do all that lies in their power; but after he was brought home from the Infirmary, the mere trying to move him caused such weakness and suffering, that he was allowed to lie until a large bedsore had formed, and his sufferings much increased. The Bible Woman directed them to apply to the nurses, who took with them a waterbed, and went immediately. He was so terrified that it was almost impossible to do anything; it was only by telling him that the nurses were quite used to such things, and had often done them in the Hospital, that he consented. When it was done, and almost without pain, he looked up and said, 'When I saw ye's come in, I felt just as if I was going to be hanged,' which was always after the subject of a little joke.[25]

5. The Queen's Golden Jubilee

After 1889 the ambitions and expectations of the nursing associations were radically altered. In 1887 Queen Victoria had celebrated her Golden Jubilee, acclaimed by a people who regarded her with some astonishment and with deep affection. Women subscribed to the Women's Jubilee Offering, raising a sum of £82,000. After due consideration Her Majesty decided to use the money for the welfare of nursing and nursing establishments. On 20 September 1889 Queen Victoria's Jubilee Institute for Nurses was formally inaugurated by Royal Charter. There had been much controversy about the exact nature of the service to be provided. In the end both William Rathbone and Florence Nightingale were satisfied with a scheme which was to enlarge the horizons of the voluntary nurse-training movement by making it into a nationwide district nursing programme.

The Queen had a special interest in Scotland, partly because her daughter Princess Louise had recently married the Marquis of Lorne. Scotland and Ireland were at her insistence accorded the autonomy of separate councils for the co-ordination of nursing services.

As a result of the Queen's commitment to district nursing, it became the loyal duty of her subjects to bestir themselves and meet Her Majesty's wishes in terms of nursing services for their local communities. The movement became astonishingly widespread. By 1899[26] no fewer than 92 nursing associations were affiliated as branches to the Queen Victoria's Jubilee Institute for Nurses in Scotland. Virtually all these associations had been formed in the last decade of the century. With fewer than ten exceptions, the honorary secretaries were women, who were the social leaders of their local societies. The Duchess of Argyll ran the Inveraray branch, the Countess of Home the Douglasdale branch. The activities of branches were co-ordinated by the Scottish branch of the Queen Victoria's Jubilee Institute for Nurses, based in Edinburgh. It aimed at establishing and maintaining standards of service, training and salaries, and played a significant role in the expansion of district nursing services into all parts of Scotland.

The nursing profession was built up by women as a service to humanity and was unique among women's efforts towards professional involvement in that it 'possessed a negative advantage not shared by any other women's cause, educational, professional or political; it did not stimulate female competition in any male preserve'.[27] Notwithstanding that nursing was a secondary role in medical treatment, it was vital.

Care was needed in recruiting and then in training the new nurse. As an Edinburgh doctor urged: 'Spend the greatest strength in finding the right women and training them; when in office they will go beyond what you would require of them.'[28] It has been this ability 'to go beyond' which has always been the mark of an altruistic profession. As Mrs. Rebecca Strong of the Glasgow Royal Infirmary expressed it when addressing her nurses in 1893: 'If you follow these, the noble objects of your profession, in a proper spirit of love and kindness to your race, the pure light of benevolence will shed around the path of your toils and labours the brightness and beauty that will cheer you onwards and keep your steps from being weary in well-doing.'[29]

6. The female aspect

The rise of the nursing profession is an important part of the history of nineteenth-century women. It was their first mass assault upon a profession. They did not at first challenge the doctors directly, but offered themselves instead as auxiliaries. Soon there was to be a demand from women to be

Q

doctors also (see chapter 10, section 4, above), but the two were distinct. A male medical profession could carry on without women doctors, but by the 1880's it could make little real progress without women nurses. The Protestant outlook had enclosed women ever more tightly in the home; nursing offered an escape. Unmarried middle-class women, formerly totally dependent upon the homes of their fathers and brothers, could now find a new freedom in nurses' residences. However tough the matron might be, the residence offered a new life to women formerly constricted within the role of family spinster. Fathers and brothers, for their part, could only be persuaded to let such defenceless women out of their care if they were placed in the protective environment of the residences.

Such women were not paid much more than the domestic servants whom they formerly had at their beck and call. But they did receive money that was their own by virtue of having earned it. Because of the low level of their wages (even when residence was taken into account), they provided a kind of subsidy for the system, and without this combination of dedication and an urge to gain greater freedom the nursing response would have been very much less and medical services correspondingly arrested. In short the philanthropists, by their actions in helping to promote the nursing profession, drew upon a formerly wasted resource of work power, and at the same time wrought significant change in the role of women.

7. The sociology of the emergence of a profession

The conditions of emergence of a profession can be very powerful in determining its shape. This was certainly true of nursing. A number of interesting phenomena were involved.

The first of these had to do with the role of the hero. In this case there were two, Florence Nightingale and the Queen herself. Miss Nightingale dramatised a great national deficiency and dedicated much of her life to repairing it. She marks the entry of the major propagandist and the national lobbyist upon the health scene. Her reputation and her persistence had no parallel in the medical profession, nor perhaps in any other aspect of national life. But she did not seek to prepare the medical world for the implementation of the surgical revolution, for this she could not foresee. Her fight was against inefficiency; she was a kind of humanitarian Benthamite. It was round the lead given by her that the philanthropists could rally. The Queen in 1889 provided the second great impetus, making provision comprehensive.

Through the heroic role played by Miss Nightingale there emerged nursing as a national phenomenon in a way that no other side of medicine had done. Initiatives in other matters had been *ad hoc*, consisting of the formation of this institution or that, as described in chapters 8 to 12, but the nursing revolution was by way of being a national 'cause', a response affecting medicine as a whole and assimilating to it as an integral element.

By the same token, the nursing revolution was something largely powered from outside the medical profession. The doctors themselves were not capable of generating it. After all, they were busy men, working within limited resources. The very difficulties that confronted them, stemming from the lack of support services of which nursing was the chief, limited their capacity to think in terms of a radical new development. The nursing revolution had, therefore, to be largely exogenous, an interaction between Miss Nightingale and her associates and the philanthropists. Of course the pattern of a great many separate local initiatives had to develop in nursing as elsewhere, but there was a unity of intent, displaying itself in the drive to establish professional status for nurses.

NOTES

1. Woodham Smith, C., *Florence Nightingale* (London 1951); Huxley, E., *Florence Nightingale* (London 1975).
2. Bell, J., 'The Surgical Side of the Royal Infirmary 1854-92', *EHR*, Vol. I, 1893, 26-30.
3. See Jorns, A., *The Quakers as Pioneers in Social Work* (1931), and *Memoir of the Life of Elizabeth Fry*, edited by two of her daughters (London and Philadelphia 1847), ii, 405. It was from the Institution of Nursing Sisters (1840) that Florence Nightingale drew her nurses when she went to the Crimea.
4. Donnison, 1977, 68.
5. Anon., *Experimental Nurse Training at Glasgow Royal Infirmary* (Edinburgh HMSO, 1963), 1.
6. Nightingale, F., *Suggestions on the subject of Providing and Organising Nurses for the Sick Poor in Work-house Infirmaries* (London 1867), quoted in *Experimental Nurse Training . . .*, 1.
7. Bell, J., *loc. cit.*, 1893, 26-30.
8. *GRI*, AR (Glasgow 1880), 8-9.
9. *GMJ* (Glasgow 1878), 82.
10. Stewart, A. M., 1878, 11.
11. *GH*, 13 April 1906.
12. *GMJ* (Glasgow 1878), 85.
13. Abel-Smith, B., 1960, 25.
14. Logan Turner, E., 1937, 210.
15. *Ibid.*, 279.
16. Gordon, J. E., 'Distinguished British Nurses of the past. Mrs. Rebecca Strong — pioneer and centenarian, 1843-1944', *Midwife, Health Visitor and Community Nurse*, December 1975, Vol. II, 396.
17. See Strong, R., *Reminiscences* (London 1935).
18. See chapter 8, section 3.
19. Strong, R., 1893, 2.
20. *GMJ* (Glasgow 1888), 40.
21. McGeorge, 1889, 38.
22. Simey, 1951, chapter 5.
23. *Association for Providing Trained Nurses for the West of Scotland*, 4th AR (Glasgow 1879).
24. This home subsequently became the McAlpine Nursing Home in Hill Street and has recently been re-built as the Nuffield McAlpine Nursing Home in Beaconsfield Road in the west end of Glasgow.
25. *GMJ* (Glasgow 1878), 79.
26. Burdett, H. C., 1899, 685-688.
27. Stocks, 1960, 177.
28. *EMJ* (July-December 1886), 66.
29. Strong, 1893, 1.

PART V

Residence and Remedy

14
The Prostitutes

1. Residence as a basis for remedy

THE philanthropy of piety involved going out to those in need and reaching
into their lives, their setting and their homes. Similarly with education, where
the problem was to provide a range of facilities beyond those of the home. The
philanthropy of health was also based upon the principle of the extension of
facilities which the family could not provide.

But there was a range of challenges which seemed to require a different kind
of response, namely the provision of a substitute for the home itself. There
were three principal cases of this: the prostitutes, the orphans, and those
requiring special treatment such as the deaf, the blind and the crippled. In
these three areas the philanthropists, in order to remedy and ameliorate, took
women, children and sometimes men into direct care. But in no case was the
provision of surrogate homes the end of the matter: all three ranges of institution were intended to restore their occupants to society able, so far as possible,
to function as responsible citizens.

2. The philanthropic attack on prostitution

Philanthropists, however fastidious, could not ignore the presence of prostitutes[1] on the streets of Victorian cities. In the climate of the time it was a
shameful thing, reflecting on the middle-class vision of the woman as
daughter, wife and mother, and hence a deep affront to cherished values.
Moreover it raised frightening questions about Scottish manhood pre-marital,
marital and extra-marital. The high moral tone set by the Queen's court after
her marriage in 1840 reinforced the evangelical urge to attack what was
referred to obscurely as the 'Great Social Evil'.

Given the enormous expansion of the towns in Scotland and the consequent
social upheaval, the increase in prostitution was no doubt inevitable. Wage
rates paid to women were so low that many thousands were forced into prostitution, seasonally, temporarily or permanently, in order to survive. No consideration was given to the economic problems facing many women, except by
radicals like Owen and Engels. Yet the fear of the corrupting influence of such

women in society generated much attention. Bringing the problems of prostitution into public view was part of the new moralism;[2] the eighteenth-century laxity towards personal behaviour could no longer be reconciled with nineteenth-century evangelicalism. In the interests of both civic order and public health, reformers sought ways of dealing with fallen women.

The men who involved themselves in this type of work were self-impelled philanthropists.[3] Their personal commitment on behalf of the women of the streets was made in the name of their Christian conscience. Yet almost certainly their choice of charitable object reflected their own ambivalent attitudes. Although they were no doubt pure in their conscious motives, there could be a vicarious satisfaction in contact with sinful women. And yet moral courage was called for if there were to be any philanthropic response to a pressing problem.

The evangelicals were determined to clean up the streets of Scottish cities. This could be done in four main ways. There were attempts to alert public opinion by investigation, discussion and proposals aimed at generating higher standards of social and sexual behaviour in society at large. Means were sought of diverting women from the profession. In the face of the inevitable failure of prevention, attention turned to cure in the shape of Magdalene Societies and Asylums. Finally, campaigns were mounted for a stricter law by the promotion of various Police Acts to regulate the trade through civic authority. There was a complicated interaction between these four levels of response, varying with time and place.

All this, of course, fell far short of an attack on the basic nature of the problem: the philanthropists could do little more than act to suppress symptoms.

3. The publicists

The Scottish Victorian campaign against female prostitution was opened by two individuals, one medical and one clerical, in Edinburgh and Glasgow respectively. In 1842 William Tait,[4] a young doctor published *Magdalenism*.[5] The first edition was quickly sold out and the second was presented to the public in the same year by a gratified author. At almost the same time Dr. Ralph Wardlaw, a senior and respected Independent minister in Glasgow, as a result of 'a requisition signed by about 40 ministers of the Gospel and 11,000 fellow Christians', was prevailed upon to give four *Lectures on Female Prostitution*.[6] These were delivered in Glasgow in 1842 before a distinguished gathering of gentlemen, including the Lord Provost. They were regarded as so important that they were repeated to another appreciative audience in Edinburgh. The books by Tait and Wardlaw are long and laboured, using the same widely quoted figures which cannot be substantiated, but they give some idea of how the problem was viewed:

Table 35

Visits to houses of ill-fame in Glasgow, 1842

Number of Houses of ill-fame	450
Average Number of prostitutes (4 in each house)	1,800
Number of bullies or fancy men	1,350
Mistresses of said houses	450
Total living on prostitution	3,600
Number of men visiting each house weekly	80
Number visiting the 450 houses	36,000
The girls in the third or lowest class Houses receive on an average from each visitor 1/– making the sum weekly of	£1,800
Robberies 2/6d. weekly from each is the lowest average	4,500
Spent on drink 2/– weekly for each visitor	3,600
Total for Prostitution weekly	£9,900
Making a total annually of	£514,800

Source: Wardlaw, R., *Lectures on Female Prostitution* (Glasgow 1842), 122

For Edinburgh Dr. Tait quoted figures of between three and six thousand prostitutes in the city, although he suggested a figure of some 800 working full-time. He further speculated on 'sly' prostitutes, women in sedentary occupations or domestic servants or widows secretly selling their services. From these categories he derived a further 1,160 prostitutes.[7]

All the figures quoted by Wardlaw and Tait were guesswork, with a strong element of hearsay. This has not prevented more recent scholars from seizing eagerly upon them in an attempt to illustrate Victorian sexuality. But so far as Victorian Scotland was concerned, the accuracy of the figures was largely irrelevant. Both Tait and Wardlaw intended to shock, and in this they succeeded. They felt that the need for action was so imperative that some exaggeration was justified. A dual moral standard ensured that prostitution was seen by such men as a female failing, a viewpoint emphasised by the paucity of references in the writing of the day to the effect of male demand on the market.

In the sense of attempting comprehensive surveys, Tait and Wardlaw seem to have had no real Scottish successors. There are works by Bryce of Glasgow[8] and List of Edinburgh,[9] but Bryce especially is more concerned with the Magdalene institutions than with investigating the problem. There was, too, a set of articles in the *Scotsman* in the 1860's.[10] The Magdalene Societies in their Annual Reports produced their horror stories of social abandonment, seduction and death, with the procuresses prominent. In England the writings in the 1860's and 1870's of Dr. William Acton, a medical man of wide practical experience of the problem of prostitution, provide a better picture than was made available in Scotland, but even Acton's inquiries fall short of the Chadwickian kind of investigation conducted into other social questions. In the

Scottish case perhaps the first sign of a scientific approach came with the evidence of Margaret Irwin of the Glasgow Council for Women's Trades on the housing of working women in 1903.[11]

The philanthropists as investigators of prostitution were, therefore, not conspicuously successful and they may indeed have contributed to dubious statements made by subsequent authors. In addition to the emotive and attitudinal aspects of the subject, it was a difficult one from the data point of view — prostitution was hard to define and systematic observation was impossible to make. Even such a basic source as the reports of Chief Constables are full of ambiguities. Yet men like Tait and Wardlaw did succeed, to some degree, in making the public aware of the matter.

4. The Magdalene Asylums in Edinburgh and Glasgow

Magdalene Asylums were functioning in both Edinburgh and Glasgow by the second decade of the nineteenth century. They remained in existence for many years, providing shelter and retraining for hundreds of girls. At no time were they able to accommodate more than a fraction of those who might have been thought to be at risk according to the tables of Wardlaw and Tait. They were linked in Glasgow with the Lock Hospital, and in Edinburgh with the Lock Wards of the Royal Infirmary, for no diseased girl was supposed to be admitted to the Magdalene Asylums. Such Asylums were originally 'voluntary' charities, but from the powers which they took and used they came to be thought of as penal institutions. Increasingly in the later nineteenth century they became the instruments of the police, for by the Local Police Acts magistrates were encouraged to commit to them girls convicted of loitering and soliciting. Despite this they remained essentially philanthropic institutions.

The Edinburgh Magdalene Asylum was founded as part of the Philanthropic Society House in the Canongate in 1797. It remained on the same site for nearly 70 years, and was continually the object of much banter and rude humour. From the beginning, visiting ladies played a part in the inspection of the house. Their reports were full of the domestic detail, inconsequential and amateurish. 'The pot for the family's use' seemed to them to be too heavy, and 'in our apprehension exceeds the ability of any two women in the house to lift it off the fire, with its contents'.[12] This sympathetic attitude cannot have lasted long, for the visiting ladies were soon writing that 'The girls ought to be tasked'.[13] Later they asked 'how far it might be proper to try some stricking (sic) punishment in the house'.[14]

By the 1860's the directors knew that a new and larger building was required. But they were unable to settle on a site. The matter was resolved by Dr. Alexander, a generous benefactor, as well as the most active member of the Board. He found a site at Dalry and undertook most of the negotiations with the contractors, organised a bazaar and donated £1,000 to the new building. The move to the new site took place without incident on 2 April 1864, and the board of managers were pleasantly surprised at the ease of the operation.[15]

In Glasgow schemes to found a Magdalene Asylum around 1800 were abortive, but in 1812 a plan was put forward by the Glasgow Society for the Encouragement of Penitents, money was collected, and land was bought. A House was built (to the designs of James Cleland), in the north of the city, adjacent to the Glasgow Lunatic Asylum on Dobbies Loan, and it was opened on 9 February 1815: 'The interior is fitted up with every suitable accommodation for the matron, the committee and 34 penitents.' The House had two objects which might well have conflicted, 'one being to befriend boys in Bridewell and provide employment for them on leaving it, and the other to reclaim young females who had gone astray'.[16] The work with the boys was not successful and was soon abandoned. Between 1815 and 1840 the Magdalene received about 800 'penitents', and although many 'certainly belied the profession of penitence', there was also 'the most encouraging success'.[17]

By 1840 many young women and girls were being committed to the jail or the Bridewell in Glasgow for drunkenness, rowdiness and soliciting. In 1840 it was decided to establish a House of Refuge for Females, as distinct from the Magdalene, to supplement, by further private philanthropy, the facilities for committal by the Magistrates of women who came before them. But to some it seemed foolish to duplicate the facilities and a proposal was made to enlarge the well-established Magdalene so as to accommodate all the girls, whether committed or not, in one institution. It found favour.

Under this new arrangement three classes of women were to be admitted:

1. Females of more mature age, but under 25 years of age.
2. Females who may be committed to the jail and Bridewell, and who express a desire to be received into the Asylum.
3. Young Females who may, from extreme want and destitution, be in danger of being led astray.[18]

In 1840, as a consequence of the amalgamation, the Glasgow Magdalene ceased to exist, and from 12 October the Female House of Refuge effectively took its place. The acceptance of 'criminals' into the institution manifestly discouraged other girls. The genuine 'penitent' ceased to apply to the House of Refuge, which rapidly assumed the character of a penal institution. There were further complications: in 1838 a new initiative had been taken on behalf of juvenile delinquents (boys) in the form of a House of Refuge for them. It was soon suggested to the Secretary of the Magdalene, John Wright, that the two Houses of Refuge should be placed under the same management. He agreed, and the two organisations were brought together in 1841 by Act of Parliament. But there continued to be two institutions, one in Parliamentary Road for females, and one north of Annfield Place off Duke Street for males, which, under a common board of management, were supported partly by the rates and partly by voluntary annual contributions. Most of the young men and women entering them were committed by the Magistrates of the city.

A second society, similarly named the Glasgow Magdalene Institution, was established in 1859. It was widely believed that the association of the criminal elements in the House of Refuge discouraged those girls who might have applied to a Magdalene for succour and retraining. J. D. Bryce, who had been associated with the problem in Glasgow for many years, wrote persuasively in favour of the new Society.[19] It aimed to achieve 'the suppression of the resorts of profligacy, the abatement of the various agencies which contribute to the prevalence of prostitution in the City, and to provide temporary homes for females who have strayed from the paths of virtue'. The members thus constituted themselves as a kind of vigilante society who also ran a residential Asylum for reformed prostitutes.

The second Magdalene Society had a further objective not associated with its predecessor: this was 'the Repression of vice', as well as 'the Reformation of Penitent Females'. The preventive aspect was placed under a Repressive Committee. In the Society's Report of 1864, five years later, great prominence is given to 'the Repressive or Preventative branch, as being in itself the more important of the two'.[20] But it is difficult to believe that approaching women in the streets, in the manner of Mr. Gladstone, with a view to talking them into better ways had much success. Moreover, though the accompanying idea of saving fallen but penitent females was still credible, those who concerned themselves with this work were by the 1860's less optimistic than formerly.

The Society eventually opened two homes. One, located in Stirling Road, provided initial training. Suitable girls were later transferred for a full 3-year course to the Magdalene Asylum proper at Lochburn, Maryhill, built on an appropriately remote site beyond the Forth and Clyde Canal. In 1859 J. D. Bryce had advocated a series of small homes (on the cottage homes principle) rather than one large one, but the idea was rejected on grounds of economy and convenience.

Girls were usually in their late teens when admitted, and although accurate figures are rare, Bryce gives the following for the Glasgow Magdalene Asylum:

Table 36

Ages of girls admitted to Glasgow Magdalene Asylum between 1851 and 1859

	1851	1852	1853	1854	1855	1856	1857	1858	1859	Total
Under 16	7	4	2	2	1	2	2	6		26
Between 16 & 20	31	35	32	16	29	36	32	41	6	258
Over 20	9	11	20	17	14	19	10	16	7	123
	47	50	54	35	44	57	44	63	13	407

Source: Bryce, J. D., *The Glasgow Magdalene Asylum* (Glasgow 1859), 32.

By 1864 there were reported to be four institutions catering for such women in Glasgow,[21] and there were no doubt a similar number in Edinburgh. By 1901 there were reported to be as many as nine homes for 'penitents in Edinburgh'.[22] Many new small organisations anxious to help women at risk had become involved with this type of residential work.

5. Life in the Aslyums

The girls were admitted to the Magdalene Asylums at their own request and application, although many were encouraged by clergymen and others to apply. They were interviewed, often at great length, and their careers to date were taken into account. The committee tried to judge how genuine was the desire to reform; it tried to distinguish between girls from a rural setting who had been led astray, and those who had followed a 'career' of prostitution. In theory the first were to be accepted, while those who were 'hardened' were refused, but in practice committees could be easily hoodwinked.

The medical examination was a further hurdle. No girls were ever intentionally admitted who were diseased, otherwise disabled or pregnant. Infected girls were to be treated first in the Lock Hospital. But correct diagnosis proved very difficult, and in practice all types of sufferers were from time to time admitted. The committee also had to be convinced of the genuineness of the penitence. As the Edinburgh Magdalene Minutes report, 'Ann Johnson, aged 19 brought up in the Orphan's Hospital, was seduced about a year ago, now showing strong symptoms of contrition deserved to be admitted into the house — engaged to conform to its rules and if allowed willing to remain for four years.'

There were many girls who, once in, wanted out. The sequence seemed to be that girls desperate to find a haven were keen and applied for admission. They therefore presented as good a case to the interviewing committee as they could. The managers hastily dismissed those who were ill or troublesome, but those fit, well and amenable found it easy to get in and very hard to get out until the committee thought proper.

The girls entered into another world as they passed through the doors of the Magdalene Asylum. The Glasgow managers, 'being aware that the objects of this institution could not be obtained amid the bustle of active life have enclosed above an acre of ground by a high wall'. It was often policy to keep new arrivals in solitary confinement until they had settled down. Its duration varied, but it must have proved a sad shock to girls fresh from the noisy overcrowded houses of either Glasgow or Edinburgh.

On arrival they were given a hot or cold bath and issued with a uniform dress so that their outward appearance was completely changed. After 1834, when there was serious trouble in the Edinburgh Asylum, another practice was instituted: 'In order to repress that desire to get out, so often manifested at a very early period after admission, it was agreed that in future everyone on being admitted shall have her head shaved; as it is not probable that they will wish to leave the house in this state, it is hoped that the interval between the time of being shaved and the hair getting a length which they would like to appear in will afford opportunity of instilling into their minds some religious principle, which should they wish to go out may be of benefit on their again exposing themselves to the world.'[23] The cumulative effect of these assaults was intended to be similar to that of shock treatment. Everything associated with their previous loose life was to be abandoned and they were to turn their minds away from former enjoyments to the more sober realities of regular routine.

Once they were resident they were allocated to some form of work, usually heavy domestic labour, especially washing. The Edinburgh Magdalene Asylum was in effect an enormous laundry in which most of the girls laboured. The Glasgow Magdalene in its early days employed its girls 'in making Clothes for the Institution, sewing, tambouring, knitting, etc.' This kind of activity was almost always unproductive and indeed an expensive waste of good materials: 'Several of the Women, at their admission, had everything to learn, and had not only been idle, but ignorant of useful employment.'[24] Sewing could so easily be botched that they were soon switched to the laundry, but even there matters did not always run smoothly. Heriot's Hospital in Edinburgh complained to the Managers of the Magdalene that 'their clothes are badly washed and ill-done up: some of them much injured and the markings taken out by using Chloride or lime or some other chemical substance and a good many things lost altogether'. The matron responded with a tart denial and made an effective counter charge: 'They have very little cause for complaint . . . considering the state in which they are sent to the Asylum; hands scarcely being able to clean them.'[25] Laundry work continued to the end of Victoria's reign to be the industrial outlet for residential homes for 'fallen women'. Indeed the earnings from the laundry rapidly became the most important form of income. In 1901 they were:

	Income from Laundry	From other sources
Edinburgh Magdalene Asylum	£5,847	£493
Edinburgh Industrial Home for Fallen Women	£1,649	£158

Unfortunately for the girls, such institutions were excluded from inspection when the Factory Act of 1895 was passed. Some disquiet was expressed about the conditions under which the girls laboured. The Rev. Arthur Bruickman, who was Assistant Chaplain at St. Andrew's Home, Edinburgh, Chaplain at St. Agnes Hospital for the Fallen, and Chairman of the Church Mission for the Fallen, expressed his concern that the hours of work were 'irregular and long, especially in the laundry . . . Self-supporting homes need extra inspection, the temptation being to overwork the girls.'[26] All the domestic chores of the House were undertaken by the inmates, which seemed reasonable, as most of the girls would enter domestic employment. But factory jobs were more popular with the girls despite being regarded frostily by the managers.

The education given in the Magdalenes was based on Bible-reading, and the managers sought thereby to inculcate the evangelical traditions of the times. Life was indeed divided between work and prayer; meals and leisure time were short and attendance at morning and evening prayers was obligatory. Only religious pursuits were followed on Sundays, when ministers of the established church and 'Dissenters friendly to the Institution, have had the goodness to perform Divine Service in the Chapel of the Asylum'. In fact the chapel could be a source of charitable revenue. If a popular minister could be persuaded to preach, the chapel was crowded by many of the middle classes anxious to hear an inspired discourse, and perhaps there was a bonus in the form of a *frisson* of excitement caused by the proximity of the penitent women. Charity sermons were preached on anniversaries and holidays; these also provided revenue. The religious life of the Asylum community was organised by the Chaplain, who taught and exhorted the girls as well as planning these important fund-raising services.

The administration of the Asylum was a dual concern. A group of gentle-men acted as a managing committee, with which lay the main power; but ancillary women's committees existed in both Edinburgh and Glasgow. Perhaps in Edinburgh the women were given more scope: their reports as visitors were, in the early days, entered in the minute books. In Glasgow the ladies were restricted to a more limited role as collectors: 'The thanks of the Society were moved to those ladies who kindly interested themselves in procuring subscriptions for the Society.'[27]

The crucial appointment was that of the matron. She was usually a widowed woman of middle years, accountable to the managers, but exercising her own considerable authority. The managers appointed from among their own number a day or weekly committee which conscientiously visited the House. Some Managers gave a great deal of time to this; their well-meant daily interference must have proved a constant trial. If the matron were effective, she soon established her supremacy, and only a short-sighted committee would risk antagonising her. She was the lynch-pin of the establishment, creating tone and atmosphere as well as setting standards of efficiency. At first the matron coped on her own, but additional staff were soon necessary. If the washing were to be done properly or the 'white seams' sewed straight, constant watchfulness was essential. Two supervisors, who were responsible for the work done in the sewing and washing departments, were appointed. A porter or porteress was also necessary. Constant effort was required to keep the girls in and the curious out.

But the numbers involved in the Magdalene system were very small (see Table 37). Of those discharged, a handful went directly into domestic service (pre-sumably to places found by the institution); about half went to 'relations' and rather less than half 'left wilfully'. That is to say that out of the thousands of women at risk in Scotland only a few were, at any time, living in the Magdalene Asylums of Glasgow or Edinburgh. Even of these small number J.

Table 37

Glasgow Magdalene Asylum: admissions and discharges between 1851 and 1858

	1851	1852	1853	1854	1855	1856	1857	1858		Total
Inmates at the beginning of the year	55	47	65	54	68	64	57	54	27	
Admitted during year	39	68	43	49	40	50	41	36	25	391
Total	94	115	108	103	108	114	98	90	52	
Discharged during year	47	50	54	35	44	57	44	63	13	407
Remaining at close of year	47	65	54	68	64	57	54	27	39	

Source: Bryce, J. D., *The Glasgow Magdalene Asylum* (Glasgow 1859), 32.

D. Bryce wrote, 'Experience shows that of those leaving thus hopefully not more, perhaps, than a half, stand the trial of the world, and prove to be cases of lasting reformation.' To the pious evangelical the numbers may have been irrelevant, but to society at large the effort could hardly be said to be crowned with substantial reward. The Magdalene system made hardly a marginal difference to the problem of prostitution. But it is highly revealing of philanthropic attitudes.

6. Prostitution and the Police Acts

With the limited success of the publicists, the preventive persuaders and the Magdalene redeemers, it was inevitable that the most important form of control was seen as the law and the police.

The police indeed helped on the 'preventive' side. Part of the evangelical campaign of the city missionaries involved searching through the slums of the city at night for girls willing to be saved; William Logan,[28] one of the most assiduous night-walkers, always asked for and received police assistance in his midnight perambulations.

But there were increasing demands for more serious attacks on the problems of immorality, for prostitutes themselves were often believed to be associated with thieves and other anti-social elements in society. During the course of the second half of the century measures were taken to curb such undesirable activities. The General Police and Improvement (Scotland) Act[29] of 1862 was a wide-ranging piece of legislation designed to give enabling powers to burghs in Scotland to undertake a variety of tasks provided the citizens agreed. Among its many provisions (in Part V, Section IX) were those which could be taken against 'places of public resort and disorderly houses' and the persons associated with them. The measures included substantial fines and committal to prison if the offences persisted. The involvement of the police meant that prostitutes could, from the 1860's, be driven from the streets. Various burghs adopted the relevant sections of the 1862 Act. Greenock promoted the

Greenock Police and Improvement Act in 1865, so that the police chief could write, 'Prostitution still exists to a large extent in our midst, but it is neither so flagrant nor so offensive as it was previous to November 1865.'[30]

Glasgow and Edinburgh both acted to remove these women and their associates from the streets. By the Glasgow Police Act of 1856 police could take action against those who harboured prostitutes as well as those keeping a disorderly house. But the results seem meagre: in 1860, 12 men and 50 women were convicted of harbouring prostitutes.[31] In Edinburgh, by the Municipal and Police Act of 1879, brothels were closed and prostitutes turned out. But not everyone agreed that police action would be effective. Francis Cadell[32] remarked, 'the effect of such short-sighted legislation can only be to increase prostitution, disease and demoralisation.'[33]

The result of the Police Acts was an official pursuit of the prostitute, varying in form and severity among the cities of Scotland, but uniform in its ineffectiveness.

7. Employment, wages, marriage and prostitution

Throughout Victoria's reign the fundamental causes of prostitution continued untouched and uninvestigated. It was nurtured by the low wages paid to almost all women in gainful employment. While some of these women no doubt consorted with thieves and criminals, many were victims of a society which exploited women. Local employment opportunities and seasonal demands for female labour affected the supply of women for immoral purposes. The break-up of rural society and the presence of women on the urban labour market created conditions of over-supply. Employers pushed down women's wages with ease; few women could earn enough to keep themselves independently. Those who lived with family and friends fared best, for they enjoyed a hidden subsidy.

Both Wardlaw and Tait recognised the problem. Wardlaw believed that Edinburgh, with a smaller industrial base and therefore fewer factories, fared worse than other towns. He wrote: 'In Edinburgh there is not employment for above two thirds of the working female population, and in . . . the circumstances of Dundee, Glasgow and Paisley furnishing fewer prostitutes to Edinburgh in proportion to their population than the other large towns in Scotland, is sufficiently explained by these being manufacturing towns and providing much more employment.'[34] Dr. Tait referred to seasonal employment, or the lack of it, swelling the ranks of those willing to prostitute themselves. As he explained, 'In summer there are one-third fewer than in winter; and in the autumn the number is still further diminished.' In addition Dr. Tait refers to the part-time prostitute: 'These belong generally to the class of dress-makers, sewers, bonnet-makers, book-stitchers, shop girls, house servants and fish-wives.'[35] Professor James Miller[36] spoke very plainly: 'It is a shame that honest industrious able-bodied women, labouring with painful industry from morning to night, or oft-times far into the night cannot make a living; and may, from this cause alone, be driven into vice and self-abasement.' In Aberdeen it was recognised by some that 'the stoppage of the manufactories' caused by 'the pressure of the times' led to 'great and protracted suffering before the unhappy victims yielded to the temptations by which they were assailed'.

It was widely believed in early Victorian times that prostitutes followed a short, hectic career to the grave. Tait accepted that 'Perhaps not less than a fifth or a sixth part of all who have embraced a life of prostitution die annually.' But he was probably wrong. William Acton, the most widely known English authority, took a more optimistic line: 'It was a popular error that these women died young, and made their exit from life in hospitals and poor-houses. The facts were not so. Women of that class were all picked lives, and dissipation did not usually kill them. They lived a life of prostitution for two, three or four years, and then either married, or got into some service or employment and gradually became amalgamated with society.'[37] Acton continued: 'Prostitution is a transitory state through which an untold number of British women are ever on their passage.'

It is only fair to Tait to say that the re-absorption into respectable society of women forced to become temporary prostitutes may have been easier in England. Indeed the rigid social mores of Scotland which damned a girl who had once sinned may have made it difficult for her to re-enter conventional society.

The campaign against the prostitute was so bitter and long-lasting because she represented an attack on marriage and the family. Robert Owen had horrified Dr. Ralph Wardlaw by his comments on the restrictive nature of marriage when he wrote in the early 1840's 'that the present marriages of all the world are the sole cause of all the prostitution, of its incalculable grievous evils'.[38] Both marriage and the family had to be protected at all costs, for they were the bulwarks of society, protecting the nation not only from sin but from social chaos.

NOTES

1. There are serious difficulties about defining prostitution, although most would agree that it usually involved indiscriminate or promiscuous sexual relationships for which reward in cash or kind is given. See Benjamin, H., and Masters., R. E. L., *Prostitution and Morality* (London 1965), Morton, R. S. *Venereal Diseases* (London 1966), and Morton, R. S., 'Some Aspects of the Early History of Syphilis in Scotland', *British Journal of Venereal Diseases* (1962), 38.175. Dr. Ralph Wardlaw defined it as follows: 'The evil then . . . is *the illicit intercourse of the sexes*. The female who submits to this is guilty of prostitution. The very first offence is prostitution.' Wardlaw, R., 1842, 17. His harsh view was most likely the general one of respectable society in nineteenth-century Glasgow.
2. Young, G. M., 1936, 4.

R

3. The most famous of these was W. E. Gladstone who, throughout his adult life, dedicated some of his leisure time to this type of work, and who was given nick-names including 'Daddy do nothing' and 'Old glad eyes'; see Marlow, J., *Mr. & Mrs. Gladstone* (London 1976), 250.

4. Tait, W., Edinburgh. LRCS, 1842, surgeon to the Midwifery Dispensary at High School Yards, Edinburgh, and house surgeon to the Edinburgh Lock Hospital in 1841.

5. From Mary Magdalene, a native of Magdala, Tiberias. The Magdalen Hospital in London was founded in 1758. See Dingley, R., *Proposals for Establishing a Public Place of Reception for Penitent Prostitutes* (London 1758); Rodgers, Betsy, *Cloak of Charity* (London 1949).

6. Wardlaw, 1842.

7. Tait, W., 1842, 9.

8. Bryce, J. D., 1859.

9. List, A. C. C., 1861.

10. Strachan, J. M., 'Immorality in Scotland', *Scotsman*, 20 May, 2, 7 June 1870.

11. *Glasgow Municipal Commission on the Housing of the Poor* (Glasgow, n.d. but 1903).

12. PSHR, 16 May 1799.

13. *Ibid.*, 30 May 1799.

14. *Ibid.*, 19 May, n.d. but probably 1800.

15. EMAM, 13 April 1864.

16. Bryce, J. D., 1859, 3.

17. *House of Refuge for Females, Parliamentary Road, Glasgow*, AR (Glasgow 1840), 3.

18. Bryce, J. D., 1859, 4.

19. *Ibid.*, 35.

20. *Glasgow Magdalene Asylum*, AR (Glasgow 1864), 7.

21. EMAM, 2 May 1864.

22. See Roxburgh, J. R., *Edinburgh Philanthropic Red Book* (Edinburgh 1901).

23. EMAM, 17 January 1835.

24. Cleland, J., 1816, 251.

25. EMAM, 27 March 1863.

26. *Life in the Laundry*, Fabian Tract No. 112 (London 1920), 10.

27. *Glasgow Magdalene Asylum*, AR, 22 June 1820, 13.

28. Logan, W., 1843, and 1871.

29. 25 and 26 Victoria, Cap. 101.

30. Logan, W., 1871, 94.

31. *City of Glasgow Police Returns* (Glasgow 1860), 8-9.

32. Francis Cadell was Lecturer in Venereal Disease in the University of Edinburgh.

33. Cadell, F., 1881, 3.

34. Wardlaw, 1842, 108.

35. Tait, 1842, 2, 3.

36. Miller, J., 1859. Professor Miller held the Chair of Surgery in the University of Edinburgh and was much concerned with pietistic and medical charities.

37. Acton, W., *Prostitution* (London 1857). See also Parent-Duchatelet, A. J. B., *De la Prostitution dans la ville de Paris . . .* (Paris 1837).

38. Morton, A. L., *The Life and Ideas of Robert Owen* (London 1962), 161; the quotation is from Owen, R., *Lectures on the Marriage of the Priesthood of the Old Immoral World*, 4th ed., 1841.

15

Reformatories, Ragged Schools, Industrial Brigades and Training Ships

1. The challenge of abandoned or fugitive children

WITH the growth of urbanised living in Victorian Scotland came a great increase in the numbers of unattached children in the city streets, orphaned, abandoned, or fugitives from bad homes. Sad products of temporary or unstable liaisons, or victims of family misfortune, they scrummaged for a living by begging, by petty theft or by busking. If their ballad singing and cartwheel turning failed to produce contributions from the passers-by, they were forced into pilfering to keep themselves alive. Many of those who survived developed a remarkable resourcefulness, but they became a plague in the towns where they lived. Apart from their skills in begging or stealing, they knew nothing. Because of their way of life they were so dirty and ragged that no respectable person could tolerate their proximity. And of course they were permanently hungry. Before their restoration to civil society could even begin, they had to be fed, regularly and plentifully, washed and cleaned and their infested clothing replaced. Thereafter it was possible to consider their education and training for a job.

Officers of the law in the growing urban complexes of Scotland were increasingly disturbed by the failure of society to offer any constructive programme for these boys and girls, trapped in their own ignorance and unable because of their disadvantages to move into any worthwhile activity. Both in Glasgow and Aberdeen there arose a plea for some ameliorative reform (see below). A few enthusiasts decided to try to feed and educate the children.

The ostensible provision for such children lay in the poor law. But it was ill attuned to their needs; indeed the street arabs were fugitives from all official intervention. An entirely new range of initiatives was required to do any good with these ragamuffins and in Victorian society only the philanthropists could provide it.

They did so in various ways based on the residential or supervisory principle coupled with agencies for the generation of a sense of identity, both in personal and in group terms. The chief of these were the Ragged Schools (or 'Reformatories'), Houses of Refuge, Industrial Brigades and Training Ships.

2. The Ragged Schools

The Ragged Schools began as an educational project, and initially they were not residential: young people entered them in early morning and were kept until late evening. Attendance was ensured by the provision of three meals a day. But almost at once the organisers found that they had pupils who had nowhere to go at night. So lodgings had to be arranged. This inevitably resulted in all sorts of marshalling problems. It was a formidable step from the Ragged Day School to the residential institution, and in many cases it was taken with the aim of simplifying the complications of education, without due appreciation of the additional difficulties of providing residences and their attendant problems.

These residential institutions were all run by voluntary bodies. They continued to be so considered, despite the later involvement of state money and state inspection and some state control. Voluntary operation was being officially encouraged as late as 1896, when the inquiry of that year stated: 'Whatever credit, therefore attaches to these institutions may be said to belong to the voluntary managers . . .'[1]

Scotland produced two philanthropic leaders of the Ragged School movement, Sheriff Watson of Aberdeen and the Rev. Thomas Guthrie of Edinburgh.

3. Sheriff Watson in Aberdeen

The Ragged School movement in Scotland was largely the work of Christian evangelicals. They held the same sort of views as Lord Shaftesbury, who was much involved with the movement in England.[2] In Scotland, however, the Ragged Schools quickly developed into Industrial Schools and Reformatories, while many in England continued to be small feeding schools. The Scottish initiative for Ragged Schools came from Sheriff Watson, one of a group of Aberdeen evangelicals. He, disturbed by the number of children brought before him for petty offences, and being unwilling to commit them to the Bridewell (the common prison), came to the view that positive action should be taken.

The 'Children's Sheriff' recognised that conventional barriers would have to be crossed to reach these children. He soon identified the areas of need; as he wrote, 'We have seventy-five children in process of cleansing, scrubbing, dressing and feeding', while they were taught a useful trade. His friend, Alexander Thomson (1798-1868), another Aberdeen evangelical, insisted that 'It is manifest mockery to offer a starving child training or instruction, without first providing him with food.'[3]

At an enquiry instituted by the police in Aberdeen in June 1841, it was revealed that 280 children under 14 years of age maintained themselves in the city by begging or stealing, and that 77 had been committed to prison for one crime or another in the previous year. It was for these children that Watson's schools attempted to cater. The first was promptly founded following the report. Their motto was 'Train up a child in the way he should go and when he is old he will not depart from it' (Proverbs XXII, 6). They aimed also to inculcate a modest success ethic: 'To give (a boy) any thing like the prospect of equality, in the bustling struggle of life, with those whose lot has been within the easy reach of these attainments, he must be taught reading, writing and arithmetic; without these, he can never rise above the lowest level in society constituted as that of Britain now is.' But religion was paramount. As Alexander Thomson explained, the Bible was to be the source of educational inspiration: 'Lastly, however, and principally, he must be furnished with ample religious instruction, drawn from the pure source of the Bible alone.'[4] This was provided by much missionary effort.

The working day was punctuated by three substantial meals. But any one of these was forfeited if the child were not in school for that part of the working day which preceded it. In the initial stages of training it was not too difficult to find simple tasks which the boys could do, but it was a constant problem to find 'industrial training' which would be of value once the 'reformatory' period was over. The managers favoured trades such as shoe-making, tailoring, printing and gardening. Education, diet and industrial training were thus combined: in Aberdeen the title *Industrial Feeding School* was used.

There was considerable controversy over the residential principle. Many believed that better results ensued when children were under continuous care. But Sheriff Watson himself did not take this view. He claimed that children, far from being influenced by bad conditions at home, acted as a leavening agent with their elders. 'It was proved,' he wrote, 'that parents had been greatly improved by the influence of their children.'[5] Those of strong Christian faith continued to press for daily rather than residential attendance at Industrial Schools on the grounds that the family unit should remain inviolate.

The Aberdeen Industrial Schools became a focus of controversy after the Disruption in 1843. When Sheriff Watson's Female Industrial School was opened in 1843 it was almost immediately in trouble and was re-organised into two units to satisfy the demands of the Free Church.[6]

4. Rev. Dr. Thomas Guthrie in Edinburgh

Sheriff Watson was the quiet hero of the Industrial Feeding Schools in Aberdeen. But the real publicist for Scotland as a whole was the Rev. Dr. Thomas Guthrie of Edinburgh. He espoused the cause and made it his own, pleading eloquently, 'What teacher could have the heart to punish a child who has not broken his fast that day? What man of sense would mock with books a boy who is starving for bread? Let Christian men answer the Lord's question;

. . . "What father if his child asked for bread, would give him a stone?" And what is English grammar, or the Rule of Three, or the ABC to a hungry child but a stone?'[7] Guthrie's flood of pamphlets was well calculated to arouse the sympathies of the reader, based as they were on appeals to save the perishing children of the slums.

As a result of the great stir caused by the publication of Guthrie's *Seed-Time and Harvest or a Plea for Ragged Schools*, the Ragged or Industrial School Association was formed in 1847 in Edinburgh. Mr. Smith, Governor of the Edinburgh prison, one of the many law officers who supported the movement, wrote, 'During the last three years, 740 children under fourteen years of age had been committed to this prison for crime. Of that number 245 were under ten years of age.'

Within the first year three Ragged Schools were opened in Edinburgh: Ramsay Lane, Castle Hill (105 boys), 533 Lawnmarket (90 girls), and Warriston Close (70 children under 10 years of age). Food, education and industrial training were given. Clothing was necessary if on entry applicants had to be bathed and stripped of their verminous rags. In the beginning shelter was provided only if a child had no home. The committee organised 'lodgings with respectable parties who take charge of them at night and report upon their conduct'.[8] But arranging for lodgings was not easy and 'respectable parties' were increasingly difficult to find, so that organisers of Ragged Schools were soon pushed into providing residential premises.

The Association was conceived on a high moral plane, being 'Founded in love, attended with hope, . . . calculated under the blessing of God, to lead directly to grace and peace.' But discord appeared with dramatic suddenness. The rock on which the movement foundered was the nature of the religious teaching. The Association had originally welcomed all children, regardless of their possible religious affiliation. But in so doing it fell foul of the hierarchy of the Roman Catholic Church, which believed that many of the scholars came from Catholic families and so should receive Catholic religious instruction if they were to receive instruction at all. This response was offensive to Guthrie and his supporters and led to many meetings and much correspondence in the *Scotsman*. Thus the endemic religious debate that haunted education programmes generally, overtook the Ragged Schools. The issue at stake was a simple one. Although the Christian education offered in the Ragged Schools in Edinburgh was non-denominational, it was Protestant. Would Rev. Guthrie allow the religious teaching to be organised by both protestant ministers and catholic priests? He would not. Compromise was unlikely on so emotive a subject.

The outcome was the establishment in 1848 by the Roman Catholics of the United Industrial Schools of Edinburgh, in competition with the original Ragged School Association. The President was Lord Murray and the Vice-President Bishop Carruthers, the Roman Catholic Bishop of Edinburgh. Religious education was to be handled by two committees representing the protestants and the catholics and was to be completely divorced from the secular teaching of the schools. This dispute became a *cause célèbre* in the Edinburgh of the day and provoked much bitter comment.

In retrospect the intransigence of both presbyterian and catholic philanthropists over this matter may seem obsessive and obtuse, but it was deeply rooted in the history of the country. Moreover, starving Irish families, victims of the famine, were pouring into Scotland, and although larger numbers settled in Glasgow and the West of Scotland, many thousands searched for work and livelihood in Edinburgh. No doubt they included pious catholic families with close and genuine affiliation to their church who were not, as Guthrie tended to imply, lapsed catholics whose allegiance to their church was nugatory. Thus the heated response of the catholic community in Edinburgh was perhaps not so perverse as its opponents implied.

5. The Glasgow House of Refuge for Boys

Sheriff Watson was not the only Scotsman whose concern for the boys of the street arose directly from his connection with the law and the prison system. As early as 1829, William Brebner, Governor of Glasgow City Bridewell, pleaded for a new institution to take over the punishment and reform of juvenile prisoners.[9] At this time young offenders, if convicted, could only be housed in the Bridewell. Mr. Brebner's plea was supported by Mr. Miller, the Superintendent of Police. As a result there was a public appeal which produced the handsome sum of £10,000. The managers were able to commission Mr. Bryce to design an institution which was erected on a site to the north of the east end of Duke Street. The doors of the Glasgow House of Refuge for Boys opened on 18 February 1838.

It seems almost certain that from the beginning Glasgow magistrates committed convicted young offenders to the Refuge.[10] Numbers grew very rapidly; soon there were 200 boys in residence. The importance of the Refuge, and the speed with which it became an integral part of the city's provision for delinquents, soon brought the realisation that though the voluntary principle could be instrumental in founding the home, it could not sustain it. Steps were taken in 1840 to obtain an Act of Parliament to raise a small assessment from the rates to support the Refuge; the Act was passed in 1841. However, the amount raised by the assessment fell short of the requirement and philanthropy was again appealed to: 'Another subscription was entered into — forty-six gentlemen agreeing to contribute £10 a year each for three years.'[11]

Thus financed, the future of the Boys' House of Refuge was assured. The magistrates and police made full use of its facilities. Boys were mostly committed for stealing or picking pockets, for many had 'a great desire for sweetmeats and shows'.[12]

The Refuge proposed to make three kinds of provision for each boy:

1. To give him such intellectual training as will fit him intelligently to act his part in whatever circumstances Providence may be pleased to place him.
2. To train him to industrious habits, by learning such trades or occupations as will afterwards enable him honourably to support himself in the world; and
3. To aid him in acquiring a good moral character, and in sending him back to the world an honest and useful member of society.

The Refuge was the first 'Reformatory' established in Scotland, and so predates both the Ragged and Industrial Schools, both of which had 'reforming' intentions. The only other such institution in Britain at the time was the Juvenile Prison at Parkhurst (1838), to which selected boy prisoners could be sent for their 'effective punishment and timely reformation'.[13] The aims and objectives of the Glasgow Refuge were basically similar to those of the Ragged Schools. But because the Glasgow Refuge was a hybrid, combining elements of the philanthropic and the municipal, it was not consciously thought of as a model for the Ragged Schools. The Glasgow initiative, therefore, does not deprive Sheriff Watson of his status as the initiator of Ragged Schools.

Notwithstanding the existence of the Glasgow Refuge, there was a strong move for Ragged or Industrial Schools to be organised in the city. The first such school in Glasgow was opened in 1847 in the building occupied by the Night Asylum. But in 1850 premises were erected in Rottenrow which acted as a centre for all the Ragged School children. Glasgow at this date did not make any attempt to house the children.

Glasgow reformatory facilities were enlarged after 1859 when the Buchanan Institution was founded. James Buchanan had left charitable money for 'Ragged School' purposes providing the city would co-operate with his trustees and supply a building. It became a hybrid institution, with philanthropic and public money, and with aims similar to those of the Ragged Schools. It was regarded favourably in Glasgow at the time as 'a bold attempt to meet the case of the lowest class in society'. The Institution was conducted on the 'social principle', the boys going home at night. In his trust deed Buchanan laid on the city of Glasgow the obligation of providing and maintaining a building for his Institution. It thus became a joint responsibility of the city and the trustees, by negotiation between the donor and the city corporation.

Many of the Buchanan boys were being brought up by widowed mothers, who were glad to have them fed and educated by the Institution. The industrial training was usually shoe-making, tailoring and carpentry, although few continued in their trade after they left. The work produced was not readily saleable, so that the industrial departments operated at a loss. Indeed in the end most of the items made were used to clothe the scholars themselves. The general education given to the boys was criticised by the Assistant Commissioner on Endowed Schools and Hospitals who examined the pupils in February 1874.[14]

6. Government intervention

Ragged Schools appealed greatly to sheriffs and police officers throughout Scotland, for every town had its quota of waifs and strays wandering the streets and living by their wits. Thoughtful citizens were favourably impressed by the Aberdeen initiative when they read how the streets of that city were no longer cluttered with children begging and stealing in order to survive. It was an attractive cause: for the belief that the young were malleable and could be reformed without too much difficulty was very popular. Therefore Glasgow, Perth, Dundee, Dumfries, Ayr, Paisley, Stranraer, Inverness and Arbroath as well as Aberdeen and Edinburgh all had Ragged or Industrial Schools by 1853.

But when the initial excitement had died away the underlying problem was revealed: it was one of discipline. Although starving children were prepared to give up their freedom for three substantial meals a day, the regimen soon palled. Each school day was some twelve hours long. It included, say, five hours of industrial employment and four hours of education, with three hours for meals and recreation, all under strict discipline. Children began to truant in large numbers, although this was partly disguised by other hungry children willing to take the vacated places. Having an industrial school with a constant turnover of scholars meant not only that the young were inadequately educated, but also that 'industrial' production was held up, as new training had constantly to be given. This became particularly serious because the financial viability of such schools depended on the amount of income received from the workshops, as well as from the voluntary subscriptions. It was also frustrating and discouraging for the teachers and organisers.

Strong pressure built up to transform these day schools into residential institutions. This was a fundamental shift of position. It represented the acknowledgement of a change to authoritarianism and coercion and affected both Industrial Schools (for children under 14) and Reformatories (for those over 14). School authorities had to go to various lengths to 'persuade' the inmates to stay, for they were always 'eloping'. The outcome was the direct involvement of the forces of law and order and the committal by the authorities, as delinquents, of children and young persons to Industrial Schools. The Schools, begun with such high hopes, became in fact penal institutions.

Because of the apparent need to protect society from these troublesome young people, it seemed a satisfactory solution to incarcerate possible juvenile offenders. In 1855, therefore, the government acted in Scotland (though not in England) to give legal status to these Reformatories. Under Act 17 and 18 Victoria cap. 74 — Dunlop's Act — they could be registered (and inspected?), and the courts were authorised by statute to commit convicted youngsters to them, instead of to prisons.

The Glasgow authorities did not turn their Ragged Schools into residential schools until after 1855. A revised Act was passed in 1866; the numbers of

children thereafter committed to the care of the Industrial and Reformatory
Schools Society of Glasgow increased rapidly:

1866	256
1867	291
1868	459
1869	615

The growth in numbers so strained the accommodation of the schools that
measures had to be taken to secure larger premises. A site of 16 acres, the
estate of Mossbank, was obtained at Hogganfield. The boys moved to the new
building and the girls remained at Rottenrow. By December 1870 there were
646 inmates in the homes, 407 boys and 221 girls; in addition there were 4 boys
and 14 girls there voluntarily (or put there by their parents). Despite the
apparent official takeover, these institutions still collected subscriptions and
had the full panoply of managers of the philanthropic society.

When the Reformatory and Industrial Schools Committee presented its
report to both houses of Parliament in 1896, the system of Industrial (Day and
Residential) Schools and Reformatories was an extraordinary amalgam of
voluntary and statutory elements. There were in Scotland 6 reformatories for
boys, 2 for girls, 11 Industrial Schools for boys, 7 Industrial Schools for girls,
plus 3 day industrial schools in Glasgow. Voluntary contributions were still an
essential element of their finances, although more so in Scotland than in
England. James G. Legge, one of Her Majesty's Inspectors, commented that
'Private subscriptions and legacies in Scotland in the aggregate are proportion-
ally higher than in England . . . a few fortunate schools get more than they
absolutely need while others get scarcely anything . . . and have to resort to
too free use of such things as bands of pipers, dancers, trick performers . . .
with a view to bringing in a profit . . . Other less fortunate schools with less
enterprise are endeavouring to drag along on little more than the Government
grant.'[15]

The Committee on Reformatory and Industrial Schools of 1896 declined to
recommend that the voluntary managers be replaced by state administration.
As they explained, 'The greatest blessing that could be conferred on the
schools would be that more and more interest should be taken in them by
persons of refinement, education and benevolent interest not merely in the
financial and administrative affairs of the school, but in the life of the school,
in the superintendent, staff and children.'[16]

When Victoria died, the state was still working in tandem with the benevolent in running many of the Industrial Schools and Reformatories for young
people. Those citizens who continued to give their time and money to such
activities were performing an important philanthropic function in safe-
guarding institutions always open to abuse.

7. The Industrial Brigades

In the 1860's, although the Industrial Schools, Ragged Schools and Reformatories had been at work for nearly a generation, the cities of Scotland were still swarming with young boys who survived by begging or thieving or by holding horses, carrying parcels, selling matches or cleaning shoes. In London 'Brigades' had been established, such as the Shoe Black Brigade, which provided boys with some stock-in-trade and rudimentary elements of a uniform. They were thus made to look more respectable and more attractive to clients. In Scotland such Brigades were organised by William Quarrier of Glasgow, David Harris of Edinburgh and Sheriff Watson of Aberdeen.

William Quarrier wrote to the *Glasgow Herald* on 20 November 1864, praising the Shoe Black Brigade in London and reminding Glasgow readers that such an organisation was much needed in the city. The Lord Provost supported Quarrier, and at a public meeting sponsored by him the Glasgow Shoe Black Brigade was launched. Fifteen boys were recruited. They were measured for their outfits, supplied with the necessary equipment and sent out to seek business. A night school was established in Jamaica Street where 'an old soldier, who had the reputation of being a good disciplinarian, was appointed schoolmaster',[17] but the veteran succumbed to drink and had to be dismissed.

Quarrier, enthusiastic about the success of his efforts, soon expanded and organised both News and Parcel Brigades. The boys were provided with bags and articles of uniform so that they could be recognised while going about their business. They handed over their whole earnings to the Brigades and received a fixed wage in return. Later a hostel at 114 Trongate was opened to house those who were homeless.

In Edinburgh in September 1867 David Harris called a meeting of interested parties to see if there were sufficient support for the establishment of a Brigade in that city. His ambition was to develop an after-care service for those boys over the age of fourteen who had already been trained in Ragged Schools. As this would have been confined to a rather narrow range of boys, the proposal was extended to include those 'street arabs' who were over the age of fourteen and had not been in Industrial Schools. There was some confusion over the aims of the Edinburgh Brigade (which also had a residential home). Dr. Guthrie eventually became a supporter of the Brigade. As he explained, 'No boy is to be received into the Brigade who is admissible into the Ragged School. In that way you avoid coming into collision with the Ragged School.'[18]

The Edinburgh organisers regarded their Brigade as a stepping stone towards something better (see Appendix VII for their regulations). As the *Scotsman* reported, 'The chief object of the movement is to reclaim these boys as quickly as possible from an idle street life, and those who give promise of improvement are only employed as shoe-blacks until better, more constant, and more skilled work can be procured for them. Thus two of the boys have

got situations in chemists' shops, where they have every prospect of advancement, others have been sent to grocers, others to bakers, one has gone to the
drapery business, another is a clerk, another a blacksmith, another a painter,
another a stone-mason and one — spoken of as a remarkably fine fellow —
has gone to sea.'[19]

These Brigades were of minor consequence because they enlisted very few
boys. Only a fraction were willing to sacrifice their freedom for the discipline
imposed by Brigade membership. The organisers of Ragged Schools and Industrial Schools (who most often imposed a twenty-four hour control on their
inmates) were worried that the Brigades would damage their intake by
appealing to boys whose dislike of restraint would keep them on the streets. It
was a groundless fear. In any case the men organising the groups could only
cope with a small proportion of the boys running around the towns.

Yet the Brigades did have a role, not only in helping one element of the out-
casts of the cities, but indirectly in focusing attention on the continuing
problem of 'street arabs'. Quarrier knew very well the limitations of his
Brigades. Despite the favourable publicity which they had received when
started, they might merely be placing boys in petty jobs without permanent
prospects. Quarrier in consequence moved from the Brigades to homes for
orphans and then quickly into the field of emigration (see chapter 16 below).

8. Training Ships

The Training Ship as a method of teaching young men was introduced after
the Crimean War (1854-56), when the extent of British naval unpreparedness
was revealed. The system was officially established by Admiralty Circular on
1 September 1857, first in the *Illustrious* and later in the more commodious
Britannia.[20] At first it was intended for cadets who would in course of time
become midshipmen and were officer class. But the idea of making 'the
training ship, school and ship into one seemed a good one, readily adaptable
to other types of boy'. So the *Arethusa*, attached to Lord Shaftesbury's Ragged
Schools, began work as a training ship in 1866.

In the years following, Scottish philanthropists took up the idea and acted
with vigour so that by the 1890's Scotland had at least four such vessels of its
own. The *Mars* was based at Dundee, and the *Empress* and the *Cumberland*[21]
were at the Gareloch (from May 1869). In addition the *James Arthur*[22] was
firmly established (on land) at William Quarrier's Homes at Bridge of Weir.

Although the Training Ships were normally anchored at some sheltered and
convenient place, they did not put to sea with their complement of boys. The
training in seamanship was usually done in a sea-going tender attached to the
mother ship. For boys attached to the *James Arthur*, experience on water was
gained by working with 'two small boats' on the Gryffe (the local stream,
where boys were taught rowing and how to manoeuvre boats under sail).

Stephen Jeans described the *Cumberland* as 'an institution which, in its proved results, has done more than all the rest of our industrial institutions put together to reform our Street Arabs'.[23] At the end of 1878 the *Cumberland* had 348 boys on board. Captain Alston reported to the executive committee that 'Of these 348, two-thirds were found to be fatherless, half motherless and one-third orphans; 90 fatherless and destitute, 120 going about idle, 138 frequenting bad company and commencing criminal courses.'[24]

Although William Quarrier's aim was 'to train the best boys in the Homes to be working missionary seamen for the mercantile navy', this laudable objective was not met so often as the organisers would have wished. There was considerable discussion in the 1890's when it was revealed that less than half the boys assigned to the *Mars* and the *Empress* subsequently signed on as seamen:

Table 38

Number of boys from training ships who went to sea in 1893 and 1894

	1893		1894	
	Boys Discharged	*Sent to Sea*	*Boys Discharged*	*Sent to Sea*
Empress	107	52	119	62
Mars	125	47	121	48

Source: Reformatory and Industrial Schools Committee, c.8204 (London 1896), Appendix XLI.

There was correspondence in the *Times* (25 October 1895) when Captain Nicholette R.N., retd., proposed a ten-point plan to give boys more interest in what they were doing. He suggested: 'That each industrial training ship should have attached to her (and this is absolutely indispensable) a sea-going tender to give the lads the practical training in blue water, and to bring them into actual contact with the conditions of a sailor's life.'[25] For without any such practical service at sea, the *Empress* and the *Mars* could be regarded as prisons, keeping the boys isolated on board instead of in a reformatory on land. With the harsh discipline and rigorous regimen, it was not perhaps surprising that many young men were confirmed in their dislike of the sea and a sea-going career, a highly perverse outcome.

The industrial training ships were indeed part of the reformatory system, and similarly from 1855 gradually came under government control, although encouragement was still being given to private donors. But, as will be seen from the following table, their contributions were of the order of a mere ten per cent.

Table 39

Source of funds for industrial training ships in 1893 and 1894

	1893		1894	
	Treasury and other grants	*Private Subscriptions*	*Treasury and other grants*	*Private Subscriptions*
Empress	£7,542 14s. 3d.	£740 18s. 6d.	£6,605 10s. 9d.	£662 14s. 0d.
Mars	£8,222 4s. 2d.	£994 4s. 0d.	£6,832 14s. 2d.	£800 19s. 10d.

Source: Reformatory and Industrial Schools Committee, c.8204 (London 1896), Appendix XLI.

Indeed, by the last decade of the nineteenth century the training ships were virtually state-supported, although the *James Arthur*, being on Quarrier's estates, was not in receipt of public money.

9. Voluntary effort and government takeover

The organisation of the Ragged School movement in its early years owed much to evangelical zeal. Its leaders, like Sheriff Watson and the Rev. Dr. Guthrie, drew their inspiration for the work from the Christian faith. But for many years the jealousies and hostilities of sectarian religion split the movement, and although the Buchanan Institution, Glasgow was an exception (and much teaching and training was done in the name of the Christian faith), in general religion was a source equally of stimulus and of strife.

The reformatory movement in Scotland resulted from a philanthropic initiative optimistically organised by evangelicals who hoped to redeem the children of the Scottish slums. Led by Sheriff Watson and Dr. Guthrie, they were anxious to maintain the Ragged Schools as a non-residential institution. However, disciplinary problems led most philanthropic supporters to accept the need for greater authoritarianism within the Ragged School movement, and the institutions became residential, a crucial change which shifted the emphasis from care to reform; the subsequent involvement of the state completed the process as the Ragged Schools became part of the penal system.

NOTES

1. *Report on Reformatory and Industrial Schools*, c.8204 (London 1896), 104.
2. Battiscombe, 1974, Chapter 13.
3. Thomson, A., 1847, 7.
4. *Ibid.*, 8.
5. *TNASS* (Glasgow 1874) (London 1875), 276.
6. Angus, 1912, 63.
7. Guthrie, 1847, 2/7. There was a *Second Plea* (1849), and a *Third Plea* (1860).
8. *Edinburgh Original Ragged or Industrial School Association*, AR (Edinburgh 1848), 12, 13.
9. Brebner, 1829.
10. Cleland, J., 1837, 18.
11. *Glasgow Reformatory Institution, Boys' House of Refuge*, 20th AR (Glasgow, 1858), V.
12. The Boys' House of Refuge, Glasgow, admissions book 1851-52 (GUL Mss Gen.1017).
13. Manton, J., *Mary Carpenter and the Children of the Streets* (London 1976), 9.
14. *RCESH*, c.1123 (Edinburgh 1875), 290-296.
15. *Reformatory and Industrial Schools*, c.8204 (London 1896), Appendix XXXIV.
16. *Report on Reformatory and Industrial Schools*, c.8204 (London 1896), 104.
17. Gammie, A., *William Quarrier* (London n.d.), 53.
18. Harris, 1873, 29.
19. *The Scotsman*, Monday, 2 March 1868.
20. Charles Dickens, *All the Year Round*, 8 October 1859, 559.
21. 'The Cumberland is a handsome line-of-battle ship, of originally 70 guns; has carried the flags of various Admirals on several foreign stations and was engaged in the Baltic and the Russian War.' Earl of Shaftesbury, *Speeches in Glasgow* (Glasgow 1871), 79, and J. Stephen Jeans, *Western Worthies* (Glasgow 1872), 78.

22. The *James Arthur* was donated by his widow, who gave £3,000 for its construction. It was opened on 1 March 1887.
23. Jeans, 1872, 78.
24. Earl of Shaftesbury, *Speeches . . . in Glasgow* (Glasgow 1871), 79.
25. *Report on Reformatory and Industrial Schools*, c. 8204 (London 1896), Appendix XLI.

16

Orphanages

1. A new beginning

THE orphan had always provided what was perhaps the classic challenge to the residential principle. For children without homes must clearly be provided with such. But pressing though the need might be, notable as some early initiatives were, and appealing though children were to the philanthropically minded, the traditional provision, as surveyed by the Commissioners of 1872, was far from satisfactory (see chapter 1, section 4 above). It was fragmentary and unsystematic, and was often all too subject to the strongly disciplinarian inclinations of philanthropic sponsors and managers.

Large orphanages, which isolated children from the communities, had become increasingly unpopular after 1850. The misgiving spread, that such children, having grown up in a closed community, would have difficulty in adjusting to life in the real world. The 'cottage home' offered an alternative. In the late 1870's such small-scale homes were started in Wales and England (first in Neath and Birmingham) to rear orphan children in family groups with foster parents. In Scotland the greatest innovator in this sense was William Quarrier.

Later 'scattered' homes were advocated, in which the children lived with foster parents in ordinary houses in an ordinary street and attended the local school. In the earlier part of the century the boarding-out of orphans had had a bad press, and many shocking cases of exploitation had come to light. But there were so many children who needed care. As a result, although many philanthropists favoured 'cottage homes' or 'scattered' housing for orphans, from the late 60's boarding out was permitted (though reluctantly) and within 20 years it was being encouraged.[1] In general terms, therefore, boarding out became in the later nineteenth century the method most used by local authorities. But private benevolence continued to provide residential homes, and despite the increase in the role of the local authority, such homes were then (and are still) an integral part of the social provision for orphans.

2. William Quarrier

William Quarrier (1829-1903) was the paladin of Scottish evangelical philanthropists from the 1870's to the end of the century.[2] He never failed to launch his annual report without a Biblical quotation. His favourite was, 'In as much as ye have done it unto one of the least of these, ye have done it unto me.' He began trying to save those waifs and strays who were homeless on the streets of Glasgow by organising night shelters. All his accommodation was quickly oversubscribed. Having soon learned the limitations of his small early hostels, he swiftly organised an apparently unrestricted outlet for his charges. By associating himself with emigration schemes to Canada, he was able to evolve a broad one-way road from city streets to Canadian farmlands. The fortuitous combination of circumstances arising from labour surplus in Scotland and labour dearth in Canada was to last for over twenty years before the Government of the Dominion began to reconsider its 'open door' policy. Thereafter emigration schemes continued (right up to the 1960's), although more closely scrutinised and on a more modest scale.

Quarrier also knew that only a proportion of the children — the healthiest and strongest — would be able to emigrate and that he was bound to attract to his care many orphans who were diseased and disabled. Nothing daunted, he embarked upon an ambitious plan for a children's village at Bridge of Weir, which included not only cottage homes for normal children but special homes for cripples, T.B. patients and incurables.

Quarrier adopted the role of prophet: he believed he had a pact with God. His faith ensured that God would provide whatever was necessary. This meant that Quarrier could embark upon expensive and grandiose schemes requiring large capital expenditure in the sure knowledge that adequate support would be forthcoming. He thus exerted the strongest and most complete moral black-mail on all his supporters, and of course he was never disappointed.[3] He published annually from about 1870 'diaries' of his activities, which consisted of long, detailed entries of gifts which were presented each day of the year. The problems of his helpers handling the gifts (other than money) of varying quantities of potatoes, petticoats, porridge or pens must have been for-midable. Quarrier claimed never to have appealed to the public for support: all his income came in the form of unsolicited gifts. Nevertheless the pressure which he put on his friends and indeed the society of his day to support his en-deavours was impressive.

William Quarrier was born in Greenock in 1829. His father, a seaman, died while at sea, of cholera. His mother moved to Glasgow to try to bring up her two children where she believed there would be better opportunities for employment. They were desperately poor and the boy suffered much in his childhood; he resolved that if ever he were wealthy he would remember the poor children on the streets. He became a journeyman shoemaker, and in time opened his own shops all over Glasgow, 'becoming one of the first multiple shop-owners in the city'.[4]

He became a member of Hope Street Baptist Church and thus deeply involved with evangelical work. He was a founder member of the Glasgow Abstainers' Union (1856) and also an admirer of the social work of Josephine

Butler. During these middle years he 'never for a moment lost sight of the cause to which he had dedicated his life . . . the cry of the children was ever sounding in his ear'.[5]

As a result of a poignant incident of a small match-seller whose stock and earnings had been stolen, William Quarrier wrote on 30 November 1864 to the *Glasgow Herald*, extolling the virtues of the London Shoe-Black Brigade. Shoe Black and Parcels Brigades were subsequently established in Glasgow and Edinburgh (see chapter 15). Despite the usefulness of these Brigades, they were only a palliative.

Quarrier believed that what was needed was a Night Refuge for Children. With the co-operation of the City Improvement Trust he obtained part of Dovehill Church and adapted the upper part of it for his purpose (the lower part was used as a soap factory). He was thus able to receive homeless children and feed and rest them overnight. From these small beginnings, in 1871, he built up his astonishing empire. By 1873 he had in Glasgow the Children's Night Refuge at the Mission Hall, East Graeme Street, a boys' home at Govan Road, Cessnock, and a girls' home at 93 Renfield Street. But Quarrier was hunting for something more permanent. His search was difficult: should he look for a home in the centre of the city where temptation loomed, or seek a more isolated place where the children might feel strange and be more likely to run away, but where, as Rev. Norman MacLeod put it, they would hear the lintie sing? The Old Mansion House of Cessnock in Govan became available; it was then in rural surroundings and had upwards of three acres of land. By 1873 the boys were established there. The girls were later moved to Newstead and Elmpark Homes, both situated in the neighbourhood of Cessnock House.

3. The Orphan Homes of Scotland, Bridge of Weir

Although William Quarrier was always resident in the West, his commitment to homeless children came to embrace the whole of Scotland. Missionaries and others were constantly bringing him abandoned children. Thus his catchment area was wide and the demands made upon him great. He was only able to fulfil these obligations by means of his continuing schemes of emigration. In the early 1870's, when his life's work was beginning to take shape, children accepted into care were allocated to the homes in the city and in Govan. But for the large-scale plans which were forming in Quarrier's mind, a rural location was essential: as he explained:

> I would like to see an Orphanage established near Glasgow, on the cottage principle, to which children from any part of the country could be sent. By the cottage principle I mean a number of cottages built near each other; say ten, each capable of accommodating twenty to thirty children, with a father and mother (of sterling Christian character) at the head of each household; a schoolhouse in the centre; also a central workshop; the father of each family to be able to teach a different trade, such as tailor, shoemaker, joiner, printer, baker, farmer, smith, etc; the mother to do the working for each household, with assistance if needed. Boys from the

tailors household, wishing to learn shoemaking could be sent to the shoemakers workshop . . . The children would all meet together at school and church . . . It is desirable to keep up the family and home feelings amongst the children, and we believe this cannot be done in large institutions, where hundreds of children are ruled with the stringent uniformity necessary where large numbers are gathered together for years. A small farm near Glasgow would do for the purpose of building the cottage homes.[6]

Although many thought William Quarrier too ambitious, he persisted. After some difficulties he bought the farm of Nittingshill, Bridge of Weir. Quarrier planned two cottage homes and a central workshop building. Soon donors accepted financial responsibility for each of the two homes. The work proceeded apace and the opening ceremony took place in 1878, when the central building and two cottages were available for use. Within ten years there was a village colony of 29 units. There were by then 20 cottages, together with other general purpose buildings including the central building, laundry, workshops and bakehouse. Another donor presented the money necessary to build 'Homelea', a house for the Quarrier family at the entrance to the estate. Quarrier had gradually relinquished his own shoe business; the pressing needs of his extraordinary charity concerns had so increased. In 1882 he finally withdrew from a business which had been so neglected as to become progressively unprofitable. Thereafter he and his family were supported, as indeed were his homes, by the day-to-day generosity of charitable supporters.

Over and over again Quarrier's unbounded faith (or moral blackmail) was to triumph. By the time of his death in 1903 the colony consisted of:

Table 40

Quarrier's Orphan Homes, Bridge of Weir:
Cottage Homes built before William Quarrier's death in 1903

1.	Broadfield Home	20.	Kintyre Home
2.	Glasgow Home	21.	Marshall Home
3.	Dalry Home	22.	Lincoln-Garfield Home
4.	Dumbartonshire Home	23.	Edinburgh Home
5.	Ebenezer Home	24.	Jehovah-Jireh Home
6.	Washington Home	25.	Sagittarius Home
7.	Aberdeen Home	26.	Ayr Home
8.	Greenock Home	27.	Renfrewshire Home
9.	Anderston Home	28.	Sabbath School Home
10.	Paisley Home	29.	Smith Memorial Home
11.	Cessnock Home	30.	Michael Rowan Home
12.	Mizpah Home	31.	James Wilson Home
13.	Leven Home	32.	Ebenezer Maclay Home
14.	Overtoun Home	33.	Killearn Home
15.	Montrose Home	34.	Glenfarg Home
16.	Mitchell Home	35.	Hatrick Home
17.	Allan Dick Home	36.	Macfarlane Home
18.	Somerville Home	37.	Peddie Alexander Home
19.	Ashgrove Home	38.	John Robertson Home

'Oswald' Home for Invalid Girls   'James Arthur' Training Ship on Land
'Elim' Home for Invalid Boys   Poultry Farm Home for Boys

Table 40 (continued)

Administrative, etc.

Central Building	The School and Teachers' House
Gatehouse	'Carsemeadow' Farm Buildings
'Homelea' (the Founder's Home)	Bakehouse, Joiner's Shop, etc.
The Stores and Greenhouse, etc.	Cobbler's and Paint Shop, etc.
Laundry, Blacksmith's Shop, etc.	Fire Station and Stables, etc.
The Church	'Rozelle' — Workers' House.
City Orphan Home, Glasgow	'Fairknowe' Canadian Home, Brockville,
'Benthead' Seaside Home, Ardnadam	Ontario

The Consumption Sanatoria — 7 Buildings

Pavilion I	Disinfector House
Pavilion II	House: 'Hope Lodge'
Executive Building	House: 'Hebron'
Power House	

The Colony for Epileptics

Lands of Hatrick purchased 1902

Source: Gammie, A., *William Quarrier* (London, n.d., c. 1936), 157.

Inevitably there were those who resisted Quarrier's appeals. They found him a meddlesome busybody. More explicitly, members of the Catholic Church complained that he collected Catholic children and forced them to become Protestants. A Roman Catholic priest took him to court, on the grounds of alleged detention of a child, but lost his case and was unsuccessful on appeal. The decision was not surprising, given the strength of Protestant feeling in Scotland together with the support for a man of Quarrier's activity and reputation.

Other disputes arose. Quarrier did not calculate that he would have to pay rates. The authorities in Glasgow did not levy rates in respect of his properties there, but the County Council in Renfrewshire were less benevolent. Despite Quarrier's artful argument that he could not comply because 'none of our givers have ever spent a penny towards paying them, showing that they do not believe in either the justice or fairness of doing so', the local authority proceeded against him. He appealed to them personally at their meeting in Paisley, but 'There was a great lack of sympathy with the work.' The Renfrewshire authorities persisted in taxing his charitable properties, and though Quarrier took the matter to the Court of Session, he lost his case.

This quarrel had an important sequel. The original plan for the homes had included a schoolhouse as an integral part of the complex, but with the enforcement of the rate payment Quarrier was contributing, among other things, to the cost of public education. He embarrassed the authorities by marching all his 500 children to the village school where he demanded their admission. Reason later prevailed, and by a compromise agreement the Renfrewshire County Council accepted responsibility for the staffing and finances of the school on Quarrier's estate. School teachers, who were not members of the community, thus brought fresh outside influence to bear on the children.

There were problems associated with Quarrier's open-door policy for homeless children. Many came whose health was irreparably damaged; they could not respond to the simple benefits of good food, fresh air and clean accommodation. Many were consumptive. There was no official provision for such children. For the wealthy suffering from tuberculosis it was fashionable to flee from cold northern climes and seek sun and warmth further south. Much could be done to alleviate distress and prolong life by placing patients in sanatoria where a fresh air regime was combined with good food and much rest. Quarrier, undeterred by grey skies and heavy rainfall at Bridge of Weir, resolved to do something. He visited the consumption hospital in Ventnor, Isle of Wight and other similar places in the south and then announced his proposed plans for a sanatorium in Scotland. Within a month (December 1893) he had received promises of almost all the £7,500 required. He was fortunately able to buy the farm adjoining the Orphan Homes, at Carsemeadow, and proceeded to build. The memorial stone was laid by Sir William Arrol on 5 September 1894, and although there was delay (purportedly because of the installation of especially modern drainage), the Sanatorium was opened for patients on 27 May 1898. The building of a second Sanatorium was almost immediately undertaken and again money poured in; it was opened at a cost of £10,000 on 5 September 1900, named 'The Door of Hope'. These institutions created by private benevolence and enthusiasm have latterly passed into public hands.

William Quarrier's last initiative was the founding of a Colony of Mercy for Epileptics, opened in 1903. Seventy-five years later this Epilepsy Centre remains 'the only National Home in Scotland' caring for such sufferers. The Centre 'does its best to keep up-to-date with modern thinking in the medical, social and occupational care of epileptics'.

4. Into the Homes: Out to Canada

The success of Quarrier's work was based on his original plan, stunning in its simplicity, of using his orphan homes as halfway houses between the Scottish slums and the Canadian prairie. It was a superb piece of planning. For about twenty years (from 1871-1893) it worked to the benefit of Scotland and Quarrier's reputation. At first Quarrier (and Dr. Barnardo) operated through Miss Annie Macpherson. Her Distributing Homes in Canada were at Belleville and Galt, Ontario, and Knowlton, Quebec. From them the children might be placed in Ontario, or anywhere in Canada: later Quarrier organised emigration schemes directly on his own.

But there were difficulties. Quarrier believed that his boys and girls were efficiently vetted before emigration; indeed he and his senior assistants often travelled out with the pioneering groups who were welcomed to the Province of Ontario with offical teas and suitably phrased speeches. Nevertheless, those receiving the children were always more conscious of the shortcomings of their charges than were those despatching them, and much was made by the Canadians of the need for the immigrant children to have more training. Most of them went to farming families, the girls as domestic servants and the boys as labourers; inevitably, some did badly in Canada and, at the extreme, became criminals. Gradually the belief spread that the immigration schemes for Scottish orphans brought a bad element into the country. In 1893 the provincial legislature of Ontario (to which province Quarrier had sent almost all his children) passed a Children's Protection Act. Later, further legislation was enacted 'to regulate the immigration into Ontario of certain classes of children'.[7] From 1893, therefore, Quarrier had to work in co-operation with officials from the province. Quarrier disliked and resented this interference, but from the Ontario government's point of view it was essential.

Was Quarrier himself entirely honest in the presentation of his case? He was an environmentalist believing that Canada would provide a promising life for his charges. But he must have known that some at least would cause difficulties. Moreover Quarrier was adroit in his arguments with officialdom. When he was wrestling with the local authority over the rating of his Homes, he claimed relief on the grounds that they should come under the category of Sunday Schools and Ragged Schools which were exempt. In other circumstances he would have hotly denied that his Homes contained delinquent, or Ragged School, children.

Quarrier's achievement was very important, saving many of the poor children of the cities of Scotland. He built up a formidable reputation for himself which no doubt brought its own satisfactions. He also provided much needed young workers for Canada. At the same time he saddled himself with diseased and disabled children, to whose needs he responded with characteristic energy.

Quarrier's Homes have continued to be run as an independent institution by a Council of Management, although since the Social Work Act of 1968 most of the children are sent to Quarrier's by local authorities. Therefore the Homes have remained hybrid, owing some, especially financial, support to those bodies who send the children as well as much to the voluntary character of the children's village at Bridge of Weir.[8]

There were other philanthropic orphanages founded in Scotland in addition to those of Quarrier. At Saltcoats, The Glasgow United Evangelistic Association established its Homes for Destitute Children which were opened in 1873. About 80 destitute children were 'housed, fed, clothed, educated and fitted — the girls for domestic service, and the boys for different trades'. No doubt the regimen was strict and the standards rigid. 'The utmost economy is exercised, the cost of keeping a child being (in 1892) somewhat under £9 per annum.'

The problem of rearing orphan children is one which all societies have had to face. The many and diverse principles suggested as bases for solutions reflect the persistence of the problem. Some solutions appear more fashionable than others at any one time, and this leads to varied initiatives coming from strong-minded dedicated individuals. The philanthropist has continued to play a significant role in the provision of residential homes for orphan children, while the local authority has increasingly taken responsibility for organising boarding out and fostering arrangements.

NOTES

1. Bruce, 1968, 117.
2. In all his work with orphans William Quarrier seems to have been a disciple of Charles H. Spurgeon, the great Victorian preacher who dominated the Metropolitan Tabernacle in London. Spurgeon had launched in 1866 the Stockwell Orphanage, which could be regarded in many ways as a model for the Orphan Homes at Bridge of Weir. See Spurgeon, C. H., *Autobiography*, Vols. III and IV (London 1899 and 1900).
3. Lord Rowallan's grandfather was one of the regular donors, as he explained: 'He (Thomas Corbett) gave very large sums to Mr. Quarrier's Orphan Homes. Mr. Quarrier was Scotland's Dr. Barnardo and an honoured friend in the Corbett household. We were repeatedly told of the 'miracle', when he wanted to extend his work for orphans in the early days. He worked out in his mind how much money he would need. But divine providence must have established telepathy, for the next day a cheque for exactly the right amount arrived, unasked for, from my grandfather!' Rowallan, *An autobiography of Lord Rowallan K.T.* (Edinburgh 1976), 5.
4. Gammie, n.d., c. 1936, 37.
5. *Ibid.*, 45.
6. *Ibid.*, 94-95.
7. Letter from James Burges of the Distributing Home, Fairknowe, Brockville, Ontario, in Quarrier, 1897, 48-49.
8. See *Quarrier's Homes*, AR, 1976-77.

17
Remedial Homes for the Disabled

1. Residential homes for the deaf[1]

THE teaching and training of deaf (and often dumb) children in Victorian Scotland depended almost wholly on philanthropic initiative, for although the community was responsible for basic maintenance of the disabled, under the terms of the poor law, this involved no remedial work. After the Education Act of 1872 both parents and School Boards had some responsibilities for the deaf thrust upon them, but these were taken up reluctantly. For the most part it continued to be the availability of the eleemosynary provision which encouraged the deaf to communicate and lead useful lives.

By 1837 there were residential schools for deaf and dumb children in Edinburgh, Glasgow and Aberdeen. The Edinburgh Society had been founded in 1810, and after many financial difficulties was by the 1830's doing valuable work. The Aberdeen Society was initiated in August 1817. The Glasgow Auxiliary Society (July 1814), which collected funds and pupils in the West and sent them to Edinburgh, was replaced in January 1819 by the Glasgow Society for the Education of the Deaf and Dumb.

The basic problem in educating deaf children was that because they could not hear they could not speak. It was assumed therefore that deafness and dumbness went together. They might make sounds, but these bore little resemblance to normal conversation and indeed often seemed to listeners to be more bestial than human. Thus deaf individuals were usually placed with lunatics, beyond a soundless barrier which in earlier days none could penetrate.

The first Scot who attempted to enter into the problems of the deaf was George Dalgarno[2] of Aberdeen. He wrote as early as 1680 'Of a deaf man's capacity to speak' and demonstrated a hand alphabet. The first instruction in Great Britain specifically for deaf and dumb children was undertaken in Edinburgh by Thomas Braidwood (1715-1806), who ran a private academy there from 1760 to 1783 at Craigside House, St. Leonard's Hill, and later at 93-95 Dumbiedykes Road. Mr. Braidwood's pioneering work with the deaf apparently included teaching the deaf to speak. It must have gained considerable notoriety in the Edinburgh of the day and James Boswell recounts Dr. Johnson's reaction to the subject of the conversational abilities of the deaf children. 'Pray can they pronounce any *long* words?' asked the sage. Mr.

Braidwood informed him that they could, upon which Dr. Johnson wrote down one of his *sesquipedalia verba* (words half a yard long), which was pronounced by the scholars, and he was satisfied.[3]

The Braidwoods made their living from this work. They were apparently generous of their time and expertise and took in children whose parents could not afford the full fees. In July 1769 an anonymous writer suggested in the *Scots Magazine* that a charitable institution should be established in Edinburgh under Thomas Braidwood's guidance, but unfortunately nothing came of this and the Braidwoods, apparently discouraged, left Edinburgh for London, where they settled at Grove House, Hackney, Middlesex.[4]

After a lapse of some 27 years a new beginning was made in Edinburgh in 1810. The inaugural meeting of the Edinburgh Institution for the Education of the Deaf and Dumb was held on 3 June 1809, with the Duke of Buccleuch in the chair and the Lord Provost in attendance. Launching funds were forthcoming, but the Institution was always chronically short of money in its early years.[5] John Braidwood (of the Hackney School, the grandson of Thomas) was invited to come as teacher in charge in 1810. But he proved unstable, and left hurriedly, perhaps with some of the funds. He was succeeded by Robert Kinniburgh, who was sent to London and reluctantly accepted by the Braidwoods for training. The Braidwoods were generally unwilling to teach their methods. They apparently used the oral method to train the deaf to speak.

Kinniburgh made the first move westwards when in July 1814 he brought some of his Edinburgh pupils to demonstrate their abilities in Glasgow. This form of exhibition of the achievements of teacher and pupils was a common way of arousing interest, and was often used as a means of fund-raising. The visit to Glasgow was fortunate, and Kirkman Finlay (then Lord Provost of the city) gave his active support. Dr. Muir and Mr. Andrew Tennant became Secretary and Treasurer of a Glasgow Auxiliary Society. The Edinburgh Committee favoured the idea of auxiliary committees in Glasgow and elsewhere. By this means they hoped to channel all the funds available in Scotland for deaf children's education to their own Institution. Glasgow subscribed £500, and was thereby enabled to send 10 children to the Edinburgh School from 1815.

Further demonstrations took place in Glasgow (November 1815) and later in the North. The Northern tour was extensive: Dundee, Arbroath, Montrose, Stonehaven, Aberdeen, Banff, Elgin, Forres, Inverness, Dunkeld and Perth were visited. Auxiliary societies were set up in Perth and Inverness. At Aberdeen matters turned out unexpectedly. The audience was enthusiastic, so much so that it rejected the idea of being auxiliary to Edinburgh and pressed on with a Society for the Education of the Deaf and Dumb in Aberdeen (26 August 1817). Dundee also had a flirtation with independence, but by 1826 was again sending deaf children to the Institution in Edinburgh through the activities of a Dundee Auxiliary Committee.

Glasgow's position as an Auxiliary soon became unsatisfactory. The

Edinburgh School was crowded (it had 50 pupils by 1818) and the Glasgow committee had great difficulty in choosing the most worthy of the many applicants for their places at Edinburgh. On 14 January 1819 a public meeting was called and the Glasgow Society for the Education of the Deaf and Dumb was instituted. Funds came in readily (over £2,000 in the first few weeks of the appeal), and a site on the Barony Glebe was procured,[6] where the building was ready and occupied by 1821; 45 pupils were enrolled and John Anderson (who had been running a private school for the deaf in the city) became headmaster, with two assistants.

All the early charitable development for the care of deaf children took the form of residential boarding establishments.[7] Opinions were strongly held that deaf pupils required to live in with their teachers so that they could obtain the benefit of learning as much in leisure hours as during the school day. The isolation of these children within their home environment perhaps encouraged the boarding school system.

A new school was opened in Dundee for deaf children on 9 March 1846. It was at first a private venture of Mr. and Mrs. Drysdale, but the next year it was taken over by a philanthropic organisation. By this time there was sufficient interest and support from the local community for the establishment of the Dundee Association for the Education of the Deaf and Dumb.[8] It was always a small school, catering for some 30 children in 1850 and perhaps only 20 in 1880. In 1866 Mr. James Key of Lochee left a substantial legacy to the school sufficient to finance board and residence for 10 children. When Drysdale died in 1880 his nephew, James Barland, became headmaster. He was deaf, as Drysdale had been. The school jogged along but did not do any outstanding work. Its finances were never sufficient to pay good wages and thus attract enterprising staff.

In 1850 Donaldson's Hospital was opened in Edinburgh.[9] It came to occupy an important role in the education of the deaf. The founder had intended to establish an orphan hospital of the traditional kind, but at the suggestion of one of the governors, Mr. George Forbes, the purpose was widened to include the deaf. This was a remarkable broadening of 'founder's intent'. Forbes argued that James Donaldson's Trustees were in no way breaching the terms of their trust, because although the deaf were not mentioned, neither were they excluded. The governors were favourably disposed towards the suggestion and consulted both Robert Kinniburgh, who had recently retired from the Edinburgh School, and Duncan Anderson of the Glasgow School, as to the propriety of educating hearing and deaf children separately but within the same institution. Both headmasters approved of the plan, especially as there were known to be deaf children living in various parts of Scotland with no chance of proper education and training. Thirty deaf children were admitted in October 1850.

The Royal Commission of 1872, established to enquire into the endowed schools and hospitals of Scotland, examined and received evidence from

Donaldson's as well as from other such institutions in Scotland and they accepted the change of use which Donaldson's governors had made in 1848. They noted that the governors had recently increased the proportion of places reserved for deaf mutes.[10] But they criticised the principle of residential schools, to which they were unequivocally opposed. Subsequently considerable alarm was raised by the Educational Endowments Commission in the late 1880's, which tried to force Donaldson's to abandon the residential principle. In the event, no action was taken, and Donaldson's was able to carry on as before as an institution rearing deaf children.

But the admittance of numbers of deaf pupils to Donaldson's Hospital from 1850 had a deleterious effect on the original Edinburgh Institution for the Deaf and Dumb. Donaldson's was a wealthy foundation; parents were anxious to secure admittance there for their deaf children. The numbers attending at the Edinburgh Institution accordingly dropped during the 1850's from 70 to 45. This was unfortunate, for elsewhere in Scotland there may have been deaf children who were not known about and therefore were excluded from special attention. The Edinburgh Institution continued to take day pupils as well as boarders and by the mid-1850's claimed that there were 50 Auxiliary Societies in Scotland supporting its work.

The Glasgow School continued to flourish under the guidance of Duncan Anderson. But by 1860 the building on Barony Glebe, which had seemed so spacious when it was built, was overcrowded and the location had rapidly deteriorated as the town expanded. There was a clear need for a move. The generous well-wishers of the school responded to an appeal. The new building at Langside,[11] designed by James Salmon, Snr. in a florid Italian style, cost £18,000. Some £8,000 was subscribed at once and £5,000 was obtained from the sale of the old building. The debt of £5,000 which remained was quickly paid off.[12] The school moved there in 1868 whereupon Duncan Anderson retired. He had been a distinguished headmaster deeply involved in the welfare of his pupils. He was succeeded by John Thomson and later Dr. W. H. Addison. A swimming pool was built at Langside in 1881 and a gymnasium in 1883, in recognition of the needs of deaf children for physical education.

The small school at Aberdeen under the headmastership of Franklin Bill (1859-1881) provided education for the deaf in the North-East. The headmastership of Mr. A. Pender from 1881-1919 was important because he was the hearing child of deaf parents, who did not attempt to speak until he was admitted to Donaldson's. He was strongly opposed to oral methods of teaching; he remained in charge at Aberdeen at the very time when 'silent' teaching was falling into disrepute. Aberdeen usually had about 20 pupils in residence who were charged £16 a year for many years. When there were day pupils their fees were £1 10s. per quarter.

Thus by the opening of the twentieth century Edinburgh had two institutions for the deaf, of which Donaldson's was by far the wealthier. Glasgow was doing sterling service also. The smaller institutions at Aberdeen and

Dundee carried on as boarding establishments until 1920 (Aberdeen) and 1947 (Dundee), when they amalgamated with day schools for the deaf in their respective towns.

In the early nineteenth century and during the first half of Victoria's reign, methods of teaching deaf children to communicate were almost without exception based on methods in linear descent from those of Dalgarno. This 'silent' system was directly taken from French experts (Dr. Sicard and others), who dismissed the notions of trying to get the deaf to articulate sounds for themselves and insisted upon elaborating upon the sign language. The Scots schools for the deaf in Edinburgh, Aberdeen, Glasgow and Dundee were all teaching this way. Headmasters, often themselves from the ranks of deaf pupils, were products of the silent system and could not conceive of a system of oral instruction, far less help to teach it. They had never heard language themselves and were sceptical of other teaching systems which involved persuading deaf pupils to make sounds which they could not hear. They argued first and last for sign language which was 'the first language of infancy'.[13]

The oral method involved a long and arduous teaching process of one teacher to one pupil. The child had to be able to see the movement of the tongue before he could essay the various sounds. There was no cumulative progress by imitation; each step had to be patiently and painfully taken by teacher and copied by student. This meant slow progress, sometimes very discouraging to both parties.

Alfred Large, headmaster of Donaldson's deaf department from 1863 to 1899, led the fashion in Victorian Scotland for the 'combined method', in which finger spelling was used initially, after which attempts were made to get pupils to speak. This type of compromise reinforced the hold of the silent method. Results came easily and encouraging progress could be made with finger spelling. The oral methods were heartbreakingly slow, and once finger spelling had been learned, pupils rarely persevered with proper speech. Moreover the new methods were expensive: 'In this department of education (articulation and lip-reading) Mr. Thomson requires about double the price charged for the ordinary kind of education.'[14]

Both England and Scotland lagged behind at this stage. In the world outside, the old French system of Abbé de l'Epée was being overtaken by the so-called German system of Heinecke, by which painstaking attention was given to the positions of the mouth in making different sounds. Mirrors and diagrams of the mouth and tongue were used.

In September 1880 an International Congress of Teachers of the Deaf was held in Milan. There were over 200 delegates, and Italy and France were well represented. After long and vigorous discussions of methods to be used, the following resolution was passed: 'The Congress, considering the incontestable superiority of speech over signs in restoring the deaf and dumb to society, and in giving them a more perfect knowledge of language: declares — That the

Oral Method should be preferred to that of signs for the education and instruction of the deaf and dumb.'[15]

The combined system hung on, despite its dismissal by all major international authorities.[16] The conservatism of the residential schools for the deaf perhaps reflects the closed inner world of this type of boarding institution. This, combined with self-perpetuating boards of governors, kept well in check by authoritarian headmasters, helps to explain the reluctance to move from well trodden ways.

Young women were coming into the profession from the 1880's, specially trained in the new methods at the newly established College at Ealing in London. But in Scotland they were only usually able to obtain poorly paid posts in the day schools, and thus were prevented from making any impact on the methods used in the large, prestigious, male-dominated boarding schools.

At the census of 1851, the first to elicit such information, 21,155 persons were counted as deaf and dumb in Scotland.[17] No further official recognition of this category and its problems took place until the Education Act of 1872, when both School Boards and parents had imposed on them the obligation of educating all children including categories like the deaf and dumb. As a result of the 1872 Act, some School Boards felt it their duty to take action, and three day schools were set up. These were the Greenock (1883), Dundee (1885) and Glasgow (1886) Day Schools for the Deaf. At last teachers could bring new expertise to the job, but it was still argued that residential institutions gave more concentrated oral instruction and produced better results.[18]

The only previous official involvement had been through the Board of Guardians. Under the Poor Law (Scotland) Amendment Act of 1845 the parochial board of each parish was empowered to contribute to the maintenance of deaf and dumb children. This covered only pauper children, and problems soon arose. Nevertheless this shouldering of responsibility, however hesitantly, was to lead to further state involvement and eventually to state commitment. But this specialised field has continued to be shared by state and private enterprise. Notable successes were scored by men like Dr. James Kerr Love who, appointed Honorary Aurist to the Glasgow School in 1890, discovered that 95% of the children in the School had some residual hearing, however slight.[19]

In all education involving the deaf, tremendous efforts must be made with each individual student. There can, in the initial stages, be no common ground or common progress. Each pupil is isolated behind the barrier of his affliction and it must be the teacher's aim to surmount this as completely as possible. Any method of teaching the deaf depended on a great deal of one-to-one teaching. In order to ease the workload of the teacher, the monitorial system of using senior pupils to help more junior ones (then much in vogue in ordinary schools) was often used.

It was Duncan Anderson (1832-80), the headmaster of the Glasgow School, who brought a fresh mind and some imagination to deaf education. He introduced the study of drawing and botany, organising a botanical garden and a museum at the Institution.

There were three main ways of seeking to make the children economically independent. They could be given industrial training while resident in school, they could be apprenticed when their time in school was finished, or they could be sent out of school for technical training while still resident and completing their education. The third method of combining technical with general education was rare in the nineteenth century. Education in drawing and art-work was the exception, often leading to career prospects.

Work as draughtsmen, and in printing, photographing and various process engraving trades was often available.

Residential training was attempted from the beginning. Tailoring and shoemaking were most popular. Boys could also be taught how to work on the land, starting with the vegetable garden of the institution itself. Yet residential training was fraught with problems. The shoes and the clothes could not be sold unless they were of reasonable quality. A master craftsman was needed to supervise each type of work, and unless a particularly gifted man was found who could stimulate the boys and encourage good work, the results could be unfortunate.[20]

Boards of governors faced with ruined materials and poorly trained boys often preferred to apprentice boys to outside masters. Most schools for the deaf had an apprenticeship fund which enabled their boys to be formally indentured to good masters. Once initial prejudice had been overcome, deaf boys were popular employees. Their affliction was a difficulty, but if communications could be established they were usually found to be sober and conscientious workmen.

Girls were less of a problem. They were taught all branches of housework, washing, laundering, sewing and mending skills which could be of use in the most usual occupation, domestic service, to which they were likely to go. 'Of the pupils who left in June 1878 14 are girls who are now employed as follows:— Four as dressmakers, one as a milliner, two as weavers, and the others as domestic servants or assisting in homework.'[21] Thus these deaf girls received the type of education and training suited to their sex, regardless of their deafness.

As far as industrial training and therefore apprenticeship was concerned, headmasters came to believe that it should not be attempted until after the children had left school. Alfred Large, the headmaster who dominated deaf education at Donaldson's for so many years, stated to the Royal Commissioners:

> The allotted time at school, five years to accomplish all this necessary work, is far too short, for it must be borne in mind that the deaf mutes only commence to acquire language upon entering the school.[22]

The humanitarian urge of a few provided a system of residential institutions for the deaf in Victorian Scotland. Official provision by the School Boards was then rare.[23] Benevolence still retained a role which was unlikely to be replaced. The combined method of teaching finally gave way to oral methods, and this has enabled many deaf to live constructive lives apparently little hampered by their disability.

2. The training and education of the blind

Humanitarian concern for the blind was readily aroused, for although many blind had never been able to see, the affliction was often imposed on the individual in a sudden and arbitrary fashion after illness. With the primitive diagnostic techniques available, the causes of blindness were not really known. In the eighteenth century some curious reasons were listed in society reports; many were thought to have lost their sight 'by small-pox' and one or two 'by headache', or 'gradually by cold'.[24] The philanthropic response was initially to appeal for charitable funds sufficient to set up blind asylums.[25]

The objectives were clear, namely to establish workshops within the asylum, and to prepare the blind for employment which would make them independent. Such people would thus keep themselves, and would not become chargeable to the poor rate on which, as disabled persons, they had an incontrovertible claim. To this end asylums for the blind were established in Edinburgh, Glasgow, Aberdeen and Dundee. In these charitable institutions men and women were trained to undertake a variety of useful trades. But success was limited; those who could become financially independent after leaving were regarded as prize pupils. The parallel priority was to offer the chance of spiritual redemption by encouraging them to 'read' for themselves the holy Scriptures.

The Edinburgh Asylum for the Blind was founded in 1792 'for the relief of the indigent and industrious blind'. In its first years men were taken for training in various trades. Later women were also accommodated. The emphasis on useful employment produced a wide variety of goods, including 'mattresses and cushions, of hair, wool and straw, baskets and mats of all kinds, onion and other nets, hair gloves for rheumatisms'.[26]

The Glasgow Asylum for the Blind was opened in March 1828. It was the result of the initiative of John Leitch who, himself partially sighted, bequeathed £5,000 to provide a purpose-built asylum. The chief sponsor in Glasgow was Mr. John Alston of Rosemount, who became 'the Prime Mover of the Institution'. He prepared a pamphlet on the Glasgow Asylum and on teaching the blind, from the sale of which the Asylum made a useful profit. The Glasgow institution was originally under the charge of a Matron, a Chaplain and a Porter; in 1834 a Superintendent, Mr. Matthew Semple, was appointed. The work of the Asylum was divided between its School of Industry for Adults and its School of General Instruction. For admittance to both a sum of money was payable. In the case of the School of Industry £2 5s.

was the entrance fee, or working without income for three months. For school-children the charge was £6 6s. per year. In addition subscribers had rights of recommendation.

As with the deaf, the problems of educating the blind exercised the ingenuity of early nineteenth-century teachers. It was recognised that the blind could develop a refined sense of touch and that learning of letters and numbers would have to come through a development of this skill. To this end two blind young men in the Edinburgh Asylum (Messrs. Milne and Mcbeath) invented an extraordinary method. A series of variegated knots was tied in twine, each different knot representing a letter, the twine was wound on a cumbersome frame and the blind, by feeling the knots, could thus 'read'. This method was also used in Glasgow, where it was claimed that 'Children of eight years of age can read the Gospel of St. Mark, and other passages of Scripture with con-siderable facility.'[27] But this type of machine was bound to be replaced by other less unwieldy means. The raised dot alphabet rapidly came to the fore. Louis Braille perfected his type in 1829, but there were many other experimenters. Gall's alphabet was well known in Scotland, although John Alston (the Glasgow treasurer in 1835) was critical, for 'The blind children acquire the alphabet but the letters soon disappear with the using.' Alston himself produced his own alphabet which was much favoured in Glasgow, but the local speciality was bound in the end to give ground before other systems like Moon's type or Braille.[28]

The strength of any blind asylum depended on the variety of its occupa-tions. By 1835 the Glasgow Asylum had men, women, boys and girls under-taking a wide range of jobs. Adults worked by day in the Asylum, while boys and girls were resident, undergoing training for a craft as well as being educated. The tasks undertaken by the women and girls were the usual domestic ones. They did sewing, winding and knitting as well as making up clothes and performing domestic tasks. The men made baskets, mattresses and rope, and undertook weaving, flax dressing and sack printing. The boys added net making to their other accomplishments. The non-resident workers received a weekly wage, while the children had their board and residence.

The census of 1851 for the first time collected information as to the number of blind prsons living in Scotland: 3,010 were counted.[29] But fewer than 100 were resident in the blind asylums. Perhaps as a result of the disclosure of the figures, the Mission to the Out-door Blind for Glasgow and the West of Scotland was set up in 1859. By 1893 this organisation was employing seven Missionary Teachers caring for 1,293 blind persons. Attempts were made to teach reading 'in the raised type', and to borrow books from a free lending library, as well as to help them to support themselves and 'generally to ameliorate their conditions'.[30]

Blind persons who lived in or near the four largest cities of Scotland were more likely to be assisted than those in smaller towns or the countryside. After the 1872 Education Act, School Boards and parents had a responsibility to educate blind children, but were slow in allocating funds. Parochial boards could have assigned funds for this purpose, but they disputed that they were required to educate the blind. The Secretary of the Scotch Education Board (Mr. H. Craik) was critical of such local bodies for their failure to respond to the problem.[31]

3. Homes for the mentally and physically disabled

Because mental deficiency was regarded as a disgrace rather than a disease, many parents refused to accept that their child was 'special'. Pre-industrial rural societies often supported such 'naturals' as long as they were harmless. These people often became displaced as rural societies broke up, and they gradually drifted into care. It was always impossible to number this class of defectives, many of whom remained hidden. Only when residential facilities were opened did potential patients become visible. Distinctions between mental deficiency and (temporary?) mental illness were not readily made until the later nineteenth century when classification of mental disorders had developed and doctors were more skilled in diagnosis. Before this time both mentally and physically disabled people could be classified as lunatics (see chapter 9, section 2, above).

The humanitarian involvement usually stemmed directly from those who had personal experience of defectives. This direct concern stimulated the necessary professional interest and enquiry into various types of handicapped persons. The process of classification of mental states, a necessary preliminary to effective treatment, began. Mental abnormality and physical disability were the two basic categories, but they could be subdivided much more accurately as professional psychiatrists became more involved.

The first action in Scotland on behalf of the mentally deficient was that of Sir John and Lady Jane Ogilvy who, in 1852 on their estate outside Dundee, resolved to establish the Baldovan Institution[32] (now called Strathmartine) for the education and treatment of mentally defective children. At first, normal children and subnormal children were educated together, in the hope that the normal children would encourage the deficient. Unhappily the reverse happened. When the Institution was opened on 6 January 1855 it employed methods similar to those of Dr. Guggenbuhl in Switzerland, for 'Life in the fresh air, exercises and plenty of good food were combined with education and training.'[33] By 1904 an enlarged Institution was licensed to accommodate 160 children. It later worked closely with the psychiatric department of St. Andrews University Medical School.

The Scottish National Institution at Larbert (Stirlingshire) was opened in 1863. It was centrally situated so as to serve the most populous part of the country. It grew out of a private home originally operated in Edinburgh by Dr. and Mrs. Brodie at Gayfield Square. From 1855 the Brodies had run the

Edinburgh Idiot Asylum as a profit-making concern. The location of such an asylum in the city was unsatisfactory. Eventually Brodie was successfully established as Physician Superintendent of the new Institution at Larbert. Dr. Brodie was succeeded in 1871 by Dr. William Wotherspoon Ireland.[34] He was one of the early advocates of special schools and special classes for retarded children. From 1881 to 1914 there was no resident medical superintendent at Larbert, a layman being preferred, but after 1914 this was reversed.

The mentally handicapped received attention in the 1850's and 1860's, before the physically disadvantaged. But in the 1870's the latter also attracted the efforts of philanthropists. In the West of Scotland the Association for Aiding Infirm Children was set up in 1874 and soon opened the Eastpark Homes on Maryhill Road. The Association had originally intended to visit the homes of crippled children and give some sort of education and encourage various other activities. The home conditions in which such children lived, however, were so bad that the committee was forced to undertake the trouble and expense of a residential home.

But a major figure was soon to appear on the philanthropic scene. This was Miss Beatrice Clugston. Under the auspices of the Scottish National Society for the Relief of Incurables (1874) she set up the Association for the Relief of Incurables of Glasgow and the West of Scotland. It had a dual role, to visit and assist such people in their own homes, and also to provide residential care 'for people labouring under chronic or incurable disease'. Sufficient funds were collected to build Broomhill Home, Kirkintilloch (1875). It had accommodation for 62 patients in 1881 and for 100 by 1893. The privileges of the subscribers continued, although they had been restricted and were expensive. A subscriber who wished to nominate to a bed had to donate the enormous sum of £1,000 to do so. In addition there were 200 out-patients or pensioners. These homes still exist and are used for similar purposes by the National Health authorities.

The development of professional psychiatry enabled constructive treatment and education to be given to mentally handicapped persons so that the philanthropists could begin to operate. Similarly new techniques for the physically disabled opened the door to them. Both were greatly helped by teachers who, through philanthropic provision, were able to spend a great deal of time with each individual. The whole of this effort was voluntary and philanthropic until the passing of the Education Act of 1872. The new School Boards then became involved, though not very effectively. The School Boards had the duty of ensuring education for all children, regardless of their disabilities; for many years after 1872 they struggled with the general problem of providing day schools for all the normal children in their area. Only slowly did they begin to ponder the need to provide for children who, because of disability, were unable to attend daily at school. Eventually the local authorities did begin to cope with disabled children, but this is an area where there will always be scope for the private philanthropic institution.

NOTES

1. Watson, T. J., A History of Deaf Education in Scotland, Edinburgh Ph.D., 1949.
2. Dalgarno, G., *Didascalocophus* (Oxford 1680), reprinted in *The Works of George Dalgarno* (Edinburgh 1834). At the instigation of Dugald Stewart, Dalgarno's works were reprinted by the Maitland Club. Stewart believed that others had plagiarised Dalgarno's ideas (as indeed they had), and that his work was so rare that it might never be referred to. 'Dalgarno was born at Old Aberdeen and bred in the University at New Aberdeen; taught a private grammar school . . . in Oxford, for thirty years and died of a fever aged sixty years or more in August 28, 1687.' (Introduction to Maitland edition, X).
3. Boswell, J., *A Tour to the Hebrides*, 11 November 1773.
4. In 1792 the Old Kent Road Asylum for the Deaf and Dumb was opened in London as a charity and Braidwood's nephew, Joseph Watson, was appointed the first principal.
5. The house opened in Rose Street but moved to Chessels Court (the old Excise Office of Scotland) in October 1814. In 1823 the Deaf and Dumb Institute was in the Canongate between St. Mary's Wynd and St. John's Street, but by 1833 it had removed to Gabriel's Road near Claremont Place.
6. At 38 Parson Street.
7. There were three other early but short-lived day schools for the deaf in Scotland. John Mitchell ran a school in Paisley between 1830 and 1842. At Perth, George Hutton conducted a successful school from 1819 to 1859 and in Edinburgh the day school opened in 1837, but amalgamated with the Edinburgh Institution in 1845.
8. The Dundee School was at Sunnyside House, 15 Bucklemaker Wynd from 1848 to 1870, when it moved to Dudhope Bank, Lochee Road.
9. James Donaldson of Broughton Hall in the County of Edinburgh died on 9 October 1830. He left some £125,377 to provide a hospital like the Orphan Hospital, Edinburgh or John Watson's Hospital.
10. This they had been enabled to do by the Endowed Institutions (Scotland) Act, 1869.
11. This building is still in use, now the original building of Langside College.
12. *Society for the Education of the Deaf and Dumb*, AR (Glasgow 1868).
13. Anon., *The Edinburgh Messenger . . . regarding Deaf and Dumb* (Edinburgh 1845), 16.
14. *Glasgow Society for the Education of the Deaf and Dumb*, 58th AR (Glasgow 1879), 8.
15. Arnold, T., 1881, XIV.
16. *Ibid.*, XXXVII.
17. *Census of Great Britain in 1851* (London 1854), 80-81.
18. *Report of the Committee of Council on Education on schools for the Blind and Deaf 1896-97*, HMSO, C.8608 (London 1897), 16.
19. *The Glasgow Institution for the Deaf*, AR (Glasgow 1891).
20. *Edinburgh Institution of the Deaf*, AR, 1840 (Edinburgh 1840). By 1840 200 boys had passed through the Edinburgh Institution. Their occupations are given as follows:

Shoemakers	44	Tailors	35	Farm servants 17	Weavers	11
Clerks	9	Cabinet		Engravers 5	Blacksmiths	5
Labourers	5	makers	6	Masons 3	Cork cutters	3
Stocking		Saddlers	3			
weavers	3					

21. *Glasgow Society for the Education of the Deaf and Dumb*, 58th AR (Glasgow 1879), 4.
22. *RCESH*, 1st Report (Edinburgh 1873), 621.
23. In England, by the Elementary Education (Blind and Deaf Children) Act 1893, School Boards were required to provide schools for disabled categories. By 31 August 1896, there were 91 such schools, catering for 3,004 deaf children (1,699 day scholars and 1,305 boarders); see *Report . . . on Schools for the Blind and Deaf*, HMSO, C.8608 (London 1897).
24. *Edinburgh Asylum for the relief of the indigent and industrious blind*, AR (Edinburgh 1810).
25. Other asylums for the blind were Paris (1784), Liverpool (1791), Bristol (1793), Dublin (1799), London (1800), Norwich (1805) and York (1835). See Alston, J., *Statements of the Education, Employment and Internal Arrangements adopted at the Asylum for the Blind, Glasgow* (Glasgow 1836), 8.
26. *Edinburgh Asylum for . . . the indigent and industrious blind*, AR (Edinburgh 1816).
27. Alston, 1836, 7.

28. See *Royal Commission on the Blind, the Deaf and Dumb* (London 1889).
29. *Census of Great Britain in 1851* (London 1854), 78.
30. *Glasgow Charitable and Philanthropic Institutions* (Glasgow 1893), 8.
31. *Royal Commission on the Blind, the Deaf and Dumb*, HMSO (London 1889), Questions 19790-20,001, 731.
32. *Handbook to the charitable institutions of Dundee* (Dundee 1875).
33. Henderson, D. K., 1964, 74.
34. See Ireland, 1877.

PART VI

The Philanthropy of Housing

18
The Transient Tenant

1. The two challenges

THERE were two respects in which the Victorian philanthropists of Scotland became involved in housing. The first was in relation to the floating population, those at the bottom of the income and employment scale. This was the most pressing aspect of the problem: the one which struck the public attention as homeless people wandered the streets. The second related to the long-run inadequacy of the housing supply for the working classes. How could the philanthropists act here?

2. The housing crisis

Much has been written about the squalid and unhealthy housing of the industrial cities during Victoria's reign. Conditions then prevailing have drawn scholars to the field as to a magnet.[1] There has been much indignation concerning the conditions in which people lived. But the philanthropists of the day were also seriously concerned with the general deterioration of the urban environment. As early as 1818 in Glasgow, Professor Graham, Regius Professor of Botany, was searching for solutions when he wrote:

> An important step towards ventilation would be affected, if we could even open up the lanes in which the lower classes live. In Glasgow, the hovels which they inhabit are collected into dense masses of very great size between some of the larger streets. I believe it would greatly add to the healthiness of the place, if some improvements I have talked of were effected, and straight and wide streets carried in different directions through these depositories of wretchedness. It would not I think be easy to devise a more judicious charity, than the building of houses for the poor on an approved plan, and in a good situation.[2]

But action on the necessary scale required that new authorities and powers be created and wielded in a way which would have been quite unacceptable at the time. Indeed it is hard to resist the conclusion that the law of necessary deterioration had to operate in Scottish Victorian cities before any action could be mounted. Ameliorative measures could only be undertaken when need had become urgent and capable of expressing itself politically.

But the housing crisis in Scotland was compounded by a series of invasions by homeless and destitute persons from the Highlands and Ireland who poured into the cities, overwhelming what primitive social services there were. To these homeless hordes, the quality of the houses they occupied in Glasgow or Edinburgh was of little consequence, provided they could find work and food. Many of them had come from primitive dwellings in rural settings. They brought with them a ready acceptance of the low housing standards characteristic of overcrowded cities. The one-roomed 'house' was home to thousands of Scottish families. The Committee on Housing for the Working Classes of the Free Church of Scotland used some of the information gathered from the Census of 1861 to report that 'In Scotland there are 7,964 houses without windows, and 226,723 houses of only one apartment, proving that nearly one million of the people of Scotland, or one third of the entire population, are living in houses of one room.'[3]

Many philanthropists, especially from the class of civic leaders, business and commercial men, involved themselves in attempting to house the homeless. Their first attempts were to aid those who were peripatetic, wandering within Scotland to find work, and took the form of Night Asylums and Lodging Houses. Such ventures were intended for workers and their families who were on the move, for transients were believed to comprise a major proportion of the homeless. The provision made for their temporary overnight accommodation reflects the acceptance by contemporary society of a permanent peripatetic element among the working classes. Perhaps there was an inter-class misunderstanding here, for the men, women and children who were unsettled regarded the urban centres where work was often plentiful as their ultimate destination, while their intending benefactors continued to regard them as transients.

3. The Night Asylum and the Strangers' Friend

Night Asylums for the Houseless were philanthropically established in Glasgow (1838), Aberdeen (1840), Edinburgh (1842) and Dundee (1882) to provide overnight accommodation for those 'on the road'. These included labourers seeking work, women and children put out of their homes, single women without friends and many of both sexes and all ages travelling in search of something better. Night Asylums were a sensible and practical response to industrialisation with its demand for a mobile population and its disruption of traditional family support. They were busier at the end of Victoria's reign than ever before.

The Night Asylum, the Poor House and the Lodging House were the three main provisions for transients. The Superintendent of the Asylum accepted people who were not eligible for the Poor House; he in turn sent on some applicants, armed with a 'line', to the Poor House. The Night Asylum movement remained strong in Scotland because 'Our Poor Law makes no provision for this class and therefore shelter and food have to be provided by private benevolence.' It would seem that the class of people who claimed Night Asylum accommodation in Scotland were in England accommodated in the casual wards attached to the various Poor Law Unions.

Although they were privately financed charities, the Night Asylums came to be *de facto* part of the semi-official provision of overnight shelter. They were popular with the police, who were glad to know of a place to which to send wandering strangers. In Aberdeen the Night Shelter remained part of the House of Industry and Refuge. In Dundee, prior to the establishment of the Night Asylum, police officers could sometimes be persuaded to receive the homeless into the police office where they dozed around the fire through the night. In most large cities each evening the police marshalled the queue of applicants for the Night Asylums. In general relations between the police and the Night Asylum staff were friendly and harmonious, although individual incidents could lead to dispute. On 10 January 1871, the Superintendent of the Edinburgh Asylum expressed his indignation:

> On the night of 27 December, Margaret Thomson and Mary Walker were apprehended by the police, and charged with being drunk and incapable, the lieutenant on duty did not think they were drunk enough to lock up, but ordered them to be put in to the Reception Room of the Asylum, although told by the officers that they were not cases for that charity. In the morning when I saw them, they were not then sober, and during the night they made the floor of the reception room in such a filthy state with vomitting, wine and human excrement that a scavenger had to be engaged to clean it out — Margaret Thomson is 28 years of age, common prostitute, she was turned out of the Asylum on the previous evening beastly drunk. — Mary Walker is 44 years of age, a brothel messenger; both are known at the Asylum, being regular pests, when they have drink.[4]

The Glasgow Night Asylum was opened in the Old Granary in St. Enoch's Wynd (Argyll Street) on 28 May 1838. Once success had been ensured, new enlarged premises were built in North Frederick Street and opened in 1847. It was one of those charitable ventures strongly supported by the Lord Provost and senior Magistrates. There were thirty-six Directors who exercised a supervisory control; this took the form of one of them always being on duty as the evening's intake was admitted. Apparently this system worked efficiently. Nor did the Directors become forgetful of their duties with the passing of the years; as one witness reported in 1903, 'There are thirty-six directors . . . and practically there is one director on duty every night of the year along with the Superintendent.'[5]

In Aberdeen the Night Refuge was opened in 1840 as a branch of the House of Industry and Refuge (1836). It remained a small unit within the larger institution, although overnight accommodation was increasingly sought in the later years of Victoria's reign.

The town of Edinburgh made provision in that general utility building, Queensberry House, for a House of Refuge (for semi-permanent occupants) and a Night Refuge for those on the move. The Edinburgh Night Asylum was founded by philanthropists in 1842 as an additional facility and continued to serve the itinerant population until the twentieth century.

The Curr Night Refuge was opened in West Bell Street, Dundee in 1882. The initiative followed a letter from the chief constable bemoaning the lack of such a facility.[6] Mr. Dewar wrote, 'There are always many persons in need of a night's shelter and a wholesome meal, which if provided, may tide over a temporary necessity . . .' From 1876 arrangements had been made for such casuals to stay overnight in a common lodging house but, although thousands had been accommodated in this way, the demands for a proper Night Asylum continued. It proved of great value to migrant workers and others in need of temporary shelter.

Applications were made in person each night to the Night Asylum officers. If accepted (and almost everyone was except known troublemakers), the applicant was entitled to soup and bread in the evening, floor space and perhaps a blanket overnight, and oatmeal porridge and buttermilk in the morning before departure. Occupants were only supposed to stay one or two nights. The Saturday night intake was kept until Monday morning.

Night Asylum managers were inevitably drawn into the problems of their clients, and so found themselves providing additional services. In Glasgow they were alarmed at the numbers of 'respectable females without means or friends and out of place or work'. To provide for some of these women on a long-term basis they established a House of Industry (1 January 1842). The women did sewing work to pay for their keep. But after the first enthusiasm there were few applicants.

In Edinburgh the Night Asylum had grown out of the Strangers' Friend Society (1817). The object of this sort of Society was to provide temporary assistance to strangers and genuine travellers. In Edinburgh this was coupled with keen anxiety to remove them from within the city bounds to prevent them from becoming a burden on the poor rates. The Strangers' Friend Society organised journeys out of Edinburgh for those stranded, obtaining tickets from steamboat and railway companies 'at less than their ordinary fares', and so made a small budget (between £150-£200 per annum) go a long way. The Society was based for many years at 84 High Street, where its officials interviewed applicants for aid. A crisis in their affairs came in 1869 when the activities of the Edinburgh Improvement Trust rendered their property 'ruinous and untenantable'. At this date they offered to amalgamate with the Night Asylum, whose objectives seemed to them to be similar. A joint body emerged in 1871 known as the Edinburgh Night Asylum and Strangers' Friend Society. This sensible amalgamation enabled the Strangers' Friend Society to survive. It continued to vet its applicants and provide them with tickets, although some clients apparently failed to depart unless actually seen off by the officers of the Society.

In Dundee they were perhaps more practical and more realistic. Instead of trying to reverse the process of workers streaming into the cities by sending them home, they tried, after 1882, to organise 'a labour bureau in connection with the refuge, where employers of labour and those in search of work might be brought into contact with one another'. This attempt at a labour exchange reveals an appreciation of the problem of improving the labour market. The Dundee managers also felt that 'A labour yard would be valuable which would be much taken advantage of, by men and women who are out of employment and who would be only too willing to give their work in return for food and shelter until more profitable employment could be found for them.'[7]

The only detailed insight into the workings of a Night Asylum after 1900 appears in the evidence of the Superintendent and the Hon. Treasurer of the Glasgow Night Asylum, who appeared before the Glasgow Municipal Commission on the Housing of the Poor. From this it is clear that they were becoming alarmed at the increase in numbers of persons applying to them.

Table 41

Night Asylum, Glasgow: total overnight stays, 1838-1902

Year	Men	Boys	Women	Girls	Total	Grand Total
1838-97	790,667	178,925	826,894	176,152	1,972,638	
1898	32,333	5,925	21,823	5,656	65,107	
1899	33,207	4,746	21,996	5,478	65,427	
1900	36,402	4,645	23,825	5,446	70,318	
1901	45,076	5,747	27,959	6,523	85,305	
1902	42,330	4,851	23,802	5,698	76,681	
	980,015	204,209	946,299	204,953	2,335,476	2,335,476

Source: Glasgow Municipal Commission on the Housing of the Poor (Glasgow 1904), 481.

In 1902 the Glasgow Night Asylum appears to have been housing over 210 persons per night.

The Table of nationalities gives some idea of the proportion of Glasgow citizens who sought shelter as well as of Scots from outwith the city. It also reveals the number of Irish who looked to the Night Asylum.

Table 42

Night Asylum, Glasgow: place of origin of people admitted, 1838-1902

Year	Glasgow	All other parts of Scotland	England	Ireland	Foreign	Total	Grand Total
1838-97	692,007	747,945	124,004	392,873	15,809	1,972,638	
1898	28,067	20,575	3,655	12,103	707	65,107	
1899	28,099	19,549	3,712	13,450	617	65,427	
1900	29,198	21,858	3,238	15,379	645	70,318	
1901	36,757	26,076	3,656	18,129	687	85,305	
1902	32,818	22,868	3,820	16,589	586	76,681	
	846,946	858,871	142,085	468,523	19,051	2,335,476	2,335,476

Source: Glasgow Municipal Commission on the Housing of the Poor (Glasgow 1904), 481.

There seems no doubt that the philanthropic provision of temporary overnight shelter supplied by the Night Asylums in Scotland was a substantial contribution to communities seriously overstrained by large numbers of temporary residents.

4. The Model Lodging House

The other possible place of shelter for the temporary resident in a Scottish Victorian city was the lodging house. Men and women who owned or rented larger property were quickly engaged in the lodging house business, encouraging hundreds to sleep, for a small fee, in crowded beds or in a cramped space on the floor. There were no standards and no control; men and women who had come to Central Scotland from the black (windowless) houses of the Highlands and from Ireland were glad of anywhere to sleep and make contacts. As James Watson explained, '. . . a large portion of the dwellings of the poor in the Wynds and Streets upon the south side of the Trongate, in the High Street, Gallowgate, Calton consist of lodging houses, and constitute the very worst parts of these localities.'[8] In Glasgow, before the really serious influx of the famine-driven population from Ireland, Dr. Cowan, one of the city's District Police Surgeons, stated the case plainly enough: 'The lodging-houses are the media through which the newly arrived immigrants find their way to the fever hospital and it is remarkable how many of the inmates . . . coming from lodging houses, have not been six months in the city.'[9]

Various philanthropists, looking at the housing scene in Glasgow, Edinburgh or Aberdeen, and shocked at the overcrowding, believed that they could do better. They entered the lodging house business to try and provide clean, wholesome, well managed accommodation at reasonable overnight fees. The Edinburgh Lodging House Association was founded in 1841, with the modest ambition of adapting old houses for lodging house purposes. The Association opened its first house, for 70 men, in the West Port (1844). Later a tiny house was opened in Rattray's Close, Cowgate (1847) for 8 men; but this proved too small and premises in Merchant Street were converted in 1849 for 76 men.

The Glasgow response came rather later, but was on a much bigger (and more expensive) scale.[10] The Glasgow Association for Establishing Lodging Houses for the Working Classes was begun in 1847 with the ambition of providing 5,000 beds a night.[11] In Mitchell Street it opened 'a house of four floors, with accommodation for about 60 individuals. In this house the lodger can procure a comfortable and clean bed for 3d., and a wholesome and plain breakfast or supper for 2d; he can sleep securely, having a place perfectly private.' Later the Association opened in McAlpine Street, where in 1858 family rooms were provided at 1s. per night rent. But this house was so small that the Association quickly purchased property in Greendyke Street, where it altered the buildings and extended them. The Glasgow Association reported on their Greendyke Street venture with some pride,

> In 1855 the Glasgow Association at their Greendyke Street venture, accommodated 45,200 people (maximum 46,000), they handled 770 every week (maximum 800) and 124 every night (maximum 128).[12]

This success was so marked that the Association was encouraged to undertake new ventures. It was anxious to supply lodgings for women as well as men, and so obtained sites in Carrick Street (women) and McAlpine Street (men) and there built two new hostels. These were opened with high hopes in April 1857. But in October 1857 the Western Bank of Scotland crashed, creating a great business crisis in Glasgow and the West of Scotland.[13] Many were thrown out of work and the new hostels were not as immediately successful as might have been expected. The overall figures were gloomily discussed in the annual report:

	1860	*1861*	*Decrease*
McAlpine Street (men)	58,671	56,086	2,585
Greendyke Street (men)	45,749	45,492	257
Carrick Street (women)	25,231	25,913	682 increase[14]

In order to preserve standards at all, the inmates were subjected to close discipline. The Directors liked to use phrases like 'Liberty Hall', but inmates might have chosen other titles. In 1885 the regulations in force in Glasgow were:

1st.   That every man pay for his bed before being admitted.
2nd.   No one admitted in a state of intoxication.
3rd.   No intoxicating drinks allowed on the premises.
4th.   No swearing or indecent language; no fighting or uproarious conduct of any kind allowed.
5th.   Cleanliness in habits and person to such an extent as the nature of their employments admits of.[15]

These 'working people's hostels' also had regular prayer meetings. Evening prayers and Sunday services were organised by willing churchmen. Although attendance at these was not compulsory, no doubt absence would not go unnoticed. The general regulations were enforced by superintendents who must have been tough and authoritarian to survive. For example: 'High wages and perquisites — about £100 per annum all found — attracted men like a Drill Sergeant of the Third Argyll Rifles, appointed in 1878 from over 100 applicants to be superintendent at Portugal Street.'[16]

The Corporation of Glasgow, fearful of the common lodging houses' reputation as a source of infection during the fever epidemics, were anxious to raise standards. In 1866 the Glasgow City Improvement Trustees secured considerable powers which were reinforced by the Public Health (Scotland) Act of 1867. In 1870 the first sanitary inspector was appointed and in the same year corporation officers started to inspect lodging houses.

Over the next twenty years the Corporation of Glasgow gradually took over and became owner of some thirteen Model Lodging Houses. The Corporation in law exerted considerable authority and found it easier to have the 'Models' directly under its control. As can be seen from Table 43, Glasgow Corporation had taken over or opened on its own behalf six 'models' for women by 1891.

Table 43

Glasgow Corporation Model Lodging Houses in 1891

		Inmates	Irish born
Model Lodging Houses	(Drygate)	296	88
	Greendyke	294	114
	Clyde Street	360	91
	McAlpine Street	337	86
	N. Woodside Road	352	131
	Hydepark Street	361	117
	Portugal Street	345	117
(Females) —	Russell Street	133	24
	Watson Street	121	27
	Watson Street	427	119
	Watson Street	558	142
	Gt. Hamilton Street	397	96
	Clyde Place	179	41
Total in Model Lodging Houses		4,160	1,193

Source: Laidlaw, S., *Glasgow Common Lodging Houses and the People Living in Them* (Glasgow 1956), Appendix II.

The Lodging House Associations had long tried to accommodate working women, and this demand Glasgow Corporation had attempted to meet. There was a special problem in housing women, for women's wages were disgracefully low and few could afford even the modest fees. As Margaret Irwin said in 1903, in reply to the question, 'How do single women pay the current rent?' — 'I am afraid that it is a mystery, they simply starve, year in and year out.'[17] Many women had to live crowded in with relatives where they received a hidden subsidy from living *en famille*. Some women living in lodging houses were forced into prostitution when jobs were scarce; it was very easy for the houses to become branded as houses of ill-repute. Strict supervision was required. But once Glasgow had taken over responsibility for them, they had a good reputation. Mary Higgs, writing later, put the matter plainly: 'Those who have visited the Glasgow Lodging House testify that it is well conducted, and that Municipal control means well-regulated hours and entire absence of the degradation, vice and uncleanliness inevitably associated with the common lodging house.'[18]

The only figures which show the cost of the Women's Lodging House relate to the year 1872:

Table 44

Outgoings at the Women's Lodging House, Glasgow, in 1872

Matron's Salary	£70 0 0		Fire Insurance	£5 0 0
Harmoniumist	5 0 0		Bedding	18 0 0
Servants	261 4 2		Repairs	68 0 0
Fuel	94 0 0		Telephone	4 0 0
Gas	43 0 0		Manager's Office	22 0 0
Water	23 0 0		Interest	253 0 0
Rates and Taxes	124 0 0		Entertainments	8 0 0
Washings & Furnishings	154 0 0		Depreciations	90 0 0
			Total	£1,242 4 2

Source: Higgs, M., and Hayward, E., *Where Shall She Live?* (London 1910), 204-5.

The record of the philanthropists in providing temporary accommodation for a mobile population in Victorian Scotland through the medium of the Night Asylum and the Model Lodging House is impressive. At this level of provision the relationship between the city authorities (usually acting through the police) and the philanthropic manager was close and harmonious. In Glasgow, where the problem of the houseless was most acute, the town council was responsive to the demand and moved quickly into taking overall responsibility for model lodging houses.

The demand for this temporary accommodation showed no signs of slackening at the end of the century, and this led to some questioning of the function of both the Night Asylums and the Lodging Houses. Many persons began to think that they had encouraged a vagrant population which had made a way of life out of such temporary shelter.

NOTES

1. Gauldie, E., *Cruel Habitations* (London 1974); Tarn, J. N., *Five per cent Philanthropy* (London 1973); Butt, J., 'Working class housing in Glasgow, 1851-1914', in Chapman, S. D., ed., *The History of Working Class Housing* (Newton Abbot 1971); Best, G., 'Another part of the Island', in Dyos, J., ed., *The Victorian City* (London 1971).
2. Graham, 1818, 64.
3. *GAFCS* (Edinburgh 1863), report on Houses for the Working Classes, 3.
4. ENAM, 10 January 1871.
5. *GMCHP* (Glasgow 1904), question 10202, evidence 478-489.
6. *Dundee Advertiser*, 19 September 1882.
7. Anon., *Curr Night Refuge for the Homeless* (Dundee 1882), 6.
8. *GALH*, AR (Glasgow 1847), 4.
9. Quoted in Baird, C. R., *Report on the general and sanitary condition of the working classes and the poor in the city of Glasgow* (Glasgow 1841), 21.
10. The Glasgow initiative came from a group of businessmen who were also civic leaders, including James Watson and John Blackie. See Jeans, J. Stephen, *Western Worthies* (Glasgow 1872), 155-157, and Laidlaw, S., *Glasgow Common Lodging Houses and the People Living in Them* (Glasgow 1956).
11. *GALH*, AR (Glasgow 1847), 6.

12. *Ibid.* (Glasgow 1855), 4.
13. Checkland, S. G., 1975, 446-9.
14. *GALH*, AR (Glasgow 1857), 6.
15. *Ibid.* (Glasgow 1855), 5-6.
16. Butt, J., 'Working-class Housing in Glasgow, 1851-1914', 64, in Chapman, S. D., ed., *The History of Working Class Housing* (Newton Abbot 1971).
17. *GMCHP* (Glasgow 1904), Miss M. Irwin question 11453, evidence 523-537.
18. Higgs and Hayward, 1910, 204-5.

19

The Housing Debate

1. Permanent housing: the philanthropic response

EVEN more serious than the problem of shelter for transients was the general condition of working-class homes. Philanthropists turned their attention to the provision of permanent accommodation in the form of housing for those workers who lacked clean and decent homes. These concerned men sought to plan and build 'model' dwellings of various types, intending to demonstrate to commercial house builders the possibilities of relatively low-income housing. Unfortunately for the exercise, the commercial men were perhaps more hard-headed than the philanthropists. Although the 'models' were demonstrated in the four major cities of Scotland, the expected stimulus to private enterprise housing for the workers never materialised.

The problem of housing has basically two parts, namely the provision of site services, including water and sanitation, and the building of the shell in which people live. Because of the killing epidemic diseases which swept British cities in the nineteenth century, vigorous action had to be taken to meet the first of these requirements by community action. The state intervened, encouraging the local authorities to develop their own schemes to tap water supplies from abundantly supplied rural areas and to lay drains to collect and dispose of sewage. A sanitary inspectorate was built up to ensure that the rules were adhered to. But once this had been done, the financial pattern of housing building changed. Prior to the introduction of these modest standards, houses could be put up speculatively by builders who could hope to sell or rent at a profit. Such houses were often mere shelters from the wind and weather. The only amenity built into them was a fireplace and a chimney. Otherwise they were boxes, with tiny rooms and thin dividing walls. With the insistence upon sanitary arrangements and the provision of water supply, higher standards were imposed, and building regulations became increasingly complex. Small builders, the principal suppliers of working class houses, recognising that even the simplest regulations cost them time and money, abandoned constructing cheap houses and resorted to alterations, over-building and in-filling. They thus operated on the existing housing stock rather than adding to it.

The problem was compounded by the rise in the cost of urban land. Cheap land for housing, near city centres, no longer existed. Land values rose as offices and factories competed for convenient inner city sites. Before the advent of cheap local workmen's trains and trams, houses had to be within walking distance of work, and the crisis of availability of land coincided with the rapid rise of city populations in Victorian Scotland.

There were several groups of philanthropic activists in the field, each with its solutions. They included both churchmen and practical businessmen, both of whom demonstrated their 'model' solutions. The churchmen were strong advocates of the patriarchal family system, and wanted each family to have a home of its own. Inspired by the Biblical injunction, 'Enter into thy closet to pray', they resisted the use of one-roomed houses and the bothy system (whereby unmarried farm-workers lived communally), neither of which allowed any privacy. This Bible-based housing policy was advocated by James Begg of Edinburgh (1808-1883), who believed that 'The most important physical remedy for the woes of man is a comfortable and wholesome dwelling.'[1] Begg was supported by Hugh Miller (1802-1856), who brought much publicity to the campaign through his editorship of *The Witness*. Under the churchmen's influence terraces of respectable working men's houses were built in Edinburgh, but the movement never became more than an interesting experiment.

More practical business philanthropists, often linked to the civic leaders' group, launched schemes for encouraging working men to build or rent better houses. The provision of permanent housing depended upon raising sufficient capital at a low rate of interest. The usual way of doing this was for wealthy subscribers to build up a fund for charitable purposes, of which housing was one. The plan was that once the money was available it could be invested in building new houses which, when rented, would provide enough revenue to service the property and provide a return on the capital investment. This '5% philanthropy' was heavily criticised for its apparent ungenerousness, demanding as it did such a return on money supposedly charitably provided. But the practical good sense of Victorian businessmen did not allow them to consider the use of capital without a proper return. The Artisans' and Workmen's Dwelling Companies run on 5% philanthropy were intended to be 'models' or examples to builders. It was therefore of fundamental importance that they adopted principles of sound business management. Without the element of profitable return there was no way speculative builders could possibly be encouraged to emulate the activities of the philanthropic builders.

In addition there were disciples of Octavia Hill working in Scotland along entirely different (although basically philanthropic) lines. She was an ameliorist, working on the principles of sound property management, together with the encouragement of tenant self-discipline. She needed relatively little capital, used volunteer labour, and attempted to manage working-class housing effectively and efficiently so as to provide support for her tenants. Her colleagues managed the properties by collecting rents regularly and on time, attending to repairs promptly, and achieving a high standard of maintenance.

U

The development of this kind of work in Scotland was undertaken by the Kyrle Society in Glasgow and the Social Union in Edinburgh. This type of experiment is perhaps more properly classified as social work and as such is discussed in chapter 20, section 2, below.

But these societies were small and experimental, and no great movement grew out of them. The aspiration of owning the family home was rare and was too big a challenge for most Scottish working-class families to face. Only workmen paid regularly, and in specially favourable employment, could risk the obligations which house ownership brought. Nor was there any encouragement for the wage earner to remain a house owner. House taxes were high; in addition, if the threat of unemployment became a reality, men who were house owners were discriminated against by relief and poor law committees on the grounds that they were not destitute and had an asset which they could realise.[2]

2. Building societies

Middle class activists were keen to encourage working men to organise societies through which they could accumulate funds and build their own houses, or buy houses already built. These societies were not necessarily intended to be philanthropic ventures. They were based rather on self-help, although many were indebted to the leisured classes for their initiation and organisation.

The Edinburgh Working Men's Building Association (1860) and the Edinburgh Co-operative Building Company Ltd. (1861) were apparently established and organised by working men without the executive or financial intrusion of the middle classes. The Edinburgh Trades Council encouraged the Working Men's Building Association. The Co-operative Building Company grew out of the 1861 stonemasons' strike and lock-out. Both Societies were successful in helping workers to save and to build and occupy their own houses. No doubt they were helped by the tradition of co-operation in Edinburgh.

The Dundee Working Men's Houses Association Ltd. was more typical. It was founded in 1864 (following a visit to the city of Dr. James Begg) to secure 'the providing of dwelling houses within the Town of Dundee suited for the occupation of the working classes; the acquisition of land . . . the purchase of houses already built . . . and the letting, sale or disposal of said houses'.[3] 1,043 shares of £1 each were subscribed by 113 shareholders, and 53 of these shares were reported to be held by working men, the other 930 shares being taken by 'merchants and others'. Donations of £130 18s. were also received. Ten two-storey tenement houses (containing four units in each block) were built for sale in Blyth Street. Unfortunately the prosperity which Dundee had enjoyed during the American Civil War ended abruptly, leaving some of the Blyth

Street houses unsold and empty. The prices had to be reduced before they could be disposed of.

3. Workmen's dwellings

Yet another venture was launched in 1890. The Glasgow Workmen's Dwelling Company was established with a capital of £40,000. This body was fortunate in that the secretary was John Mann junior, a chartered accountant, who had worked in London as well as Glasgow and whose enthusiasm for housing schemes of this nature caused him to give a good deal of his time to them. The new tenements built by the Society were intended for respectable families. Of four or five storeys, they were constructed of brick, with balconies, concrete lintels and facings. Each house was 'fitted with bed frames, kitchen range, dresser, coal box, gas fittings, water supply and (in joint use with one other tenant) water closet on the balcony'.[4] They also had a chute for the disposal of rubbish together with ample washing house accommodation.

Perhaps of even greater interest was the policy of the Company in reconstructing poor property badly in need of repair. The four properties chosen for this demonstration were all 'ticketed' houses. That is to say they had been condemned by Glasgow Corporation as overcrowded, and a small metal plaque giving the legal maximum of people had been nailed to the door of each house. The Corporation action ended here; ticketed houses were still habitable but were under a kind of notice that the Corporation might eventually clear the site. No previous attempt had ever been made by the city authorities or the

Table 45

Glasgow Workmen's Dwelling Company Limited: new houses built

Property	Number of Houses				Club Rooms and Halls	Totals	Annual Gross Rental
	1 Rooms	*2 Rooms*	*3 Rooms*	*4 Rooms*			
Cathedral Court, Rottenrow	8	48	1	—	1	58	£548
Greenhead Court, Bridgeton Cross	131	56	1	—	1	189	£1,355
Reconstructions Property							
Ardgowan Place, Southside formerly Bolton Street	57	33	1	—	2	93	£603
Dundas Court, Brown Street, Port Dundas	30	35	2	—	1	68	£408

Source: GMCHP, John Mann, jr., precognition, para. 15, 393.

philanthropists to rehabilitate dilapidated houses. But in so doing the Workmen's Dwelling Company were following advice given by Octavia Hill, who advocated minor improvements to property rather than wholesale re-housing.

In April 1903 John Mann gave evidence of the activities of the Company to the Glasgow Municipal Commission on Housing of the Poor (see Table 45).

4. A philanthropic failure?

The philanthropic stimulation of permanent house building as a result of 'model' house building was not a success in Scotland. An enormous gap remained between houses provided and houses required. The examples set by the philanthropists were not sufficient to stimulate emulation.

The housing philanthropist was a middle-class individual with means, leisure and a good education. By devoting his skills to the Model Housing Association he made use of his business experience and contacts and so could surmount the planning hurdles which yearly became more formidable. At no time were his services costed; they therefore remained hidden, appearing in no balance sheet. The private builder who was to be enticed into emulating the philanthropist found that there was no real 'model' for him to follow, as his costs would have to include the hidden subsidies which the philanthropic experimenter provided but left out of the cost calculation.[5]

Building societies in Scotland, whether organised by workmen or their masters, were never really successful. There were many reasons for this. Few workmen thought of themselves as property owners; most did not wish to take on such onerous obligations and did not want to occupy the houses provided for purchase because they were larger than they wanted to pay for. As the Property Investment Association explained, it 'found that those few workers who used its resources usually sold their property on completion of payments, and bought inferior houses to live in themselves'.[6] Workers were never secure enough, had little or no reserves or insurance and so, with relatively few exceptions, could not commit themselves to house buying. In yet another sense, house purchase was too big a step for working class families to take, for the houses available were often in areas of a better class, demanding a major and unpopular move for families from their own communities. Middle-class philanthropists encouraged the artisan class to accept their standards. As Robert Q. Gray has explained of the skilled artisan in Edinburgh, 'The accumulation of savings was thus often linked to the hopes of moving to superior housing.' But few felt sufficiently secure to embark upon so major an undertaking as house buying.

It took many years for the middle classes to recognise that many workers suffered from acute poverty and that on the wages which they earned they could not hope to pay a regular rent for decent property. In the end the only way out was for the local authority to build municipal housing at low rents supported by public money. But throughout Victorian times there was a 'subsidy barrier'; few middle-class taxpayers could conceive of a system whereby working-class tenants would be liable for only a part of their rent. Nor was this blindness confined to the middle classes.

There were two enquiries into the problems of housing the poor in Glasgow. Reports were published in 1890 and 1902-3. The earlier investigation was set up by the Glasgow Presbytery of the Church of Scotland, the second by Glasgow Corporation. Two Socialists, Bruce Glasier[7] and Joseph Burgess,[8] gave evidence to these commissions. Their reactions to questions concerned with the housing of the poor were very different. Glasier emphasised the economic problems of low-paid unskilled labour. He quoted costs of upkeep in various residential homes; he claimed that a pauper in the City Poor House cost £15 16s. 11d. per year, while in Duke Street Prison it was £17 18s. 1d. Even a child at Quarrier's Home cost £12. 15s. From this he concluded that no workman in low paid or erratic employment could hope to keep a family cleanly or decently on £1 a week. When asked about the responsibility of Glasgow Corporation to build houses for the poor he replied, 'I think it is the very first duty of the Corporation to undertake it.'[9] Joseph Burgess, a Yorkshireman, newly arrived in Glasgow, was not so clear. His evidence mainly concerned the need for Glasgow to build 'self-contained cottages'. He did not understand the prevalence of the continental-type tenement in Glasgow and consistently undervalued it. But when questioned about the financing of housing schemes for the workers, he contended that 'There is no necessity in any housing scheme for housing any class at the expense of the citizens.' When further pressed by Professor Glaister who asked, 'Is it your opinion . . . that you do not approve of any housing scheme that comes upon the rates?' Burgess answered, 'I do not.'[10]

That Burgess, a leading Socialist both in his native Bradford and in Glasgow, had not accepted the need for subsidised housing suggests that the idea was slow to take root. Both Enid Gauldie[11] and Anthony Wohl[12] suggest that not only did philanthropic housing do nothing to solve the Victorian housing problem, but that the existence and publicity for 'philanthropic' housing measures merely delayed the adoption of subsidised municipal housing. The argument here is that the philanthropists were wrongly accused, for although their remedies were not effective, the real obstacle to housing progress was the unwillingness of Scottish voters to accept any further burden on the rates.

Indeed when Glasgow Corporation did start building 'model' housing in the 1890's it was intended for policemen and public servants, respectable families who had regular wages and who would be a credit to the flats. Neither the philanthropists nor anyone else succeeded in housing the irregularly paid of Victorian and Edwardian times, who so often combined lack of skills with ill-health and other disabilities. It took the First World War to reconcile the nation to the idea of subsidised housing.

NOTES

1. See Begg, J., 1866.
2. See Gray, R. Q., 1977.
3. Gauldie, 1974, 203.
4. *GMCHP,* John Mann, jr., precognition, para. 6., evidence 391-411.
5. Gauldie, 1974, Chapter 20.
6. *Ibid.,* 206.
7. Bruce Glasier, an architectural draughtsman, was at this time Secretary of the Glasgow Branch of the Socialist League.
8. Joseph Burgess, Labour councillor for Townhead Ward, Glasgow, Labour journalist and lecturer, candidate for Parliament, Leicester by-election 1894, general election 1895, a founder of the Independent Labour Party, Labour organiser at Leeds, came to Glasgow in the same capacity 1899, member of Scottish Workers' Labour Representative Committee, 1899-1903, commissioned by I.L.P. to study English Housing and report to this committee.
9. *Glasgow Presbytery Church of Scotland Commission* (Glasgow 1891). Glasier's evidence 179-189 (GUL Bf76.d.3).
10. *GMCHP,* Joseph Burgess, question 5658, evidence 254-279.
11. Gauldie, 1974, 235.
12. Wohl, 1977, 177-178.

PART VII

The Philanthropist Challenged

20

The Approach to Professionalism

1. The need for a new beginning

THE effort by the middle classes both in England and Scotland to place charity on some kind of systematic basis began in the late 1860's. By this time a multiple challenge was apparent. It was necessary to base charity on a set of principles; this involved a theory of entitlement which in turn rested upon a theory of society. Secondly, the need for data, so important in the promotion of Chadwickian legislation, was now apparent in terms of the voluntarist principle: social investigation was imperative. Thirdly, there was serious overlap in the services provided; this meant not only waste, which was serious enough, but also the debauching of the poor through what was called 'indiscriminate charity' or 'giving money without thought'. Finally, dedication and the amateur principle in social work were no longer enough; training and professional status were required. At the same time it was necessary to extend the social work labour force by the recruitment, on a new scale, of women.

2. The Charity Organisation Society

In 1869 there was established in London the Society for Organising Charitable Relief and Repressing Mendicity.[1] It became generally known as the Charity Organisation Society. The COS brought a new dimension to the attack upon the problems of poverty. Its organisers recognised that most philanthropists and charity workers were basically ignorant of the extent of the social problems which confronted them. In consequence the Society involved itself in serious fact-finding, and so helped to inaugurate the age of social enquiry. Its members, having thus armed themselves with knowledge, attempted a more ambitious diagnosis of social problems. They also called for certain forms of social amelioration. They were, indeed, a major source of information and opinion for the government. The members of the COS were therefore the forerunners of modern social workers. They were able to be such partly because they especially encouraged women to involve themselves. Middle-class girls and women were searching for outlets in the form of education and employment, and were slowly forcing their way into the universities and colleges. In all this there was an interplay between England and Scotland.

The Edinburgh Association for Improving the Condition of the Poor was founded in 1868.[2] It anticipated the COS in the new approach to charitable work and was influenced by both Thomas Chalmers and the Elberfeld System.[3] The Association divided the city into 28 districts, within each of which 'visitors' were to pursue their enquiries about the needs of individuals and families. They were to avoid 'an inquisitional or magisterial air'. But after the first flush of enthusiasm in 1869, when the Association was able to publish the names of members and officers of all its district committees, volunteer effort fell away. By 1873 systematic visitation had had to be suspended. As Rhona Morrison stresses, the failure of volunteers to come forward in Edinburgh on a sufficient and sustained scale undermined this attempt at a systematic approach to charitable relief. She also emphasises the point, rarely made, that at Elberfeld, citizens had a legal obligation to 'volunteer' for service with the Poor Law; there were sanctions hanging over them if they failed to do their stint.

The Edinburgh Association for Improving the Condition of the Poor was renamed *The Help* in 1893. It continued to work along traditional lines. Because of the inability of the able-bodied poor in Scotland to claim a legal right to relief, the Scottish societies, including that of Edinburgh, had a wider responsibility than the COS branches in England. They were under constant pressure, especially after the annual conference of the COS in Glasgow in 1897, to become affiliated to the nationwide movement. In 1900 the first edition of *The Edinburgh Philanthropic Year Book* was published, modelled on the *COS Annual Charities Register and Digest*. C. S. Loch (1849-1923) had become Secretary of the COS in 1875, a post which he held until 1914. He was a Scotsman, and was anxious to reconstruct the Edinburgh organisation. This was eventually done in 1906, when the Edinburgh Association was reconstituted as the Edinburgh Charity Organisation Society.

In Glasgow the Association for Organising Charitable Relief and Repressing Mendicity was set up in 1874. Its object was to achieve 'the proper distribution of Charitable Relief and the promotion of the Welfare of the Poor, without regard to creeds'. As in London and Edinburgh, these objectives were to be attained by the careful investigation of the circumstances of all applicants for charity, the granting of small loans to persons who might be in temporary difficulty, and the examining of the claims of those societies soliciting public support by providing reliable information about them.

The Aberdeen Association for Improving the Condition of the Poor was set up in 1870 on Charity Organisation Society principles. It continued to work until after the Second World War, when it was re-organised as the Aberdeen Council for Social Services. All, indeed, of the COS branches eventually underwent this change.

'Careful investigation' represented a new element, a new 'scientific' approach to the exercise of charitable functions in Scotland as in England. Greater care and sensitivity to social problems led directly to the emergence of the social worker as an essential component of social provision. The Charity Organisation Society implied a criticism of the accounting methods and casual procedures of earlier days. Its first two objectives, the investigation of cases of need and the granting of small loans, were adopted because they involved direct and searching investigations. The organisers of benevolent societies that benefited from the COS enquiries were warm in their praise: the Glasgow Angus and Mearns Benevolent Society, for example, said: 'We would here take the opportunity of stating publicly the indebtedness of this Society, and no doubt of many other similar societies, to the Glasgow COS for the excellent and prompt help it is always ready to give to societies as well as individuals in investigating such cases and furnishing thoroughly reliable information, and thus preventing imposture.'[4] The COS in England and in Scotland achieved its objectives with the aid of a new class of social worker. In Glasgow the COS employed an investigating agent who did the fieldwork and reported weekly to the Council of the Society. In 1876 it first published a booklet listing the charities of the city, which has since been frequently re-issued.

But despite its novel approach, the COS in Scotland was not so forward-looking as it pretended to be. The prophet of the COS in Scotland was Thomas Chalmers. Many references were made to his work in St. John's Parish, Glasgow, as if it had been a triumphant success. The Society might usefully have enquired more closely into the figures which supporters of Chalmers so readily quoted. Part of Chalmers' claim to be remembered rests on his attempts to stimulate interest in direct social enquiry as undertaken by parochial deacons and his insistence on treating the family as a unit. For this he must be given credit. But a closer scrutiny of his efforts to cut down the amount granted for poor relief in St. John's reveals some curious accounting.[5]

The Scottish COS made a disappointingly small impact, at least in terms of its objectives. As the *Glasgow Herald* wrote at the time of the seventh annual meeting: 'To carry out the original idea of (their) founders the societies ought to occupy the whole ground; their operations should be coterminous with those of charity itself. It is not possible to regard the movement as really successful and completely efficient as long as it is only the hobby of a few enlightened individuals, and is regarded with jealousy and even disfavour by a large section of the community.'[6] The COS did make more or less systematic enquiry about other societies, seeking to discover unnecessarily high administrative costs and to investigate organisations that were exploiting the public. Inevitably this inquisitorial approach was deeply resented, making the COS unpopular with many charities.

But much more fundamental were the old attitudes towards the poor. The organisers of the COS were ameliorists par excellence, imbued with so many ideas of self-help that they unhappily lost sight of the basic problems of poverty. They continued to think in the patronising terms of the early days.

They were hostile to the introduction of the old age pension in 1908 because it was 'indiscriminate'. Some earlier supporters of the COS who recognised the inherent limitations of this sort of piecemeal treatment of the poor moved on to found the Fabian Society in 1884. This new venture had as its watchwords 'Educate, Agitate, Organise.'[7] The Socialist movement in general believed in the inevitability of class struggle: it induced a radical change in the outlook towards charity. In its view working men and their families were quite right to refuse charity and should demand much more from the community as of right. Higher wages were believed to be essential in order that the working family could from their own resources supply their own needs.

The COS was thus overtaken by new ideologies which attacked the very roots of its philosophy. Fundamental to its creed was the problem of definition: how could the deserving poor be differentiated from the un-deserving? The COS failure to discover how to distinguish between the two reflected the intransigent nature of the problem. But the COS was aware of its failure to make the impact in Scotland which it had hoped for. Its members included a number of University teachers in Glasgow led by Professor William Smart, first holder, from 1896, of the chair of Political Economy. They made efforts to encourage new initiatives. But the pattern within the COS appears to have been unchanged; the condescension of the middle class toward the workers seemed to remain. The organisers of the Scottish COS's were following the traditional pattern of behaviour towards the downtrodden, coming dangerously close to patronising them. Their efforts to deal with the challenge of rationalisation are dealt with below in chapter 21, section 2.

The relations between the Scottish and the English COS reflected the differing circumstances of the two countries. In Scotland, because there was no legal provision for the able-bodied under the poor law, the COS there tended to be somewhat more generous in its giving. Loch, on the other hand, wanted the system of charitable relief to follow more or less uniform principles throughout Britain. The national conferences of the COS held in Glasgow in 1897 and in Edinburgh in 1902 did bring about closer collaboration with London.

Soon there were other initiatives. In 1888 James Burn Russell (the Medical Officer of Health for Glasgow) had published *Life in One Room*; it caused a great stir, stimulating discussion and concern about social welfare. In 1889 the Glasgow Social Union was formed. It was intended to stimulate friendly contact between classes and to break down class barriers. It was thus very different in spirit from the COS, seeking to bring the classes together in mutual interaction. In addition it was to undertake a wide range of ameliorative measures such as the Children's Sabbath Dinner (1874), the Children's Day Refuges (1875), the Children's Fresh-air Fortnight (1888), and the Poor Children's Dinner Tables.

There were two other departures. One was the Kyrle Society, and the other the University Settlements. Both of these new developments were pioneered by women. They brought a difference in social philosophy and a breath of practical good sense into a charitable scene much hidebound by old ideas, and led on to new fields of social caring in housing management and general social work with problem families.

3. **The Kyrle Society**

The Kyrle Society in London was founded early in 1876 by Miranda and Octavia Hill.[8] Ruskin had not only helped with Miss Hill's first housing projects, but his conviction that beauty should be part of everyday life remained an important influence on her work.[9] The first Kyrle Society in Scotland was probably in Edinburgh. It became a training centre 'which sent workers to Perth, Dundee and Glasgow'.

The Glasgow Kyrle Society was founded in 1882. 'Its object shall be to bring the influences of natural and artistic beauty home to the people.' Modelled directly on the parent society, its intention was to provide better homes by better housing. This was to be combined with an awakening of a sense of beauty, together with the teaching of a range of skills, that would make it possible for families to embellish the homes provided. The Society had six sections, Music, Decorations, Sanitary Aid, Wood Carving, Housing of the Poor, and Window Gardening. Under the Music Section a very successful choir was set up which provided concerts for charitable organisations all over the city every year. The Decorations Committee organised the painting of murals and such in church halls.[10] Its work in 1894 was primarily in the Mission Halls at 384 Garscube Road, where 'We decided to decorate the principal Hall with Scriptural pictures, the subjects chosen being the parables, as it is exclusively used for Evangelical Meetings and Sunday School teaching. A smaller hall in which Sewing and Mothers Meetings are held, we hung with bright pictures of a secular kind.'[11] Window gardeners provided bulbs for schools and old people, and flowers during the summer; lectures were organised to promote good health.

The Housing Section was probably begun about 1889. Among the leading figures from the beginning was Miss Marion Brodie Blackie of the distinguished Glasgow family. She administered three properties for the Kyrle Society in 1894-5. These were at 4 West College Street, Anderston; George Court, Brook Street, Mile End; and Cathedral Court, Rottenrow. The first of these had been entrusted to her by Alexander Ferguson and Company, whose principal, Alexander Ferguson, was converted to the idea of scientific housing management. The other two belonged to the Glasgow Workmen's Dwellings Company (see chapter 19, section 3, above). By 1903 Miss Blackie had added properties at Bridgeton and Cowcaddens. Miss Blackie reported on her work to the Glasgow Municipal Housing Commission in 1903. At that time she had ten lady rent collectors in her team, who enforced simple but strict rules. All tenants had to deposit a month's rent in advance before they could obtain a tenancy. Once rents were set, they were always collected on a Monday morning; failure to pay rent for one week meant eviction. Arrangements were made for a rota of tenants' wives to undertake the cleansing of common stairs, passageways and w.c.'s. Much emphasis was placed on tenants fulfilling their duties to the small community in which they lived. Miss Blackie recommended the employment of a caretaker in each block of houses, as he could do small maintenance jobs promptly and so keep the property in good order. He could also have a disciplinary function, keeping the tenants in check, if necessary. But good caretakers were difficult to find, and could themselves generate problems. Miss Blackie permitted herself a mild joke in her evidence: 'I sometimes say the caretaker is a caremaker.'[12]

The Kyrle Society's Housing Section was inevitably on a small scale, dealing with the respectable poor and providing comfortable, clean and quiet accommodation at a reasonable rent. It was making necessary educative explorations in a field where they were badly needed. But its work could be no more than a token. It was always short of volunteer women rent collectors and good caretakers. It could not hope to do more than launch an experiment. At that time it had no imitators. One commentator sympathetic to the work of the Society was sadly dismissive of its influence:

> The Kyrle Society is endeavouring by gifts of flowers and paintings to elevate and beautify the homes of the poor — a noble aim; but it is to be feared that it is a process that will take a very long time to produce much fruit.[13]

Notwithstanding the apparent failure in the short run, the principles of good housing management, of resident caretakers and of concern for tenants were all essential lessons which municipal landlords subsequently had to learn.

4. The University Settlement movement

Whereas the COS was a middle-class response launched in the late sixties, the Settlement movement came from the same element of society in the eighties. It was an attempt to bring to bear the energies and training of university students and graduates upon the problems of the poor. This was to be done by going to the industrial slums and establishing 'Settlements' where young men could live among the poor. By lecture programmes and other means wider horizons would be opened to those whose minds were confined. In this way links could be forged between the universities and the working population.

The originator was Arnold Toynbee of Balliol College, Oxford, who died as a young man in 1883. His scheme was taken up by the Rev. Samuel A. Barnett, Vicar of St. Jude's, Whitechapel, who proposed in 1883 'To establish a University Colony in East London where men might live face to face with the actual facts of crowded city life, might gain practice and experience in social questions, and strive to ennoble the lives and improve the material condition of the people.' Men at the Universities of Oxford and Cambridge took up the proposal enthusiastically and a Universities Settlement Association was formed. Its two main objectives were:

> 1. To provide education and the means of recreation and enjoyment for the people in the poorer districts of London and other great cities; to enquire into the condition of the poor, or to consider and advance plans calculated to promote their welfare; and

> 2. To acquire by purchase or otherwise, and to maintain a house or houses for the residence of persons engaged in or connected with philanthropic or educational work.[14]

The Settlement, Toynbee Hall, was to be the base for all these activities. The educational courses, no doubt valuable in themselves, disappeared fairly soon. This was partly because of the extension of public education. Such courses were, however, incorporated later in various university extra-mural departments.

In Glasgow there were three Settlement initiatives. The first was largely due to Professor William Smart. After a visit to Toynbee Hall in London he published an account of its work advocating a Settlement in Glasgow. His arguments were threefold. In the first place he was confident that a group of young men living in a Settlement would not only do good work in its immediate neighbourhood, but also that they themselves would benefit from the enrichment of community life. Secondly, he envisaged the Settlement as an outpost of the University itself, where University Extension Lectures could be held. As he expressed it in his pamphlet: 'It is surely not creditable to our University that there is not a single class held in the evening, nor any attempt made to get at the mass of people. As a consequence there is considerable bitterness and hostility towards the University.' Thirdly, he wanted to encourage 'social intercourse' between the residents in the Settlement and those in its environs. As a result of Smart's enthusiasm, the Glasgow University Settlement Association was formed in November 1886. Smart was the Treasurer and the moving spirit. He rented part of a building in Townhead erected by the Workmen's Dwelling Association (of which he was a Director), and there established the Association and its Settlement, named from 1897 Toynbee House. It became the base for the Glasgow Kyrle Society.

In this work Smart was supported by many within the University, including the Principal, John Caird. As Caird wrote: 'From the outset we have tried to make Toynbee House a centre of social work in the district. Members of the Association, grouped together as "families", undertook to get gradually associated with residents and to invite them to social gatherings . . . Every one now acknowledges that this kind of work is most essential to knit the various classes of the community together, and to extend the blessings of civilization to all.'[15] The Men's Club, the Literary Society and Library were very successful. Smart was skilful in persuading University professors and others to lecture and debate. Many men must have found new horizons opening to them, and pursued their own education further as a result. The range of topics was very wide, including (in 1897-98) 'The Engineers Lock-out, Agricultural Depression, Taxation of Land Values, Three-fold Option, Eight-hours Day, Co-operation, Equality and Should the Lifeboat movement be under State Control.' Professor Smart's contribution was perhaps primarily in this kind of University Extension teaching.

There was much social and cultural activity, including a choir, gymnastics, elocution and violin classes under Herr Romisch. In addition there were 'Drawing Rooms' where social evenings were held, organised by supporters of the Settlement. Hugh Roberton first came to public notice as leader of the Toynbee House Choir. Girls' and women's classes were also held primarily for sewing and dressmaking.

An ancillary venture was based upon Toynbee House. This was The Queen Margaret Lecture Guild. Its members were the women students of Queen Margaret College in the University of Glasgow. Its objects were to organise short courses of lectures, together with summer reading, for working women and girls. Arts courses were normally of at least six lectures, Medicine of at least three. In 1896 the women organised fourteen courses of Arts lectures and three on medical subjects. The medical courses were normally given free by sympathetic lecturers, men who were already helping to teach the women of Queen Margaret College. The courses of summer reading were intended for working girls as well as others. At the end of the summer, essays were presented which were subsequently 'examined' and prizes were awarded. In 1896 the annual prize was won 'by a girl who is employed in a factory from six to six'. Thus the enthusiasm of these young women enabled a handful of working girls to have some vision of higher education. The Guild is of special interest not so much because of the amount of work done but because of the courage of the women who ventured to tempt their sisters beyond the parameters of the sewing circle.

The second Glasgow venture was the Students' Settlement. It grew out of the University Missionary Society[16] (1821), an old-style body. Its motto was, 'The Harvest truly is great' (Matthew 9, 37). Its evangelical inspiration was reflected in its co-operation with the University Total Abstinence Society. Although it was supported by money collected from students in all faculties of the University, the students who volunteered their time were almost all Divinity men. They assisted the paid missioner. When, after 1870,[17] the University had moved to Gilmorehill, and the Missionary Society had difficulty in finding a new site for its operations, Professor Henry Drummond (1851-1897) urged that a Settlement[18] be established. It opened on 28 November 1889 at Garscube Cross. A four-storey building, formerly the store of the iron foundry that lay behind, it was known locally as the 'Roon' Toll'.[19] The Garscube Cross Settlement consisted of fifteen residents, together with many part-time volunteers. The Settlers ran the house themselves, although the Finance Committee was run by older men. Difficulties arose with the Missionary Society and it moved out of the premises in 1894.[20] Perhaps the Society's energies were sufficiently engaged in the overseas mission work which the combined Scottish universities were doing in Kalimpong and Sikkim.[21] The Student Settlement was seriously weakened during the First World War, but it survived until 1926. When given notice to quit its rented premises, it closed. It is difficult to judge its impact. Its primary purpose was religious conversion, so that its priorities were different from those of the other two Glasgow Settlements. The Students' Settlement had no connection with Smart's Glasgow University Settlement at Toynbee House.

The third venture of this kind derived from Queen Margaret College, which had been founded in 1883 to enable women to obtain a higher education. The Settlement movement appealed to its students and graduates for two main reasons: it made it possible for them to undertake social work, and it gave them somewhere to live. Women whose families and friends were anxious about girls living away from home could be reassured if they were living in the Settlement under the guardianship of a warden. In May 1897 the Queen Margaret College Settlement Association was founded, the first women's Association in Scotland.[22] It was 'to promote the welfare of the poorer people, chiefly of the women and children in the Anderston district of Glasgow'.

Thanks to the generosity of Mrs. Lander and her sister Miss Allan, premises in Port Street and Elliot Street, Anderston were acquired. The Settlement was opened by Principal Story on 3 March 1901. At first the residents consisted of the Warden and 'the lady doctor in charge of the Western branch of the Maternity hospital and the women students working under her during part of the year'.

The Queen Margaret Settlement was to be far and away the most successful in Glasgow. It housed and manned the office of the Anderston Charity Organisation Society. The close association between the two bodies reflected the commonsense, practical view of the Queen Margaret women. They believed strongly in 'rationalised' charity and were anxious to associate themselves with the work of the COS. Indeed the COS found its most productive role in Scotland in its co-operation with the Queen Margaret Settlement.

The Anderston Charity Organisation handled in the early years about 255 cases a year. These were (between December 1899 and November 1900) treated as follows:

Not assisted	88
Referred to local institutions and private individuals	66
Employment given	49
Lines for homes and infirmaries	12
Grants of money, clothing or groceries	92
Loans	25
	332

The figures are important, but much more significant was the method of handling each case:

> On Mondays and Thursdays we are in the office at 66 Port Street from 11 am. till 2 pm. to receive applicants; these are chiefly sent to us by clergymen, employers of labour, and private individuals, but a steadily increasing number come of their own accord. We begin by asking the names of all the family, their occupations and earnings; then we find out the rent of the present house, the factor's name, the previous addresses of the family, and as many particulars as possible regarding church connection, birthplace, relatives, income, debts, and prospects. When all this and a great deal more has been noted down, we have a pretty fair estimate of the person we are dealing with, but it takes a long time and plenty of patience and tact to draw out a clear account of their history and difficulties, and to grasp the essential points of the story. We then write a concise statement of the circumstances of the family, the chief causes of poverty, and the best means of giving relief. We also write to reliable sources, always including the parish authorities for information regarding character and conduct, and in cases of sickness and accident we get a doctor's opinion. The papers are next handed to an investigator, who visits the home, verifies or contradicts the statements made to us, and learns as much as he can about the applicant's past and present life.[23]

The Society/Settlement often refused to give money, 'but we try never to drop people without putting them in touch with some agency fitted to deal with them'.[24] The women were certainly indefatigable in ferreting out other agencies who might take responsibility for some of their cases. It was a very sophisticated form of social service which they offered. Because of the arduous demands of the work, it was from the beginning hampered by lack of volunteer labour.

The second arm of the work was the Anderston Collecting Savings Bank. The workers in this scheme presented themselves every Monday morning at the homes of provident working families to collect their small savings. Once £1 had been saved, the thrifty client was transferred to the Glasgow Savings Bank. In 1899 there were 9 collectors and 237 depositors. Once the business matter of savings had been completed, the 'bank ladies' were encouraged to take an interest in the family and enquire about their activities. A great deal of advice was no doubt given. The 'bank ladies' spent a great deal of time collecting comparatively small sums of money: 'From January 1900 to the end of October 1900 £104 7s. 3½d. was deposited and £88 16s. 6d. withdrawn.'[25] But the amount of time needed for this type of commitment was very great and the Settlement was always keen to recruit new collectors.

The third activity undertaken was that of caring for invalid children. This started with home teaching. While the School Boards had a statutory obligation to provide elementary schooling for all children, those who were unable to attend school because of ill-health were perforce excluded. In addition the Settlement organised visits to convalescent homes and boarding-out homes under the auspices of the Fresh-air Fortnight Society. It arranged for visiting by nurses of the Sick Poor Nursing Association. The initial list of invalid children's names and addresses was supplied (unofficially) by courtesy of the Head Inspector of the School Board. A school for invalid children was opened on 1 October 1901; children unable to cope with the rough and tumble of ordinary school-life attended daily. The School Board and the Cripple League of Kindness were associated with this work. The Glasgow School for Invalid Children was modelled on that at the Passmore Edwards Settlement in London and was the first in Scotland. In this way statutory bodies like the School Board were encouraged to extend their commitments, urged on by the voluntarists who saw a pressing need. Health visiting also expanded in this manner in Glasgow.

A member of the School Board suggested that the Settlement women should organise playground games for children. These were arranged at Bishop Street School on Saturday mornings. The idea of play as a constructive pastime for working children was foreign to many parents, and some opposition had to be overcome. Nevertheless this project was successful, with enthusiastic children enjoying the games so arranged.

More and more ideas for further services to the poor living in Anderston were constantly being aired. Many were implemented and the Settlement and its work grew from strength to strength. The Queen Margaret Settlement, by the time of the First World War, was running a milk depot for the Corporation, and had established a nursery school and a training centre for nursery school teachers. Free legal aid was pioneered later. The Settlement's efforts to find employment for working-class women through its Skilled Employment Committee were taken over by the Anderston After-care Committee of the Glasgow Labour Exchange.

Although the Queen Margaret College Settlement Association organised conferences and lecture courses on social work, it was felt by 1909 that something more systematic should be attempted. Accordingly QMCSA, the COS and the Glasgow Union of Women Workers (later augmented by the Scottish Christian Social Union and the University Students' Settlement) organised lectures, with tutorials and an examination. In February 1912 a School of Social Study and Training was established with a Diploma Examination to follow. The school aimed to provide social workers in the following categories:

1. Workers, both voluntary and paid, in connection with Settlements, Charity Organisation Society, Children's Care Committees and other agencies doing work among the poor.

2. Public officials: Assistant inspectors of poor, those engaged in various branches of municipal service, Labour Exchange officials, and secretaries of Juvenile Advisory Committees, Inspectors and officials appointed under the Insurance Act.

3. Organisers and Secretaries of Trade Unions, Co-operative Societies, Friendly Societies, etc.

The Edinburgh initiative came somewhat later than that of Glasgow. The University Settlement[26] there started in 1905, at a location in Surgeons' Square, with a few residents. It was organised by an all-male committee and attracted a few male students to live in. As in Glasgow, the warden and the resident members arranged a wide selection of activities such as Saturday evening concerts, boys' clubs and men's clubs. The women students, especially those of the Women Students' Christian Union, organised work for women and girls in the Waverley Buildings. A women's committee of the Settlement Association was shortly set up. The organisers were aware of the need to use the Settlement as a 'training ground for the study of social questions by men who will be called upon in the future to play their part as citizens'. They were eager to attract recruits. With the coming of the war in 1914 the women took over more responsibility, and for the first time a female warden and secretary, in the person of Miss Grace Drysdale, became the effective centre of the work. After the war the Settlement and the University's School of Social Study, believing that their aims were broadly similar, united. But the marriage was dissolved in 1925 when it had become clear that their objectives and aims were not so similar as had been hoped. An appeal was launched in 1926 for substantial funds to rebuild the premises in the High School Yards near the Old College.

5. Women in social work and the advent of professionalism

The Settlement movement, especially as represented by the work of the Queen Margaret Association in Glasgow, had perhaps two major effects.

Though the idea was initially male, it provided a great release for female energies and ingenuity. It would be erroneous to suggest that the women's basic attitudes to the social problems of the city were different from those of the men, but their enthusiasm, their practical ability, and even their novelty value, enabled them to make a link between earlier charitable effort and the newer form of social work. The growth point of voluntary effort lay in developing a brand of modern social work; this the newly educated women, needing to find outlets and eagerly embracing their opportunity, provided. No doubt their outlook was hortatory and maternalistic. But their emphasis on working for women and children created an important precedent, and one which was to push them and the community generally into much greater concern with maintaining standards of good health. Their recognition of needs, and their skill in developing modest schemes to satisfy them, deserved the warmest commendation. Almost all they pioneered as pilot schemes was eventually taken over by public authorities.

The second great consequence of their efforts was the creation of Schools of Social Work. It was by this route that true professionalism was to come as, in association with the universities, training and professional status were provided. Though most were religious women still, the emphasis was shifting from the philanthropy of piety to practicality and professionalism.

NOTES

1. Mowat, 1961.
2. Morrison, 1968.
3. Davy, J. S., *The Elberfeld System of Poor Relief: A report to the Local Government Board* (London 1888).
4. Spence, S., *The Glasgow Angus and Mearns Benevolent Society* (Glasgow 1895), 6.
5. Cage, R. A., and Checkland, E. O. A., 'Thomas Chalmers and urban poverty: the St. John's parish experiment 1819-1822', *Philosophical Journal*, Vol. 13, No. 1, Spring 1976, 37-56.
6. *GH*, 20 December 1890.
7. Shaw, G. B., *The Fabian Society: its early history* (London 1892), 4.
8. 'Kyrle' came from Alexander Pope's *Man of Ross* who, with small means, beautified his surroundings.
9. Bell, 1942, 248; Wohl, 1977, chapter 7; and Gauldie, 1974, chapter 19.
10. '. . . The Kyrle Society were willing to aid in decorating our hall, and the superintendent was authorised to get done whatever painting or cleaning might be necessary to enable the Kyrle Society to begin', University Missionary Society, Minute Book, 20 November 1889.
11. *Glasgow Kyrle Society*, AR (Glasgow 1895).
12. *GMCHP* (Glasgow 1904), 369.
13. *AHR*, 1886, 17.
14. Smart, W., 1886, 5.
15. *Toynbee House*, AR (Glasgow 1897), 3.
16. Originally entitled The Association of Theological Students in the University of Glasgow. See Minute Books, GUL Ms gen. 1434-1439.
17. The Missionary Society was defunct from December 1870 to 15 March 1872.
18. At Garscube Cross was based a Workmen's Club as well as a Total Abstinence Society. See UMA Minute Book, 12 December 1893.
19. Cunnison, J., 'Casual recollections of the Student Settlement', *The College Courant*, Martinmas 1955, 31.
20. Wishing to resort to old style mission work, it resolved: 'that this Society disassociate itself herewith from the Glasgow University Settlement and united organisations, and set for itself the accomplishment of some definite work that will abide in a tangible form as a witness and result of its operations, and that the work take the form of the formation of a congregation.' UMA Minute of 15 December 1893. The UMA subsequently worked in Wellwood, Raeberry Street, Maryhill and Dennistoun Church.
21. 'The Treasurer reported that, approximately, the total income for the year had been £555 and the expenditure £198. From the balance the committee agreed to recommend the general meeting to vote £260 to India.' UMA Minute Book, 14 March 1890.
22. *QMCSA* records, GUA.
23. *Anderston COS*, AR (Glasgow 1900), 9.
24. *QMCSA*, AR (Glasgow 1900), 9.
25. *Ibid.*, 11.
26. See EUS records in EUL.

21
Civic Action and the Question of Rationalisation

1. The civic contribution

THE Victorian philanthropist epitomised the spirit of his age. Especially in the cities he was the successful individual who regarded himself as having followed the precepts of Samuel Smiles in *Thrift* and *Self-help*. In so doing he had amassed a fortune, part of which he was then ready to disperse, but on his own terms, for the good of the community. He tended to be linked with civic authority, being a civic leader or the associate of such. The relationship and balance of power between philanthropy and the city changed in emphasis during the course of the long reign of Victoria. The active generosity of the philanthropist was prominent in the larger urban centres, especially in Glasgow, Edinburgh, Aberdeen and Dundee. Elsewhere in Scotland charitable effort ran along more traditional, unadventurous lines; there were few new initiatives. At first glance it might appear that the philanthropic contribution to Victorian social progress was arbitrary and idiosyncratic, depending on the whim of the individual donor. And so to some extent it was, although philanthropists were influenced not only by their friends and peers but also by the newspapers, journals and pamphlets of the day, which were ever ready to espouse good causes and stimulate the philanthropic propensity to give.

Local government in Scotland had been re-organised in 1833; in 1888 the Local Government Act brought municipal authorities up to date. The new town councils in general were a source of power to mercantile and professional interests. Such men often had a strong sense of civic pride, administering their cities with zeal and authority. The philanthropic presence, whether in the sense of men having money to bestow on good works, or of men with professional expertise which they wished to dispense for the good of the community, was an essential part of increasingly powerful civic authority (see chapter 7, section 6, above).

It was in the interest of the town council to encourage the philanthropist as far as possible for, in a society which made no official provision for social casualties except through the Poor Law, any charitable monies could be a valuable addition to social provision.

311

Civic authority in pre-industrial Scotland had recognised the value of charitable societies by granting them status by the award of a Seal of Cause.[1] This formula, designed to give legal identity (and a monopoly within the city) to the craft guilds, was extended to include eleemosynary societies. Such a grant implied official approval and recognition. By the nineteenth century the seal of cause had become obsolete. But other methods of showing civic commendation were practised. Town councils (and the Trades' House and the Merchants' House if they existed) showed their approval of selected charities by allocating an annual contribution to their funds. The provost and other civic representatives accepted honorary positions on boards of management of the larger charities *ex officiis*. The provost or his nominee would also occupy the chair at the annual general meeting of important bodies. The Royal Infirmaries, Royal Lunatic Asylums, orphanages, reformatories, missions and many other church societies could expect to receive this sort of official approval. Temperance societies, small and unpopular at the beginning of the reign, became very powerful and could by the end of the century also command this type of civic recognition.

The differences between Edinburgh and Glasgow affected their respective charitable responses.[2] Edinburgh, the capital, was primarily a professional city, with strong and vocal professional classes, entrenched and deeply conservative. It was also the centre of church organisations, including those of the Church of Scotland, the Free Church and the United Presbyterian Church. Though many Victorian churchmen were more concerned with theological than with social problems, the churches produced philanthropic activists, both clerical and lay. Perhaps the ruling classes of Edinburgh, confident after a long period of power and influence, were less willing to involve themselves charitably. For in Edinburgh charitable initiatives could fail for lack of support. The attitude of the Scottish landed class, with its strong Edinburgh connection, was not always clear, probably because its loyalties were divided between the capital, containing their town houses, and their landed estates where they felt they really belonged. Thus the lesser Scottish landed gentry may have felt that their charitable obligations lay at their home bases, and Edinburgh charities may have suffered from this. The great aristocratic families did support charitable effort in Edinburgh and at home; certainly their names appear regularly on appeals which circulated widely. Whether they did so in proportion to their means is another matter.

Glasgow, the commercial capital of Scotland, had few contacts with the traditional landed class. The initiative for ameliorative social action there rested squarely upon the commercial, merchant and industrial classes. It may be that Glasgow's merchants were less well established and less secure, and that these characteristics promoted a greater propensity to give. In addition, successful men in Glasgow came from a stratum of society deeply imbued with the evangelical ethos which almost automatically projected them into the charitable world. 'Generous Glasgow' was a well-known phrase, and appeals made in the city rarely fell on deaf ears. Through both philanthropic and civic initiatives Glasgow's record in the field of social progress in the nineteenth century represents a notable response to enormous and intractable problems. Much of Glasgow's reputation as a great and warm-hearted city stemmed from the immense civic pride of her citizens in her status as 'second city of the empire'.

However, even in Glasgow they did not entirely eschew the snobbish appeal of the aristocratic. Miss Beatrice Clugston, and others like her, used the names and presence of grand titled personages at the head of her appeals. Most of the sumptuous Grand Bazaars and Fancy Fayres (held in the new civic palace of the Glasgow City Chambers) were so patronised. This tendency may have been reinforced by the marriage of Queen Victoria's daughter Princess Louise to the Marquis of Lorne, the heir to the Duke of Argyll, in 1871.

Aberdeen and Dundee were smaller enclaves, vigorous in tackling their own problems, and led by active commercial interests with a strong sense of civic pride. Aberdeen especially had its own group of evangelistic businessmen who gave a strong lead to many charitable enterprises there. But they were also led, in name at least, by the local landed aristocracy, whose names topped the philanthropic lists.

The relationship between the philanthropic world and civic authorities is perhaps most clearly seen over problems of law and order. With the rapid growth of population in Scottish cities in the nineteenth century there was a large increase on the streets of social casualties of all kinds. Humanitarian considerations demanded that something should be done to provide for such men, women, boys and girls, other than in the bridewell. A number of movements were started which were primarily philanthropic, but which almost from the beginning came to be used as part of the offical provision. Ragged Schools, started by Sheriff Watson in Aberdeen because he so disliked committing child vagrants to the bridewell, were of this kind (see chapter 15, section 3, above). Other shelters and refuges were of this nature, hoping to attract voluntary residents, but quickly becoming convenient homes for delinquents. The Magdalene Asylum hoped to attract 'penitent females', but again civic authorities were not slow to make use of them for women on the streets who were troublesome and came to the attention of the authorities (see chapter 14 above). The interplay between voluntary and statutory elements was thus of great importance. The role played by contributors was significant, for by their annual subscriptions, their donations and endowments, they preserved their fellow citizens from rate increases, and helped develop hybrid forms combining philanthropy and the rates. The Glasgow House of Refuge for Boys was something of an exception; charitably founded in 1838, it continued to attract private monies although partly supported by a 1d. rate levied in the city from 1841 (see chapter 15, section 5, above). This mixed status was also accorded to the many Ragged Schools built in Scotland, which were charitably supported and managed although officially registered and recognised by Dunlop's Act of 1855.

The police too found it convenient to co-operate with many charitable bodies. They aided the superintendents of the Night Asylums in controlling the queues of people waiting to enter each night. They had access to hospitals and often guided women to the Lying-in and the Lock Hospitals. In this regard they were sometimes fulfilling one of their traditional roles of looking after the 'stranger poor'.

There was also a growing field of public health, arising from the need to provide effective medical services to cope with fever epidemics. This was public provision, funded by the rates. But it is worth noting that the doctors who chose to serve in the public health spheres were often motivated in part at least by humanitarian considerations. The role of the doctor as philanthropist is one which might repay further study. The medical profession had long given free treatment to the poor, and the continuing commitment of men like Professor W. P. Alison in arousing public sympathy for the poor was very real. The involvement of men like James Burn Russell as first full-time Medical Officer of Health to Glasgow from 1872-1898 is a reminder of how an unknown and untried public service could attract men motivated by the urge to serve the community. Perhaps the essential element for such men was their Christian faith, encouraging them to choose a sphere of action which rendered direct service to their fellow citizens.

Following the Education Act of 1872, the School Boards began to organise elementary education. But they left to the philanthropists higher, technical and university education (see chapter 6 above). There was liaison with the local authority; civic pride ensured that local educational institutions were supported. There were greater expectations too about leisure activities, and libraries and art galleries and parks became attractive propositions. Carnegie's use of philanthropic initiative as a stimulus to municipal action transformed the public library world in the course of a decade.

The enthusiasm and optimism of the philanthropist led to a commitment to social experiments, some of which could be philanthropically sustained, and some of which were bound to cause the municipality to become involved. The philanthropist by his initiatives may have hastened civic action by about thirty years. In so far as he provided finance from his own resources for any work from which the city benefited, he saved public money and thus helped to keep the rates low: from the general middle-class point of view this was perhaps the most acceptable action any citizen could take.

2. The challenge of rationalisation: the voluntary versus the municipal principle

It was inevitable that, by the latter part of Victoria's reign, the need to rationalise philanthropic effort in Scotland should arise. There was the question of wasteful overlap in provision, together with its opposite, namely serious gaps. Could some kind of generalised pattern be established which would obviate both? In addition to the problems of waste and omission on the supply side, there was concern also about those demanding assistance: fears were strong among many philanthropists that the undeserving were drawing upon the system, and that this was made easier by the lack of co-ordination of the many services provided.

Two co-ordinating functions were envisaged. The milder had to do with the collecting of information about the services available, an obvious first step, so that each charitable organisation could act in a full knowledge of what others were doing. But could the matter be pushed further in the direction of rationalisation? The greatest difficulty was to arrive at the principle that should govern any programme of co-ordination. There were two possibilities: one was functional, and the other was geographical and familial. The functional approach would begin, for example, with health provision; a survey would be made of existing arrangements, and then plans would be drawn for their integration. But such a programme had obvious difficulties, the greatest of which had to do with the vested interests embodied in the many institutions large and small, powerful and weak. The geographical-familial approach took the form of reviving the principles of Thomas Chalmers by dividing the city into districts, within each of which a careful surveillance would be kept of individual and family need.

There was also the problem of *aegis* and control. Should rationalisation, on whatever principle chosen, be done under voluntary auspices, or under the municipalities, or under some combination of the two?

By 1897, when the COS held its sixth annual conference in Glasgow, there had been a good deal of discussion of these matters.[3] They became indeed the principal theme of the conference. The Glasgow COS had shortly before divided the east end of the city into districts, much as Chalmers had done. It was conscious of the Berlin arrangements by which that city had been divided into 234 districts cared for by 2,259 voluntary workers co-operating with the Town Council. The principal speaker on this theme was Professor Henry Jones (holder of what had once been Adam Smith's Chair of Moral Philosophy). He did not discuss functional integration, for this in the prevailing Scottish context was out of the question. His concern was with the district system as it might be extended and strengthened by local government. He believed that 'The municipality of Glasgow had shown such practical intelligence in its dealings with social problems that it would be able to select persons who would perform the work of charity in an effectual manner.' The city would thus become the organiser of effort and selector of workers. In addition, powers would be given to the city 'not to supplant or extinguish, but to regulate, direct and organise individual charity, so that no broken or innocent citizen shall lack bread in our midst'.

But Jones thought the time was not yet ripe for the municipality to take the lead. The first requirement was that the philanthropic organisations themselves come together; it was necessary that every charity in the city should recognise 'the need of working in harmony with the COS'. Before any rationalisation, much less municipalisation, could be considered, all philanthropic effort must be brought together, voluntarily, under a single organisation.

C. S. Loch, the London Secretary of the COS, certainly favoured the role of co-ordinator for his Society. But he rejected municipal leadership outright: 'An elective corporation or municipal body,' he insisted, 'could neither provide the training nor strengthen the inspiration. Associated charity could do both.' With such a view held at the heart of the COS, it was impossible to move in the direction of municipal initiative.

So it was that one of the great limitations of the voluntary principle became obvious. It was incapable of generating a sufficient degree of co-operation between philanthropic ventures such that the next step, that of integration with local government, could take place. The tentative division of Glasgow into districts by the COS was carried no further: the other Scottish cities did not even get thus far. The voluntary principle could not get beyond the *ad hoc*, generating its myriad of initiatives: it was incapable of evolving into a systematic service either under a co-ordinating charity like the COS, or under city government. Order in the operation of social services, if it were to come at all, had to be imposed by the state, a prospect abhorrent to most philanthropists. In this regard Scotland, in spite of the tradition of municipal action in Glasgow, was in the same position as the rest of Britain.

NOTES

1. By the grant of a Seal of Cause, societies were made corporate bodies with perpetual succession and the right to hold property.
2. See Smout, T. C., 1969, chapter XV.
3. *Charity organisation and relief societies of the United Kingdom, May 1897* (Glasgow 1897).

PART VIII

The Voluntarist Balance Sheet

22

How Successfully Was Need Met?

1. Provision versus need

IT is not easy to sum up the supply response of the Victorian philanthropists to the social problems that confronted them. Of the range and diversity of what was provided there can be no doubt. But how adequate was it when set against need?

Such a question at once poses difficulties in terms of assumptions. Should the philanthropic performance be judged against the removal of all social suffering, or only some part of it? Clearly any notion of 'total' response is inappropriate — no society has ever succeeded, or even tried, to be totally comprehensive, not least for the reasons that the philanthropists feared, namely the dangers in such a society of loss of moral fibre and of the willingness to work, together with the generating of an insatiable demand. If we think of less than full relief from social ills, then how much less would be right?

In spite of these difficulties, however, is it possible to make a distinction in this matter between quantitative and qualitative achievement? On the quantitative side it is plain that in some aspects the inadequacy of provision was so great as to be gross. By this test the two major areas of default were medicine (let alone nutrition) and, especially, housing. In these two cases, when what was provided is set against what was needed, the shortfall is patent. In education, though there was delay in providing systematic elementary teaching, and the weaknesses of secondary education were plain, the indictment is perhaps not so serious. Indeed when the failures of education today in terms of working-class areas are taken into account, any simple criticism of Victorian provision seems unjustified.

On the qualitative side the verdict is much more favourable. With so much activity in so many varied fields, a kind of learning process was generated by the philanthropists, both particular and general. By their direct involvement in so many problems they were performing an exploratory role. To have had so large a part in the development of the hospital and health system was a remarkable achievement. The philanthropists, indeed, appear in retrospect as a necessary stage in the development of the industrial system on market principles. When the time came to invoke the state in one area after another, the philanthropists were often the providers of such experience and data as

318

there were, as well as themselves being among the invokers.

So much for the attempt at a general verdict. But it is necessary to look more closely at the five main headings of this book, namely the philanthropy of piety, education, health, the use of the residential principle for care, cure and custody, and housing.

2. The philanthropy of piety

Any judgment one might make of the enormous range of philanthropic activities inspired and sustained by evangelical piety depends, of course, on one's scheme of values. If the evangelical religious philosophy and objectives are accepted, then the effort to promote them is laudable. If the pietistic value scheme is rejected, then it follows that attempts to proselytise in its favour were wrong. The matter is, in this sense, irreducible.

Those who approve of Christianisation in this form would argue that to provide a system of belief and reassurance to those upon whom life bore heavily was itself good. Moreover, we must not blame philanthropic individuals for what may have been a failing of their class. There remains of course a second question, namely that of means: was it right to make religious appeals to people who were deprived and bemused, accompanying such appeals with material incentives like meals and medicine? Those who take a humanist, agnostic or atheist view would, of course, reject pietistic effort as being a means of imprisonment and perversion. Those who move in a socialist direction would insist that the relief of misfortune was a communal responsibility, to be discharged through the state. But even such people would have to make a judgment as to whether pietistic effort, though having its bad side, was on balance, in some aspects, and for some of the time, good.

One thing is clear: the state disengaged itself from piety, as was plain from its refusal to back church extension in the 1830's. Perhaps this proposition should be cast in a different form, namely that in the Scottish case no religious group or syndicate of groups was able to gain sufficient control of the state to use it for pietistic purposes. In this sense there was no 'established church' in Scotland and no state money for religion. And yet the state, in dealing with education, had to take account of the power configuration that related one church to another, and the conflicts between them.

In quantitative terms the philanthropic enterprises that were religiously based were far and away the most numerous. Or, if one were to argue in a counter-factual way, without religious impetus it seems likely that very little would have been done. But in spite of the range of activities, did pietistic philanthropy Christianise the masses? The answer, in general, can only be in the negative, for it proved impossible to 'church' the working classes. And yet, though the adult males might be outside religion, there was the impact upon the women and children. Especially through the Sunday Schools there was a wider dissemination of literacy and religion. For good or ill, the Sabbath was preserved. The Bible Societies distributed enormous numbers of Scriptural writings — they were, indeed, the 'dispensaries' of the system, providing a basic service. The temperance movement, with its evangelical basis, became a part of working-class life, for everyone knew of its activities; a not insignificant number of men and women responded to its appeal for a new beginning, indeed a new life. In many areas temperance work mixed the classes, bringing a measure of social cohesion, though no doubt it was a case of cultural impact 'downward' from the middle classes. Temperance work could moreover provide working-class leadership as well as an extended cultural outlook, rather as Methodism had done.

In the case of home missions it is true that the missionaries to the working classes became discouraged and retreated to a less exposed position by caring for particular categories of workers, and by offering other attractions in the form of entertainments. But even here there was a form of achievement: Bible Women and Bible Women Nurses, together with Colporteurs, were people from the working classes seeking to improve the lot of their own kind. There can be no doubt, also, that the medical missions and the Deaconesses did much good, epitomising Christ's own mission of healing and prayer.

The blind impact of the evangelicals on Gaelic culture provides in Scotland an ethnic aspect of philanthropy: the mission to Christianise was an absolute, so that no thought was given to cultural damage.

Churches and churchmen launched many initiatives designed to alleviate conditions in the towns. But they were at no time able to lead the vanguard, demanding radical changes to remedy deteriorating urban conditions. Indeed harsher comments have been made of the Church of Scotland. The Reverend Professor Henry Reid of Glasgow University charged in a lecture in 1904 that 'Her clergy were . . . little more than chaplains in the central fortress of power, wealth and privilege . . . who not only failed to champion the causes associated with the oppressed and the underprivileged but were amongst their most heated opponents.' This relative failure of the churches was fundamental; it indicates challenges which could not be met adequately by the efforts of isolated men, or even by organised religious groups. For some purposes only the state would do.

With the relative failure to Christianise the working classes, church philanthropy increasingly turned in a 'softer' direction, namely to those who were, or who aspired to become, church members. Here the philanthropic initiatives of the church were remarkably successful: Sunday Schools, Boys' Brigades, YMCA's and many other groups received much support. Funds were benevolently subscribed for an enormous variety of endeavours. A wide range of people were committed to an active participatory role at many levels. And yet the involvement of the more ambitious and more articulate members of the community in church work and church subscriptions may have received a disproportionate amount of publicity in press and journals, exaggerating their achievements.

An intriguing aspect of all this is the power of the ideas based upon Chalmers' work and writings. His influence indeed pervaded Scottish social thought and action through much of the nineteenth century. To the district idea, which he had inherited from the traditions of the Church of Scotland, he gave a new insistence — it turns up time and again. His emphasis on the need to work in terms of the family, using family case work carried out by dedicated social workers, is another continuum. Thirdly, his unwillingness that able-bodied persons should acquire a claim on the state for maintenance had powerful effects on outlook both in Scotland and England. Indeed Chalmers was, so far as the English were concerned, the Scottish voice on social welfare.

All the while the churches had to fight a drift away from them. The re-appearance of the revivalist movement in the 1870's can be seen as an attempt to reduce the numbers of 'the unchurched masses'. The promise of salvation was held forth in a highly theatrical manner, using rousing oratory and heavy rhythm (hymnal and martial) in an endeavour 'to bring man to Jesus'. Revivals took on the fervour of crusades, and many new religious bodies were spontaneously established. The new concept of caring, which the Salvation Army brought to its appeal, was intended to embrace the sinners as well as the saved. Much of this work was undertaken in 'tent' halls and mission halls, outside the established and other churches in Scotland.

The philanthropy of piety does not, therefore, lend itself to any simple, gratuitous verdict. It must be disaggregated into its diversity. Only if one has that fierce clarity of outlook which allows a condemnation of the whole effort out of hand is an easy verdict possible. But whether approved or not, pietistic philanthropy had profound effects upon Scottish Victorian life.

3. Education

The two fields in which the philanthropists made their greatest contributions in Victorian Scotland were education and the supply of health services. In both cases it was necessary for philanthropic providers to relate to vocational professionals: in education the teacher was, of course, the direct supplier of the service, and, in health, the doctor. But in both aspects the state was seriously deficient. In the case of education in its elementary form, the state did from 1872 rationalise the piecemeal provision and to other parts of the system it brought a measure of order and support. The case of medical provision was in striking contrast; there the state left matters inchoate until 1946.

At the elementary school level, prior to 1872, there was an extraordinary mixture of provision, including parish schools of the traditional kind (with a legal claim upon the heritors for support), General Assembly (Church of Scotland) schools, and schools run by subscription and as private ventures. After 1843 the new Free Church set about building its own school system; the Roman Catholics also provided for the children of their faith. In this mélange the philanthropists were of course involved, but they had no distinctive role. There was a profusion of minor philanthropic endowments to assist pupils, often founder's kin. With the 1872 Education Act these passed to the new School Boards.

On this pattern of elementary education the philanthropists acted in two principle ways. The Dick Bequest was a demonstration of the improvements possible when a system of reinforcement of the skills and incentives of teachers was operating. Secondly there were the wealthy charity hospitals or boarding schools, chiefly in Edinburgh. So rapidly did their endowments appreciate that they were made vulnerable by their riches to public criticism. Accordingly the wealthiest, Heriot's, set up a range of day schools in the poorer areas of the city: the Edinburgh Merchant Company under the Act of 1869 sought to widen their facilities in the same direction. It is possible to view the Heriot's programme as a means of taking the public pressure off a charity school so that, by providing facilities outside itself, it could remain intact. There may be some analogy with the Royal Infirmaries and the Royal Lunatic Asylums, both of which sought to preserve themselves from being overrun, the Infirmaries by fever patients and the Asylums by the pauper poor. In any case, even with the new Heriot's day schools the principle of selection by merit was gaining ground; this apparently egalitarian principle could work in reverse, for any system of examinations inevitably favours the children of the middle classes. A philanthropist like Provost Duncan McLaren would seem to have been genuinely motivated by an urge to promote popular education, but the system was always exposed to the danger of a return to élitism. The Commissioners after 1872 made an effort to see that charitable monies were used to spread benefits lower down the class structure, but the middle classes continued in possession of most of the benefits.

Indeed in the case of grammar school education élitism was the accepted principle. The government combined this with a form of equity: it flatly recognised that secondary education was an affair of the middle classes, and so thought it only fair that the middle classes should pay for it by a combination of fee paying and philanthropic giving. Even the new Higher Class Schools placed under the School Boards were to be without public money, except such as might come from the 'common good' funds of the burghs, fees or philanthropy. These schools were the best hope of a more egalitarian system, but they were a disappointment to their promoters. Thus it was that secondary education, always a middle-class provision, largely for middle-class boys, continued as before. Even the intervention of the new Commissioners in the 1880's did little to change this. Philanthropy thus played a large, though perhaps unintended, part in the preservation of class distinction through the educational system. Only with the intervention of the state around 1900, in the person of Sir Henry Craik, did the Higher Class Schools begin to be a reality; the Act of 1908 provided a new financial base.

But the grammar schools did not exhaust the secondary sector. There was also the problem of secondary education of a scientific and technical kind. In spite of almost frantic pleas to the government to repair the serious gap in Britain's educational system, the matter was left to the philanthropists. The range of new technical colleges that appeared in Scotland's cities was a philanthropic achievement. Though local authorities were given power to allocate certain sums for this purpose, they were petty. Only with the Education Act of 1908 was public money made available on a significant scale.

In the case of the universities, as with elementary education, the pattern was complex. The three oldest universities inherited pre-reformation church resources (though these were slender); Edinburgh was the creation of the Town Council and so was locally funded. The state made its first contribution in the form of the eighteenth-century regius chairs, intended to introduce new disciplines. Its second came after 1858 with a pattern of modest grants. But, throughout, the mainstay was philanthropy augmenting students' fees by donations, and paying fees through bursaries. Even when it came to the two greatest undertakings, the removal and renewal of Glasgow University and the founding of the University College of Dundee, much of the finance came from private giving, half of it in the case of Glasgow and the whole of it in the case of Dundee. In general, as with secondary education, the state wished to be as passive as possible, with the philanthropists making the principal provisions.

The philanthropic achievement in the field of education was, then, one of more or less continuous supply of funds, with bursts of larger generosity for special projects. Reciprocally, the role of the state was, by and large, with the exception of elementary education, confined to minor augmentation, together with, especially from the 1870's onward, some effort to bring a measure of order into the system.

4. Health

There can be no doubt that the philanthropic achievement in the field of health was a major one. It is impossible to assess the quantitative effect of philanthropic effort on the health record of Victorian Scotland, because of the multiplicity of circumstances including incomes, family budgeting, diet and housing. But there can be no denying that the philanthropists accomplished much, namely the erection of a range of institutions, with the Royal Infirmaries and Royal Asylums at the centre, and the specialist hospitals, the dispensaries and the supportive services as intermingled peripheries, all sustained by the new nursing profession. Of course they could only do these things in collaboration with the professional medical men; the philanthropists were indirect providers of services through sponsorship, finance and management. The philanthropists had to work through a medical profession that was one of the most powerful of established interests, veiled in mystique and feared even by persons of power. But the provision of medical facilities was an indispensable function of philanthropy when the state saw its role in such matters in minimal terms.

But public sector action was not altogether absent and, of course, it had to increase as industrialisation and urbanisation proceeded. On the private side there was a dualism (philanthropists and doctors); in terms of public action there were three sets of participants. The public functions lay between the poor law, with its responsibilities as defined or implied, the municipalities as re-organised from the 1830's and the new race of Medical Officers of Health coming into being from the 1860's. The poor law, especially after 1845, required the guardians to care for the pauper sick, including the lunatic: they were responsible for the individual residuals. Poor law hospitals thus came into being. The municipalities were made responsible for meeting major challenges in the form of epidemics; their response was to set up fever hospitals. Both poor law and fever hospitals were inferior affairs, without medical prestige. The Medical Officers of Health, employees of the local authorities, had a general watching brief for the health of the community as a whole, concerning themselves with sanitation, condition of foodstuffs and the like. Though excluded from the charmed circle of the Infirmaries, they could become a centre of real power and initiative. The evolution of the voluntary system must therefore be seen in the context of simultaneous developments in poor law hospitals, municipal fever hospitals and the actions of the Medical Officers of Health.

In health provision, as in the other areas of philanthropic activity, piety was a powerful and compelling motive. But, in general, the functions to be per-formed in the Infirmaries, specialist hospitals, dispensaries and so on were secular. Because they were performed by professionals they had no pietistic content or conditions. Though many of the doctors were themselves evan-gelical, this did not intrude into their professional functions.

Private sector medicine was undoubtedly strongly impregnated with élitism. The philanthropic middle class could not stand against the inherent trend in the medical world toward hierarchy and authority. Indeed, as in the case of education, very few of them would think resistance to this to be proper. It is true that in the conflicts over the use of subscribers' lines the philanthropic managers would sometimes insist upon nominating patients, but by and large they did not, and indeed could not, challenge professional authority. At least this was so in terms of the great Infirmaries; there may have been somewhat more scope in the specialist sector, but it of course consisted of small units where hierarchy could not thrive (though autocracy could). In any case the philanthropic supporters of the Infirmaries shared the view that, as the teaching hospitals, and as the places where medical progress took place, they should become centres of excellence where outstanding men should be left to rule. The authority of the medical men in the Infirmaries proved to be self-confirming: by 1900 the managerial role of the philanthropists was fading.

The Infirmaries were the greatest beneficiaries of the practice of ritual giving. As this, in the long run, was the best source of funds, the Infirmaries were thus placed in a very strong position. They offered a cause that was un-ambiguously accepted as good, one from which the dissensions of religion had been largely excluded, and to which high secular status was attached.

The Royal Lunatic Asylums, being concerned with the mind rather than the body, stood outside the general system. It became clear, however, that an important link existed between mind and body: the successes of the Royal Asylums lay largely in treating those who needed rest and nutrition, together with those who needed to be removed from stressful situations in the home or elsewhere. Moreover, though mental health was separate from physical health, and evolved along its own lines, there was a parallelism, in that the Royal Asylums, like the Royal Infirmaries, were the focal elements, with various outlyers, especially the district asylums and the lunatic wings of the poor houses. This meant that the philanthropists were crucial in lunacy as in general health. There was, however, a difference between the two kinds of provision. The Asylums attracted middle-class patients before the Infirmaries did. Indeed, in terms of patients, the Asylums, unlike the Infirmaries, were subject to an early tendency to become middle-class institutions, a trend confirmed by the provision of separate facilities for pauper lunatics as at the Edinburgh Royal and the Crichton Royal. There was in the case of lunacy no breakthrough analogous to the surgical revolution, though the Asylums shared in the benefits of the nursing revolution. But, as with the Infirmaries, there was a strong trend for a hierarchy of authority to develop.

The sponsorship of the specialist hospitals brought the philanthropists into relationship with different doctors, namely those who wished to become medical entrepreneurs on their own account. The philanthropists here performed what was in effect an exploratory function, seeking to deepen knowledge by the subdivision of diseases. By virtue of such division they and the specialists could launch their enterprises on a small scale; the specialisms were thus open-ended in terms of entry. But the specialists could only specialise in terms of philanthropic acceptability. Some kinds of treatment were not attractive to sponsors and givers, as for example lying-in hospitals or venereal disease cases; others found a wide sympathy, as with children's diseases (once the argument over the residential principle was settled), and tuberculosis and cancer. But the specialists were active to greater or lesser degrees on all fronts, pushing their way into acceptance by the medical profession, and altering the profession as they did so. Hospitals for female diseases provided a double opportunity for women: as philanthropists to gain a footing in hospital management, and as doctors to gain opportunities to practise.

The dispensaries were the 'popular' aspect of the system, scattered about the cities, bringing medicine within the reach of a high proportion of the population. They were extraordinarily cheap to run, in terms of cost per patient, subsidised as they were by voluntary and student labour. It may be, however, that the very low level of cost per patient reflected a low level of service.

Certainly there was no attempt at elaborate diagnosis and sustained treatment. It was the fairly superficial aspects of accident or ill-health that were dealt with, no doubt with the aid of placebos. Even so, the dispensaries may well have been the most effective part of the system in cost-benefit terms, the points at which the philanthropic pound sterling did most good, certainly until the surgical revolution was well advanced.

But they were subject to criticisms, which were of two kinds. Firstly there was the charge that they patronised and manipulated the poor. It may well have been that to reach the level of throughput that was attained, this was unavoidable. By the same token there may have been a temptation to treat people in a highly impersonal way. The second charge was that the dispensaries, with their crowds of miscellaneous sick, were unclean and unsafe, centres for the propagation of disease. This their protagonists strenuously denied.

The cottage hospitals were another case, similar to that of the specialist hospitals, where the established medical profession was hostile. But here also small-scale beginnings were part of the nature of things, so that there was open entry. A demonstration effect could be produced, bringing with it general acceptability. Even so it was between the Royal Infirmaries and the often tiny cottage hospitals that the greatest differences in size and atmosphere obtained. The Infirmaries stood for the economies of scale, high collective prestige and a structured community of doctors; against this there was daunting size, authoritarianism and inflexibility. The cottage hospitals epitomised intimacy of scale, reassurance, local affection and care by the family physician; against this was the limited range of skills and equipment at their disposal, and the danger of decline if the philanthropic managers lost interest.

The nursing revolution provided a facility common to all medical provision; it provided an enormous extension of support services, both in terms of size and skill. It widened the labour force that could be drawn upon by bringing women, in large numbers, into medicine. With nursing, the philanthropists, perhaps losing ground in the operation of the Infirmaries, renewed their vitality. The nursing bottleneck could only be broken from outside the work of male doctors. The necessary initiative came through the intervention of heroic female figures like Florence Nightingale and the Queen herself, together with a mustering of general philanthropic zeal. In producing the new kind of nurse, the philanthropists had to confront an educational problem, investigating the means whereby training could be provided.

5. The residential principle

The Victorian philanthropists were instrumental in taking a wide and varied range of people into care. The assessment of such action can proceed in two steps, namely a consideration of the validity of the residential principle in general, followed by a view of its application in particular cases.

The case for residence rested on two main factors, namely the need for care and protection, and the need for guidance and discipline. There were many categories of people who, by virtue of their condition, could not care for themselves, and whose families could or would not accept the burden. Such people had to be protected and provided for. If not brought into care they often remained unnoticed by the authorities and so by society, and thus were beyond the reach of philanthropy or the state. Even if maintained in the family home, they were often in effect prisoners, immobile 'cabbages' whose condition bore even more heavily on the rest of the family. Indeed the mother, already under stress, could be broken, and the family itself shattered. On the side of guidance and discipline a residential context could supply a sustained communal framework, together with a range of instruction. The disabled of various kinds could be provided with specialised care and facilities. The School Boards too often defaulted on their responsibilities in this direction, especially in the earlier years after 1872, making philanthropic action all the more necessary.

But there were powerful arguments raised against the residential principle. These, like the arguments in favour, were of two kinds. The first had to do, in effect, with institutional living *versus* the family home. The second was concerned with the likely trend of conditions in the residences. One of the chief of the first category of argument was that the real effort should be to sustain the family and the home, rather than to remove from it those it could not handle. This view was expressed particularly strongly over the children, some people insisting that children in the home could, indeed, redeem it, or at least act as a cohesive element. The acceptability of this argument depended, of course, on the philosophy held of family life. Moreover there was the economy aspect — retention in the home meant that a much higher proportion of social cost was borne by the family rather than by philanthropy or the state. The home, also, in the view of many philanthropists, offered greater independence, as against the rules and confinement of institutions. People withdrawn into a residence, it was argued, lose their capacity to live and function in society.

The second kind of objection to the residential principle had to do with the dangers of repression and perversion. Necessary discipline could too easily become autocratic, morbidly feeding upon itself. Just as fatigue and frustration could produce resentment and even violence in the family home, it could do so in an institution, but in a compounded way. At the same time, the staff whose morale was thus put under such pressure might not be the most appropriate people to be subjected to such a test. Necessary discipline could thus become unnecessary rigour and finally abuse, the kind of sequence to which closed societies are all too prone. One further adverse circumstance was sometimes present, namely religious jealousy. There were quarrels between Protestants and Catholics over the use of the residential principle as a proselytising device;

in short the question of the custody of the minds of the children, and even of adults, as well as of their bodies, could arise.

But these are general arguments. It is necessary to see residential practice in terms of its components. In the case of the prostitutes it would seem that if anything at all was to be done the residential principle was inescapable. It prolonged the period of convalescence after infected women had spent their time in the Lock Hospitals, providing regular hours and meals. There was also the possibility of learning an alternative employment, though this was relatively slight. Perhaps most important of all in the minds of the philanthropists was the opportunity for contrition and for escape from an otherwise closed circle. It is hard to see any high level of achievement in applying the residential principle to prostitution. But for the pious philanthropist, with his or her sense of the absolute sanctity of every soul, even a single life changed meant success.

The same notion of the absolute value of the individual applied to reformatories, ragged schools and training ships. Their success rate may not have been high relative to the problem of the street arabs, but there were indeed cases that turned out well. Just as with the prostitutes, the residential principle was a form of protection for society against anti-social conduct, in this case among boys and youths. Because of this there was a natural path of evolution for such institutions, especially the reformatories, in the direction of becoming part of the system of public punishment. Thus the hope of redemption and re-education ran up against the repository principle, making it difficult to maintain any sort of inspiration. The training ships were highly disciplined communities, sometimes with counter-productive results.

In the case of orphans, who were in the nature of things homeless, there could be no appeal to the principle of attempting to restore family home life. The choices were three: either large institutions with large-scale buildings and mass corporate living, or the cottage homes principle of the Quarrier kind, or the practice of putting orphans out to foster parents in private homes. Residential institutions, both large and small, perhaps provided the context in which the philanthropist was most obviously visible and powerful. In such a situation he did not feel himself obliged to co-operate with the professionals, as in hospitals or schools, but could give his own theories full rein. Quarrier's principle was a halfway house, rejecting the monolithic institution and seeking to generate the atmosphere of the home. Its success depended in no small measure on the personal drive of Quarrier himself. But local authorities did not adopt Quarrier's plan of establishing cottage homes. It would seem that something like a vogue operates in the matter of the treatment of orphans, swinging to and fro between the residential and the fostering principles.

It was with the disabled that the residential principle had its greatest success. In dealing with persons of this kind some sort of protective environment, accompanied by training, was essential. Because there were successes in the treatment of the deaf and dumb, the blind, and the disabled, morale could be maintained. Teachers and taught were confronted with real challenges, in the sense that at least a degree of success was possible, acting as a continuous reinforcement of incentive. In consequence training skills were generated among the staff, sustained by the sense of shared success.

The most difficult cases were, of course, the lunatics. The mental hospitals were confronted with two sets of problems, those having to do with the incurables, and those relating to patients who could respond to treatment. So far as the incurables were concerned the asylums were mere repositories, with all the dangers of a self and mutually reinforcing deterioration among patients and staff.

6. Housing

The problem of housing as it confronted the Victorian philanthropists had two aspects — the provision of shelter for transients, and the challenge of the great shortfall in working-class housing supply. With the first the voluntarist principle had considerable success, with the second very little.

As with so many of the emerging challenges of industrial society, the transient in search of work was first cared for by voluntary action. The Night Asylums and the Strangers' Friend were spontaneous responses in a field in which the state and the municipalities had defaulted. These organisations were soon in close relationship with officialdom, for there was nowhere else for the police to send wandering strangers who had no claim on the workhouse. But the Night Asylums remained independent bodies. A more far-reaching philanthropic response came through the Model Lodging Houses. The lodging houses run for profit were often terrible places; various philanthropic groups came to the conclusion that such provision could be organised with proper facilities and supervision. Here was another considerable success. Middle-class organising ability, freely given, greatly eased the situation. But in this case success was to cause the philanthropic principle to be superseded. So important a facility did the Model Lodging Houses provide, and so large did their clientele become that in Glasgow, the largest Scottish city, the municipality took them over.

Permanent housing supply for the workers was a much more difficult matter. In this field the philanthropists could neither provide the means, as they had done with medicine, nor push the state toward systematic provision, as with education. There were indeed optimists among the philanthropists, like Octavia Hill and her Scottish followers, who believed that by reducing house costs through efficiency of management and good tenant behaviour, the gap between working-class incomes and rents could be closed. But this solution, consistent with the working of the market economy, though it had some success, and produced minor demonstration effects, could make no impression where relief was most needed, namely at the bottom end of the income scale. The only escape lay through subsidy. But this was unacceptable.

On 29 July 1904 the Glasgow Municipal Commissioners on the Housing of the Poor presented their report. They thereby concluded an inquiry based upon a serious effort to collect evidence, and to come to terms with the condition of the city's housing. The witnesses called had included the Corporation's own local civil servants, superintendents of model lodging houses, private landlords and owners of farmed-out houses. Men and women active in the philanthropic housing field were also heard in force, representing the City Mission, the Charity Organisation Society, the Queen Margaret Settlement, the Sabbath School Union, the Salvation Army, the Kyrle Society, the Glasgow Workmen's Dwelling Society and the Night Asylum. The Commissioners thus had available the philanthropic view of housing shortly after the death of Victoria.

Their report reflected the confusion of the community on how best to deal with the problems of working-class housing shortage. It stressed not so much the lack of houses, but the inability of the poor to pay economic rents. But the members of the Commission were not able to face up to a commitment to a housing subsidy. They declined to express 'any opinion upon the general policy of Municipal Housing'. Indeed the questions and replies show vividly how great was the dilemma to be faced. Peter Fyfe, Chief Sanitary Inspector for Glasgow, returned again and again in his evidence to the low wages of the semi-drifting population, insisting that the Corporation should build some houses for them. But his ideas on how to pay for such dwellings were confused. Despite the fact that many people working with the poor recognised that casual workers of both sexes did not earn enough to obtain and keep a permanent home of their own, Commissioners refused to consider putting housing costs on the rates. There was indeed a subsidy barrier.

Philanthropic housing has recently been blamed for conditioning middle-class opinion, so that effective housing solutions were delayed. Both Gauldie and Wohl refer to the inhibiting effect of philanthropic housing theory and programmes. There was really very little housing, in Scotland, provided by philanthropists; such as there was seems unlikely to have affected the outcome. But there may indeed have been an effect on official attitudes that frustrated action. Perhaps the greatest obstruction to public sector housing was a moralism which deplored the living habits of the non-respectable poor, particularly their drinking. It was argued that if they would drink less they could pay an economic regular rent and subsidy could thus be avoided.

The Glasgow Commission made recommendations to demolish insanitary and 'illegal' houses which did not conform to the standards which the city applied at that date. But the members of the Commission knew they could not advocate such ruthless action without making some suggestion about re-housing. They therefore proposed the building of some 4,000 houses. 'Under the powers of The Glasgow Corporation Act 1897 and the Glasgow Corporation (Water and General) Order Confirmation Act 1902', the Corporation should undertake the building 'of tenements of one or two apartment houses'.

But these were to be 'reserved exclusively for respectable people of the "poorest class" as defined by the former Act, preference being given to those dispossessed and to the most necessitous; such houses to be situated, if possible, near to the area of dispossession, and to be under carefully selected caretakers'. This was a very cautious proposal. In the event there was no significant change in attitude toward housing the poor until after the First World War.

7. The philanthropic outlook and performance

Typically, the philanthropists were not radicals. They took the prevailing form of society for granted, along with its gross inequality of incomes. Their energies were devoted not to remaking society, but to alleviating the condition of its current casualties and repairing the gaps left in social provision by the market system. By and large they sought solutions that would not disturb the market allocation of incomes and wealth. Indeed when it came to the shortfall in the supply of houses for labouring families, the adverse relationship between earnings and rents was their great problem. They tried to meet it by getting house-building and operating costs down, and by improved working-class budgeting. In a sense the middle-class philanthropists, in seeking to confine their assistance to the deserving poor, made themselves the protectors and protagonists of a set of social sanctions within which it was intended the working classes should live. To the fundamental tensions in society most Victorian philanthropists, by and large, seemed oblivious: it did not enter their heads that a society could function on any basis other than by all its members espousing a particular set of values, namely those which they themselves held. Theirs was not a conflict model of society, but one of co-operation augmented by ameliorative action. For the Victorian middle class, in short, philanthropy was inherently conservative. Indeed this clarity of mind was part of their strength.

And yet, in a sense, there was an egalitarian element in their outlook. Though there was no thought of a state-implemented redistribution of wealth and incomes, there was among many philanthropists a real urge to improve social mobility by education and other means. But the potential for so doing was thought of within pretty narrow limits. There was little real hope that upward social osmosis would affect those at the bottom of the system. Those who in the last decades of the nineteenth century found this outlook inadequate tended to pass into one or other of the available expressions of socialism.

It may be that the philanthropists were most successful when they could act in empathy with a set of professionals, as in health provision and education. Conversely, where no such alliance was possible, because of the absence of professionals the philanthropists were least effective, as in the application of the residential principle and in housing. Whatever the truth in this regard, it is clear that philanthropic action and the spread of professionalism were in close interaction.

The general characteristics discussed above were shared by the Scottish philanthropists and their English counterparts. But the Scots, though they achieved much, did so largely on an imitative and emulative basis, rather than by invention and innovation. Time and again the story is one of borrowing ideas from the larger world, especially England. No doubt relative size and isolation had a good deal to do with this. Chalmers and his outlook perhaps provide the great exception to this generalisation: there can be no doubt that he ranks as a major figure. But he was deeply rooted in the pre-industrial past where a hard attitude to pauperism and a pervading pietism stood side by side. Indeed the principal Scottish philanthropic pioneering activities arose from that characterisitc quality of Scottish society, namely its pietistic aspect. It was this that lay behind the founding of the Young Men's Christian Association and the Boys' Brigade. But even when adopting ideas from elsewhere the Scots showed striking vigour, much of it deriving from evangelical zeal.

23

Lessons Learned and Lessons Lost

1. The continuity question

THE final set of questions that arises, and in a sense the most interesting, has to do with the relationships between the past and the present. Is it possible to deduce from the philanthropic provision made by the Victorians and Edwardians, and the behaviour associated with it, lessons that have meaning for the 1980's?

Two generalised attitudes are possible. It can be argued that the discontinuities in social experience have been so great as to deprive the past of any significant relevance to the present. The antithetical view is, of course, that continuity in a real sense has indeed been present, and that a consideration of the voluntarism of the preceding age has a value in terms of contemporary problems.

The discontinuity case rests on the argument that the relationships between social groups or classes, and the dynamics within and between them, have altered so greatly since the nineteenth century that no comparison is useful, at least for policy purposes. This change greatly accelerated, it is said, in the 1950's and 1960's, and assumed new forms, or at least new emphases. A release of new consciousness then took place, out of which came a demand for a participatory society, infused with a new communalism. This amounted to a repudiation of the philanthropic/voluntarist principle as it had been practised in the past. The one-way relationship operating downward from the people of substance, education and leisure, to the working classes, was rendered obsolete. The workers would henceforth look after themselves, evolving their own responses, institutions and ethos. With the prospect of labour redundancy on a massive scale, it becomes all the more important that a new and sound sense of individual and communal identity be found, lest alienation destroy us. Whereas the evangelical philanthropists of the past believed that the impact of the new technology, at which they in their day also marvelled, had to be controlled in humility before God, the new view rests upon the possibility of humanist populist self-comprehension and control. With this set of assumptions the entire nature of things has changed.

This approach leaves a good many questions unanswered. There has long been a debate among Marxists and non-Marxists alike as to the nature of the

333

working classes. It is generally recognised that, apart from the purposes of shorthand or rhetoric, the working class is not homogeneous. At the bottom are those who can scarcely be expected to ameliorate their own condition, being demoralised by it — Marx's *lumpenproletariat*. At the top are the skilled men with high earnings. These are sometimes referred to as the 'labour aristocracy', in approval by those who see progress in terms of the values of the middle classes permeating downward (self-help and respectability), and in disapproval by those who regard the labour aristocracy as capitulating to a class not its own, and thus damaging the possibilities of working-class solidarity and, more recently, communalism. Between are the true proletariat of the Marxist tradition, who carry the power of change, either in the revolutionary or the communal sense. If this kind of class disaggregation is thought plausible, then what has happened is a redefinition of the *locus* from which 'leadership' must come. It is now indigenous to the working class, but it is nevertheless 'leadership'.

There are further difficulties. Whatever the stratification of the working classes and the implications flowing therefrom, there is also the question of structure. For effective action some kind of structuring must take place. Of course there are those who deny or minimise this necessity. But the anarchist view in this regard may place too great a degree of confidence in the ability of groups to choose and promote ends without the provision of some kind of structure.

There are, of course, organisational forms which are the product of long historical evolution. The two most important are those at the political level, especially the Labour Party, and those at the industrial level, the trade unions. A good deal of disillusionment is current about the first. There are problems, too, about the second. Trade union officials often find themselves at variance with their shop stewards and rank and file. The union leader is sometimes accused of remoteness, complacency and autocracy, just as the philanthropist has been. The problem of mutual identification, as between those making decisions and those affected by them, is present. Structure, so necessary for effective action, can thus get in the way of effective communication. For structure is the parent of authority. Manipulation of one group by another is thus always likely to re-emerge. There can be no question that the philanthropists in their way manipulated the working classes, but so also do working class leaders.

The latest attempts to escape from structure are centred upon two kinds of effort. There are firstly those experiments aimed at generating a spontaneous communalism (if indeed this is not a paradox). Remarkable examples of this have appeared in Scotland and elsewhere, where a high degree of spontaneity is present. But even these require support in the form of public funds; as soon as this is envisaged, the situation is made subject to *de haut en bas* decision, making it not all that different from the kind associated with the philanthropists. The difference is that whereas in the philanthropic context success depended upon well-meaning but alien people of means taking up the matter, and often acting effectively in doing so, in the state-welfare context it is a question of gaining support from politicians and officials, with their control of the public purse, and with their elaborate institutional organisation and complex political susceptibilities. The preference as between the philanthropic and the state principles is much affected by the value preferences of the individual. What is plain is that neither is both self-acting and self-correcting. Both the philanthropists and the state can use their position in a constructive way, but both can be insensitive and sometimes obtuse about the feelings of those being helped.

The Community Councils are the second form of the attempt to escape from the constraints of structure. They are intended to promote a new kind of response on the part of those affected by public action, by bringing 'representatives' into discussion, both as commentators and initiators. The object is to assist community formation, especially in working-class areas, so that a sense of identity and a capacity for self-organisation may be promoted. But these persons may well not be the product of any optimal principle of choice. It may be difficult, also, for them to maintain their dynamic.

From the foregoing it is apparent that a case for continuity as between the philanthropy of the past and the situation of the present can be made. It rests on the reasoning that certain universals are present in terms of the need to structure, but to do so in a manner consistent with the objectives to be attained. If these include spontaneity and communal feeling, as in the modern age, the problem is greatly compounded.

2. The components of continuity

The question of continuity is perhaps best approached not in general but in more particular terms. Though there are few direct, positive, clip-on lessons to be learned from Victorian and Edwardian philanthropy, a study of nineteenth-century voluntarism does provide a number of aspects and interdependencies, arising from direct experience, that may help in forming judgments about welfare provision in the last quarter of the twentieth century.

It is perhaps right to begin with the most difficult aspect of all, namely the problem of rationalising the pattern of philanthropic provision. The attempts by the COS to bring order into philanthropy are still of interest. There the irreducible difficulty was encountered of generating a sufficient sense of common purpose for a generalised consensus to emerge to which all bodies would subsequently conform, sacrificing their idiosyncrasies to the larger good. This is a permanent dilemma for voluntarism, with its atomistic initiatives. It is related to the role of the hero — the dominant and activating personality who is essential to get things started and sustain them. By the nature of things such people are not natural collaborators, but are obliged to follow their compelling urges, with varying degrees of assertiveness or subtlety. In Victorian times there was sometimes a self-identification with God (the motto of Quarrier's Homes was 'A father of the fatherless of God'). Such people are essential for the health of society: it is important that the conditions that produce them are not impaired. The initiatory hero of earlier times is sometimes succeeded by the obverse type, the administrator who is artificially set in his ways. He is no less difficult to integrate.

The problems of rationalising, while still maintaining a real but integrative set of objectives, do not disappear when the state takes over the components and seeks to synthesise them into a system. Medical provision and education are the two great examples. When the infirmaries, the asylums, the specialist hospitals, the dispensaries, the cottage hospitals and nurses' training and provision were merged by the National Health Act of 1946, the problem of the relationship of the parts and of sharing of resources between them did not, of course, disappear. The parts could be allowed to cohere loosely for a time, especially when general resource constraints were not too severe in the 1960's. With the public purse opened, not surprisingly the provision itself increased apace. But when inflation arrived, the rationalisation problem took on a new dimension. The Resource Allocation Working Party began in 1975 the task of setting up a governing formula. A situation antithetical to *ad hoc* philanthropic provision had been reached. But it may be that those seeking the new kind of solution would be aided in their judgment by a knowledge of the working of the system in its formative, philanthropic years.

In education too, the attempt to tidy up has proceeded a long way. Its principal component is the comprehensive principle. Wholly private education has been left untouched, but grammar school education is rapidly being assimilated to comprehensiveness. So there exists no halfway house. Educational rationalisation has been pursued not primarily for resource allocation reasons, as in the case of health provision, but for reasons deriving from the politically prevailing social philosophy. In both cases, however, the spirit of tidying up has been dominant. It may be that some appreciation of the historical preliminaries would be useful here also.

In order that violence be not done to real values, thought should be given to the terms upon which the voluntarist and the collectivist principles could and should co-exist. Beveridge before 1914 believed that 'the vast network of voluntary self-help organisations should themselves no longer be seen as alternatives to state action, but should be brought into co-operation with the machinery of the state'.[1] Much of the framework of voluntary action to which Beveridge referred has disappeared, but the problem of relating voluntary and state activity remains.

In all this the needs of the recipients should play a major part. *The Times* stressed the limitations to which even the state is subject: 'Welfare bureaucracies have proved themselves expensive and inflexible. Without a steady growth of national wealth they cannot offer more than a basic minimum of provision for the disadvantaged. By their nature they are in danger of reducing their beneficiaries to a state of passive anonymity.'[2] It is natural for doctors now, as in the past, to prefer controlled environments, with themselves the controllers: people are pushed out of their homes and into hospitals for maternity and other services; there is danger that big hospitals will break down the district system. The Chalmerian insistence upon the district principle may still have relevance. Though the philanthropic provision of the past could also bring hierarchy and the manipulation of people as things, there was value in the attempts made to decentralise initiatives and to reach the family in the home, through the dispensaries and district nursing. Centrifugalism was a danger then as now. The parent of the schoolchild, the patient in the hospital, the family in subsidised council housing, have no more rights of say in education, hospital treatment or housing arrangements that affect them now than they had under the philanthropist. In theory the emergence of the state as provider in place of the private benefactor should have given the ordinary citizen more control. In practice this has not happened. The ordinary man in the street has to re-enter the lists if he is to wrest back a share of control over the services which affect his life.

The problem is compounded by the necessary restrictions on the actions of components of the system. The Victorian and Edwardian philanthropic managers did manage. The responsibility for the institution and its working was directly theirs, and had to be discharged. They were not part of an elaborate system of representation and formal accountability, binding them to other bodies and exempting them from real responsibility, but were wholly autonomous. The contests and conflicts of hospital boardrooms, for example, were of a kind to try philanthropic mettle as these men took their part in regulating affairs at the core of the most formidable of all professions, especially in the first three-quarters of the nineteenth century. It continues to be necessary that management bodies be given a degree of autonomy such that they feel that they are meaningful. At the same time they must not be to too great a degree the nominees of the political parties.

A special problem of management exists where the residential principle is involved. Now, as in the past, two problems are present. One has to do with the scale of residential institutions and the division of function between them and the fostering principle. Some Victorian philanthropists had learned the counter-productive aspects of large and frightening orphan institutions. They had experimented, too, with fostering. They had discovered the difficulties that arise when the foster parents themselves require continuous surveillance. Secondly, there was the problem of the dumping ground — what to do with those wholly unable or unwilling to behave in a social manner. The philanthropists under the COS banner exempted themselves from this aspect. They did so by adducing the distinction between the deserving and the undeserving. Clearly if the latter category had any meaning at all it included the anti-social. From the COS point of view they were the responsibility of the state, for they could only be dealt with through coercion, threatened or applied.

A good many Scottish philanthropic enterprises did not draw so tight a distinction. Nevertheless moral judgments were part of the stock-in-trade of the Victorian philanthropist; today the passing of such verdicts upon other men and women is regarded by society as being wrong (another paradox, for this is itself a moral judgment). But wherever we stand on moralism, some judgments seem to be called for in terms of the public sector allocative process. Housing is the great example. The justification for a judgment of behaviour today derives not from morality, but from social engineering, for example in the creation of stable tenant communities when the local authority is the landlord. But does the adoption of social engineering as a warrant for manipulation really dispose of moralism? For so long as sanctions are used, they can only be justified as enforced on persons judged to be responsible for their actions. Now, as in Victorian times, tidying up messes means manipulating those who make them.

All philanthropic enterprises, like those of the state, are confronted with the problem of renewal. How is it possible for an organisation to adjust itself to its task after it has been involved in it for a considerable time? Two possibilities exist. Renewal may come from within, or it may be imposed from without. Internal self-renewal in any generalised sense did not often occur in the philanthropic field. It was the possibility and sometimes reality of external scrutiny that brought some degree of change. The Royal Commission (Scotland) on Endowed Schools and Hospitals of 1872 is perhaps the leading case. It brought about a significant measure of change, though of a limited kind. Perhaps surprisingly, the other large area of philanthropic provision, namely health, was not made the subject of public inquiry; the only exception to this was the Lunatic Asylums (Scotland) Act of 1857, setting up Commissioners. Indeed it seems almost to be a characteristic of the organism to develop protective devices against external intervention.

The philanthropic driving force in Victorian times was evangelical religion. Humanism has now infused and indeed largely taken over the churches. The approach through faith and guilt has largely gone. This was already beginning by the late Victorian times as churches, especially the English nonconformists, stressed social responsibility. This at least has meant that religious controversy no longer impedes social provision. What has been lost by the fading away of the pietistic drive? Has it really disappeared, or does it represent some fundamental urge? A good many modern religious sects seem to be seeking a synthesis of belief in the non-material with the urge for social regeneration.

There can be no group of people whose demise has been more frequently heralded than the philanthropists. But at each stage of official activism the philanthropists have re-formed and appeared in new fields, as involved as ever. As Beveridge remarked, 'Time after time philanthropy is seen breaking in on official routine, unveiling evils, finding fresh channels for service, getting things done that would not be done for pay.'[3] Indeed we are rapidly approaching the state of affairs when in terms of cost alone the unpaid volunteer must be encouraged, for voluntarism is a cheap source of energy. The Wolfenden Committee suggested in 1977 that 'The scale of human resources that can be tapped is indicated by the report's calculation that in man hours the voluntary organisations make at least as great a contribution as all the paid staff in local authority social services departments.'[4]

This, of course, relates to the attempts to professionalise the social services. Though it has been necessary for professionalism to emerge, it may be that there is danger that this trend is going too far in claiming exclusive competence for those with 'qualifications'. The reservoir of help upon which the Victorians drew may thus be left unused. Perhaps social workers themselves must be given a new role, not so much to deal with individual cases as to mobilise community initiatives. Certainly philanthropic energies should be harnessed by the state and the local authority; this perhaps can best be done by providing relatively small sums of money for voluntary philanthropic purposes.

The process of professionalisation was continuous in Victorian times as central government legislated and local government administered in matters formerly in voluntary hands. Local rates rose inexorably, and with them the number of local civic servants who were developing careers previously located within the philanthropic sector. Many of these changes took place with the approval of philanthropists, who were not in principle averse to official takeover. Philanthropic zeal may well have been part of the motivation of the new range of local government officers.

The classic philanthropic roles still need to be filled, namely the monitoring of provision, looking for gaps, the acting as a watchdog on the state as it operates on people's lives, the exploration of entirely new possibilities, the performance of the promotional and propagandist functions, and the taking of direct action. A consideration of the responses made by the Victorians, in addition to helping our understanding of an earlier phase of our society, may entertain, and perhaps in some measure may instruct, those who have inherited the challenge of social welfare.

NOTES

1. Harris, J., 1977, 102.
2. *The Times*, 23 November 1977.
3. Beveridge, 1948, 301.
4. *The Times*, 23 November 1977.

x

APPENDICES

Appendix I

(See chapter 1, p. 21)

The Old Man's Friend Society

Treasurer's Account 1838

Debit

1838

Jan. 1	To Cash in Glasgow Bank		£330 0 0
	—Balance in Treasurer's hands		17 12 4
	—Proceeds of Sermon by the Rev. H. Moncrieff		21 13 0
Feb. 1	—Interest from Glasgow Bank		9 2 6
23	—Legacy from the late Thos. Norris	£250 0 0	
	Less, Legacy Duty and Stamp receipt	£26 5 0	223 15 0
Nov. 15	—Donation from a Gentleman who recommended an inmate to the Asylum		5 0 0
Dec. 31	—Fines from Justice of Peace Court, at sundry times during 1838		13 3 0
	—Amount of Subscriptions and Donations		283 13 6

Credit

£903 19 4

1838

Dec. 31	By 52 weeks' relief and occasional payments	£420 8 6
	—Advertising Annual Sermon, Printing Report, &c.	12 3 6
	—Religious Institution Rooms for 12 meetings	1 4 0
	—R. McCulloch for Collecting Subscriptions	10 17 0
	—Paid for 20 Doz. Shirts	25 5 0
	—Expense attending support of Asylum	111 3 10
	—Cash in Glasgow Bank	315 0 0
	—Balance in Treasurer's hands	7 17 6

£903 19 4

Glasgow, 19th January, 1839.

Compared with the Books and found correct,
(Signed) WILLIAM FLEMING,
GEORGE GILLESPIE.

The Old Man's Friend Society

Treasurer's Account 1846

Debit

1845

Dec. 31	To Amount of Subscriptions & Donations	£203 0 0
	—Parochial Aid for inmates of Aslyum including board, &c.	332 15 9
	—Proceeds of Work done in Asylum	41 6 11
	—Cash Found in Donation Box	2 4 6
	—Fines from Justice of Peace Court	3 7 6
	—Balance due the Treasurer	109 17 3

£782 11 11

Credit
1845

Jan. 1	By Balance due to Treasurer		£20 7 1
Dec. 31	—Ordinary Provisions		494 17 1
	—Servants' Wages, Rent, Insurance, collecting Subscriptions		84 9 7
	—Gas, Coal, and Water		31 11 2
	—Shirts, &c.		8 14 3
	—Printing, Stationery, Advertising and Postages		17 7 1
	—Medicine		5 13 6
	—Allowance to out-door Pensioners		119 12 2
			£782 11 11

Glasgow, 10th March, 1846. — We have examined the foregoing Account, compared the entries with the different vouchers, find the whole correct, and the Balance due to the Treasurer to be One Hundred and Nine Pounds, Seventeen Shillings and Threepence.

(Signed) CHARLES WATSON,
MATHEW FAIRLEY.

The Old Man's Friend Society

Treasurer's Account 1878

December 31, 1878

To Board of Inmates, Private and Parochial			£866 1 11
—Subscriptions and Donations			407 0 10
—Rents—Dean Street Property	£101 0 0		
,, —Rottenrow Property	37 0 0		
			138 0 0
—Interest on Bonds and Feu-duties			889 14 10
—Income Tax returned			11 8 10
—Refuse Sold			£5 0 0
		Ordinary Revenue	2317 6 5
—Legacies, as per subjoined list			1017 13 7
—Donation Aged Women's Home			50 0 0 .
			£3385 0 0

December 31, 1868

By House Expenses, Food, Wages, &c.			£1295 18 5
—Repairs, Alteration, &c.			302 1 5
—Assessments and Local Taxes			19 11 10
—Printing Reports, Stationery, &c.			15 4 6
—Medical Attendance and Medicine			53 18 6
—City Mission			30 0 0
—Pensioners—Fortnightly	£561 1 6		
,, —Quarterly	155 10 0		
,, —Half-Yearly	125 0 0		
			841 11 6
Insurance			5 1 0
—Feu duty—Balmanno Street			5 9 1
—Collecting Subscriptions and Rents			23 9 2
		Ordinary Expenditure	£2592 5 5
—Additional Cost of New Buildings			513 6 0
—Deposit Repaid John Lymburn on leaving Asylum			100 0 0
—Lodged in Union Bank per Pass Book	£2660 3 3		
—Drawn from ,, ,, ,, ,, ,,	2494 5 7		
			165 17 8
—Balance due Treasurer, 31 Dec. 1877	198 15 4		
— ,, ,, ,, ,, ,, 1878	194 4 5		
			13 10 11
			£3385 0 0

Glasgow, 17th March, 1879. — We have examined the accounts of the Old Man's Friend Society, from 1st January to 31st December 1878, and compared Vouchers and Bank Books and found all correct. The amount at credit of the Society in the Union Bank of Scotland is Three Hundred Pounds (say £300), and the amount due the Treasurer is One Hundred and Eighty-five Pounds Four Shillings and Fivepence (say £185 4s. 5d.).

(Signed)　HUGH BROWN,
MATTHEW PETTIGREW.

The Old Man's Friend Society

Legacies Received during 1878—

	£	s.	d.
Late Robert Napier, Shandon	100	0	0
,,　Miss Elizabeth Cameron — balance	130	16	11
,,　J. Dunsmore	349	16	7
,,　Miss Ramsay Walker	45	13	1
,,　Andrew Wilson	50	0	0
,,　James Taylor	18	0	0
,,　Miss Leichman	93	3	4
,,　Malcolm Brown	200	0	0
,,　Lady Cunningham Fairlie	30	4	8
	£1017	13	7

Appendix II

(See chapter 3, p. 72)

Regulations of the Glasgow Sailors' Home in 1858

Respecting terms

Men will have to pay 14s. a week for living at the Institution. Apprentices will pay 10s. 6d. a week.

Officers availing themselves of superior accommodation will be charged 18s. a week. All exclusive of Washing.

When a men has entered his name as a Boarder, the charge for his Board will go on, unless he give notice to the contrary to the Superintendent.

If a man on leaving the Home, after the settlement of his account, wishes to deposit any Property in charge of the Institution, he is carefully to pack it up, place his name and number upon it, and give the Superintendent the necessary information respecting it, when it will be kept till his return, but at his risk.

Should any Property, be left in the Home without such notice, the Institution will not be answerable for it, and it will be sold at the expiration of two years, and proceeds, after deducting expenses, carried to an Account for Unclaimed Property.

If a Boarder goes away in debt, leaving property in the Home, it will be sold at the expiration of six months, and the proceeds applied in payment of the debt.

Respecting conduct

All swearing and improper language, so unbecoming the character of a man and so dishonouring to God, must be entirely avoided in this place.

Drunkenness, that disgraceful vice, which sinks a man below the beasts that perish, and which is so contrary to order and decency, cannot be permitted.

All quarrelling and abusive language must be guarded against; and a respectful manner towards those who superintend the Institution will be expected of every man.

No Smoking can be allowed in the Bed-Rooms, or other places than those set apart for the purpose.

No Lucifers, Matches, or Candles, can be allowed in any of the Bed-Rooms under any pretence, and the Gas Lights there must be put out if the Inmate goes to bed before Eleven o'clock.

No Spirits, Wine, or other Intoxicating Liquors, will be permitted to be brought into or used in the House.

Respecting hours

Morning Prayers will be offered up in the Reading Room at Half-past Eight o'clock each Morning throughout the year, and Evening Prayers at Nine o'clock each evening. It cannot be considered creditable to any man who will absent himself from the worship of God.

The Street Door will be opened at Five o'clock in the Morning, and locked at Eleven o'clock at Night. No one can be admitted after that hour except by the Watchman.

On Week-days, — Breakfast will be on the table at Nine o'clock, Dinner at Two, and Tea at Half-past Six.

On Sundays, — Breakfast at Nine, Dinner at One, and Tea at Five.

For the sake of regularity, it is hoped the Men will be punctual at the appointed hours for Meals.

By order   WM. TEER, Supt.

Source: Glasgow Sailors' Home, First Annual Report (Glasgow 1858).

Appendix III

(See chapter 9, p. 170)

An Account of the CEREMONY, which took place on the 2nd day of August, 1810, at laying the Foundation Stone of the Glasgow Asylum for Lunatics.

The FOUNDATION STONE of the Glasgow Asylum for Lunatics, was laid by the Honourable the Lord Provost, acting Provincial Grand Master for the Lower Ward of Lanarkshire, in presence of the Magistrates, Public Bodies, Mason Lodges, and Contributors to the Institution. At Twelve o'Clock, noon, the several parties assembled in St. George's Church, when the Rev. Dr. Macgill, one of the Ministers of this City, delivered the preceding Discourse.

Immediately after Divine Service was concluded, the Procession moved down Buchanan Street, along the Trongate, up the High Street, along the Rottenrow, and down Taylor Street, to the Site of the Building, in the following Order:—

A Band of Music, Drums, etc.
The Town Officers, in Scarlet Uniforms and Halberts,
The Magistrates, in full Dress, with their Staffs of Office,
The Town Clerks,
The Town Council, three and three;
The Town Officers of Paisley,
William Jamieson, Esq. ⎫
James Whyte, Esq. ⎬ Magistrates of Paisley;
Robert Hart, Esq. ⎭
The Officers of the Barony of Gorbals,
Robert Ferrie, Esq. ⎫
David Niven, Esq. ⎬ Magistrates of Gorbals;
William Mills, Esq. ⎭
Council of Gorbals, three and three;
The Beadles of the City Churches,
The Ministers of the City and Neighbourhood, in their Gowns and Bands,
A Deputation of Two Members from each of the Church Sessions,
The Officer of the Merchants' House,
The Dean of Guild, in full dress, with his Staff of Office,
The Members of the Merchants' House, three and three,
A Band of Music, Drums, etc.
The Officer of the Trades' House,
The Convener, in full Dress, with his Staff of Office,
The Members of the Trades' House, three and three,
The Rev. John Ritchie, Chaplain to the Trades' House, in his Gown,
The Colours of the late Regiment of Trades' House Volunteer Infantry, supported by the Captains
    Meikle and Lyon, formerly of that Regiment;
The Officer of the Incorporation of Hammermen,
Deacon Napier, and the Master-Court of the Incorporation of Hammermen, three and three;
The Officer of the Incorporation of Tailors,
Deacon Ross, and the Master-Court of the Incorporation of Tailors, three and three;
The Officer of the Incorporation of Cordiners,
Deacon Craig, and the Master-Court of the Incorporation of Cordiners, three and three;

The Officer of the Incorporation of Maltmen,
Visitor Hunter, and the Master-Court of the Incorporation of Maltmen, three and three;
The Officer of the Incorporation of Weavers,
Deacon Buchanan, and the Master-Court of the Incorporation of Weavers, three and three;
The Officer of the Incorporation of Bakers,
Deacon Marshall, and the Master-Court of the Incorporation of Bakers, three and three;
The Officer of the Incorporation of Skinners,
Deacon Nicol, and the Master-Court of the Incorporation of Skinners, three and three;
The Officer of the Incorporation of Wrights,
Deacon McCallum, and the Master-Court of the Incorporation of Wrights, three and three;
The Officer of the Incorporation of Coopers,
Deacon Scott, and the Master-Court of the Incorporation of Coopers, three and three;
The Officer of the Incorporation of Fleshers,
Deacon Scouler, and the Master-Court of the Incorporation of Fleshers, three and three;
The Officer of the Incorporation of Masons,
Deacon Paterson, and the Master-Court of the Incorporation of Masons, three and three;
The Officer of the Incorporation of Gardeners,
Deacon Hamilton, and the Master-Court of the Incorporation of Gardeners, three and three;
The Officer of the Incorporation of Barbers,
Deacon Campbell, and the Master-Court of the Incorporation of Barbers, three and three;
The Officer of the Incorporation of Dyers and Bonnet-makers,
Deacon Cassels, and the Master-Court of the Incorporation of Dyers and Bonnet-makers, three
    and three;
Mr. Cowan, one of the Teachers of the Trades' House Free School, in his gown;
The Directors of the Trades' House Free School, three and three;
The Officer of the Faculty of Physicians and Surgeons,
The Preses & Faculty of Physicians & Surgeons, three and three;
The Officer of the Faculty of Procurators,
The Dean and Faculty of Procurators, three and three;
The Officers of Police, in their full uniform,
Captain Mitchell, the Superintendent of Police, with his Medal and Badge of Office,
The Commissioners of Police, with their Batons of Office, three and three;
The Officer of the Lunatic Asylum,
The Committee, the Managers, and the Contributors to the Institution, three and three;
A Band of Music, Drums, etc.

GRAND LODGE OF SCOTLAND

The Grand Tyler, with a drawn Sword;
Two Grand Stewards, with Rods;
Compass and Level, carried by two Operative Brethren;
Two Grand Stewards, with Rods;
Square, Mallet, and Plumb, carried by Operative Brethren;
Two Grand Stewards, with Rods;

| Silver Cup, | Cornucopiae, filled with | Silver Cup, |
| filled with Wine; | Corn and Corn Stalks; | filled with Oil; |

Two Grand Stewards, with Rods;
Two Inscription Plates, carried by Operative Brethren, on one of which is inscribed:—

TO RESTORE THE USE OF REASON,
TO ALLEVIATE SUFFERING, AND LESSEN PERIL,
WHERE REASON CANNOT BE RESTORED,

THE

GLASGOW ASYLUM FOR LUNATICS,

was erected by Public Contribution.

By the Favour of Almighty God,

The Honourable JAMES BLACK,
Lord Provost of Glasgow

Acting Provincial Grand Master of the Lower Ward of Lanarkshire,

LAID THIS FOUNDATION STONE,

On the Second Day of August, MDCCCX

AERA OF MASONRY, 5810,

And 50th Year of the Reign of our most Gracious Sovereign,

GEORGE THE THIRD;

In Presence of the Committee, consisting of

Robert Cleghorn, M.D.
John Craig, Esq.
Robert McNair, Esq.
George Rutherford, Esq.
John Mair, Esq.
James Cleland, Esq.

and

William Jamieson, Esq., Chief Magistrate of Paisley,
And of the other Managers and Contributors to this Asylum;

William Stark, Esq., Architect;
Thomas Smith and Alexander Hay, Contractors;
Robert McNair, Esq., Treasurer;
William Cuthbertson, Esq., Secretary—

Which Undertaking may the Supreme God bless and prosper.

———

(Similar civic ceremonies were mounted for many charitable occasions.)

Source: MacGill, Stevenson, in Appendix to *On Lunatic Asylums: a discourse delivered on 2nd August 1810, previous to laying the foundation stone of the Glasgow Lunatic Asylum* (Glasgow 1810).

Appendix IV

(See chapter 12, p. 216)

GRAND BAZAAR

THE PROMOTER AND DIRECTORS
of the
WEST OF SCOTLAND CONVALESCENT HOMES
DUNOON

Have arranged to hold a Bazaar on a Large Scale in aid of the above Institution, in the CITY HALL, Glasgow (the use of which has been kindly granted by the Hon. the Lord Provost and Magistrates), on the 1st, 2nd, 3rd and 4th November, 1871.

Under the immediate Distinguished Patronage of:—

Her Royal Highness Princess Louise, Marchioness of Lorne
The Most Noble the Marquis of Lorne
His Grace the Duke of Argyll
Her Grace the Duchess of Argyll
His Grace the Duke of Roxburghe
Her Grace the Duchess of Roxburghe
The Right Honourable the Earl of Glasgow
The Right Honourable the Countess of Glasgow
The Right Honourable the Countess of Dunmore
The Right Honourable the Lady Octavia Shaw Stewart
The Right Honourable the Lady Alice Louisa Ewing
The Right Honourable the Lady Elizabeth Harvey, Castlesemple
The Right Honourable the Lady Isabella Gordon, of Aikenhead
The Right Honourable the Lady Charlotte Fletcher
The Right Honourable the Lady Caroline Charteris
The Right Honourable the Lady Belhaven and Hamilton
The Right Honourable the Lady Dunfermline
The Honourable Mrs. Hope
Lady Colebrooke, of Crawford
Lady MacDonald of Lockhart, of Lee and Carnwath
Lady Campbell, of Garscube
Lady Emily Hamilton, of Dalziel
Lady Coats, of Woodside and Auchendrane
Mrs. Rae Arthur, Park Terrace, Glasgow
Mrs. Baird, of Cambusdoon, Ayrshire
Mrs. Buchanan, of Drumpellier
Mrs. Campbell, of Camis Eskan
Mrs. Grahàm, Langley House, Prestwich, and Urrard House, Pitlochrie
Mrs. William Hozier, of Tannochside
Miss Smith, of Jordanhill
Mrs. Whitelaw, Gartsherrie House.

349

NB. — with reference to the above, special attention is directed to the Letters printed at the close of this Pamphlet. The Names and Addresses of the Stallholders and Work Receivers will be advertised shortly.

Source: Clugston, Beatrice, *West of Scotland Convalescent Sea-side Homes . . . for the purpose of stirring up the community of Glasgow and the West of Scotland to greater efforts for the working classes in times of sickness and distress* (Glasgow 1871).

Appendix V

(See chapter 12, p. 217)

Gifts to the Mission Coast Home, Saltcoats, in 1878

MANY societies published in their annual reports lists of gifts received from benefactors. The catalogue below is a typical example.

Presents to the Home

5 Large Kettles — Mr. Lindsay, Glasgow. 1 Cart Turnips — Mr. Wyllie, Border. 1 Cart Turnips — Mr. McKinnon, New England. Parcel of Books — Mrs. Fyfe, Glasgow. Parcel of New Underclothing — Mrs. Barr, Fenwick. 1 Bag Rice — Mr. James Philips, Glasgow. Parcel of Books — Mr. A. Marshall. 6 Fire Shovels — Mr. Coats, Sanquhar. Barrel of Flour — Mr. Charles Smith, Stevenston. 3 Bags of Potatoes, and 3 Bags Chaff — Mrs. McIsaac, Parkend. 1 Jigot Mutton and 1 Roast Beef — Mr. John Crawford, Saltcoats. Parcel of Tea and Bag Oranges — Mrs. Orr, Saltcoats. Parcel of Tea — Mr. R. Barclay, Saltcoats. 1 bag Feathers with £1 10s. for Ticking, and 6 Brace of Rabbits — Miss Brown, Lanfine. Parcel of Buns — Mr. R. Black, Saltcoats. Parcel of Sheets and Sheeting — Miss Fairlie, Kirkmichael Manse. 2 Parcels of Clothing — Rev. Dr. Edwards, Glasgow. Parcel of Clothing and Boots — Mrs. Alexander, Partick. 3 Parcels Books — Anonymous. 1 Boll Meal — A Friend. 3 Hams and 2 Cheese — Mr. Whiteford, Stewarton. Parcel of Clothing, and Supply of Herrings, given by Mr. Elliot, Saltcoats. Supply of Marmalade and Jam — Mrs. Cunninghame, Pavilion, Ardrossan. Parcel of Tea, Sugar, Buns, and Books — Mr. McFarlane, Glasgow. Large Parcel New Clothing — per Miss Morrison, from Ladies at Hillhead. 112 lbs. Marmalade — John Gray & Co., Glasgow. Large Supply of Plants and Seeds — Mr. Samson, Kilmarnock. 9 Bags Potatoes — Mr. James Gray, Glasgow. 6 Fire Shovels, and Scripture Bed Mat — Anonymous. Parcel of Books — Miss Smith, Saltcoats. Parcel of *Good Words* and *Chambers' Journals* — Mr. McKnight, Plain, Kilmaurs. Large Supply of Jelly and Jam, Vegetables and Flowers — Mrs. Brown, Monkcastle. Box of Preserves — A Friend, Kilmarnock. 1 Bag of Rice — Mr. John Gloag, Largs. 10 Night Shirts, 60 Flannel Slips, 3 Bed Covers, and 24 Sheets — Mrs. Gloag, Largs. Parcel of Clothing — Miss Boyle, Skelmorlie, per Mrs. Gloag, Largs. 2 Parcels Books, 12 Towels, and Parcel of Bed Linen — Mrs. Moon, per Mrs. Gloag. 2 Parcels Clothing — Miss Adam, Tour, by Kilmarnock. Parcel of Clothing — Mr. John Edwards, jun., Glasgow. A Mangle, Writing Desk, and Bath — Mrs. Richardson, Glasgow. 12 lbs. Tea — Mr. Alex. Pollock, London Street, Glasgow. 1 Cart Turnips — Mr. Cunninghame, Auchenharvie. 1 Bed Mat, and other useful articles — Mr. H. Banks, Stevenston. 1 Load Meal — Mr. Tyre, Maqueston, Thornhill. 1 Bag Carrots — Mr. Alex. Fleck, Saltcoats. Bread Cutter, and Green Mower — Mr. R. Miller. Parcel of Publications, monthly — League Office, Glasgow. 2 Nos. Christian Cabinet, monthly — Mr James Taylor, Edinburgh. Number of Parcels, Periodicals, &c. — Anonymous.

Source: 13th Annual Report of Mission Coast Home, Saltcoats, 1879.

Appendix VI

(See chapter 15, p. 249)

Regulations of the Glasgow Boys' House of Refuge (founded 1838)

THESE regulations appeared in full in each year's annual *Report of the Glasgow Boys' House of Refuge*, off Duke Street. Whether they had any application to everday life in the home is hard to say, but they must have impressed possible subscribers.

REGULATIONS FOR TEACHERS

TEACHERS! It is impossible to over-estimate the importance of your office. Yours is pre-eminently the vocation of training your youthful charge for both worlds. You need peculiar qualifications — firmness blended with love, decision with gentleness. In undertaking your office, see that you have counted the cost. Your daily duties call for daily self-denial. You must live by prayer. You cannot take a step without it. Your own strength is weakness. Through Christ you can do all things. Your moral influence in the school is omnipotent. If on the side of rectitude, regularity, and order, the children will emulate your virtues; if on the contrary side, who can estimate the disastrous consequences. Seek to realize the value of the precious souls entrusted to you. Yours is the task to mould them for immortality. You possess a plastic power whose efficacy cannot fail — Bible truths uttered by loving lips from earnest hearts. School instruction — the Teacher's words and looks, fresh and vivid, associated with the parents' — survive when the winter of old age had chilled almost all beside. How important that these be SACRED recollections! Those entrusted to you have, in most instances, either lost their parents, or it had been better for them they had never seen them. This makes your task doubly responsible. You have not only to implant proper principles, but to eradicate evil ones. But the seed you sow shall never die. It will bear fruit in eternity. Live then by faith. Whether you see it or not, a rich harvest SHALL be reaped. Be a hero in God's work. 'Fight the good fight of faith.' Your warfare will at last be crowned with victory.

The following Regulations are appended more as a few suggestions to aid, than as complete rules to regulate you.

1.   Seek to realize the momentous importance of your office.
2.   Enter upon the discharge of your daily duties with much fervent prayer for divine blessing.
3.   Remember that yours is the training of immortal spirits for the highest destinies of which they are susceptible.
4.   Be earnest. Be hopeful. Work for God. Consider the magnitude of your enterprise. Apply your undivided energies to its execution.
5.   Have faith in the promises of God's word that they will all be verified in the experience of the earnest believing spirit. 'Train up a child in the way he should go; and when he is old, he will not depart from it.' 'My word goeth forth out of my mouth shall not return unto me void, but shall accomplish that which I please, and prosper in the thing whereto I sent it.'
6.   Give a daily Bible lesson, and strive to impress the minds of all your children with the supreme importance of loving, reverencing, and practising the holy precepts of the Word of God.
7.   Make sure that you possess the primary and indispensable element of a qualified teacher — deep and genuine piety.
8.   Strive to co-operate with the Governor in bringing the children to a saving knowledge of the Lord Jesus.
9.   With the view of rendering your teaching efficacious, acquire a complete control over your children while you possess their entire confidence.

10.   Your duties are peculiarly trying on your temper, therefore endeavour to unite melting love with unflinching decision in the exercise of discipline.

11.   Let order and regularity pervade the whole arrangements and routine of your School.

12.   Be punctual. Teach your boys punctuality. Let them know that irregularity of attendance cannot be tolerated, and if tolerated would injure themselves through life.

13.   Acquaint yourself as soon as possible with the names, respective characters, and dispositions of your boys. You need not be reminded that your treatment of each must vary according to peculiarity of circumstances.

14.   Endeavour to ground the boys well in the common elements of education, being (with few exceptions) all the learning that they will ever receive.

15.   Endeavour to make your instruction as interesting as possible, that their attention and sympathies being enlisted they may regard their education with pleasure, and make corresponding progress therein.

16.   Keep a careful account of each boy's attendance and diligence at the School, with the progress he is making. You will render a Quarterly Report to this effect to the Governor, which is engrossed in his books, and submitted to the Directors.

17.   Teach your children politeness. Whilst you are kind and familiar, let them never intrude by coarseness or vulgarity. Their previous habits expose them very much to this evil.

18.   Enforce cleanliness and tidiness as to person, clothes, books, and School furniture. This is indispensable in a well-regulated class-room.

19.   Make your boys march in order to and from the School, and when changing their classes. In no instance allow them to jump over the seats or act disorderly.

20.   See that each boy has laid past his books, cap, &c., in the proper place. Many of the impediments that retard the success of the Teacher would be removed by attention to such minor points as these.

21.   Continually impress on the children the importance of valuing their present opportunities for improvement. Their minds are volatile. They need 'line upon line, and precept upon precept.' They look to you for instruction.

22.   In reproving or checking for faults committed, make reference to the Bible as your authority, thereby impressing upon the minds of the children the sacred majesty of the Word of God.

23.   See that the School Regulations be constantly carried out; and with this view cause one of your Monitors to read them aloud, at least once in the week, in the presence of the whole School.

REGULATIONS FOR ASSISTANTS

ASSISTANTS! Your designation delineates your duties. You contemplate one day to superintend a Reformatory. Enter now on your great work with all your heart. Be in earnest. Pray much. Labour much. Believe much. God will be with you. The cause demands and deserves your entire energies. You are a fellow-labourer with God. You desire to dive into the sea of human depravity and corruption, to bring thence gems to adorn the diadem of your Redeemer. Persevere. God will bless your labours. 'My word that goeth forth out of my mouth SHALL not return unto me void, but shall accomplish that which I please, and prosper in the thing whereto I sent it.' The Bible is your sheet anchor. Religion is your mighty lever. Philosophy is your handmaid. 'They that honour me I will honour.'

The following Regulations are designed to supplement, not supersede, your own plans of usefulness. The Governor will always be delighted to co-operate with and aid you. May you be 'wise in winning souls'.

1.   Begin, conduct, and close your work daily in the spirit of prayer.

2.   Endeavour to realize the conviction that nothing comparatively is effected for your youthful charges until they are converted unto God.

3.   Pray, labour, look for conversions.

4.   Endeavour to adopt God's appointed means to effect God's work, therefore prayerfully study the Bible as your great model in all things.

5.   Inspire love and reverence for the Bible in the mind of your charge, and see that the daily portion be duly committed to memory.

6.   Study the characters and dispositions of each of the children entrusted to you, and adapt your instruction and dealing to him accordingly.

7.   Never despair of the recovery and salvation of the most degraded and vicious under your care.

8.   Deal personally with each one entrusted to you; pray with and for him; gain his confidence; convince him, by your earnestness and affection, that you seek his temporal and eternal welfare.

9.   Endeavour to impress him that his sins have not only dishonoured God, but injured himself, and exposed him to present and future misery. But

10.   Show him that God is merciful, and that there is hope for him through sincere 'repentance towards God and faith towards our Lord Jesus Christ'.

11.   Inspire him with hope. Show him that while the past may be dark and dreary, the future is pregnant with promise and bright with hope.

12.   Instil the love of industry into the mind of your youthful flock. Show them that honest labour is not less an appointment of Heaven than a condition of human happiness.

13.   Inculcate constant habits of Obedience, Truthfulness, and Industry on your charge; and see that the Masters are regular and punctual in giving the daily marks for these qualities to their boys.

14.   See that order, punctuality, and cleanliness prevail in your regular inspection of the Workshops, Dormitories, and other parts of the Institution.

15.   Teach the children to love one another, to cultivate a kind and obliging disposition towards each other.

16.   In visiting the Dormitories entrusted to you, conduct the worship occasionally, hear and explain the daily verses, give such directions as may enable the Monitors to discharge their duties efficiently, and take a note each visit of the state of the Ward in your Dormitory Report.

17.   A large amount of your success, under God, being dependent on the manner in which the Monitors discharge their duties, take a special interest in them; advise, encourage, and train them for their difficult and interesting work. And,

18.   As the ranks of the Monitors are constantly thinned by their being discharged from the Institution as reformed boys, be always watching for suitable ones to occupy their places, making them at first assistants, and then training them to their important duties.

19.   Issue no commands unless you see that they are punctually and promptly executed.

20.   Expect difficulties, and be prepared, in God's strength, successfully to overcome them.

21.   Give your whole heart to your work; the task of rescuing the fallen can only be achieved by prayer, patience and perseverance. 'Be not weary in well-doing, for in DUE SEASON you shall reap if you faint not.'

22.   When you need to correct for faults, watch your temper; do not give way to passion. Convince the erring that you seek his good. A few kind loving words will seldom fail in melting the obdurate, and so aid in reforming him.

23.   Never let a boy at large in a sour or sullen state of mind. He prevents his own improvement, and does much to impede the improvement of others. He must be brought to a right state before you give him up, and an energetic master never fails.

24.   Do not hold out bribes for well-doing or industry. The children should be made to feel that they are to do right from a sense of duty.

25.   Little encouragements should be occasionally given — such as a holiday, a visit to the Coast, Botanic Gardens, prizes for excelling at their School, Trade, &c., in conjunction with moral improvement — but these should be sparingly and judiciously bestowed.

26.   Always give prominence to goodness rather than cleverness, and encourage excellence in moral character rather than in intellectual display.

27.   Teach the children gratitude, contentment, and civility. Show them the bearing of these principles on their future life.

28.   Take special interest in the new inmates. For the first few months generally decide the character they are to sustain while in the Institution. Loving words and looks then impress them that they are come among friends who are concerned for their welfare.

29.   When any of your boys are on the sick list, be earnest to impress their minds with the importance of possessing 'the one thing needful'. These are seasons especially pointed out by providence for directing the soul to eternal things. 'Before I was afflicted I went astray, but now I keep thy word.'

30.   On week days you will take a share of the duties of the school-room. Endeavour to acquire the best system of teaching. No one can be an efficient Superintendent of a Reformatory unless he has had considerable experience in School management.

31.   On the Sabbath you will assist the Governor in the duties of the sacred day. Special efforts

Y

must then be made on behalf of the boys' eternal interests. In addition to training them to the regular habit of attending Divine Worship in the Institution and elsewhere each boy, as far as possible, must be made the subject of individual catechising and instruction.

32.   Make yourself thoroughly acquainted with all the arrangements of the Institution, and suggest improvements when you think them necessary. The Governor will be glad to consider them carefully.

33.   Consult freely with the Governor as to the best mode of training the boys, and qualifying yourself for your deeply important work. He will gladly sympathize with you in your difficulties, and communicate to you the result of his experience.

34.   Make the glory of God in the salvation of the souls of 'the little ones' committed to you, the supreme object of your life, and 'WHATSOEVER THINE HAND FINDETH TO DO, DO IT WITH THY MIGHT; FOR THERE IS NO WORK, NOR DEVICE, NOR KNOWLEDGE, NOR WISDOM IN THE GRAVE WHITHER THOU GOEST.'

REGULATIONS FOR MASTERS OF WORKSHOPS, OR FAMILY FATHERS

MASTERS AND FAMILY FATHERS! Consider your solemn responsibility. You are engaged in training immortal souls for both worlds. Whether you will or not, the boys under your care will take from YOU the character of their destiny. Are YOU punctual, upright, and diligent? THEY will become so. Are YOU the reverse? THEY will follow your example. They are with you the principal portion of the day. If you follow out and inculcate the lessons they have been receiving from the Governor and at School, the result cannot but be favourable; if otherwise, you will be the means of their ruin. You occupy much the position of a parent. The Directors and the Governor repose great confidence in you. Discharge your important trust with fidelity. Become thoroughly acquainted with EACH of your boys. Find out his disposition. Ascertain the entrance into his heart. Gain his confidence. Show that you CANNOT give him up till he is reformed.

The following regulations will assist you. Ponder and pray over them.

1.   Endeavour to enter on your responsible duties daily in a spirit of prayerful dependence on the divine blessing.

2.   As the Word of God gives directions for the life that now is, as well as for that which is to come, make the Bible your constant study, to guide you in discharging with fidelity your important trust.

3.   Unite kindness and firmness in your treatment of the boys.

4.   As they are specially placed under your care for acquiring a knowledge of some trade or handicraft, strive, by exciting their emulation and interest, to make them thoroughly masters of it.

5.   Impress upon them constantly the necessity of combining honesty and integrity, with proficiency at their respective trades and occupations.

6.   Study the characters and dispositions of your youthful charge, and adapt your instructions to them accordingly.

7.   Teach them habits of politeness and respect towards their superiors, love and kindness towards their equals.

8.   Be punctual yourself, and teach punctuality to your boys. On no account allow them to be behind the appointed hour in being present at their workshops.

9.   Inculcate implicit and cheerful obedience to all your commands, it being understood that these are always just and reasonable.

10.   Avoid irritation and passion, and when you need to report a boy for misconduct, show that you do it with grief, but that his welfare demands it.

11.   Consult freely and frequently with the Governor about the best mode of managing your boys, and especially regarding any one who may be troublesome. He will always be glad to co-operate with and assist you.

12.   Train your boys to habits of neatness and cleanliness, as regards their workshop, clothes, and person; having a place for everything, and everything in its place. On no account allow them to appear with unwashed hands or faces, or with clothes torn or out of order.

13.   Allow no talking in your shop during work hours, except what is necessary in asking the tools from one another.

14.   When your shop is out of work, apply to the Superintendent of the department for more; and when a boy is waiting for a job, let him read for the benefit of others. Never allow a boy to remain idle.

15.   Give the daily mark for Truthfulness, Obedience, and Industry, to each boy under your care, according as he merits it, with scrupulous conscientiousness. Neglect, partiality, or want of firmness here, may do incalculable and irreparable mischief to the boy's future destiny.

16.   In all your intercourse with your charge, let them witness on your part, straightforwardness, sincerity, and christian principle. If you act otherwise, no one can estimate the amount of damage you inflict upon them.

17.   Do nothing yourself by stealth, and allow none of your boys to do it. The Governor's visits are never dreaded by a well-conducted shop.

18.   Be particularly watchful to check, in your boys, every tendency to dishonesty and deception, whether in look, word, or action.

19.   When you have made yourself thoroughly acquainted with the character and disposition of your boys, appoint the best behaved among them as a Monitor; whose duty it will be to assist you in the management of the rest, and to act for you in your necessary absence.

20.   On the ringing of the bell at night, you will march your boys in order to the lavatories, see them thoroughly washed, and then delivered over to the receiving officer; in all such marching, the Monitor will walk at the front, and yourself at the rear of the boys.

21.   At your turn to superintend them on the Play-ground, see that they all enjoy themselves with the utmost freedom, laying no restraint on them, except such as is necessary in preventing wrong-doing; hearty energetic play is good for their body and mind.

22.   Impress on them the importance of observing the rules of the Institution, of conducting themselves in a becoming manner, of cherishing feelings of gratitude to God for placing them in such favourable circumstances, and of using every effort to improve these.

GENERAL RULES

BOYS! These rules are designed to make you happy. They aim at your welfare for both worlds. You are in the House to do you good. The Masters are your friends. Consider them as such. Permit them to aid you in your efforts for self-improvement. Without your earnest co-operation, no training will benefit you.

The following rules will help you to remember your duty. Reflect on them. They are only some out of many which the Bible will point out to you. Pray to God, for Christ's sake, 'to teach you all things'.

I.— CULTIVATE EARLY PIETY.
'I love them that love me; and those that seek me early shall find me,' —   —   Prov. viii. 17.

II.— HONOUR THE BIBLE.
'Search the Scriptures,'   —   —   —   —   —   —   —   —   John v. 39.

III.— LOVE THE LORD'S DAY.
'Remember the Sabbath day, to keep it holy,'   —   —   —   —   —   Exodus xx. 8.

IV.— BE PRAYERFUL.
'Pray without ceasing,'   —   —   —   —   —   —   —   —   1 Thess. v. 17.

V.— WATCH THE STATE OF YOUR HEART.
'Keep thy heart with all diligence; for out of it are the issues of life,' —   —   Prov. iv. 23.

VI.— BE HUMBLE.
'God resisteth the proud, but giveth grace unto the humble,'   —   —   —   James iv. 6.

VII.— CULTIVATE DECISION OF CHARACTER.
'Choose you this day who ye will serve; . . . but as for me and my house, we will serve the LORD,'   —   —   —   —   —   —   —   —   Josh. xxiv. 15.

VIII.— BE OBEDIENT.
'Obey them that have the rule over you,' —   —   —   —   —   —   Heb. xiii. 17.

IX.— BE TRUTHFUL.
'Lie not one to another,'   —   —   —   —   —   —   —   —   Coloss. iii. 9.

X.— BE HONEST.
'Thou shalt not steal,'   —   —   —   —   —   —   —   —   Exod. xx. 15.

XI.— BE INDUSTRIOUS.

'The hand of the diligent maketh rich,' — — — — — — Proverbs x. 4.

XII.— BE CAREFUL.

'Gather up the fragments that remain, that nothing be lost,' — — — John vi. 12.

XIII.— RISE EARLY.

'Love not sleep, lest thou come to poverty,' — — — — — Proverbs xx. 13.

XIV.— PRACTISE SELF-DENIAL.

'If any man will come after me let him deny himself,' — — — — Matthew xvi. 24.

XV.— BE GRATEFUL.

'In every thing give thanks,' — — — — — — — — 1 Thess. v. 18.

XVI.— BE BENEVOLENT.

'Do good unto all men,' — — — — — — — — Gal. vi. 10.

XVII.— BE CONTENT.

'Godliness with contentment is great gain,' — — — — 1 Timothy vi, 6.

XVIII.— GUARD AGAINST ENVY.

'Envy is the rottenness of the bones,' — — — — — — Proverbs xiv. 30.

XIX.— AVOID SWEARING AND PROFANE LANGUAGE.

'Swear not at all,' - - - - - - - - - - Matthew v. 34.

XX.— BEWARE OF EVIL COMPANIONS.

'My son, if sinners entice thee, consent thou not,' — — — — Proverbs i. 10.

XXI.— BE ORDERLY AND REGULAR.

'Let all things be done decently and in order,' — — — — — 1 Cor. xiv. 40.

XXII.— BE PUNCTUAL.

'To every thing there is a season,' — — — — — — — Eccles. iii. 1.

XXIII.— BE POLITE.

'Honour to whom honour is due,' — — — — — — — Romans xiii. 7.

XXIV.— CULTIVATE GOOD TEMPER.

'Anger resteth in the bosom of fools,' — — — — — — Eccles. vii. 9.

XXV.— GUARD AGAINST COVETOUSNESS.

'Beware of covetousness,' — — — — — — — Luke xii. 15.

XXVI.— BE PERSEVERING.

'Be not weary in well doing,' — — — — — — — 2 Thess. iii. 13.

PRACTISE CLEANLINESS.
DO EVERY THING AT ITS PROPER TIME.
PUT EVERY THING IN ITS PROPER PLACE.
USE EVERY THING FOR ITS PROPER PURPOSE.
NEVER PUT OFF TILL TO-MORROW WHAT YOU CAN DO TO-DAY.

REGULATIONS FOR CHAPEL

1. As it is a solemn act to engage in God's worship, it is expected that seriousness, earnestness, and a becoming deportment, will characterize every one present; and

2. As no worship is acceptable before God, unless it be performed by the heart, and through the mediation of Jesus Christ, every one should commence by secretly asking God's Holy Spirit to enable him to perform it aright.

3. The bell rings for worship at 8 o'clock in the morning, when every boy will drop his work, and join his rank, preparatory to going to the Chapel.

4. On orders being given, the boys will march to the Chapel, taking their seats in silence, and prepare for the worship of God.

5. Each boy will have the regular psalm and chapter prepared before the commencement of the worship, and will take part in the singing and other services.

6. The morning worship being concluded, the boys will march in order to the Breakfast Hall, and at night, after the evening worship, to the Dormitories, except on the evenings devoted to the Lectures, Examinations, Music, &c.

7. No talking of any kind, nor sleeping, on Sabbath, while in the Church or Chapel, nor any noise made with the hands or feet, is allowed.

8. Every boy will simultaneously repeat, at the morning worship, the daily text of Scripture, when notice is given by the Governor, or the person conducting the service.

9. Every boy will sit with his back to the seat, and will not lean upon the book-board with his arms or hands, or be listless or inattentive while the worship is being conducted.

10. No boy should rise to the singing till the lines are distinctly read, not sit after prayer till the person conducting the worship has closed.

11. Every boy will simultaneously repeat, at the morning worship, the daily text of Scripture, when notice is given by the Governor, or the person conducting the service.

12. Each boy is expected, on Sabbath evenings, to give the texts and portions of the sermons heard through the day, whether in or out of the House, and to repeat the seven verses of Scripture committed to memory during the week.

REGULATIONS FOR SCHOOL

1. All the orders of the Teachers should be punctually and promptly obeyed.

2. Every boy ought to be regular and punctual in his attendance, entering the School along with his class, and in no instance staying away without special permission to do so.

3. Politeness and becoming respect, both in speech and behaviour, towards the Teachers, should at all times characterize the boys; therefore, all rudeness and incivility of any kind, ought to be entirely unknown in the School.

4. Every boy will cultivate feelings of affection and regard, and avoid unkind or injurious treatment towards each other.

5. Diligence and activity must characterize each boy as well during School hours as at his trade; therefore, no talking or trifling of any kind can be allowed.

6. No one will begin a new page in Writing, nor a new rule in Arithmetic, until he has obtained permission from the Master. Every boy ought perseveringly and thoroughly to master all his lessons.

7. As every boy ought to take special care of his own books, he is not to meddle with, nor take those of another. No book to be taken out of the School without liberty to do so; and there must be no waste of the ink-bottles, slates, pencils, or pens.

8. Every boy ought to appear at School clean and tidy in his person and clothes; and no spitting on the floor or desks, or other nuisance, are on any account tolerated. The Class-rooms will be kept clean during the week, and washed on Saturdays by the Classes meeting in them. Boys will do this by rotation: at the same time, every boy ought to feel a pleasure in seeing the rooms in a clean and comfortable condition, and it ought to be the constant effort of all to keep them in this state.

9. Every boy should enter and retire from the School in a quiet and orderly manner, taking special care to clean his feet on entering, so that the Class-rooms may be kept clean and tidy. All writing or marking on books, desks, or walls, is prohibited; and boys ought to be very careful not to put their feet upon the heating apparatus, and not to meddle with the window blinds or cords, or any other part of the School furniture. Care should be taken that the brushes and dusters are put back in their proper places, and that the pails, &c., are properly cleaned and set aside for the week.

10. As the future prosperity in life of each boy will greatly depend upon the use he has made of his opportunities to acquire a competent education, it is expected that he will diligently improve his present privileges.

REGULATIONS FOR DORMITORIES

1. In the morning, every boy is to rise immediately on the ringing of the First Bell, at half-past 5 o'clock. He will wash himself thoroughly, comb his hair, make his bed, and leave it clean and tidy.

2.   The Monitor, with his Ward, will silently ask God's blessing and guidance on the duties of the day.

3.   On Sabbath mornings the Monitors, along with their Ward, will take special cares to implore God's blessing on the solemn duties of the sacred day.

4.   Every boy, in addition to the daily worship in the Ward, is expected to cultivate the duty of secret prayer.

5.   The boys of each Dormitory, when ordered by the Monitor, will march into the Gallery, the Monitor going out last, after seeing that the windows are thrown open, the beds neatly made, the shoe-horns in their place, and the Dormitory left in good order; when they will be ready, on the ringing of the Second Bell, to march to the back-ground in order.

6.   No quarrelling, angry words, improper language, or any other unseemly conduct, to be on any account allowed in the Ward. Should the Monitor fail in reporting such conduct, he renders himself liable to be disgraced from his post.

7.   On the command being given, the boys of each Gallery will march in order to meet their Masters in the back-ground at 6 o'clock, the Monitor going last.

8.   The Captains in charge of the Galleries will march at the head of the other boys, and take their place in their respective Galleries, observing strict order as the boys pass into their Dormitories.

9.   Each boy will enter his respective Dormitory in order, the Monitor going in last.

10.   During the time of Worship in the Ward, which consists of singing, reading a portion of the Scriptures, and prayer, good conduct and becoming seriousness will characterize each.

11.   On the nights appointed for general reading, each boy will get a Library Book to himself, which he is to read silently; and when the Monitor is instructed to read for the benefit of all, earnest attention is enjoined.

12.   The Bibles and Library Books to be carefully preserved, and no writing or marks of any kind to be put upon them, and no injury to be done to the beds, the bed-clothes, or any part of the furniture in the Ward.

13.   On mending nights, each boy will carefully mend his stockings and clothes; no one to appear in the ranks with his clothes in bad order.

14.   The Monitor will hear regularly the daily verse repeated by each boy, and faithfully report to the Assistant any one who has neglected to learn it.

15.   In cases where a boy cannot read the verse, the Monitor will appoint a boy to assist him; all to be willing cheerfully to render that assistance in turn.

16.   It is the duty of the Monitor to preserve thorough order in his Dormitory, therefore the boys must render prompt obedience to his instructions. Should any boy notwithstanding continue to mar the harmony of the rest by disorder, the Monitor will instantly report the case to the Assistant, who will either settle or remit it to the Governor, as he shall see necessary.

17.   After the ringing of the Second Bell, the gas will be turned off, and complete silence will prevail for the rest of the night.

Appendix VII

(See chapter 15, p. 253)

Industrial Brigades: Regulations and Rules, 26 February 1876

'The following Regulations and Rules for the Home were approved by the Directors of the Edinburgh Industrial Brigade, and may be found useful elsewhere:—

These to be signed by each boy, after being read over and fully understood.

Having been admitted to the Brigade on my own application, I agree to obey the directions of the Superintendent in all matters relating to the proper administration of the Institution, and specially I agree to rise in the morning when called, to wash and dress myself, and make up my bed neatly and cleverly; to attend morning and evening worship when not necessarily prevented; to conduct myself at meals, at worship, and in school, in an orderly and becoming manner; to abstain from all swearing and indecent language; to do my utmost to satisfy my employers; to account for all the wages I receive, and not to leave my service without previously informing the Superintendent; to attend the week-day and Sunday evening school, and church or chapel once a day at least on Sunday; and, lastly, I agree not to leave the Brigade on any account, without a day's previous notice to the Superintendent — all which, for the good of the Institution, I promise faithfully and honestly to perform.

..........................Boy's name signed here.

....................................Witness.'

RULES

1. Every boy on entering shall have the admission line read over to him, and shall be made to understand its import, and shall then sign it.

2. Every boy shall treat the Superintendent with respect, and give implicit obedience to his orders, and shall also behave in a proper and kindly manner to the other inmates.

3. The boys shall be called in time to get ready for their work; and when called they shall immediately rise, wash and dress, and make up their beds neatly and tidily.

4. All the boys shall attend the week-day evening classes, unless when prevented by out-door employment, or specially excused by the Superintendent.

5. No boy shall be excused for leaving his employment, without having previously informed the Superintendent, and given a satisfactory reason for his intention to do so.

6. Every boy must return to the Home immediately on leaving his work, and at all times give a faithful account of his earnings.

7. The greatest propriety of conduct shall be required in the Home (especially at meals), in the school, and during divine worship — all being made clearly to understand that it is only by such conduct that there can be either real usefulness or happiness in the establishment.

8. Every boy shall be present at family worship, unless when excused by the Superintendent. Every boy shall attend a place of worship on Sunday forenoon, and be present at the Home service in the afternoon at two o'clock (the best thanks of the Directors are due to those ladies who have so kindly volunteered to play the harmonium at this service) and evening at eight.

9.   Any boy staying out all night may be dismissed; and any boy leaving the Home, without leave asked and given, shall not be allowed to come back without the consent of the Superintendent.

10.   Any boy who is guilty of the wilful breach of any of the above rules, and continues to offend after being warned by the Superintendent, shall be brought before the Judicial Committee, for admonition or dismissal.

11.   Any boy who has been admonished, and again offends in the like manner, shall be dismissed.

12.   Any boy who commits any criminal offence shall be conveyed before the sitting magistrate, with the view of getting him sent for five years to a Reformatory.

13.   The Superintendent is authorized to punish any boy who disobeys an order, behaves in a riotous and disorderly manner, or stays out late at night, by confinement in the cell for any period not exceeding two days.

Schedule of Application for Admission

EDINBURGH INDUSTRIAL BRIGADE,
72 Grove Street, Fountainbridge

No. _____________   Case of ____

Residing ____

____

1.   Place of birth, and if the birth is registered, state where . . . .

2.   Age. . . . .

3.   Length of time resident in Edinburgh . . . .

4.   Are parents alive? If not, what was their occupation, and who has taken charge of the boy since their death . . . .

5.   Give names of parents, and of all the family, and state how employed, and the amount of their weekly earnings. . . . .

6.   Are they in receipt of parochial relief? If so, state the amount. If applied for and refused, state the reason . . . .

7.   Reference for inquiry . . . .

8.   Has the applicant ever been at work, at what, and amount of wages? . . . .

9.   What school has applicant attended (if any) and for how long? . . . .

10.   Can applicant read and write?. . . . .

11.   Contributions, if any, from whom, and at what rate? . . . .

Note: It is computed that the Society will lose upon each boy £4 per annum beyond the amount of his wages. It is to be hoped that friends taking an interest in a particular boy may subscribe or otherwise raise the amount.

DECLARATION TO BE SIGNED BY THE BOY.

I ____faithfully promise to be cleanly, kind to the other boys, obedient and respectful to the masters, and be at all times careful to maintain the good character of the Brigade.

Case refused on account of ____

Case admitted on ____

Left on ____on account of ______________________

DECLARATION BY PARENTS, IF EITHER ARE ALIVE.

________________________________hereby declare that________________________________ enters the Edinburgh Industrial Brigade with our full approval and consent, and we pledge our-selves not to interfere with his management, nor to remove the boy without the consent of the Directors, or paying up the loss the Institution may have sustained through his wages being inadequate to meet his expenses, as shown by the books kept by the Superintendent. And we promise to give every assistance in our power to the Directors in their efforts for the boy's good.

Signed____

(A rhyme, no doubt considered useful in attracting subscribers):

The Shoeblack Brigade

'Weel, grannie, there was nae tobacco to spin
This morn whaur I howpt a bit trifle to win,
And the bobbies hae cried doun the match-sellin' trade,
And little at horse-haudin' is to be made;
See I wi' vexation could grutten ootricht
To think I should bring ye nae bawbees the nicht,
When 'twas my guid luck to meet Jamie Dillap—
Yon callan ye thocht aye a pushin' wee chap.

'"Man, Dawnie," cried Jamie, "here's stunnin' news noo;
I've just pairted wi' Curly an' Sawnie McClew,
Wha bouncin'ly tell me their fortune is made,
For they've been ta'en on in the Shoeblack Brigade.
'Twad seem that some big anes had met an' agree't
To try an' tak some o' us kids aff the street,
An' mak' us shoeblacks—and they're wantin' a lot—
Sae, Dawnie, let's aff tae their office like shot."

'Awa' to the office we skirted wi' speed
To see an they ony mair laddies micht need,
And the manager, seemin' to fancy our looks,
Spak kindly; and, writin' our names in his books,
Speered wha we belangt tae? had e'er we dune ocht?
Wi' wha, an' at what sort o' bizness we'd wrocht?—
A' whulk bein' answered, he'd trust us, he said;
Syne fitted us out for the Shoeblack Brigade.

'He gied us our tools, and appointed our stance,
And bade us march aff to our duty at ance;
An' though my stance be na the best i' toun,
It isna the warst ane, I wager a croun.

'I brushed like a hatter, and yesterday's rain,
The streets makin' glaury, did add to my gain;
And though it was late ere to wark I gaed there,
Ere gloamin' I polished my twenty-twa pair.

'An' grannie, I polished them aff a' sae clean,
That in them our Tam micht his shadow hae seen;
An' had I my brushes an' bleck here the noo,
I'd gar your auld shoon look as bonnie's when new.
Some gentlemen, Curly says, whiles gie them mair
Than's charged—that's a penny for brushin' ilk pair,
O whilk our kind manager gies us our wheck;
For to get a' our winnins we couldna expeck.'

Source: David Harris (F.S.S. Edinburgh), *A Plea for Industrial Brigades, as adjuncts to Ragged Schools* (Glasgow 1873), 56-60.

Bibliography

List of contents

1. Annual Reports
2. Minute Books
3. Newspapers and Periodicals
4. Official Reports
5. Other Reports
6. Books and Pamphlets
   A. Before 1837
   B. 1837-1901
   C. 1902-1978
7. Theses

THE principal source of primary material is the records of the philanthropic and charitable societies. Many of these collections are now in the hands of library and archive departments throughout Scotland, others remain in society offices. Sometimes whole series of annual reports and minute books are available, in other cases only one report or minute book survives.

1. **Annual Reports**
   Dates of founding are given if known.

Aberdeen
   Female Penitentiary (1842)
   Female School of Industry (1843)
   General City Mission (1853)
   Hospital for the Relief of Persons Labouring under Incurable Disease (1857)
   Industrial School Association (1850)
   Institution for Deaf and Dumb (1819)
   Institution for the Employment of Women (1860)
   Ladies' Sanitary Association (1859)
   Lodging-house Association (1849)
   North-East Coast Mission (1858)
   Oldmill Reformatory School (1857)
   Temperance Society (1845)
   Town and County Association for Teaching the Blind at their Homes (1880)
   University Missionary Union (1836)

Aberdeenshire
   Association of Ladies for the Rescue of Fallen Women (1862)

Ayr
   Sabbath School Union

Dumfries
   Dumfries and Maxwelton Education Society

Dundee
> Baldovan Institution (1855)
> Charity Organisation Society (1885)
> Convalescent House, William Street, Forebank
> Curr Night Refuge, West Bell Street (1882)
> Flower Mission to the Sick Poor (1887)
> Home for Friendless Children (1876)
> Home for Incurables (1879)
> Homeopathic Dispensary for the Medical Relief of the Sick Poor (1876)
> Industrial Schools Society (1847)
> Institution for the Blind (1869)
> Ladies' Union in the Interest of Young Women and Girls (1884)
> Mission to the Outdoor Blind (1867)
> Orphan Institution (c. 1823)
> Royal Lunatic Asylum (1820)
> Social Union (1887)
> Society for the Prevention of Cruelty to Children (1890)
> Society for the Relief of the Indigent Sick (1819)
> Working Boys' Home (1887)

Edinburgh
> Angus Club (1841)
> Ayrshire Club (1854)
> Benevolent and Strangers' Friend Society (1817)
> Bible Society (1809)
> Blind Asylum (1792)
> Chalmers Hospital (1864)
> Fountainbridge Medical Dispensary (1870)
> Gratis Sabbath School Society
> Health Society
> House of Industry
> Ladies' Association on behalf of Jewish Females (1840)
> Lock Hospital (1835)
> Maternity Hospital (1793)
> Medical Missionary Society (1841)
> New Town Dispensary (1815)
> Ragged Schools (1847)
> Royal Edinburgh Asylum for the Insane (1813)
> Royal Public Dispensary and Vaccine Institution (1776)
> Edinburgh Sabbath School Teachers' Association (1848)
> Society for the Relief of the Destitute Sick of Edinburgh (1785)
> Society for the Support of Gaelic Schools (1811)
> Edinburgh University Settlement (1905)

Fife
> Fifeshire Society

Glasgow
> Abstainers' Union (1854)
> Angus and Mearns Benevolent Society (1838)
> Association for Higher Education of Women (prospectus 1879)
> Association for Providing Trained Nurses (1875)
> Asylum for the Blind (1827)
> Asylum for Lunatics (1814)
> Auxiliary Bible Society (1812)
> Auxiliary Society of Glasgow for Support of Gaelic Schools (1812)
> Baptist Missionary Society (1815)
> Benevolent Society for Destitute Sick (1832)

Bible Society (1805)
Boys' Brigade (1883)
Boys' House of Refuge, Duke Street (1838)
Calton and Bridgeton Association for Religious Purposes (1815)
Central Dispensary (1889)
Charity Organisation Society (1874)
City Mission (1826)
College of Science and Arts (1823)
Continental Society (1826)
Deaf and Dumb Institution (1821)
Discharged Prisoners' Aid Society (1858).
Dispensary for Skin Diseases (1861)
Eye Infirmary (1824)
Gaelic Mission (1866)
Grove Street Institute (1859)
House of Shelter for Females (1850)
Industrial School Society (1848)
Kyrle Society (1882)
Lodging Houses Association (1847)
London Missionary Society, Glasgow Auxiliary
Magdalene Asylum (1858)
Medical Training Home for Lady Missionaries (1890)
Archibald Millar's Charity School for Girls (1795)
Mission to the Out-door Blind (1860)
Missionary Society of the University of Glasgow (1821)
National Bible Society of Scotland (1860)
New Vennel School Society (1840)
Night Asylum for the Houseless (1838)
Old Man's Friend Society (1812)
Protestant Institute for Female Orphans (1825)
Protestant Laymen's Association (1852)
Queen Margaret College Settlement Association (1897)
Royal Infirmary (1794)
Royal Infirmary Dorcas Society
Royal Lunatic Asylum (1814)
St. Matthew's Home for Orphan and Destitute Children (1854)
Sabbath Evening School Youths' Union (1818)
Sabbath School Union (1837)
Sailors' Home (1858)
Seaman's Friend Society (1825)
Society for Bettering the Condition of the Poor
Society for Education of Deaf and Dumb (1829)
Society for Promoting Christianity among the Jews (1821)
Society for the Prevention of Cruelty to Animals (1856)
Society for the Rescue of Young Women and Children
Total Abstinence Society (1852)
Union for the Care and Help of Girls and Women
University of Glasgow, Association of Students in the University of Glasgow in aid of
    Missionary Exertions (1821)
The University Lying-in Hospital (1792)
University Settlement, Toynbee House (1885)
West Coast Mission (1855)
Western Infirmary (1874)
Western Public Dispensary (1853)
Young Men's Christian Association (1824)

Greenock
    Greenock Bible Association
    Greenock Charity School
    Seaman's Friend Society (1819)
    Society for the Promotion of Temperance (1830)
    Total Abstinence Society

Kirriemuir
    Kirriemuir Gratis Sabbath School Society (1817)

Perth
    Murray's Royal Asylum for Lunatics (1827)

Scotland
    Society in Scotland for Propagating Christian Knowledge (1709)
    Scottish Permissive Bill and Temperance Association (1858)
    Western Scottish Temperance Union

2. Minute Books and Original Papers

Airdrie Female Benevolent Society
Blantyre Lodging House
Dumfries, Crichton Royal Institution
Dundee, Baldovan Institution
       Bannatyne Home of Rest
       Curr Night Refuge
       Johnson's Charity
Edinburgh, Governess Benevolent Institution
       Magdalene Asylum
       Medical Mission
       Night Asylum
       Royal Society for the Relief of Indigent Gentlewomen
       University Settlement
Glasgow, Baillie's Institution
       Eye Infirmary
       Independent Order of Rechabites
       Lying-in Hospital
       North Parish Washing Green Society
       University Lying-in Hospital
       Queen Margaret College Settlement Association
       University Missionary Association
       Victoria Infirmary
       Western Infirmary

3. Newspapers and Periodicals

Aberdeen Journal
Adviser (issued by Scottish Temperance League)
Aberdeen University Review
College Courant (University of Glasgow)
Dundee Courier
Edinburgh Christian Instructor
Edinburgh Evangelical Magazine
Edinburgh Medical Journal
Edinburgh Review
Free Church Record

Glasgow Herald
Glasgow Medical Journal
League Journal (issued by Scottish Temperance League)
Monthly Repository
North British Advertiser
North British Daily Mail
North British Review
Rechabite Magazine
Scots Magazine
Scotsman
Scottish Reformer (issued by Scottish Permissive Bill and Temperance Association)
Scottish Temperance Journal
Scottish Temperance League Register and Abstainers' Almanac
Social Reformer
Taits Magazine
Temperance Society Record
Transactions of the Gaelic Society of Inverness

4. Official Reports

Only the more important reports are listed.

1831 — Inquiry into the state of the Universities of Scotland, (310) XII.

1832 — Sabbath Observance, laws and practices, SC, HC report (Sir Andrew Agnew). Minutes of evidence and appendix, (697) VI.

1834 — Intoxication among working classes, SC report, minutes of evidence, appendices (J. S. Buckingham), (559) VIII.

1835 — Municipal Corporations (Scotland), Commissioners' general report (J. B. Greenshields) and local reports, (30) XXIX and (31).

1836 — Municipal Corporations (Scotland), Commissioners' local reports, parts II and III, appendix to general report, (32) XXIII, 33, 34.

1837-39 — Reports of Commissioners to inquire into opportunities of public religious worship

1st	1837	(31)	XXI	9	6th	1839 (153)	XXIV	1
2nd	1837-8	(109)	XXXII	1	7th	1839 (154)	XXV	1
3rd	1837-8	(113)	XXXIII	1	8th	1839 (162)	XXVI	1
4th	1837-8	(112)	XXXIII	273	9th	1839 (164)	XXVI	607
5th	1839	(152)	XXIII	1				

1837 and 1839 — Inquiry into the state of the Universities of Scotland, RC, Evidence Edinburgh, (92) XXXV; Glasgow, (93) XXXVI; St. Andrews, (94) XXXVII; and Aberdeen, (95) XXXVIII (1837): University of Glasgow, report (1839), (175) XXIX.

1842 — Sanitary condition of the labouring population of Scotland, local reports HL, XXVIII.

1844 — On the administration and practical operation of the Poor Laws (Scotland), RC, including minutes of evidence, (557) XX, (563) XXVI, (543).

1846 — Public Houses (Scotland), SC report (Forbes Mackenzie), (457) XV.

1854 — On Public Houses, SC of HC, minutes of evidence, (XIV).

1857 — Lunatics and Lunatic Asylums (Scotland), RC report (A. E. Monteith), (2148) V.

1860 — On the licensing system and sale of excisable liquors in Scotland, report and minutes of evidence, XXXII, XXXIII.

1865-67 — Schools in Scotland, RC, 1st and 2nd reports and minutes of evidence (Duke of Argyll), (3483) XVII, (3845) XXV, Glasgow, (3845) II, appendices, (3850) XXV.

1867-68 — Education, scientific instruction (B. Samuelson), (432) XV.

1867-68   Police (Scotland), county and burgh police systems, SC, HL (Earl of Minto), report, minutes of evidence and appendix, (486) IX.

1867-68   Schools in Scotland, RC, 3rd report, burgh and middle class schools, (4011) XXIX.

1868-69   On the poor law, Scotland, SC, HC; proceedings, minutes of evidence, appendix and index, (301) XI, 1.

1873-75   Endowed Schools and Hospitals (Scotland), RC, 1st report c755, 2nd report c976, 3rd report c1123.

1877   On intemperance, SC, HL (Duke of Westminster), 1st report and minutes of evidence, (171) XI; 2nd report, (271); 3rd report, (418).

1880-90   Endowed institutions in Scotland, Commissioners' 1st report, 1880, c2493, XXIV, 459; 2nd report with evidence, 1881, c2790, XXXVI, 237; 3rd report with appendix, 1881, c3076, XXXVI, 1019.

Educational endowments (Scotland) Commission appointed subsequently, 1st report, 1884, c3995, XXVII, 1; 2nd report, 1884-5, c4329, XXXII, 1; 3rd report, 1886, c4664, XXVIII, 1; 4th report, 1887, c4981, XXXIII, 1; 5th report, 1888, c5312, XLI, 841; 6th report, 1889, c5641, XXXII, 569; 7th report, 1890, c5957, XXXI, 763.

Endowed institutions in Scotland, in terms of the Endowed Institutions (Scotland) Act 1878 on higher education, distribution of grant, 1881, c2768, XXXVI, 1.

There are also hundreds of schemes and provisional orders for the management of local education endowments in Scotland.

1882-84   Technical instruction, RC (B. Samuelson), 1st report, c1371, XXVII; 2nd report Vol. I, c3981, XXIX; 2nd report, Vol. II, c3981-1, XXX; 2nd report, Vol. III, c3981-11, XXXI; 2nd report, Vol. IV, c3981-111, XXXI; 2nd report, Vol. V, c3981-IV.

1884   Housing of the working classes, RC (Sir C. W. Dilke), 2nd report (Scotland), c4409, XXXI, 1.

1888   Science and technical education in certain schools in Scotland, c5590, LV.

1889   On the blind, deaf and dumb of the United Kingdom, RC, evidence and appendix, c5781, XIX, XX.

1895   Habitual Offenders, Scotland, departmental committee, report, minutes of evidence, c7753, XXXVII and c7753-1, XXXVII.

1895   Lunacy (Scotland), increasing prevalence of insanity, GBCLS, supplement to 36th AR, c7610, LIV.

1896-98   Reformatory and industrial schools committee, Home department report, 1896, c8204, XLV; report, 1897, c8290, XLII, minutes of evidence, XXXVIII.

1899   Liquor licensing laws, RC, final report, XXXV.

1899   Inebriate reformatories in Scotland, departmental committee, report, minutes of evidence, c9175, XII.

1909-10   On the poor laws and relief of distress, RC, Cd.4798.

Vol. VI. Minutes of evidence, with appendices relating to Scotland.

Vol. XV. On the administrative relation of charity and the poor laws, . . . and potential utility of endowed and voluntary charities in England and Scotland, 1909, Cd.4593, XLII, 677.

Vol. XXVI. Documents relating more especially to the administration of charities, 1910, Cd5078, LIV, 1.

Vol. XXIX. On the methods of administering charitable assistance, . . . prepared by the Committee on Church Interests appointed by the General Assembly of the Church of Scotland, 1910, Cd.5243, LIV.

Vol. XXX. Documents relating especially to Scotland, 1910, Cd5440, LIV, 595.

1952   On the law and practice relating to charitable trusts (Lord Nathan), Cmd.8710.

5. Other Reports

Aberdeen kirk session, presbytery and synod of, selections from the records, Spalding Club, Aberdeen 1846.
Board of supervision of relief of the poor in Scotland, AR from 1847.
General Board of Commissioners of Lunacy for Scotland, AR from 1857.
General Assembly of the Church of Scotland
    AR of committees including education, home missions, sabbath schools, Christian life and work, temperance.
    Deficiencies in the means of education for the poor in certain large towns in Scotland, 1836.
    On the management of the poor in Scotland, 1839.
    Presbyterial and parochial reports on the state of education in Scotland, 1842.
General Assembly of the Free Church of Scotland, Proceedings of.
Glasgow Municipal Commission on the housing of the poor, Glasgow 1904.
National Convention for the Prohibition Movement of the Liquor Traffic, papers and proceedings, Newcastle 1897.
New Statistical Account of Scotland, Edinburgh 1845.
Presbytery of Glasgow: report of commission on the housing of the poor, in relation to their social condition, Glasgow 1891.
Report by a committee of city elders in Edinburgh, regarding the proposal for a commutation of the annuity tax and other funds for the support of the Edinburgh clergy, Edinburgh 1837.
Statistical Account of Scotland (Sir John Sinclair), Edinburgh 1795.
Third Statistical Account, Edinburgh 1950-1966.

6. Books and Pamphlets

A. *Before 1837*

Adams, A. M., *Sketches from life* (Glasgow 1835).
Anon, *State of the Society in Scotland for the Promotion of Christian Knowledge* (Edinburgh 1741).
    Memorial — containing account of erection of the Edinburgh Charity Work-house (Edinburgh 1742).
    A short account of the use, progress and present state of the Society in Scotland for propagating Christian Knowledge (Edinburgh 1748).
    Address to the reverend the clergy of Scotland from the Managers of the Vaccine Institution at Edinburgh (Edinburgh 1803).
    Rules of Archibald Miller's Charity Schools for Girls (Glasgow 1812).
    Edinburgh, Regulations of the Edinburgh Lunatic Asylum (Edinburgh 1816).
    Report of the Society for promoting the religious interests of the poor of Glasgow and its vicinity, or Glasgow City Mission (Glasgow 1827).
    Charter of incorporation in favour of the Dundee orphan institution (Dundee 1830).
    Town's hospital of Glasgow (Glasgow 1830).
    Edinburgh City Mission (Edinburgh, n.d. c. 1832).
    An historical account of the Orphan Hospital of Edinburgh (Edinburgh 1833).
    Observations on the moral condition of the lower orders in Edinburgh (Edinburgh 1834)
    Church Accommodation in Scotland, statement relative to — in answer to the representations in the circular of the moderator of the General Assembly by the Scottish Central Board for Vindicating the rights of Dissenters (Edinburgh 1835).
    Voluntary church society, lectures on church establishments, by Rev. W. Anderson and Dr. Wardlaw (Glasgow 1835).
    Brief historical sketch of the origin and progress of the Glasgow Deaf and Dumb Institution (Glasgow 1835).
    Report by a committee of city elders regarding the proposal for a commutation of the annuity tax and other funds for support of the Edinburgh clergy (Edinburgh 1837).
Arnott, H., *History of Edinburgh* (Edinburgh 1816).
Battie, W., *A Treatise on Madness* (London 1758).

z

Bell, B., *Treatise on Lues Venerea* (Edinburgh 1793).

Bellers, J., *An Essay towards the improvement of Physick in 12 proposals: The Assigns of J. Sowle* (London 1714).

Bentham, J., *Panopticon, or the Inspection house* (London 1791).
    Management of the Poor (Dublin 1796).

Bilby, T., and Ridgway, R. B., *The infant teachers' assistant or scriptural and moral lessons for infants* (London 1835).

Boswell, James, *The Journal of a tour to the Hebrides, with Samuel Johnson* (London 1786).

Brebner, W., *A Letter to the Lord Provost on the Expediency of a House of Refuge for Juvenile Offenders* (Glasgow 1829).

Buchanan, M. S., *History of the Glasgow Royal Infirmary* (Glasgow and London 1832).

Buckingham, J. S., *Drunkenness — speech on the extent, causes and effects of drunkenness* (London 1834).

Chalmers, T., Pauperism (*Edinburgh Review*, Edinburgh 1817).
    Considerations on the system of parochial schools in Scotland, and on the advantage of establishing them in large towns (Glasgow 1819).
    The Importance of Civil Government to Society, and the duty of Christians in regard to it (Glasgow 1820).
    The Christian and civic economy of large towns (Glasgow 1821).
    A speech . . . explanatory of the measures which have been successfully pursued in St. John's parish, Glasgow, for the extinction of its compulsory pauperism; with an appendix (Glasgow 1822).
    Scripture references: designed for the use of parents, Sabbath School Teachers and private Christians (Glasgow 1822).
    Speech delivered 24 May 1822 to the General Assembly of the Church of Scotland (Glasgow 1822).
    Statement in regard to the pauperism of Glasgow, from the experience of the last eight years (Glasgow 1823).
    Churches and Chapels: or the necessity and proper object of an endowment, being the subject of a speech recently delivered before the Presbytery of Edinburgh (Glasgow 1834).
    The cause of church extension (Edinburgh 1835).
    On the distinction between parochial and congregational and between endowed and unendowed churches (Glasgow n.d.).

Clason, P., *Considerations on the propriety of erecting the Chapels of Ease in the parish of St. Cuthbert into parish churches, and on the necessity of increasing the church accommodation: with a statement of the means by which these objects may be accomplished* (Edinburgh 1833).

Cleland, J., *Specification of the manner of building and furnishing an Asylum for Magdalenes* (Glasgow 1813).
    Annals of Glasgow, comprising an account of the public buildings, charities and the rise and progress of the city (Glasgow 1816).
    Enumeration of the inhabitants of the city of Glasgow (Glasgow 1823).
    Statistical tables relative to the city of Glasgow (Glasgow 1823).
    Enumeration of the City of Glasgow and the County of Lanark (Glasgow 1831).

Collins, W., *Statistics of the Church Accommodation of Glasgow Barony and Gorbals with accompanying observations, with an appendix* (Glasgow 1836).
    On the harmony between the Gospel and Temperance Societies (Glasgow 1836).
    The Church of Scotland and the poor man's church (Glasgow n.d.).

Colquhoun, P., *A treatise on Indigence* (London 1806).

Dalgarno G., *Didascalocophus, included in the Works of George Dalgarno of Aberdeen*, The Maitland Club (Edinburgh 1834).

Dingley, R., *Proposals for establishing a public place of reception for penitent prostitutes* (London 1758).

Duncan, A., *Observations on the operation and use of Mercury in the Venereal Disease* (Edinburgh 1772).
    A proposal for establishing a lunatic asylum in the neighbourhood of the city (Edinburgh 1792).
    Reports of the practice in the clinical wards during November and December, 1817, January, May, June, July, 1818 (Edinburgh 1818).

A letter to Sir William Fettes affording demonstrative evidence that much great benefit will arise from improving the Royal Infirmary by the establishment of a Lock Hospital and an hospital for incurables, than by beginning a new rival infirmary (Edinburgh 1825).

Duncan, H., *An Essay on the Nature and Advantages of Parish Banks: together with a corrected copy of the Rules and Regulations of the Parent Institution at Ruthwell* (Edinburgh 1815).

Dunlop, J., *On the Wine System of Great Britain* (Greenock 1831).

Artificial Drinking Usages of North Britain (Greenock 1836).

Edinburgh Bible Society, *Statement and Second and Third Statements by the Committee relative to the circulation of the Apocrypha by the British and Foreign Bible Society* (Edinburgh 1825-6).

Statements of dissentient members of the Committee in reference to its operation from the British and Foreign Bible Society and publication of its 2nd statement (Edinburgh 1826).

Fleming, W., *An address on behalf of the Glasgow Seamen's Friend Society* (Glasgow 1836).

Graham, R., *Practical Observations on Continued fever with some remarks on the most effective plans for its suppression* (Glasgow 1818).

Gray, A., *National Security Savings Bank* (Glasgow 1836).

Halliday, A., *A letter to the Rt. Hon. Lord Binning, M.P.* (Edinburgh 1816).

Halliday, Sir A., *A general view of the present state of lunatics and lunatic asylums in Great Britain and Ireland and in some other Kingdoms* (London 1828).

Harriston, W., *The City Mission or Glasgow in miniature* (Glasgow 1824).

Harvey, A., *On the Voluntary principle in relation to National Responsibility and the religious instruction of the poor* (Glasgow 1835).

Henderson, W., *Address to the Inhabitants of Aberdeen respecting the Medical Attendance of the Poor at their own Houses* (Aberdeen 1822).

Howard, J., *Account of Principal Lazarettos in Europe* (Warrington 1789).

Kirkwood, J., *A copy of a letter anent a project for erecting a library, in every presbytery, or at least county, in the Highlands, from a reverend minister of the Scots nation now in England, to a minister of Edinburgh, with reasons for it, and a scheme for Erecting and preserving these libraries* (Edinburgh 1702).

Proposals made by Rev. James Kirkwood in 1699 to found public libraries in Scotland. Reprinted . . . from rare copy in the Free public library, Wigan, with introductory remarks by W. Blades (London 1889).

Knox, J., *History of the reformation of religion* (Glasgow 1761).

Lettsom, T. C., *Medical memoirs of the General Dispensary in London 1773-1774* (London 1774).

Hints designed to promote beneficence, temperance and medical science (London 1801).

McFarlan, D., *On the duty of prayer as connected with the day of fasting* (Glasgow 1835).

MacGill, S., *On Lunatic Asylums, a Discourse delivered August 2, 1810, previous to laying the Foundation stone of the Glasgow Lunatic Asylum* (Glasgow 1810).

Remarks on Prisons (Glasgow 1810).

On Elementary Education (Glasgow 1811).

A Sermon delivered at Glasgow on the opening of the Magdalene Asylum (Glasgow 1815).

Discourses and essays on subjects of public interest (Edinburgh 1819).

A sermon preached on behalf of the Church Accommodation Society (Glasgow 1834).

MacNish, R., *The Anatomy of Drunkenness* (Glasgow 1827).

Marshall, A., *An address delivered on August 24, 1832, the day observed as a Jubilee on account of the passing of the reform bill* (Glasgow 1832).

Morison, A., *Cases of Mental disease, with practical observations on the medical treatment* (1828).

National Education Association of Scotland, *Declaration of principles adopted by National Education Association of Scotland at a public meeting* (Edinburgh 9 April, 1805).

Poole, R., *An Essay on Education applicable to Children in general: the defective, the criminal; the poor, the adult and aged* (Edinburgh 1825).

A letter to A. Duncan Snr., regarding the establishment of a new infirmary (Edinburgh 1825).

Rose, G., *Observations on Banks for Savings* (London 1816).

Stark, W., *Remarks on public hospitals for the cure of mental derangement* (Edinburgh 1807).

Remarks on the construction of Public Hospitals for the Cure of Mental Derangement (Glasgow 1810).

Stewart, W., *Society for the promotion of temperance* (Greenock 1830).

B. *1837-1901*

Aberdeen Education Trust, Minutes for years 1889, 1890, 1891, 1893 (Aberdeen n.d.)

Acton, W., *Prostitution, considered in its moral, social and sanitary aspects in London and other large Cities and Garrison Towns* (London 1870).

A.H.R., *Domestic legislation or how to elevate the homes of the poor* (Glasgow 1886).

Alexander, W. L., *A Discourse of the qualities and worth of Thomas Chalmers, DD., LL.D.* (Edinburgh 1847).

Memoirs of the life and writings of Ralph Wardlaw (Edinburgh 1856).

Alison, W. P., *Observations on the Management of the poor in Scotland* (Edinburgh 1840).

Remarks on the Report of Her Majesty's Commissioners on the Poor Laws of Scotland (Edinburgh 1844).

Alston, J., *Statements of education, employments and internal arrangements of Asylum for Blind, Glasgow, with a short account of its founder* (Glasgow 1846).

Anon., *History of Sunday* (London n.d.)

Statement relative to the Orphan Hospital (Edinburgh 1838).

The Medical Missionary Society in China (Canton, China, 1838).

Report of the Managers of the Charity Work-house, on the Lunatic Asylum (Edinburgh 1842).

Lectures on the social and physical condition of the people; by five parish ministers of Glasgow (Glasgow 1843).

The Edinburgh messenger . . . regarding Deaf and Dumb (Edinburgh 1845).

Aberdeen Railway Company: debate on running of Sabbath trains (Aberdeen 1849).

Sabbath passenger trains, report of the great public meeting held in the City Hall of Glasgow . . . for the purpose of expressing approval of . . . discontinuing the running of passenger trains on the Lord's Day (Glasgow 1847).

Temperance and Teetotalism: an inquiry (London 1847).

Sunday Trains on the Edinburgh and Glasgow railway: reasons why we voted for the resumption of Sunday trains (Glasgow 1847).

Sunday Trains: reply to the review of Professor Eadie of the reasons why we voted for the resumption of the Sunday trains (Glasgow 1847).

Industrial Schools, their origin, development and success (Dundee n.d.).

Lectures on Medical Missions (Edinburgh 1849).

Regulations and Bye-Laws of Murray's Asylum at Perth (Perth 1850).

The Lintie o' Moray (Forres 1851).

The Sunday steamer: remonstrance of the Established Presbytery of Glasgow with the answer of the owners of the steamer, Emperor (Glasgow 1853).

Addresses to medical students delivered at the instance of the Edinburgh Medical Missionary Society, 1855-56 (Edinburgh 1856).

Constitution and Rules of the Aberdeen Hospital for the Relief of persons labouring under Incurable Disease (Aberdeen 1857).

(L.N.R.), *The Missing Link, or Bible Women in the homes of the London Poor* (London 1859).

The Glasgow Highland Society (Glasgow 1861).

(Lewis, D.), *The History of the Temperance Movement in Scotland* (Edinburgh 1860).

Sabbath traffic on the railways (Glasgow 1865).

Norman's Blast (Edinburgh, Glasgow & Aberdeen, 1866).

An account of Hutcheson's School in Glasgow (Glasgow 1867).

Inaugural ceremonies in honour of the opening of the Fountain Gardens, Paisley (Paisley 1868).

Seventh Earl of Shaftesbury's visit to Glasgow, full report of the meeting of the Glasgow Working Men's Sabbath Protestant Protection Association (Glasgow 1871).

Statement by the Directors of the Edinburgh Medical Missionary Society of the occurrences which led to and followed the resignation of Mr. W. Burns Thomson, the former Superintendent of their Dispensary and Training Institution (Edinburgh 1871).

Joint Hospital, Abstract of Agreement . . . of Burghs of Partick, Hillhead and Maryhill for the erection and Maintenance of a joint Hospital for the treatment of patients under the Public Health (Scotland) Act 1867 (Glasgow 1874).

Sabbath Labour at iron-works; Two reports by the Sabbath Observance Committee of the Free Synod of Glasgow and Ayr (Glasgow 1875).

Handbook to the Charitable Institution of Dundee (Dundee 1875)

Great demonstration against the opening of museums and art galleries etc. on Sabbath (Glasgow 1880).

Edinburgh Health Society, Health lectures for the people (Edinburgh 1882).

Curr Night Refuge for the homeless, Dundee (Dundee 1882).

Robert Gordon's College in Aberdeen, Minutes of General Courts and of Committees, Vols. I, II, III, 1883-85 (Aberdeen 1885).

Memoirs and portraits of One Hundred Glasgow Men (Glasgow 1886).

(James Erskine, M.B.), *The Abuse of our Medical Charities* (Glasgow 1886).

History of the Glasgow Night Asylum for the Houseless from origin till Jubilee (Glasgow 1887).

Report of proceedings at the official inspection by the Lord Provost, Magistrates and Council of Belvidere Hospital as finally completed 4 March 1887 (Glasgow 1887).

Report of proceedings at the opening of the Baillie's Reference Library, September 1887 (Glasgow 1887).

How the poor live, the vagrant 'lackalls' (Dundee 1888).

The poor of Glasgow and how to help them with suggestions for forming a Glasgow Social Union (Glasgow 1889).

The Present Condition and Future Organisation of the Volunteer Force (London 1891).

The Elder Park, Govan: an account of the gift of the Elder Park and of the erection and unveiling of the statue of John Elder. With notices of the lives of David Elder and John Elder and historical sketches of Govan (Glasgow 1891).

Glasgow Charitable and Philanthropic Institutions (Glasgow 1893).

Rules and Regulations of Glasgow Royal Infirmary (Glasgow 1894).

Catalogue of the National Gallery of Scotland under the management of the Board of Manufactures (Edinburgh 1895).

The Grove Street Institute, record of a year's work among the masses in a great city (Glasgow 1895).

The Glasgow and West of Scotland Technical College: notes upon the history and objects of the College (Glasgow 1895).

Charity Organisation and Relief Societies of the United Kingdom, 6th Annual Conference (Glasgow 1897).

(Bunyan, John jnr.), *The Drunkard's Progress* (Glasgow n.d.).

Sabbath Traffic on Railways, being report of proceedings of Glasgow presbyteries (Glasgow 1865).

Tradesmen's Association Advancing the interests of the Church (Edinburgh n.d.).

Royal Hospital for Sick Children, 45 Scott Street (Glasgow n.d.).

Arnold, T., *Method of Teaching the Deaf to Speak* (London 1881).

Arnot, W., *Autobiography of the Rev. William Arnot and Memoir by his daughter* (London 1877).

Bache, A. D., *Report on Education in Europe* (Edinburgh 1839).

Baillie, D., *Donaldson's Hospital* (Edinburgh 1872).

Baillie, G., *Trust Deed, for the endowment and management of Baillie's Institution* (Glasgow 1864).

Baird, C. R., *Report on the Sanitary regulation of Glasgow* (Glasgow 1841).

   Report on the general and sanitry condition of the working classes and the poor in the city of Glasgow (Glasgow 1841).

Balfour, G. W., 'How the Royal Hospital for Sick Children was founded', *EHR*, Vol. 1 (Edinburgh 1893), 35-41.

Barclay, H., *Memoir of Mr. George Baillie, the founder of Baillie's Institution* (Glasgow 1873).

Barr, T., 'The Hearing of School Children', *The Schoolmaster*, September 1889.

Bayne, P., *The Life and Letters of Hugh Miller*, Vol. 1, (London 1871).

Bedford, F. W., *History of George Heriot's Hospital by William Steven, D.D.*, revised and enlarged by Bedford, F. W. (Edinburgh 1859).

   'The Hospital System of Scotland' in *TNASS*, Edinburgh meeting 1863 (London 1864).

Begg, J., *Report in regard to the state of pauperism in the parish of Liberton, with suggestions for improving it* (Edinburgh 1839).

   Pauperism and the Poor Laws (Edinburgh 1849).

Scotland's demand for electoral justice (Edinburgh 1857).
Happy Homes for Working Men and how to get them (Edinburgh 1866).
The causes and probable remedies of pauperism in Scotland (Edinburgh 1870).
The ecclesiastical and social evils of Scotland (Edinburgh 1871).
Workmen's Houses — an address in the City Hall, Glasgow, January 26, 1875 (Glasgow 1875).
Bell, G., *Day and Night in the Wynds of Edinburgh* (Edinburgh 1849).
Bell, J., 'The Surgical side of the Royal Infirmary', *EHR*, Vol. 1 (Edinburgh 1893).
Bell, J., & Paton, J., *Glasgow, its municipal organisation and administration* (Glasgow 1896).
Binnie, T., *Memoir of Thomas Binnie, builder in Glasgow* (Glasgow 1882).
Black, W. G., *Scottish Parochial Law* (Edinburgh 1893).
Blaikie, W. G., *Heads and hands in the world of labour* (London 1865).
Better days for working people (London 1867).
The preachers of Scotland (Edinburgh 1888).
After fifty years (London 1893).
Recollections of a busy life — an autobiography (London 1901).
Blyth, Rev. R., 'Scottish Sabbath Schools' in *TNASS*, Edinburgh meeting 1863 (London 1864).
Bonar, A. R., *The Church of Scotland's duty to the masses* (Edinburgh 1857).
Booth, W., *In darkest England* (London 1890).
Boyd, W., 'Colportage in Scotland' in *TNASS*, Edinburgh meeting 1863 (London 1864).
Brewster, P., *The Chartist and Military Discourses* (Paisley 1843).
The plague of patronage (Paisley 1860).
Bristowe, Dr. and Homes, Mr., *The Hospitals of the United Kingdom* (HMSO 1864).
Brown, T., *Annals of the Disruption* (Edinburgh 1893).
Browne, W. A. F., *What Asylums were, are and ought to be, being the substance of Five Lectures delivered before the Managers of the Montrose Royal Lunatic Asylum* (Edinburgh 1837).
Bryce, J. D., *The Glasgow Magdalene Asylum, its past and present: with relative facts and suggestions* (Glasgow 1859).
Buchanan, G., 'Glasgow Royal Infirmary: reminiscences', *GMJ*, Vol. 42 (1849).
Buchanan, R., *The school master in the Wynds* (Glasgow 1850).
The Spiritual Destitution of the Masses in Glasgow; its alarming increase, its fearful amount, and the only effectual cure (Glasgow 1851).
Church Extension, the City's spiritual wants and the Christian church's duty: an address at the City Hall of Glasgow (Glasgow 1871).
Buckingham, J. S., *Autobiography of James Silk Buckingham* (London 1855).
Buckie, F., *Vital and Economical Statistics of the Hospitals for the Year 1863* (London 1865).
Burdett, Sir H. C., *Cottage Hospitals* (London 1880).
Burdett's Hospitals and Charities 1899 (London 1899).
Hospitals and Asylums of the World (London 1891-3).
Burns, R., *Memoirs of the Rev. Stevenson Macgill, D.D.* (Edinburgh 1842).
Burns, R. F., *The life and times of Rev. Robert Burns, D.D.* (Toronto 1872).
Butler, J., *Campaign for repeal of the Contagious Diseases Act 1866* (1869).
Woman's Work and Woman's Culture (London 1869).
Personal Reminiscences of a Great Crusade (Edinburgh 1889).

Cadell, F., *The Contagious Diseases Acts* (Edinburgh 1881).
Caldwell, J., *Education in Scotland: containing reference to School Board education and abolition of school fees* (Glasgow 1886).
Educational Endowments in Glasgow (Glasgow 1886).
Campbell, J., *Memoirs of David Nasmyth, his labours and travels in Great Britain, France, United States and Canada* (London 1844).
Carmichael, J. 'The Edinburgh Royal Hospital for Sick Children', *EHR*, Vol. 4 (Edinburgh 1896).
Carnegie, A., *A gospel of wealth* (London 1890).
Cassells, J. P., 'On teaching the dumb to speak — being remarks on the best mode of educating children who are totally deaf but not *dumb* or who are deaf *and* dumb', *GMJ*, 1878.
Caughie, D., *The Glasgow Infant school magazine*, 1st & 2nd series (Glasgow 1869).
Chalmers, T., *On the sufficiency of the Parochial System without a poor rate for the right management of the Poor* (Glasgow 1841).
Churches and schools for the Working Classes (Edinburgh 1846).

Posthumous Works, edited by Rev. W. Hanna, 9 vols. (Edinburgh 1847-9).
The Works of Thomas Chalmers, D.D., 25 volumes (Glasgow n.d.).
Chambers, R., *Traditions of Edinburgh* (Edinburgh 1847).
Charteris, A. H., *Life of Rev. James Robertson* (Edinburgh 1863).
Address at the opening of the Deaconess Hospital (Edinburgh 1894).
Christie, J., *The Medical Institutions of Glasgow* (Glasgow 1888).
Christison, R., *The Life of Sir Robert Christison, Bart.* (Edinburgh 1885).
Cleland, J., *Statistical facts descriptive of the former and present state of Glasgow* (Glasgow 1837).
Rise and progress of the city of Glasgow (Glasgow 1840).
Clouston, T. S., 'New Craig House, Royal Edinburgh Asylum', *EHR*, Vol. 3 (Edinburgh 1895).
Clugston, B., *West of Scotland Convalescent Sea-side Homes, Dunoon, being a short account of their present position and capabilities of extension and use* (Glasgow 1871).
Homes of refuge for the stricken . . . a short account of a visit to Putney and other hospitals for incurables (Glasgow 1874).
Cockburn, H., *Memorials of his Time* (Edinburgh 1856).
Collins, W., *The Harmony between the Gospel and the Temperance Societies* (Glasgow 1851).
Corder, Susanna, *Life of Elizabeth Fry: compiled from her journal, as edited by her daughters* (London 1853).
Cowan, R., *Vital Statistics of Glasgow* (Glasgow 1840).
Cox, Sir James, 'On the Condition of the Insane in Scotland, as influenced by Legislation', *TNASS*, Edinburgh meeting 1863 (London 1864).
Craik, J., *A Discourse: preached on Thursday, 15 November, 1849, day of National thanksgiving* (Glasgow 1849).
Craven, J. B., *Descriptive Catalogue of the Biblioteck of Kirkwall* (1683) (Kirkwall 1897).
Crawford, J., *The history of defensive organisation from the earliest times to the volunteer movement of 1859 with a sketch of volunteer progress to 1863* (London 1878).
Dale, W., *The State of the Medical Profession in Great Britain and Ireland* (Dublin 1875).
Davy, J. S., *The Elberfeld system of Poor Relief: A report to the Local Government Boards* (London 1888).
Dickson, W. P., *Biographical notice of William Euing* (Edinburgh 1875).
Drummond, H., *The ascent of man* (London 1894).
The Greatest Thing in the World and Other Addresses (London 1897).
Stones Rolled Away (London 1900).
Drysdale, C. R., *On Treatment of syphilis, and other diseases without mercury: being a collection of evidence to prove that mercury is a cause of disease, not a remedy* (London 1863).
Prostitution medically considered (London 1866).
Duncan, Alexander, *Memorials of the Faculty of Physicians and Surgeons of Glasgow* (Glasgow 1896).
Duncan, E., *A plea for an hospital on the south side of Glasgow* (Glasgow 1878).
Duncan, G. J. C., *Memoir of the Rev. Henry Duncan, D.D.* (Edinburgh 1848).
Duncan, J. M., *On the mortality of childbed* (Edinburgh 1870).
Dundee, *Charters, Writs of Royal Burgh of Dundee, the Hospital and Johnston's Bequest 1292-1880* (Dundee 1880).
Dunlop, J., *The Philosophy of Artificial and compulsory drinking usage in Great Britain and Ireland . . . with copious anecdotes and illustrations* (London 1839).
Finlayson, J., *Glasgow Hospital for Sick Children* (Glasgow 1888).
Flint, R., *Socialism* (London 1895).
Gairdner, W. T., 'The Edinburgh Royal Infirmary in the 'Fifties', *EHR*, Vol. 2 (Edinburgh 1894).
Gibson, G. A., 'The Deaconess Hospital, Edinburgh', *EHR*, Vol. 3 (Edinburgh 1895).
Gillespie, A., *Buchanan Institution* (Glasgow 1871).
Goadby, E., *The Gothenburg Licensing System* (London 1895).
Gordon, J. E., 'Distinguished British nurses of the past. Mrs. Rebecca Strong — pioneer and centenarian, 1843-1944', *Midwife, Health Visitor and Community Nurse*, December 1975, Vol. II, 396.
Gordon, M. M., *What is a medical mission?* (Aberdeen 1868).
Grainger, S., 'Sketch of the history of the Royal Infirmary and of the development of clinical teaching', *EHR*, Vol. 1 (Edinburgh 1893).
Grant, Sir A., 'The endowed hospitals of Scotland', *Recess Studies* (Edinburgh 1870).

Grant, J., *Old and new Edinburgh*, 2 vols. (London 1882).
Greig, J., and Harvey, T., *Report on the State of Education in Glasgow* (Edinburgh 1866).
Guthrie, D. K., and C. J., *Autobiography of Thomas Guthrie, DD., and memoir by his sons, 1803-1873* (London 1874-5).
Guthrie, T., *A Plea for Ragged Schools, or Prevention better than cure* (Edinburgh 1847).
    A Plea on behalf of Drunkards against drunkenness (Edinburgh 1851).
    A City's Sins and Sorrows (Edinburgh 1857).
    Autobiography of Thomas Guthrie (London 1874-5).
Halliday, Sir A., *A letter to Lord Robert Seymour* (London 1839).
Hanna, W., *Biography of Thomas Chalmers, D.D., LL.D.* (Edinburgh 1852).
Harris, D., *A Plea for Industrial Brigades, as adjuncts to Ragged Schools* (Glasgow 1873).
Henderson, T., *Savings Banks of Glasgow: one hundred years of thrift* (Glasgow 1936).
Hodder, E., *Sir George Burns, Bart: his times and friends* (London 1890).
Howie, R., *Churches and Churchless in Scotland* (Glasgow 1893).
Hunter, R., *History of the Missions of the Free Church of Scotland in India and Africa* (London 1873).
Hutchinson, J., *Syphilis* (London 1887).
Ireland, W. W., *On Idiocy and Imbecility* (London 1877).
Jeans, J. S., *Western Worthies* (Glasgow 1872).
Jex-Blake, S., *Medical Women* (Edinburgh 1872).
Johnston, J., *The rising tide of irreligion, pauperism, immorality and death* (Glasgow 1871).
Kennedy, W., *The School Boards of Scotland: their relation to Higher Education* (Glasgow 1883).
Kettle, R., *Temperance Memorials* (Glasgow 1853).
Lamond, H., *The Constitution and rules and regulations of the Glasgow Royal Infirmary* (Glasgow 1867).
Lamond, R. P., *The Scottish Poor Laws: examination of their policy, history and practical action* (Edinburgh 1870).
Laurie, S. S., *The Dick Bequest* (Edinburgh 1890).
    Report on Hospitals (Edinburgh 1868).
    On the Educational Wants of Scotland (Edinburgh 1881).
Lees, J., *A Treatise on the Poor Law of Scotland* (Edinburgh 1847).
Leggatt, W., *An account of the ten years educational experiment among destitute boys conducted in the Buchanan Institution, Glasgow* (Glasgow 1871).
Lennox, C., *Henry Drummond: A Biographical Sketch* (London n.d. but 1901).
Lewis, D., *The Gothenburg and Bergen Schemes: should they be introduced into Britain?* (Edinburgh 1895).
Lewis, G., *The filth and fever bills of Dundee* (Dundee 1841).
    Scotland a half educated nation? (Dundee 1839).
    The Pauper bill of Dundee (Dundee 1841).
    The Church in the fire (Dundee 1841).
    History of the Temperance Movement in Scotland (Edinburgh n.d. but c. 1860).
List, A. C. C., *The two phases of the Social Evil* (Edinburgh 1861).
Littlejohn, H. D., *Report on the Sanitary Condition of the city of Edinburgh* (Edinburgh 1865).
Loch, C. S., *Charity Organisation* (London 1892).
    Methods of Social Advance (London 1895).
Logan, W., *An exposure of female prostitution in London, Leeds, Rochdale, and Glasgow* (Glasgow 1843).
    Moral Statistics of Glasgow (Glasgow 1849).
    The Great Social Evil (1871).
    Early Heroes of the Temperance Reformation (London 1873).
Lorimer, J. G., *On Sabbath profanation* (Glasgow n.d.).
    The Poor Man's Church defended or popular objections answered (Glasgow n.d.).
Lowe, J., *Historical sketch of the Edinburgh Medical Missionary Society* (Edinburgh 1892).
MacAulay, G., *The Lord's Law and Day* (Glasgow 1866).
MacCandlish, J. M., *A Study of Christian Socialism* (Edinburgh 1898).
MacColl, D., *Work in the Wynds* (London 1867).
McFarlan, D., *Railway travelling on the Lord's day indefensible* (Glasgow 1841).
Macgeorge, A., *The Royal Hospital for sick children and its dispensary* (Glasgow 1889).

MacGill, H. M., *The life of Hugh Heugh, D.D.* (Edinburgh 1852).

Macgill, S., *Discourses with a biographical memoir* (Glasgow 1844).

Mackie, J. B., *The life and work of Duncan McLaren*, 2 vols. (Edinburgh 1888).

MacLaren, D., *Facts regarding the seat rents of the city churches of Edinburgh: in seven letters . . . with an appendix of documents* (Edinburgh 1840).

MacLean, M., ed., *Archaeology, Education, medical and charitable institutions of Glasgow* (Glasgow 1901).

MacLeod, D., *Non church going and the housing of the poor* (Edinburgh 1888).

Memoir of Norman MacLeod (London 1886).

Christ and Society (London 1893).

MacLeod, J. N., *Memorials of the Rev. Norman MacLeod* (Edinburgh 1898).

MacLeod, N., *The Lord's Day* (Glasgow 1865).

Simple truth spoken to working people (London 1867).

Reminiscences of a Highland parish (London 1891).

Mann, H., *Education in Great Britain* (from Census of 1851) (London 1854).

Mapother, E., *The Medical Profession* (Dublin 1868).

Marshall, A., *The duty of attempting to reconcile the unenfranchised with the enfranchised classes* (Edinburgh 1841).

Mason, T., *Glasgow Public and Private Libraries* (Glasgow 1885).

Masterman, N., *Chalmers on Charity* (London 1900).

Matheson, A. S., *The Church and social problems* (Edinburgh 1893).

Matheson, J. J., *Memoir of Greville Ewing* (London 1843).

Meikle, W., *The Savings Bank of Glasgow: its origin and progress* (Glasgow 1858).

The Penny Savings Banks of Glasgow: their formation and management (Glasgow 1871).

Members of the University, *The University of Glasgow: its position and wants* (Glasgow 1900).

Menzies, Allan, *The Dick Bequest* (Edinburgh 1854).

Menzies, T., 'The Royal incorporation of Hutcheson's Hospital in the city of Glasgow', *TNASS*, 1874 (London 1875).

Merrick, G. P., *Report to H.M. Commissioners on Discharged Prisoners' Aid Societies* (c.8299) (London 1897).

Mill, J. S., *On the Subjection of Women* (London 1869).

Miller, H., *Thoughts on the Educational Question, or the Battle of Scotland* (Edinburgh n.d.).

My schools and schoolmasters (Edinburgh n.d.).

Miller, J., *Prostitution in relation to its cause and cure* (Edinburgh 1859).

Mitchell, W. (Edinburgh), *The Working Men's Missionary, being the memoir of William Mitchell, City Missionary, Edinburgh* (Edinburgh 1874).

Mitchell, W. (Glasgow), *Rescue the children* (London 1886).

Neglected Children in our towns and cities (Glasgow 1891).

Twelve years' experience of day industrial schools in Glasgow (Glasgow 1892).

Morison, A., *Outlines of Lectures on the Nature, Causes and Treatment of Insanity* (London 1848).

Morren, N., *The national church, a national blessing* (Edinburgh 1844).

Morris, E., *History of the temperance and teetotal Societies in Glasgow* (Glasgow 1855).

Munro, Rev. A., *Sore Nipples and Nursing* (Aberdeen 1861-2).

Murray, D., *A Plea for Stirling's Library* (Glasgow 1894).

Napper, A., *On the advantages derivable to the medical profession, and the public, from the village hospital* (London 1866).

National Education Association of Scotland, *Report of proceedings at the public meeting of the Friends of National Education in the Music Hall, Edinburgh* (Edinburgh 25 January 1854).

Neilson, W. M., *Glasgow Technical College* (Glasgow 1880).

Nichols, G., *A History of the Scotch Poor Law* (London 1856).

Nicol, J., *Vital, Social and Economic Statistics of Glasgow, 1881-1885* (Glasgow 1885).

Vital, Social and Economic Statistics of the City of Glasgow, 1885-1891 (Glasgow 1891).

Nightingale, F., *Introductory notes on Lying-in institutions* (London 1871).

Notes on Nursing: what it is and what it is not (London n.d.).

Notes on nursing for the labouring classes (London 1876).

One of themselves (James Frame, iron store-keeper), *Essay on the Advantages of Savings Banks to the Working-classes* (Edinburgh 1851).

O'Reilly, J. B., *In Bohemia* (Boston 1886).

Paisley, R., *Address to the Presbytery of Glasgow* (Glasgow 1839).

Parent-Duchatelet, A. J. B., *De la Prostitution dans la ville de Paris* (Paris 1837).

Parker, P., *Statements respecting hospitals in China preceded by a letter to John Abercrombie* (Glasgow 1842).

Perry, R., *Observations on the Sanitary State of Glasgow* (Glasgow 1841).

Philip, R. W., 'The Victoria Hospital for Consumption, Edinburgh', *EHR*, Vol. 3 (Edinburgh 1895).

Pinnington, E., *The Art Collection of the Corporation of Glasgow* (Glasgow 1898).

Poole, R., *Memoranda regarding the Royal Lunatic Asylum, Infirmary and Dispensary of Montrose* (Montrose 1841).

Quarrier, W., *A Narrative of facts relative to work done for Christ in connection with the Orphan Homes of Scotland, Destitute Children's Emigration Homes, and City Home and Mission, Glasgow, for 14th year ending 31st October 1885* (Glasgow 1885).

    A Narrative of facts relative to work done for Christ . . . for Twenty-sixth year, ending 31st October 1897 (Glasgow 1897).

Rae, J., *Reformatories; their history and management* (Glasgow 1867).

Ramsay, G. G., *Glasgow and the West of Scotland Technical College: Allan Glen's School and Technical Institution* (Glasgow 1888).

    Glasgow and West of Scotland Technical College (Glasgow 1896).

Rankin, J., *Handbook of the Church of Scotland* (Edinburgh 1888).

Rankine, W. J. McQuorn, *Memoir of John Elder* (Edinburgh 1871).

Rathbone, W., *The History and Progress of District Nursing* (London 1890).

Reid, W., *Temperance memorials of the late Robert Kettle consisting of selections of his writings on the temperance question. With a memoir of his life* (Glasgow 1853).

    Our National vice (Glasgow 1858).

    Woman's Work and Woman's Weal (Glasgow 1860).

    Memoirs of William McGavin (Edinburgh 1884).

    Total abstinence from intoxicating liquors an essential element in the moral training of the young (Glasgow n.d.).

    Patience needed; or, the duty of temperance reformers at the present crisis (n.p., n.d.).

Richmond, Sir D., *Corporation of the City of Glasgow, notes on Municipal Work November 1896-November 1899* (Glasgow 1899).

Rivington, W., *The Medical Profession* (Dublin 1879).

Robinson, H., *The Whole Truth and Nothing but the truth about the Social Evil* (Edinburgh 1866).

Ross, W., *The Sabbath made for man* (Edinburgh 1865).

Roxburgh, J. R., *Edinburgh Philanthropic Red Book* (Edinburgh 1901).

Russell, J. B., *Report of the City of Glasgow Fever Hospital* (Glasgow 1867).

    Report upon uncertified deaths in Glasgow (Glasgow 1876).

    The vital statistics of Glasgow (Glasgow 1886).

    On some sociological aspects of sanitation (Glasgow 1887).

    The house in relation to public health (Glasgow 1887).

    Life in one room: or, some serious considerations for the citizens of Glasgow (Glasgow 1888).

    The children of the city: what can we do for them? (Glasgow n.d.).

    On the 'ticketed' houses of Glasgow . . . (Glasgow 1888).

    The evolution of the functions of public health administration in Glasgow (Glasgow 1895).

Sabbath School Teacher, a working man of Glasgow, *The Sabbath on the Rock* (Edinburgh 1867).

Scottish Council of the Liberation Society, *Statistics relating to the Established Church in Scotland* (Glasgow 1888).

Scotus, *The Scottish Poor Law* (Edinburgh 1870).

Sellar, A. C., *Manual of the Education Act for Scotland* (Edinburgh 1872).

    Scotch Educational Progress 1864-1887 — An Address (Glasgow 1887).

Seton, A. H., *Allan Glen's School: the first Technical College* (Glasgow 1894).

Shaftesbury, Earl of, *Speeches of the Earl of Shaftesbury in Glasgow* (Glasgow 1871).

Shaw, G. B., *The Fabian Society, its early history* (London 1892).

Simpson, A. R., 'Sketch of the history of the Royal Maternity and Simpson Memorial Hospital', *EHR*, Vol. 1 (Edinburgh 1893).

Simpson, J. Y., *Henry Drummond* (Edinburgh 1901).

Smart, W., *Toynbee Hall. A short account of the Universities Settlement in East London, with suggestions for similar work in Glasgow* (Glasgow 1886).
   Women's Wages (London 1891).
Smiles, S., *Self-help* (London 1859).
   Thrift (London 1892).
Smith, G. Adam, *The Life of Henry Drummond* (London 1899).
Smith, J., *Our Scottish Clergy; 56 sketches* (Edinburgh 1849).
Smith, J. G., *The laws of Scotland relating to the Poor* (Edinburgh 1867).
Smith, T., *Memoirs of James Begg* (Edinburgh 1885).
Spence, S., *The Glasgow Angus and Mearns Benevolent Society* (Glasgow 1895).
Spurgeon, Mrs. C. H., *C. H. Spurgeon's Autobiography*, 4 vols. (London 1897-1900).
Stevenson, T. G., *Edinburgh Merchant Company Hospital* (Edinburgh 1874).
Stewart, A. M., *Romish Nurses: with an appendix . . . containing letters to the managers of the Glasgow Royal Infirmary* (Glasgow 1878).
Stewart, H. D., *Statistics of Insanity: Crichton Royal* (n.p., n.d.).
Stirling, F., *The Failure of the Forbes MacKenzie Act* (Glasgow 1859).
Strachan, J. M., 'Immorality in Scotland', *Scotsman*, 20 May, 2 June, 7 June 1870.
Strang, J., *Bursaries, Schools, Mortifications and Bequests* (Glasgow 1861).
Strong, R., *Introductory remarks on practical classes on ward work* (Glasgow 1893).
Struthers, G., *The History of the rise, progress and principles of the Relief Church, embracing notices of the other religious denominations in Scotland* (Glasgow 1843).
Swete, H., *Village hospitals and their position with regard to County Infirmaries, Unions and the professions* (London 1866).
Symington, W., *A sermon to students and young men* (for the Edinburgh University Missionary Association) (Edinburgh 1843).
Tait, W., *Magdalenism: An Inquiry* (Edinburgh 1842).
Thomson, A., *Industrial Schools, their origin, rise and progress in Aberdeen* (Aberdeen 1847).
   Social Evils: their causes and their cure (London 1852).
Thomson, J., *Life, lectures and writings of William Cullen, M.D.* (Edinburgh 1859).
Thomson, W. Burns, *Medical Missions* (Edinburgh 1854).
   The City Arabs (London 1858).
   Medical Missions: an address delivered at the Mildmay park conferences (London 1869).
   Reminiscences of Medical Missionary Work (London 1895).
Tiffany, F., *Dorothea Lynde Dix* (Boston 1890).
Tuke, D. H., *Reform in the Treatment of the Insane* (London 1892).
   Early history of the Retreat, York (London 1892).
Vernon, E. R., *A narrative of the Royal Scottish Volunteer Review in Holyrood Park, August 7, 1860* (Edinburgh 1860).
Walker, A., *A history of the Workhouse in Aberdeen* (Aberdeen 1883).
   Robert Gordon. His Hospital and his College (Aberdeen 1886).
Walker, N. L., *Robert Buchanan, D.D., an ecclesiastical biography* (London 1877).
Wardlaw, R., *Lectures on female prostitution: its nature, extent, effects, guilt, causes and remedy* (Glasgow 1842).
Waring, E. J. *Cottage Hospitals, their objects, advantages and management* (London 1876).
Watson, W. West, *Vital Social and Economic Statistics of Glasgow for 1876* (Glasgow 1877).
Watson, J. L., *Life of Robert Smith Candlish, D.D.* (Edinburgh 1882).
Weir, W., *Address on the origin and early history of the Faculty of Physicians and Surgeons of Glasgow* (Glasgow 1864).
Wellwood, J., *Norman MacLeod* (Edinburgh 1897).
Wilson, C., *On the Expediency of Founding an Hospital for the Diseases of Children, with notes on Continental Children's Hospitals* (Edinburgh 1859).
Winskill, P. T., *The comprehensive history of the rise and progress of the temperance reformation* (Warrington 1881).
   The Temperance Movement and its Workers, a record of social, moral, religious and political progress (London 1893).
Wright, A., *The history of Education of the old parish schools of Scotland* (Edinburgh 1898).
Wylie, J. A., *Disruption Worthies* (Edinburgh 1881).

C. *1902-1978*
Abel-Smith, B., *A History of the Nursing Profession* (London 1960).
    The Hospitals, 1800-1948 (London 1964).
Adams, W. G. S., *A report on library provision and policy* (London 1915).
Aitken, W. R., *A History of the public library movement in Scotland to 1955* (Glasgow 1971).
Anderson, J. W., *Sir William T. Gairdner: an appreciation* (Glasgow 1913).
    Four Chiefs of Glasgow Royal Infirmary: Rainy, Buchanan, Fleming, Gairdner (Glasgow
        1916).
Angus, M., *Sheriff Watson of Aberdeen* (Aberdeen 1913).
Anon, *Life in the laundry, Fabian tract, No. 112* (London 1902).
    Scottish licensing laws as embodied in the Licensing (Scotland) Act 1903 (Glasgow 1903).
    *The Glasgow and West of Scotland Technical College. Notes upon the history and objects of
        the College* (Glasgow 1905).
    Handbooks of Glasgow charities (Glasgow 1876, 1881 and 1907).
    Scottish Permissive Bill: an historical retrospect (Glasgow 1908).
    British Association, Handbook of Dundee (Dundee 1912).
    Glasgow School of Social Study and Training (Glasgow 1912).
    Municipal Glasgow: its evolution and enterprises (Glasgow 1914).
    History of the Hutcheson's Hospital and School 1881-1914 (Glasgow 1914).
    Historical Sketch and Laws of the Royal College of Physicians of Edinburgh (Edinburgh
        1925).
    Edinburgh University, Bicentenary of the Faculty of Medicine 1726-1926 (Edinburgh 1926).
    Lister and the Lister Ward (Glasgow 1927).
    Centenary of the Total Abstinence movement in Scotland (Glasgow 1932).
    Edinburgh Institute Melville College Centenary (Edinburgh 1933).
    Edinburgh public libraries 1890-1950, a handbook and history of sixty years' progress
        (Edinburgh 1951).
    Airdrie Public Library: A century of reading, 1853-1953 (Airdrie 1954).
    Experimental Nurse Training at Glasgow Royal Infirmary, HMSO (Edinburgh 1963).
    Glasgow Public Libraries, 1874-1966 (Glasgow 1966).
    Aberdeen Savings Bank (Aberdeen 1967).
    Health in brief, NHS, Statistics (Edinburgh 1974).
    The Hamilton Bequest (Glasgow 1977).
    The Mitchell Library 1877-1977 (Glasgow 1977).
Armstrong, A., *The Church of England, the Methodists and Society, 1700-1850* (London 1973).
Ayers, G. M., *England's first State Hospitals and the Metropolitan Asylums Board, 1867-1930*
        (London 1971).
Barbour, G. F., *Church and Nation in Scotland today* (Edinburgh & London 1930).
Barclay, J. B., *Edinburgh* (Edinburgh 1965).
Battiscombe, G., *Shaftesbury: a Biography of the Seventh Earl, 1801-1885* (London 1974).
Bell, E. M., *Octavia Hill* (London 1942).
    The Story of Hospital Almoners (n.p. 1961).
Benjamin, H., and Masters, R. E. L., *Prostitution and Morality* (London 1965).
Best, G., *Mid-Victorian Britain 1851-75* (London 1971).
Beveridge, W. H., *Unemployment: a problem of industry* (London 1909).
    Voluntary action: a report on methods of social advance (London 1948).
Bieler, A., *The Social humanism of Calvin* (Geneva 1961), this translation Richmond, Virginia,
        1964.
Binfield, C., *George Williams and the YMCA: a study in Victorian social attitudes* (London 1973).
    So down to prayers: studies in English nonconformity 1780-1920 (London 1977).
Blackwell, E., *Essays in medical sociology* (London 1902).
    Medicine and Society in America (New York 1972).
Blanco, R. L., 'The Attempted Control of Venereal Disease in the army in Mid-Victorian England',
        Journal of the Society of Army Historical Research, 45 (1967).
Bone, T. R., *Studies in the history of Scottish Education 1872-1939* (London 1967).
Boog Watson, W. N., *A short history of Chalmers Hospital* (Edinburgh 1964).
Booth, C., *Life and Labour of the people of London 1889-1903* (London 1904).
Branston, W. T., 'A History of Parliamentary Grants for Education', *Scottish Educational Journal*,
        July 1953.

Bready, J. Wesley, *Dr. Barnardo, Physician, Pioneer, Prophet: Child Life Yesterday and Today* (London 1930).

Bremner, R. H., *American Philanthropy* (Chicago 1960).

Bremner, R. L., *The Housing Problem in Glasgow* (Glasgow 1903).

British Medical Association, *The Book of Glasgow* (90th annual meeting) (Glasgow 1922).

Brockbank, E. M., *The Foundation of Provincial Medical Education in England* (Manchester 1936).

Brotherston, J. H. F., *Observations on the early public health movement in Scotland* (London 1952).

Brownlee, J., *Biographical Sketch of the late James B. Russell* (Glasgow 1905).

Bruce, M., *The Coming of the Welfare State* (London 1968).

    The rise of the Welfare State: English Social Policy 1601-1971 (London 1973).

Bruce, W. S., *Social aspects of Christian morality* (London 1905).

Buchanan, A., *Life of James Wallace Anderson, M.D.* (Glasgow 1914).

Buckley, K. D., *Trade Unionism in Aberdeen 1878-1900* (Edinburgh 1955).

Burleigh, J. H. S., *Church History of Scotland* (London 1960).

Burns, W. L., *Age of Equipoise* (London 1964).

Butt, J., 'Working class housing in Glasgow, 1851-1914', in Chapman, S. D., ed., *The History of Working Class Housing* (Newton Abbot 1971).

Cage, R. A., and Checkland, E. O. A., 'Thomas Chalmers and Urban Poverty: The St. John's parish experiment in Glasgow, 1819-37', *The Philosophical Journal*, Spring 1976, Vol. 13, No. 1, 37-56.

Cairns, D. S., *David Cairns, an autobiography* (London 1950).

Calvin, J., *Tracts and Treatises on the reformation of the church:* this edition by Thomas F. Torrance (Edinburgh 1958).

Cameron, Sir H. C., *Reminiscences of Lister* (Glasgow 1927).

Campbell, A. J., *Two centuries of the Church of Scotland, 1707-1929* (Paisley 1930).

Campbell, Richardson, *Rechabite History* (Manchester 1911).

Campbell, R. H., *Scotland since 1707* (Oxford 1971).

Cant, R. J., *The University of St. Andrews* (Edinburgh 1970).

Canton, W., *A History of the British and Foreign Bible Society* (London 1904-06).

Carpenter, S. C., *Church and people 1789-1889* (London 1933).

Caw, J. L., *The National Gallery of Scotland* (Edinburgh n.d.).

Chadwick, E., *Report on the Sanitary Condition of the labouring population of Great Britain* (1842: reprinted with introduction by M. W. Flinn, 1965).

Chalmers, A. K., ed., *Public health administration in Glasgow: a memorial volume of the writings of J. B. Russell* (Glasgow 1905).

    The health of Glasgow 1818-1825 (Glasgow 1930).

Chalmers, T., *Problems of Poverty*, ed. H. Hunter (London 1912).

Chambers, W. D., *A History of Murray Royal* (Perth 1927).

Checkland, S. G., *Scottish Banking: a history 1695-1973* (Glasgow 1975).

    The Upas Tree, Glasgow 1875-1975 (Glasgow 1976).

Chesler, P., *Women and Madness* (London 1974).

Clark, I. M., *A History of church discipline in Scotland* (Aberdeen 1929).

Clark, K., *Churchmen and the Condition of England 1832-1885* (Cambridge 1973).

Clarke, W. K. Lowther, *A History of the SPCK* (London 1959).

Clow, W. M., *Dr. George Reith, A Scottish Ministry* (London 1928).

Collins, E. T., *The History and Traditions of the Moorfields Eye Hospital* (London 1929).

Compston, H. F. B., *The Magdalen Hospital* (London 1917).

Comrie, J. D., *History of Scottish Medicine*, 2 vols. (Edinburgh 1927, 1932).

Cormack, A. A., *Poor Relief in Scotland* (Aberdeen 1923).

    District nursing in Scotland, Peterculter, Aberdeenshire (n.p. 1965).

    Susan Carnegie, 1744-1821, her life of service (Aberdeen 1966).

Cowan, J., *From Glasgow's Treasure Chest* (Glasgow 1951).

Cowan, R. M. W., *The Newspaper in Scotland 1815-1860* (Glasgow 1946).

Craig, Archibald, ed., *The statue of Mrs. John Elder, Govan . . . together with some account of the Elder Free Library, the Elder Cottage Hospital, and the Cottage Nurses' Training Home and an obituary notice of Mrs. Elder* (Govan 1912).

Craig, W. S., *John Thomson: pioneer and father of Scottish paediatrics 1856-1926* (Edinburgh 1968).
  History of the Royal College of Physicians of Edinburgh (Oxford 1976).
Crawford, J., 'Two miners' libraries in the '70's', *Library Review*, Vol. 23 (1971-1972), 14-17.
Cresswell, C. H., *The Royal College of Surgeons of Edinburgh* (Edinburgh 1926).
Davie, G. E., *The democratic intellect: Scotland and her universities in the nineteenth century* (Edinburgh 1961).
Diack, W., *History of the Trades Council and the Trade Union Movement in Aberdeen* (Aberdeen 1939).
Dock, L., *A History of the nursing profession* (London 1912).
Donnison, J., *Midwives and Medical Men* (London 1977).
Drummond, A. L., and Bulloch, J., *The Scottish Church, 1688-1843: the age of the moderates* (Edinburgh 1973).
  The Church in Victorian Scotland, 1843-1874 (Edinburgh 1975).
  The Church in late Victorian Scotland, 1874-1900 (Edinburgh 1978).
Dunlop, J., *Autobiography of John Dunlop*, ed. by J. G. Dunlop (London 1932).
Easterbrook, C. C., *Chronicle of Crichton Royal 1833-1936* (Dumfries 1940).
Eaves-Walton, P. M., *The Royal Infirmary of Edinburgh, 1729-1900* (Edinburgh 1968).
Erskine, J., *Old Glasgow Hospitals* (Glasgow 1905).
Fairbairn, A. M., 'The Scottish Church and the Scottish people', *The Contemporary Review*, Vol. LXXIX (January 1901), 129-152.
Fergus, A. F., *The origin and development of the Glasgow School of Medicine* (Glasgow 1911).
Ferguson, T., *The dawn of Scottish Social Welfare* (Edinburgh 1948).
  Scottish Social Welfare (1864-1914) (Edinburgh 1958).
Ferguson, W., *Scotland 1689 to the present* (Edinburgh 1968).
Ferrier, J., *The Greenock Infirmary 1806-1968* (Greenock 1968).
Finzi, J., King, C., and Boover, D., eds., *Volunteers in Hospital* (London 1971).
Fishlow, A., 'The Trustee Savings Banks 1817-1861', *Journal of Economic History*, Vol. XXI, No. 1, March 1961, 26-40.
Fleming, J. R., *A History of the Church in Scotland 1843-1874* (Edinburgh 1927).
  A History of the Church in Scotland 1875-1929 (Edinburgh 1933).
Flinn, M. W., *Public health reform in Britain* (London 1968).
  British population 1700-1850 (London 1970).
Foucault, M., *Madness and Civilisation* (New York 1965).
Friedson, E., *The Hospital in modern society* (New York 1963).
  Profession of Medicine (New York 1970).
Fyffe, P., *Housing of the labouring classes* (Glasgow 1899).
Gammie, A., *William Quarrier and the Story of the Orphan Homes of Scotland* (London n.d.).
Garlick, P. L., *The wholeness of Man* (London 1943).
Gauldie, E., *Cruel Habitations* (London 1974).
Gibbon, F. P., *William A. Smith of the Boys' Brigade* (London n.d.).
Gibson, A. J. H., *Stipend in the Church of Scotland* (Edinburgh 1961).
Gibson, G. A., *Life of Sir William Tennant Gairdner* (Glasgow 1912).
Gibson, H. J. C., *The history of Dundee Royal Infirmary 1789-1948* (Dundee 1948).
Glasse, J., *The relation of the Church to Socialism* (Edinburgh 1900).
Gordon, A., *The Life of A. H. Charteris (1835-1908)* (London 1912).
Grant, J. M., *et al*, eds., *St. Leonard's School 1877-1927* (London 1927).
Gray, B. Kirkman, *A History of English Philanthropy* (London 1905).
Gray, R. Q., *Labour Aristocracy in Edinburgh* (London 1977).
Guthrie, D., *The Royal Edinburgh Hospital for Sick Children 1860-1960* (Edinburgh 1960).
Haldane, E. S., *The British Nurse in peace and war* (London 1923).
Hamilton, J. T., *Greenock Libraries, a development and social history 1635-1967* (Greenock 1967).
Hamilton, T. W., *The temperance reformation in Scotland with special reference to John Dunlop and Greenock: a century of work and progress 1829-1929* (Greenock 1929).
Hammond, J. L., and Barbara, *James Stansfield: a Victorian Champion of sex equality* (London 1932).
Handley, J. E., *The Irish in Scotland 1798-1845* (Cork 1943).
  The Irish in modern Scotland (Cork 1947).

Harper, J. W., *The Social ideal and Dr. Chalmers' contribution to Christian economics* (Edinburgh 1910).

Harris, José, *William Beveridge: a biography* (Oxford 1977).

Harrison, B., 'Philanthropy and the Victorians', *Victorian Studies*, 1966.
     Drink and the Victorians (London 1971).

Harrison, J., *Merchant Company and its schools* (Edinburgh 1920).

Hayter, A., *Opium and the Romantic Imagination* (London 1968).

Heasman, K., *Evangelicals in Action* (London 1962).
     'The Medical Mission, and the Care of the Sick Poor in Nineteenth Century England', *Historical Journal*, Vol. VII, No. 2, 1964.

Heeney, B., *Mission to the Middle Classes, the Woodard Schools* (London 1969).

Henderson, D. K., *The evolution of psychiatry in Scotland* (Edinburgh 1964).

Henderson, T., *The Savings Bank of Glasgow* (Glasgow 1936).

Henderson, T. B., *The History of Glasgow Dental Hospital and School 1879-1959* (Glasgow 1960).

Hendry, J. D., *A Social History of branch library development* (Glasgow 1974).

Higgs, M., and Hayward, E., *Where shall she live?* (London 1910).

Highet, J., *The Scottish Churches* (London 1960).

Hillcourt, W., *Baden-Powell: two lives of a hero* (New York 1964).

Hodgkinson, R. G., *The Origins of the National Health Service: the medical services of the New Poor Law, 1834-1871* (London 1967).
     Science and public health (London 1973).

Horn, D. B., *A short history of the University of Edinburgh* (Edinburgh 1967).

Horne, H. O., *The Assets of the Small Saver* (Aberdeen 1937).
     Insch and Upper Garioch Savings Bank, 1838-1938 (Aberdeen 1938).
     Ellon Savings Bank 1839-1939 (Aberdeen 1939).
     Forres Savings Bank 1839-1939 (Aberdeen 1939).
     Savings Banks at Kintore and Inverurie (Aberdeen 1939).
     Stonehaven Savings Bank 1838-1938 (Aberdeen 1939).
     A History of Savings Banks (London 1947).

Hutchins, B. L., and Harrison, A., *A History of Factory Legislation* (London 1926).

Huxley, E., *Florence Nightingale* (London 1975).

Irving, G., *Dumfries and Galloway Royal Infirmary, the First Two Hundred Years 1776-1975* (Dumfries 1975).

Jardine, M. B., *The Chapbook of the Rottenrow* (Glasgow 1913).

Jeal, T., *Livingstone* (London 1973).

Jennett, B., 'Sir William Macewen, 1848-1924, pioneer Scottish neurosurgeon', *Surgical Neurology*, Vol. 6, No. 2, August 1976, 57-60.

Johnston, T., *History of the Working Class in Scotland* (Edinburgh 1920).

Jones, G. Stedman, *Outcast London* (Oxford 1971).

Jones, K., *Lunacy, Law and Conscience 1744-1845*, (London 1955).
     Mental Health and Social Policy 1845-1959 (London 1960).
     History of the Mental Health Service (London 1972).

Jones, Sir Henry, *Social responsibilities: lectures to business men* (Glasgow 1905).
     The working faith of the social reformer and other essays (London 1910).
     The principles of citizenship (London 1920).

Jones, S. J., *Dundee and District* (Dundee 1968).

Jones, W., *The expectation of life in Glasgow* (Glasgow 1925).

Jordan, W. K., *Philanthropy in England 1480-1660* (New York 1959).

Jorns, A., *The Quakers as pioneers in Social Work* (London 1931).

Kaufman, P., *Libraries and their users: collected papers in library history* (London 1969).

Kelly, T., *Public Libraries in Great Britain before 1850* (1966).

Keir, D., *The House of Collins* (London 1952).

Kerr, J., *Scottish Education, School and University* (Cambridge 1913).

Kerr, J. M. M., *Historical Review of British Obstetrics and Gynaecology* (Edinburgh and London 1954).

Kidd, W., *Dundee past and present* (Dundee 1909).

Laidlaw, S., *Glasgow Common Lodging Houses and the people living in them* (Glasgow 1956).

Lang, J. M., *The Church and its social mission* (Edinburgh 1902).

Larrabee, E., *The Benevolent and Necessary Institution, The New York Hospital 1771-1971* (New York 1971).

Laqueur, W., *Religion and Respectability* (London 1976).
Laurie, S. S., *The Dick Bequest* (Edinburgh 1904).
Lister, J., *The collected papers of Joseph, Baron Lister* (London 1909).
Lloyd-Jones, I. D., 'Glasgow University Settlement, 1897-1966', *College Courant*, 1967.
Macadam, E., *The new philanthropy* (London 1934).
McAlpine, I., and Hunter, R., *Three Hundred Years of Psychiatry 1535-1860* (Oxford 1962).
    George III and the Mad Business (New York 1969).
McCaffrey, J. F., ed., *Shadow, Midnight Scenes and Social Photographs* (Glasgow 1976).
MacCallum, M., *Religion as Social Justice* (Glasgow 1915).
MacDonald, D. F., *Scotland's Shifting Population* (Glasgow 1937).
McDonald, J. C. M., 'History of Dr. Gray's hospital, Elgin', *Medical History*, April 1976, 174-175.
MacGregor, J. B., *The Scottish Presbyterian Polity* (Edinburgh 1926).
MacGregor, M. B., *Towards Scotland's Social Good: a Hundred Years of Temperance Work in the Church of Scotland* (Edinburgh n.d. but c. 1949).
MacInnes, J., *The Evangelical Movement in the Highlands of Scotland* (Aberdeen 1951).
MacKenzie, A. M., *The Kingdom of Scotland* (London 1940).
    Scotland in Modern Times (Edinburgh 1947).
Mackenzie, Norman, *The First Fabians* (London 1977).
MacKenzie, W. M., *Hugh Miller: a critical study* (London 1905).
McKeown, T., *Medicine in Modern Society* (London 1965).
Mackie, J. D., *The University of Glasgow* (Glasgow 1954).
MacKinnon, J., *The Social and Industrial History of Scotland* (London 1921).
MacLaren, A. A., *Presbyterianism and the Working Class in a mid-nineteenth century city* (London 1974).
    (ed:) *Social Class in Scotland: past and present* (Edinburgh 1976).
MacLean, N., *The Former Days* (London 1945).
McLeary, G. J., *The Maternity and Child Welfare Movement* (London 1935).
Maclennan, D., *Is local option a failure?* (Glasgow 1924).
McNeil, J. T., *The History and Character of Calvinism* (New York 1954).
McPherson, J. M., *The Kirk's care of the poor* (n.p., n.d.).
McQueen, L., and Kerr, A. B., *The Western Infirmary, 1874-1974* (Glasgow 1974).
McRoberts, D., ed., *Essays on the Scottish Reformation 1513-1625* (Glasgow 1962).
Manton, J., *Mary Carpenter and the children of the streets* (London 1976).
Marlow, J., *Mr. and Mrs. Gladstone* (London 1976).
Marwick, W. H., *Economic Developments in Victorian Scotland* (London 1936).
    'Social Heretics in the Scottish Churches', *Records of the Church History Society*, Vol. XI part III, 1953, 227-239.
Mathieson, W. L., *Church and Reform in Scotland* (Glasgow 1916).
Mechie, S., *Church and Scottish social development 1780-1870* (London 1960).
Metcalfe, W. M., *John Neilson's Institution* (Paisley 1902).
Milne, G. P., 'History of Midwifery in Aberdeen', *Medical History*, April 1978, 205-206.
Monro, J., 'Remarks on Dr. Battie's treatise on Madness, 1758', reprinted in *Psychiatric Monographs*, Series No. 3, 1962.
Morgan, A., *Rise and Progress of Scottish Education* (Edinburgh 1927).
    Makers of Scottish Education (1929).
Morrison, R., *The Help, an Account of the Edinburgh Association for the Improvement of the Poor 1868-1906* (Edinburgh 1968).
Morton, A. L., *The Life and Ideas of Robert Owen* (London 1962).
Morton, R. S., 'Some aspects of the early history of Syphilis in Scotland', *British Journal of Venereal Disease*, 1962.
    'The Sibbens of Scotland', *Medical History*, 1967.
    Venereal Disease (London 1972).
Mowat, C. L., *The Charity Organisation Society, 1869-1913. Its Ideas and Work* (London 1961).
Murray, I., *The Victorian Infirmary of Glasgow* (Glasgow 1947).
Neill, S., *A History of Christian Missions* (London 1964).
New, C. W., *Life of Henry Brougham to 1830* (Oxford 1961).
Newman, C., *The Evolution of Medical Education in the Nineteenth Century* (Oxford 1957).
Newsholme, Sir A., *International Studies on the Relation between the Private and Official Practice of Medicine, Vol. III, England and Wales, Scotland and Ireland* (London 1931).

Nield, K., *Prostitution in the Victorian Age: Debates on the Issue from Nineteenth-Century Critical Journals* (1973).

Oakley, C. A., *The Second City* (Glasgow 1946).

O'Neil, J. E., 'Finding a policy for the sick poor', *Victorian Studies*, 1964.

Owen, D., *English Philanthropy* (London 1965).

Parry, N. and J., *The Rise of the Medical Profession* (London 1976).

Patrick, J., *A short history of the Glasgow Royal Infirmary* (Glasgow 1940).

Payne, P. L., *Studies in Scottish Business History* (London 1967).

Pelling, H., 'Religion and the nineteenth century British Working-Class', *Past and Present*, No. 27, 1964.

Porter, I. A., *Alexander Gordon, M.D., of Aberdeen, 1752-1799* (Edinburgh 1958).

Poynter, F. N. L., and Keele, K. D., *A Short History of Medicine* (London 1961).

Poynter, F. N. L., ed., *The Evolution of Hospitals in Britain* (London 1964).
Medicine and Science in the 1860's (London 1968).

Rae, J. A., *The History of Allan Glen's School 1853-1953* (Glasgow 1953).

Reid, H. St. Clair, *An Analysis of the Temperance (Scotland) Act 1913 with introduction, excursus and appendix containing the act, regulations, applied enactments and forms* (Edinburgh and Glasgow 1920).

Reid, R., *Observations on the structure of Hospitals for the treatment of lunatics* (new edn. London 1964), Hunter, R., and Macalpine, E., eds.

Riddell, W. J. B., *The Ophthalmic Institution 1868-1968* (Glasgow 1968).

Robertson, D., *The Princes Street proprietors and other chapters in the history of the Royal Burgh of Edinburgh* (Edinburgh 1935).

Robertson, E., *Yorkhill Story* (Glasgow 1972).

Robertson, P. L., 'The finances of the University of Glasgow before 1914', in *History of Education Quarterly*, Winter 1976.

Rodger, B., *The Cloak of Charity* (London 1949).

Rorie, D., *The Book of Aberdeen* (Aberdeen 1939).

Rothstein, W. G., *American Physicians in the Nineteenth Century* (Baltimore 1972).

Rowallan, Lord, *An Autobiography of Lord Rowallan* (Edinburgh 1976).

Russell, G. W. E., ed., *Sir Wilfred Lawson: a memoir* (London 1909).

Sanderson, M., *The Universities and British Industry 1850-1970* (London 1972).

Saunders, L., *Scottish Democracy 1815-1840* (Edinburgh 1950).

Scotland, James, *The History of Scottish Education* (London 1969).

Scott, G. R., *A History of Prostitution from Antiquity to the Present Day* (London 1954).

Shaw, J. E., *Local Government in Scotland* (Edinburgh 1942).

Sheman, J., *Voluntary Service in Seven Hospitals in Scotland* (Edinburgh 1969).

Silver, P. and H., *Education of the Poor: The History of a National School 1824-1974* (London 1974).

Simey, M. B., *Charitable Effort in Liverpool in the Nineteenth Century* (Liverpool 1951).

Smart, W., *The Housing Problem and the Municipality* (Glasgow 1902).

Smith, R. Mudie, *The Religious Life of London* (London 1904).

Smout, T. C., *A History of the Scottish People 1560-1830* (London 1967).

Sorsby, A., 'Defunct London Eye Hospitals', *British Journal of Ophthalmology* (1936).
'Nineteenth Century Provincial Eye Hospitals', *British Journal of Ophthalmology* (1946).

Spencer, J. A., *Management in Hospitals* (London 1967).

Stalker, H., *Murthly Hospital 1864-1964: a Centenary History* (Perth 1964).

Stocks, M., *A Hundred Years of District Nursing* (London 1960).

Strong, J., *A History of Secondary Education in Scotland* (Oxford 1909).

Strong, R., *Reminiscences* (Edinburgh 1935).

Tait, A. C., 'History of Crichton Royal', *Medical History*, Vol. XVI, 1972.

Tait, H. P., *A Doctor and Two Policemen, the history of the Edinburgh health department, 1862-1974* (Edinburgh 1974).

Tarn, J. N., *Five per cent Philanthropy* (Cambridge 1974).

Thomas, K., 'The Double Standard', *Journal of the History of Ideas* (April 1959).

Thompson, J. D., and Goldin, G., *The Hospital: A Social and Architectural History* (New Haven 1975).

Thomson, A. M. W., *The History of the Glasgow Eye Infirmary 1824-1962* (Glasgow 1963).
The life and times of Dr. William McKenzie, founder of Glasgow Eye Infirmary (Glasgow 1973).

Todd, M., *Sophia Jex-Blake* (London 1918).

Tuke, S., *Description of the Retreat* (new edn. London 1964, ed. Hunter, R., and Macalpine, I.).

Turner, A. Logan, *Story of a Great Hospital, the Royal Infirmary of Edinburgh 1729-1929* (Edinburgh 1937).

Underwood, E. A., *Boerhaave's Men at Leyden and After* (Edinburgh 1977).

Vicinus, M., *Suffer and Be Still: Women in the Victorian Age* (Bloomington 1972).

Ward, J. T., 'The factory reform movement in Scotland', *Scottish Historical Review*, Vol. XLI, No. 132, October 1962, 100-123.

Watson, D., *The Scottish Social Union and how it came to be formed* (Glasgow 1901).
    The Heritage of Youth (London 1903).
    A Mile-end Chronicle (Glasgow 1903).
    Social problems and the Church's unity (Edinburgh 1908).
    Social advance — its meaning, method and goal (London 1911).
    The Social expression of Christianity (London 1919).
    Chords of Memory (London 1936).

Watt, H., *The Published writings of Dr. Chalmers*, privately printed 1943.
    Thomas Chalmers and the Disruption (Edinburgh 1943).

Watt, O. M., *Stobhill Hospital, the first seventy years* (Glasgow 1971).

Webb, S. and B., *The State and the Doctor* (London 1910).

Webb, R. K., 'Literacy among the Working Classes in nineteenth century Scotland', *Scottish Historical Review*, No. 116 (October 1954).

Wickham, E. R., *Church and People in an Industrial City* (London 1957).

Wohl, A., *The Eternal Slum* (London 1977).

Wood, Grace Chalmers, *Dr. Chalmers and the Poor Laws, a comparison of Scotch and English pauperism and evidence before the committee of the House of Commons* (Edinburgh 1911).

Woodham Smith, C., *Florence Nightingale* (London 1951).

Woodward, J., *To Do the Sick No Harm: A Study of the British voluntary hospital system to 1875* (London 1974).

Woodward, J., and Richards, D., *Health Care and Popular Medicine in England in the Nineteenth Century* (London 1977).

Wright, R. S., *Fathers of the Kirk* (London 1960).

Young, G. M., *Victorian England: Portrait of an Age* (London 1936).

Youngson, A. J., *The Making of Classical Edinburgh* (Edinburgh 1967).

7. Theses

Boyd, K. McK., The Theological Presuppositions of Scottish Church Pronouncements on Sex, Marriage and the Family 1850-1914 (Edinburgh Ph.D., 1973).

Brackenridge, R. D., Sunday Observance in Scotland 1689-1900 (Glasgow Ph.D., 1962).

Burnet, G. B., The Rise, Progress and Decline of the Quaker Movement in Scotland (Glasgow Ph.D., 1937).

Bussey, O., The Religious Awakening of 1858-60 in Great Britain and Ireland (Edinburgh Ph.D., 1947).

Cage, R. A., The Scottish Poor Law 1745-1845 (Glasgow Ph.D., 1974).

Kirkland, W. M., The Impact of the French Revolution on Scottish Religious Life and Thought with special reference to Thomas Chalmers, Robert Haldane and Neil Douglas (Edinburgh Ph.D., 1951).

McCaffrey, J. F., Political Reactions in the Glasgow Constituencies at the General Elections of 1885 and 1886 (Glasgow Ph.D., 1971).

Macdonald, H., Public Health Legislation and Problems in Victorian Edinburgh with special reference to Dr. Littlejohn as Medical Officer of Health (Edinburgh Ph.D., 1971).

McFarlan, D. M., Religious Teaching in Nineteenth Century Scotland (Glasgow Ph.D., 1951).

Paterson, A., A Study of Poor Relief Administration in Edinburgh City Parish between 1845 and 1894 (Edinburgh Ph.D., 1974).

Paton, D. C., Drink and the Temperance Movement in the Nineteenth Century (Edinburgh Ph.D., 1976).

Pennington, C., Mortality, Public Health and Medical Improvements in Glasgow 1855-1911 (Stirling Ph.D., 1977).
Smith, D. C., The Failure and Recovery of Social Criticism in the Scottish Church 1830-1950 (Edinburgh Ph.D., 1963).
Tyler, W. E., The Development of Scottish Public Libraries (Strathclyde M.A., 1967).
Watson, T. J., The History of Deaf Education in Scotland from 1760 to 1939 (Edinburgh Ph.D., 1949).
Wilson, N., The Sociology of a Profession: the Faculty of Advocates (Edinburgh Ph.D., 1965).

Index

Notes: Collected entries: INSTITUTIONS, SOCIETIES, STATUTES
'p.' means *passim*; 'n' means note

Abel Smith, Brian, *quoted*, 222 & n
Aberchirder, 212, 213
Abercrombie, Dr John, 81
Aberdeen, 7, 8, 13, 127, 285, 311, 313, 365,
    see also under INSTITUTIONS *and*
    SOCIETIES
    charity hospitals, 108, 109
    children, 182, 246-7, 251, 266, 267, 269-70,
        273
    convalescent homes, 214
    Dick Bequest, 105-7, 116
    dispensaries, 200, 202
    higher education, 119, 122, 124-8 p.
    hospitals, 153-4 p.
    housing, 285
    industrial schools, 60
    lunatic asylums, 168-9 p.
    medical mission, 82
    Milne Bequest, 107-8, 116
    orphanages, 16 p., 17, 60, *see also* children
    prostitution, 243
    recreation, 141-2, 145, 146
    savings, 134 p.
    specialist hospitals, 182-4 p., 187, 189, 190,
        192
Acton, Dr William, 234, 243
Acts of Parliament, *see* STATUTES
Adam Brothers, 156
Adams, Dr A. M., 24 & n, 207 & n
Adams, Professor W. G. S., 143 & n
Adamson, Dr John, M.D., 209, 210
Addison, Dr W. H., 269
aged persons, charities for, *see under* IN-
    STITUTIONS *and* SOCIETIES
Agnew, Sir Andrew, 43-4
agricultural and industrial training homes,
    see under INSTITUTIONS
Agriculture, Scottish Board of, 60
Airdrie, 37
Aitken, Dr, 144
Albert, Prince Consort (d. 1861), 142, *quoted*
    145-6 & n
alcohol, *see* temperance movement
Alexander, Dr, 235-6 & n
Alexandria, 57
Alison, Dr W. P., M.D., 81, 202 & n, 314

Allan, Miss, 306
Alloa, 211, 221 p.
Alston, Captain, of *Cumberland*, 255 & n
Alston, John, 273, *quoted* 274
America, 51
Anderson, Duncan (1832-80), 268, 269 p.,
    271-2
Anderson, John, 268
Anderson, Rev. John, D.D. (d. 1796), 51-2,
    122
Anderson, Rev. Peter, 69
Anderson Robertson, Dr John, 84
Anderston, 204, 302, 306 p., 307
Anne, Queen, 73, 138, 155-6
Annual Charities Register & Digest (C.O.S.),
    299
Annual City Hall Lectures in Glasgow, 51, 53
Annuity Tax, in Edinburgh (1809-70), 36 & n
Anstruther, Fife, 211
anti-Semitism, 43
Apocrypha controversy (1820s), 40-1
Arbroath, 251, 267
Arethusa (ship), 254
Argyll, Duchess of, 216, 227
Argyll, Duke of, 56, 216, 312
Armitage Bridge, 57
Arrol, Sir William, 263
art galleries, 6, 132, 143-6, 148; *see also under*
    INSTITUTIONS
Assimilating Bill (1876), 96
Associations; *see under* SOCIETIES
Astwick, Bedfordshire, 137-8
asylums, *see under* INSTITUTIONS
Asylums, District or Parochial (Table 23),
    175
Ayr, 19, 37, 57, 59, 119, 175, 251

Baikie, William, 138 & n
Baillie, George (d. 1973), 140-1 & nn
Baillie, Lady Grisell, 86, 88
Baillie's Trust, 140-1 & n
Ballingall, Sir George, 195
Balmanno, Dr John, 173
Banff, 14 & n, 105, 116, 175, 200, 267
'bank ladies', 307 & n

banks; *see under* INSTITUTIONS: *Savings*
Baptists, 47
Barland, James, 268
Barnardo, Dr, 263
Barnett, Rev. Samuel A., 9, 303-4
Barony Church, Glasgow, 47
Barr, Miss Agnes, 187
Battie, Dr William, M.D., 167
Baxter, Sir David, 124, 147
Baxter, Dr John Boyd, 130 & n
Baxter, Miss Mary Ann, 130 & n
Bearsden, 217
Beattie, Dr, 92 & n
Bedlam; *see under* INSTITUTIONS
Begg, Dr James (1808-83), *quoted* 291 & n,
    292
Beith, Ayrshire, 57
Bell, Joseph, *quoted* 219 & n, *quoted* 220 & n
Bell Bequest, 116
Belleville, Ontario, 263
Belmont Castle, Meigle (1931), 60
Belvidere, Glasgow, 153, 169
benevolent societies, 21-6 & nn, 68; *see also
    under* SOCIETIES
Bentham, Jeremy, 170
Berlin, 189, 197, 315
Beveridge Report, 336, 338-9 & n
Beza, Theodore (1519-1605), 43
Bible and Tract Societies, 22, 30, 32, 39-41,
    61, 90, 320; *see also under* SOCIETIES
bible classes, 51, 70
bible women, 32, 38, 77, 78 p., 79, 83, 85,
    320; *see also* Deaconesses
bible women nurses, 80, 82, 85 p., 87, 320;
    see also Deaconess nurses
Bill, Franklin (1859-81), 269
bills, *see under* STATUTES
Binford, Miss, 210
Binnie, Thomas, 37 & n
Bird, Robert, 191
Birkbeck, Dr George, 122
Birmingham, 258
Blackie, Miss Marion Brodie, 302-3
blind asylums, 273-5; *see also under*
    INSTITUTIONS: *homes for disabled
    children*
Board Schools (after 1872), 18, 26; *see also*
    SCHOOL BOARDS
boarding schools (Charity Hospitals); *see
    under* INSTITUTIONS: *Charity Hospitals*
Borstal lads, 60
Boswell, James, 74
bowling greens, 98
Boyd, Rev. William, *quoted* 78 & n
boys' clubs; *see under* SOCIETIES, *clubs for
    boys and girls*
Bradford, 295
Braidwood, John 267

Braidwood, Thomas (1715-1806), 266, 267 p.
Braille, Louis (1809-52), 274
Brebner, William, 249
bridewell, 236 p., 249, 313
Bridge of Allan, 60
Bridge of Weir, 254, 259, 260-1, 263, 264
Bridgeton, 302
'British Workman', Dundee (teetotal public
    house), 98
Brodie, Dr and Mrs, 275-6
Broomielaw, 44, 72 p., 98
Browne, Dr W. A. F. (1805-85), 173 & n
Bruickman, Rev. Arthur, 239
Bryce, J. D., 234 & n, *quoted* 237 & n, *quoted*
    241, 249
Buccleuch, Duke of, 138, 267
Buchanan, Dr Andrew, *quoted* 194
Buckingham, James Silk, 94
building societies, 292-3; *see also under*
    SOCIETIES: *workmen's dwellings*
Burdett, Henry C., 200, 201, 212-3, 215
Burgess, Joseph, 295 p. & n
Burgesses, 15 & n, 18
Burgh and Middle Class Schools, 112, 117;
    see also under INSTITUTIONS
Burn, William, 170, 171-2
Burnet, Sir John, 192
Burns, George, 44
Burns, John, of Castle Wemyss, 8, *quoted* 56
    & n
Burns, Dr John, 47 & n
Burns Line ships, 44
Burns, Mrs, 69
Burns Thomson, Dr William (1821-93), 81-2
    & nn, 85 p., 89, 217, 218
Burrell, Sir William, 145
Bute, Marquis of, 129
Butler, Josephine, 259-60

Cadell, Francis, 195 & n, 242 & n
Caird, J. K., 187 & n, *quoted* 304-5
Caithness, Earl of, 137
Calton, Glasgow, 47, 285
Calvin, John (1509-64), 31, 43
Calvinism, 31 p. & n, 66
Cambridge, 304
Cameron Corbett, A., 96
Campbell, James, of Tulliechewan, 8
Campbell, Lady, of Blythswood, 191
Campbell, Louis E., 140
Campbell, Sheriff Substitute, of Paisley,
    quoted 94 & n
Campbell, Dr William, 189 & n
Canada, 60, 259
    Distributing Homes for orphans in, 263-4
cancer, 183, 197-8, 325; *see also under* IN-
    STITUTIONS: *Specialist Hospitals*

Candleriggs, 60
Candlish, Robert, 32
Canongate, Edinburgh, 154, 175, 235
Carey, William (1761-1834), 66
Cargill, Baillie John, 169
Carlyle, Thomas, *quoted* 129
Carnegie, Andrew (1835-1919), 130, 137, 142-3 & nn, 314
Carnegie, Susan, 5, 168, *quoted* 169 p. & n, *quoted* 172 & n
Carnegie United Kingdom Trust (1913), 143
Carruthers, Bishop, Roman Catholic Bishop of Edinburgh, 248
Castle Douglas, Galloway, 212
Cathkin Braes, Glasgow, 146
Catholic Church, 73, 262, 321
catholic nurses, 161, 222
Census (1861), 281
Cessnock, Govan, 260
Chadwick's Sanitary Report (1842), 153, 234, 298
Chalmers, Rev. Dr Thomas (1780-1847), Moderator of the Free Church of Scotland, 3, 13, 32-7 p. & nn, 47 & n, 49, 81, 158, 299, 300, 315 p., 321, 332, 337
chaplains, sea-going, 44
Charity: considered, 1-9, 26; *see* Philanthropists *and* philanthropy; *see also under* INSTITUTIONS *and* SOCIETIES
    church, for members only, 1
    financing, 7-9
    in kind, 23
    motivation of, 4-6, 7
    municipal and state, *see* State and Municipal
    nature of, 1-3
    organising principle of, 4
    phasing, 3-4, 23
    range of 5, 6, 7
Charity Hospitals (boarding schools); *see under* INSTITUTIONS
Charity Organisation Society, 1, 3, 86 & n, 298-301, 315-6, 330, 335, 337; *see also under* SOCIETIES
Charles I, King, 36
Charteris, Rev. Professor A. H. (1835-1908), 59, 85 & n, 86 p., *quoted* 88 & n
Charteris Hospital, Kalimpong (1893), 86
children: *see also under* INSTITUTIONS *and* SOCIETIES
    blind, deaf and dumb, homes for, 6, 266-75
    day refuges for (1875), 301
    Fresh-air Fortnight for (1888), 71, 218, 301
    hospitals, 188-191
    Sabbath Dinner (1874), 301
choirs, Glasgow, 99
Christianity, 4, 36 & n
Christie, Provost Alexander, 169 & nn

Church of England, 66
Church Extension Movement (1830), 30, 32-9 & nn, 61, 90, 93
Church Extension Programme in Scotland (1835-9) (Table 4), 35
Church of Scotland, 12, 21, 30-3 p., 35, 37 p., 44-7, 50, 58, 60-2, 66, 74, 312
    Association for Promoting the Interests of, 53
    attempt to regain welfare initiative, 59-61
    clergy, pay of, 36
    Commissioners, 34-6
    Deaconesses, 84-8
    General Assembly of, 32, 50 & n, 59, 86, 321
    Life and Work Committee, 60, 86
    Schools, 104 & n, 321
    Social Work Committee (1804), 59, 60 p.
    'the poor man's church' (Collins), 34
City of Glasgow Bank failure (1878), 5, 53
City Improvement Trust, 260
City Missions, 66-71; *see also under* SOCIETIES: *religious*
Cleghorn, Dr Robert, 173
Cleland, James, *quoted* 67 & n, *quoted* 68 & n, 236
clergy, pay of, 36
'clergy and churchmen', 30 & n
Clinical Study and Treatment of Sick Children, The (1898) (Dr John Thomson), 190
Clough, Mary Ann, 55
Clouston, Thomas Smith (1840-1915), 173
clubs for boys and girls, 62; *see also under* SOCIETIES
Clugston, Miss Beatrice, 5, 70, 216 p. & nn, 276, 313
Coats, Thomas, 147 & n
Cockburn, Henry, *quoted* 203 & n
cocoa and coffee houses, 98
Coldstream, Berwick, 212
Coldstream, Dr John, 81
Colebrook, Thomas Edward, 117
College of Science and Arts, Glasgow: Students and their courses 1881 (Table 16), 123
Collins, Elizabeth, *quoted* 33 & n
Collins, William I (1789-1853), 33-5 p. & nn, 92 p. & nn, 93, 94 & n
colporteurs, 32, 41, 78 p. & nn, 79, 320; *see also under* SOCIETIES
Commissions: *see under* Royal Commissions
Community Councils, 335
Conan Doyle, Sir Arthur, 219
Confession of Faith, 74
Congregational Church, 47
Connal, Dr J. G., 84
consumption, 183, 197-8, 325; *see also under*

INSTITUTIONS: *Specialist Hospitals*
convalescent homes, 5, 6, 70, 214-18; *see also under* INSTITUTIONS
Corbett, A. Cameron, 96
C.O.S. Annual Charities Register and Digest, 299
cottage homes, 328; *see also under* INSTITU-TIONS
cottage hospitals, 6, 209-13, 325, 326, 336; *see also under* INSTITUTIONS
Cottage Hospitals 1880 (Table 32), 212-3
Coutts, F. and Sons, 216
Cowan, Dr, *quoted* 285 & n
Cowcaddens, 301, 302
Cox brothers, 147
Craik, Sir Henry, 120, 122, 275, 322
Crichton, Mrs Elizabeth Grierson, 168, 171-2 & nn, 173
Crichton, James, 171 & n
Crieff, Perthshire, 138
Crimean War (1854-56), 54, 85, 219, 222, 254
Crown Endowment of Universities, 126-8
Cullen, Dr William, 156 & n
Cumming, Dr Elder, 37
Cumnock, 212
Cunningham, Andrew, 129
Cupar, Fife, 175, 211, 212

Dale, David (d. 1806), 40 & n, 192
Dalgarno, George, 266 & n, 270
Dalry, 235
Darvel, 37
Darwin, Charles (1809-82), 52
Davidson, J. H., M.D., 202
Day Schools
Deaconess nurses, 84-8 p.
Deaconesses, 84-8 & nn, 320
deaf, residential homes for the, 266-73; *see also under* INSTITUTIONS
Dean (a place near Edinburgh), 17
Denny, Stirlingshire, 212
dental hospitals, 196-7; *see also under* IN-STITUTIONS: *Specialist Hospitals*
Dewar, Dr, 193
Dewar, Mr, *quoted* 283
Dick Bequest (1833), 105-8 & nn, 116, 322
Dick, James (1743-1828), 105, 146
Dingwall, 211-2
Discipline, First Book of (1560), 14
dispensaries, 6, 200-8, 323, 325-6; *see also under* INSTITUTIONS
  general, 202-5
  Infirmary, 205-6
  medical mission, 206
  provident, 206-7
  specialist hospital, 206
  study and teaching, 200

Dispensaries, Scottish, in 1899 (Table 28), 200
Disruption, The (1843), 37 p., 44, 74, 90, 104, 247
Dissenters, Scottish, Central Board of, 35-6 p.
Distributing Homes in Canada for orphans, 263-5
District Asylums, 175-6 (Table 23), 178
District Social Meetings, 38
Dixon, Edward Maxwell (1829-89), 122-3 p. & n
Donald Collection, 145 & n
Donaldson, James, 110, 268-9
Donaldson's Trust, 268, 269
Douglas of Grangemuir and Dunino, Lady, 210
Douglas, Samuel, 18
Douglasdale, 227
Dowie, Lance-Corporal Alex, 57 & n
Drummond, David (Lord Madertie), 138
Drummond, Professor Henry (1851-97), 5, 58-9, 305
drunkenness, *see* temperance movement
Drysdale, Miss Grace, 309
Drysdale, Mr (d. 1880), 268 & n
Duddingston, 114, 175, 218
Dufftown, Banffshire, 213
Duke Street Prison, Glasgow, 295
Dumbarton, 19, 200, 213
Dumfries, 13, 18, 19, 119, 153, 154, 168 p., 171 p., 173 p., 175, 251
Dunbar, 137
Duncan, Andrew, M.D. (1744-1828), 167 & n, 169, 172, 173, 195
Duncan, Rev. Henry (1744-1846), 133 p. & n, 135 & n, 137
Duncan, James Matthews, 185
Dundee, 7, 13, 311, 313, 323, 366; *see also under* INSTITUTIONS and SOCIETIES
  boys' brigades, 57
  'British Workman' (teetotal public house), 98
  building societies, 292-3
  cabmen's shelter, 69
  children, 267, 268, 270 p., 273, 275
  church extension, 37
  higher education, 119, 120, 122, 124-5
  hospitals, 153, 154
  housing, 59-60 p.
  lunatic asylums, 168, 169 p., 175
  mission work, 302
  night refuge, 283-4
  orphanages, 16
  prostitution, 242
  recreation, 142, 145
  sailors' home, 72
  specialist hospitals, 182, 183, 184, 188 & n

training ship, 254
Dunfermline, 142, 143, 213
Dunkeld, 154, 267
Dunlop, John, 92 p. & nn, 93, 94 & nn
Dunoon, 69, 70, 214, 215, 216 p., 349-56; *see also under* INSTITUTIONS
Dyer, Henry (1848-1918), 122 & n

Ear hospitals: *see under* INSTITUTIONS
East (and West) Lothian, 40
Ecclesiastical Polity (Hooker), 106
Edinburgh; *see also under* INSTITUTIONS, SOCIETIES *and* STATUTES
   benevolent societies, 22 p., 24, 299 p., 301, 302
   Bible and Tract Societies, 22-3, 40 p., 41 p.
   boys' brigade, 57
   building societies, 292, 294
   charity, 1, 7, 8, 13 p., 15, 311, 312
   charity hospitals, 18, 19, 108, 109-114, 116
   children, disabled, 266-70 p., 273-6 p.
   church extension, 34, 37-9 p.
   convalescent homes, 214 p., 215, 217-8
   day schools, 322, 323
   dispensaries, 201-4 p., 325
   general hospitals, 21, 153, 154, 156, 159, 163, 176, 183, 220, 223, 323
   higher education, 119, 121-2, 124, 126-8 p., 322
   housing, 60, 308-9
   lunatic asylums, 166-7 & n, 168, 169, 172-5 p., 178, 323, 325, 326
   missions, 66, 67 & n, 73, 74, 80-2, 206
   night asylums, 281, 282, 283, 285, 291
   nursing training, 220-3 p., 226, 227
   orphanages, 16-18 p; *see also* charity hospitals
   prostitution, 233-40 p., 242 p.
   ragged children, 246, 247, 248-9, 251, 253 p. & n, 254, 260, 272
   recreation, 137, 142, 144, 145-6
   savings banks, 133-4 p.
   specialist hospitals, 179, 183-5 p., 188, 189-90, 192, 194, 195, 197, 323
   temperance, 94
   Universities, 126, 127, 128, 308-9, 323
Edinburgh Medical Journal, 189
Edinburgh Philanthropic Year Book (1900), 299
Education, 14-16, 18, 104-30, 321-3, *see also* Acts of Parliament *and* Royal Commissions; *see also under* INSTITUTIONS, Knox, *and* SOCIETIES:
   Board Schools, 18, 26, 104
   charity hospitals, 16-18, 26, 108-12, 113-8 p
   children, disabled, 6, 266-76

   day schools, 116-8
   endowments, 15-16 & nn, 18-20, 25-7 p., 105-18 p & nn, 322
   ragged schools, 7, 109 & n, 245-56, 264, 312, 313, 328
   recreation, 6, 132-48
   secondary schools, 118-20, 322-3
   Sunday schools, 46-8, 49-50, 62
   technical schools, 121-6
   Universities, 126-30, 323
Education Board of Scotland, 275
Education Department of Scotland, 120, 125
Education, General Endowments available in Scotland in 1875 (Table 15), 116
Elberfeld, 299 & n
Elder, Isabella, 147 & nn
Elder, John, 129, 147
Elgin, 25, 114, 119, 154, 168, 169, 170, 174, 175, 267
Elie, Fife, 217
Ellon, 37
employment bureaux for women (1929), 60
Emslie, Mrs Mary, 17-18 & nn
Endowed Hospitals in Edinburgh by 1872 (Table 13), 113
Endowed Hospitals in Scotland in 1872 excluding Edinburgh (Table 14), 114
Engels, 232
Epée, Abbe de L' (1712-89), 270
epilepsy, 262, 263
Episcopalian Church, 47
Erskine, Sir James (d. 1845), 144
Esquirol, J. E. D. (1772-1840), 172
Established Church of Scotland, 51; *see also* Church of Scotland
Etty, William, 144
Euing, William (d. 1874), 72, 144
Evangelical Movement, 4, 5-6, 30-3, 39, 41, 46
   prostitution and, 233, 240
Eventide Homes, 60; *see also under* INSTITUTIONS: *aged and homeless, homes for*
Ewing, Greville, 67
eye hospitals: *see under* INSTITUTIONS: *Specialist Hospitals*

Fabian Society (1884), 4, 301 & n
Falkirk, 213
farming for destitute men, 50
Ferguson, Alexander, 302
Ferguson, Alexander and Company, 302
Ferguson's Bequest, 19
Fergusson, Robert (poet) (d. 1774), 166-7
Fettes College, Edinburgh (1864), 18, 108, 113
fever hospitals, 69, 153, 159; *see also under* INSTITUTIONS: *General Hospitals*

Finch, John, 92
Findlay, Alex, 96
Finlay, Kirkman, Lord Provost of Glasgow, 267
First Book of Discipline (1560), 14, 15
First World War, 295, 306, 330
Fleming, J. G., M.D., 20-1
Fliedner, Fredericke, 219
Fliedner, Theodor, 219
Forbes, George, 268
Forbes, John, 133, 169
Forbes, Sir William, 133
Forfar, 187
Forgue, Aberdeenshire, 211, 212, 213
Forres, 25, 213, 267
Forth and Clyde Canal, 55, 237
Fountainbridge, Edinburgh, 188
France, 51, 54, 270
France, Emperor of, 54
Free Church of Scotland (1843), 37, 41, 43, 47 p., 51, 90, 312, 321
   first Moderator of (Chalmers), 56
   manse fund, 37
   Sustentation Fund, 37
   Tron Church, 47
   Working classes, Committee on Housing for (1861), 281 & n
Free College Church Mission Authority, 57
Fry, Elizabeth, 219 & n
Fyfe, Peter, 330
Fyvie, Aberdeenshire, 211, 212, 213

Gaelic, 73-7 p., 320; *see also* SOCIETIES: *Religious*
Gairdner, Andrew, 16
Galashiels, 213
Gall's Alphabet for the Blind, 274
Gallowgate, Glasgow, 285
Galt, Ontario, 263
Gareloch, 254
Garibaldi (1807-82), 193
Garscube, Glasgow, 305
Gartloch, 175
Gartnavel, 170
Gauldie, Enid, 295 & n, 330
Gee, W. M., 58
General Hospital provision in Edinburgh and Glasgow (1899) (Table 19), 159
George III (d. 1820), 166 & n
Germany, 192
Gibson, Joseph, 184
Gilbert, Graham (d. 1877), 144
Gilbert Scott, Sir George, 129
Gillespie, James; *see under* INSTITUTIONS
Gilmorehill, Glasgow, 305
girls,
   clubs for; *see under* SOCIETIES

delinquent, homes for (1908), 60; *see also under* INSTITUTIONS
orphanages for (1913), 60; *see also under* INSTITUTIONS
Girvan, 37
Gladstone, Mrs, of Liverpool, 75 & n
Gladstone, William E. (1809-98), 115, 121, 135-6, 237
Glaister, Professor, 295
Glasgow; *see also under* INSTITUTIONS *and* SOCIETIES
   aged, homes for, 19-21, 69, 70
   benevolent societies, 22, 23 p., 24-6
   Bible and Tract Societies, 40 p., 41
   boys' brigade, 54, 58-9, 320
   charity, 1, 3, 7, 8, 13 p., 299, 300, 301, 302, 311-6 p. & nn, 330
   charity hospitals, 16, 18, 108
   children disabled, 266-74 p. & nn, 276, 307-8, 325
   church extension, 33-4, 35 p., 37 & n
   church welfare, 60
   convalescent homes, 69, 70, 71, 214-8 p.
   dispensaries, 83, 201, 202, 204-6 p., 209, 323, 325, 330
   general hospitals, 23, 69, 129, 153, 154, 156-63 & nn, 183, 221, 312, 322, 323, 325, 326, 336
   Great Western Cooking Depot, 98
   higher education, 119, 121, 122-4, 125, 314, 322, 323
   housing, 280, 292, 293-4, 295 & nn, 302-7 p. & nn, 327, 329, 330
   lodging houses, 60 p., 285-8 & nn, 329
   lunatic asylums, 69, 168, 169, 172, 173, 174, 176, 312, 322, 323, 325, 336
   missions, 44 p., 45, 66-70 p. & nn, 72 p., 73 p., 76, 77, 81, 82 p., 83-4, 87, 206, 312
   night asylums, 281, 282, 284, 329, 330
   nursing training, 86, 87, 220-7 p. & nn, 326, 336
   orphanages, 8, 259-60 p. & nn, 264, 312, 328
   prostitution, 233-8 p. & nn, 241, 242 p.
   ragged children, 245, 249-54 p. & nn
   recreation, 139-41, 144-5 p. & nn, 146 p., 147
   Religious Institution Rooms, 41-3
   religious societies, 55-8
   savings banks, 134 p., 135, 136 p. & nn, 307
   specialist hospitals, 69, 152, 180, 181, 183-8, 190-7 p., 206, 222, 224, 323, 325-6, 328, 336
   Sunday schools, 47, 49
   temperance, 92 p. & nn, 93, 94-9 p. & nn
   Universities, 126, 127 p. & nn, 129-30, 186, 303-4, 320, 323

Settlement Movement, 303-9 & nn, 330
YMCA, 50-3, 320
Glasgow Central Dispensary, cases dealt with, 1893 (Table 30), 210
Glasgow Dental Hospital, Patients, 1886-88 (Table 27), 196
Glasgow Herald, 253, 260, 300 & n
Glasgow Magdalene Asylum, Admissions and Discharges, 1851-8 (Table 37), 241
Glasgow Magdalene Asylum, Ages of Girls admitted to, 1851-9 (Table 36), 237
Glasgow Medical Missionary Society, statement of income, 1872 (Table 8), 83
Glasgow Royal Infirmary, annual subscriptions, 1842-58 (Table 20), 162
Glasgow YMCA Annual City Hall Lecture Programme, 1861 (Table 7), 52
Glasier, Bruce, 295 & n
Glen, Allan (1778-1850), 122, 123
Gordon, Robert; *see under* INSTITUTIONS: *Charity Hospitals and Mechanics' Institutes*
Gothenburg System, 95 & n, 100
Govan, 60, 96, 147 & nn, 175, 195, 260 p.
Graham, Professor, *quoted*, 280 & n
Graham Gilbert Collection, 144
grammar and secondary schools, 14, 117, 118-20 & n, 322; *see also under* INSTITUTIONS: *Education*
Grant, Sir Alexander, 116-7 & n
Grantown, 114, 213
Gray, Rev. John, 138
Gray, Robert Q., *quoted* 294
'Great Social Evil'; *see* prostitution
Greenock, 18, 37, 40, 43, 71, 92, 109, 119, 153, 175, 182, 242, 259
Guggenbuhl, Dr, 275
Guilds of Play, 86 & n
Guthrie, Rev. Dr Thomas, 5, 32, 109 & n, 246, *quoted* 247-8 p., 253, 256 p.

Hackney, 267
Haddington, 119, 138, 175
Haddington, Earl of, 202
Haddo, 212, 213
Haddo, Earl and Countess of, 213
Hamilton, Dr Alexander, 184
Hamilton Bequest, 145 & n
Hamilton and Brandon, Duke of, 204
Hamilton, James, 184
Hamilton, Sir William, *quoted* 172 & n
Handyside, Dr Peter (1808-81), 81
Hanoverians, 73
Harris, David, 253
Harvey, Rev. Alex, *quoted* 35-6 & n
Hawick, 213
health, 323-6

health visitation of infants, 86 & n
Heinecke, 270
Henderson, T. B., 196
Henderson, Dr W., *quoted* 189 & n
Henry, Dr Robert, 138
Hepburn, Captain (Merchant Navy), 44
Heriot, George, 15, 18, 108 p., 117; *see also under* INSTITUTIONS: *Charity Hospitals*
Heriot's Day Schools, Edinburgh, 1859 (Table 11), 110
Heriot's Day Schools, Edinburgh: occupations of fathers, 1859 (Table 12), 111
Higginbotham, Mrs Mary Orrell, 225
Higgs, Mary, *quoted* 287 & n
Higher Class Public Schools, 115 p., 116-20 p. & nn, 322; *see also under* INSTITUTIONS: *Education*
Highlands and Islands of Scotland, 25-6; *see also under* SOCIETIES
  drift to the cities from, 281, 285
  libraries, 138
  mission work in, 73-7, 78
Hill, Lieutenant James R., 57
Hill, Lieutenant John B., 57
Hill, Miranda, 302 & n
Hill, Octavia, 291, 302 & n, 329
Hillhead, Dumfries, 171, 175
History of Temperance (Edward Morris), 91
Holmes, Sherlock, 219
Holyrood Park, Edinburgh, military parade (7 August 1890), 55 & n
Home Bell, Professor Oswald, M.D., 210
Home, Countess of, 227
Home Department, Scottish, 60
Home Medical Missions, 81 & nn, 320; *see also under* SOCIETIES
Hope, William, 170
Hopetoun, Earl of, 204
Horne, *quoted*, 128 & n, 136
Horner, Leonard, 124
hospitals; *see under* INSTITUTIONS
Houses of ill-fame in Glasgow, visits to, 1842 (Table 35), 234
housing; *see also under* INSTITUTIONS and SOCIETIES
  aged and homeless, 19-21, 59, 60, 69-72 p., 154, 342-4, 345
  children, 26, 108-10, 246-52, 254-6, 258-65, 266-76 p., 328, 352-60
  lunatics, 165-72 p., 174-6, 346-8
  permanent, 280, 329-30
  temporary, 280-8, 329-30
housing for the working classes of the Free Church of Scotland, 281 & n
Howard, John, 167 & n
Hunter, Ian, 55 & n
Hunter, William, 55 & n
Huntly, Aberdeenshire, 213

Hutcheson, George and Thomas, 19-20 p. &
nn, 122, 140 & n
Hutcheson's Trust, 19-20, 122, 140 & n
Hutton Bequest, 19

Industrial brigades, 253-4
infirmaries (general hospitals); *see under* IN-
STITUTIONS
Innerpeffray, Perthshire, 138
INSTITUTIONS, 365-9; *see also* SOCIETIES
*Aged and homeless, homes for; see also
Night Asylums, and Seamen*
Balmanno House, Glasgow (formerly
Old Woman's Home, Dean Street), 21
Broomhill Homes, Kirkintilloch, 69, 70
Eventide Homes, 60
Hutcheson's Hospital, Glasgow, 19, 20
& n
Old Man's Asylum, Glasgow, 69
Old Man's Friend Asylum, Rottenrow,
Glasgow (c. 1837-40), 20, 21 p.
Old Woman's Home, Dean Street,
Glasgow (1877), 21
Powfoulis Home for Aged Persons,
Belmont Castle, Meigle (1926), 60
*Agricultural and Industrial Training
Homes; see also Ragged Schools*
Cornton Vale Farm, Bridge of Allan
(1907), 60
Humble Agricultural Labour Home for
Boys (1865), 60
Labour homes at Ayr, Dundee,
Edinburgh, Paisley, Peebles, Perth,
59, 60
Maberley Street Home, Aberdeen
(1905), 60
Art Galleries, 6, 132, 143-6, 148
Aberdeen Art Gallery (1885), 145
Dundee City Museum and Art Gallery
(1872), 145
Glasgow Art Gallery (1902), 144-5 p. &
nn
McLellan Galleries, Glasgow, 144
National Gallery of Scotland (1859),
144, 145-6
Royal Institution (1819), 144 & n
Royal Scottish Academy (1826), 144 & n
Charity Hospitals (Boarding Schools), 18,
108-13, 116; *see also Orphanages*
Aberdeen Female Orphan Asylum (1840-
91) (*later* Girls' High School), 17-18 &
nn, 114
Aberdeen Hospital for Boys (1818), 16
Aberdeen Hospital for Boys and Girls
(1739), 114
Aberdeen Hospital for Girls (1828), 16
Brooklands Hospital, Kirkpatrick-
Durham, 114

Christ's Hospital, London, 108
Educational Institute for Young Ladies,
Melville House, Edinburgh, 112
Elgin Institution (1815), 114
George Heriot's Hospital, Edinburgh
(1624), 18, 108 p., 109, 111 & nn, 112,
113, 116, 117, 239, 322
George Stiell's Hospital, Tranent (1822),
114, 117
Glasgow Institution for Orphan and
Destitute Girls (1825), 18 & n
Hutcheson's Hospital, Glasgow, 108
James Schaw's Hospital, Prestonpans
(1789), 114, 117
Louis Cauvin's Hospital, Duddingston
(1833), 114, 117
Merchant Company Schools,
Edinburgh:
Daniel Stewart's Hospital (1814), 108,
111-113 p., 117
George Watson's Hospital (1738), 108,
111-113 p., 117
James Donaldson's Hospital (1850),
18, 108-110 p., 113, 117, 268, 269,
270
James Gillespie's Hospital, 108, 111,
112 p.
John Watson's Hospital (1759), 18,
108, 113, 117
Orphan Hospital (1727), 16-17 p. &
nn, 108, 113, 117, 238
Trades Maiden Hospital (1704), 108,
113, 117, 190
Merchant Maiden's Hospital, Edinburgh
(1695), 108, 111 & n, 112, 113, 117
Morgan's Hospital, Dundee (1861), 114
Morham Institute for Boys (1913), 60
Muirhead's Hospital, Dumfries (1753),
18, 114
Orphan and Destitute Female Children's
Hospital, Aberdeen (1849)
Robert Gordon's Hospital, Aberdeen
(1732) (*later* Robert Gordon's College
(1881), *now* Robert Gordon's Institute
of Technology), 108, 109 & n, 114,
124
Royal Orphan Institution, Dundee
(1815), 16, 114
Samuel Douglas Free School, Newton
Stewart (1789), 18, 114
Scott Institution, Greenock (1838), 18,
108-9, 114
Shaw's Hospital, Aberdeen (1807), 114
Speyside Charity School (1795), 114
Spier's Hospital, Ayrshire, 114
Wood's School, Newburn by Largo
(1659), 18
Convalescent Homes, 5, 6, 70, 214-8

Aberdeen Convalescent Hospital, Cults (1897), 214
Arbroath Convalescent Home, Jennyswell (1891), 214
Busby Convalescent Home, 214
Convalescent Home of the Northern Infirmary, Lochend, Inverness, 215
Corstorphine Convalescent Home, Edinburgh (1867), 214, 216
Dundee Convalescent Home, Barnhill, 69, 215
Dundonald Convalescent Home, Kilmarnock, 215
Edzell Convalescent Home, 215
Eidda Convalescent Home, Culter, Aberdeen, 214
·Gilmerton Children's Convalescent Home, Edinburgh (1881), 215
Gilmerton Ravenscroft Convalescent Home, Edinburgh (1878), 215
Glasgow Convalescent Home, Lenzie (1865), 214, 215, 216 & n
Hawthornbrae Convalescent Home, Duddingston (1897), 214, 218
Kilmun Sea-Side Convalescent Home for the Poor (1867), 99, 215, 217 & n
Lady Hozier Convalescent Home, Lanark (linked to Glasgow Western Infirmary) (1891), 214, 215, 217
Northern Counties Convalescent Homes, Tradespark, Nairn (1882), 215
Ochiltree Convalescent Home, Ayrshire (1881), 215
Paisley Convalescent Home, West Kilbride (1886), 215
Ravenscraig Children's Convalescent Home, Eaglesham (1890), 215
Saltcoats Mission Coast Home (1866), 71, 214, 215, 216-7, 218, 351
Schaw Convalescent Home, Bearsden (linked to Glasgow Royal Infirmary), 215
Victoria Infirmary of Glasgow Convalescent Home, Brooksby, Largs (1897), 214, 215
West of Scotland Convalescent Seaside Homes, Dunoon (1869), 69, 214, 215, 216 p., 349-50
Cottage Hospitals, 6, 209-13, 325, 326, 336
Alloa, Clackmannanshire (1868), 211
Castle Douglas, Galloway, 212
Coldstream (and Dispensary), Berwick (1888), 212
Cranleigh, Surrey (1859), 209
Crimond, Aberdeen (1866), 211
Cumnock (1883), 212
Cupar, Fife, 212
Denny, Stirling, 212

Dumbarton (1890), 213
Dunfermline (1894), 213
Falkirk (1887), 213
Fleming, Aberlour, Banffshire (1895), 212
Forgue, Aberdeenshire (1875), 211, 212, 213
Forres, Moray (1892), 213
Fyvie, Aberdeenshire (1880), 211, 212
Galashiels (1893), 213
Garrick, Stranraer, Wigtownshire (1892), 213
Grantown (Ian Charles) (1884), 213
Haddo House, Tarves, Aberdeenshire (1883), 212, 213
Hawick (and Dispensary) (1884), 212, 213
Johnstone, Renfrewshire (1893), 212, 213
Jubilee, Huntly, Aberdeenshire (1889), 213
Kirkcaldy (1890), 213
Kirkcudbright (1897), 213
Lewis, Stornoway (1896), 213
Mackinnon, Skye, 213
Moffat, Dumfriesshire, 213
Mull (1892), 213
Rose Innes, Aberchirder, Banffshire (1892), 212
Ross Memorial, Dingwall (1873), 211, 212
St Andrews Memorial, Fife (1865), 209, 210-11 & n, 213
Sister Margaret, Jedburgh (1896), 213
Stephen, The, Dufftown, Banffshire (1888), 213
Thomas Hope, Langholm, Dumfriesshire (1896), 213
Turner Memorial, Keith, Banffshire (1880), 212, 213
Victoria, Rothesay, Bute (1894), 213
West Highland, Oban (1896), 213
Dispensaries, 200-8, 323, 325-6, 336
Aberdeen Royal Infirmary Dispensary (1781-1948), 205-6 & nn
Aberdeen Vaccine and Lying-in Dispensary (1823), 200
Banff Dispensary (1842), 200
Dumbarton Eye Dispensary, 200
Dundee Eye Dispensary (1836), 200
Edinburgh:
Cowgate Dispensary (1858), 81-2 p., 85
Dispensary for Women and Children, 201
Eye Dispensary (1822), 201
Fountainbridge Dispensary (1830), 204, 366
Fountainbridge Street Dispensary

(1830), 204
Homeopathic Dispensary for Women and Children, 201
Hospital and Dispensary (1878), 201
Lying-in Institution, 201
Medical Missionary Society's Dispensary (1884, rebuilt 1877), *later* Livingstone Memorial Mission's Training Institution, 82 & n, 201, 206
New Town Dispensary (1815), 201, 202 p. & n, 203 p. & n, 204
Overseas Medical Mission Dispensary, Malcolm Kerr House, 82
Port Hopetoun Public Dispensary, 204
Provident Dispensary (1878), 204
Richmond Street Dispensary (c. 1875), 204
Rose Street Dispensary (c. 1875), 204
Royal Public Dispensary and Vaccine Institution (1776), 201, 202 p. & n, 203 & n, 204
Skin Diseases Dispensary (1890), 201
Women's Dispensary (1887), 201
Women's Dispensary in Chalmers Institute (1870), 201
Forbes Dispensary, Inverness (1832), 201
Glasgow:
Anderston Medical Mission Dispensary, 206
Bellahouston Dispensary (1892), 201
Central Dispensary (1889), 201, 205
Cowcaddens Medical Mission Dispensary, 206
Grove Street Mission Dispensary, 70 & n, 84, 206
Missionary Society Dispensaries:
Nelson Street (c. 1868), 83, 206
North Street (1875), 206
South Coburg Street (1875), 206
Public Dispensary (1874), 201
Royal Infirmary Dispensary, 206
Skin Diseases Dispensary (1861), 201
Tradeston Dispensary (1892-98), 187-8
Western Public Dispensary, Anderston (1853), 204 & n, 366
Jedburgh Dispensary (1807), 201
Kelso Dispensary (1777), 201, 202
Montrose Infirmary Dispensary, 205 & n
Education, 104-30; *see also under* STATUTES
Day Schools, 116-8; *see also Charity Hospitals*
Grammar and Secondary Schools, 118-20;
Aberdeen New Grammar School, 119
Ayr Academy, 119

Dumfries Academy, 119
Dundee High School, 119, 120, 125 p. & n
Edinburgh High School, 119
Elgin High School, 119
Glasgow High School, 119, 123
Greenock Academy, 119
Haddington Burgh School, 119
Inverness Academy, 119
Madras College, St Andrews, 119
Montrose Academy, 119
Paisley Grammar School & Academy, 119
Perth Academy, 119
Stirling High School, 119
Mechanics' Institutes and Technical Schools, 121-6
Allan Glen's Institution, Glasgow (1853), 122-4 & nn
Anderson's College, Glasgow, 122, 124
Atkinson Institution, Glasgow, 124
College of Science and Arts, Glasgow, 122, 123-4
Dundee Mechanics' Institute (1871), 124-5
Dundee Technical College and School of Art (1911), 125 p. & n
Edinburgh School of Arts (1821) (*later* Watt Institution and School of Art, *now* Heriot-Watt University), 125
Glasgow Mechanics' Institution (1823) (*later* College of Science and Arts, 1879), 122
Glasgow School of Art and Haldane Academy, 125
Glasgow and West of Scotland Technical College (*later* Royal Technical College, *now*, University of Strathclyde, 1962), 124 p., 125
Gray's School of Art, Aberdeen, 125
Robert Gordon's College, Aberdeen, 124, 125
Young Chair of Technical Chemistry, 124
Universities, 126-30; *see also* STATUTES
Aberdeen University (1494), 126, 127 & n, 128 p.
Anderson's University, Glasgow, 193
Cambridge University, 304
Dundee University (University College, Dundee (1881), united with St Andrews 1897, separated 1967), 130, 323
Edinburgh University (1582), 82, 106, 116, 126-9 & nn, 137, 144, 154 & n, 158, 173, 308-9, 323

Glasgow University (1451), 26, 122, 126-30 p. & nn, 140, 154 & n, 184, 185, 186, 192, 197, 304, 305, 306, 320, 323
Heriot-Watt University, Edinburgh, 125
Oxford University, 127, 138, 143, 303, 304
St Andrews University (1411), 126, 127 & n, 128 p., 130
Strathclyde University, Glasgow (*formerly* Royal Technical College), 124
University College, London, 157
General Hospitals and Infirmaries, 21, 152-63, 169, 178, 183, 206, 214, 322-6 p., 336; *see also* Lunatic Asylums
Aberdeen Poors' Hospital (1741), 13, 16, 134 & n, 154 p.
Aberdeen Royal Infirmary, 153, 154, 169, 183 & n, 187 & n, 193, 205-6
Allen's Hospital, Stirling, 19
Barony Parish Hospital, Springburn (1853), 159
Belvidere Hospital (1870), 69, 153, 159
Canongate Poor House, Edinburgh (1871), 153
Chalmers Hospital, Edinburgh (1864), 82, 85, 158 & n, 159, 366
City Hospital for Infectious Diseases, Edinburgh, 159
Colinton Mains Fever Hospital, Edinburgh (1903), 153
Cowane's Hospital, Stirling, 19
Deaconess Hospital, Edinburgh (1894) 60, 80, 88 & nn, 158, 159
Dumfries Hospital, 153, 154
Dundee Royal Infirmary, 153, 154, 169, 183 & n, 187, 223
Edinburgh Charity Workhouse (1742), 13, 154, 159, 166, 175
Edinburgh Fever Hospital, 159
Edinburgh Poor Law Hospital, 159
Edinburgh Royal Infirmary (1729), 21, 153, 154, 155 p. & nn, 157, 158, 159, 163, 165, 183 & n, 189, 190, 192, 195, 214, 216, 220, 222, 223 & n
Elgin Hospital, 154
Fever and General Hospital, Glasgow (1887), 159
Glasgow Poor Law Hospital, 159
Glasgow Royal Infirmary (1792), 23 & n, 129, 153, 155-8, 159, 160 p., 161-3, 165, 183 & n, 190, 193, 206, 220-22, 223-4, 367
Glasgow Town's Hospital (1733), 13, 154 p., 159, 169
Glasgow Victoria Hospital (1881), 159, 214, 368

Glasgow Western Infirmary (1874), 129, 156-7, 158, 159, 184, 186, 193, 214, 217, 368
Gray's Hospital, Elgin, 170 & n
Greenock Hospital, 153, 194
Greenock Infirmary, 195
Inverness Hospital, 153
Kennedy Street Fever Hospital, Glasgow (1865), 159
Leith Hospital, 153, 154
Magdalene Hospital, Edinburgh, 154
Montrose Infirmary, 153
Paisley Hospital, 153, 154
Perth Hospital, 153
Ruchill Fever Hospital, Glasgow (1900), 159
St George's Hospital, Dunkeld, 154
St Thomas's Hospital, London, 219-20 & n, 223
Spittal's Hospital, Stirling, 19
Trinity Hospital, Edinburgh (1461), 16
Homes for disabled children:
blind children, 273-5
Aberdeen Asylum for the Blind, 273
Dundee Asylum for the Blind, 273
Edinburgh Asylum for the Blind (1792), 273 & n, 274
Glasgow Asylum for the Blind (1828) (including the School for Industry for Adults and the School of General Instruction), 273-4 p., 366
deaf and dumb children, 266-273
Aberdeen School for Deaf and Dumb Children (1819), 269, 270, 366
Craigside House Academy for Deaf Children, Edinburgh (1760-83) (*later* at Dumbiedykes Road), 267, 268, 270
Donaldson's Hospital (from 1850), 268 & n, 269 p., 270, 272
Dundee Day School for the Deaf (1885), 271
Dundee School for the Deaf and Dumb, 271
Ealing College for the Deaf and Dumb (1886), 271
Glasgow Day School for the Deaf (1886), 271
Greenock Day School for the Deaf and Dumb (1883), 271
Hackney School for the Deaf and Dumb (1769), 267
School for Deaf and Dumb Children, Barony Glebe, Glasgow (1821), 268 p. & n, 269, 270, 271
School for Deaf and Dumb Children, Langside, Glasgow (1868), 269
mentally and physically disabled children, 275-6

Baldovan Institution, near Dundee (1855) (*now* Strathmartine Institution), 275 & n, 366, 368
Broomhill Home, Kirkintilloch (1875), 276
Colony of Mercy for Epileptics, Bridge of Weir (1903), 263
Eastpark Homes for Infirm Children, Glasgow (c. 1874), 276
Scottish National Institute, Larbert, Stirlingshire (1863), 275-6
Strathmartine Institution, *formerly* Baldovan Institution, 275
Libraries, 6, 132, 137-43 & nn, 148
Aberdeen Mechanics' Institute Library (1824), 141-2 p.
Airdrie Library (1853), 142
Albert Institute, Dundee (1869), 142
Baillie's Institution Library, Glasgow (1887), 140-1 p. & n
Bibliotheck of Kirkwall (Baikie Collection) (1684), 138 & n
Carnegie Libraries, 142-3 & nn
Edinburgh Mechanics' Institute Library (1825), 141, 142 & n
Elder Free Library, Govan, 147
Glasgow Central Lending Library (1912), 139 & n
Glasgow Public Library, 139
Haddington Burgh Library (1729), 138
Innerpeffray Library, Perthshire (1694), 138
Jeffrey Reference Library (c. 1902), 140
Kirkwall Free Library, 138
Leadhill Reading Society (The Miners' Library) (1741), 138 & nn
Linlithgow Burgh Library (1790), 138
Mitchell Library, Glasgow (1877), 125, 139-40 & nn
Orkney Library, 138
Stirling's Library, Glasgow (1804) (amalgamated with Glasgow Public Library 1871), 139 & n
Wanlockhead Library (1756), 138 & n
Lunatic Asylums (Mental Hospitals), 152, 165-76, 174-6, 178, 312, 322, 323, 325, 326, 336
Aberdeen Lunatic Asylum (1800), 168, 169, 174, 176, 325
Argyll and Bute District Lunatic Asylum, Lochgilphead (1893), 175
Ayr District Asylum (1869), 175
Baldovan Asylum for Imbecile Children, near Dundee (1853), 175, 366, 368
Banff District Asylum, Ladybridge, Woodpark (1864), 175
Bethlem Hospital, Moorfields (Bedlam) (1247), 167

Crichton Institution for Lunatics, Dumfries (1839) (*later* Crichton Royal Lunatic Asylum, 168 p., 169, 170-2, 173-6 p., 323, 325
Dundee Lunatic Asylum (1820), 168, 169, 174, 176, 366
Edinburgh City Bedlam (part of Charity Workhouse), 166
Edinburgh Idiot Asylum, 276
Edinburgh Royal Lunatic Asylum (1813), 165, 168, 169, 171, 173, 174, 175, 323, 325, 366
Elgin District Asylum (1832), 175
Elgin Pauper Lunatic Asylum (1835), 168, 169, 170, 174
Fife and Kinross Lunatic Asylum, Cupar (1866), 175
Gartloch Asylum and Hospital for the Insane, Glasgow (1896), 175
Glasgow District Asylum, Woodilee, Lenzie (1875), 175
Glasgow Lunatic Asylum (1814) (*later* Royal in 1824), 154, 165, 168, 169-70 p. & nn, 174, 176, 236, 323, 325, 346-8, 367, 368
Govan District Asylum, Hawkhead, Paisley (1895), 175
Govan Parochial Asylum, Merryflats, Govan (1875), 175
Greenock Parochial Asylum, Smithson (1879), 175
Haddington District Asylum (1866), 175
Inverness District Asylum (1864), 175
James Murray's Royal Asylum for Lunatics, Perth (1827), 168, 169, 170 & nn, 171, 174 p. & n, 176, 323, 325, 368
Lanark District Asylum, Hartwood, Shotts (1895), 175
Midlothian and Peebles District Asylum, Roslin Castle (1874), 175
Montrose Lunatic Asylum (1782), 168 p., 169 & n, 173, 174, 176, 325
Paisley Burgh Parochial Asylum, Riccartsbar, Paisley (1876), 175
Perth District Asylum, Murthly (1864), 174
Retreat, The, York (1792), 167 & n, 170
Roxburgh, Berwick and Selkirk District Asylum, Melrose (1872), 175
St Luke's Hospital, London (1751), 167
Scottish National Institution for the Education of Imbecile Children, Larbert, Stirlingshire (1862), 175
Southern Counties Asylum, Hillhead, Dumfries (1849), 175
Stirling District Asylum, Larbert (1869), 175

Mental Hospitals; see Lunatic Asylums
Model Lodging Houses:
 Bridgeton (c. 1903), 302
 Carrick Street, Glasgow (for women), 286
 Cathedral Court, Rottenrow (1815), 302
 Cowcaddens (c. 1903), 302
 George Court, Glasgow (1815), 302
 Greendyke Street, Glasgow (1855), 285-6
 McAlpine Street, Glasgow, 285
 Merchant Street, Edinburgh (1849), 285
 Mile End, Glasgow (1815), 302
 Mitchell Street, Glasgow (c. 1847), 285
 Rattray's Close, Cowgate, Edinburgh (1847), 285
 West College Street, Anderston (1815), 302
 West Port, Edinburgh (1844), 285
Night Asylums and Strangers' Friend, 7, 281-5, 288, 314, 329, 330; *see also* Aged and homeless, homes for
 Aberdeen Night Shelter (1840) (part of House of Industry and Refuge from 1836), 281, 282, 283-4 & n
 Curr Night Refuge, Dundee (1882), 281, 283-4 & n, 366, 368
 Edinburgh Night Asylum (1842), 281, 282 & n, 283, 368
 Edinburgh Night Asylum and Strangers' Friend Society (1871), 283 p.
 Glasgow Night Asylum, St Enoch's Wynd (1838), 200, 281, 282, 284 p., 330
 House of Industry for Women, Dundee (1842), 283
Nurses: Homes and Training Schools, 219-29, 336; *see also* SOCIETIES
 Alice Mary Corbett Memorial Nurses' Home, Edinburgh (1906), 222 & n; *see also* Glasgow Samaritan Hospital for Women
 Bethnal Green Hospital, London, 85-6
 Chalmers Hospital, Edinburgh (for Bible Women Nurses), 85, 366
 Deaconess Hospital, Edinburgh, 88
 Edinburgh Royal Infirmary New Nursing Department, 223
 Glasgow Maternity Hospital, Nurses' Training Department, 187, 224 & n
 Glasgow Sick Children's Hospital Nurses' Home, 224 & n
 Glasgow Training Home for Nurses (1873), 225 p. & n
 Grove Street Mission Medical and Surgical Department, 84, 87
 Lady Missionaries' Training Home, Glasgow, 80, 84, 87 p., 367

 Livingstone Memorial Medical Missionary Training Institution, Edinburgh, 82 & n, 206
 Maternity Nurses' Home, Dundee, 187 & n
 Medical Training Home for Lady Missionaries, Glasgow (*formerly* Missionary Nurses' Training Home, Dennistoun), 80, 86, 87
 Mildmay Mission for Deaconesses, 85-6 & n
 Missionary Nurses' Training Home, Dennistoun; *see* Medical Training Home for Lady Missionaries
 Nightingale Training School for Nurses, St Thomas's Hospital, London, 219-20 & n, 223
 Queen Victoria's Jubilee Institute for Nurses, Edinburgh (1889), with branches at Douglasdale and Inveraray and 92 affiliated associations, 226, 227
 'Red Home' (Nurses' Home), Edinburgh (1892), 223
 St Mungo's Medical College, Glasgow (1889), 157, 224
Orphan Homes, 8, 26, 258-65; *see also* Charity Hospitals and Homes for disabled children
 Boys' Home, Cessnock, 260
 Carsemeadow Sanatorium (1898), 263
 Children's Night Refuge, Glasgow, 260
 Colony of Mercy for Epileptics (1903), 262, 263
 Door of Hope Sanatorium, Carsemeadow (1900), 263
 Elmpark Home for Girls, 260
 Girls' Home, Renfield Street, Glasgow, 260
 Homes for Destitute Children, Saltcoats (1873), 264
 Morham School for Boys (1913), 60
 Newstead Home for Girls, Cessnock, 260
 Old Mansion House, Cessnock, 260
 Quarrier's Orphan Homes, Bridge of Weir, 261-2
Parks and Recreation Grounds, 6, 132 p., 146-8
 Aberdeen Links, 146
 Dundee: Baxter Park (1863), 146; Lochee Park (1899), 147; Maxwell Park, 146-7
 Edinburgh Royal Parks, 146
 Elder Park, Govan (1885), 147 & n
 Glasgow: Alexandra Park, 146; Cathkin Braes, 146; Glasgow Green, 146, 147; Kelvingrove Park (1852-4), 146, 147; Queen's Park, 146-7 & nn

Paisley: Fountain Gardens (1886), 147 & n
Ragged Schools (Reformatories), 7, 109 & n, 245-56, 264, 312, 313, 328
  Aberdeen Female Industrial School (1843), 247, 365
  Aberdeen Industrial Feeding School, 247
  Buchanan Institution, Glasgow (1959), 250, 256
  Castlehill, Lawnmarket and Warriston Close, Edinburgh (c. 1848), 248
  Glasgow House of Refuge for Boys (1838), 249-50 & nn, 313, 353-60 p.
  Juvenile Prison, Parkhurst (1838), 250
  United Industrial Schools, Edinburgh (Roman Catholic) (1848), 248; *also ragged schools* at Arbroath, Ayr, Dumfries, Dundee, Inverness, Paisley, Perth, Stranraer, 251
training ships, 245, 254-6, 328
  Arethusa (1866), 254
  Britannia, 254
  Cumberland, Gareloch, 254, 255
  Empress, Gareloch, 254, 255 p.
  Illustrious, 254
  James Arthur, Bridge of Weir, 254 p., 256, 261
  Mars, Dundee, 254, 255 p.
Religious; see also under SOCIETIES
  Christian Institute, Glasgow (1877), 42-3
  Grove Street Mission Halls (1865), 70, 367
  Religious and Charitable Institution House, Glasgow (1820), 42-3
  YMCA, Glasgow, 1841
Rescue Homes for Women, 7, 60, 232-43
  Dalry (1864), 235
  Edinburgh Industrial Home for Fallen Women, 239
  Edinburgh Magdalene Asylum (1797), 154, 195, 235-41 p., 239 & nn, 240, 313, 368
  Glasgow Female House of Refuge (1840), 236 p.
  Glasgow Magdalene Asylum, Maryhill (1815-40), 195, 235-41 p., 313, 367
  Glasgow Magdalene Institution (1859), 237 & n
  House of Refuge for Females, Glasgow, 236 p., 237
  Morham Rescue Home for Women (1907), 60
  St Agnes Hospital for the Fallen, Edinburgh, 239
  St Andrew's Home, Edinburgh, 239
  Uddingston Industrial and Lodging Home for Women (1907), 60
Savings, 6, 18, 132-7
  Banks:
    Bank of England, 134, 135
    British Linen Bank, 134
    City of Glasgow Bank, 5
    Glasgow Provident Bank (1815), 134
    Royal Bank of Scotland, 134
    Western Bank, 135, 286 & n
  Savings Banks:
    Aberdeen Savings Bank (in Poors' Hospital), 134 p. & nn
    Anderston Collecting Savings Bank, 307
    Edinburgh Savings Bank (1813), 133, 134 p., 135
    Edinburgh Society for the Suppression of Beggars; *see* Edinburgh Savings Bank
    Glasgow Glass Works (1834), 136
    Glasgow Savings Bank (1834), 135, 136 p. & nn
    Hood's Cooperage, Glasgow, 136
    Kerr & Co.'s Nailery (1841), 136
    Monkland Iron & Steel Works (1840), 136
    National Security Savings Bank, 135, 136
    Olde Wynd Savings Bank, Glasgow (1850), 136 & n
    Penny Banks, 136 & n, 137
    Post Office Savings Bank, 135
    Ruthwell Savings Bank, 133 p., 134
    Trustee Savings Bank, 135, 136
Seamen's Homes, 71, 72; *see also* Aged and homeless, homes for
  Glasgow Sailors' Homes, Broomielaw (1857 & 1869), 72 p., 367
  Mariners' Asylum (later Home), Greenock (1850), 72
  New Bethel Reading and Recreation Rooms (1884), 72
  Sailors' Home, Dundee (1879), 72
Specialist Hospitals, 152, 158, 178-98, 200, 202, 323, 336
Cancer and Consumption:
  Consumption Hospital for Scotland, Bridge of Weir (1896), 182
  Glasgow Cancer Hospital (1890), 180, 197; *see also* Royal Cancer Hospital
  Glasgow Cancer and Skin Institution (1886), 180, 197 & n
  Royal Cancer Hospital, Glasgow (1912), 197
  Victoria Hospital for Consumption and Diseases of the Chest, Craigleith House, Edinburgh (1894), 179, 197
  Victoria Tuberculosis Dispensary, Edinburgh (1887), 197
Children, 179, 180, 181, 188-91, 325; *see also* Women
  Edinburgh Hospital for Sick Children

(1860, rebuilt 1903), 189-90 p. & n
Hôpital des Enfants Malades, Paris (1802), 189
Royal Aberdeen Hospital for Sick Children (1877), 182, 190-1 & n
Royal Edinburgh Hospital for Sick Children (1859), 179
Royal Hospital for Sick Children, Glasgow (1883), 180, 190-1 & nn, 224
Sick Children's Dispensary, Graham Street, Glasgow (1888), 180, 191
Dental, 196-7
Edinburgh Dental Dispensary (1860); see Edinburgh Dental Hospital
Edinburgh Dental Hospital (1880), 179
Glasgow Dental Dispensary and School (1885) (affiliated to University of Glasgow, 1947), 180, 196-7
Eye and Ear, 179, 180, 182, 191-4
Aberdeen Ophthalmic Institution (1835), 182, 192
Edinburgh Eye, Ear and Throat Infirmary (1834), 179, 192
Glasgow Ear Dispensary (1872), 193, 194
Glasgow Ear Hospital (1800), 181, 193, 194 p.
Glasgow Ear and Skin Dispensary, 193
Glasgow Eye Infirmary (1824), 69, 180, 191-2 & n, 367, 368
Glasgow Ophthalmic Institution (1868-92), 180, 192-4 p.
Greenock Eye Infirmary (1880), 182
Women, 179-82, 183-8, 325
Aberdeen Maternity Hospital (1896), 184
Dundee Maternity Hospital (1899), 184, 187
Edinburgh General Lying-in Hospital (1793), 183, 184, 366
Edinburgh Hospital and Dispensary for Women and Children, Fountainbridge (1878), 179, 188 & n, 366
Edinburgh Royal Maternity and Simpson Memorial Pavilion (1793), 179, 184, 185
Glasgow Hospital for Diseases peculiar to Women (1877), 180, 188 & n
Glasgow Lying-in Hospital (1834), later Glasgow Maternity Hospital after 1874, 180, 183, 184, 185, 186 p. & n, 192, 224, 368
Glasgow Maternity Hospital; see Glasgow Lying-in Hospital

Glasgow Samaritan Hospital for Women and Agnes Barr Dispensary, Tradeston (1886), 181, 187 & nn, 188, 222
Glasgow (University) Lying-in Hospital (c. 1792), amalgamated with Western Infirmary 1878, 180, 184-5, 186 p., 366, 368
Private Hospital for Women, Dundee (1896), 182, 188 & n
Royal Maternity and Simpson Memorial Hospital, Edinburgh (1879), 184, 185
Women's Private Hospital, Glasgow (1903), 188
Venereal Disease, 7, 183, 194-6
Lock Hospitals, 194-6 & nn, 235, 314, 328
Edinburgh Lock Hospital (1835), 194-6 & nn, 195 & n, 238, 368
Edinburgh Royal Infirmary (Lock Wards), 235
Glasgow Lock Hospital (1805), 180, 194 p. & nn, 195 p. & nn, 235, 238
International Exhibition, Glasgow (1888), 145
Intoxication, Select Committee on (1834), 94 & nn
Inveraray, 56, 227
Inverness, 13, 57, 76, 119, 153, 154, 175, 201, 251, 267
Ireland, drift to Scotland from, 281, 284, 285
Ireland, Dr William Wotherspoon, 276
iron foundries (Glasgow), 55
Irwin, Margaret, 235, quoted 287 & n

Jacobite rebellions (1715 and 1745), 73 & n
James VI and I, King, 108, 155
Jardine, Dr George (1742-1827), quoted 156 & n
Jardine, Dr R., quoted 186
Jarvie, Corporal John R., 57 & n
Jeans, Stephen, quoted 255 & n
Jedburgh, 201, 213
Jeffrey, Robert (d. 1902), 140
Jex-Blake, Sophia, M.D. (1840-1912), 188 & n, 201
John Elder Chair of Naval Architecture (1883), 129
Johnson, Samuel, 74, 266-7 & n
Johnston, Rev. James, quoted 83 & n, quoted 200 & n
Johnstone, Renfrewshire, 212, 213
Johnstoun, John, 156 & n
Joint Subscription Committee (Glasgow and the West), 129
Jones, Professor Henry, 315 p.

Jones, Kathleen, *quoted* 166 & n
Judaism, 2

Kaiserworth, Germany, 85, 219
Kalimpong, 86, 306
Keith, Banffshire, 212, 213
Kelland, Professor, 105
Kelso, 201, 202
Kelvingrove, Glasgow, 145, 146
Kerr, Dr John Guthrie, 123
Kettle, R, 92 & n
Key, James, 268
Kidston, William, *quoted* 97 & n
Kilmarnock, 57
Kilmun, 99
Kincardine, 108
Kinnaird, Lord, 96
Kinnear, Dr, 216 & n
Kinniburgh, Robert, 267, 268
Kinnoull Hill, 170
Kirkcaldy, 213
Kirkcudbright, 19, 213
Kirkintilloch, 69, 70
Kirkwall, 138
Kirkwood, James (1650-1708), 137-8 & nn
Knowlton, Quebec, 263
Knox, John (c. 1505-72), *quoted* 14-15 & n, 31
Koch, Robert, 197

Labour Exchange, Glasgow, 308
Lady Missionaries, 86, 87 p· *see also* Deaconesses
Lambeth, H. A., 99
Lamond, Robert Peel, *quoted* 13 & n
Lanark, 19
Lancaster, Henry H., 117
Lancet, The, 193
Lander, Mrs, 306
Langholm, Dumfriesshire, 213
Langside, Glasgow, 269
Lansbury, George, M.P. (1859-1940), 4
Laqueur, Walter, 46 & n
Larbert, Stirlingshire, 175, 275-6
Large, Alfred, 270, *quoted* 272
Laurie, Professor S. S., 107 p., 111, 117
Laurieston, 37
Lawson, Sir William, of Brayton (1829-1906), 96
Leadhills, 138
Lectures on Female Prostitution, 1842 (Dr Ralph Wardlaw), 233
Lectures on the Nature, Causes and Treatment of Insanity, 1848 (Alexander Morison), 172
Legge, James G., 252
Leitch, John, 273
Leith, North and South, 153, 154, 175

Lenzie, Dunbartonshire, 175, 214, 215, 216; *see also under* INSTITUTIONS
Lewis, 143
libraries, 6, 132, 137-43, 148; *see also under* INSTITUTIONS
Life in One Room, 1888 (James Burn Russell), 301
Linlithgow, Marquis of, Governor of Victoria, 193
Lintie o' Moray (poem), 25 & n
List, Dr, 234
Lister, Joseph (1827-1912), 157 & nn
Little Brick Builders, The (poem) (Robert Bird), 191 & n
Little Skye, Victoria, Australia, 76
Liverpool, 44, 75, 81, 92, 224
Livesey, Joseph, 92 & n
Livingstone, Dr David (d. 1873), 82
Loch, C. S. (1849-1923), 299, 301, 316
Lochee, 268
Lochgilphead, 37, 175
Lock hospitals, 195, 314, 328; *see also under* INSTITUTIONS: *Specialist Hospitals*
Lodgings and Employment Committee, 53
Logan, David, 140
Logan, William, 241 & n
Lord's Day observance, 44; *see also* Sabbath and Sunday observance
London, 54, 57, 67, 81, 82, 108, 172, 267, 298
Lorne, Lord, 227, 313
Lorne, Marchioness of (Princess Louise), 197, 216, 227, 313
Lothian, East and West, 40
Louise, Princess; *see* Lorne, Marchioness of
Love, Dr James Kerr, 271
Lowe, Peter, 155
'Lucky Mackintosh', *quoted* 24 & n, 68 & n
lunatic asylums, 165-8, 312, 322, 323, 325, 336; *see also under* INSTITUTIONS
Lunatic Asylums, Local Authority, in Scotland in 1899 (Table 23), 175
Lunatics in Scotland at 1 January 1858 (Table 22), 174
Luther, Martin (1483-1546), 43
Lyell, Dr, 83, 85 & n
Lying-in hospitals, 183-7, 314, 325; *see also under* INSTITUTIONS: *Specialist Hospitals*

McAlpine, Miss, 225 & n
McBeath, 274
Macdonald, Alexander, 140, 145
Macdonald Bequest (1897), 145
MacDougall, Professor, 105
Macewen, Professor Sir William (1848-1924), 157-8 & n, 224

Macgill, Rev. Stevenson, *quoted* 170 & n
MacKeith, Alexander, 55 & n
Mackenzie of Seaforth, 75
Mackenzie, William (1791-1868), 191-2
MacLagan, D., M.D., 202
McLagan, P., 96
McLaren, Duncan, Lord Provost of Edinburgh (1815-54), 94 & n, 110, 322
Maclean Bequest, 116
McLellan, Archibald (1796-1854), 144 & n
MacLeod, Rev. Dr D., *quoted* 23, *quoted* 75-6
MacLeod, Rev. Dr Norman (1812-72), 44-5 & nn, 61, *quoted* 146 & n, 260
McNair, Robert, 169
McNeill, Sir John, 174
Macpherson, Miss Annie, 263
McPherson, Donald, 140
Maberley, 60
Madertie, Lord; *see* Drummond, David
Madhouses (Lunatic Asylums); *see under* INSTITUTIONS
Magdalene Asylums, 7, 154, 195 & n, 235-41, 313; *see also under* INSTITUTIONS
Magdalenism, 1842 (William Tait), 233
Maine Law, 95, 100
Manchester, 57, 92
Mann, John, 294
Manse Fund (Free Church), 37
Martin, William, 55 & n
Marx, Karl, 334
Marxism, 333-4
Mary of Gueldres, 16
Maryhill, Glasgow, 55, 90
maternity hospitals, 183-7; *see also under* INSTITUTIONS: *Specialist Hospitals*
Medical Missions (William Burn Thomson), 81
Medical Officers of Health, 153, 324; *see also* School Boards
Medical Training Home for Lady Missionaries, Glasgow (Table 9), 87
Meikle, William, 136 & n
Melbourne, Lord, 171
Melrose, 175
mental hospitals (lunatic asylums); *see under* INSTITUTIONS: *Lunatic Asylums*
Menzies, Professor Allan, 107
Merchants' Houses, 27, 154
Mesmer, Friedrich Anton (1743-1815), 172
Milan, 270
Mile End, 302
Mill, Sergeant George, 57
Millar, Archibald, *quoted* 15 & n
Miller, Hugh (1802-56), 291
Miller, Professor James (1812-64), *quoted* 82 & n, *quoted* 242 & n, 243
Miller, M., Superintendent of Police, Glasgow, 249
Miller, W. M., 99
Milne, 274
Milne Bequest (1841), 107-8, 116
Milne, Dr (d. 1841), 108
Mission Coast Home, Saltcoats, number of patients admitted 1866-78 (Table 34), 217
mission study circles, 86 & n 17
missionary movement, 65-79; *see also under* SOCIETIES: *religious*
  city missions, 66-71, 77
  in the Highlands, 73-7
  for the Outdoor Blind, 274
  to seamen, 71-3 & nn
missions, home, 59, 78, 320; *see also under* SOCIETIES: religious
missions, medical, 80-9, 206, 320
missions in poor areas, 37
Mitchell Bequest, 139-40
Mitchell, Stephen (1798-1874), 139-40 & nn
Mitchell, William, 78 & n
Mixed Endowments available in Scotland in 1875 (Table 2), 19
Mizpah Band, 71
model lodging houses, 285-8, 329; *see also under* INSTITUTIONS
Model Lodging Houses, Glasgow Corporation, in 1891 (Table 43), 287
Moderates (a sect), 32
Moffat, Dumfriesshire, 213
Moffat, Rev. Dr, 82 & n
Moir, James, 140
monastic system in schools, 109 & n
Monkland, 136
Monro, Alexander, 155
Monteath, George C. (1788-1828), 191-2
Montrose, 119, 153, 168-9 p., 173, 205, 267
Montrose, Duchess of, 191
Montrose, Duke of, 191
Moody (1837-99) and Sankey (1840-1908), hymn writers, 56, 70
Moon's type for teaching the blind, 274
Moral Alphabet (rhyming), 48 & n
Moray, 25, 105, 116
Morgan, Alexander, *quoted* 104 & n
Morham, 60
Morison, Alexander (1779-1866), 172, 173
Morning Star (ship), 72 & n
Morris, Edward, *quoted* 91, 93
Morrison, Rhona, 299
Mortality of Childbed, 1870 (James Matthews Duncan), 185
Mother's Catechism, The, 74
Mothers' Meetings, 38
motivation (of charity), 4-6, 12
Mountstephen, Lord, 213
Muir, Dr, 267
Mull, 212, 213

Muncie, Mr, 49 & n
municipal charities; *see* State and Municipal
   Charities
Murdoch, Ja., M.D., 52
Murray, Sir James, 145, 170
Murray, Lord, 248
Murthly, 175

Nairne, Dr Stuart, 187
Napoleon III (Emperor of France r. 1852-70),
   54
Napoleonic Wars (1813-14), 192, 219
Napper, Albert, 209
Nasmyth, David (1799-1839), 42, *quoted* 49
   & n, *quoted* 51 & nn, 52, 67 p. & nn, 216
National Debt, 134, 135; *see also* savings
   banks
National Health Service (1948), 6, 82, 88,
   153, 276, 336
Nationalism, Scottish, 77
Neath, 258
Neilson, Montgomery, *quoted* 121 & n
New Testament, 39, 74
Newburn, 18
New Town Dispensary, Edinburgh, patients
   treated 1815-42 (Table 29), 203
Newton, by Largs, 16
Newton Stewart, 114
Nicholette, Captain, R. N., *quoted* 255 & n
Nicol, James, *quoted* 147 & n
Night Asylum, Glasgow; place of origin of
   people admitted 1838-1902 (Table 42), 284
Night Asylum, Glasgow: total overnight
   stays 1838-1902 (Table 41), 284
night asylums, 7, 281-5, 288 p., 314, 329,
   330; *see also under* INSTITUTIONS
Nightingale, Florence, 185, 216, 219 p. & n,
   quoted 220 & nn, 226-7, 228 p., 229, 326
Norman's Blast (poem) 1866, 45 & nn
Nuffield Foundation, 9
nursing, associations and training; *see under*
   INSTITUTIONS *and* SOCIETIES

Oban, 213
Ogilvy, Lady Jane, 275
Ogilvy, Sir John, 275
old people, charities for, 18-21; *see also under*
   INSTITUTIONS *and* SOCIETIES
Old Wynd, Glasgow, 47, 136
Ontario, Province of, 263-4
ophthalmoscope, invention of, 192
O'Reilly, J. B., *quoted* 24 & n
Origin of Species, The (Darwin, 1859), 52
Orkney, 138, 143
Orphan Homes, Quarrier's, at Bridge of Weir
   prior to 1903 (Table 40), 261-2

Orphan Homes, of Scotland Annual Report,
   8
orphanages and orphan homes, 8, 16-18, 26,
   258-65; *see also under* INSTITUTIONS
Orr Ewing, Archibald, of Ballinrain, Dean of
   Guild, 129
Owen, Robert, 232, 243
Oxford, 127, 303, 304

Paisley, 59, 60, 119, 122, 147, 153, 154, 175,
   242, 251
Panopticon, prison plan, 170, 172
Paris, 121, 172, 193 & n, 189
Parker, C. S., 117
Parker, Dr Peter, 80 & nn
Parkhurst Juvenile Prison, 250 & n
parks and recreation grounds, 6, 61, 146-7,
   148; *see also under* INSTITUTIONS
parochial asylums, 175-6, 178; *see also under*
   INSTITUTIONS
parochial schools, 14, 105, 112, 115, 118
Passmore Settlement, London, 308
Paterson, Lance Corporal Robert, 57 & n
Paton, Dr, 58
Paton, David C., *quoted* 100 & n
Paton, James, 59
pauper lunatics, 170
pauperism, 'compulsory'?, 36
paupers, 15, 36, 170
Payne, P. L., *quoted* 136-7 & n
Peebles, 59, 60
Peel, Viscount Rt. Hon. Robert, 97, 171
Pender, A., 269
penny-savings bank movement, 136-7 & nn;
   see also under INSTITUTIONS
Penzance, 57
Permissive Bills, *see under* STATUTES
Permissive Bills, Votes of Scottish Members
   (Table 10), 96
Perth, 24, 59, 60, 119, 153, 154, 168, 169,
   170, 174 p., 251, 267, 302
philanthropists and philanthropy; *see also*
   INSTITUTIONS, SOCIETIES,
   STATUTES *and* Royal Commissions
   charity organisation, 1-3, 86, 298-316, 330,
      337, 386
   children, orphan and ragged, 8, 16, 18, 19,
      26, 59, 60, 69, 108-13, 116, 239, 245-56,
      258-68, 312, 313, 322, 328, 361-4
   clergy and churchmen, 30, 39, 64
   clubs for boys and girls, 54, 56-9
   considered, 2, 4-6
   doctors, role of, 158-60, 172, 173
   education:
      day schools, 116-8
      grammar schools, 14, 115-20 p., 322
      mechanics' institutes and technical
         schools, 121-6

universities, 126-30
endowments (and bequests), 19-20, 105-8, 113, 114, 116, 122, 139-41, 143, 322
evangelical, 30-2
financiers and managers, 160
government involvement, 4, 12-14, 134-5, 153, 154, 174-6, 251-3, 295, 311-4, 324, 330-1
health:
  cottage hospitals, 6, 209-13, 315, 326, 336
  convalescent homes, 5, 6, 69, 70, 99, 214-8, 349-50, 351
  disabled children, 266-76, 325, 328
  dispensaries, 200-8, 323, 325-6, 336
  general hospitals and infirmaries, 21, 152-63, 169, 178, 183, 214, 322-6, 336, 337
  lunatic asylums, 152, 165-76, 174-6, 178, 312, 322, 323, 325, 326, 329, 336
  Magdalene asylums, 7, 154, 195, 235-41, 313
  nurses' training, 86-8, 219-29, 336
  specialist hospitals, 152, 158, 178-98, 200, 202, 206, 323, 324, 325, 328, 336
housing:
  temporary (lodging houses and night asylums), 7, 281-5, 288, 314, 329, 330
  permanent (workmen's), 281, 291-5, 302-9, 329-30
missions:
  city, 66-71, 77
  in the Highlands, 73-7, 78
  home, 59, 65, 77-8, 320
  medical, 80-9, 206, 320
  for the outdoor blind, 274
  in poor areas, 37
  seamen's, 71-3
  moral judgements, 338
  motivation, 4-6
  nurses' training, *see* health
  outlook and performance, 331-2
  piety, 30-64, 319-20
  prostitution, 232-44
  publicists, 233-5, 242
  rationalisation, 314-6
  recreation, 6, 99, 132, 137-48
  residential principle:
    for care and attention, guidance and discipline, 326, 327
  savings, 6, 18, 132-7
  temperance, 6, 56, 59, 91-101
  voluntarist balance sheet, 318
Philip, Robert, 197 & n
Philp Bequest, 116
Piety, rise and fall of, 61-2
Piety as a programme, 30-64
Pinel, Philippe (1745-1826), 172, 173

Pinnington, Edward, *quoted* 145 & n
Pittenweem, Fife, 211
'pledge' (abstinence), 92
Police Office, Glasgow, 68
Pollokshaws, Glasgow, 60
Polson, Alice Mary, 222 & n
Polton, East Lothian, 217
Polwarth, Lord, 60
Poole, Richard, M.D., *quoted* 168 & n
Poor Children's Dinner Tables, 301
Poor Christian and the Church, The (poem), 38-9 & n
poor houses, 281, 295; *see also under* INSTITUTIONS
Poor Law Board, 174
poor law hospitals, 324; *see also under* INSTITUTIONS
Poor Law Union, 282
poor rates, 130 & n
poor relief, 12-14
Poors' Hospitals, 154; *see also under* INSTITUTIONS
Port Glasgow, 40, 73
Possilpark, Glasgow, 55
Presbyterian Church (est. 1560), 31
Presbytery of Glasgow, 44, 45
Preston, 92
Prestonpans, 114
pre-Victorian charities, 12-27, 180
Primitive Methodist Church, 47
prostitution ('The Great Social Evil'), 232-44, 328
  life in asylums, 238-41; Police Acts, 241-2; philanthropic attack, 232-3; publicists, 233-5; rescue homes for fallen women, 232-43; *see also under* INSTITUTIONS
public libraries; *see under* INSTITUTIONS
Public Libraries Report by Select Committee of the House of Commons (1849), 138
public sector charities; *see* State and Municipal Charities
Pyper, Dr, 105

Quakers, 2, 219
Quarrier, William (1829-1903), 5, 8, 182, 253 p., 254, 255, 258-65, 295, 328, 336
questionnaires, 22

Ragged children 5, 245-56
Ragged Schools (reformatories), 69, 109, 264, 312, 313, 328; *see also under* INSTITUTIONS
Ramsay, Professor George Gilbert, 122 & n, 141
Ramsay, John, 117, 141
Randolph, Charles, 129

Rathbone, William IV, 224 & n, 226
recreation grounds; *see under* INSTITU-
  TIONS
Reformation, Scottish, 15, 30
reformatories, 7, 312, 328; *see also under*
  INSTITUTIONS
Reformed Presbyterian Church, 37, 47
Reformer's Gazette, The, 54-5
Regional and Family Name Societies active in
  Glasgow in 1881(Table 3), 25
Reid, Rev. Professor Henry, 92 & n, *quoted*
  320
Reid, James, 145
Reith, Mr, 56
Relief Body, 67
Religious and Charitable Institution House,
  Glasgow, Societies based on, in 1836
  (Table 5), 42
Religious Institution Rooms, Glasgow, 41-3
religious instruction in Scotland, Com-
  missioners for, 34 p.
religious societies; *see under* SOCIETIES
Renfrew, 19, 262
renovations, 26-7
rescue homes for women; *see under* IN-
  STITUTIONS
Resource Allocation Working Party (1975),
  336
Ritchie, Rev. Dr John, *quoted* 36, 92 & n
Robertson, Dr J. Anderson, 84
Robertson, Rev. James (d. 1860), 37 & n
Robinson, Sir Charles, *quoted* 144-5 & n
Roman Catholic Church, 1, 84, 221, 248-9,
  321-2
Romish, Herr, 305
Rose, George, *quoted* 133 & n, 134, 135
Rosebery, Lord, 117
Roslin Castle, 175
Rothesay, 37, 213
Rottenrow, Glasgow, 20, 170, 186, 194, 195,
  250, 252, 302
Royal Commissioners of the Church of
  Scotland, 14, 34, 35, 37; *see also* Church of
  Scotland
Royal Commissions:
  Burgh and Middle Class Schools (Argyll
    Commission) (1868), 111, 117
  Endowed Schools and Hospitals (1872), 3-
    4, 9, 17, 18, 26, 112, 113-4, 116-18 & nn,
    122, 123, 124, 268-9, 338
  Endowed Schools and Hospitals (Scotland)
    (1874), 116-7
  Endowed Schools and Hospitals (Scotland)
    (1878), 117
  Higher Education (Bryce) (1895), 121
  Housing of the Poor, Glasgow (1904), 284,
    294, 330
  Liquor Licensing Laws for Britain (1896),
    97
  Poor Laws (1906), 4
  Reduction of the National Debt, 134-5 & n
  Technical Education in Britain (Samuelson)
    (1884), 121, 123 & n
Royal Infirmaries, 312, 322, 323-4, 336; *see
  also under* INSTITUTIONS
Royal Lunatic Asylums, 312, 322, 323-4,
  336; *see also under* INSTITUTIONS
Ruskin, John, 302
Russell, Dr James Burn, Medical Officer of
  Health, Glasgow, *quoted* 204 & n, 205
  p., 301, 314
Ruthwell, Dumfriesshire, 133, 134
Ruthwell Savings Bank, Deposits made
  between 1811 and 1814 (Table 18), 133

St Andrews, 119, 126, 127, 128, 130, 209,
  210, 211, 213
St Clement's Church, Glasgow, 37-8
St Cuthbert's Church, Glasgow, 59, 175
St George's Church, Glasgow, 72
St James's Free Church, Glasgow, 83
St John's Parish Church, Glasgow, 3, 33, 330
St Jude's Church, Whitechapel, 303
St Petersburg, 189
Sabbath, Committee for Promoting the
  Better Observance of the, 42, 43 & n
Sabbath Defence, 30
Sabbath Evening Discourses, 98-9
Sabbath Evening Schools, Glasgow (1816),
  47 & n
Sabbath observance, 43, 44, 47, 49, 61, 62,
  72, 146
Sabbath Protection Association, Working
  Men's (1850), 43-5
Sabbath Schools; *see* Sunday Schools
Sabbath School Teachers, 49
Sabbath School Union, Glasgow (1853), 47;
  see also under SOCIETIES
Saints Everlasting Rest, The, 74
Salmon, James, snr., 269
Salonika, 193
Saltcoats, 71, 215, 216-7, 218, 264, 351
Salvation Army, 321, 330
Sandeman, David (1814-87), 122 & n
Sandyford Church, Glasgow, 37-8
Sanitary Report, Chadwick's (1842), 153
Sankey, *see* Moody and Sankey
Saturday Evening Concerts, 98-9
savings banks, 6, 18, 132-7 & nn; *see also
  under* INSTITUTIONS
School Boards (1872), 17, 62, 104, 107, 112
  p., 115, 118, 119 p., 123, 130, 132, 142,
  266, 271, 272, 274, 276, 307-8, 314, 322 p.,
  327
Schools; *see under* INSTITUTIONS
Science and Art Department, South
  Kensington, London, 53

Scots Magazine, The, 267
Scotsman, The, 189, 234, 248, 253-4
Scott, Sir Giles Gilbert, 129
Scott, John Oldrid, 129
Scott, Sir Walter, 53
Scottish Dispensaries in 1899 (Table 28), 200-1
Scottish poor relief system, 13
Scottish Universities, Annual revenue received in 1875 from endowments (Table 17), 128
Scripture, divine inspiration of, 52
Seal of Cause, 25, 312 & n
seamen, 43-4, 71-3; *see also under* INSTITUTIONS *and* SOCIETIES
secondary schools, 107, 118-20; *see also under* INSTITUTIONS
secularism, 30
Seed Time and Harvest or a Plea for Ragged Schools (Rev. Dr Thomas Guthrie), 248
Self-Help (Samuel Smiles), 311
Sellar, A. Craig, 115 & nn, 117, 119, *quoted* 127-8 & n
Semple, Matthew, 273
Seton Brown, William, 216
Settlement Laws, 23
Shaftesbury, 7th Earl of (1801-85), 52, 56 & n, 70, 246, 254
Shanks-Schaw, Miss Marjory, 215, 217
Shetland, 143
Shoe Black Brigades, 253, 260; *see also under* SOCIETIES
Shotts, 175
Sicard, Dr, 270
Sikkim, 306
Simpson, Sir James Y., 185
Sinclair, Dr, 223
Skae, Dr David, 173
Skilled Employment Committee, 308
Skye, 213
Smart, Captain, 69 & n
Smiles, Samuel, 311
Smith, Adam, 315
Smith, Robert, 184
Smith, William, 5
Smith, Sir William Alexander (1854-1914), 56-8 p. & nn
Smithston, 175
social problems, range of, 6-7
SOCIETIES (including Associations and Organisation), 365-9; *see also* INSTITUTIONS
  Benevolent, 21-6 & nn; *see also Religious Societies and Missions*
    Argyllshire Society, Glasgow, 25
    Brown's Society (1769), 25
    Buchanan Society, Glasgow (1725), 25
    Church Life and Work Committee, 60

Early Closing Association, 52
Edinburgh Benevolent and Strangers' Friend Society (1817), 22, 23, 283, 329, 366
Edinburgh Lodging House Association (1841), 285
Edinburgh Society for the Relief of the Destitute Sick (1785), 22-3 & n, 366
Fabian Society (1884), 4, 301 & n
Female Benevolent Society, Glasgow, 22
Glasgow Aberdeenshire Association (1858), 25
Glasgow, Angus and Mearns Benevolent Society, 300 & n, 366
Glasgow Ayrshire Society (1761), 25
Glasgow Caithness Benevolent Society (1837), 25
Glasgow Celtic Society, 25
Glasgow City Improvement Trust, 260, 286
Glasgow Dumbartonshire Benevolent Society, 25
Glasgow Dumfriesshire Society, 25
Glasgow Eaglesham Friendly and Educational Association, 25
Glasgow, Galloway and Dumfriesshire Society, 25
Glasgow, Moray and Banffshire Friendly Society, 25
Glasgow Northern Highland Benevolent Society (1836), 25
Glasgow Orkney and Shetland Benevolent Society (1837), 25
Glasgow Society for Benevolent Visitation of the Destitute Sick and others in extreme poverty (1823), 22, 23 & n, 42, 366
Glasgow Society for Bettering the Condition of the Poor, 22, 367
Glasgow Society for establishing lodging houses for the Working Classes (1847), 285
Glasgow Stirlingshire and Sons of the Rock Society, 25
Gorbals Benevolent Society, Glasgow, 22
Graham Charitable Society, 25
Greenock Seamen's Friend Society (1819), 43, 368
Highland Society of Glasgow (1727), 25-6 p. & n, 122
Kilmarnock Benevolent Society of Glasgow (1855), 25
Kintyre Club (1825), 25
Lochwinnoch Benevolent Society, 25
Magdalene Societies, 233, 234, 237
North Parish Washing Green Society, Glasgow (1792), 23 & nn, 368

Old Man's Friend Society, Glasgow (1812), 20-1 & n; Asylum (1837), 20; Asylum (1840), 20-1; Treasurer's Accounts, 342-4

Perthshire Charitable Society, Glasgow, 24, 25

Philanthropic Institute, 49

Property Investment Association, 194

St George Benevolent Society in Scotland (1844), 25

Scott Institution, Greenock (1838), 18

Society of Friends, 167

Tweedside Charitable Society (1813), 25

Bible and Tract, 22, 30, 32, 39-41, 61, 90, 320; *see also* Religious Societies

British and Foreign Bible Society, London (1804), 40 p., 41
    Auxiliaries: East Lothian (1809), 40; Edinburgh (1809), 40 & n, 41; Glasgow (1805 and 1811), 40

National Bible Society of Scotland (1861), 40, 41

Women's Bible Society (England), 41

Charity Organisation, 1-3, 86 & n, 298-301, 308, 315, 316, 330, 337; *see also* Benevolent

Aberdeen Association for Improving the Condition of the Poor (1870) (*now* Aberdeen Council for Social Services), 299

Anderston After Care Committee of the Glasgow Labour Exchange, 308

Anderston Charity Organisation Society, 306-7

Association for Organising Charitable Relief and Repressing Mendicity, Glasgow (1874), 299, 300 p.

Bishop Street School, 308

Charity Organisation Society, London (1869), 1-3, 86 & n, 298-301, 308, 315, 316, 330, 337

Cripple League of Kindness, 86, 308

Edinburgh Association for Improving the Condition of the Poor (1868), 299 & n (*renamed* 'The Help' *in* 1893, *later* Edinburgh Charity Organisation Society *in* 1906)

Edinburgh Charity Organisation Society (1906), 299 & n

Edinburgh University Settlement (1905), 308 & n, 366, 368

Fabian Society (1884), 4, 301 & n

Garscube Cross Settlement, Glasgow (1889), 305

Glasgow Charity Organisation Society (1890), 315, 316, 330, 367

Glasgow Kyrle Society (1882), 302, 367

Glasgow Social Union (1889), 301

Glasgow Union of Social Workers, 308

Glasgow University Settlement Association, Toynbee House (1886), 304-6, 367

'Help, The'; *see* Edinburgh Association for Improving the Condition of the Poor

Kyrle Society, Glasgow (1882), 302-303

Queen Margaret College Settlement Association (1897), 306 p. & nn, 307, 308 p., 309, 330, 367, 368

Salvation Army, 330

Sick Poor Nursing Association, 307

Society for Organising Charitable Relief and Repressing Mendicity (1869); *see* Charity Organisation Society, London

Universities Settlements Association, Toynbee Hall, London, 303, 304

University Students' Settlement, 308

Children, blind, deaf and dumb; see also INSTITUTIONS

Aberdeen Society for the Education of Deaf and Dumb Children (1817), 2, 266, 267

Association for Aiding Infirm Children (1874), 276

Dundee Association for the Education of the Deaf and Dumb (1846), 268 & n

Dundee Auxiliary Committee for the Education of the Deaf and Dumb (1826), 267, 268

Edinburgh Institution for the Education of the Deaf and Dumb (1810), 267 p., 268, 269

Edinburgh Society for Deaf and Dumb Children (1810), 266, 267

Fresh Air Fortnight Society, 307

Glasgow Auxiliary Society for Deaf and Dumb Children (1814-19), 266-8 p.

Glasgow Society for the Education of the Deaf and Dumb (1819), 266-9 p., 367

Inverness Auxiliary Society for Deaf and Dumb Children, 267

Mission to the Outdoor Blind, Glasgow (1859), 274, 367

Perth Auxiliary Society for Deaf and Dumb Children, 267

Children, disabled mentally and physically; see also under INSTITUTIONS

Association for aiding Infirm Children (1874), 276

Association for the Relief of Incurables (1874), 276

Industrial and Reformatory Schools Society, Glasgow, 252, 367

Ragged or Industrial School Association, Edinburgh (1847), 248 p., 366

Scottish National Society for the Relief
of Incurables (1874), 276
Clubs for Boys and Girls; see also Religious
Societies
Boys' Brigade (1883), 56-9, 367
Boys' Life Brigade (1889), 58
Boy Scouts (1908), 58
Catholic Boys' Brigade, 58
Church Lads' Brigade (1890), 58
Girls' Guildry (1900), 58
Girls' Life Brigade (1902), 58
Glasgow Volunteer Rifle Corps (1859),
54
Jewish Lads' Brigade, 58
Cultural; see also under INSTITUTIONS
Association for the Promotion of Art
and Music, 145
Glasgow Tonic Sol-fa Choral Society, 99
Leadhills Reading Society (Miners'
Library) (1741), 138 & nn
Royal Institution (1819), 144
Royal Scottish Academy (1826), 144
Royal Society of Arts, 125-6
Industrial Brigades, 253-4, 361-4
Edinburgh Industrial Brigade, 253-4 p.,
361-4
News and Parcels Brigades, 253, 260
Shoe Black Brigades, 253, 260
Medical, 154-8, 160, 187, 196, 200, 202,
224; *see also under* INSTITUTIONS
Edinburgh University Faculty of
Medicine (1720), 155 p., 156, 157
Forfar Medical Association, 187
Glasgow University Faculty of Medicine,
154, 155-6 & nn, 157 p.
Glasgow University Faculty of
Physicians and Surgeons (1599) (*later*
Royal College of Physicians and
Surgeons of Glasgow, 1865), 160 p.,
196, 202
Royal College of Physicians, Edinburgh
(1681), 154 & n, 155, 157
Royal College of Physicians and
Surgeons of Glasgow (1599), 154 & n
Royal College of Surgeons, Edinburgh
(1505), 154 & n, 155, 157, 196, 200
Royal Infirmary Medical School,
Glasgow (1875) (*renamed* St Mungo's
Medical School, 1889), 157, 160, 224
& n
St Andrews University Medical School,
275
St Mungo's Medical School, Glasgow,
see Royal Infirmary Medical School
Nurses' Training, 86-8, 219-29; *see also
under* INSTITUTIONS
Association for Providing Trained
Nurses for the West of Scotland (c.

1845), 225 p. & n
Association for the Training of Nurses,
Edinburgh (c. 1862), 223
District Nursing Association, Liverpool
(1859), 224-5
Glasgow Sick Poor Private Nursing
Association (c. 1875), 225 p., 307
Kaiserworth Institution, 219 & n
North Argyll Nursing Association, 212
Royal Scottish Nursing Association,
Edinburgh (1872), 225
Religious, including Missions, 41-5, 54-6;
see also Benevolent Societies
Association for Promoting the Interests
of the Church of Scotland (1832), 33
Band of Hope, 38
Better Observance of the Sabbath, Com-
mittee for Promoting, 42, 43
Christian Institute, Glasgow (1877), 42,
71
Church Mission for the Fallen, 239
Colporteurs' Society, Scotland (c. 1850),
78 p.
Congregational Young Men's Mutual
Improvement Societies, 51
Edinburgh Association for Sending
Medical Aid to Foreign Countries
(1841) (*later* the Edinburgh Medical
Mission Society), 80-2
Edinburgh City Mission (1832), 66, 67 p.
& n
Edinburgh Medical Mission Society
(1841), 80-2, 217, 366, 368
Edinburgh Social Union, 292
Edinburgh Women Students' Christian
Unity, 309
Evangelisation Society, London, 70
Free College Church Mission, 56-7 & nn
Glasgow Aberdeenshire Association
(1858), 25
Glasgow Church Building Society, 33,
34
Glasgow City Mission (1826), 42, 66-7 &
nn, 68-71 p. & nn, 77, 329, 330, 367
Glasgow Foundry Boys' Religious
Society (1865), 55-7 & nn
Glasgow Friendly Society (cabmen), 69
Glasgow Medical Missionary Society,
80, 82-4 & nn
Glasgow Sabbath School Union (1837),
47, 330, 367
Glasgow Seamen's Friend Society (1822),
42, 73, 367
Glasgow Social Union, 301
Glasgow Society for the Encouragement
of Penitents, 236
Glasgow Sunday School Union (1837),
47, 367

Glasgow Theological College, 58
Glasgow United Evangelical Association (1874), 271 p.
Glasgow University Missionary Society (1821), 305-6 & n, 367
Glasgow Young Men's Christian Association (1841), 51, 52, 53 & n, 367
Glasgow Young Men's Society for Religious Improvement (1824), 51, 52
Greenock Seamen's Friend Society (1819), 43-4 & n, 71-2, 368
Grove Street Mission, Glasgow (1865), 70, 84, 367
Inverness Auxiliary Gaelic Schools Society (1818), 76
London City Mission (1825), 67 & n
Medical Missionary Society in China, 80
Peace Society, 58
Philanthropic Institute, 49
Port Glasgow Auxiliary Society to the Society for the Propagation of Christian Knowledge in Scotland, 73
Queen Margaret Lecture Guild, Glasgow, 305
Religious and Charitable Institution House, Glasgow, Societies based on (1836), 42
Religious Institution Rooms, Glasgow (1821), 41-3, 61
Scottish Christian Social Union (1901), 59 & n, 308
Shipwrecked Fishermen and Mariners' Royal Benevolent Society, Glasgow (1839), 73 & n
Society of Friends, 167
Society for the Propagation of Christian Knowledge in Scotland (1709), 16, 73-7, 78, 104 & n, 138
Society on Sunday Sailing (1834), 43-4
Society for the Support of Gaelic Schools, Edinburgh (1811), 75-7 & nn
Society for the Support and Management of Sabbath Schools in Glasgow (1787), 47
Sunday School Union, Glasgow (1837), 47, 58, 367
Sunday Schools, 46-50
Voluntary Church Association (1834) (later Scottish Central Board of Dissenters), 35
West of Scotland Protestant Association, 221-2 & n
Women Students' Christian Union, 309
Working Man's Sabbath Protection Association, 43
Young Men's Christian Association, London (1844), 6, 30, 50-3; see also Glasgow Young Men's Christian Association

Young Men's Religious Society, 49
Temperance, 6, 56, 59, 90-101; see also under INSTITUTIONS
British Temperance Association, England, 95, 97
Church of England Temperance Society, 58
Glasgow Abstainers' Union (1856), 98-9 p., 217 & n, 259, 366
Glasgow Abstinence Society (1838), 93
Glasgow Radical Temperance Society (1836), 92-3 & nn
Greenock Temperance Society (1829), 92
Maine Liquor Law League, 95
Scottish Permissive Bill and Temperance Association (1858), 95-6 & n, 97, 368
Scottish Temperance League (formerly Scottish Temperance Union), 93 p. & n, 95 & n
Scottish Temperance Union (1838); see Scottish Temperance League
Temperance Society (cabmen), Glasgow, 69
Total Abstinence Society, University of Glasgow, 305, 367
United Kingdom Alliance (1853), 96
Workmen's Dwellings, 291-5
Dundee Working Men's Houses Association Ltd (1864), 292-3 & n
Edinburgh Co-operative Building Company Ltd (1861), 292
Edinburgh Lodging House Association (1841), 285
Edinburgh Working Men's Building Association (1860), 292
Glasgow Association for Establishing Lodging Houses for the Working Classes (1847), 285, 367
Glasgow Workmen's Dwelling Company (1890), 293-4, 302, 304, 330
Kyrle Society, Glasgow (1882), 292, 301-3 p., 304, 330, 367
Social Union, Edinburgh, 292
Specialist Hospitals in Aberdeen, Dundee and Greenock, 1899 (Table 26), 182
Specialist Hospitals in Edinburgh, 1899 (Table 24), 179
Specialist Hospitals in Glasgow, 1899 (Table 25), 180
Spence, Miss, 225
Speyside, 18
State and Municipal Charities, 3-4, 7, 61
Stark, William, 169-70, 171
STATUTES,
Acts of Parliament:
Children:
Children's Protection Act, Ontario (1873), 264
Dunlop's Act (Act 17 & 18 Victoria

Cap 74), 251, 313
Social Work Act (1968), 264
Education:
   Allan Glen's Institution Act (1876),
      122 & n
   Education Act (1872), 15, 46, 76, 104,
      107, 108, 112-115, 116, 118, 119 &
      nn, 130, 141-2, 266, 271, 274, 276,
      314, 321, 322 p.
   Education Act (1878), 118
   Education Act (Scotland) (1908), 120,
      125, 126, 322, 323
   Education and Local Taxation
      Account (Scotland) Act (1892), 120
   Educational Endowments (Scotland)
      Act (1882), 124, 141
   Endowed Institutions (Scotland) Act
      (1869), 111, 112, 322
   Gas Trust and Local Taxation
      (Customs and Excise) Act (1890),
      140 & n
   Hutcheson's Act (1873), 20 & n
   Local Taxation (Customs and Excise)
      Act (1890), 120, 125
   Scottish Universities Act (1858), 127
   Technical Instruction Act (1889), 121,
      125
   Technical Instruction Act (1892), 121
   Technical Schools (Scotland) Act
      (1887), 121
   Universities Act (1858), 127 & n, 128-
      9, 156
   Universities Act (1889), 128-9
Health:
   Dentists' Act (1878), 196
   National Health Act (1946), 336
   National Insurance Act (1911), 207
   Public Health (Scotland) Act (1867),
      286
Housing:
   Glasgow Corporation Act (1897), 330
   Glasgow Corporation (Water and
      General) Order Confirmation Act
      (1902), 330
   Local Government Act (1888), 311
Libraries:
   Free Public Library Act (1871), 141,
      142 & n
   Free Public Library Act (1872), 141,
      142 & n
   Public Libraries Act (1871), 141, 149
      & n
   Public Libraries Consolidation
      (Scotland) Act (1887), 149 & n
   Public Libraries Consolidation
      (Scotland) Act amended (1899), 149
      & n
   Public Libraries Act (England) (1864),

   148 & n
   Public Libraries Act (England, Scot-
      land and Wales) (1886), 148 & n
   Public Libraries (Scotland) Act (1854),
      148 & n
   Public Libraries Act (Scotland) (1867),
      149 & n
   Public Libraries (Scotland and Ireland)
      Act (1853) 139, 148 & n
Liquor:
   Forbes Mackenzie Act (1853), 94 p. &
      n
   General Police and Improvement
      (Scotland) Act (1862), 241 & n
   Licensing (Scotland) Act (1903), 97
   Liquor Acts (1756, 1793, 1808), 93
   Private Police Act, Glasgow (1890), 97
   Temperance (Scotland) Act (1913), 97,
      100 p.
Lunacy:
   Lunatic Asylums Act (England)
      (1853), 167, 174
   Lunatic Asylums (Scotland) Act
      (1857), 174 & n, 338
Poor Law:
   Poor Law Amendment Act (1845), 13,
      26, 154, 174, 311
   Poor Law (Scotland) Amendment Act
      (1845), 14, 271
Parks:
   Public Parks Act (1859), 146
Savings:
   Post Office Savings Bank Act (1861),
      135-6
   Savings Banks Act (1835), 135 p.
Women:
   Factory Act (1895), 239
   Glasgow Houses of Refuge, Act
      combining (1841), 236-7
   Glasgow Police Act (1856), 242 & n
   Greenock Police and Improvement
      Act (1865), 242 & n
   Municipal and Police Act, Edinburgh
      (1879), 242
Bills related to,
   Assimilating Bill (1876), 96
   Licensing Boards Bill (1876), 96
   Permissive Bills (1864), 69, 70, 71, 73,
      74, 75, 76, 95-7 & nn
   Poors' Fund and Assurance Office Bill
      (1807), 135
   Sunday Closing Bills (1876), 96
   Suspensory Bills (1876), 96
Statutory Secondary Schools, 119, 120 & n
Stewart, A. M., 221 & n
Stewart, Daniel (d. 1814), 117
Stirling, 19, 119, 175
Stirling, James, 94-5 & n, 138 & n

Stirling, Walter (d. 1791), 138, 139 & n
Stirling Maxwell, Sir John, 146
Stirling Maxwell, Lady, 188
Stonehaven, 267
Stornoway, 213
Story, Principal, 130
Stranraer, 213, 251
'street arabs', 245, 254, 255
Strong, Mrs Rebecca (1843-1944), 223-4 & nn, *quoted* 227 & n
Sun Foundry, Glasgow, 147
Sunday Observance
   Sunday railway trains, 44
   Sunday Schools, 30, 46-50, 54, 55 p., 58, 62, 65, 80, 90, 264, 319, 320
Sunday School enrolments and density in Great Britain 1851-1911 (Table 6), 50
Sunday School Magazine, 49
Sure and Steadfast (motto of Boys' Brigade), 57
Suspensory Bills (1876), 96
Switzerland, 275
Syme, Professor James, 157, 219

Tait, William, 233 & n, 234-5 & n, *quoted* 242 & n, *quoted* 243 p.
Tarves, Aberdeenshire, 213
Taylor, Mrs, 223
teachers of the deaf, International Congress of, Milan (1880), 270
technical schools, 121-6 & n; *see also under* INSTITUTIONS: *Education*
temperance bills (1875-6), 96
temperance hotels, 98
temperance movement, 6, 56, 59, 90-101; *see also under* SOCIETIES
'Temperance Ships', 72
Tenant, Andrew, 267
Tennant, Sir Charles, 5, 8
Tennant, Corporal John, 57 & n
Tharsis Sulphur & Copper Mine Company, 124, 218
Thompson, E. P., *quoted* 46 & n
Thomson, Alexander, 246, *quoted* 247 & n
Thomson, John, M.D., 202, 269, 270
Thomson, Dr John (1856-1926), 190 & n
Thrift (Samuel Smiles), 311
Torrie, 144
Towers, Dr James, 184-5, 186
Towers, Dr John (d. 1834), 184-5, 186
Townhead, Glasgow, 304
Toynbee, Arnold (d. 1883), 303
Toynbee House Choir, 305
trade corporations, 19
trade unions, 334
Trades Houses, 27, 154, 185, 312

Tradeston, Glasgow, 96, 187 & n
'Training Ships', 254-6, 328; *see also under* INSTITUTIONS
   Source of Funds 1893-4 (Table 39), 255
   Number of Boys who went to sea from 1893-4 (Table 38), 255
Treatise on Madness (1758) (Dr William Battie, M.D.), 167
Tron Free Church, Glasgow, 47
Trongate, Glasgow, 19, 285
tuberculosis, 183, 197-8, 325; *see also under* INSTITUTIONS: *Specialist Hospitals*
Tuke, William (1732-1822), 167 & n
Turner, J. W., 202

Uddingston, 60
unemployment bureaux, 60
Unitarian Church, 2, 122
United Associated Synod, 67
United Original Seceders, 47
United Presbyterian Church, 47, 51, 312
Universities, 14, 126-30, 323; *see also under* INSTITUTIONS *and* SOCIETIES
University Extension Lectures, 304
University Settlement Movement, 303-9; *see also under* SOCIETIES
Urban Assessments in Scotland, entered into and not revoked (Table 1), 13

Vaughan Bequest (1900), 144
venereal disease, 183, 192, 325
   hospitals for, 7, 194-6; *see also under* INSTITUTIONS: *Specialist Hospitals*
Ventnor, Isle of Wight, 263
Victoria, Queen, 4, 19, 55 & n, 62 p., 73, 169, 216, 226-7, 228, 232, 252, 330, 326
Vienna, 189
Volunteer Movement in Britain, 54-9; *see also under* SOCIETIES: *clubs for boys and girls*

Wanlockhead, 138
Wardlaw, Dr Ralph, 92, 233 & n, 234-5, 242, 243
Waring, Dr, *quoted* 209
Washington Browne, G., 190
Waste (poem), 48 & n
Waterloo, Battle of (1815), 54
Watson, Rev. David, 37-8 & n, 59-61 p. & n
Watson, James, *quoted* 285 & n
Watson, John, 18

Watson, Sheriff (The Children's Sheriff), 5,
  246-7 p. & nn, 249, 250, 253, 256 p., 313
Watt, James, 124
Webb Beatrice (1858-1943) and Sydney, 4,
  quoted 88 & n, 89, 207 p. & n
Webster Trust, 120
Wesleyan Methodists, 47
West Lothian, 40
Whitbread, Samuel, 135
Wigtown, 19
Williams, George, *quoted* 51 & n, 52
Wilson, Carfrae, 57
Wilson, Charles, 170
Wilson, Dr Charles (1804-84), 189 & n
Wilson, John, 96
Witness, The, 291
Wohl, Anthony, 295 & n, 330
Wolfe, John Reissburg (d. 1904), 192-3 & nn,
  330
women,
  delinquent, homes for; *see* INSTITU-
    TIONS: rescue homes
  employment bureaux for, 60
  hospitals for, 179-82, 183-8, 325
  hospitals staffed by, 187-8

Magdalene asylums for, 235-243
medical training of, 219-29
pensioners outnumber men (1869), 19
in social work, 309
Women's Jubilee Offering, 226
Women's Lodging House, Glasgow, Out-
  goings in 1872 (Table 44), 288
Wood, Sir Gabriel, 72
Wood, John, M.D., 20-1
Workmen's Dwelling Company Ltd,
  Glasgow, new houses built (Table 45), 293
Wright, John, 236
Wylie, Sergeant William H., 57 & n

York, 170
York, Duchess of (Elizabeth, née Bowes-
  Lyon, b. 1900, Consort of King George
  VI), 60
Young, Dr James, 124, 184 p.
Young, Lord, 119
young men's societies, 30, 49, 50-5; *see also*
  under SOCIETIES